Metis Pioneers

D1260580

Marie Rose Delorme Smith and Isabella Clark Hardisty Lougheed

Metis
Pioneers

DORIS JEANNE MACKINNON

The University of Alberta Press

Published by

The University of Alberta Press
Ring House 2
Edmonton, Alberta, Canada T6G 2E1
www.uap.ualberta.ca

LIBRARY AND ARCHIVES CANADA
CATALOGUING IN PUBLICATION

MacKinnon, Doris Jeanne, author
    Metis pioneers : Marie Rose Delorme
Smith and Isabella Clark
Hardisty Lougheed / Doris Jeanne
MacKinnon.

Includes bibliographical references
and index.
Issued in print and electronic formats.
ISBN 978-1-77212-271-8 (softcover).—
ISBN 978-1-77212-363-0 (PDF).—
ISBN 978-1-77212-361-6 (EPUB).—
ISBN 978-1-77212-362-3 (Kindle)

    1. Smith, Marie Rose, 1861-1960.
2. Lougheed, Isabella Clark Hardisty.
3. Métis women—Alberta—Biography.
4. Métis women—Alberta—History.
I. Title.

FC109.1.A1M33 2017   971.004'9700922
C2017-905169-5
C2017-905170-9

First edition, first printing, 2018.

Copyediting by Kirsten Craven.
Proofreading by Joanne Muzak,
Michael Lahey.
Indexing by Judy Dunlop.

This project was funded in part by the
Alberta Historical Resources Foundation.

The University of Alberta Press gratefully
acknowledges the support received for its
publishing program from the Government
of Canada, the Canada Council for the
Arts, and the Government of Alberta
through the Alberta Media Fund.

Canadä   Canada Council   Conseil des Arts
          for the Arts   du Canada

Alberta
Government

For Camille Joseph Robinson

A scholar living the life of a labourer—you taught me the value of hard work and humility.

For Alma Juliette Robinson

An artist living the life of a labourer—you taught me that to plant a garden is to believe in tomorrow.

Contents

IX   Acknowledgements

XI   Note on Terminology

XV   Note on Sources

XVII   Note on Names

XIX   Introduction

1   1 | Being and Becoming Metis

25   2 | The Ties That Bind

71   3 | Gracious Womanhood

127   4 | With This Economy We Do Wed

189   5 | Trader Delorme's Family

227   6 | Queen of the Jughandle

285   7 | Fenced In

325   8 | Many Voices—One People

349   Notes

465   Bibliography

507   Index

Acknowledgements

THERE ARE MANY PEOPLE who have blessed me with their support for my research and for my desire to share the stories of these two amazing women. First, I would like to thank Peter Midgley at University of Alberta Press, both for his enthusiasm for this book and for his relational style of editorial work.

During the journey that culminated in this book, there were many who offered their support and advice. Those include the anonymous readers of this book whose suggestions served to inform and improve my research and writing. My supervisors and committee members at the University of Calgary provided invaluable expertise to the research and writing of the dissertation that formed the working document for this book, namely Drs. Heather Devine, George Colpitts, Warren Elofson, and Donald B. Smith. To Dr. Smith, I acknowledge the tremendous resources on Isabella Clark Hardisty Lougheed that he shared with Lougheed House National and Provincial Historic Site and Museum, which so enriched my research. To Donald McCargar, I acknowledge the continued support for my research into the life of his great-grandmother, Marie Rose Delorme Smith.

I acknowledge the Social Sciences and Humanities Research Council, the Eleanor Luxton Historical Foundation, and the Queen Elizabeth II Graduate Scholarship Fund for their support of my research.

Finally, I remain eternally blessed by the support of my family.

x

THE PARLIAMENT OF CANADA, by way of the Constitution Act, 1982, section 35, used the term "Métis" in recognition of the Aboriginal status of people of Indigenous and Euro-North American ancestry who were not included as "status Indians" under the federal Indian Act. While section 35 did not define the term "Métis," leaving that task to the courts, provision was made to include "Métis" people as distinct Aboriginal people. Over a century earlier, the French version of the Manitoba Act, 1870, used the distinction "*des Métis residants*," while the English version described the residents as "half-breeds," suggesting that there were two separate and distinct groups. However, from that point on, references in Canadian legislation no longer made the distinction between the two groups.[1] In Alberta, where Marie Rose Delorme Smith and Isabella Clark Hardisty Lougheed spent their adult lives, the first political body organized by the Metis, in 1932, bore the name L'Association des Métis d'Alberta et des Territoires de Nord Ouest. That name was later changed to the Metis Association of Alberta, and then to the Métis Nation of Alberta.[2]

The variety of names used to describe people of Indigenous and Euro-North American ethnicity, from half-breed, *bois brulé*, *gens libres*, country-born, freemen, mixed-bloods, and Iroquois freemen, has not led even today to a general consensus on the best term to describe the Metis. In 2013, a federal court ruled (and the Supreme Court upheld in 2016) that "non-status Indians" and the Metis could be considered "Indians" under subsection 91 (24) of the Constitution Act of 1867.[3] At least one scholar argues that this proliferation of terminology has led to the "constructed vocabulary" that suggests that "the Métis" might "encompass mixed individuals...It is important to note that scholars have not reached consensus on the use of the term 'Métis.'"[4] (It is also important to note that the Metis themselves have not reached consensus on the most appropriate use of the various terms.) Recently, many scholars have chosen to use the unaccented "Metis" as an acknowledgement that these communities had, and continue to have, diverse and expansive kin connections and were not always rooted to a particular place.[5] In my earlier publications, I used the term "Métis." However, my research since those earlier publications confirms, for me, that the term "Metis" has become more inclusive and thus more appropriate. Therefore, this book uses the term "Metis" to describe people of Indigenous and Euro-North American ethnicity, unless it appears differently in the direct quotations of other researchers, or in contemporary publications, or in the words of Marie Rose and Isabella themselves.

In addition to the issues surrounding terminology, it is important to note that this book focuses on Metis identity and not on Metis nationhood or national consciousness. For a long time in Metis historiography, there existed a Red River myopia, in which the argument states that a distinct Metis identity and nationalism emerged in response to conflicts with outsiders, largely in the Red River area, such as those in 1816 (referred to by some as the Battle of Seven Oaks), and in 1869–1870 (referred to as the Resistance by some), as well as the broader conflict in 1885 (referred to by some as the Northwest Uprising). This focus on Red River has fuelled the notion of a "singular Metis consciousness and national identity."[6] There has often been a general consensus that a sense of Metis nationhood solidified as a result of the conflicts in the Red River, beginning in 1816 and specifically fuelled by the North West Company. However, there is more appreciation now for the fact that there was a distinct Metis identity and culture in geographic areas not only in the Red River region but also in areas removed from the Red River.

In reality, if there had not been a pre-existing distinct Indigenous identity among the Metis in 1816, the North West Company would have had little success in instilling a sense of Metis nationhood. In the end, the intent of this book is to examine the lives of two particular Metis women who lived their adult lives away from Red River, and not to examine in any depth the history of the Red River area (nor the concept of Metis national consciousness). However, references are made when they help to understand the formative years of Marie Rose and Isabella and how those experiences informed their adaptive strategies during the transitional period after the fur trade.

The term "Aboriginal," as it is referenced in the Constitution Act of 1982, was intended to include First Nations, Metis, and Inuit. Much of Canada's historiography, when referring to Aboriginal people, has included the same groups as the Constitution Act, while many have referred to other groups as non-Aboriginal, particularly for the historical period when there was not yet a country of Canada. More recently, many scholars have replaced the term "Aboriginal" with "Indigenous" in recognition that their history is not bound by national borders. For the purposes of this book, unless appearing in direct quotations, the term "Indigenous people" will be used in reference to groups of people that are either First Nations, Metis, or Inuit. In recognition of the 1980 Declaration of First Nations by hundreds of chiefs and the subsequent re-establishment of the National Indian Brotherhood as the Assembly of First Nations in 1982, the term "First Nations" will be used as a general term to refer to Indigenous people who are not Metis or Inuit, while specific nations will be referred to by their names, such as Cree. The term "Euro-North American" will be used to refer to those people who interacted with Indigenous people who were not Indigenous themselves.

NO HISTORICAL RESEARCH is ever complete. This is especially true when researching the lives of Canada's Indigenous people, particularly because their history has been an oral one and because, even during the fur trade era, there were few written documents produced by and about Indigenous people. Indeed, this truth about no historical research being complete also extends to Indigenous people, such as Marie Rose Delorme Smith and Isabella Clark Hardisty Lougheed, who were both literate and who, as adults, experienced the transitional period after the fur trade when the society of the North West became reliant on paper transactions in the late nineteenth and early twentieth centuries. While we must recognize that it is necessary to rely on documented sources in historical research, this book relies in small part on oral history (the recollections of a single person rather than oral tradition),[1] and in large part on documents written by and about Marie Rose and Isabella within the context of the times in which they lived. However, due to their own censorship of the documents left behind, it is sometimes necessary to rely on reasoned speculation, while always acknowledging that more sources may yet be found.

In relating the life stories of Marie Rose Delorme Smith and Isabella Clark Hardisty Lougheed, historians of Indigenous history face persistant challenges. While Marie Rose left a good number of written documents, those documents were silent about a fair bit of her own history. On the other hand, no documents written by Isabella have been located other than one letter, and, in the few interviews she granted, there was no mention of her Metis ancestry. While both women spoke only briefly to the contemporary press, that press was acutely interested in their lives. Admittedly, there was more interest by the press in Isabella than in Marie Rose, specifically because of the Senate position of Isabella's husband, James Lougheed. However, as Marie Rose's position as a respected homesteading pioneer solidified, she was sought out for numerous interviews.

Note on Sources

Note on Names

MANY OF THE WOMEN discussed in this volume had multiple
names as they moved through childhood into adulthood and on to
marry different partners. For simplicity, I have chosen to maintain
their names as they relate to the various stages of their lives. Mary
Anne Allen Hardisty Thomas, for example, is referred to as: Mary
(Anne) Allen when discussing her childhood and young adult life;
Mary (Allen) Hardisty when discussing her life while married to
William Hardisty; and Mary (Hardisty) Thomas when discussing
her life after her marriage to Edwin Stuart Thomas. The various
names used will be cross-referenced in the Index.

MARIE ROSE DELORME SMITH was born in 1861 to Urban
Delorme and Marie Desmarais in the Red River. The Delorme
family was of French-Metis ancestry and its members were
primarily fur traders and buffalo hunters. My initial publication,
*The Identities of Marie Rose Delorme Smith: Portrait of a Metis Woman,
1861–1960* (2012), which examined Marie Rose's documents and
numerous other primary sources, revealed a multifaceted Metis
identity.[1] Although not confirmed by Marie Rose, early in the
research it became clear that her family included Urbain Delorme
Sr., a man referred to as "*le chef des prairies*," and descended of the
North West Company tradition. The Delormes were wealthy and
were always politically active in the Red River area. Yet, from my
vantage point, Marie Rose appeared to distance herself from her
birth family, the Delormes, and the fact that they were involved in
the conflict in the Red River region in 1869–1870 as well as the
conflict in 1885. It appeared that Marie Rose negotiated her own
identity less through ethnicity than through pure survival strategy.[2]
Whatever her survival strategy, there was some indication in her

manuscripts that Marie Rose remained tentative about her public identity. It was also clear that, in public, she sought to subsume her Metis ethnicity.

The second subject of this book is Isabella Clark Hardisty Lougheed, who was also born in 1861 to Metis parents, William Hardisty and Mary Anne Allen. Although her Metis fur trade family had connections with the Red River area, her father's responsibilities as a chief factor with the Hudson's Bay Company (HBC) meant that Isabella spent her formative years in the northern Mackenzie district. In Isabella's case, she left few written documents, but, as a married woman who settled in southern Alberta, Isabella became the focus of much media attention. Thus, there are a number of primary sources available that help us understand how she negotiated her Metis identity. As with Marie Rose, there is evidence that, in public, Isabella sought to subsume her Metis ethnicity.

This book assumes a rare methodology and presentation in that it compares the lives of two Metis women for whom the comparison may initially seem illogical, based on the fact that one was of French-Metis ancestry and one of Anglo-Metis ancestry. Scholars of the Metis people have not reached a consensus on who might rightfully identify as Metis. There are some who argue that the Metis emerged as a people in the geographic area of the Red River, and specifically after the conflicts in 1816, 1869–1870, and 1885, while others argue that identity for the Metis was more about "webs of kinship" than it was locale.[3] The perspective that Metis identity can be traced only to those who were connected to the locale of Red River would then disqualify Isabella as a Metis person, and would relegate her as an Indigenous person, who was, at best, "in between" the Indigenous and the Euro-North American worlds. The in-depth research that was conducted to support this book confirms that Metis identity and culture were diverse but inclusive, and that Isabella's ethnicity was undeniably Metis.

Indeed, although a cursory look at Marie Rose and Isabella suggests that there might be few similarities in the adaptation of their Metis culture and identity after the end of the fur trade, there were actually a striking number of parallels in their lives. This close comparative study confirms that their parents valued daughters alongside sons, that both were privy to formal educations, that both of their families were involved in finding suitable Euro-North American husbands for their daughters, that both assumed active roles in the transitioning economies, and that both manipulated the fluid boundaries of identity. Indeed, both women were linked to Indigenous people, and both showed themselves to be intelligent, resourceful, and strong women whose lives are living testaments to the role of Metis women in the construction of the Prairie West.

In order to gain an understanding of the society in which Marie Rose and Isabella negotiated their adult identity, it is important to understand the changing social landscape as the fur trade was drawing to a close at the end of the nineteenth century. The western plains that would officially become Alberta in 1905 served as a colonial settlers' space in which Indigenous people would eventually be relegated to occupying small tracts of land. Ideologies such as social gospel and beliefs in an edenic promised land left little space, both physical and literal, for Indigenous people who were increasingly seen as uncivilized and unsuited for success as farmers or business people in the emerging capitalist society. Geographical boundaries became more important, as did "racial" boundaries, which engendered beliefs in degrees of "Indianness" and questions about who could rightfully identify as "Indian" or "Metis," with the answers often coming by way of government legislation. As a belief in the boundaries of race solidified, questions about Metis identity created challenges. Were they mixed-blood, were they Indigenous, to which community did they belong, did they belong at all or were they forever to reside in between other peoples, and would subsequent generations be less Metis and more Euro-North American?

My earlier publications focused only on Marie Rose Delorme Smith, examining the four main roles that the research to that point indicated, those of historical character, of folk historian, of author, and of a person who became one of the first homesteaders in southern Alberta.[4] This book necessarily relies on some of the biographical data uncovered during the research for my earlier publications,[5] as well as on some of the previous analysis (particularly of Marie Rose's writing as it related to her identity). However, although my earlier research raised many questions, the scope of that research did not address in any depth how Marie Rose created a persona that allowed her to portray herself as a homesteading pioneer in the Anglo-dominated society that emerged in the Prairie West as new settlers

arrived. There was also the question about the survival strategies of other Metis women who had settled away from the Red River area. Another question was whether Metis women of the fur trade were able to maintain their fur trade kinship connections, and whether those connections actually assisted or hindered their transition into the new society.

Given that Metis identity during the fur trade was embedded in webs of kinship, there was a clear question that emerged about how that identity was maintained or subsumed by Metis women, depending upon the ability of the men in the family group to transition successfully. There was also a question about whether French-speaking Metis women were able to transition as successfully as English-speaking Metis women. Another question that emerged was that of the role that Metis women assumed in the building of the Prairie West—how specifically did they contribute to the community-building organizations that were so crucial to the transition?

Although the research that supported my earlier publications did not delve into all of these questions, the information available about Marie Rose suggested that these questions could be addressed in a broader study. This was particularly so if a comparative study could be undertaken of Marie Rose's life and that of another woman of Metis ancestry, especially an English-speaking woman from the Hudson's Bay Company tradition. The indication was that much could be learned about the history of Metis women, and of their community of connections on a broader level, by undertaking close comparative case studies of individual Metis women. It was also clear that a study such as that which supported this book could inspire similar comparative research. At this point, few scholars have undertaken a comparative close case study of Metis people (particularly women) born of the two variants of fur trade society, the French-Metis and the country-born. Yet, because the history of the Metis people is complex and ecompasses so much of particularly western Canada, and because the sources are often difficult to identify, it is important that we study the Metis people on an individual basis.[6]

The editors of a recent collection of essays, while focusing on ethnic groups rather than way of life, suggest that "Métis" is not a "signifier of a particular population situated in a particular time or place."[7] Another recent study concurs with an analysis of Metis ethnicity that does not focus on geography. That study argues that ethnicity is culturally constructed, and that ethnic groups, particularly in modern settings, are "constantly recreating themselves and ethnicity is continuously reinvented in response to changing realities."[8]

Indeed, this study of Marie Rose and Isabella confirms this to be the case. For these two Metis women, their identity was far more complex than "place." Their stories raise questions about the permeable boundaries of identity for many other Metis people during the transitional period after the fur trade, and indeed in contemporary society, as there is no consensus on the "idea of being Métis in Canada today."[9] As was the case for Marie Rose and Isabella, some contemporary narratives by Metis women note that there was a silence about Metis identity in their own lives.[10] It is important to remember that Metis identity was never static. Rather it was (and continues to be) negotiated and renegotiated, attesting to the "diversity, fluidity, resilience and silence of Metis identities."[11]

In terms of methodology, this book relies on some of the same sources as women's narratives and biography. However, although more sources have been identified for Marie Rose and Isabella than for many other Metis women, there are relatively few compared with other historical subjects. As Sarah Carter and Patricia McCormack note in their recent collection, encountering passages in the "sometimes somnolent and stuffy world of archival and documentary research is exciting, rewarding—and frustrating." This is because, while the few references to Indigenous women in traditional historical sources "provide glimpses and bonds to place, and they breathe life into and connect us with the past[, they] also leave us wanting more."[12] If we are to have a broad understanding of the lives and experiences of Indigenous women, both during the fur trade and during the transitional period that followed, relying on women's narratives, while expanding our resource base, is critical.

While biographies are rarely used as the basis for scholarly arguments, biography has become a useful tool for women's history, and increasingly for less well-known women. However, it is clear that "much remains to be done to heighten awareness of the diversity of women" and to apply comparative approaches.[13] Biographies can tell us a great deal about the history of the average woman by providing a wealth of specific information about the life course of differently positioned women, whose lives can then be viewed collectively and comparatively.[14] As Jean Barman notes, focusing on the lives of individual women can lead us to question older interpretations and larger historical contexts.[15] Yet women's biography has been underused as a tool that actually presents very real opportunities to understand the histories of Alberta women in general.[16] Perhaps this underuse is due to the fact that biographies often focus on "extraordinary" rather than ordinary people, and that Canada's collective history has often identified more extraordinary men than women. Because they can be removed from the larger debates, such as the conflicts between French Metis and Anglo-Metis, biographical studies make important contributions to understanding the early twentieth-century history of Metis women, not only on an individual basis but on a broader level.[17]

While it is a micro-history of two women, and thus relies on some methodologies of biographical writing, this book is not a "great woman" approach to history, as biography often is. It is important to define biography in broad terms when writing about Indigenous women in particular, given the paucity of traditional sources.[18] It is also important not to romanticize the lives of Marie Rose and Isabella in an effort to portray them as "great" or extraordinary women, as biography sometimes tends to do. Marie Rose and Isabella were women who struggled with the pressures of raising families, and with partners who were often away. They were forced to negotiate their identities in environments that were becoming increasingly Anglocentric. In fact, during the time in which Marie Rose was likely writing many of her manuscripts, in the early 1900s, the Ku Klux Klan (KKK) chapters, whose targets in western Canada were primarily Roman Catholic and French-speaking residents, were particularily active in southern Alberta. Klan membership was strong in some districts, such as Calgary, which had three hundred members, and there were "chapters in three communities within 25 miles of the city."[19] For Marie Rose, there were many realities to consider as she wrote her manuscripts and "wrote out" parts of her history. For Isabella, her son Norman attended schools in which the schoolmasters held the opinion that the "Red Men of the West" did not care to work, due to innate characteristics as shiftless vagrants.[20] Indeed, the reality of history is that it is multidimensional and must be viewed along its "vital edges."[21]

By looking closely at their lives we can see the "vital edges" where Marie Rose and Isabella mixed, clashed, or cooperated with those around them. Perusing these "vital edges" where they came together with settlers and other Indigenous people provides traces that help us understand how Marie Rose and Isabella were able to publicly obscure their Metis identities and to recreate themselves as homesteading pioneers. Examining the relationships that Marie Rose and Isabella had with members of their changing communities also helps us understand their labour, the work involved in raising their children, and the unpaid service work they undertook, work that is so critical in organizing and maintaining social institutions as new societies emerge.[22] Conversely, it is important to study aspects of their new society that lend themselves to providing an intimate look at both Marie Rose and Isabella.

That intimate look at Marie Rose and Isabella confirms that they formed not only marital partnerships with Charlie Smith and James Lougheed, respectively, but that they also formed business partnerships that helped their families to negotiate and succeed in the changing economy. In fact, it is difficult to fully understand the history of Marie Rose and Isabella without an understanding of their life partners. It is also true that, in the study of people of the past, we can never really know the "structure of feeling"[23] of a particular era, and thus aspects of a person's history, without examining the cultural components of the era in which historical subjects lived. Thus, it is important not only to understand Charlie Smith and James Lougheed, but also to get a sense of Marie Rose's and Isabella's kinship networks and how they adjusted to the changing culture during the transitional period at the end of the fur trade.

Given her own manuscripts, rather than study Marie Rose primarily from the perspective of legal documents and newspaper reports, as we, for the most part, must do with Isabella, there is an opportunity to understand Marie Rose's history from her own perspective. However, because Marie Rose chose to reveal only some aspects of her history, and because Isabella left few documents, the analysis of both Marie Rose and Isabella at some point becomes somewhat abstract in the sense that we must allow for the zones of silence, and we must allow for both Marie Rose's and Isabella's clear desire to create enhanced personae as important members of their transitional society.

The ensuing comparison of Marie Rose and Isabella answers some of the important questions about their experience as the fur trade drew to a close, and exposes some of the questions that should be examined in the history of other Metis women and men. Specifically, just as territorial boundaries were important to the Metis consciousness at various times during the fur trade, individual land ownership for Marie Rose and Isabella assumed a level of significance in the new economy. In regard to their ability to adjust to that new economy, it appears that Isabella, the Anglo-Metis woman, rose above those challenges with more ease, at least financially. At the same time, both women continued to rely on aspects of the Metis culture of their youth, and they both maintained contact with their fur trade family networks that were so crucial during the fur trade era. Yet both did establish fictive kinship connections with members of their society that they knew were important to the new economy. Their ability to build new community connections speaks to the fact that both Marie Rose and Isabella continued to contribute social capital to their respective partnerships in the way that Metis women at the height of the fur trade had contributed. Yet, in the end, both felt the need to either suppress or repackage the Metis identity and culture that had sustained both of their fur trade families and that, in many ways, continued to sustain them.

The research that supports this book confirms that comparative studies can provide insight into the lives of other Metis women during the transitional period, and it raises questions about the possibilities for the study of the Metis men in their fur trade families. We know that Marie Rose had two brothers and that Isabella had four brothers who survived into adulthood, but we do not really know at this point in the research what became of those siblings. When Isabella hosted royalty and other important guests at her grand home, were her Metis siblings, cousins, or mother present? When Marie Rose hosted the businessmen and political figures of southern Alberta at her ranch, were her Metis siblings, cousins, and mother present? There is some documentation of where both Marie Rose's and Isabella's brothers settled after the end of the fur trade. However, there has yet to be uncovered information that speaks to their ability to transition, and to the history of Marie Rose's and Isabella's own children.

There is also the question of the other Metis women who were Marie Rose's and Isabella's neighbours in the early pioneer sedentary communities of southern Alberta. Did they forge connections with influential Euro-North American people as a way to accommodate the difficulties that their Metis identities presented, as had Marie Rose and Isabella? Did other Metis women continue to rely on the Metis culture and identity in the private sphere as a way to transition? Like Marie Rose and Isabella, were they important figures in the transitional period in the late nineteenth and early twentieth centuries, when the fur trade gave way to a sedentary economy based on agriculture and industrialized commerce? These questions about other Metis women and men cannot be answered in the context of this book, but they remain important areas of future study.

1

Being and Becoming Metis

IN ORDER TO UNDERSTAND both how Marie Rose and Isabella transitioned in a changing world, and how Canadian society has accessed some of its historical knowledge about Metis people, it is important to speak briefly about the changing focus for historians. It was only in the 1980s that scholars acknowledged that the Metis had survived the end of the fur trade era as a "people" with their own identifiable culture and distinct history. Early histories of the Metis were largely subsumed within the history of the fur trade, and most scholars saw them as an ethnic group unable to thrive beyond the fur trade. While this chapter cannot undertake a complete annotated bibliography of the rapidly changing field of Metis historiography, there are pivotal works that help explain the trends that contributed to the historical process that has enabled and assisted close case studies of Metis women such as this one, and provide opportunity for continuing this type of study.

Beginning in the 1930s with the work of Harold Innis,[1] through to Arthur Ray's work in the 1970s,[2] the economy of the fur trade was the primary focus for historians. In the transitional period of Metis historiography that began in the 1970s, scholars such as Sylvia Van Kirk,[3] Jennifer Brown,[4] and Jacqueline Peterson[5] expanded Indigenous history to focus on the role of Metis women who lived during the fur trade era. John Foster's work on the emergence of the Metis as a distinct cultural group was also published during this period.[6]

The focus on fur trade company corporate cultures evolved to examinations of kinship links for Metis people, with work by scholars such as Lucy Eldersveld Murphy,[7] Tanis Thorne,[8] and Susan Sleeper-Smith, who also expanded the geographic focus from Red River to the Great Lakes area of what is now northwestern Indiana and southwest Michigan.[9] Sleeper-Smith explored the thesis that Indigenous women who married French men actually assumed a role as cultural mediators and negotiators of change when they established elaborate trading networks through Roman Catholic kinship connections that paralleled those of Indigenous societies.[10] It was evident that these women did not "marry out," but rather that they incorporated their French husbands into a society structured by Indigenous custom and tradition.[11] Thus, these Metis women did not reinvent themselves as French but rather enhanced their distinct Metis identity. Van Kirk also argued that, from an Indigenous perspective, the process of women marrying fur traders was never regarded as marrying out.[12] Rather, these marriages were important means of incorporating traders *into* existing kinship networks, and traders often had to abide by Indigenous marital customs, including the payment of bride price.[13] These scholars were able to demonstrate that Metis women made significant contributions to the fur trade. However, there has yet to be a significant number of studies that examine the important roles Metis women played in the transition from the fur trade economy to the industrialized sedentary economy that replaced it.[14]

More recently, scholars of Indigenous ancestry, such as Heather Devine[15] and Brenda Macdougall,[16] used geneaological reconstruction and biographical methodologies to examine Metis identity formation in geographic areas that expanded beyond the Red River area. Martha Harroun Foster, whose research also expanded beyond the traditional fur trade era that had previously been studied by many historians, noted that some Metis women in the Spring Creek community of Montana used kinship networks (and practices such as godparenting) as a way to consolidate more recent trade relationships to ensure their families' prosperity, and in essence reaffirm existing Metis networks.[17] The Spring Creek Metis, former fur traders, became business people in the new economy, and tended to extend their kinship networks through such practices as asking non-Metis associates and neighbours to serve as godparents for their children.[18]

Harroun Foster notes that as the kinship network of the Spring Creek Metis expanded, and came to include more non-Metis members, the terms the Metis used to identify themselves became more complex. Thus, terms like "breed," once common, became more private, so that few Metis people remembered using the terms "half-breed" or "Metis" outside of the family. Yet self-identification as Euro-North American could, but did not necessarily, represent a rejection of a Metis identity or Metis kin group.[19] For this group of Montana Metis, although a private Metis identity survived, that identity became increasingly complex, multilayered, and situational, but nonetheless remained rooted in the kinship networks first established as part of fur trade culture.[20]

In reality, for families of the Canadian fur trade that might have various "tribal relatives," as well as Euro-Canadian family members, Metis ethnicity was often inclusive enough to encompass and accept all members of the family. Kinship links between culturally distinct groups enabled accommodation and subsequently influenced tribal politics in many geographic areas when settlement by Euro-North Americans occurred.[21] Because there was very little opportunity between the late 1890s and the 1920s to publicly identify as Metis, it was not unusual for most Metis during that time to identify as either "Indian or white," while privately nurturing a Metis identity. History confirms that it has always been an integral aspect of the Metis culture to allow a web of kinship ties to enrich rather than to destroy a sense of unique ethnicity.[22] Kinship systems often allowed the Metis to sustain their identity in a safe, supportive atmosphere, even if those identities had to be enjoyed only in the private realm.

In Canada, the Metis were often forced to enjoy their identity in the private realm due, in part, to the fact that Metis identity has not always been open to individual choice. At various times in Canadian history, by way of the Indian Act, treaty negotiations and enforcement, and scrip regulations, the government determined who was "status Indian" and who was Metis. It is entirely possible that some Metis in Canada, as in the United States, found they could be "white *and* Métis or Métis *and* Indian with sincerity and apparent ease."[23] In a study of her own "French-Indian" ancestors who settled in the Willamette Valley, Melinda Jetté concluded that

> *they were not exclusively American, Indian, French-Canadian, or métis, but were all of these things at different times and in different places...there was a process of negotiation that went on throughout their lives...the family navigated a place for itself amidst a unique set of cultural traditions.*[24]

Despite observations such as those by Harroun Foster and Jetté in regard to the continuity of Metis culture and identity, some scholars had previously argued that fur trade society was abruptly replaced by a new economy. The first scholar to conduct an in-depth study of Canada's Metis people, Marcel Giraud, helped to create (in historiography) a stereotypical Metis character unsuited to function in the new economy,[25] and a belief that deficiencies in Metis culture were a result of miscegenation.[26] In the same way, W.L. Morton, often seen as the first regional historian of the Canadian Prairies, believed that

*when the agricultural frontier advanced into the Red River Valley
in the 1870s, the last buffalo herds were destroyed in the 1880s, the
half-breed community of the West, la nation métisse, was doomed,
and made its last ineffectual protest against extinction in the
Saskatchewan Rebellion of 1885.*[27]

Despite viewing the Metis as doomed people, Morton saw what
he believed to be the "two strongly defined currents" emanating
from unions between HBC men and Indigenous women, and those
between the French traders and Indigenous women. However, he
also acknowledged a sense of unified identity, in that "the children
of both streams of admixture had bonds of union in a common
maternal ancestry and a common dependence on the fur trade."[28]
Nonetheless, for Morton, there was a clear break between fur trade
society and that which replaced it, and there was really no place for
the Metis in the new economy.

In reality, the research that forms the basis of this book confirms
that there was distinct and identifiable continuity from the fur
trade economy with the new sedentary agricultural and commercial economy. Furthermore, the view that Red River was unstable
exaggerates the weaknesses of the community and thus under-
estimates the abilities of its residents and the kinship webs that
extended from that community into the transitional era. By the
late 1850s and into the 1860s, Red River was already becoming integrated into the wider world, and many of the Metis had adjusted
to new economic opportunities and adopted characteristics of an
entrepreneurial class. These entrepreneurs were found among both
French- and English-speaking Metis.[29] The idea that the Metis were
a people "in between" two cultures, which still persists for some
today, ignores the reality that the fur trade engendered its own
diverse people with their own unique and diverse culture. The view
that the Metis were not equipped to survive in the new economy
that emerged after the end of the fur trade ignores the fact that

Metis culture thrived in the capitalist institution of the Hudson's Bay Company,[30] a company that had absorbed the North West Company and established the foundations of the new order. In reality, the lessons that fur trade children learned from their Metis culture could have facilitated the transition for the majority of them had there not been other mitigating factors.[31]

One of the most visible early examples of continuity between the fur trade economy and the new economy was John Norquay, the Metis man who served as premier of Manitoba between 1879 and 1887.[32] The main priority for Norquay's government was to foster economic development by building railway lines, public works, and municipal institutions, as well as assuming debt for construction activity.[33] While some may have seen Norquay's defeat in 1888 as the end of the old order in Red River, Norquay was, in fact, a "creature of the new age," given his dedication to economic development according to the principles of industrial capitalism.[34] In reality, the primary reason Norquay clashed with John A. Macdonald, Conservative prime minister at the time, was not because he was a Metis of the old order, or even because he was Liberal, but because he attempted to establish a competing rail line to the Canadian Pacific Railway in order to satisfy the growing concerns of a broad cross-section of Manitoba's population.

By 1886, near the end of Norquay's time as premier, and just one year after the conflict in 1885, the population of Manitoba had grown substantially, from 60,000 in 1881, to 109,000.[35] It is true that, by this time, many Metis had moved further west and north, where rapid settlement by newcomers only occurred after 1896. However, the reason for this exodus by the Metis had less to do with economy than with the influx of Euro-North American settlers who were less than tolerant of racial equality. In addition, the long-distance supervision by the federal government over the vast North-West Territories (and the imposition of its new land use regulations) presented challenges for all residents. Despite the challenges, many of the Metis who were forced away from Red River were able

to re-establish themselves on prosperous farms along the South
Saskatchewan River and in permanent settlements that featured
merchants, mills, farms, and churches. This is further evidence of
Metis adaptation to economic changes.[36]

In reality, both incoming settlers and the Metis were forced to
negotiate new economic challenges, including recessions, such as
that in 1882, which saw many new immigrants leave Canada. The
emigrants included some Metis who went to Dakota and Montana.
Out-migration continued to be a cause for concern on the prairies
until the 1900s. Also, not unlike the new settlers in their struggles
with the changing economy, the Metis had concerns regarding
Ottawa's policies addressing territorial rights. Widespread concern
about property rights by the majority living in the area was one of
the motivating factors in the political agitation that led to the
armed conflicts in 1885. Although this conflict came to be viewed
as a Metis uprising, in reality, Frank Oliver, editor of the *Edmonton
Bulletin*, had argued in 1884 that "rebellion alone" would force the
central government to heed concerns in the North West.[37] As many
have since noted, government inefficiency led many new settlers to
join the initial protests that eventually culminated in the fighting
in 1885.

Because the fighting in 1885 has come to be seen as an
Indigenous action that arose only out of Indigenous concerns, the
view that Indigenous people were unable to adjust to new economic
and environmental realities persisted for some time in historiography. However, in a broadly based macro study published in 1996,
Frank Tough provided solid evidence that Indigenous people were
prepared to alter tradition by participating in the Euro-North
American economy when mercantilism gave way to industrialism.
For example, in the late 1800s, the export of new staples, such as
fish, lumber, and cordwood from northern Manitoba, represented a
diversification of activity for Indigneous people.[38] History demonstrates over and over that, when allowed, Indigenous people were
able to maintain viable economies by incorporating their labour

into new resource industries and responding to new markets.[39] It was because Indigenous people did not have control of the land that they remained dependent on the needs of the metropolis and on the decisions of government agents and Euro-North American business interests.[40] Some historians have demonstrated that, even when Indigenous people were successful workmen, they were still not masters of their own destiny in ways that they had been when traditional territorial boundaries were respected, and in ways that Euro-North American settlers were.[41]

Territorial boundaries were an important component of Metis history in the North West. It is also true that Central Canadians increasingly saw land as the West's best resource. Eventually, the practice of informal land occupancy that had been enjoyed by the Metis over vast areas of the North West gave way to a formalized system managed by the Dominion Land Survey and the free hold tenure system. Land for settlement space and resource wealth was so important to the annexationist plans of Central Canada that it remained in the control of the Department of the Interior (which also controlled immigration and administered Metis scrip)[42] when the territory, and later the western provinces, were formed.

The threat to traditional territorial land was an integral issue that united many Anglo- and French Metis when they challenged the incoming annexationists in 1869–1870. The man who emerged as the leader of that resistance, Louis Riel, was not opposed to diversifying the economy, but he correctly saw that land ownership was integral for the future survival of the Metis. For Riel, it was more a question of who would determine and benefit from diversification of the Metis economy and land. The issue of land became even more complicated for the Metis than for those Indigenous people, now defined as First Nation,[43] given the ad hoc administration of government policy with regard to extinguishing Metis title in comparison to the numbered treaty process. As Metis territorial lands were increasingly threatened during the transitional era, so, too, was their freedom to identify as distinctly Metis people.

Given that so much of the early studies of the Metis focused on the Red River area, scholars of the fur trade had long argued (and some still do) that the formation of a distinct Metis ethnicity occurred primarily among the predominantly French Metis of Red River who supported Louis Riel. While this book disputes this argument, it is important to explore Red River society in order to understand that, within that settlement, Metis identity was complex and diverse. For example, the fact that more and more HBC men retired to the Red River from posts throughout fur trade country, rather than return to their "home country," suggests that they were beginning to see themselves not as a mixed people but as distinct Indigenous people, with families that would not be welcome in the home territories of their fathers. Even if they had never lived in Red River, many HBC men (like Isabella's father) sent their children to Red River so they could be educated alongside other Indigenous children. As more company men chose to stay in fur trade country, and more of them married British women who came to fur trade country after the 1840s, Anglo-Metis women were increasingly less likely to view themselves as English. Thus, by the mid-nineteenth century, the term "half-breed" had come to encompass people of Indigenous ancestry from both fur trade traditions.

The distinctions that some have identified based on two fur trade traditions could be blurred. For example, there was a noted trend in census documents for the Red River area that indicated intermarriage in the community between the various groups of Metis people was "guided by social and economic factors [and] integrated one partner, more often the 'Native English,' into the parent Metis society."[44] Thus, despite the complexity and diversity of the Red River Metis settlement, the common bonds of culture and kinship ensured some solidarity.[45]

While there were common bonds of culture among the Metis in Red River, there were increasingly many newcomers to the region. One of those newcomers was a trader named Alexander Begg, who arrived in 1867 and who left written documents that have become useful sources to help understand the diversity of Red River society. As historian W.L. Morton concluded, Begg's text, which relied to a large degree on the records of Roman Catholic priest Father Pierre Picton, demonstrates that there was a "web of blood relationship which not only held the *métis* together, but bound the two halves of the Red River Settlement with ties that were not to be disregarded."[46]

Although there is evidence of a web of blood relationships during the fur trade era, some scholars argued that there were variances in Metis identity based on class. There were certainly class distinctions and conflict in the Red River community prior to the fighting that erupted in 1869–1870 and 1885. Irene Spry argued that conflict was based less on ethnicity than on economic class.[47] On the other hand, Fritz Pannekoek argued that much of the conflict and class distinctions in Red River society existed because of, and were exacerbated, by the clergy. Recent scholarship has expanded the study of the Metis far beyond Red River and has argued that "groups variously termed classes, tribes, people, and nations endured and adapted by transcending these national and state identifications."[48]

Whereas many believe that class is not the most appropriate comparative factor to help us understand Metis identity, it is still important to note that, when they were children growing up during the fur trade era, both Marie Rose and Isabella could be considered to be of the higher class of Metis, who either had ties to the Roman Catholic Church in Marie Rose's case, or to the Hudson's Bay Company in Isabella's case. Both were from families who could afford European-style education. As married women, both continued to rely on "webs of real and imagined kin" that could be "fashioned and refashioned" in order to succeed, and even to thrive, so they were able to maintain their status in the transitional period after the fur trade. In fact, the survival strategies that worked for Marie Rose and Isabella were not unlike the "enduring form of organizing one's larger social, economic, and political world" that the Metis relied upon at the height of the fur trade era.[49]

Although Marie Rose and Isabella were able to maintain a semblance of the class status they enjoyed during the fur trade, one of the complicating factors in relying on class to understand the Metis identity is that class distinctions in fur trade society could blur, depending on political, geographical, and external forces. For Marie Rose, her family members chose to support Louis Riel's challenge to the incoming political control imposed from Central Canada. This led to a decline in status for most of the Delorme men and their families, but no less conviction for them of Metis identity. For Isabella, it is true that her father was a chief factor in the Hudson's Bay Company. However, his entire service was in the northern Mackenzie district. While there were certainly class distinctions between HBC officers and their staff, conditions at the northern posts were often harsh, and privations many. A child of the fur trade at northern posts would not often understand themselves to be of higher status when all were expected to contribute to the provision of food and shelter, all experienced periods of severe hardship, and all classes of Indigenous people were often in close proximity for periods of time throughout the year.

Yet class distinctions were still evident and, as the fur trade progressed, class distinctions affected not only the children of HBC men but Indigenous women and their ability to maintain the positions that some had enjoyed. Unions between First Nations women and fur traders were more commonly accepted by free traders and the North West Company early in the fur trade era. However, partly to secure trade relationships and partly to ensure their own survival, the HBC officers also forged relationships with Indigenous women, and positions of status were soon reserved for Metis women over First Nations women. Class distinctions intensified further when George Simpson cast aside his country relationships for the cousin he married and then brought back from a European trip. It was after this change in Simpson's marriage partner that Isabella's father felt the need to explain his own choice of a wife who was of a lower social status.

For most Metis, more important than class were the familial links that allowed them to navigate changing opportunities. Although the more northern and western Metis people had Dene rather than Cree origins, with distinct economies and lifestyles, they had familial links with the Red River area and shared some cultural traditions.[50] The Metis of the North West also had work connections with Red River through the Portage La Loche brigades and often travelled south to trade and socialize.[51] They would have had contact with Isabella's kin. Many Metis were eventually dispersed from Red River to points further north and west, and the common bonds of culture and kin survived for many of them. Given the diverse webs of connection, the fluctuation in fortune, and the conditions at northern fur trade posts, it is plausible that people from both fur trading traditions, such as Marie Rose and Isabella, were exposed to similar aspects of Metis culture and history.

In fact, it is possible that, as historian Brenda Macdougall argues, the Hudson's Bay Company inadvertently fostered a Metis identity, and that HBC men incorporated Indigenous kinship models into the corporate model. Even though the HBC had originally forbid country unions between its employees and Indigenous women, Macdougall argued that the HBC often and increasingly assumed a role as benefactor for the Metis, and that

> local chief factors and chief traders asserted a relationship that
> firmly encapsulated it [the relationship] within the reciprocal
> family model by assuming a position that cultivated and harnessed
> the loyalty of its servants through support of their family life.[52]

It appears that Metis women often continued to rely on the HBC for supplies, support, and employment even after their company partners were no longer in the picture, suggesting that some Metis believed the HBC was a component of the reciprocal family model.[53] As early as 1824, the HBC was insisting that families of employees residing at posts in the Mackenzie district pay for their board.[54]

While this suggests that the company may still have been trying to discourage country unions at the managerial level, it also suggests that company officials were very aware that country unions with Indigenous women were common and, indeed, necessary.

Even though these unions were necessary and common, by the early nineteenth century, the company was finding that the family life of its officers was becoming burdensome, and interpersonal relations difficult to manage. Although the wives and children of HBC servants had provided invaluable assistance as an informal but necessary labour pool, they could also have a negative impact on company profits by draining local resources and serving as conduits for illegal trade networks through their family networks.[55] These were some of the very reasons that the governor of the HBC, George Simpson, had originally opposed the relationships. However, it is also why his policies changed after 1821, when there was an increasing need to care for abandoned and distressed families. Thus it was that the Red River Colony became a designated retirement community for company men and their families.

The kinship webs established and maintained by many HBC men suggest that they came to view themselves as family men first and company men second, while their children increasingly self-identified as Metis. Susan Armitage's research determined that, although some HBC men did retire to Montreal and England, leaving behind their country families, as early as 1845, a

> surprising number [chose to] retire where they were...John McLoughlin, who retired in 1845, was following the example of a number of former HBC employees who, with their Indian wives, were the first settlers in the agriculturally rich Willamette Valley of Oregon in the 1820s. Here, then, was a multiracial social network of men, linked by kinship and common work histories, who chose in retirement to become settlers—subsistence farmers.[56]

It is plausible that many who have in the past been referred to as the "country-born," Isabella included, increasingly internalized a distinctly Metis identity.

Although HBC culture engendered a distinct ethnicity, that culture was not static and the history of people of Metis ancestry in the North West was diverse due to the different origins of their ancestors, as well as the many geographic areas in which they lived.[57] Yet, one recent scholar argues that the term "Métis" should be used to refer specifically to those Indigenous people who can trace their history to the "buffalo hunting and trading Métis of the northern Plains, in particular during the period between the beginning of the Métis buffalo brigades in the early nineteenth century and the 1885 North West Uprising."[58]

However, to use this narrow categorization disregards the connection of many Metis to the earlier fur trade. More importantly, it relegates an analysis of Metis people who do not fit neatly into the events-based (the Northwest Uprising or the Battle of Seven Oaks) perspective to a discussion of race and degrees of mixedness. Such categorization positions them as people "in between" rather than as rightful members of the "nation" of Metis. Indeed, as Nicole St-Onge and Carolyn Podruchny argue, "[d]efinitions of Metis that rely on the ingredients of buffalo hunting, practicing Roman Catholicism, speaking French, and wearing woven sashes imply that Metis cultural traits are static, exclusive, and singular, thus precluding cultural change and the creation of diverse ranges of Metis cultural expression."[59] According to the Manitoba Métis Federation in 1983, Metis culture and identity were formulated by way of a wide variety of commercial and domestic forms of living, such as those listed by St-Onge and Podruchny, as well as through "socials, music, jigging, country food, art, religious beliefs." This organization also lists one component of Metis culture and identity as "historical knowledge."[60]

Yet historical knowledge, most often connected to the fur trade, may be very different for a Metis person born in Red River, like Marie Rose (who acknowledged listening to the oral history of her Metis mother), than for one born at a fort in the northern Mackenzie district, like Isabella (who spent her formative years with a northern Metis mother). Neither instance may be more or less indicative of the retention of Metis culture and identity. When we restrict ourselves to categorizing the Metis as only rightfully "Métis" if they can demonstrate a connection to the historic "Métis Nation" that emerged in Red River, we risk perpetuating the idea that Indigenous people are homogenous. It is helpful at this point to acknowledge what Theda Perdue has argued, specifically that "biographies can, in fact, serve as sifters that both separate individual women's lives and distinguish women's experiences from those of men."[61] In the same way, biographies and comparative analysis of Metis people serve to "humanize" them and confirm that retention of culture and identity occurs equally on an individual basis as it might on a collective "nationhood" basis.

While the retention of culture and identity can be difficult to assess, for women during the transitional period after the fur trade, their contributions to the family economy were often based on their cultural knowledge. Yet, for economic studies in general, many seem to have accepted the idea that what is "socially and politically valuable has to be something done within the institutional structure of the polity and done for money."[62] However, we really cannot understand economic history without understanding the contributions made by the unpaid labour of women, even if we must understand the labor for its social capital rather than for its monetary value. This is especially so for pre-industrial Canada, which functioned through a subsistence economy.[63]

Although it can be difficult to assess the monetary value of Metis women's work, which began during the fur trade era but extended into the transitional period, many Euro-North American documents reveal a vibrant trade during the fur trade era in the items produced by Metis women.[64] In addition, while post journals can provide no specifics on the unpaid labour of women and children, the company did pay a price for family labour in that it became a benefactor by administrating wills and pensions, operating a transportation system, providing retirement advice, and dispensing rations.[65]

In terms of the economic roles of Metis women, their detailed family stories reveal that those roles allowed them a sense of continuity with their past.[66] Not only did the practical skills of Metis women afford them that continuity but their skills also helped their families to transition to the new economy. Further, when Metis women participated in the shifting economy in ways such as providing traditional clothing to newcomers, they assumed roles as cultural brokers, as they had during the height of the fur trade.[67] The roles of Metis women, their skills, and their elaborative kinship networks that facilitated trade in the earlier period later served to transform the impersonal exchange process characteristic of capitalism into a socially accountable process.[68] Yet few women who contributed the unpaid labour vital to the success of both the fur trade and the transitional economies of the North West, such as Marie Rose and Isabella, viewed their own roles as significant enough to record details of their lives with the intention of passing them on to a public archive.

To understand the value of Marie Rose's and Isabella's unpaid labour, and how they underwrote the costs of establishing the joint estates they maintained with their husbands, it is important to understand the value of both of their Metis families in establishing a sound base for beginning married life to Euro-North American husbands. While Isabella was born at a northern fur trade post and she spent her formative years there, she had the benefit of formal education at Wesleyan Ladies' College in Hamilton, Ontario. After leaving that eastern school and returning to the North, Isabella spent another number of years in fur trade country before moving to Lachine, Quebec, when her father retired. After her father's death in 1881, Isabella returned to the North West to live with her uncle, Chief Factor and Senator Richard Hardisty, who helped facilitate her marriage to James Lougheed, a man without important family connections of his own and little understanding of survival in the early Prairie West. In fact, until his marriage, James's fledgling law practice experienced difficulties in securing funds from outside sources for investment and expansion. Shortly after his marriage, James joined Isabella's uncle as a partner in various business ventures and, soon after this partnership, James and Isabella began to amass large land holdings in Calgary.

In regard to Isabella Hardisty Lougheed's stature, the young Thomas Hardisty remembered that the first time he saw his aunt, Isabella, a woman of Anglo-Scot Metis descent (i.e., "country-born"), she had the aura of royalty.[69] Despite periods of real privation in the northern fur trade, Isabella's family was part of fur trade aristocracy and she later assumed the aristocratic title "Lady Belle Lougheed" of Beaulieu (Lougheed) House, bestowed upon her when her husband, Senator James Lougheed, was knighted. Like Jughandle Ranch, where Marie Rose and Charlie Smith settled, Beaulieu House was also built on the open prairie, but, as one of Calgary's first sandstone homes, it was elaborately furnished to reflect the growing wealth and prestige of the Lougheeds. An ambitious young lawyer from a working-class family of Irish immigrants based in Toronto, James had every reason to believe he would benefit from his marriage into Isabella's kinship network, which included Richard Hardisty and Donald A. Smith (Lord Strathcona), two of the wealthiest men in the North West. Not long after his marriage, James found himself in the fortuitous position of assuming the Senate post previously held by Richard Hardisty, who had died suddenly.

Although he was an outsider to the transitional economy after the fur trade, James Lougheed's Senate post and his acceptance into the Hardisty web of kinship enabled the couple to amass that large estate. They served as community leaders and were involved in all aspects of community-building activities. Isabella's father, William Hardisty, had left an estate, which was eventually managed by James. For all intents and purposes, James had indeed become a "company man."

Like James, Charlie Smith, Marie Rose's husband, was an outsider to fur trade country. It was Marie Rose who had kinship links to Metis society and thus to the fur trade economy. Marie Rose was born in Saint François Xavier, Red River, to Urbain Delorme Jr. and Marie Desmarais,[70] both of Metis ancestry. Marie Rose's early culture was as the daughter of a free trader and part-time farmer who set out regularly on hunting and trading brigades. As a young girl, Marie Rose spent a large part of her life either traversing the plains with her family or living on the small plot of land in the Red River area. She was then enrolled in the convent in Saint Boniface, where she learned to read and write in French and English. Shortly after her time in the convent, when she returned to a more traditional Metis lifestyle on the plains, Marie Rose's mother arranged a marriage for her. The financial agreement reached between her mother and robe and whiskey trader Charlie Smith saw Marie Rose become his wife and ranching partner in exchange for fifty dollars.[71]

Not long after they were married, Marie Rose and Charlie became among the first to transition from trade in buffalo robes to cattle ranching. They began their new life together by driving cattle from Montana to what would become the district of Macleod in southern Alberta. Eventually, British and Canadian investors followed, establishing ranches in the foothills, so that by 1886 there were over 100,000 cattle in the region.[72] Writing in the early twentieth century, Marie Rose referred to herself at various times throughout her manuscripts, when she spoke of those early days of her marriage, as the "Queen of the Jughandle." As an adult somewhat removed from fur trade society, she earned that title after she and Charlie staked a homestead they named Jughandle Ranch.

While it is clear that Marie Rose continued, out of necessity, to rely on the skill set she learned as a child, and on her Metis Delorme family, it is also evident that she desired a role as an important member of the changing West. Thus, it was necessary to build a community of connections that would allow Marie Rose to create a new persona as a homesteading pioneer. In fact, it was her community of connections that clearly came to her aid when Charlie died without having mastered the skills necessary to succeed (and to help his children succeed) in a society increasingly reliant on paper transactions.

The last half of the nineteenth century, when Marie Rose and Isabella were negotiating their identies as married women, was critical to the history of North America. It was a time when both Canada and the United States were attempting to establish separate and distinct countries and linear boundaries, in part by encouraging Euro-North American settlers into the border areas. In addition to these geographic boundaries, there was an increasing desire to erect racial boundaries.

However, despite a desire to erect racial boundaries, those boundaries remained fluid for some time, given that settlement of the prairies was not immediate or consistent.[73] For example, on the one hand, one newly arrived settler to southern Alberta, Mary Inderwick, was "pleased to note" in 1883 that "squaws were not allowed" to attend the ball at the North West Mounted Police barracks at Fort Macleod. On the other hand, Inderwick noted that "half-breeds" were allowed to attend,[74] suggesting that the class distinctions that emerged in the latter part of the fur trade persisted.[75] It is of note that Inderwick's often racist comments in regard to Indigenous people were made in documents that were intended for her audience of family members and acquaintances in the east. In the privacy of her own diary, Inderwick revealed little of either racism or admiration; she simply recorded the fact that she shared her space with Indigenous people.[76]

The presence of so many people of Metis ancestry made it diffi-cult to maintain the boundaries that newcomers in the emerging society of the North West might have sought to establish. It may be that, for many newcomers, ethnic boundaries had to be maintained in other ways, perhaps by reinforcing the social distance, and by coming to view Indigenous people as "other." Maintaining bound-aries may have been seen to be increasingly important—the arrival

of more Euro-North American women in the North West coincided
with treaties and the growth of ranching, which led to the establishment of more Euro-Canadian institutions.[77]

Yet, until the late nineteenth century, the Euro-North American
women who arrived in the North West were, for the most part,
"spatially isolated on ranches." Given this isolation, and that it was
it was "rare to see two or three together at one time,"[78] the degree of
social change that Euro-North Americans could effect during the
late 1800s is debatable. In 1882, former Red River resident Alexander
Begg (by then a southern Alberta rancher) reported that he had seen
"scarcely a house between Fort McLeod and Fort Calgary."[79] When
Mary Inderwick arrived in Calgary in 1883, she wrote that the town
was "very nice but it is a village of tents framed in Indians and squaws
in plenty."[80] It was not until the 1890s, a time when there were few
Euro-North American women in the West, that federal officials started
actively encouraging agricultural settlers to southern Alberta in
order to replace the large land lease companies.[81]

It was in the 1880s, before the arrival of the large numbers of
settlers, that Marie Rose and Charlie Smith settled in the Pincher
Creek district and Isabella married James Lougheed in Calgary, and
thus a time when Indigenous people outnumbered new settlers,
and when those new settlers were spatially isolated. The slow
settlement was no doubt due to the fact that the region seemed
farther from "civilization" and remained difficult to access until the
Canadian Pacific Railway was completed.[82] Yet, while the last spike
that connected Canada "from sea to sea" was driven in in 1885, and
boosterism promoted the West's wide open spaces and limitless
land,[83] the fighting in Duck Lake between the Metis and government
troops still gave the impression the North West was a harsh and
inhospitable place.

By the time that Euro-North American women had established
a permanent and more visible presence in the larger centres of
Alberta in the early twentieth century, Isabella and Marie Rose

had already established themselves as matriarchs of their own extended families. Their roles as matriarchs represented an important aspect of the construction of the Prairie West, as did the roles of other Metis women. Researchers Judith Hudson Beattie and Helen M. Buss use the example of Isabella's mother, Mary Allen Hardisty, to argue that her situation "illustrates an important part of Canada's settlement. The line of succession from Indigenous and European grandparents to Canadian prairie dweller is not an unusual one."[84] In this regard, Beattie and Buss astutely identify the continuity from fur trade to sedentary industrialized agriculture and commerce. While Mary Allen was an orphaned daughter of a Euro-North American man and his Indigenous wife, and she spent the bulk of her life at northern posts living one of the traditional fur trade lifestyles, her daughter went on to become one of the most influential women in the new society of the North West. Indeed, Beattie and Buss could just as easily have included Marie Rose in their assessment of succession to prairie dweller. Despite her lack of monetary wealth, Marie Rose gained some recognition as an important pioneer of the plains and a "first lady" of her community, who by the time of her death attracted the attention of local media in the new West.

While Marie Rose's and Isabella's adult lives followed somewhat different economic and social trajectories, and they occupied different segments of the new society's class groups, at another transitional time in their lives, when both became widows, their financial situations again had some similarity. Marie Rose Smith and Isabella Lougheed were widowed in 1914 and 1925, respectively, when the West was experiencing very difficult economic times. Both had to bury a number of their children, Marie Rose twelve of seventeen and Isabella three of six. As a widow, Marie Rose became an independent property owner and gained a reputation as an amateur author/historian, and she continued to mingle with southern Alberta's community leaders. In fact, she had taken over the management of family finances well before Charlie's death in 1914. While she was able to survive (sometimes in real poverty) through a number of activities, such as taking in boarders and working as a midwife, Marie Rose did eventually have to live with members of her extended family, both in Lethbridge and in Edmonton, until she died.

After James died in 1925 and his sons were left to manage his and Isabella's vast estate, the greatest global economic downturn ever experienced wreaked havoc on Prairie real estate values. Because the bulk of the Lougheed estate was in real estate, Isabella and her sons faced financial ruin, and Isabella died virtually penniless. It was only out of respect for her long-standing contributions to the new western economy and society that the municipality of Calgary allowed Isabella to remain in her stately home until her death. This meant that, even after she lost all of her material wealth, Isabella was able to carry on as Lady Lougheed of Beaulieu House, continuing to entertain high-ranking dignitaries who visited Alberta, and continuing in her commitment to various philanthropic and social groups.

It is interesting that both Isabella and Marie Rose were interviewed not long before their deaths and both were described using similar adjectives. To their contemporaries, Isabella and Marie Rose were both pioneers and colourful characters. Indeed, circumstances had brought Isabella and Marie Rose to southern Alberta and enabled both of them to create personae as homesteading pioneers. This experience was very likely common among many other Metis women and men at the time. For many Metis, while the move to southern Alberta after the fighting of 1885 was partly motivated by economic factors, it was also motivated by social factors.

Two of the social factors that led to the exodus from Red River, and contributed to Marie Rose's and Isabella's success, were Metis customs whereby families traditionally lived close to kin groups and also incorporated outsiders in a way that would enrich the web of kinship. For many Metis, the period after 1885 afforded them the opportunity to stake homesteads in southern Alberta because that district was slow to attract newcomers. Diane Payment concludes that, when the Metis established communities in new geographic areas at the turn of the twentieth century, "family, culture, and lifestyle" continued to "shape and distinguish Metis society." Relying on current interviews with Batoche Elders, Payment identifies what she calls an "enduring hidden pride in their Métis heritage."[85] Using a degree of reasoned speculation, we can see that, although there was a need to supress their Metis identities, both Marie Rose and Isabella felt that enduring hidden pride.

The fact that a pride in Metis ancestry remains "hidden" in the private realm for many Metis even today gives some sense of the need for Marie Rose and Isabella to obscure their own ethnicity those many years ago. Their ability to obscure that ethnicity gave Marie Rose and Isabella not only a sense of power but a heightened sense of their own uniqueness as they helped to construct the new Prairie West. It is clear also that both always recognized the value of their early culture, regardless of the level of their material wealth. This is particularly so later in life as the wealth each had acquired sank to desperate lows, but it is also evident at the beginning of their married lives, when they lived in areas that were slow to attract newcomers and when they relied out of necessity on their early fur trade culture and kin connections. These two Metis women served as agents of transition as the fur trade gave way to a new economy. Marie Rose Delorme Smith and Isabella Clark Hardisty Lougheed were important contributors to the construction of the Prairie West in the same way that many other Metis women surely were, but whose lives have yet to be studied.

2

The Ties That Bind

ISABELLA HARDISTY LOUGHEED'S contemporaries acknowledged the link between the old economy of the North West and that
which eventually replaced it. In 1922, the periodical *Saturday Night*
featured "Lady Lougheed" in its series, entitled "Canadian Women
in the Public Eye." The article noted that

> Thirty-nine years ago a young girl came to visit her uncle, who was
> a Hudson Bay factor, and who had been sent by the great Hudson's
> Bay Co. to establish a trading post, at the Junction of the Bow and
> the Elbow rivers...Her uncle whom she visited was the late Senator
> Hardisty, the first senator of the North West Territories, and of the
> well-known family of Hardisty that had been so intimately connected
> with the Hudson Bay development in the McKenzie and Saskatchewan
> river districts...At that time a new country was just awakening...
> And the young girl who visited her uncle in that unpretentious log
> home in the summer of '83 was destined to see an amazing feat of
> civilization.[1]

The article continued that the story of Lady Lougheed's life had "all the background of romance, adventure and hardship of the pioneer life of the frozen north—on down to the comforts and civilization of the 'Boom Days'"[2] There is no doubt that this article romanticized Isabella's early life. Yet it does demonstrate that even her contemporaries believed that she, much like Indigenous women who lived when the fur trade economy dominated, was destined to serve as agent of transition. For Isabella, the transition was from the fur trade to a sedentary agricultural economy increasingly reliant on paper transactions. As the article pointed out, the transition period was very short:

> *From the humble first home of her married life she has lived long since in one of the most beautiful homes of the West, in a decade the flat stoney [sic] prairie "Yard" was changed into beautiful terraced grounds where Calgarians are proud to entertain many official visitors.*[3]

The newspaper identified Isabella not as an Indigenous woman but as a pioneer who had survived hard times to now enjoy civilization and "Boom Days." No doubt her membership in the Hardisty family, which continued to be important in the transitional society of Calgary where she lived her adult life, enabled this pioneer persona.

Yet Isabella spent her formative years as a daughter of the fur trade at Hudson's Bay Company posts in the northern Mackenzie district. Her mother was a Metis woman from the Pacific Northwest who appeared in the North somewhat mysteriously. For most posts in the North, kinship networks were an integral part of the company culture, and children spent a good deal of their time with those networks in close proximity. In terms of survival at northern posts, even the children of chief factors had to endure a level of privations and necessarily rely on traditional Metis skills and culture.

Isabella was one of nine children born to William Lucas Hardisty and Mary Anne Allen.[4] Her father, William Hardisty, son of the company officer Richard Hardisty and his wife, Marguerite Sutherland,[5] both of Metis ancestry, always worked in the North West with the HBC, as had three generations of Hardistys before him. Eventually, all six of Richard and Marguerite's sons served in some capacity with the HBC. For his part, William Hardisty was an officer for thirty-six years, rising to the position of chief factor for the vast Mackenzie district.

In addition to securing positions in the company for his sons, Isabella's grandfather, Richard Hardisty, ensured that all of his children received a Euro-North American education. It was in 1842, after completing his education at Red River Academy, that Isabella's father began his own career with the HBC, accepting the position of apprentice at Fort Halkett, in the Mackenzie district. At the time of his employment, William Hardisty's parish was listed as Native.[6] In 1843, William took the position of apprentice postmaster at Frances Lake (Yukon), where he served under Robert Campbell, the well-known explorer and Yukon River trader.[7] William Hardisty quickly worked his way up and, in 1848, became the clerk in charge of Frances Lake. In 1856, William became chief trader at Fort Yukon, and then transferred to Fort Resolution in 1860. It was at this post at Fort Resolution, on the shores of the Great Slave Lake, where Isabella was born in 1861.

After serving at Fort Liard from 1861 to 1862, Isabella's father moved his family to Fort Simpson so he could assume a post in charge of the Mackenzie district. In recognition of his ability to deal with the challenges faced by company traders, including provision problems and an outbreak of both measles and scarlet fever, William Hardisty received a commendation for good management and, in 1868, a promotion to chief factor.[8] Although he was successful in attaining positions of authority in the HBC, it appears that William Hardisty also had a reputation as a drinker, perhaps suggesting that his drinking was a bit more noticeable than the amount enjoyed by many HBC men.[9]

There were some recorded instances of alcohol being sent to William Hardisty. On 11 February 1867, William Mactavish wrote to Spencer Fullerton Baird, assistant secretary of the Smithsonian Institution, to say that it was perhaps best to

> *let things take their course in silence...I will say that it is contrary to rule to send spirits of any kind into McKenzie River except for medicinal purposes. So that if as a medical man you consider Hardistys [sic] ailments require something of the kind, I may tell you that packages for the Company officers are never subjected to examination by us. Hardisty is an Officer in the service and knows his duty as well as I do.[10]*

At one point, when Richard Hardisty Jr. thought his brother William might join him in Edmonton, he wrote, "I cannot say that the place will suit him if he is still given to drink—for large quantities of the abominable stuff is brought in these [days]."[11]

Regardless of this observation by his brother, it appears that, for the most part, William Hardisty was deemed quite capable in his duties. After taking charge of Fort Resolution on Great Slave Lake, William Hardisty assisted Robert Kennicott of the Smithsonian Institute in collecting specimens.[12] This activity signalled the beginning of a long affiliation between Isabella's father and the institute, as he evolved from contributor of specimens to author, when his account of the Loucheux people was published by the Smithsonian in 1867.[13] William Hardisty's description of the Loucheux reflects the anthropological analysis of the age, when he wrote of Indigenous women that

> *William Hardisty, chief factor, Hudson's Bay Company. Photo dated 1880s.*
Glenbow Alberta Museum and Archives, NA-1030-18.

Infanticide is caused by the misery of the women—at least this
the only reason they give for it...The women are literally beasts of
burden to their lords and masters. All the heavy work is performed
by them. When an animal is killed, they carry the meat and skin
on their backs to camp, after which they have the additional labor
of dressing the skin, cutting up the meat and drying it. They are the
drawers of wood and water; all the household duties devolve upon
them...In the summer the man uses a small light hunting canoe,
requiring very little exertion to propel it through the water, while
the poor woman is forced to struggle against the current in a large
ill-made canoe, laden with all the baggage, straining every nerve to
reach a particular place pointed out beforehand by her master.[14]

William Hardisty's expressed opinion, his education, and his
intentions to acculturate his children to Euro-North American
standards do not, however, negate the fact that Isabella's father
undoubtedly internalized a great deal of Indigenous culture.
While it was noted in an 1854 letter between traders that William
Hardisty was regarded as "efficient" at his post, the letter also
continued that Isabella's father had "completely mastered the
Youcon dialect," and that he spoke the "Chipewyan tongue" with
great ease.[15] In 1860, the Smithsonian researcher, Robert Kennicott,
visited Fort Resolution when William Hardisty was at that post,
and Isabella's father might have been surprised that Kennicott later
referred to him as a "native with some Indian blood." Regardless,
Kennicott appears to have appreciated Hardisty's help, for he
implored Professor Baird to be sure to send Hardisty some books.[16]

The wives of Hudson's Bay Company men also assisted
researchers and, on at least one recorded occasion, Kennicott
noted that Mrs. Hardisty called him out to look at four pelicans.[17]
By 1864, when Kennicott again reported on his time in fur trade
country, William and Mary Hardisty were at Fort Simpson. At the
time, according to Kennicott's journal, Mary was given the use of
James Lockhart's "old Youcon dogs" to "drive about with,"[18] so she

could maintain her "Rabbit Snares."[19] It was also in 1864 that James Lockhart noted,

> Mr. Hardisty has every wish to collect and render whatever assistance he can in furthering the objects and views of the Smithsonian Institution, but unfortunately he has suffered so much from sore eyes all last winter and spring, that he could attend to nothing. He is now recovered, and promises great things for next year.[20]

Only two years after this letter, in 1866, Isabella's father was ill again and reportedly "very narrowly escaped being carried off by Scarlatina last Autumn," at a time when the servants lost many of their children.[21] William Hardisty's bouts of illness, and the duties that often took him away from the post, meant that Mary Allen Hardisty was the primary caregiver of her children for extended periods.

Clearly, Mary Allen Hardisty relied on her Metis skill set when she cared for her family at the northern posts, often without the help of her husband. In fact, we know that women in the North possessed a "skilled repertoire" that included serving as interpreters and diplomats, preparing pelts, making clothing and snowshoes, transporting furs, and even procuring food for the company's stores.

Other material details of Isabella's early years at the northern posts are scarce. However, there is one memoir of life in the North published by Charles Camsell, which allows for some understanding of Isabella's daily life.[22] Camsell was born at Fort Liard in the Mackenzie district and relied on his memories of his time in the North for his book, in which he tends to romanticize the duties of the HBC men. For example, he wrote,

> No officer would take the smallest item for his private use without marking it against his own private account…These men were the men who were responsible for law and order in the north country since I was a child, and it is worth noting that in the 180 years since

the first fur trader went into the north country there was never at
any time any unrest among its native people.[23]

Despite his somewhat idealistic portrayal of the North, Camsell
provides some of the details of his early childhood, when he lived at
many of the same posts just a few years after Isabella's family had
left. Regarding those northern posts, Camsell wrote that most of
them were

more or less alike—a small cluster of log huts surrounded by a picket
fence, situated in a clearing in the northern forest, usually at some
strategic point or at a good fishing place on the river. All were on
streams navigable for canoes, because the rivers were the highways
and only in the winter time was travel customary or even possible
over land.[24]

Describing Fort Liard, where Camsell lived until he was six years
old, and where William Hardisty was posted in 1861, the year of
Isabella's birth, Camsell wrote that it was "occupied in the first
place only by the fur traders and their entourage of Indians or half-
breed servants, from four to a dozen people in all." He continued,
"In every direction other than the river, the post was surrounded by
impenetrable northern forest, in which there were only a few roving
bands of Indians who came into the post only three or four times
a year to exchange their furs for necessary supplies of tea, tobacco
and hunting and trapping equipment."[25]

Given the isolation and close contact with Indigenous people,
it is no surprise that HBC men concerned for the future success of
their children would often send them away for education so they
might be suited for work with the company in the case of boys, or
for marriage to company men in the case of girls. However, it is
also a given that the children of fur traders at these northern posts
would be exposed to primarily the culture of Indigenous people
during their formative years.

One of the aspects of culture familiar to children of company men was the reliance on country food. Often, supplies at these northern posts had to be anticipated for and requisitioned one year in advance, with the post manager allowed little in the way of imported food other than flour, sugar, and tea. The balance of the dietary requirements had to be met in-country, and thus consisted mainly of fish, rabbit, moose, caribou, or wild fowl, and a limited amount of garden produce for posts that were were established in more fertile areas, unlike Fort Rae or Fort McPherson which were built on bare rock. In the case of Fort Liard, Camsell wrote that the climate and soil allowed gardens to produce a great variety of vegetables, and its fields to yield wheat, oats, and barley.[26]

In terms of connection with the outside world, mail arrived twice per year, once by boat and the other by dog team. Camsell noted that, despite the long winters, there were "many occasions throughout the winter for fun and pleasure at Fort Liard."[27] Yet, as he continued,

> only one who has lived through the long cold winter of the far North can really appreciate the meaning of spring; not only the feel of it, but the smell of it...at every trading Post from the Saskatchewan River to the Arctic Ocean, the Post's journal recorded first of all the arrival of the first goose and, second, the break-up of the river.[28]

Speaking of his early childhood days, likely similar to Isabella's, Camsell recalled,

> life at Fort Liard or Fort Simpson as at every other northern trading Post, was simple, but, as I recall it, not unpleasant. Certainly there was lots to do, and we made our own fun. Spring and fall were the busy seasons. In the springtime, gardens had to be planted and boats built and repaired...Spring also was the time for making syrup from the birch trees and soap from wood ashes and grease. In the fall, fuel and fish and other food had to be put up for winter, and

snowshoes, toboggans and other winter gear overhauled. Summer,
for those who remained at home and did not make the trip to the
Long Portage, was the season of relaxation and enjoyment. Winter,
on the other hand...was a period of great activity...Everyone at the
Post had a line of traps or rabbit snares which he visited once a
week...Indoors there were games of cards, checkers or chess, and on
special occasions a dance.[29]

Fort Simpson, which Camsell wrote about, is where Isabella's
father was posted from 1862 to 1877, and it served as headquarters for the entire Mackenzie district. The length of time at Fort
Simpson and its importance to the region suggest it is the posting
of which Isabella might have had the most memories. According to
Camsell, Fort Simpson was "beautifully situated on an island at the
junction of the Mackenzie and the Liard Rivers." The buildings were
laid out in a square with an open side facing the river. In the centre
of the square was the office building, which housed the chief factor.
During Camsell's time, there were five buildings around the square.
One was a storehouse with a museum of stuffed animals upstairs.[30]
The front building on one side of the square was the "Big House,"
the residence for all senior officers and their families ("Big House"
was interestingly the name that her contemporaries eventually used
to refer to the mansion that Isabella lived in as a young married
woman in Calgary). On the main floor of the Big House in the
North was found a great dining hall in which staff took their meals,
and which also served as a dance and reception hall. The upstairs
housed a library and a recreation room for playing cards, chess,
checkers, or billiards. No doubt, having access to all of these activities would allow the children of the chief factors to enjoy a sense of
their own distinctiveness.

Yet the activities that Camsell recalls enjoying as the child of
an HBC man would often necessarily have included the children of
the various Indigenous people who frequented the northern posts.
This is especially so if their mothers were, as in the case of Isabella,

Indigenous women raised in northern fur trade country who would not likely be directing their children to spend their entire time with the books and checkerboards found inside the Big House. In fact, even if the children of company men spent a good portion of their time in the Big House, William Hardisty confirmed in his letter to Miss Davis at Red River (quoted at length later in this chapter) that "Indian children" were always "about the house."[31]

Camsell and Isabella had both been sent from northern fur-trade country to school. Camsell left Fort Simpson in 1884 at the age of eight; Isabella undertook that same journey in approximately 1868. Although Camsell had the luxury of boarding the train from Qu'Appelle to Winnipeg for the final leg of his journey, it was still a journey that took from the start of June until September to complete. Parts of the trip were no doubt the same for both Isabella and Camsell, that is, the brigades travelled in "fair or foul" weather, for sixteen hours per day, at times navigating "one hundred miles of...stormy waters...then 180 miles up the winding, muddy Slave River to the foot of the rapids at Fort Smith."[32] During the long journey, travellers camped on the beach with only mosquito nets for shelter, and endured portages across sandy, forested plains and across swamps and muskegs, with the sound of the "noisy Red River cart...heard for miles."[33]

While Camsell's memories of his time in the North and his journey out are of a somewhat later time than Isabella's, Father Émile Petitot provides one of the most detailed accounts of life in the Far North during the time when Isabella was a young child. Although Petitot's time was spent primarily living among Indigenous people rather than at company posts,[34] he interacted with HBC men on a regular basis. While Petitot "deplored the Company's racist policies and sharp business practices," it is said that he held many individual HBC men in "high regard and friendship."[35]

Petitot likely had such a friendship with William Hardisty, for he noted that, when he had occasion to call on the hospitality of the commander of Fort Norman, Nichol Taylor, a letter of introduction from Isabella's father had "warmly recommended" Petitot.[36] On several occasions, the translators of Petitot's manuscripts refer to his choice of various names for Hardisty Lake, once as Kia-go-tpié,[37] and once as Large Flat Leaves.[38] Petitot wrote that, when he travelled to the shores of lakes Yanéhi and Inton-tchộ-kka, he gave them the names of "Tozelli and Hardisty."[39] Given that the translators of his manuscripts judged him to be a French nationalist throughout his life, and a man whose primary concern was promoting his own accomplishments, Petitot's decision to honour the Hardisty family by naming a lake for them confirms a friendship, as well as the importance of the Hardisty family in the North.

In addition to the writing of Petitot and Camsell, there is another source of information about the social history of Isabella's youth. Between 1845 and 1848, artist Paul Kane journeyed many thousands of miles crossing the Prairie West, and is thought to be "unequalled by any other artist on the continent in his time," for his "superb eye for recording the historically important."[40] At a time when Isabella's uncle and father were company men, Kane was at a gala ball at Fort Edmonton in 1847, when

> white, Metis and Indians alike, joined in festivities...dressed with
> bright sashes and ornamented moccasins...Highland reels were
> squeaked out by a fiddler. One of Kane's partners was a young Cree
> girl, "who sported enough beads round her neck to have made a
> pedlar's fortune."[41]

This excerpt suggests that HBC men were often exposed to the same social customs that have more commonly been attributed to the Red River Metis. Despite the fact that Isabella's father always served at more northern posts than Fort Edmonton, there was undoubtedly time for merriment. In fact, newspapers reported that Isabella remembered well how to dance the Red River Jig long into her adult life,[42] so she certainly would have observed this Metis custom as a child first-hand on several occasions.

In terms of geography, there was a great deal of difference between some of the posts that Kane visited and those where Isabella lived. Edmonton House, where Kane enjoyed the lusty celebrations put on by the HBC, was always more of a presence than any of the locations where Isabella's father served. Compared to Edmonton House's three thousand acres, Fort Resolution was a mere twenty acres, Fort Norman ten acres, Lapierre House ten acres, Fort Liard three hundred acres, and Fort Simpson one hundred acres.[43]

The complement of men varied greatly from post to post as well. Although there was a fur trade aristocracy, which the Hardisty family clearly belonged to, at most posts the complement of men was often small, rendering distinctions of social status impractical.[44] Of the women he observed at many of the posts, Kane wrote that they found ample employment

> making moccasins and clothing for the men...doing all the household drudgery, in which the men never assist them. The evenings are spent round their large fires in eternal gossiping and smoking.[45]

Thus, when they lived at northern posts, which Isabella's father always did, even if they might have enjoyed the benefits and special status of belonging to the family of the chief factor, clearly Isabella and other fur trade children were expected to take part in some work duties. There is also no doubt that they spent evenings around the fire enjoying the "eternal gossiping and smoking" of the Metis culture, and that they were certainly subjected to many privations.

As testament to the privations and sometimes difficult situations that Isabella experienced at the northern posts, an examination of William Hardisty's correspondence confirms the many outbreaks of illness in the North, when often

> the non-Native HBC servants were afflicted, including W.L. Hardisty at Fort Simpson. In 1866 [when Isabella would have been five years old], reports poured in throughout the winter as the death toll mounted.

The residents of Peel River post were in "a most pitiful condition,"
with most of the best hunters dead and so many orphaned children
that the survivors could scarcely manage to care for them.[46]

In 1867, the winter following this outbreak, Hardisty estimated the
death toll in the Mackenzie district at one thousand, and pleaded
with the HBC to send a doctor: "Let us however for mercy's sake
endeavour to save the remnant of these poor people who survive."[47]

In addition to his concern for health care in the North, Isabella's
father often bemoaned the lack of education his wife, Mary Anne
Allen, had received. In a letter to Sir George Simpson, governor of
the HBC, dated 10 November 1857, Hardisty explained not only his
recent marriage to the seventeen-year-old Mary Anne Allen but also
the emphasis he placed upon formal education:

I was up at Fort Simpson in August and got married there in a very
offhand way to a Miss Allen—she is an orphan, her parents having
died when she was an infant—her education has been very neglected,
and it is my intention to send her to school for a year or two. It is a
very unusual thing to send a Wife to school and no doubt will cause
a laugh at my expense, but I don't care a fig and won't mind the
expense, so long as she is enabled thereby to act her part with credit
in the society among which she is placed—as for the rest, the woman
who I consider good enough to live with, is good enough for my
friends to look at.[48]

Researchers Judith Hudson Beattie and Helen Buss conclude
that William Hardisty did follow through on his plans to educate
his wife, and that she became an "educated elite of fur trade
society."[49] However, there appears to be no formal written record
of Isabella's mother attending any educational institution, and no
letters have been found that were written by her, which suggests
that she received little or no formal education. In fact, William
and Mary Hardisty were married in 1857, and their first surviving

child was born in 1858, followed by another in 1861, and another in 1862. There is no way to know if any children were lost in between these births, which was often the case in early fur trade marriages. Further, in 1869, William still held his wife and her lack of education responsible for problems with his children. In a letter to Miss Davis, the mistress of the school at Red River, William apologized for his children's behaviour:

> I have to thank you for the trouble you must have had with him [Richard]. It is very difficult in this District to keep the children away from the Indians who are always about the house & my children labour under this further disadvantage that their mother has no education. I am generally absent from them all summer, and at intervals during winter, so that they are to be pitied more than blamed for their mischievous habits. I hope therefore that you will excuse them if they are not so good or so well behaved as those who have educated mothers to instil virtuous habits into them from their infancy & to teach them the rudiments of their education...I am willing to recompense you for the extra trouble.[50]

William Hardisty was always concerned with formal education for his family, and there is some evidence that he was anxious to have a convent school built in the Mackenzie district. In a letter to Hardisty from Roman Catholic Bishop Henri Faraud in 1863, the bishop "assured the chief trader he would try to bring the Grey Nuns north not later than the summer of 1865, provided Hardisty helped build them a suitable house." William may have assisted in the building, since nuns were brought to Fort Providence in 1867.[51] Possibly, Mary Allen Hardisty went there for some education, but all indications are that she never left fur trade country for an extended period of time to attend school, as her husband had initially hoped. In addition, as William confirms in this letter, "Indians" were always close at hand, and he was away a good deal of the time, including most of the summers and intervals in winter.

Further, he notes that his wife had no education, and no ability to instil "virtuous habits" in her children. Thus, with her father away so much of the time, and her mother likely having no Euro-North American education, it is reasonable to assume that much of Isabella's early role modelling was from her Metis mother, and that she had ample exposure to Indigenous culture as a child.

Despite her primary parenting role due to his own extended absences, in an 1870 letter, William was still complaining about his wife, this time to the woman who had married his brother, Eliza McDougall Hardisty:

> *I wish my Mary had your kind and gentle way, for I am sure there is the making of a good respectable father of a family in me, if managed in the proper way. It is true I am getting rather crabbed as I increase in years, which makes it all the more necessary to receive a few [sic] to make me a good boy.* [52]

William's letters suggest that, in regard to raising his children, he felt he was at a disadvantage because he had chosen to marry an Indigenous woman, unlike his brother Richard.[53] It is important to note, though, that William's letters, in which he despaired over his wife's shortcomings, were written during the latter part of the fur trade era in the later nineteenth century, when attitudes toward miscegenation were hardening.

Despite the shifting perceptions of mixed marriages (which was not the case for William and Mary Hardisty, as both were Indigenous), William Hardisty's desires to correct his wife's short-comings with Euro-North American education were hampered by the same reality that early fur traders came to understand. Indigenous women possessed a wide range of skills that were critical for survival in fur trade country. With the privations of the North and his extended periods away, William likely soon realized that he could not spare his wife for a "year or two," as he had intended so that she might receive a formal education, even as near at hand as Fort Providence.

In addition to the changed attitudes generally, William's desire to educate his new wife may have been influenced by the feelings that his own father expressed in a letter to his son Richard. In it, the senior Hardisty wrote,

> When I received your letter, I received one also from William, and in it he tells me of his marriage with a Miss Allen from the Columbia. It is a pity she has no education, but I hope William will set to work and educate her himself, as he is well able to do it.[54]

In another letter to William's younger brother Richard, Richard Sr. again implored his son to be cautious about a marriage partner himself, and perhaps revealed that he was not so pleased in William's choice: "I hope you will not think of marrying any girl who is not the Daughter of a respectable family. I do not wish to interfere with you in your choice, but hope you will make a good choice."[55]

While it was a concern for his father and certainly was a sentiment that William Hardisty himself expressed, specifically that he undertook his marriage to a Metis woman in a "very offhand way," William did come to express in his letters what was becoming the commonly held view of such unions. In a letter to James Grahame, dated 19 August 1877, William wondered if the condition of the Indigenous people, who he referred to as "miserable wretches," and who were afflicted with one of the many epidemics that swept the North West, had been brought on by intermarriage.[56] Given that William felt it necessary to apologize for his wife, it is quite likely that he shared (at least publicly) the views of country unions expressed in traders' journals. However, perhaps William Hardisty privately appreciated the Metis culture that many of the HBC families embraced, for it was his expressed desire that Isabella receive her entire education at Red River, where she could be among other HBC children, rather than at Wesleyan Ladies' College in Ontario, which she eventually attended.

While Isabella's time at the eastern school is discussed later, it speaks to William's appreciation for fur trade culture that he wrote in a letter to Miss Davis, the head of the Red River school that Isabella had briefly attended, that "I can never thank you or pay you enough for your kindness and attention to my little girl—whom I fully intended from the first should have finished her education under your direction—had her health permitted."[57] When Isabella did return to the North after her time at school in Ontario, it was only a few years before her father retired from his post with the HBC. In 1878, Isabella's father moved his family to the home of his brother-in-law, Donald A. Smith, in Winnipeg.

Donald Smith had first encountered the Hardisty family when he served in the Esquimaux Bay district of Labrador, where Richard Sr., Isabella's grandfather, had also served. Immediately upon his arrival at Lachine, Richard Hardisty was transferred with his family to the Esquimaux Bay district of Labrador, as Donald Smith had been a short time earlier.[58] After Richard Hardisty was transferred out, Donald Smith assumed the position of chief factor, and soon thereafter married Isabella's aunt, for whom she was named, in the fashion of the country. The district was to be the home of Donald and Isabella Smith for some twenty years.[59]

Donald Smith eventually rose to the position of family patriarch when Isabella's grandfather, Richard, died on 13 October 1865 (when Isabella was just four years old and living at Fort Simpson).[60] Records indicate that Smith not only managed many of the investments for his fur trade family but also served as witness for many of their important events such as funerals and marriages.[61] In fact, Smith always assumed responsibility for helping his Hardisty family and thus was always as good a family man as he was a company man. As noted, after retirement, William Hardisty and his family had spent time at Donald A. Smith's mansion, known as

Silver Heights, near Winnipeg, before moving to Lachine.[62] Smith
mentioned William's plans in a letter to Chief Factor MacFarlane,
dated 26 December 1878, where he wrote, "I saw Wm. L. Hardisty
in Winnipeg the other day. He intends, I believe, settling down at
Lachine next spring and will spend the present winter at my place
at Silver Heights."[63]

While at Silver Heights, Isabella's father demonstrated some of
the same hosting skills that Isabella would later rely on when she
established her position in the new North West. William Hardisty
reportedly "gave splendid parties according to the stories which
rapidly spread among the HBC fraternity."[64] The following year,
William moved his family to Lachine, Quebec, as planned. According
to a letter written by his brother Richard, he continued to be
concerned for William's drinking while in Lachine, writing that he
hoped William would move to a rural area, for "By all accounts it
will be better for him to be away from any place where he can get
liquor for I hear he goes into it pretty freely."[65] William Hardisty did
not have the opportunity to complete a planned western trip after
he moved to Lachine, "for he died of erysipelas on 16 January 1881."[66]

When William died in 1881, his brother Richard Hardisty was
still chief factor for the Saskatchewan district, and was managing
his own growing estate, as well as supervising an addition to the
"Big House" at the fort in Edmonton.[67] It appears that together
Donald Smith and Richard Hardisty, in addition to facilitating a
suitable marriage for Isabella shortly after her father's death, eventually shouldered the burden of caring for Isabella's less responsible
or able siblings.[68] Shortly before his death in 1889, Richard was
working with Smith to assist Mary Hardisty McPherson, who was
widowed and hoping to re-establish herself in the North West with
her family. Smith acknowledged Richard's information about the
"idle Lads" of Mary Hardisty McPherson's but nonetheless committed
five hundred dollars per year for her care.[69]

When Isabella's youngest brother George was temporarily
confined to an asylum in 1884, Donald Smith agreed to cover those

expenses.[70] Later, Richard brought George back to Edmonton with him, where correspondence between Richard and his brother Joseph indicated that, in Joseph's opinion, George's main problem was in leading an "indolent life."[71] Despite concerns about indolence, it appears that both Donald A. Smith and Richard Hardisty continued the tradition established during the fur trade of caring for all members of their kinship network. Although caring for members of families was perhaps not unlike the behaviour of most newcomers to the North West, for the Hardisty family, it was a tradition of their culture born of three generations of fur trade service at northern posts for the Hudson's Bay Company.

While there are not as many details about the Hudson's Bay Company family of Isabella's mother, Mary Anne Allen, it is clear she was born into at least the first generation of an HBC family. Mary Anne Allen was born at Fort Vancouver on 10 August 1840, the daughter of an English man, Robert Allen, and an Indigenous woman, Charlotte Scarborough.[72] Robert Allen had joined the HBC on 31 October 1829, at Portsmouth, Hampshire, sailing shortly thereafter for the Northwest Coast on the brig *Isabella*.[73] At one point, in an undelivered letter to Robert Allen, his mother, Mary, expressed her dismay at not having received any money or word from her son in over two years.[74] It is not clear if Robert Allen ever did contact his mother, but he and his wife Charlotte Scarborough did name their daughter (Isabella's mother) Mary Anne, perhaps after Robert's own mother.

Isabella's grandmother, Charlotte Scarborough, may have been the daughter of Captain James Scarborough and Paly Temalkimi Tchinouk, christened Anne Elizabeth.[75] While there is some question of her parentage, discussed shortly, Charlotte was raised by James and Anne Elizabeth Scarborough. James Scarborough's first contract of service was, interestingly, also aboard a ship named the *Isabella*, in 1829.[76] Before his marriage in 1838, James Scarborough was promoted to commander of the ship, the *Cadboro*,[77] despite complaints that, as first mate on the *Cadboro*, "he did not command that respect as an officer which he ought; that it was said he was given to Liquor."[78] Regardless, Isabella's great-grandfather, Captain Scarborough, was later honoured by having his name used to represent geographic areas, an honour Isabella herself would eventually enjoy in the new society of the North West. Previously known as Chinook Hill, Scarboro Hill (sometimes spelled Scarborough Hill), on the Washington side of the Columbia River, near the town of Chinook, was named in honour of the captain who hailed from Scarborough Head, England.[79] According to a brief article about him in 1947, Captain Scarborough was believed to be among the first "white settlers in the state of Washington." This news report continued that Scarborough took a land claim in 1844, on the edge of the Indigenous fishing village of Chinookville.[80]

The area around Chinookville in the Pacific Northwest was where the first fur trade children were born to Chinook women who inhabited the lower Columbia River Valley, as had Mary Anne Allen in her early formative years.[81] Many of the part-Chinook fur trade children, like Mary Anne Allen, lost their connection to their Chinook kin, who often rejected them,[82] and thus do not fit the more common image of "half-breed" living in between two cultures.[83] The Chinook people, although they promoted unions between their women and fur traders to facilitate trade, did not look favourably on the children of these unions and felt they belonged with the fathers. Thus, much of the history of these fur trade children remains a mystery.

Some of those mysteries persist in Isabella's family. It is not clear when Charlotte Scarborough Allen, Isabella's grandmother, died, but Robert Allen, her grandfather, died in 1845. As alluded to earlier, there is some mystery surrounding the parentage of Charlotte Scarborough and the subsequent care of her daughter (Isabella's mother), Mary Anne Allen, who was five years old when she was apparently orphaned. Regarding Charlotte's parentage, according to a copy of the Catholic Records, James Scarborough and Anne Elizabeth "of the tribe of the Tchinouk" were married on 30 October 1843, and, at the time, had a "legitimate child James aged

18 months."[84] Records indicate that James Scarborough Sr. came to the North West in 1829. Thus, he could not have had a daughter born in fur trade country old enough to marry by 1840, when Robert Allen married Charlotte Scarborough. So, perhaps, Robert Allen's wife, Charlotte, was the daughter of Paly Temalkimi Tchinouk by another man prior to her marriage to James Scarborough. If Charlotte was not James Scarborough's natural daughter, then it is perhaps more understandable that Charlotte's own daughter, Mary Anne Allen, was not cared for by James Scarborough after the deaths of her parents, even though he served as executor of Robert Allen's will and was named as guardian to his children.[85]

While Edwin Ernest Rich's research suggested that the children of Robert Allen and Charlotte Scarborough (likely the step-daughter of James Scarborough) lived with James Scarborough until his death in 1855, the Catholic Records only make note of two boys, Edwin and Robert, living with James Scarborough. These two boys were eventually cared for by James Birney.[86] We do know that Mary Anne Allen was not living with James Scarborough by the time she was six years old but rather was living near Fort Dunvegan in northern fur trade country, where she was baptised.

The history of the man who would eventually be entrusted with the care of Mary Anne Allen's siblings, James Birney, perhaps sheds some light on how Mary Anne Allen appeared at Fort Dunvegan. Birney was born in Scotland and came to Canada at the age of sixteen "to take service in the North West and later in the Hudson's Bay Company. He was stationed at various western posts, but chiefly at Astoria," and, in 1845, he retired to Cathlamet.[87] Although schools at Fort Vancouver in the mid-1800s were likely not up to European standards, there is record of James Birney having attended Fort Vancouver School from 1835 to 1837. Perhaps Birney's education would have confirmed for James Scarborough his suitability to raise Mary Anne Allen's brothers.

There is also some documentation that indicates that James Scarborough viewed James Birney's home as suitable in another way.

In an interview conducted sometime in approximately 1937, a woman named Sarah Scarborough noted that her husband's father was a captain in the British army, and that the Bible given to her mother and father recorded several marriages, including that of James Allen Scarborough to Annie Elizabeth Scarborough and that of Robert Scarborough and Jane West. In the interview, Sarah mentioned that school was held at the home of James Birney, the "only white family here."[88] Although some, including James Scarborough, may have considered James Birney's family to be "white," according to the Catholic Records, James Birney was married to Charlotte Beaulieu, a "metisse from Red River," a woman of

> much ability and independent spirit. She was no less celebrated than her husband for the grand style in which they entertained their guests in their big house on the hill at Cathlamet. Thirteen children were born to them.[89]

There was clearly a connection between Mary Anne Allen's grandfather James Scarborough and James Birney and his Metis wife Charlotte Beaulieu. There are also a number of records held by the Catholic Church that help shed some light on life in the home of James and Anne Elizabeth Scarborough and on the subsequent early experience of Mary Anne Allen.[90] Over the years, numerous infants were baptised in the home of Mary Anne Allen's grandfather, James Scarborough. Some were listed as the children of James and Charlotte Scarborough, and some had parents who were listed as slaves. In addition, on 10 July 1852, a priest provided the Sacraments over the deceased wife of James Scarborough, Anne Elizabeth Scarborough, aged about forty.[91] One year after the death of his wife, on 28 July 1853, another child, Therese, daughter of a female slave, was baptised at the home of James Scarborough.[92]

The series of births and baptisms in the home of James Scarborough and the practice of slave trading in both the Chinook culture and the early culture of the HBC may perhaps be the only indications of how Isabella's mother, Mary Anne Allen, came to be in the North, where she eventually married William Hardisty. The Chinook people were a coastal trading people known to deal in slaves, buying them from southern Oregon and California Indigenous people and selling them to more northerly tribes along the Pacific Coast.[93] Fur trader Alexander Ross noted that slaves performed important functions in the Indigenous economy of the lower Columbia: "Slaves do all the laborious work...and a Chinook matron is constantly attended to by two, three, or more slaves." Slaves were not only food producers—the ethnographies of the Chinook, Haida, and Tahltan contain accounts of slaves hunting—but also served as "units of exchange."[94] Some argue that, by 1843, "everything in the Native world had a price: fur, provisions, labour, slaves, women, and land."[95]

In fact, there is record of some Hudson's Bay Company employees of different ranks and backgrounds marrying or living with First Nation or Metis women of "all classes and cultures, from slaves to nobles."[96] There were accounts of the HBC men keeping slaves at the western headquarters and "Fort Vancouver's traditions of labour and slavery were also carried over into the Willamette settlement... Many settlers married liberated slaves or ones they had bought."[97] In 1836, as a precursor to negotiations for the Oregon territory, William Slacum wrote in his report for the American government that

> Many instances have occurred where a man has sold his own child... Women, who are said to be the owners of the slaves, are frequently bought themselves by the men with whom they live, when they are mere children.[98]

In addition, James Douglas noted there were slaves at Fort Vancouver and that "some are children of tender age."[99]

James Birney and his wife Charlotte Beaulieu Birney had a connection to Mary Anne Allen and cared for her brothers, Edwin and Robert. The Birneys may also have cared for Mary Anne when she became orphaned at a young age and prior to her being sent to the North. According to the notes on the biographical sheets held by the Hudson's Bay archives, Mary Anne Allen remembered other brothers and sisters living in Oregon when both of her parents died. Her guardian after her parents died was to be her grandfather, Captain Scarborough, along with trustee A.C. Anderson.[100] In fact, after Robert Allen and his wife, Charlotte, died, most of the children, except Isabella's mother, appear to have remained in Washington Territory.[101] Since Scarborough, Mary Anne Allen's grandfather and guardian of her siblings, did not die until Mary Anne was sixteen years old, it is still more curious how she found herself at Fort Dunvegan when she was so young.

Whatever the circumstances of her arrival in the North, Mary Anne Allen was only with her guardian and grandfather a short time after her parents' deaths. Robert Allen died in Chinook, Oregon, on 7 March 1845, and Mary Anne, Isabella's mother, was baptised at Fort Dunvegan, in present-day Alberta,[102] one year later on 10 August 1846, when she was approximately six years old.[103] Mary Anne Allen married William Hardisty in the summer of 1857,[104] which would have made her seventeen when her husband was chief factor in charge of Fort Yukon.[105] According to his letter, William married Mary Anne Allen at Fort Simpson, one of the HBC's main centres of distribution and administration.[106] As noted, it is not clear how Isabella's mother went to the North. The only thing that is absolutely clear is that William Hardisty (although Indigenous himself) thought his wife to be of a lower order.

By the time William Hardisty advised his superior, George Simpson, of his marriage in 1857, Simpson had long since deemed it necessary for the advancement of his own career in the HBC to abandon his various Indigenous partners and to finally bring his British-born cousin, Frances, to fur trade country as his wife in 1830.[107] This likely helped Simpson, as the highest-ranking officer, to portray himself as the model of decorum, discipline, and gentlemanly character. It is likely that, in order for the company to maintain its patriarchal structure at fur trade posts, and given that so many of the servants were now taking country wives, officers like Simpson felt it necessary to take Euro-North American wives and turn their backs on their own Indigenous wives and their children. Although the long custom of unions between company men and Indigenous women continued, Simpson's new policy no doubt convinced men like Isabella's father that they now had to explain their choices of marriage partners if they were Indigenous.[108]

It is evident that William Hardisty felt the need to explain his reasons for choosing a Metis woman, or as he described her, an "ignorant girl." Hardisty clearly hoped Simpson would see his decision as a better option than "keeping a mistress," as others were doing,[109] as he noted in another letter to Simpson. In this letter, William now wrote that Mary Anne Allen was of "reputable parentage" (although still admitting she was not educated). Whatever the circumstances of Mary Anne 's appearance in the North, it is not likely that William would have noted that information in any correspondence but preferred to refer to his wife as simply an ignorant girl. In this correspondence, William continued,

> We—the officers of McKRr have been greatly scandalized of late, by one of our Colleagues Keeping a Mistress-, and not being certain which I might be allowed to leave this district, I considered it better to marry even an ignorant girl, than pine away in solitary misery at the Youcon—or disgrace myself, and the service to which I belong, by imitating the example set us by Mr C.T. Ross...I have been more comfortable and happier since my marriage than I have been at any time during the last 10 or 12 years. Even the absence of my wife would be less unpleasant & more bareable [sic] than the consciousness of being single, unthought of, and uncared for, by any one.[110]

> Mary Anne Allen Hardisty Thomas, sometime after her 1881 marriage to Edwin Stuart Thomas. Photo dated 1880s. Glenbow Alberta Museum and Archives NA-2758-1.

Whether he really believed she was an ignorant girl, it appears that Mary Anne Allen was a suitable and competent partner to help William Hardisty at the northern posts where he always worked. Given she was there at such a young age, Mary Anne would have adjusted from a lifestyle reliant on fishing and trading, common to the coastal Chinook people, to a hunting lifestyle and, indeed, to all aspects of northern Metis culture. Yet, despite her early acculturation as a Metis living in the North, Mary Anne eventually once claimed she was French,[111] perhaps partly due to William's apparent need to explain his marriage choice. Regardless, there appears to be only one photo of Mary Anne that was preserved, and that photo, along with her documented history, belies her claim of French ancestry.[112] Yet the fact that she chose to identify as French on at least one occasion may harken back to her early connection to the wife of James Birney, Charlotte Beaulieu, who had ties to the important French Metis northern fur trading family.

Mary Anne Allen's exposure to an important northern Metis fur trading family may also speak to her feelings about sending her own daughter away from fur trade country to be educated. Although it is common knowledge in fur trade historiography that HBC men sent their children away to be educated, as did most of the Hardisty family, there is little to indicate how Indigenous women such as Mary Anne felt when they were forced to watch their young children leave fur trade country. In one documented case, Johnny Grant recalled that his Metis mother, Marie Anne Breland, insisted that her husband Richard Grant not send her children away, to which he agreed.[113]

In Isabella's case, she was sent to Red River to attend school at a young age, so either her mother shared William Hardisty's desire that their children acquire the skills that would allow them to succeed in Euro-North American society, or she may simply have not had much say in this decision. Either way, there were surely some concerns with a young child being so far removed from her family,

and this is likely why William Hardisty expressed a clear preference for a school in Red River rather than the Ontario school that
Isabella eventually attended. In regard to the culture with which
Isabella was familiar, it is true she was born at Fort Resolution,
an isolated post on the south shore of Great Slave Lake,[114] so she
cannot be considered a "Red River Métis." Yet the majority of
residents at this northern post with which Isabella would have
had contact were Dene or Metis, and both of her parents were
Indigenous. Clearly, some of the culture she encountered at Red
River would have been familiar to Isabella, given that

> In such centres as Fort Smith, Fort Chipewyan, Fort Simpson, and
> Fort Liard, the Métis formed an integral part of the community...
> These people carried the culture, values and personal identifications
> of the southern Métis; they...deemed themselves a distinct social
> group.[115]

In addition to the northern Metis who frequented the posts,
several Dené people traded and served as provisioners at posts where
Isabella's father served, primarily the Chipewyan, the Slaveys, the
Yellowknives, and the Dogrib.[116] Given the great distances these
people travelled, it was common to establish camps near the posts
for extended periods. This gave the children of HBC men ample
opportunity to associate with many Indigenous people. While summer
tended to be a period of inactivity at many of the northern posts,
often mission-trading complexes remained viable throughout the
year and were hosts to large temporary gatherings. For example, one
report refers to a gathering of three hundred Indigenous people at
Fort Rae.[117] In addition, the Fort Simpson journal for the period 1862
to 1865 records the presence of Reverend W. Kirby and the baptism
of several Indigenous babies, often with William and Mary Hardisty
serving as godparents.[118] Their participation again suggests some
socialization with visiting groups.

In addition to the lack of educational facilities, perhaps it was this socialization and the recreational pursuits in the North that convinced Isabella's father that it was best for his daughter to live elsewhere, but in a culture with which she was familiar. On one occasion, William Hardisty wrote to his Euro-North American sister-in-law, Eliza McDougall Hardisty, and bemoaned the lack of care given by his wife. There is no way to know what occupied Isabella while at the northern posts, but she undoubtedly joined in some traditional activities alongside her mother (particularly when she returned to the North as a teenager), such as dressing skins, gumming canoes, and making moccasins, clothing, fishnets, and snowshoes.[119]

In fact, records kept by Europeans during the late nineteenth century demonstrate that the subsistence sector of the fur trade required that domestic work be done by women, some of which also included fishing, snaring, gathering, and gardening. Missionary records suggest that children participated in the drying of meat and preparing of skins, as well as in hunting and fishing. Women and children at the various posts also often engaged in hauling firewood, sometimes from great distances depending upon the remoteness of the post.[120] While there were distinct class differences among HBC men, these divisions were no doubt blurred when families faced starvation conditions. Given the remoteness of the northern posts, fur traders were required to rely on locally available raw materials and thus to be fairly self-sufficient and open to adopting many of the Indigenous customs.[121] There were even instances when fort employees lived with the Indigenous population in the bush when provisions were low at the posts.[122] However, there is no indication from Isabella that she and her family lived in the bush during times of privation.

Although she may not have actually lived in the bush, the attempt to groom Isabella to "gracious womanhood" at European-styled schools would have faced some challenges, given the realities of survival strategies in the North. While Isabella's mother tended to her traplines, and her father to company business, what were the young ones doing? This was a concern for William, who surely worried about the freedom his children had in "running wild."[123] No doubt many HBC men had similar misgivings about their children adopting an Indigenous way of life that was increasingly viewed as "primitive, heathen, and dangerous."[124] William Hardisty was familiar with the dangers of living in the North, and he was well aware of the family dynamics of the northern Metis.

The Beaulieu family, one of the most prominent Metis families in the North, was very familiar to William Hardisty. While Isabella eventually named her grand mansion Beaulieu (the house referred to by locals in Calgary as the "Big House"), it is difficult to ascertain any specific reason why she chose a name that became culturally significant to the Metis in the North. The Beaulieus were independent fur traders who were a major contact for Red River traders, and who had long-established kinship links with the Chipewyan.[125] For a time, the HBC had eventually secured the allegiance of "Francois *père et fils* in 1863 to act as traders for the Company. The Beaulieus held out for a time, but when their shipment of trade goods failed to arrive in 1866, they finally agreed to cooperate with the HBC."[126] This assessment suggests the HBC had long recognized the importance of the Beaulieu family in northern fur trade country.

There was a time when the Beaulieu men were of special assistance to William Hardisty. Francois Beaulieu II had once restored order to the fur brigade under the command of a young William Hardisty. According to Father Louis Menez, who served for years at Saint Joseph's Parish in Fort Resolution, when the fur brigade rebelled near Salt River, Beaulieu, the

> *old dictator came, pulled his long knife and pretended to shave his tobacco plug. "Get back to your boat and give no more trouble to your chief" he told the rebels who were in their boats. They feared*

Beaulieu's knife. Hardisty gave the old rascal a suitable present for his trouble.[127]

Although "Old Beaulieu" might have saved William's life, by 1869, Isabella's father felt it necessary to advise William McMurray of the HBC about his concern that Francois Beaulieu, the son of Old Beaulieu, might be tampering with "Our Indians in favour of the Free Traders—His brothers also whose contracts expire next spring are speaking of going to Lac La Biche in the interests of the opposition." Hardisty continued that the Beaulieus should be "treated with the utmost rigour, and should not on any account be employed hereafter."[128] In early 1870, William Hardisty again expressed his feelings regarding the Beaulieu men:

> *As for Beaulieu & his sons I wish to have nothing to do with them & have always said so, altho [sic] I thought it would quiet the old man, & prevent him from doing mischief if he received a small pension, especially as he had been allowed good wages before by Christie & Campbell—tho otherwise left free to do as they pleased— As to his being of any use to us in "R" it is simply ridiculous—my only object in keeping his sons in the service hitherto was to keep them out of mischief & to prevent their joining the opposition, but I always fully intended to dismiss them on the first symtoms [sic] of dishonesty or disloyalty to the Co.—& from the complaints of those immediately connected with them now there is very little hopes that any of them will be continued in "R" after next spring.*[129]

Many of the Metis, particularly the Beaulieus, with their large families, were sometimes seen as a threat to the HBC. As early as 1860, the company sought to replace the Metis with single men, whether Scotsmen, Canadians, or Iroquois.[130] In 1872, Donald A. Smith and Richard Hardisty corresponded about using the Yukon River and portages between the Bell River, East Rat River, and Peel River in order to transport all freight from the Mackenzie and

Athabasca districts, thus hopefully reducing expenses by half and allowing a discharge of "Indian voyageurs, all expensive servants... and all those married with families."[131] Reportedly, in 1875, William planned to send the Metis

> boatmen with large families out of the district as their contracts expired. This was not entirely an economizing move. Hardisty feared that the Metis with their intricate web of relationships would "join in plotting mischief against the Company or their Officers," or intrigue with the Indians, or join the opposition freetraders.[132]

As Martha McCarthy notes, in the southern Mackenzie region, a

> Métis society of descendants of the voyageurs was a well-recognized entity. They spoke French, were Roman Catholics, and considered themselves a distinct social group. Their long presence in the north, their mobility from one post to another, and their intricate web of relationships gave them a familiarity with the region as a whole which was uniquely Métis.[133]

By the time of the 1875 report by William Hardisty, this most powerful of the northern Metis families had lost its "patriarch," when Old Beaulieu died as a result of one of the devastating epidemics of scarlet fever and measles that swept through the North in 1872.[134] No doubt some welcomed Old Beaulieu's death. During the final takeover of the North West Company by the HBC, François Beaulieu, referred to by the Oblates as "the patriarch" or "Le Bonhomme Beaulieu," had engaged in the violent struggle between the two companies, even becoming involved in a plot to kill HBC man John Clarke, for which he was to receive Clarke's wife and property.[135] Although he did eventually come to work with the HBC, Beaulieu remained a free trader to the end, and his ties to the Oblates "always caused some suspicions at the HBC that the priests supported his freetrading."[136] Thus, the Beaulieu family had two strikes against them in the eyes of most HBC men—not only were they free traders but they were Roman Catholic as well.

Despite the eventual enmity, and as was the case when William's men were cautioned by Old Beaulieu, there is more evidence of an earlier congenial relationship between William and some of the Beaulieu family. In the daily journal for Fort Simpson from 1862 to 1865, when Isabella was approximately two to six years old, a man referred to as "King Beaulieu" made regular visits to the post.[137] At times, the loads of fish delivered by King Beaulieu would no doubt relieve long periods of privation, as post journals often noted that berry-picking expeditions led by Mary Hardisty, and no doubt including Isabella, sometimes yielded only a "very small quantity collected."[138] On one occasion, Isabella noted that she and her siblings were sent with their mother to another post because they faced starvation. The times when food was scarce are corroborated in the diary of Selina Cox Bompas, wife of Bishop William Bompas, who served at Fort Simpson in the 1870s when Isabella was a young girl. The diary suggests there were times when the residents of that HBC post were very near starvation.[139]

Given these privations, post journals noting that "King Beaulieu arrived with 3900 fish from Big Island"[140] might make a lasting impression upon a young girl, but they might also seem quite ordinary. On another occasion, when "Mr. Hardisty had a long 'Council' with the Indians, regarding the price paid at Fort Rae for furs...King Beaulieu was his most efficient interpreter."[141] While William eventually demonstrated much disdain for some of the Beaulieu family, he also recognized their importance in the North, as would Isabella.

Yet, given Isabella's eventual determination to establish herself as the grand lady of the new society in the West, it is difficult to believe she would have openly embraced a name known for its significance to the Metis history and culture. It could be, as some have speculated, that "Beaulieu" was chosen as the name for Isabella's palatial home simply because it meant "beautiful place" in French.[142] Or it could be that, given their emerging roles in the new economy, the name "Beaulieu" was chosen by both James and Isabella because of its links to European aristocracy.[143]

That Isabella was able to become "Lady Lougheed" of Beaulieu House is due, in part, to the fact that her mother and father sent her away from northern fur trade country to be educated in Euro-North American schools. It was perhaps even more important for William to ensure that his daughter was educated, given he was not able to provide his wife with a formal education and that she was of a "lower position." The fact that her husband considered her to be of a lower position may have induced Mary Hardisty to desire that Isabella be educated and thus lend her support to her young daughter undertaking such an arduous journey out of fur trade country.

As an adult, speaking of her journey out of the North to attend the school operated by Miss Davis near present-day Winnipeg, Isabella recalled for her interviewer that she first set out by York boat,

> walking portages of ten and twelve miles through mosquito-infested areas, voyaging down the Saskatchewan River via Fort Carleton and Prince Albert, and overland by prairie Schooner. On this trip she caught scarlet fever and for a year and a half afterward lay ill in bed. Then her grandmother, who was living at Lachine, Quebec [where many HBC men retired] sent for her.[144]

Although she was speaking by this time as Lady Lougheed, Isabella still seemed intent on reminding her contemporaries that she was, at the very least, a pioneer capable of walking portages and of surviving privations.

Today, there sits a plaque outside of Isabella's first school in Red River identifying it as Twin Oaks. To Miss Davis and her students it was known as Oakfield. As the plaque explains, the house was built in the mid-1850s to serve as a residence for a private girls' school operated by Matilda Davis until 1873.[145] The girls at Miss Davis's school were primarily daughters of HBC men, sent there to be educated as English ladies by a woman who had become one herself when she left fur trade country to attend school in Europe. To that end, the girls were taught French, music, drawing, dancing, needle work, and deportment.[146]

It is not clear exactly how long Isabella attended Miss Davis's school, since there is only record of tuition for the year 1867.[147] While Isabella's father expressed a preference for her to be educated in Red River, shortly after arriving there to attend Miss Davis's school, Isabella became ill and was sent to Lachine to be cared for by her grandmother. Isabella would have been around six years old at that time. It was in the same year that tuition was paid for her at the Red River school, 1867, that Isabella's grandmother Marguerite Sutherland Hardisty reported in a letter to her son Richard that Isabella was in Lachine, and that she had "improved wonderfully since she arrived, the cough she was so much troubled with has almost entirely left her."[148] Isabella remembered that, after she became ill while at Miss Davis's school, the man who escorted her to Lachine from Red River was the son of the man who had built Whitby Ladies' College in Ontario.[149] Whoever that man was, he likely had a role in Isabella later being sent to Wesleyan Ladies' College in Ontario.

While Isabella was at the school in Ontario, her father wrote a letter to Miss Davis, explaining the reason for her departure. Following the lengthy quotation included earlier, William went on to express regret that Isabella had "gone back in everything, and what is still more to be regretted, she has lost a good deal of that religious feeling and firm reliance on her Creator that she learnt [sic] from you."[150] There is further indication that William and his family did not feel the quality of the education, or at least the cultural experience, at Wesleyan Ladies' College measured up to that offered at Miss Davis's school. Thomas Hardisty wrote to Miss Davis, complaining that he did not think Isabella was improving much. Rather, he said,

*if I may judge from her writing...it is not so good as when she came
down here [Montreal] last fall. Anyway I know if she were my
daughter I would never send her to a school such as she is at just
now—for the reason that there are too many scholars and the
teachers can never look after all of them properly.*[151]

One might think the Hardistys, with their adherence to the
Protestant faith and the value of work and education for both sons
and daughters, would appreciate a more liberal education like that
offered at Wesleyan. Perhaps William was primarily concerned
about Isabella because she was so far removed from other children
of the fur trade, most of whom remained in Red River.[152] At the
time of William's letter to Miss Davis in 1870, "Bella" was in Lachine
for a visit during a school break, and her father again expressed his
concern for his daughter, in particular that she may become a
"woman of the world." He wrote,

*Bella was quite well—her cough had entirely left her—but they were
spoiling her by allowing her to pass her holidays with too many
different families. She will form no real or lasting friendship and
settle down at last into a mere woman of the world.*[153]

Perhaps some of William's concerns were born of the fact that
Isabella had left her immediate family at a relatively young age and
that she was so far removed from northern fur trade country. There
is some indication that Isabella may have had a brief visit from either
her father or mother in 1868, when both were in Lachine to bury their
young son, Edward Stewart Hardisty,[154] but she would not have
enjoyed many visits from them. On one occasion, when Isabella was
approximately twelve years old, Donald A. Smith referred to "little
Isabelle" in his letter to Richard Hardisty in December of 1872, noting
that "all at Lachine are well as are also those of my own household."[155] Although Isabella was not in the North with her parents,
when she was not at school she was being cared for by Marguerite

Sutherland Hardisty, another woman of Metis ethnicity familiar with HBC fur trade culture.

Though she was in close contact with her grandparents while she was at school, being separated from her parents must have been difficult for Isabella. While there do not appear to be any letters remaining that she might have written home while she was away at school, there is one from her cousin, young Richard Hardisty, written while he was at school in Europe. In a letter addressed to "my dear father," postmarked Merchiston Castle, Edinburgh, 28 October 1885, and signed "your loving son," Richard expressed not only his desire to please his father but implored him to write:

> I wish you would write to me I have not had a letter from across the ocean for nearly seven weaks [sic] and so now if I was to get a letter I would feel so much better because it seams [sic] so dul [sic] to see the other boys getting their letter and I standing and looking at them reading and I have nothing to do so I wish you would write as often as you can...I would feal [sic] a great deal better so pleas [sic] write...Perhaps you are to [sic] busy to write but if you are surly [sic] Ma or Clara are not too busy...I wish you would write to Mr. Rogerson and tell him all you would like me to do.[156]

We might assume that Isabella shared some of the same sentiments of loneliness expressed by her cousin Richard when she found herself so isolated not only from her parents who remained in the North West but from her culture. School calendars confirm that Isabella was one of only a few students at Wesleyan from northern HBC country, while most others came from Ontario, Quebec, or the United States.[157]

Perhaps William was aware of some of Isabella's challenges in her new school. In a letter to Eliza McDougall Hardisty, William again expressed his concern that Isabella would become too worldly:

You did not say much about my little girl. It is a theme I never hear
of poor child [sic] they are knocking her about very much and I fear
[she] will become worldly minded and superficial, a kind of cosmo-
politan lady of the world, with hosts of acquaintances, but few real
friends in the proper sense of the term. She was very attentive to her
religious duties when she left Miss Davis [sic] school but I was sorry
to observe that she became less so after she went to Canada. I have
not had a line from Dr. Rice or even Mr. and Mrs. Wright about
Bella since I left Canada and she herself is so nervous and frustrate
[sic] that she cannot write an intelligible letter. She is always in
such a hurry to get to the end of it in fact it is altogether illegible
and unintelligible. I have told her now that she must try to write a
good plain hand before she attempts a running hand. Her ideas go
faster than her pen and the poor girl makes a sad mess of it but she
may improve as she grows older.[158]

Again, William bemoaned the shortcomings he saw in his own wife
when compared to Eliza, writing, "I wish my Mary had your kind,
gentle way."[159]

In 1872, while still at Wesleyan, Isabella was again mentioned
in a letter from Marguerite Sutherland Hardisty to her son Richard.
In the letter, Marguerite referred to Isabella's mother as Mrs.
William, for whom Bella was sending a "small parcel." The letter,
which suggested that Marguerite was aware of her granddaughter's
unhappiness at Wesleyan, went on to say that William had written
his mother advising that he "thought of removing his daughter
Bella from Hamilton, but as he did not intend staying much longer
in the service, he thought it hardly any use to do so."[160]

There is some correspondence that suggests Isabella stood out
as "different" while at Wesleyan, which likely contributed to her
unhappiness and the nervousness her father noted. Reports about
Isabella surfaced later when a few of the alumnae also returned
to the West after they left Wesleyan.[161] It is from one alumna in

particular that we learn about some of the students' perspectives on Isabella. In the annual report of 1962–1963, Louise Purchase

> read an interesting paper on the life of her mother who was Nettie (Janet) Coatsworth, daughter of Emerson Coatsworth, [and who] attended the Hamilton Ladies College from 1875–1879. She empha-sized the influence of her years in the college on her life as a pioneer mother and community leader on the prairie in Saskatchewan.[162]

Purchase went on to explain that her mother, Nettie Coatsworth, received her Mistress of English Literature Degree from Wesleyan. Apparently, Nettie often shared with her daughter fond memories of visiting prominent Hamilton homes with her classmates, and parading to "Church (Centenary) with classmates and teacher." According to Purchase, her mother recalled that fellow classmate, Isabella Hardisty, now "Lady Lougheed, wife of Senator Lougheed, [was the] daughter of an Indian chief. Her name was Bella Hardisty. She attended in Mother's time."[163] Where the girls at Wesleyan got the idea that Isabella was the daughter of an "Indian chief" is not clear, but they were clearly aware that she was Indigenous and "different."

In 1927, the *Hamilton Herald* alluded to the different classes of girls that attended Wesleyan, when it referred to tuitions that ranged from "$143 per annum to $275." The newspaper concluded, "One could imagine the arrogant misses of that time boasting that they were on the $275 course to some poor lass who was paying $175 or less."[164] Many of Wesleyan's records were destroyed, thus there is no way to know the tuition her father paid for Isabella's attendance. Yet the fact she seemed to have achieved some noto-riety as the daughter of an "Indian chief" suggests she was regarded as belonging to a different class than other girls, regardless of the tuition paid. It is not totally clear what effect her "special" status had on Isabella, but she did not graduate like many of the other girls did. Rather, she returned to her family in the North in her teens.

After having been away at school in Ontario, life was no doubt different for Isabella at the northern posts. Isabella wrote in a letter to her aunt, Eliza McDougall Hardisty, that she wished to spend the next winter with her. One of the reasons given by Isabella was that she found it "hard when I cannot practise my music. I will be glad when we go out, I am sure I will sit at a piano all day long if I get a chance."[165] Eliza McDougall would not have been familiar with the lifestyle at northern posts, thus Isabella would naturally speak of something they may have in common, such as piano playing.

Yet, later in life, Isabella continued to refer to a "genteel" lifestyle when she spoke of some aspects of her youth, such as the time she had spent with her grandmother in Lachine prior to her arrival at Wesleyan. She commented that, although there had been many "privations" in her early life, she had never had to do "much hard work, having been in school, and my grandmother had had twelve servants."[166] Surely, Isabella's early years at forts Resolution, Liard, and Simpson, along with the three years spent at Fort Rae and again at Fort Simpson after her time at Wesleyan, were key periods in her life. Living at northern posts necessitated that *all* family members contribute to the physical labour required to ensure survival. These contributions were crucial—Isabella once noted a shortage of food so severe that she was sent to another post with her mother and siblings in order to survive one particularly difficult winter. It appears that, after 1821, there was often limited capacity on the part of the HBC's transportation system, meaning that the quantities of supplies sent to the Mackenzie River area were inadequate to meet the demands of Indigenous people.[167] After having been away at school in the east, the privations of the North were no doubt difficult to become re-accustomed to. When speaking to the media later in life, Isabella may not have wanted to recall those difficulties as she focused on maintaining a higher status in her southern Alberta community.

While she did not speak much about her time at Wesleyan, Isabella once reminisced,

For years and years I was the youngest of the three hundred girls who attended there. At eighteen I went back to Fort Simpson, where I lived for three years.[168]

In this instance, her recollections are inaccurate. Wesleyan has records of Isabella's attendance from 1868 to 1875.[169] Given that she was born in 1861, Isabella would have been fourteen years old when she left the college. Thus, she would have spent another three years as a young teen in fur trade country. There is some suggestion that Isabella did return to school in 1877, but no indication which school.[170] Wherever it was, it would only have been a short stay, since Isabella's father retired from the HBC in June 1878, and the family, including Isabella, arrived in Winnipeg in October to spend the winter at Donald A. Smith's residence.[171]

It is not clear if Isabella understood her Uncle Donald Smith's role in the political happenings of the North West. However, Isabella was at the eastern school when fighting erupted in the first Metis resistance in 1869. Thus, she would have been exposed to the sentiments of Canadians with regard to the Metis.[172] Also, not long after her marriage to James Lougheed, when fighting erupted again between the Metis and government troops, Isabella undoubtedly attended and then read the account of the military funeral held for her brother, Private Richard Hardisty, whose body was being sent from Moose Jaw to Winnipeg in May of 1885.[173] She was likely there on 24 May 1885 as all heard the "Toll for the Brave," when her brother was laid to rest during a funeral service that resulted in a gathering the size of which was never "before seen in Winnipeg or in the North West." During the funeral service, Isabella would have heard that the community, although mourning the dead, recognized the necessity of the losses so that the "stability of our institutions and security under good government" would continue.[174] While in

Winnipeg for the funeral, Isabella also likely read the story of the battle that led to her brother's death. It may have been ironic for Isabella to read in the newspaper that Riel's soldiers were assured of their reward in Heaven should they die, while knowing that her own brother was "shot through the head" at 8:00 P.M. on 16 May 1885, and died the following morning at 5:00 A.M.[175]

No doubt, Isabella read the tribute to Private Hardisty, published on 28 May 1885, which indicated that Richard Hardisty had lived with the Inkster family in Seven Oaks from the time he was ten until he was seventeen years of age, while he attended St. John's College. Given that he was at the school in the Red River area for so long, those who spoke of him at his funeral likely knew Richard better than did his sister Isabella. The newspaper story on Richard's death described him as "liberal, bright, chatty, cheerful and interesting...he was the life of his friends."[176] are words used to describe Richard. Despite her physical distance from her brother, the words used to describe him could also apply to Isabella, given that she made such a lasting impression as a "gracious woman" when she became first lady and primary hostess of the new North West.

The persona of the gracious woman she was cultivating likely prevented Isabella from commenting publicly about the fighting in Batoche, even though her family had been very personally involved in the politics of the day. For the most part, gracious womanhood necessitated the appearance of publicly embracing the emerging Anglo-dominated society of the new North West and refraining from political commentary. Yet Isabella's appearance always thwarted a completely successful subsuming of her ethnicity. Her facial features confirmed her Metis ancestry. Indeed, a man, who was himself familiar with attempted assimilation, Sylvester Clark Long, confirmed Isabella's ancestry. Long was better known to his contemporaries and in history as Chief Buffalo Child Long Lance, a man believed at the time to be the son of a Blackfoot chief. As Long Lance, Long, who was actually descended from black slaves, achieved some noto-riety, and many residents of the West read his words. Long Lance confirmed in writing what many already knew about Isabella but perhaps did not speak of, noting in an article for the *Mentor*, "Some of western Canada's best citizens are of Scotch and Indian descent. Lady Lougheed, wife of Sir James Lougheed, minister of the interior, is a half-breed."[177]

Aside from her physical appearance, there is a brief but rather telling assessment of Isabella's character that belies the rather simplistic conclusion that the agenda of "gracious womanhood" and the abandonment of her Metis culture were a fait accompli. According to a letter written on 11 December 1876 to her uncle, Richard Hardisty, from Fort Chipewyan, the unnamed author expressed regret that Isabella had left Wesleyan so soon. The author shared his doubts about Isabella's ability to assimilate to European-inspired gracious womanhood, saying,

> Miss Bella Hardisty is passing the winter at this place—it is to be regretted that she was removed so soon from the Canadian Institution where she was being educated—2 or 3 years longer would have turned out a highly accomplished and charming young lady.[178]

Given the isolation in which Isabella lived during a good part of her childhood, it is understandable that some who knew her as a youngster might doubt her eventual ability to succeed as a gracious woman. There is some indication that even Isabella might have felt she was not fitting in at Wesleyan, which was so far removed from her family and the northern fur posts where she spent her early childhood.

However, those who doubted Isabella's abilities to become "highly accomplished" and "charming" not only underestimated Isabella but the resilience of her family network. Like many HBC men, William Hardisty had sent his daughter to school so she would be English rather than Metis, and for the most part Isabella did not disappoint. She became the gracious "English" wife of a man who would become one of the new economy's most successful businessmen and community leaders. Yet, as an adult, she continued to rely on the extended family network of the Hardistys and on the culture that she had learned in her formative years—a culture and family that helped her to transition from a child of the northern fur trade to a respected pioneer.

3

Gracious Womanhood

IT IS SAID that the poet E. Pauline Johnson could transition before her captivated audience from "pure Indian" to "almost white," simply through a change of clothing. This may speak to the cliché that the "clothes make the (wo)man."[1]

In the only known video recording of Isabella Hardisty Lougheed, produced by Dr. Burwell James Charles,[2] Isabella, dressed in European-inspired finery, posed in front of her grand home, Beaulieu. Unfortunately, the audio portion no longer exists, but Isabella is clearly directing the activity on the grounds. The recording is not dated; however, Isabella appears to be past middle age, and thus the filming was likely done sometime in the 1930s.[3] She is of smaller stature, and her facial features reflect her Indigenous ancestry. Yet the majority of the press reports about Isabella, which often included elaborate descriptions of her attire, suggest the public persona of a woman who was not Indigenous but rather a woman who internalized the finer aspects of European-inspired gracious womanhood.

That she was able to internalize these finer aspects of graciousness does not negate the fact that Isabella became a political person, nor does it suggest she abandoned her Metis culture and history. In fact, Isabella proved adept at networking with the right people, and she demonstrated the diplomacy of an accomplished Hudson's Bay Company chief factor. She became a recognized and important public figure in her own right, with newspapers commenting on her every move, from her dancing partners to her grand home and garden, to her family connections with HBC men.

That Isabella succeeded in constructing her persona as the gracious first lady of the North West (who was nonetheless a respected pioneer) is evident. It is also evident that Isabella and James formed a highly successful business partnership. Together they helped establish many of the community-building organizations and cultural venues that were necessary for the West to portray itself as progressive and sophisticated. Yet James was a staunch Methodist with roots in Protestant groups such as the Orangemen, and he had married a woman of Indigenous ancestry. Despite the social capital her kinship group provided, there was still a need to extend a social network that would include primarily Euro-North American political and business leaders and even British royalty. With James away so much of the time, the social networking in Calgary was often left in Isabella's capable hands.

Isabella's preparation for her life as the wife of a public figure began when she was just a young girl in northern fur trade country. At a young age, she was sent away for formal educationl, trained to be a gracious woman. Given that her father had retired to Lachine, Quebec (when Isabella was of marrying age), where many of the HBC officers retired, the plan was likely that Isabella would marry in the East, and the expectation was likely that her husband would be connected to the fur trade. It was in 1879 that Isabella had left the West for what she may have thought would be the last time. However, Isabella's father died on 16 January 1881, and her mother married Edwin Stewart (also known as Stuart) Thomas, a man with far fewer connections than the Hardisty family, in Winnipeg, in August of 1883.[4]

It is not clear if Isabella was in Winnipeg with her mother between the time of her father's death and her mother's remarriage, or if she stayed in Lachine with other family members. The only indication that she was already separated from her mother was her comment made later to a newspaper, when Isabella said that her father's death

> *necessitated the breaking up of our home, and on this occasion I came to Calgary to visit my uncle...I came here in 1882, and I never went east to live again, for I was married in 1884.* [5]

If Isabella's dates are correct and she arrived in Calgary in 1882, then she and her brothers Frank and Thomas came to live with their uncle, Richard Hardisty, one year prior to her mother's marriage and one year after her father's death. [6]

According to some sources, in 1882, when Isabella likely arrived to live with him, Richard Hardisty was the wealthiest man in the North West. [7] The fact that he was so wealthy would have made the arrival of family members, and his niece in particular, noteworthy. As the North West was evolving from fur trade to sedentary economy, the arrival of young ladies was always a newsworthy event. As the local newspaper, the *Calgary Herald*, wrote, the appearance of these young ladies was akin to the arrival of "angels," bringing joy to "especially those in the legal profession." [8] Reminiscing about those early days in Calgary, Isabella recalled,

> *Those were happy days. We used to ride miles and miles around— we knew everybody—girls were few and always very popular, and our social life centered around the homes and the church. My aunt was an ardent Methodist. She was the daughter of the Rev. George McDougall, the first Methodist Missionary in the west, and she was very keen to start a Methodist church. No building could be secured and my uncle finally managed to get a large tent.* [9]

It was only a year after Isabella's arrival at Calgary, that, in the late summer of 1883, her future husband, James Alexander Lougheed, moved from Medicine Hat to Calgary.[10] Despite his Irish working-class background, when the ambitious young lawyer arrived in Calgary, James garnered a fair bit of attention. At a time when lawyers often served as brokers for business investments of all sorts, the *Calgary Herald* noted that James was seen as a "valuable acquisition to Calgary society."[11]

Although he may have been a valuable acquisition to Calgary society, James Lougheed had a fairly humble background and he arrived in the West with few assets and influential connections. He was born in Brampton, Ontario, on 1 September 1854 to a Methodist family of Scottish and Irish descent. His father was a carpenter, a trade he hoped to pass along to James. The family resided in Cabbagetown, the poor eastern section of Toronto, which was English-speaking, Protestant, and highly British and Orange in sentiment and tradition. The Cabbagetown of Lougheed's youth comprised

> lines of utilitarian frame houses, largely covered over in roughcast plaster...thinly built, lacking central heating, and boasting privies out back...a drab industrial environment with dirt, debris and fumes of factories close at hand.[12]

His mother believed that James should aspire to more than carpentry,[13] and she encouraged him to accept a position as assistant librarian at Trinity Church in Toronto. Trinity was sometimes referred to as "the Poor Man's Church," where parishioners were likely to be bricklayers, mariners, servants, and tavern keepers, with only a few listed as "gentlemen."[14] It was at this church, however, that James was encouraged by the Anglican layman, Samuel Blake (who went on to become a Member of Parliament)[15] to further his education at Weston High School.

According to the *Newsletter of the Lougheed Families of North America*, James spent his spare time as a young man attending church meetings, listening to the speeches at the House of Parliament, or fulfilling his duties as chaplain in the Orange Order, duties that included donning a white gown and carrying a Bible in parades.[16] There is no evidence of James continuing his involvement with the Orangemen when he later lived in Calgary, perhaps in part because he married an Indigenous woman with an influential kinship network.

While still in Ontario in 1877, James had studied law with the Toronto firm of Beatty, Hamilton and Cassels. In 1881, James opened his own law office in Toronto but only practised a short time before heading west in 1882 with his brother Sam. The 1880s were times of expansion in the North West, and James quickly gained an appointment to practise law in the Manitoba Court of Queen's Bench and County Courts.[17] James kept a diary for most of his adult life and, while the entries for the period when he was married to Isabella are not very detailed, the entries for his days in Winnipeg are more revealing of his personality. As a young man intent on making his fortune in the West, James was quite pleased to note everything from who preached the services to the amount he spent on his first suit, even noting in his diary the first time he wore the new suit.[18] Although he was beginning to make some good connections in Winnipeg, James was not there long. When the Canadian Pacific rail line was completed to Medicine Hat in 1883, he soon travelled to the end of that line, where he set up a general store in a tent with business partner, Thomas Tweed.[19] There is no official record of this, but Lougheed family history holds that, during this time, James reportedly met William Van Horne and secured a position as legal counsel for the Canadian Pacific Railway (CPR).[20]

Whether he made this connection or not, in the late summer, James and his brother Sam moved to Fort Calgary,[21] where James rented the back half of a log cabin for his legal practice. If James was not the first lawyer in Calgary, he quickly became the busiest.[22] It did not take much time for the enterprising young man to make even more important personal connections. In December of 1883, James was elected as one of the first stewards of Central (Methodist) United Church "at the first meeting of the quarterly official board," held at the home of Richard Hardisty.[23] Soon after, James and Isabella became a couple. No doubt it was not only her important family connections that convinced James of Isabella's suitability as a wife but also her Euro-North American education.

James's marriage into the Hardisty family was fortuitous for him. Yet, according to some newspaper articles, James often attributed his success to his mother, Mary Ann Alexander, a "beautiful Christian woman...It is said that from her he inherited his Scotch shrewdness and cleverness that characterized him in later years."[24] Mary Ann Alexander, who had given her son the middle name of Alexander, died before James went west. Thus, unfortunately, she never witnessed her son's tremendous success after he had forged ties with the Hardisty family.

Indeed, it had not taken James long after he arrived in the North West to become what some referred to as a "pedigreed Westerner through marriage" to Isabella.[25] The social significance of the marriage on 16 September 1884 was clear when the *Calgary Herald* reported,

> *Last evening, the youth and beauty of our town might be seen wending their way to the Methodist Church, where a scene of no common interest was being enacted...Before the hour the building was packed, a number having to satisfy themselves with a peep through the windows. The principals were James Alexander Lougheed, Esq., Barrister, and Miss Isabella Hardisty.*[26]

The invitations for James and Isabella's wedding indicated that the event was organized by Richard Hardisty, with no mention made of Isabella's mother. Whether or not Mary Hardisty was even at her daughter's wedding is not clear, but the invitations requested the presence of guests at the Methodist Church and then at the home of Richard and Eliza Hardisty to celebrate the marriage of their niece.[27] Newspaper reports were focused on the "youth and beauty" in attendance, so no mention is made of Isabella's mother or siblings, if they were in attendance.

At least one author believes that the union between Isabella and James was sanctioned by the elders of the Hardisty family. Popular historian J.G. MacGregor wrote,

Evidently Dick Hardisty, keeping an eye on the budding romance (between Isabella and James) had made up his mind that his brother's eldest daughter was making a good match. There is nothing to show how one of her other uncles, Donald A. Smith, regarded the union, but undoubtedly his interest in the affair would have boded well for the young couple.[28]

Regarding Richard Hardisty's wealth and stature, MacGregor continued,

Whatever it cost Dick Hardisty to send his children away to school it made little dent in his wealth. Undoubtedly he was the richest man in the western prairies and besides his mill had his hand in several other ventures.[29]

Although MacGregor's sources are sparse, Hardisty was well connected enough for it to be plausible that he was one of the wealthiest men in the West during the transitional period. In addition to his own stature as a chief factor, as a member of the McDougall family, because of his marriage to Eliza, Richard often employed and formed partnerships with other McDougall men, also a fairly wealthy group. In fact, recognizing the changing times, Richard worked "hand in hand with...David [McDougall] who competed with the Hudson's Bay Company for trade."[30] This suggests that Richard was, at least by this time, a family man first and a company man second. After his marriage, family member James soon also became Richard's close business associate.[31]

Despite the excitement generated by the marriage of the future senator to the daughter of fur trade aristocracy, James and Isabella still began married life in a small log hut next to James's law office. The only renovation was a bay window, imported from Central Canada, a renovation that served as notice to the townspeople that this couple already viewed themselves to be "distinct."[32] It is not clear if this incident precipitated a move, but, according to popular historian Grant MacEwan, the bay window continued to be an object of interest and curiosity, until the day a runaway horse veered off what is now Stephen Avenue, plunged through the window, and "landed in the middle of Mrs. Lougheed's front parlor."[33] The Lougheeds physically moved the house twice to new locations, until they finally left it to move into their grand home, Beaulieu, in 1891.[34]

Confirming Isabella had not married out of, but rather that James had married *into* an established Hudson's Bay Company family, and as though he was now a company man himself, James had chosen HBC man Charlie Parlow to stand for him as best man. In fact, when James was interviewed in 1921, he indicated he had sensed a new beginning for himself as a "company man" upon his marriage. James said,

> My wife was a Hardisty, of Lady Strathcona's family, so that, in a way, I'm a Hudson's Bay man, my father-in-law having been chief factor of the company. In early western days people spoke of "The Company" pretty much as a man from Prince Edward Island spoke in New York of "The Island," and asked "What other Island is there?"[35]

James's contemporaries noted that, when he ventured west, "Like most men who came to Calgary in those days he was not over burdened with surplus wealth."[36] Yet, by 1889, just six years after his arrival in Calgary, and subsequent marriage into the Hardisty family, the local paper could refer to James as "one of our heaviest real estate owners, having accumulated property to the extent of nearly $70,000 worth."[37] Given that the 1881 census does not even list Calgary, but rather a region identified as the Bow River, which contained "five shanties, seventy-five houses, and four hundred people, of whom fifty were women,"[38] James and Isabella's accumulation of property by 1889 was impressive.

While researching members of Isabella's kinship network, historian Donald B. Smith located what he believed to be the earliest surviving letter written by James, dated 25 November 1885. Speaking about this letter, Smith wrote,

> One can also see from this letter how the young lawyer has worked himself into the network of his wife's influential family connections, who included not only Richard Hardisty, the richest man in the Northwest Territories, but also Donald A. Smith [aka Lord Strathcona], soon to be the richest man in Canada.[39]

In this letter to Richard Hardisty, James did give some indication of the close connection he quickly developed with Isabella's uncle. After some personal details about his first-born son "growing like a weed in a potato field," James went on to speak of other family members, referring to an upcoming visit by Lord Strathcona, the "worthy driver of the last C.P.R. Spike." James also confirmed some of the investments he held with Richard Hardisty, in this case, cattle. In the same letter, James noted that his brother Sam was looking after the herd for Richard and James.[40]

Like James after him, Richard Hardisty was never elected as a representative of the North West in the Canadian government (although Richard had run unsuccessfully in the 1887 election before receiving his Senate appointment). Rather, both men took advantage of political connections, and were successful in part due to the long fur trade history of the Hardisty family. In fact, when Richard was appointed to the Senate in 1887, he continued to hold the position of Chief Factor for the Northern Department, comprising all of Manitoba, Saskatchewan, Alberta, and the Territories.[41] The fact that Richard could retain his post as an HBC man at the same time as serve in the Senate demonstrates the continuing importance of the fur trade company and its employees and their family networks during the transitional period.

As both chief factor and the area's senator, Richard was well placed to monitor changing times and to identify political and financial opportunities. According to the man who would eventually become a business partner to James, Edmund Taylor (another HBC man), it was Richard who had encouraged the HBC to expand its operation to include "Flour Mills, Lumber Mills, and caused the company to become the pioneer cattle ranchers in the North after the buffalo made their last trek southward about 1870."[42] As the senior HBC officer when settlers began arriving on the western prairies, Richard was ideally situated not only to assess material needs but also to profit personally from land speculation.

After Richard Hardisty's death, even though James soon assumed his uncle's Senate post, James and Isabella relied on Donald A. Smith as the senior patriarch of the Hardisty family. Indeed, Smith was a good connection to have, given that he was not only a friend and confidant of Sir John A. Macdonald but one of the principal shareholders of the Hudson's Bay Company, the Canadian Pacific Railway, and the Bank of Montreal.[43] Not only had James stepped into the Senate seat of his wife's uncle, but soon after his marriage he was appointed to serve as solicitor for these three companies, which helped propel Donald A. Smith to immense wealth. Thus, it was soon after his own Senate appointment on 15 October 1889 when James and Isabella's status in the North West was truly and very publicly confirmed.[44]

When Senator Richard Hardisty died in 1889 as the result of a wagon accident in Saskatchewan, James, still only thirty-five years old, was considered to be his natural successor by people who were well placed themselves. In a letter to John A. Macdonald, Reverend Leonard Gaetz, Red Deer's Methodist minister, who was a fairly wealthy land owner and fur trader by then, wrote,

> James Lougheed is a gentleman of culture, ability and position, with a thorough knowledge of, and faith in, Alberta. He is a Conservative of Conservatives, a good address, and will make a first class representative.[45]

In reality, Gaetz's first connection in the North West was not to James but to Richard Hardisty, who had helped Gaetz find a homestead in the agriculturally rich area surrounding the Red Deer River.

It is true, though, that in addition to Gaetz and the connection to the Hardisty family, Lougheed had managed to make some connections of his own. He was a personal friend of Minister of the Interior Edgar Dewdney and, while in Toronto, had also worked to help John A. Macdonald gain re-election in 1878, through his involvement with the Young Men's Conservative Club.[46] Although he followed the promise of success to what would become Alberta, it was said that James

> never forgot the traditions of the staunch old Conservative East Toronto...and, while advocating changes, he always made it plain that in his opinion the Conservative party was a true friend of the North-West...Even before 1887, when representation was given to the North West in Parliament, a Conservative Association was formed in Calgary in 1884, of which Mr. Lougheed was one of the founders and active members.[47]

It should be no surprise, then, that James always remained loyal to Macdonald during the volatile times in the 1880s, and also that he became a prominent investor in the Conservative organ, the *Calgary Herald*.[48]

After Richard Hardisty's death and his own political appointment, James acknowledged his new role as an up-and-coming patriarch in the Hardisty family, and the youngest man in the Senate chamber. In a letter to Richard's widow, James thanked her for her congratulations on his new post as senator and noted that he hoped the

> mantle of poor Mr. Hardisty, which has fallen upon me may be worn by me as worthily as it was by him. Should you ever consider that I can be of any service to you in my new position do not fail to command me in any way.[49]

Of course, it was not only James who became quite adept at picking up the mantle left by Richard when the North West experienced tremendous growth. According to news reports, both James and Isabella entertained on a regular basis from the very beginning of their married life. As Isabella recalled years later,

> Those were the days of the real western hospitality. Every New Year the men called at our homes and we used to receive from 9 A.M. until midnight, sometimes having a hundred callers. There were many privations too but we were young and did not mind them.[50]

In this excerpt, Isabella refers to the custom of receiving guests on the first day of every New Year, a custom she experienced first as a young girl at the "Big House" in the North. She clearly remembered the privations of her early married years as well, though, as she had also remembered the privations she had faced in the North.

However, the privations for James and Isabella as a married couple in Calgary were relatively short lived. As a symbol of their role as members of the aristocracy of the new West, shortly after James's appointment to the Senate in 1889, the couple began to plan the building of their grand home, Beaulieu, to which they moved in December of 1891. The sandstone mansion, located at present-day 13th Avenue and 7th Street SW, necessitated the services of Ottawa architect, James R. Bowes. It generated much attention, and, soon after its completion, the Lougheeds' grand home was profiled in the *Calgary Weekly Herald*'s "The buildings of 1891."[51] The *Calgary Tribune* described the lavish housewarming held on 16 February 1892, when James and Isabella hosted 150 guests, the "cream of Calgary and Alberta society."[52]

According to some assessments, the imposing mansion was to be an "ostentatious symbol of the new prairie wealth." James and Isabella went to such extravagances as to seek out marble cutters from Italy to build the eight fireplaces housed in Beaulieu.[53] Construction did what it was meant to do—boost the sophistication of not only the Lougheeds but also the new West. Beaulieu drew national attention, with detailed descriptions in both the *Toronto Mail* and the *Toronto Globe*.[54] Whatever the reasons behind the naming of their new mansion as Beaulieu, the extravagance was very likely meant to demonstrate the importance of the up-and-coming aristocratic and soon to be "Lady" Isabella and "Sir" James. With its "rugged sandstone walls, irregular roof line, projecting towers, iron cresting, lacy balustrades and tall chimneys," Beaulieu clearly had established new standards of elegance and sophistication, revealing not only how far the town had come in such a short time but also how far James and Isabella themselves had come.[55]

In addition to the establishment of a new mansion, James and Isabella's family was growing. On 29 July 1885, they welcomed their first son, and his name, Clarence Hardisty Lougheed,[56] served as notice of the continuing importance of the Hardisty connection.[57] On 3 February 1889, another son, Norman Alexander, was born.[58] Alexander may have been chosen as Norman's second name in honour of James's mother, Mary Ann Alexander. However, two of Isabella's brothers also shared the middle name Alexander, and thus it seems the name held some significance for the Hardisty family as well. On 19 December 1893, the couple's third son, Edgar Donald, was born.[59] Again, the middle name was no doubt drawn from the Hardisty kinship network, and arguably a man who would become

Isabella as a young mother. Photo undated. Lougheed House National Historic Site Archives.

its most influential member, Donald A. Smith. On 22 August
1898, Isabella and James welcomed their first daughter, Dorothy
Isabelle, whose middle name was chosen in honour of Isabella's
aunt, Lady Strathcona. A fourth son, Douglas Gordon, was born
on 3 September 1901. In this son's case, there is no known link to
the Hardisty family for the second name. The final child, Marjorie
Yolande, was born on 21 February 1904. "Yolande" is an interesting
choice, given that it was more commonly bestowed upon French
girls. [60]

The role of mother was one of many that Isabella assumed,
along with wife, colleague, employer, patron, leader, and hostess.
However, despite these roles, many of them very public, the first
researchers with Lougheed House National Historic Site, Trudy
Cowan and Jennifer Bobrovitz, observed that Isabella was a
"private person," and that knowing her "remains a challenge."[61] It
is true that she left few personal documents and that there are no

descendants remaining who have extensive personal memory of Isabella and James. However, by the time written records were more common, there were some family members who had specific memories. For example, the late Peter Lougheed (who served as Alberta's premier from 1971 to 1985), while having no memory of James, did recall for a local newspaper in 2001, in an article appropriately titled "A Daughter of the West Who Made a Difference," that his grandmother was an

"elegant woman in a rocking chair living out her last few years in the old house...She was elderly when we knew her," says Peter who was only eight when his grandmother died. "My main memory of her is her comment on my name. 'Peter. It's funny you named him Peter. That's the name of our dog.'"[62]

During the same interview, Donald, Peter's brother and three years his senior, recalled Isabella talking to him about those who viewed Metis leader Louis Riel as a hero: "She told me about her brother who was killed at Batoche...I remember her talking about Riel...She would be terribly upset with all this talk of Riel today."[63] The reporter's interview with Peter and Donald led him to Norman Lougheed Jr., who was eighty-six years old at the time and living in Sidney, British Columbia, and the oldest surviving descendant of Isabella and James.

Norman Jr. lived with Isabella at Beaulieu until her death, and thus was a good primary source of information. Norman's mother, Mary Stringer Lougheed, was often present at the functions at Beaulieu, and knew Isabella fairly well.[64] Norman recalled that Mary had observed that Isabella was an excellent and gracious hostess, who had a "profoundly beneficial effect" on the senator, "guiding him socially and culturally into new worlds." Mary had even concluded that Isabella was the "driving force behind James."[65] Another family member, Flora, Norman Jr.'s wife, shared her opinion with the reporter at the time that Isabella

*was a tyrant...She was definitely in charge. Mary talked a lot about
her, and about how strict she was. Mary knew a lot about entertaining—she learned it from Granny, who was an excellent hostess,
a gracious hostess. There's no doubt she was made of good stuff.*[66]

Perhaps it was Flora's detailed memories that best described Isabella,
the "gracious" woman in charge but no doubt made of "good stuff."

Although Mary had told Flora that Isabella was the driving
force behind the partnership, according to Bobrovitz, speaking to
the *Calgary Herald* in 2001, James and Isabella worked as a team:
"Individually, they could not have been as successful as they were
collectively."[67] Bobrovitz's assessment, though made by a popular
journalist, is nonetheless useful in understanding Isabella's history.
James and Isabella were immensely successful as they worked
collectively to build upon the prestigious position of the Hardisty
family in the transitional economy.

In fact, it appears James always maintained an attitude of
pragmatism when it came to marriage and the partnerships that
would lead to the most success. As a young boy attending school in
Ontario, James is said to have replied to a request to define marriage
with the following assessment: "Marriage—ah—is a corporation of
two persons, with—ah—power to increase its numbers."[68] Whether
James ever did make this exact statement, or whether it was one
of the many "tongue-in-cheek" comments attributed to James by
Prairie satirist/journalist Bob Edwards, some did come to believe
that marriage for James and Isabella was a partnership with a goal
to increase its "numbers" in terms of family fortunes.[69] Writing in
the *Calgary Herald* in 2000, David Bly noted about James,

*Everything he did seemed to advance his career and his fortune. He
met Isabella Clarke [sic] Hardisty, daughter of the late William
Lucas Hardisty, the Hudson's Bay Company's chief factor for the
McKenzie [sic] district. Isabella embodied the Canadian West. She*

was born at Fort Resolution, an HBC post, and grew up under fron-
tier conditions...Her mother was the daughter of a Metis woman.[70]

Certainly, James's achievements in the world of politics and wealth
accumulation speak to a man driven to succeed, and his marriage to
Isabella contributed greatly to his ability to do that.

We cannot understand James's success without examining
Isabella's contribution. As was often the case with unions made
during and immediately after the fur trade, success in business
depended on a productive partnership. Writing about Elizabeth
Boyd McDougall, second wife of Methodist missionary John
McDougall, MacEwan noted that, after their marriage, "from this
point forward, the husband and wife story become so interwoven
that it was difficult to relate about one without talking about the
other."[71] For James, the items of exchange became land, money, and
legal services; and Isabella's entries in the marriage's accounting
books balanced with fur trade family connections, hostess skills,
mothering skills, boosterism, and networking, all of which are difficult to measure but yet equally important to the couple's success.[72]

There is no way to accurately measure the value of Isabella's
contribution to the partnership, or the degree to which she was
involved in business decisions. However, from the time of his marriage
in 1884, when he had modest land holdings, which included a small
log house to which he brought his bride, to the time when the value
of his property reached $75,000 in 1889,[73] making him Calgary's
largest landowner, the transformation of James's social position
was quite impressive. At least one family member believes (while
noting he has nothing against James) that Isabella deserves to be
known "in her own right." Great-grandson Robert Lougheed
continues that James's decision to marry Isabella was a "very good
decision politically and economically for him...The marriage
certainly helped his law and political career."[74]

Even his legal partner noted the importance of Isabella's family
to James's career. Among John A. Macdonald's papers, there is a

note from Peter McCarthy, at the time James's law partner, in which McCarthy indicated he was "writing to encourage appt of JAL to Senate." McCarthy noted a number of attributes in favour of James's appointment, one of the first of which is not related to James's skills but that "he is a relative by marriage to Sir Donald A. Smith and also to the late Senator [Hardisty]." He continues,

> He is a personal friend of the Hon. Edgar Dewdney and along with myself has spent a considerable sum in sustaining the only Conservative organ in Alberta...he and I have within the last two weeks been forced to purchase the plant and franchises of the Calgary Herald to prevent it [going insolvent?].[75]

Certainly, the press noted that when James served in the Senate, Isabella was making a contribution to the advancement of her husband's career, both in the North West and in Central Canada. Quoting from the *Montreal Star*, the *Morning Albertan* noted in 1912,

> Quite a loss has been temporarily sustained by the official social set at the Capital by the return to Calgary of Mrs. James A. Lougheed, wife of the government leader in the Senate, who has been one of the most active and most popular official hostesses since the Borden Government came into power. Mrs. Lougheed is the mistress of one of the largest and most beautiful houses, not only in Calgary, but anywhere west of the great lakes, and it is but natural that she would desire to return to her western home as soon as her duties at Ottawa would allow.[76]

The article in the *Montreal Star* demonstrated the importance of Isabella's fur trade family, when it deemed to provide an "outline of the patriotic services of a woman whose family for two generations has contributed to the development of the Canadian west."[77] As a way to demonstrate her success, the *Star* (as reprinted by the

Morning Albertan) continued to educate Central Canadians about Isabella's links to the development of the North West, writing,

> *Mrs. Lougheed, whose maiden name was Belle Christine Hardisty,*
> *was the daughter of Lady Strathcona's brother, the late Mr. William*
> *L. Hardisty, who, in the middle of the past century, spent thirty*
> *eight years in the wilds of the Mackenzie river district, in the service*
> *of the Hudson's Bay Company...Mr. Hardisty's family spent many*
> *years in the wilds...She is an ideal hostess, full of honest fun and*
> *unassuming.*[78]

The article continued that Isabella intended to "return to Ottawa next session,"[79] a plan suggesting she understood it to be to James's advantage that she attend Ottawa regularly when Parliament was in session. Prior to the hardening of public/private spheres in the later 1800s, elite women in British North America "could play powerful roles, making or breaking the political careers of their male relatives...or promoting the political goals of their choice."[80]

Unfortunately, not much is known about Isabella's public activities until the time of her husband's political career, when her involvement in many organizations and activities became more newsworthy. However, if we are to judge by later reports in newspapers, both were always involved, as a couple, in community boosterism and building. In early prairie society, churches assumed major roles as institutions of boosterism and building, and James and Isabella were always committed members of Calgary's Methodist Church.[81] As well as his church activities, James was active as a school trustee and member of the Calgary Board of Trade.[82]

Many of James's political duties would necessarily involve Isabella's assistance, not only in Ottawa but in Calgary. One example was his work on the organizational committee for the Calgary reception of Sir John A. and Lady Macdonald in July of 1886, when they were on board the first passenger train across the country that was meant to promote the North West as an important part of the new Canada. No doubt, Isabella was present during that visit, when one of Lady Macdonald's official functions included laying the cornerstone for Knox Presbyterian Church.[83]

Because so many of James's responsibilities necessitated Isabella's hostess skills, they needed to have a home that was suitable to host dignitaries. As noted earlier, it was not long after James's appointment to the Senate that he and Isabella made plans to build Beaulieu House. Not unlike the forts of the HBC, Beaulieu became the temporary accommodations for many visitors to the North West. Some of these visitors included members of the British royal family. According to some observers, James and Isabella considered themselves to be aristocrats like those they entertained, "remaining aloof, enjoying public esteem if not public affection."[84] James was even said to sport a British accent, despite the fact that he was born in Toronto's Cabbagetown, and that he spent most of his adult life in the North West.[85] James was not alone in emulating aristocracy, for it is said that many in the ranching community "tried to represent the standards of an established landed gentry."[86]

Some of his contemporaries mocked James's apparent attempts at aristocracy. H.F. Gadsby, writing for the *Canadian Liberal Monthly*, kidded,

> One of Senator Lougheed's chief qualifications as Senate leader...is
> his rich, crusted old English Stilton accent...If any other citizen of
> Calgary than the one who collects rent from half the town said
> "ahftahnoon" instead of afternoon he would be dumped in the Bow
> River. But Senator Lougheed gets away with it...You don't look for
> an English accent with a Scotch name like Lougheed...It probably
> grew up with the Senator when he went to Calgary to grow up with
> the country. There were many remittance men in Alberta at the
> time, and accent was about the only thing they had to give away.[87]

Still, some took the aristocratic persona seriously. In 1921, when the *Toronto Star Weekly* described the Senator's presence in chambers, it noted,

> *You would say that he was an English visitor, probably an army officer, or a hunter of big game...You will be surprised to learn that... the man you took for an English visitor has lived all his life in Canada.*[88]

He may have begun a humble existence in Cabbagetown; however, after his marriage to Isabella, James was frequenting places such as the Roxborough Apartments, where he stayed while in Ottawa. The Roxborough, where many of the politicians and business elites stayed, was built in 1910 by Boer War veteran Colonel James Wood, and featured architecture that successfully portrayed "an air of British solidarity and respectability."[89]

Aristocrat or not, James was sufficiently influenced by Isabella's very social nature so that he shed aspects of the strict Methodist requirements of his early Sunday schools, such as that which forbid dancing.[90] Although both James and Isabella hosted dances at Beaulieu, it was Isabella who was exposed to the arts at Miss Davis's school and at Wesleyan Ladies' College, and it was likely her influence that led James to invest in the Calgary arts scene throughout his life. In addition to Isabella's very social nature, no doubt, the world of nineteenth-century politics, with the "noise, the whiskey, the laughter, the tobacco,"[91] not to mention the patronage and scandals that often accompanied it, also had a somewhat relaxing effect on James's strict upbringing.[92]

Despite some softening, James never strayed from the attention to self-improvement that was inspired by his strictly religious mother. He carried on with many of the activities from his youth, such as helping to organize a Literary and Debating Society in Calgary in 1882, with fellow lawyer Paddy Nolan.[93] It appears that 1882 was a "landmark" year for the arts in Calgary, when Nolan was also involved in organizing the Calgary Amateur Dramatics Association.[94] In fact, James and Isabella were always on the forefront of philanthropic organizations in Calgary. As one historian notes,

> *Calgary's business leaders were usually too busy to cultivate a lifestyle markedly different from that of their employees. Thus, social leadership generally came from churchmen, senior government officials and members of the professions. However, some individuals, like James A. Lougheed...were prominent in both business and social reform.*[95]

A committed church member and government official, James fits the normal criteria of such early social reformers, and, as his wife, Isabella assumed some of that responsibility for social reform.

As a politically active and socially conscious couple, James and Isabella were the focus of much media attention, and also the consistent subjects of commentary by the popular Prairie satirist, Bob Edwards. During the twenty years of publication of his paper, the *Calgary Eye Opener*, Edwards used humour to draw attention not only to the Lougheeds and their contemporaries but to the social injustices of his times. As historian Sarah Carter wrote, Edwards made "merciless fun of the fox-hunting and pheasant-shooting society, class distinctions, privilege and aristocracy."[96] In July 1906, when rumour had it that Lougheed would be knighted, meaning that Isabella would also earn the title "Lady," Edwards commented,

> *A knighthood is the infallible stamp of mediocrity nowadays, a sop thrown by royalty to pretentious four-flushers. Our beknighted senator will interject more "ohs" and "ahs" into his conversation than ever after he is Sir James.*[97]

Edwards chided the opportunism of the Lougheeds, noting that, when James threw his support behind a new civic centre and post office, to be located at the "foot of First street west," this would conveniently mean "a street car line down past the Sherman Grand and the new vaudeville house which the senator contemplates erecting shortly."[98]

Whatever Edwards really thought of the Lougheeds, James and Isabella were clearly adept at political manoeuvring. In 1911, the first Conservative government was elected after a long hiatus in opposition that began in 1896. Soon after that election, James was appointed a member of Robert Borden's Cabinet, as Minister without Portfolio. Then in 1915, James was appointed acting Minister of Militia and Defence, a key wartime responsibility. In July 1915, James became chair of the Military Hospitals Commission, a position he held under the Union government until 1918.[99] It was a position that likely became more personal when James and Isabella's son Clarence enlisted in 1915 for active service as a major with the Canadian Over-Seas Expeditionary Force,[100] and again in 1916 when Edgar enlisted as a lieutenant. It was reportedly for his service during the war that James was knighted on 3 June 1916.[101]

In addition to the importance of being granted the titles "Sir" and "Lady," in honour of James and Isabella's positions in the new social fabric of the West, their names were eventually bestowed upon everything from remote islands to mountains. Perhaps the most fitting tribute, though, might be that which demonstrates the importance of the linking of the Lougheed family to that of the fur trading Hardisty family. In 1906, a small central Alberta town, situated on Highway 13, ten kilometres southeast of Sedgewick, assumed the name "Lougheed" in honour of Senator and Lady Lougheed. The CPR station directly to the east of this small prairie town, at the crossing of the Battle River in former Metis buffalo-hunting territory, held the name "Hardisty," in honour of Isabella's fur trade family.[102]

Perhaps the *Calgary Herald* stated it most appropriately in December of 2001, when it wrote, "Underpinning all of Sir James Lougheed's achievements is the fact that he married well. Isabella Clarke [sic] Hardisty was truly a daughter of the Canadian West."

As the article continued, "With her connections, she could probably have done well in Toronto, Winnipeg or Montreal, but after
her father died, she chose to live with her uncle in a muddy hamlet
called Calgary."[103] As marriage and business partners, James and
Isabella very soon witnessed this muddy hamlet transform into a
showcase of boosterism for the new West, and they were themselves
catapulted into the positions of Sir James and Lady Isabella.

The quotation in the *Calgary Herald* in 2001 demonstrates that
James (more so) and Isabella have continued to be recognized as
important community builders. However, even during their own
time, many Calgarians felt they knew Isabella and James well. One
of those, William Pearce, "one of Calgary's oldest residents (who)
has known Sir James longer probably than any other person in this
city," described James as "always very industrious and aggressive."[104]
Yet, even when the political climate in the North West had changed
drastically, James's contemporaries recognized the wisdom of his
choice for a wife in the daughter of fur trade aristocracy. In fact, far
removed from the North West, James's fortuitous marriage arrangement was recognized. An article in the *Toronto Star Weekly* in 1917
noted that, among his

> *Many Wise Moves...Two years after he left his home in Toronto he
> was wise enough to take a wife unto himself in the person of a Miss
> Hardisty, whose father was a Hudson Bay factor and uncle a
> member of the Dominion Senate...Five years after this happy event
> came his real entry in public life, when, on the death of Senator
> Hardisty, through an accident of a runaway, he was the choice of
> the Government as his successor...In the Senate the Hon. James
> Lougheed may not have proved himself to be amongst its most
> brilliant members, but he has certainly been one of its ablest.*[105]

Perhaps he was not among the most brilliant members of the
Senate, and it was true that he had married well, but it is also true
that James was politically astute and knew how to invest wisely.

According to historians Donald B. Smith and David Hall, authors of James's online biography, the senator was a great supporter of business interests, and at one point he brought forward legislation that would limit the rights of workers.

Likely due in part to his business interests, James appeared to show little regard not only for the worker but for Isabella's ancestry. For example, according to Smith and Hall, James

> *shared common western conservative views about Canada's Native peoples. Canada, in his opinion, had by far the best record of any country of dealing with its indigenous peoples. He firmly believed that the First Nations required a strong paternal supervision by government. They must not be allowed to impede progress. While in opposition he had wanted the government to take power to sell Indian lands, especially when they were located close to settlements...In 1914 he strongly supported a government measure to do just that. In 1920 he vigorously advocated a bill to give government increased authority to forcibly educate and enfranchise natives.*[106]

James did say, "The Indian has not those characteristics which make it proper to leave to his discretion whether he shall assume responsibility or not." Two years after making this comment, James strenuously opposed as a retrograde and reactionary step "a measure to leave to the individual native the decision concerning enfranchisement."[107] Smith and Hall judged James's opinion of First Nation people to be negative and paternalistic, referring specifically to a debate about a bill addressing game preservation in 1894. During the debate, James stated, "The Indians in my section of the country kill indiscriminately in the close season...The most destructive element we have in that country is the Indians themselves."[108]

Whatever his sympathies, James may have been a more complicated man than many historians have acknowledged. In his role as a lawyer, James defended a range of clients, from women charged with being "keepers of houses of ill-fame"[109] in 1889, to "Dr. Lovingheart" (aka Andrew Campbell) in 1893, when he was accused of performing an abortion for a Mrs. Maggie Stevenson.[110] Charges were eventually dropped against Campbell, but he again came to the attention of police for failing to comply with the fire limit bylaw on his frame building.[111] Given James's conservative nature and that he was primarily a business lawyer, and that abortion was increasingly condemned in the nineteenth century,[112] he clearly saw his practice in pragmatic terms and defined his responsibilities generously.

An article that appeared in the 19 March 1903 edition of the *Medicine Hat News*, and again on 26 March 1903, might have potentially harmed James's reputation. The headline read,

> *King vs Lougheed: Defendant was charged with seduction under promise of marriage. On the application of the Crown, the hearing was postponed to secure necessary evidence. C.R. Mitchell for Crown. P.J. Nolan and D.G. White for accused.*[113]

The story was also reprinted in the 23 March 1903 edition of the *Calgary Herald*, with a note that Chief Justice Sifton would preside shortly over the case at the Supreme Court in Medicine Hat. Again, few details were provided, other than that "King vs Lougheed Defendant was charged with seduction under promise of marriage."[114] Two months later, the *Medicine Hat News*, under the headline "The King vs Jas. A. Lougheed" reported,

> *The accused was charged with seduction under promise of marriage, and resulted in a conviction. On the application of the Counsel for accused the Chief Justice reserved the case for the opinion of the Poll Court. C.R. Mitchell for Crown. P.J. Nolan and D.G. White for the Defence.*[115]

While it turns out that the Jas. A. Lougheed in question was twenty-three years of age,[116] and thus could not have been Isabella's husband, the local press did not appear to make the distinction.

Nonetheless, the reported conviction of a man bearing the same name appears to have had little effect on James's career, as his pragmatism, his political influence, and his law practice continued to grow. Yet it was his junior partner, R.B. Bennett, who achieved his lifelong dream of becoming prime minister, even though James may have had that same dream. If James did have any such aspirations, as some news reports suggested, they went unfulfilled. One report claims that James "was passed over for Arthur Meighen, it is said, because his wife's half-Native ancestry was too exotic for the Tory hierarchy."[117] Brian Brennan, reporting for the *Calgary Herald* in 1997, appears to have relied to a great extent on an interview with Donald Lougheed, James and Isabella's grandson, when he indicated that family members generally agreed that James wanted to become prime minister, and they even believed that Isabella had been referred to as an "Indian wife." Brennan wrote,

> *Due to the integrated nature of frontier society at the time, most found nothing unusual in what was nevertheless considered an interracial marriage because Belle was one-quarter Metis. But later, as James Lougheed's position grew, he had to face taunts about his "Indian" wife. If it bothered him, he never let it show. Belle was hailed as "first hostess of the West" as she contributed to her husband's career.*[118]

Whether there were concerns about his wife's ancestry, James's marriage strategy was likely the most prudent, even if it did eliminate him from the competition to lead the national government. Certainly, James chose the politically expedient path of accepting executive appointment to the Senate and a wartime appointment as Minister without Portfolio, rather than seeking election. James may have learned political expediency from his wife's uncle, Donald A. Smith (Lord Stathcona). It has been suggested that Lord Strathcona, married to the Indigenous Isabella Hardisty Smith, turned down an offer of a second peerage for fear of scorn over his own country marriage. So fearful was Smith of the gossip about his marriage as attitudes toward interracial marriages hardened that he arranged a private and "proper" European ceremony in New York when he and his wife were in their seventies.[119]

It is not clear whether his wife's ancestry was ever a matter of concern for James Lougheed. However, as noted earlier, he certainly seemed to pay Indigenous people little regard when the matter of their rights might interfere with business interests. In 1906, during debate in the Senate chambers, James again defended business interests over Indigenous rights, arguing that the government ought to be

> *taking to itself larger power to dispose of many Indian reserves contiguous to settlement, rendering it undesirable that the Indian should be there in the first place, and in the second place that the lands should be held from settlement...That, I might say, is becoming a matter of considerable importance to growing centres in the new provinces. Very large tracts of land are tied up immediately adjoining important centres of civilization and settlement, and it is both prejudicial to the Indians and prejudicial to settlement.*[120]

Immediately after James's argument that favoured settlement by newcomers over treaty rights, the Senate adopted Bill 194, which amended the Indian Act.[121] In 1911, James supported another motion to amend the Indian Act by way of Bill 177, in which it was deemed "a good thing for Indians to be moved from the vicinity of towns where they are exposed to vice drunkenness and immorality." This was also the amendment that made reserve land available for annexation and purchase.[122] In 1920, James defended the British Columbia Indian Lands Bill, arguing, "No other Indians have been as well looked after as the Indians of Canada."[123] He continued that British Columbia had "looked after the Indians with a parental attention." James further stated that the federal government was at no fault either, for "the treatment of the Indians by the Government of Canada has been proverbial for sympathy, for generosity, and for

Western Canada College football team, Calgary, Alberta. Front row (L–R): Norman Lougheed, C. Smith (mascot), –. Centre row (L–R): R. Oakley, H. McInnes (captain), Dr. Archibald Oswald MacRae, A. Thomas, G.E.H. Johnston. Back row (L–R): Ronald Freeman, W.J. Sharpe, M. Jaffray, H. White, W. Simpson. Photo dated 1906.
Glenbow Alberta Museum and Archives, NA-3899-2.

all that parental solicitude could do for any section of the population."[124] Later in the debates, James continued, "The Indian has not those characteristics which make it proper to leave to his discretion, whether he shall assume responsibility (i.e., accept franchise) or not."[125]

In this regard, James held the same views as those of Dr. Archibald Oswald MacRae, the principal of Calgary's Western Canada College, the very school James and Isabella's son Norman attended. According to MacRae, "The Red Man of the West has always been a difficult individual, he does not care to work, to beg he is not ashamed. In consequence he tends to become shiftless and vagrant."[126] It is reasonable to assume that both James and Isabella were aware of Dr. MacRae's views.

Given James's own expressed views of Indigenous people, it should be no surprise that Indigenous activist Fred Loft's appeals to James while he was Minister in Charge of Indian Affairs, so well-articulated, were all for nought.[127] Later, when the Conservatives were out of power and the Liberals brought forward amendments to the Indian Act, effectively doing away with forced enfranchisement, Lougheed defended his party's policies, saying,

> It seems to me that the law of 1920, which we are not altogether repealing, but which we are weakening, was a very salutary statute. The policy of that law was that the Government, of whom the Indians are the wards, would determine whether an Indian should be enfranchised...Upon every reserve there are always a certain number of restless and dissatisfied spirits who will attempt to make trouble...They want to continue in the position of wards of the nation...if we give recognition to that spirit of dependence on the Government, we shall never be able to develop our administration of Indian affairs to that stage at which we shall finally solve the Indian problems of Canada.[128]

Clearly paternalistic in some of his political views, which might suggest the same in terms of parenting style for James, there is evidence that Isabella had a somewhat more relaxed parenting style.[129] There was one very public example of the differing views on parenting that might have been embarrassing for James's political career had he been an elected official. This example occurred shortly after James had departed for Ottawa on one of his frequent trips. Despite a warning from James that Isabella and their sons should not undertake such a trip, James had no sooner left than his family took the automobile for a road trip to Banff. According to the Banff Crag & Canyon, Norman Lougheed had arrived in his "big automobile, this being the first car to enter the National Park over the coach road."[130] Indeed, the Lougheeds had undertaken their road trip at a time when vehicles were prohibited inside the park, thus their vehicle was promptly seized.[131]

Years later, Mary Stringer Lougheed, who had been along on the joyride, recalled the "hectic venture of driving through swamp, rut, and bog to get to Banff." She confirmed the trip went ahead despite the fact the senator had "put his foot down calling it foolhardy! 'The impulse of a bunch of kids and poor old granny!'" Mary noted that, after James left, the boys and Isabella immediately got busy. The car was made ready with an extra can of fuel, the tires inflated with hand pumps, and the family cook put up a "huge hamper of food, for of course there were no restaurants on the way." Mary recalled that things

> breeze [sic] along wonderfully for the first ten miles. We had
> our hats tied on with a mile of veil. Norman wore big gauntlets
> and a driving cap with goggles. The motor veils streamed behind
> in the wind. It was wonderful: a lovely sight as we approached the
> Rockies.[132]

Along with two other vehicles, the motorcade "roared by at 15 miles per hour to follow the old Indian and wagon trail west." When the two other cars lost steam, the Lougheed car "roared on alone." Dealing with eight-inch ruts and bears, the car slowed to three miles per hour, when "in front loomed an Indian wagon loaded with small fry in the back." Despite the challenges, Isabella and her sons made it to the village of Banff, where

> soon eager citizens crowded round and offered congratulations.
> The triumph of being the first car, however, was short lived...An
> RCMP officer on a horse came along with a summons. The stunned
> Calgarians saw their car impounded. It was wheeled into Brewster's
> livery stable and locked up.[133]

Not deterred by the impounding of their car, and apparently not in the least bit concerned about any political implications for her husband, Isabella and her sons

> took in some of the loveliest scenery in the world on horseback. They drifted in gaily painted canoes across lakes and down picturesque rivers. They rode through pine forest, beside swift mountain streams.[134]

Apparently, there was some leniency granted for whatever reason because, after their time enjoying the scenery, "the authorities said they could have their car back if they went directly out of town."[135]

All might have gone unnoticed by the senator, hard at work in Ottawa, had a tire not blown near Kananaskis on the way back to Calgary, when the car "veered to the right, ran off the road down a slope, and smacked into a tree."[136] After the mishap with the tire, according to Mary Stringer Lougheed, "Granny" (Isabella) showed her "pioneer heritage" by walking back the seven miles to the tiny station on the rail line. According to daughter-in-law Mary, though suffering swollen feet, Granny "surprised everyone with a tremendous show of energy," making it to the station, where they boarded a train back for Calgary.[137] According to the same article in *Golden West Magazine*, to which Mary granted the interview in 1977, "The Hardistys had battled the frontier for generations so Lady Belle was in her environment."[138] At least one researcher, who spent time reading between the lines of correspondence about Isabella, observed she had a "wild" side that eschewed the restraints placed upon her by the rigours of public life as a gracious woman in the new West.[139]

Reportedly, Lady Lougheed commented with some pleasure after the trip that "we looked like a bunch of tramps." A few days later, a train crew dragged the stranded auto onto a flatcar, leaving it on a sideline beside the main track in Calgary. Suspecting nothing, James returned home from Ottawa on the train, when, upon his approach to Calgary, he "looked out the window he could hardly believe his eyes. There, on the sideline, looking lonely and forlorn, was his prized Pope-Toledo, battered and bent!" The senator arrived home to find a "rather chastened family admitting that they had disobeyed his wishes and ended up a crocker." However, "Lady Belle soothed things down and finally the whole thing ended up with a big laugh."[140] It appears that the patriarchal attitude James displayed publicly was, at least on this occasion, shed at the doors of Beaulieu.[141]

Commenting on the difference in world view between James and Isabella, Lougheed House researcher Jennifer Bobrovitz wondered if Isabella's background as a child of the fur trade might have contributed to her desire to push the boundaries of protocol in the new North West.[142] Regardless of what contributed to it, pushing boundaries no doubt contributed to Isabella's reputation as one of the most successful and fun hostesses of the new North West.

Isabella may have had a desire to push the social boundaries, but she did work as a team with James toward realizing the goal of boosting family fortunes. Together, James and Isabella were involved in the early stages of most social initiatives and community organizations in Calgary. However, there were some clubs the couple could not join together, such as the elite Ranchmen's Club, fashioned after the British gentlemens' clubs that originated in the 1600s. For a long time Calgary's club forbade the membership of women.[143] Even though Isabella could not join the club, in February 1914, son Clarence joined James when he was also elected as a member.[144]

Although she could not join all of the same clubs as James, Isabella took her role as first lady of the transitional society seriously. One of the duties she assumed was that of greeting newcomers to Calgary. As Christian Helen Drever, one of the Drever sisters from St. John's Parish in Red River, related, when she arrived in Calgary on the train in 1886, Isabella was her first visitor.[145] Christian married J.P.J. Jephson, "pioneer barrister," while her sisters also married Calgary pioneers and community builders, one the Anglican bishop, Cyprian Pinkham, and the other, Colonel James Macleod.[146] The Drever women would join Isabella in many of her philanthropic endeavours. While Isabella made it a habit to welcome new arrivals, there is a good possibility she knew of the Drever girls already, given their attendance at Miss Davis's school in Red River.

Indeed, newspaper reports confirm an extensive social schedule for Isabella, and there are a few private details that also confirm this busy schedule. During the restoration work at Lougheed House in the 1990s, one of Isabella's dance cards was found behind the baseboard. Although the card appears to have been used later by a child to scribble on, there is a name filled in next to all twenty of the dances listed on the program, suggesting Isabella may have been on the dance floor the entire evening.[147] When the *Calgary Daily Herald* reported that Isabella was to attend the state ball in Ottawa, it made sure to mention she had been "asked to dance in the state quadrille."[148]

No doubt, it was a great pleasure for the fun-loving Isabella when, in October 1912, a young Fred Astaire and his sister Adele introduced the tango to Calgary during a vaudeville act at the Lougheed's Grand Theatre.[149] Despite concerns expressed by local clergy[150] and the officials from the local university's administration, who forbade students to take part in the tango, it was rumoured that Isabella had organized a "dansant" at Beaulieu for her daughter Dorothy on 1 January 1914, where guests reportedly partook in the tango.[151]

Clearly, Isabella, who likely did host the "dansant" for Dorothy and her friends, enjoyed playfully teasing the media. While many minute details were confirmed, such as the choice of "large yellow mums and yellow and white tulips...tea was served at 4 o'clock," as far as the tango, the *Albertan* was forced to conclude, "whether or not the tango was danced the young people had a merry time and are looking forward to another similar event this afternoon."[152] It appears that Isabella continued to host many "dansant" at Beaulieu, despite warnings such as that given by Rev. C.C. McLaurin in 1915, during an address to a Baptist convention, where he described the West as "dance crazy," and cautioned that "such worldliness and pleasure-seeking" were a "curse to the community."[153] Isabella's networking skills must have been exemplary, for there is no evidence that her reputation suffered, even though she enjoyed activities deemed a "curse" by some community leaders.

While William Hardisty had expressed concerns about Wesleyan, and it appears Isabella was lonely there, it seems she did enjoy at least some aspects of her education, which served her well as a young married woman. Clearly, she was able to apply the skills she learned at Wesleyan to enriching the social fabric of Calgary. By all accounts, Isabella was an accomplished pianist and certainly supported all aspects of Euro-North American cultural activities in Calgary throughout her life. It was no doubt her interest in the arts, garnered at Wesleyan, that inspired Isabella to establish the Grand Theatre with James in Calgary and to entertain world-renowned performers, such as Kathleen Parlow.[154]

Equally adept at official functions as she was at entertainment, Isabella attended the ceremonial laying of the cornerstone for Alberta's legislative building in Edmonton in 1909, perhaps fittingly on the site of the former home of her uncle, Chief Factor Richard Hardisty.[155] Press coverage of the event noted that the former HBC post, which overlooked the North Saskatchewan River, was perhaps one of the "most important trading posts of the Hudson's Bay Company in the then North American wilds."[156] One official commented about the continuation of HBC tradition and the importance of the site for the transition of the new West, saying,

we are after all only aiming to establish for our people the most important and imposing structure in the province upon a site, in our judgement, well suited for the purpose, and in doing so following

in the footsteps of the officers of the historic trading company who
established themselves upon the same ground some two generations
before.[157]

Like her uncle, Chief Factor Richard Hardisty, all indications are
that Isabella came to be regarded as an important public figure. Before
her attendance at the Alberta Legislature, "Mrs. Senator Lougheed"
had stood in for her uncle, Lord Strathcona, when the cornerstone
of the new Methodist Church was laid on 12 May 1904 on the corner
of what is now 7th Avenue and 1st Street East in Calgary. After a
telegram was read from Lord Strathcona, "Mrs. Lougheed stepped
forward and 'with trowel in hand declared the stone well and truly
laid.'"[158] Isabella performed this function despite the fact that
Senator Lougheed was also present. While it would not have been
unusual for women of some standing to perform official functions,
James was the one with the official designation, not Isabella.

In part due to her marriage to the new senator and in part due
to her membership in the Hardisty family, Isabella's activities came
to be closely monitored by the local press. While there was a good
deal of attention devoted to her philanthropic activities, readers
seemed just as interested in her private life. One such example was
the 1907 report in the *Calgary Daily News*, which advised readers
that Isabella and a Mrs. Grott were to holiday in Laggan.[159] In
September 1908, the *Calgary Daily Herald* informed readers that
Isabella was "At Home" for the first time since the renovations at
Beaulieu, commenting that the dining room had been enlarged and
redecorated, while the "roses are grown with wonderful success in
the rosary opening off the dining room."[160]

In typical booster fashion, newspapers referred to the "delightful
tea hour reception" hosted by Isabella in honour of His Royal
Highness the Prince of Wales, followed by an evening dinner at the
Ranchmen's Club, where James proposed the toast to the king.[161]
Reports were always peppered with tremendous detail, such as the
description of the grounds at Beaulieu during the prince's visit:

Masses of vivid flowers against the borders of green trees and foliage were an effective background for pretty light-colored summer frocks worn by the women...the reception was therefore a very informal and intimate tea party, permitting of pleasant chats with the prince and the members of his entourage. By a coincidence, it was for the most part a gathering of "old-timers" of the city—a majority of the guests having been contemporaries of Sir James and Lady Lougheed in this city for the past fifteen or twenty years.[162]

Not only does this excerpt confirm Isabella's hostess abilities (and her position as an old-timer) but it also speaks to her astuteness in contributing with a magnificent garden to the "City Beautiful" movement that swept North America in the late 1800s and early 1900s.

In addition, it surely was no "coincidence" that the majority who were invited to greet the prince were fellow "old-timers," referred to as "contemporaries of Sir James and Lady Lougheed." It was also likely no coincidence that the entire Lougheed family was on hand to greet the prince. This included young Dorothy, dressed in a "very effective gown of black with a smartly-draped tunic heavily brocaded with gold," along with Captain Edgar Lougheed and brother Douglas.[163] Bobrovitz muses that James and Isabella may have sought to extend their kinship network to include British royalty by manipulating situations that might inspire the dashing young prince to take a shining to Dorothy.[164]

Local writer Jean Leslie also suggests that Isabella and James sought to boost the importance of their own family unit by encouraging a romance between their daughter Dorothy and Prince Edward. According to Leslie, "one evening...Edward, Prince of Wales, danced into the wee hours of the morning with Lougheed's daughter Dorothy, who was an excellent dancer."[165] It is not clear if Dorothy joined Isabella when she later travelled to Banff, as did the prince, where Isabella attended the ball given there in his honour.[166] Whether or not there was a desire to expand her family network to include the prince, Isabella's connection to him certainly boosted her own social network, as did the fact that she lived in a house suitable to entertain royalty.

Given the fact that the Lougheeds lived in the "Big House," it was only natural that their home would be the venue from which the new North West welcomed many visiting dignitaries. Given the importance of Beaulieu to promoting the West, Isabella assumed an important role in the marriage partnership, as she managed the social capital that was Beaulieu House. There are many examples found in the local newspapers, reporting Isabella's superb "hostess" skills in particular. One such example was the occasion when Isabella and James hosted Nicholas Flood Davin, at which time Davin delivered a "most eloquent speech." As well as commenting on the speech, the reporter noted,

> A most enjoyable and instructive evening was wound up with a cordial vote of thanks, which called forth enthusiastic cheers to Senator and Mrs. Lougheed for the courtesy and hospitality shown by them to the members of the Liberal Conservative association.[167]

In fact, the *Herald* positively "gushed" in its 1 February 1900 edition, writing,

> Beaulieu...was last night the scene of a brilliant society event, when the Senator and Mrs. Lougheed were "at home" to their wide circle of friends and acquaintances. Entertaining at Beaulieu is the synonym for all that is best and most hospitable in Calgary's social history. Not even Government House at the territorial capital at its palmist could exceed Beaulieu as it appeared last night with its gay company of handsome women and their escorts. What less, indeed, could be expected? The appointments were in every respect perfect, the music bright and crisp, the supper unsurpassed, the dresses such as would have graced a London ballroom, and the host and

hostess doing everything they could [to] conduct to the enjoyment
of their numerous guests. Dancing began shortly after 9:30 to the
music of Mons. Augade's orchestra and was sustained with the
utmost interest until an early hour. In the spacious billiard room,
gentlemen who were no longer devotees of Terpischore enjoyed whist,
billiards, cigars and mellow conversation. The spacious rooms,
admirably designed for dancing, looked most brilliant in their floral
decorations of pink and white carnations, white Roman hyacinths
and palms.[168]

Readers could not help but be impressed by the transformation
of former fur trade country into a space that now boasted venues
equivalent to London ballrooms.

In another report speaking to Isabella's skill as a hostess, the
Calgary News Telegram confirmed that Isabella often relied on her
children for assistance when she threw open her

magnificent home to the many charitable organizations of the city,
and [its] spacious ballroom is thronged several times during the
season with the many friends of her sons. In early January 1914 Belle
held a Saturday afternoon dance jointly for her 15 year old daughter
Dorothy and her 20-year old son Edgar and their friends in the
Lougheed House tea room.[169]

With James away so often attending to Senate work in Ottawa,
the social calendar, so crucial to successful business networking
and boosterism in the early Prairie West, was left in Isabella's
capable hands.

Often, Isabella was accompanied in her leadership and hostess
role by her son Clarence, and at times other dignitaries. For instance,
when their Sherman Grand Theatre opened its doors in Calgary,
Isabella had Clarence by her side. Later, it was Mrs. Arthur Sifton
who joined Isabella.[170] If James happened to be in Calgary, he

Isabella Lougheed (front row on the left) and James Lougheed (back row, third from left). Photo undated. Lougheed House National Historic Site Archives, LHCS 2-1.

stepped right into the events that were pre-arranged by Isabella, as evidenced by the report in the *Albertan* that "Senator Lougheed, who returned to town last night from Ottawa, was able to be present." Despite James's presence, the *Albertan* still noted that it was "Mrs. Lougheed who was entertaining a box party."[171] This description does not imply that James was irrelevant, for it was noted by one newspaper that he was "not an aggressive fire-eater, but, as an executive and as a diplomat, he has few equals at Ottawa."[172] These examples do suggest, however, that it was Isabella who directed much of the couple's commitments and their role as social leaders in Calgary.

In addition to opening Beaulieu to many social events, as a member of the Imperial Order Daughters of the Empire (IODE), Isabella often opened her home for causes such as that which saw 150 guests raise funds for the Boy Scouts. All indications in the local newspapers are that Isabella enjoyed a reputation as a fun-loving hostess, in whose home guests always had a "merry" time and were left in the "happiest mood."[173] While most gatherings in the homes of Calgary's "upper" set were described as "delightful," Isabella's were most often described as "lively" events, where, for example, "Music and animated conversation were followed by several lively contested games of cards."[174]

Often, the music enjoyed at the Lougheed mansion was provided by the woman known to service men and women as "Ma Trainor." Josephine Trainor was actually a serious pianist,[175] who, after playing at Beaulieu, once recalled, "A cheer went up after the first waltz and next thing I knew the Lougheed boys had talked their mother into hiring me for their next *dansant*." Again speaking to the social events that Isabella organized, in 1914, the *Calgary Herald* reported that the "dansant" given by Isabella in honour of her daughter Dorothy proved to be "one of the smart and delightful events of the season."[176] Over seventy guests reportedly had such a "merry time" that they looked forward to another similar event very soon.[177] Isabella also helped organize a winter club, to "encourage figure and fancy skating as well as other winter sport in Calgary."[178] At the fifth annual Pioneer Association Ball in 1913, Isabella and other guests enjoyed moose steak and the orchestra's rendition of the "Red River Jig."[179]

Equally at home with old-timers or royalty, the Lougheeds were always centre stage, even opening their home so the Duke and Duchess of Connaught could make it their residence. In fact, when in Calgary, the duke and duchess, "contrary to the usual custom... requested that their host and hostess should not leave their home during the royal sojourn."[180] This unusual request by Arthur, Duke

of Connaught, son of Queen Victoria, was likely the result of the
time he had spent with Isabella earlier in Ottawa. It was reported in
March of 1912 that Isabella "was singled out for the distinction of
the Duke's company" at a dinner reception. Reportedly, at this
dinner, "the conversation was turned almost immediately to western
topics,"[181] and was surely a wonderful opportunity for Isabella to
share some of the successes of the new North West. Demonstrating
the boosterism common at the time, during this September visit by
the royals, the *Calgary News Telegram* noted,

> *Nowhere in the east can be found gardens that surpass those*
> *surrounding the Lougheed home...The sight of these gardens will put*
> *an end to that Eastern fallacy that it is impossible to grow flowers*
> *in the West.*[182]

Isabella's importance to boosterism of the West is evident in
the 1913 Special Souvenir Issue of the Calgary paper, the *Western
Standard Illustrated Weekly*. In this issue, the Calgary Women's Press
Club claimed,

> *The Last Best West is the women's west. Nowhere else in the world*
> *is the evolution worked by the great feminist movement of the last*
> *century demonstrated more strikingly.*[183]

The women of Calgary used the special issue to "call upon western
men to be 'fair and generous,'" and highlighted successful women
who ran their own businesses and farms, or who held professional
jobs. Despite the fact she did not operate her own business or hold
a "professional" job, Isabella was featured in the article as one of
these women of success. Although her ancestry was not mentioned,
Isabella was listed as one of the few "western born women."[184]

There is no doubt that Isabella became adept at boosterism by
emulating other members of her Hardisty family. Some observe that
Isabella's aunt, Isabella Hardisty Smith, wife of Lord Strathcona,

became quite well known to the British for the lavish receptions the couple hosted, to which invitations were eagerly sought.[185] Like Isabella, Lady Strathcona was the focus of much media attention, but it was not often mentioned that she was of Indigenous ancestry. However, Lady Strathcona was attacked on at least one recorded occasion in which reference was made to her ancestry.[186] This attack appeared in a letter written by the fourth Earl of Minto, appointed in 1898 as the Governor General to Canada. In the letter, the earl seemed to find everything wrong with the Smiths' accommodations when the Duke and Duchess of Cornwall and York, the future King George V and Queen Mary, visited Canada in 1901. In the letter to his brother, Minto wrote about what had long been the custom during the fur trade era—the practice of taking a country-born wife—saying, "Poor old Strathcona attempting to lead society, the ways of which he is ignorant of, with a squaw wife who is absolutely hopeless…what could he expect."[187] Despite the lack of regard paid by Canada's Governor General, Lady Strathcona was, in fact, quite successful at social networking, as was her niece Isabella.[188]

As with the media attention given to her aunt, the local press did tend to feature every detail of Isabella Lougheed's life, including providing portraits and elaborate descriptions of her attire. One example of the extensive detail, and admiration that most newspapers demonstrated when reporting on Isabella, is that which appeared in the *Calgary News Telegram* in 1912. In an article describing the opening of the Sherman Grand Theatre, built by the Lougheeds, the newspaper clearly appreciated the social value of the Lougheeds' contributions:

> *Senator Lougheed is to be congratulated and thanked for giving the city so complete and beautiful a playhouse. Its beauty, refinement, rich tapestries, soft harmonizing tones and artistic appointments combine to make it one of the most beautiful buildings in the west.*[189]

The *News Telegram* continued, "Mrs. Lougheed carried an armful of choice blossoms," while it featured a full-length portrait of Isabella in her "exquisite gown."[190] Even in 1985, detailed descriptions were repeated, such as that in the *Herald*, which described Isabella's "creamy satin gown with a five-foot train."[191]

Local newspapers clearly viewed not only her grand home but Isabella herself as a commodity to be used in the boosterism of the North West. Her success served to demonstrate the sophistication of the emerging society and economy, and quietly spoke to the success of assimilation for those who recognized Isabella's ethnicity. Whatever the agenda for other boosters in the new West, Isabella was equally adept at boosterism herself, not only of the West but of her own social network. Her role as hostess, so necessary in boosterism and community building, emanated from a demonstrated genuine capacity for relating well to most of the people she encountered and an ability to adapt, certainly attributable in part to the culture of her youth.

To understand how Isabella adapted, and thus expanded her own network, it is helpful to examine as many of the roles that she undertook as possible. One of the activist organizations in which Isabella assumed a position was the local chapter of the National Council of Women, an organization that founded a Canadian branch in 1893. At the time, the mission of the council was ostensibly directed toward improving the lives of three groups of women: immigrants, prisoners, and factory workers.[192]

Isabella and James together pledged their support for the Council of Women when they addressed one of its first meetings in Calgary. No doubt many men threw their own support behind the new initiative after James spoke to the gathering during the organizational meeting, predicting "the active sympathies of Calgary's husbands and brothers...would exceed those in any other town and cities." As might be expected, a vote on James's motion to form the local council received unanimous support.[193]

> *Lady Lougheed. Photo dated early 1900s. Glenbow Alberta Museum and Archives, NA-3232-3.*

Although the Lougheeds gave the local chapter their support, it does not appear they initiated its formation. Lady Aberdeen, the wife of the Governor General, suggests in her journal that the chapter was initiated by Jean Drever Pinkham, the Anglican bishop's wife.[194] Lady Aberdeen first met Mrs. Pinkham and a Mrs. Barwis regarding the Council of Women when passing through Calgary in August 1895.[195] Yet Isabella did lend her name and her palatial home to the organization, which she knew would serve to notify Calgarians about the importance of the council, and her own stature. In 1896, Isabella even appeared to take what might have been the bold step of accepting Lady Aberdeen's nomination to become national vice-president, District of Alberta, for the National Council of Women.[196] However, it was a position Isabella held only until the disbanding of the Calgary local just two years later in 1898. It appears that Isabella followed the same pattern with most new social and philanthropic organizations—that is, the public was aware of her involvement, but she was never linked to any controversial activities, such as the campaigns of suffragists or labour activists, which were eventually supported by the Council of Women.

While Isabella's role was most often noted as "hostess," women such as Henrietta Muir Edwards and Maude Riley, Isabella's contemporaries and leaders in the National Council of Women, were often featured in the media at rallies and political meetings.[197] For example, in 1929, when Emily Murphy's group won the Person's Case, there was a good deal of newspaper attention paid to the women of Calgary who were involved in local groups such as the Council of Women. Given her interest in current events, and her social inclination, it is unlikely that Isabella would have missed an event that generated so much interest as the one held at the Palliser Hotel to celebrate the victory for women. Yet there is no mention of Isabella in newspaper reports, and thus no way to know if she actually attended the celebration where all five women involved in the Person's Case spoke after the Privy Council struck down the Supreme Court decision denying that women were persons.[198]

When Isabella was involved in the local Council of Women activities, her role was clearly more as a diplomat than as an activist. When Lady Aberdeen appeared on a podium along with Isabella in 1895, she attempted to clarify for Calgarians the "diplomatic" purpose of the Council of Women. While she noted that the aims appeared vague, Lady Aberdeen chose rather to stress what the council was not. It was not to be a political organization that would support any particular political party. Nor was it formed with the object of gaining the franchise for women, even though some individual members may be active in that campaign. Nor was it to be seen as a religious organization, although some of its members were affiliated with churches. Thus, it was that each organization should reflect the variety of thought of the women involved, be those secular, religious, or philanthropic. Lady Aberdeen went on to ask women to answer the question, "For what is woman's mission? Is it not comprised of that good old English word mothering?"[199]

This question leaves little doubt that, in Lady Aberdeen's mind, and likely in many of those supportive of her cause, the council would be identified with a nonconfrontational form of maternal feminism, framed in diplomacy.[200] So, while Lady Aberdeen had begun with a disclaimer that she would not say what the Council of Women stood for, in the end she was very clear about her perspective of the council's ideology. Lady Aberdeen received rousing applause when she reassured the crowd that the goal was not suffrage but that, although

> woman's first priority was the home, she must carry the same
> strength of commitment into her wider mission—mothering. Her
> call to care for the orphans, the poor, the sick, the tempted and the
> erring, and to elevate social life through literature and education.[201]

This call by Lady Aberdeen to "mother" society was the one that Isabella, at least initially, answered. Unfortunately, early minute books for the Calgary chapter of the Council of Women have been

lost: thus, it is not clear how long Isabella served. Although organized by Lady Lougheed in 1894, the local chapter "did not become
firmly established until 1912," and only sporadic documents exist
until 1939.[202] While a copy of minutes for 1919 does not indicate
Isabella's attendance, it does reveal the types of issues addressed by
the council at that time, including aiming to

> *raise the standard of moving pictures, theatrical and vaudeville*
> *performances and dance halls...care for the mentally deficient...*
> *conservation of natural resources...household economics...*
> *immigration...supervised playgrounds...suppression of objectionable*
> *printed matter...minimum wages for women.*[203]

Despite a lack of evident public activism, historian Marjorie Norris
explains the importance of the Lougheeds to the local council, and
how the council as a whole took advantage of Victorian society's
means of fundraising through events such as teas, garden parties,
"at home" days and soirees. Inclusion on guest lists was

> *confirmation of one's social status, particularly if one's name*
> *appeared in the papers...Calgary's elite also prided themselves on*
> *entertaining visitors from eastern Canada, the United States and*
> *Britain, and probably the most frequently mentioned mansion was*
> *Lougheed's Beaulieu.*[204]

Irene McLachlan, a columnist for the *Calgary News Telegram* in the
early 1900s, commented on Calgary society's penchant for teas and
garden parties. Interviewed after she returned to her native America,
McLachlan commented on the work of women's clubs in Calgary:

> *Tea is the "open sesame" to the inner circle of these clubs. A round*
> *of teas composed the afternoon diversion of the average woman of*
> *position in Alberta. To the uninitiated, the most striking feature of*
> *this side of Canadian life is the endless repetition of the same thing,*

day after day, without seeming to tire the women in the slightest
degree. A week of such perpetual teas would bore an American
woman to distraction.[205]

Victorian-inspired society's penchant for teas and garden parties
certainly represented a major aspect of the social capital that
Isabella contributed to, at least if we are to judge by the numerous
accounts of her social calendar in local newspapers.[206]

While it does not appear that Isabella's involvement in the
local Council of Women was a long-term commitment, the reasons
for this may have been varied. The National Council of Women, in
the early stages, faced difficulties for several reasons. For one, the
membership "quickly came to rely on an urban elite whose mascu-
line counterparts—husbands, fathers, brothers—were often deeply
involved in the Conservative and Liberal hierarchies." The realities
of their husbands' political careers would have necessitated caution
on the part of members of the council. The second problem was that
the first national president, Lady Aberdeen, held "personal sympathies for Gladstonian liberalism," which "made her very much suspect
in Conservative circles."[207] Lady Aberdeen's personal sympathies
may have been a concern for the local Conservative Senator
James Lougheed.

Certainly, as the Council of Women assumed a more political
agenda, James would have been concerned. For example, in his political role, James was expected to comment on the franchise campaign.
During Senate debates that addressed women's rights, James defended
the government's record on equal pay, an issue that groups such as
the Council of Women was seeking to revise. In one example, James
responded to the questions posed by J.G. Turriff with the assertion,
"No distinction is made at all in the classification of employees of
the Government. I might say it is sexless."[208] However, by 1917, when
the campaign for granting the franchise for women was gaining
momentum, Senator Lougheed did finally publicly declare himself
in favour, saying,

"As for me, I am in favour of it"...The Senator explained that
the question of woman franchise was a most important one, that
without doubt all the members of the present administration
realized it, and that steps toward its accomplishment would
no doubt soon be taken.[209]

Whether concern for her husband's career was the catalyst,
Isabella did not become involved in the suffrage campaigns that
many in the Council of Women came to endorse. However, it appears
she was more supportive of extending the franchise to women than
James initially appeared to be. On one occasion, Isabella publicly
opposed a draft City of Calgary bill aimed at removing the franchise
for married women. She obviously felt strongly about this particular
issue, given it is one of the rare instances on which she commented
publicly, telling a local newspaper,

Of course I think that married women ought to have the vote.
I should think any fair-minded person would feel the same way.
I always have voted and I should dislike very much to give up the
privilege. It would not be fair. Married women have more right to
vote than single women.[210]

Isabella's views in this instance were well in line with maternal
feminists, in the sense that she believed married women were more
entitled to vote than single women. For the most part, though,
Isabella steered clear of the franchise campaign.

Although Isabella's name appeared as an executive member for a
vast number of organizations, minutes and newspaper reports
rarely quoted her, suggesting an intelligent management of image
through diplomacy. On the other hand, Isabella seemed more
comfortable with reports detailing her activities that were direct
outreaches of the Methodist Church, such as the Ladies' Aid, established in 1890.[211] The Ladies' Aid tended to reflect ideologies such
as maternal feminism, Christian imperialism, and Methodist piety.[212]

According to the Constitution of the Ladies' Aid in 1934, the primary aim continued to be to

further by every means possible the spiritual, social and material interests of the church; to assist the Pastor in his work, by visiting the members of the congregations, especially the sick and strangers, and any new members coming to the city to reside.[213]

Working with these stated goals, members of the Ladies' Aid engaged in a wide range of activities, from general housekeeping to spiritual leadership.

While Isabella committed to organizations such as the Ladies' Aid and the Council of Women, the more important ties for her may have been private and familial. However, in proto-industrial societies, the family unit was also the work unit which may explain why James and Isabella worked together so closely on many of the new initiatives in Calgary. Another joint venture was their attendance at the founding meeting of the Alberta chapter of the Victorian Order of Nurses (VON) in 1909.[214] If the conditions of health care in the new North West were not enough to induce the couple's participation, they would have recognized the value to the family network of forging links with fellow prominent citizens. In fact, Isabella's uncle, Lord Strathcona, was present at and addressed many of the inaugural meetings of the VON, and it was under his advice that they would only admit fully trained "Hospital Nurses."[215]

In addition to Lord Strathcona's support for the VON, it was Lady Aberdeen's goal that the wives of prominent men, such as senators and Members of Parliament, should be approached to serve as board members.[216] It is also understandable that Isabella was not only attracted to but excelled in the VON, given that the major method of fundraising for the order until the 1940s was, again, through garden parties, teas, and social visits.[217]

In regard to the VON at the time when Isabella and James were involved, many viewed the call to nursing as one exemplifying specifically feminine characteristics of altruism and service, making it an acceptable profession for women.[218] Perhaps this served a purpose for Isabella personally, as her specific role with the VON required more than socializing. Isabella was the first board chairperson, at a time when "board members made contributions which went beyond normal requirements of executive councils." This included driving nurses to see patients, most of whom were too poor to pay for private nurses, as well as attending the first prenatal classes as a way to boost public attendance.[219] The fact that she may have spent a good deal of time with the nurses would have given Isabella access to the working-class segment of her new society.

Again, it is not known exactly how long Isabella served in her role as chairperson of the VON, given that earlier records are sporadic. However, by the early 1920s, Isabella's name no longer appears in any of the minutes or correspondence. Why Isabella, along with women like Mrs. Roper Hull, Mrs. J. Pinkham, Mrs. J.E. Irvine, and Mrs A.M. Scott (all married to prominent men in the community), served is unknown, but it was not likely simply for the sake of networking. The words of one unnamed member of the executive provide some insight behind their motivations:

> Why are our members ready to sacrifice time, money, thought & energy...why is our presidents ever [sic] ready to drop everything and help the nurses with their various difficulties...? It is just plain love for our fellow men.[220]

Conditions in the West were desperate at times and may explain why many felt there was an absolute need for the VON. The 1905 annual report for the VON noted,

> Work of the hospitals in the West has increased tremendously during the past year...They are all overtaxed, cots being placed in the halls...I do not think the people in this part of Canada can

realize the difficulties under which the nurses work in some of the
small Western towns; no light but oil lamps, and oft-times the only
supply of water being in the basement of the building...A large
number of the patients come long distances to be treated.[221]

When she joined so many of the community-building organizations, Isabella was also doing what many of her alumnae from Wesleyan were doing in their respective communities. Minnie Buck, who later became Mrs. Colin Campbell, also moved west after her time at Wesleyan. Buck served as the editor of Wesleyan's periodical, *The Portfolio*, for a time and later went on to help found the Winnipeg chapter of the IODE, a role that Isabella assumed in Calgary.[222] It was in 1909 that Isabella joined as a member of her local chapter, serving as first vice regent and hosting most of the meetings at Beaulieu. According to the *Calgary Club Woman's Blue Book*, a public reception was held at Beaulieu on 20 October 1909, when the inaugural "meeting was happily presided over by Senator Lougheed."[223] Again acting as partners, Isabella moved that a chapter be formed, while James suggested that the name honour Colonel James Macleod, whose life motto, "Hold fast," be adopted as the chapter's motto. Calgarians seemed relatively enthusiastic about the arrival of the IODE to their community, and the *Morning Albertan* reported that a "strong chapter" was organized at the inaugural meeting held at Isabella's home.[224]

There are no existing copies of minutes found from early meetings of the IODE, so there is no way to know how much Isabella participated and who most of her fellow members were, although at the time of her death, in 1936, she was still an honorary regent of the IODE.[225] It is interesting that, other than the inaugural meeting, and the fact that she retained a ceremonial title, there is no evidence in the local newspapers that her name ever appeared as a leader of the organization, nor was she recognized at any further public functions. Given that, throughout its history, the IODE maintained working relationships with organizations such as the

National Council of Women, the Federation of University Women, the Salvation Army, the Young Women's Christian Association, the Girls' Friendly Society, and the Red Cross,[226] Isabella may have simply seen belonging as the thing to do.

While Isabella's name appeared regularly in local newspapers, it was most often in connection with her role as superb hostess for the West, rather than involvement in any sort of controversial political activism. In the tradition of "gracious womanhood," and in the spirit of boosterism, Isabella allowed her name to be used in the formative stages of many organizations but was not publicly present when controversial issues were debated, such as temperance, suffrage, and various social "problems." Thus, Isabella was not only a "gracious" woman but a skilled diplomat, well poised to play a leading role in the changing economy of the new North West but never publicly involved in what could become controversial matters.

Association with groups such as the IODE no doubt assisted in consolidating her reputation and sterling associations; it certainly "contained" the difficulties of being a woman of Indigenous ancestry.[227] In some ways, Isabella and other members became a symbol of contradiction in that they were extending help to those in need while also supporting the patriarchal and imperial practices which often helped create that need.

That contradiction is obvious in one of the few instances when Isabella granted an interview to a newspaper. In the interview with an unnamed Toronto reporter, Isabella referred to the early privations for her fur trade family in the North:

> One winter we stayed at Fort Rae...It was because of the great scarcity of food that my father told my mother that we could not possibly winter at Fort Simpson, that we would starve if we did. So in the fall my mother, three brothers, my sister and self left to winter at Fort Ray. We were given fifty pounds of flour as our share of available provisions. For seven months we lived on that and white fish from Great Slave Lake.[228]

Despite these recollections in 1922 that confirm she was not always a privileged "Lady," for the most part Isabella adhered to her new image. She continued in the same interview to tell her audience,

> *In Calgary's early days it was almost impossible to get help. The squaws and half breed women were all that were available. They could wash but could not iron, and they were never dependable.*[229]

This interview provides a rare example, in Isabella's own words, of her own management of her public image. In the North, she would have been quite comfortable with the concept of having Indigenous people "around the place" daily. Yet this is the one and only time we know for certain she had Indigenous women in her grand home in Calgary as well, and she took the opportunity to let her new community know that she thought little of "squaws" and "half breeds."

We do not really know the motivation for this rare interview or her decision to publicly criticize the Indigenous women that she had in her home (some of whom may have even been her family fur trade connections). There is also no way to know if these comments were simply meant to maintain her public image, or even how Isabella really felt about organizations such as the IODE and her role within them. However, recent historical work has challenged the assumption of the two discrete spheres of private and public, arguing that some have demonstrated how "closely linked and intertwined family, sexuality, gender, imperialism, nation and citizenship were."[230] For Isabella, the "private" was very often necessarily the "public," given that her role in the partnership involved throwing open the doors of the "private" Beaulieu to the always enquiring minds of the public. Further, along with gender, race, and class, it must be taken into consideration that all women are not the same, indeed, that all Metis are not the same, and that "identities are multiple and complex."[231]

While Isabella's networking drew her to organizations that fostered the ideology of assimilation, such as the IODE, it is also true that she was a very social woman. Fundraising for most causes at that time involved the production of pageants and plays, which many times occurred in people's homes or in church basements, or sometimes in the form of grand balls. These are all activities that would have appealed to Isabella's very social nature. When we remember that Calgary was not a large city at the time that most of these organizations were formed, and entertainment opportunities were rare, it is understandable that most leading citizens would become involved in such things as pageants and plays, no matter which organization was hosting. This is particularly true of Isabella and James, who were always on the forefront of the promotion of arts and culture. While the many causes Isabella belonged to no doubt harboured social engineering ideologies, care must be taken in ascribing the collective identity of these causes to her personally. However, one thing that can be concluded with certainty is that Isabella's active social calendar extended her women's network and helped further the success of her own family unit.

While the practical skills that she learned from her Metis mother in fur trade country helped Isabella survive in the sparsely settled Prairie West shortly after the fur trade era, Isabella's social role bore some resemblance to that of a trading chief of the Indigenous world during the fur trade era, and even more so to that of a chief factor of the Hudson's Bay Company. Isabella's diplomacy and noted skills as a hostess matched those of the most successful of trading chiefs during the fur trade era. Her abilities at leadership, diplomacy, and social convening were all integral aspects of being a fur post factor, as most threw balls and regales for their men and assumed diplomatic roles both in and outside of the post. Despite her husband's sometimes paternalistic attitude toward Indigenous people, the example that Isabella learned by observing her own Metis father, grandfather, and uncles, in fact, set James in good stead.

Clearly, Isabella's skills as diplomat and hostess began when she was a young girl in fur trade country, were honed as a pioneer during the transitional period, and were perfected as the gracious wife of Sir James Lougheed.

4

With This Economy We Do Wed

THERE WAS A SUGGESTION THAT, as a young man, James
Lougheed referred to marriage as a business partnership of sorts,
a perspective that resembled that of many Hudson's Bay Company
men at the height of the fur trade era. At the time of James and
Isabella's marriage, the HBC was still enjoying profitable business
activity and continued to be involved in many aspects of the North
West's changing economy. Subsequently, company men (and those
in their network) were well placed to continue to reap profits, not
only through company business but by becoming landowners and
investors in many new ventures.

Many of those involved in the new business environment that
developed in Alberta were connected to the Alberta-based bourgeoisie,
particularly during the period from 1885 to 1925.[1] A number of those
Alberta-based bourgeoisie very likely had ties to the fur trade, and
more specifically to the Hudson's Bay Company. Thus, the class
system that was becoming more apparent during the latter part of
the fur trade, in which those affiliated with the HBC achieved more

influential positions and thus more wealth, would persist. James Lougheed, a poor Irish boy from Toronto's Cabbagetown,[2] was able to negotiate the transitional economy as a member of one of the most influential HBC bourgeoisie families, largely because of his fortuitous marriage to Isabella Hardisty, but also in part because he was able to offer skills the Hardisty family did not possess—legal skills that would be useful in the new era of paper transactions.

Boosters of most Prairie towns, in their efforts to portray images of sophistication and progressivism, portrayed women as proper ladies and mothers, while men would be seen as "shrewd in business."[3] Isabella certainly cultivated a persona as a "lady" and James one of being "shrewd" in business. Many contemporary publications recognized James's ability to forge advantageous connections, even drawing attention to the most fortuitous—his marriage to Isabella. The extensive connections the couple then managed to forge together enabled their successful transition from Metis girl of the fur trade and young lad from Cabbagetown into one of the most powerful and aristocratic couples the North West could boast about in the late nineteenth and early twentieth centuries.

James Lougheed was able to connect with the HBC bourgeoisie at a time when many of them had used their connections in, and knowledge of, the North West to prepare for the transition that everyone knew was coming. As we know, one of James's new connections, Reverend Leonard Gaetz, promoted James's appointment to the Senate shortly after his marriage to Isabella. According to Gaetz's granddaughter, Richard Hardisty had met Gaetz at the "end of the steel" in Medicine Hat in 1883, and had driven him to Edmonton, helping him to locate a homestead in the Red Deer River valley.[4] Reverend John McDougall, another member of the Hardisty family, upon visiting the Gaetz homestead, remarked on his progress, noting,

> We came to the hospitable home of Rev Leonard Gaetz, with whom
> we camped for the night. We found our friend like one of the patriarchs

of old, with his sons and daughters, man servants and maid servants,
oxen and flocks and herds, as busy as could be, building up for his
descendants a home in this new country.[5]

Annie Gaetz, Leonard Gaetz's granddaughter, obsered that "Dr.
Gaetz must make about three extra trips to Calgary every year to
take down the furs he had taken in and to bring back trade goods."[6]
These journeys perhaps explain his connection to the Hardisty
family. Certainly, she noted that Gaetz was involved in the boosterism that led a group, which included James Lougheed, to appeal
to Ottawa for a rail link from Calgary to Edmonton.[7]

Leonard Gaetz was also to become an ardent supporter of agricultural and economic expansion in the North West. He became
well known not only in the North West but also to decision makers
in the Canadian government, perhaps because of his connection to
the Hardisty family. Gaetz's own family were poor farmers from
Nova Scotia, and were not able to provide the same connections as
the Hardisty family. Speaking to his growing importance, the Select
Standing Committee on Agriculture and Colonization called Leonard
Gaetz to Ottawa in February of 1890, so that he could offer his opinion
on the potential for agriculture in the North West. Gaetz provided a
glowing report, assuring the government,

> *I am a co-worker with you in everything that leads to the success*
> *and development of this ancient and honourable industry...It does*
> *not require and [sic] great prophetic genius to fortell [sic] the*
> *commercial possibilities that are to be found in such a district.*[8]

Gaetz, ever the booster, then provided his assessment of the possibilities in mining, timber, the limitless supply of water, and great
potential in farming, noting,

> *It does not take very great skill to raise cattle which at 28 or 30*
> *months will dress...It does not take a great deal of skill in farming.*

Even a novice like myself, in a normal years [sic] *can grow crops of grain-oats 50–75 bushels per acre.*[9]

The connection between Gaetz, McDougall, and Hardisty speaks to the emerging and important relationships between HBC men and new businessmen in the North West.

There is another example that demonstrates the close links that many fur trade "pioneers" of the North West maintained into the transitional economy. Richard Hardisty's work as chief factor often involved having to balance the needs of the company with new opportunities for his family, as more free traders operated in the 1870s. One of those free traders was David McDougall, brother of Richard's wife Eliza, and son of John McDougall. Besides trading, David joined his missionary father and brother in the cattle business as a way to supplement their missions. David operated with a group of Metis traders near Buffalo Lake in the mid-1870s, a group that included Cuthbert McGillis and his son-in-law, Addison McPherson.[10] One of the men who partnered with McPherson was none other than Charlie Smith (Marie Rose's husband), and another of the free traders who may very well have dealt with Richard Hardisty.[11]

Understanding Richard Hardisty's financial holdings sheds light on how James managed to amass personal wealth in a relatively short time. Richard Hardisty and his wife, Eliza, were leading figures in the rapidly growing West, and likely had a hand in most significant social activities and economic enterprises in Edmonton before their move to Calgary.[12] While scouting new opportunities for the HBC, Richard established his own steam saw and gristmill. He subsequently applied for timber limits in his own name, in effect setting himself up as competitor to his own employer.[13] In 1881, the *Edmonton Bulletin* reported mining activity by the HBC, which "sent a force of 9 men up to work the seam of coal on Big Island." It was at the same time that Richard took two men with him to establish another mine, this one for his own personal gain.[14]

By 1884, the lumber harvested for Hardisty and his partner, Fraser, exceeded that harvested for the HBC.[15] To power his saw and gristmill, Hardisty fired it with coal from a mine he had set up earlier near Big Island, a few miles upstream from the fort, and which he had staked near an HBC mine.[16] It is not clear whether Richard's mines ever produced large quantities of coal. However, as early as the late eighteenth century, "Europeans started burning the coal that could be found locally along the banks of the North Saskatchewan."[17] Known to Indigenous people as "burning rocks," coal eventually played a major role in the selection of the land holdings the HBC made as compensation for rights ceded to the Canadian government in 1869.[18]

Also fortuituous for Richard Hardisty is that, without waiting for official survey, he and numerous Edmontonians staked out acres of land near HBC lands.[19] By 1882, Hardisty was noting in company documents the profits that many were making in land sales, such as one example when lots originally purchased for $25 sold for $200.[20] In addition to his opportune investment in land in the North West, Richard, like so many of the Hardisty family, owned stocks in the Bank of Montreal.[21] The full extent of Richard's assets is not clear, but there is reference to a statement submitted by James, covering the period from May 1884 to April 1886. This particular statement identified several debts owed to Richard, as well as mortgages he held on various Calgary properties,[22] suggesting his cash flow was extensive.

It was the other HBC man, Richard's brother-in-law, Donald A. Smith, who handled most of Richard's investments,[23] and who eventually accumulated one of the largest personal fortunes in Canada.[24] Smith was appointed as land commissioner by the HBC in 1874, a position that was no doubt compatible with his ongoing business interests. He had begun as early as 1869 to invest his own retirement money and that of many of his fellow officers in a variety of industrial, commercial, and land development ventures. By the 1870s, Smith was also buying stock in the HBC and was subsequently elected as governor in 1889, serving in that capacity until his death in 1914, at the age of ninety-four.[25] Undoubtedly, the fact that company men like Richard Hardisty and Donald A. Smith ventured into new and independent areas of commerce contributed to their ability to transition so successfully when the HBC shifted its focus.

The HBC managed to retain a position of importance in the Bow Valley through activities other than land speculation, but it was the intense speculation on land that became a concern for company headquarters in London. There was always a question of mismanagement, and company records were often lost in the rush to expand and diversify.[26] In fact, some researchers have argued that many men trained in the fur trade were poorly equipped for business management, or that they simply did not pursue retail and government contracting.[27] It is perhaps for this reason that Smith, whose business horizons had expanded, often clashed with others in the company who were slow to respond to new opportunities.[28] Regardless of the poor business abilities of some HBC men, that was not a problem for the Hardisty men. Not only was Donald Smith adept at recognizing profitable opportunities but Richard Hardisty Sr. also left a valuable estate.[29]

It was also fortuitous for the Hardisty family that, when the CPR had located freight yard facilities in Calgary, government agencies soon followed. This federal presence meant that issues of justice, timber and grazing leases, homestead entries, and immigration were increasingly decided in Calgary,[30] a development that further facilitated new ventures for the Hardisty family. According to a memo that spoke of a "ranche" house, barn and stables, and a manager's house and fields, it appears that Richard was also involved in the new business of ranching.[31] In addition, in 1882, Richard's name was listed as one of the investors involved in the Fertile Belt-Western Ag. Co. Ltd.[32] Like Hardisty, who, by the 1880s, had substantial land holdings in Calgary, including (conveniently enough) the Dominion Lands office building,[33] James quickly began to erect commercial buildings on the open prairie.

Although her sources are sparse, Marian McKenna wrote that, by 1914, James and Isabella had acquired so much of the real estate on 7th and 8th avenues in downtown Calgary that they were paying a high proportion of assessed taxes for the city, even more than the Hudson's Bay Company and the Alberta Hotel combined.[34] The *Calgary Herald* did report, "Sir James at one time in the 1920s was said to have paid more than half the taxes in the entire city of Calgary for his land holdings were of considerable proportion."[35]

James's connection with the HBC continued, when he formed a partnership with Edmund Taylor, who was involved in the company's own plans to diversify. Taylor, James's future business partner, managed the building of a "modern retail dry goods establishment" by the HBC in Calgary. In the late 1890s, the HBC's retail outlet was the place where "customers went to see the shape of the future," and where "every country in the civilised world is represented within the walls of this sightly emporium."[36] In addition to managing the Calgary store for the HBC, Taylor had worked as an apprentice clerk, then at various trading posts in the North-West Territories prior to going into the financial business with James.[37] In 1911, Lougheed and Taylor used their connections with the HBC to build reputations as "among Calgary's most useful and enterprising citizens,"[38] when they formed Taylor and Lougheed, a company that handled mortgages, insurance, and finances.

In addition to land speculation and financing, James invested in another important aspect of Calgary's growing economy—entertainment. In 1912, construction on the Lougheed Building, a combined office block and 1,500-seat Grand Theatre, was completed. In James's absence, Isabella took in the inaugural performance on 5 February, occupying the Lougheed box.[39] According to contemporaries who remembered all three theatres in which James and Isabella were eventually involved, James "certainly looked after the young crowd."[40]

Just as certainly, Isabella looked after the "young crowd," although she is not mentioned by contemporary Leishman McNeill, who made this comment.[41] Another of the important new symbols of a progressive economy, which no doubt impressed the young crowd, was Calgary's Symphony Orchestra, launched in 1913. Isabella and James always supported the symphony,[42] and Isabella remained a member until her death.

In addition to the arts, boosters of Calgary were always determined to demonstrate that their expanding community was on the leading edge of all new innovative technology. When closed cars appeared on the streets of Calgary in 1911, they were greeted by many with laughter and called "greenhouses on wheels." However, Isabella again eschewed criticism and instead chose to set the trends. One of the largest such closed cars was that which

> came to Calgary for Mrs. Lougheed, wife of Senator Lougheed. Seven thousand dollars would buy much of any commodity in 1911 and the huge, custom-made Peerless, with driver's seat securely partitioned off, bore the same relationship to cars of later models as the cumbersome steam engine of that period bore to the handy farm tractors that followed.[43]

Boosterism and the efforts of real estate magnates and society leaders, such as the Lougheeds, had borne fruit. In 1901, Calgary's population was listed at 4,000; by 1911, it had grown to over 43,000; and, by 1916, population numbers neared 65,000. Land speculation continued as the largest industry, as evidenced by the 1913 *Henderson's Directory*, which listed 358 real estate agents in comparison to 166 grocery stores, 17 banks, and 27 hardware stores.[44]

It was only after 1910, and extensive economic activity by people such as Isabella and James, that another major industry, wheat production, soared in Alberta, propelling Calgary to the role of regional wholesale and distribution centre.[45] The Calgary Grain Exchange had already formed, in the hopes of unseating Winnipeg as the leading

Lady Lougheed, daughter Marjorie, and chauffeur in front of Beaulieu House.
Photo dated 1911. Glenbow Alberta Museum and Archives, NA-3232-6.

grain centre, a goal achieved with the opening of the Panama Canal
in 1914.[46] These developments led to rising land prices in Calgary,
which was extremely beneficial to James and Isabella, given their
extensive land holdings. In most centres, real estate speculation
was tied to boosterism. When the boosters were less active, the real
estate market tended to slow as well.[47] James, in his official capacity,
was ideally placed to be a champion booster. Further, as a lawyer, he
could play the role of middleman in real estate speculation on
behalf of others.

Most accounts of James stress his immense financial and political success, all of which occurred after his marriage to Isabella. Few
write of James's "fledgling law practice," when he first arrived in
Calgary, and the fact that he had difficulty attracting investors and
securing his own funds for investment. However, one author wrote
about James that

*Still considered a shaky venture in the mid-1880's, his law practice
experienced difficulties in securing funds from outside sources. Only
in the 1890s was his firm's financial base broadened through several
substantial loans from the Hamilton, Ontario-based Canada Life
Assurance Company.*[48]

James married Isabella in 1884, and in 1889 he was appointed a
senator. Thus, these two events occurred prior to the acquisition of
most of his wealth. It was only after he joined the Hardisty family
that James assumed many of their legal responsibilities as well.

As a legal representative for the Hardisty family, and in his
growing practice defending a wide array of clients, it is said that
James "became an effective courtroom lawyer, demonstrating
considerable skill as a cross-examiner." Adept in the courtroom,
James was equally keen in managing his extensive real estate
holdings. By 1890, he and Isabella were among the "town's largest
landholders."[49] Wisely, given his eventual disputes with partners,
he kept these holdings segregated from his law firm. In court documents filed by his former law partner in 1895, Peter McCarthy noted
that his former partner certainly knew how to succeed in the new
economy and had an "unfailing knack for knowing who would help
him in his career."[50] Surely, McCarthy would have been referring to
the most important connection that Lougheed had made—that
with the Hardisty family.

Well into the 1900s, the presence and importance of the HBC
and of its officers continued to be recognized by the citizens of
Calgary. When Isabella's uncle, Lord Strathcona, died, the *Morning
Albertan* featured a long tribute titled "Laid Down Are the Reins:
The Nations Mourn." The tribute began by expressing,

*In the passing of Lord Strathcona...the world in general and the
Hudson's Bay Company in particular, suffered a loss of which words
must fail in attempt to tell.*[51]

When Calgary's Allen Theatre showed "moving pictures" of the funeral ceremonies for Isabella's uncle three days in a row, the city declared one of those days "Hudson's Bay Day."[52] As the niece of Lord Strathcona, the social capital Isabella contributed to her partnership with James cannot be denied.

James and Isabella's many property holdings and dealings in the growing city of Calgary naturally meant they would conduct business with the HBC. One such transaction saw an exchange of land when the company planned a new "mammoth department store" in 1919. Although James played coy with the media, the *Albertan* confirmed that it was a "known fact that Senator Lougheed has recently been purchasing more property in the vicinity" where the HBC was rumoured to be considering a new location for its expansion.[53]

The fact that James appeared to have insider knowledge about the location chosen by the HBC for their expansion bears some resemblance to his earlier purchase of land that quickly increased in value when the CPR expanded in the Calgary area. Yet, when James came to the North West, it was not a given that he would succeed, and his initial relationship with the CPR was not indicative of future success. In Medicine Hat, where James first settled, he bunked with CPR engineer, P. Turner Bone. Bone once reminisced that so indignant was James at the town lot prices established by the Canada North West Land Company, a subsidiary of the CPR, that he led an "indignation meeting," in which he denounced the company.[54]

Unable to make the connections necessary to succeed in Medicine Hat, James had left for Calgary, as did Bone, where the two again bunked together.[55] In Calgary, what James had found was a town "consisting almost entirely of tents. These were all east of the Elbow River...close to the C.P.R. road-bed."[56] As Bone continued, those who had set up these tents assumed that the CPR station would be located there, but the rail company had a townsite in mind "about a mile farther west on Section 15."[57] Indeed, James had better fortune in Calgary than in Medicine Hat, and a far more cordial relationship with the CPR. According to the CPR Town Site Sales Book records, the five lots that James originally purchased in 1883 for $300 were valued at $50,000 just a few years later.[58] James purchased his land a mile west of what was at that time the centre of town. Suspicions have since been raised about James's choice of those particular lots, given that most of his contemporaries were speculating on eastern locations.[59]

It is a fact that, when James arrived at Fort Calgary, the townsite was located on the east bank of the Elbow River, near its confluence with the Bow, and most speculators were trading in east bank properties in anticipation of the coming rail lines. When the CPR subsequently announced its decision to bypass the existing townsite and build its station on the west bank, while most local businessmen were outraged, the young James Lougheed was in the "enviable position of owning much of what is today downtown Calgary."[60] Whether James had access to privileged information has not been established. However, he did continue to buy lots after the astronomical rise in the value of his first purchases, amassing thirty in all to the west of the existing townsite. No doubt sensing some resentment at his good fortune, James himself explained the growth in Calgary, writing in 1910,

> By common consent the town took root on the east bank of the Elbow...and had the then owners of section 14 taken advantage of the settlement of 1883 and acceded to the demands for sale of lots... the entire flat from the east banks of the Elbow to the west bank of the Bow would have been settled.[61]

James continued to explain that others could easily have benefitted as he did:

> In December of 1883 the Canadian Pacific Railway Company put section 15, the present site of the city, upon the market, and allowed to those who purchased lots a 50 per cent rebate, provided they

erected a building upon the lots purchased by them during the
following spring. This resulted in general migration of the town to
its present location...Before the end of 1884 the foundations of a
flourishing town had been laid. [62]

To those who questioned the resources of the area, and perhaps
addressing his aggressive construction activity, James asserted,

Calgary citizens never hesitated to take a most optimistic view of
the future, and to affirm that the development of the natural
resources of Alberta would contribute to the building up of a
promising city. The growth and success of cities are very much like
the growth and success of individuals. [63]

James was certainly more optimistic about his fortunes in
Calgary than he had been in Medicine Hat, and his attitude toward
CPR land policy had altered drastically. Most were very aware that
James Lougheed, of course, had close connections to the Hardisty
family, in addition to his new position as solicitor for the CPR.
Notwithstanding how he came about his fortunes, as justification
to those who might envy his meteoric rise in wealth and stature,
which in some ways gave him the semblance of an old world "local
patrician,"[64] James continued to explain his success by saying, "It
is frequently a problem with the public why certain individuals
succeed when there is no apparent reason why they should succeed
than that others should fail."[65]

In regard to the fortune James realized on the CPR lots, his sense
that some were suspicious of the success of land speculators in Calgary
was astute. There was a dispute between the federal government,
the HBC, and some of its former employees about previous claims
established on section 14, where most felt the townsite should be.[66]
As the solicitor for the CPR, surely James would have been aware of
the dispute, and no doubt understood the benefit to the CPR of
establishing a townsite on section 15, removed from the original

townsite. In the end, James's "gamble," though it appeared odd to many at the time, does not appear to have been a gamble at all.

A former staffer offered some insight into James's land dealing. In the autobiographical notes of Harold Mayne Daly, who was also an assistant to Sam Hughes,[67] James is described as a "dapper little man, inclined to be close in money matters and a very large holder of real estate in Calgary and Edmonton." Regarding the incredible wealth amassed by Lougheed and the young man who became his successful partner, R.B. Bennett, Daly noted that both had

> *a lot of dealings with the Department of the Interior, and made money out of government lands, which I suppose, they had a right to do, but they were not very popular with Government officials.*[68]

Whether he was unscrupulous in any of his dealings, James admitted during a conversation with Mackenzie King that "with the knowledge he now has of the workings of a Cabinet he could, were he an unscrupulous contractor, find it very easy to make millions."[69] James did amass a fair estate, so what this says about his ability to be "unscrupulous" we can only speculate.

Certainly, some members of the Hardisty family gained a reputation for such unscrupulousness, the most well known being Donald A. Smith. Smith was publicly accused by at least one Metis man of defrauding him. Johnny Grant eventually warned Smith of his intention to publish his accusations if he received no objection from his "Lordship." Apparently, Grant received no argument, for he proceeded to dictate his memoirs to family members, in which he spoke on several occasions of Smith not honouring his commitments.[70] It is plausible that Smith had made commitments to members of the Metis community, given his long career in the HBC, and Smith was certainly well connected politically. He served on the Canada Sub-Committee from 1884 to 1886, a committee that was to provide advice to HBC Land Commissioner Charles John Brydges. However, some conclude that Smith played almost "no role as advisor" to the company but rather pursued his own interests (and those of his family network), "working on behalf of friends and business colleagues—often outside proper business procedure."[71] While Smith pursued his own interests, there is some evidence that the work of the HBC land commissioner, who vigorously defended westerners' development strategies, did help boost the image of the company in the West. However, no doubt Brydges's work was made even more difficult by Smith's own priorities, which were clearly his own investments.[72]

Certainly, there were many who believed that, not unlike Donald Smith, his uncle by marriage, James Lougheed was equally committed to his own personal interests. With James's apparent "gamble" on townsites, his and Isabella's future was guaranteed.[73] Soon after the rise in value of his property, James moved his law office from its location near I.G. Baker and Co. to a new location next door to the HBC. In addition to this move, an advertisement in the Calgary Herald confirmed that James was now open for business as an agent for HBC lands.[74] His reputation for striking fortuitous deals was growing. A descendant of one of James's law partners, William McLaws, commented, "Lawyers are often the middlemen in the business world, drafting contracts and introducing wheeler-dealers to each other. And Lougheed was one of the biggest wheeler-dealers in the province, if not the West."[75] James had a hand in almost every new venture in the emerging economy, even organizing prospecting parties in the 1890s in search of gold along the Elbow River, west of Calgary.[76]

No doubt James's tremendous success and that of his partner, R.B. Bennett, would draw attention from many young lawyers seeking their own fortunes. While Calgary had five lawyers in 1884, by 1920 that number had grown to 120.[77] However, only a small minority achieved status and wealth equal to that of Lougheed and Bennett, each of whose net worth was in excess of $100,000 in the 1920s.[78] Bennett explained the prosperity available in the West:

*A young man with push and enterprise going into one of the towns
along the line of railway while having to put up with great inconvenience will make more money in a year by speculating in real estate,
and going in for life and fire insurance and a little law than he
would make in five years in Ontario.*[79]

Indeed, the main activity that transformed the Lougheed–Bennett
partnership from a small frontier practice to one that achieved a
national and international reputation was not its focus on law but
the direct investment of its members in a variety of enterprises.
Just a few of those investments included city-building operations
such as the Calgary Gas and Waterworks Co., Golden Mining and
Smelting Co., and Calgary Petroleum Products Co.[80]

Although most historians of the transitional economy pay more
attention to the presence of ranchers, merchants, farmers, railways,
and banks, lawyers were very active in financing economic development, particularly from 1884 to 1920.[81] The extensive construction
undertaken by James no doubt provided hundreds of jobs, while
creating much-needed office space and increasing the circula-
tion of money, in effect helping transform downtown Calgary.[82] By
advancing funds to ranchers, merchants, and professionals, James
assumed a key role in local and regional improvements.[83] In his role
as solicitor for many chartered banks, James facilitated credit transactions, with interest rates at the turn of the century that generated
anywhere between 8 and 18 per cent.[84] This financial activity would
have positively affected local, regional, national, and international
markets, as well as his own profit margin.[85]

Larger borrowers, like Lougheed and Bennett, were often able
to obtain preferred rates from insurance and loan companies,
which they, in turn, loaned at higher rates. In 1899, for example,
James borrowed a "substantial amount of money from the Canada
Life Assurance Company at 6 per cent, while simultaneously
charging 8 per cent for the funds he lent to a fellow barrister."[86]
In addition, Calgary lawyers were becoming increasingly tied to

the region's agricultural activity. According to records held by the Corporate Registry Archives and Calgary Land Titles Office, James made advances to ranchers in the High River, Fish Creek, and Queenstown areas during the 1890s.[87] Bennett was also involved in agriculture, becoming a director of the Calgary-based Alberta Stock Yards Company in 1910.[88]

Despite the efforts of men such as Lougheed and Bennett in trying to boost the appeal of the West by loaning funds to land speculators, even by 1909, when land rushes began, land in Alberta was still selling for only $18.20 per acre compared to $47.30 per acre in Ontario.[89] Thus, loaning on such properties, which were increasing in value almost daily, was hardly a risky proposition. It is fair to conclude that their involvement in all aspects of the economy would give lawyers, such as Lougheed and Bennett, good cause to become the primary boosters of the West.

There were those who continued to believe that, for James Lougheed, boosterism of the West was all for his own gain. Bob Edwards, the sharp-tongued publisher of the *Calgary Eye Opener*, never missed the opportunity to draw attention to James's wealth and his connections to what Edwards saw as corrupt business dealings. In 1906, a cartoon featured a likeness of James, astride a pig labelled "c.p.r.," with the caption, "Lougheed's rapid advance in life." Edwards added the sarcastic observation,

> *Lougheed is merely a* c.p.r. *solicitor of no particular note. The only note he has ever aspired to is one bearing interest at the rate of two per cent a month...The very first thing Lougheed does after receiving his pompous-sounding, but empty, appointment, is to join with some other* c.p.r. *fatheads and decry the entrance of the Hill railroads into the west. And the west shouting for increased transportation facilities! Dear, dear!*[90]

Edwards also drew attention to what he believed to be James's opportunism in forging the kinship connection to Isabella, writing,

"Lougheed's mythico-historical relationship to Lord Strathcona is a great asset, to be sure."[91] More than any other journalist of his time, Edwards earned a reputation as a "man of the people." Thus, when he drew attention to James's fortuitous marriage connection, many would have taken notice.

When it came to James's business dealings, Edwards likely articulated the sentiment shared by many who recognized that the close relationship that early lawyers such as Bennett and Lougheed shared with banks and big business was beneficial to their own profit margins. Perhaps fewer in these early heady days of expansion and boosterism recognized these relationships were often extensions of fur trade relationships, but Edwards, for one, pointed it out.

Even when recessions hit the western Prairies, many lawyers, like James, managed to retain their positions in the higher class. This no doubt led to some hostility, because lawyers were often seen as representatives of "unsympathetic banks and loan agencies who squeezed embattled farmers."[92] Further, the increasing profitability for lawyers during economic recessions because of their involvement with foreclosures, collections, insolvencies, and reorganizations bred resentment from those struggling to survive.[93] Bennett's move into the political scene was no better for his reputation. After his election as prime minister, his popularity quickly sank to record lows for a federal leader, when many came to believe he was unsympathetic to the plight of western farmers during what became the Great Depression.

Some local reporters at the time viewed James with the same disdain they did Bennett. Again, Edwards was the most vocal, reportedly calling the senator "an offensive promoter of corporation interests to the detriment of the people."[94] Edwards quoted the *Golden Star*, which noted that James would make a better sheepherder than leader of the Opposition in the Senate.[95] Despite any criticism, James never wavered in his support of both the CPR and the Conservative Party, earning him the characterization of a "machine Tory," for whom the interests of the party and the great corporations were of utmost importance.[96]

Despite the fact that many viewed him as an unwavering supporter of the Conservatives, James had developed an allegiance to the West fairly early on. When Macdonald's government had to deny the request made by a Calgary group seeking to build a new rail line in the hope of ending the CPR's monopoly, James took up the fight against the monopoly clause by petitioning Macdonald to cancel it. It is common knowledge that, by 1888, the lobbying was successful when the prime minister was finally forced to cancel the CPR's monopoly.[97] Contrary to Edwards's assessment, when James openly and publicly opposed the Conservative government and the man who had appointed him to the Senate, he demonstrated that his first loyalty had come to rest with the new North West. Yet no doubt this loyalty was not only to his kinship links in the West but to his own business interests.

James was always concerned for the success of his own family network and any new boosterism campaign that would benefit that network. Although he had at one time allied with Alberta's ranchers, when it was clear that Ottawa was preparing to transfer control of natural resources to the western provinces, James secured an amendment to Crown land lease legislation. In 1881, the Macdonald Government had established the grazing lease policy, which had allowed leases of up to 100,000 acres for twenty-one years in the dry belt. However, James, like most other boosters of his time, now embraced the new science of John Macoun, discounting the conclusions regarding Palliser's Triangle, a largely semi-arid steppe region in the Prairies, in order to encourage generous homestead grants as a way to populate the dry belt.

By 1908, the Dominion Lands Act had been altered so that odd-numbered sections between Moose Jaw and Calgary could be pre-empted, doubling the size of land granted to dry belt farmers to 320 acres, a change that "wreaked havoc with existing ranch leases."[98] Pamphleteers were quick to promote *Canada West: The Last Best West,*[99] and James was instrumental in new legislation that essentially abandoned Alberta's land leaseholders, securing an order-in-council that allowed a three-year cancellation clause for all new leases.[100] Soon after Lougheed's order-in-council was passed, during a speech in Medicine Hat, Prime Minister Arthur Meighen announced that the federal government was considering transferring to the province control of Crown lands and natural resources, withheld since the province's inauguration in 1905.[101] These federal actions set the stage for major resource speculation by businessmen like James.

It had not taken James long to begin to think like a westerner after his marriage to Isabella. To that end, he was one of the first members of the Provincial Rights Association, joining in the 1890s.[102] Not only was James a major advocate of provincial autonomy and control of natural resources but he was one of the first to invest in gas processing at Turner Valley, an investment that marked the beginning of the oil and gas industry in Alberta. In the end, James's campaign to secure natural resource control for the provinces was a profitable one for his adopted province and for his own finances. As most know, the discovery of oil at Turner Valley in 1914 became Alberta's first energy boom, and would one day establish Calgary as a major oil and gas centre.

As a way to develop the Turner Valley resources, James was involved on the ground floor and joined in the establishment of the Calgary Petroleum Products Co., which held 3,200 acres of surface and mineral rights near the gas seep at Turner Valley. To earn interest on their investment, James and the other Calgary investors agreed to spend a minimum of $50,000 developing the property.[103] It took some time to develop the resources at Turner Valley and profits were not realized until after James's death. However, James eventually retained shares in a subsidiary of Imperial Oil, Royalite Oil Company.[104] Isabella's grandsons, Donald and Peter, mused about the possibilities these shares would have provided the family had they not been sold in order to remit the succession taxes on James's estate during the depressed economy of the 1930s. Unfortunately, the bulk of James's estate was by then in real estate, and the family was not able to retain any of it, even the stately Beaulieu mansion.[105]

Despite eventual financial hardships, the Lougheeds remained integral to the transition of the North West throughout their lives. In 1903, Isabella and James began construction on the first of several commercial properties that would serve to transform Calgary from a prairie town filled with tents to a municipality that earned a reputation as "Sandstone City" in the short span of ten years. James and Isabella named their new buildings after their sons. Douglas Block, built at 339-8th Avenue SW, served as a warehouse for a wholesale grocer and was later renovated as stores and offices. The Edgar, Clarence, and Norman blocks soon followed, and the buildings today remain as valuable commercial property in the heart of Calgary.

James and Isabella made large profits from their rental properties in Calgary's commercial district. The yearly rental income in 1903 alone was in the area of $17,000.[106] A sampling of the tenants in the Lougheed buildings reveals that many of them were major companies involved in the new western economy, and speak to the extent of James's networking abilities. For example, in 1914, his tenants included Western Life Assurance Company, the Turner Valley Oil Company, and the United Farmers of Alberta. In order to finance these large projects, James borrowed from a variety of sources, which suggests that his credit rating must have at one time been one of the best in southwestern Alberta.[107]

In regard to the booming economy in which James and Isabella prospered, the high quality of building stone around Calgary stimulated the construction industry, with stonemasons among the highest paid artisans in Calgary.[108] The close proximity of sandstone proved fortuitous. Like every other new prairie town, particularly after the laying of rail lines, Calgary was initially plagued with fires, which often led to the loss of entire commercial blocks. Even in January, at times the grass was so dry that during one year "an extensive prairie fire" was witnessed "in the vicinity of the mouth of High River."[109] On Christmas day in 1900, James and Isabella lost both the Clarence and Norman buildings, the latter just recently completed. As noted in the *Herald*, James was one of the biggest losers in this fire. In addition to his buildings, he lost his entire law library. However, apparently James took a "philosophical view," and reconstruction was expected to begin the following week.[110] This suggests that, by this time, James had the ability to secure large amounts of capital very quickly.

With the extensive fires, it is little wonder that James soon turned to sandstone for his office buildings. In fact, Calgary's sandstone received national attention when a visiting reporter for the *Toronto Globe* described it as "most soft and agreeable to the eye and most hard and durable for all practical purposes."[111] In an apparent bid to give their city the aura of respectability and elitism, most up-and-coming business leaders, peddlers of boosterism, constructed their own new sandstone mansions. Most were given aristocratic names, such as Beaulieu for the Lougheeds; Langmore for William Roper Hull, magnate of ranching and real estate; and Castle-Aux-Pres for Justice Rouleau.[112]

Trudy Soby, the first director of Lougheed House National Historic Site, wrote that the nineteenth century, when the nouveau riche was overtaking the gentry, was a time of great contradictions, in which architecture produced many styles. Not long after displays of wealth and status were apparent in the east, they reappeared in the new North West.[113] While Isabella was not really a member of the nouveau riche, James certainly was, and Beaulieu did combine many architectural styles. The ostentatious and garish displays of wealth in the transitional North West elicited the following observation by one researcher:

Calgary's elite were forever revealing telltale signs of their humble origins...Calgary's Edwardian mansions were an ostentatious

Season's Greetings

Lady Lougheed

Lady Lougheed poses in her garden for her annual Christmas card. Photo undated.
Lougheed House National Historic Site Archives.

mishmash of freely borrowed and poorly interpreted styles from many historic periods. They possessed little continuity of style and exhibited little aesthetic taste. The interiors were cluttered with incongruous objects.[114]

In addition to the requisite mansion, wealth was put on parade through the mansion garden party, many of which the Lougheeds, with Isabella at the helm, hosted on a regular basis. Orchestras played while guests enjoyed tennis, croquet, or lawn bowling, and the prairie coyote hunt replaced the fox hunt for those mimicking their English brethren.[115] After the intense building campaigns that accompanied industrialism in England, the wealthy had retreated to the sanctity of their country gardens. In similar fashion, many in Canada tried to emulate British aristocracy by transforming prairie lands into "Cities beautiful," complete with elaborate gardens.[116] Lord and Lady Aberdeen had established an orchard in British Columbia,[117] and Calgary's aristocratic couple, Sir and Lady Lougheed, followed suit with a grand garden, which was to serve as the site of many lavish tea parties.

Wealth breeds wealth and the ostentatious mansions (although some may have considered them tasteless) allowed James to cultivate not only business interests but his political aspirations. In addition to his assistance with Bennett's early political career, James continued to promote his own. In the fall of 1902, he served as tour guide and advisor to Robert Borden, the newly elected leader of the national Conservative Party. As the leader of the Opposition in the Senate, James travelled with Isabella and their son Clarence to London in July of 1911, to represent Canada at the coronation of King George V and Queen Mary. After the coronation ceremony, the Lougheeds, along with a number of visiting Canadians, were guests of the British government on a tour of England, Scotland, and France. No doubt the Lougheeds enjoyed these trips abroad, which totalled ten by the end of James's career.

In October of 1911, James and Isabella's work reaped one more reward, when James was selected by Prime Minister Borden to serve in his Cabinet as Minister without Portfolio.[118] In the summer of 1914, James and Isabella received the entire entourage of the Duke of Connaught, third son of Queen Victoria, when he served as Governor General for Canada.[119] The Lougheeds had planned a trip for their guests to their home in Rocky Mountain National Park (which became Banff National Park in 1930),[120] and a stay at the Banff Springs Hotel. However, with war declared, all lavish entertainment had to be dispensed with.

Some in the Senate felt that James's executive abilities at
managing his wartime roles were second to none.[121] His service
in various posts during the war would become Sir James's "finest
hour," in that soon afterwards, in 1916, he would be decorated with
the title of Knight Commander of the Most Distinguished Order of
St. Michael and St. George.[122] After this appointment, Sir James
continued to receive prominent appointments, including serving
as head of the Military Hospitals Commission when Borden was
caught unawares by the plight of returning soldiers.[123] In assessing
his performance, First World War veteran and fellow senator,
General William Griesbach, while describing James as clever and
worthy of admiration, also described him as authoritarian.[124]
Griesbach's assessment, along with those of satirist Bob Edwards,
might give the sense that it was Isabella who was the more accomplished diplomat and the expert at managing the image of the
Lougheed–Hardisty partnership.

Yet it is clear that James became adept at diplomacy. Some
believe that "Senator James Lougheed wielded political influence
to secure favourable treatment for certain business enterprises in
which he was involved."[125] No doubt James's position would allow
him to obtain legislation favourable to local interests, as well as
to his own, such as when he secured power rights on the Bow
River.[126] James apparently did not foresee any social problems when
he lobbied for legislation in Ottawa that would secure a ten-year
monopoly for the Calgary Water Power Company, formed by Peter
Prince of the Eau Claire Lumber Company, in order to supply elec-
tricity to the city.[127]

James held the view that larger ratepayers, of whom he was
usually one of the largest, merited preferential treatment.[128] To that
end, in 1889, with his vocal support, civic elections were suspended,
and the business community chose a mayor and council.[129] With
this sort of control by the business community, it is little wonder
that social services tended to receive lower priority. Thus in 1895,
the "impetus for the first municipal hospital came not from council,

With This Economy We Do Wed

but from the Women's Hospital Aid Society,"[130] with Isabella as a founding member.

Given that private charities and churches typically met social needs at the time, it is impossible to assign a value to the contributions that these organizations, and the women who often directed their activities, made to the economy of the new North West. However, many women believed it was their responsibility, perhaps driven by boosterism efforts to a degree, to devote a great deal of time to these private philanthropic activities.

While Isabella clearly had a social conscience, demonstrated by her involvement in her community, it is important to remember that she also had a mother, siblings, and children of Indigenous ancestry. Eventually, there were appeals for assistance from those Indigenous family members when they were not able to achieve the level of economic success that was achieved by the recreated Isabella. It is not clear how much assistance Isabella provided to her mother and siblings, but she must have sensed the necessity of striking a balance as she was aware of the personal attitudes toward Indigenous people held by the staunchly Methodist and ambitious young man that James was when he headed west.

While Isabella spent her formative years with her mother, and women forged strong partnerships in the emerging communities of the new West, it is not clear how much contact Isabella maintained with her mother after her father died. Local newspapers commented quite regularly on other visitors to Beaulieu, including some of the Hardisty family, such as that in 1893 of a "Miss Hardisty of Edmonton," no doubt the daughter of Richard Hardisty.[131] Yet there was never any mention of visits by Isabella's mother. Perhaps Mary Allen Hardisty Thomas never visited Calgary, or, perhaps, it is that Isabella simply did not draw attention to any such visit.

Isabella's mother and siblings rarely receive mention in any of the documentation about the Lougheeds, making it difficult to discern how they adjusted to the new economy of the West. Yet, it is clear that Isabella and James maintained some contact with them. In 1897, at the height of gold rush fever, James reportedly "made arrangements to send a prospecting party to the Klondike by way of Edmonton—the all Canadian route. The party will be in charge of Frank Hardisty."[132] Isabella's brother Frank had been in southern Alberta earlier, in 1885, when he served with the Rocky Mountain Rangers.[133] There was no further information in the local newspapers regarding how successful James and Frank's gold prospecting venture was. However, it does not appear that Frank yielded much wealth from it, or, if he did, he was not able to retain that wealth. Nor did Frank retain any of the wealth from his father's estate, which was eventually the subject of some dispute by family members. These disputes demonstrate that Isabella's brothers, particularly Frank, were not as financially successful as she was. It would be fair to conclude that some of her siblings and her mother were destitute for large parts of their lives after William Hardisty died.

Over the course of the years, various members of the Hardisty/ Lougheed family managed William Hardisty's estate. The correspondence between Frank Hardisty and Isabella's son Clarence Lougheed during the height of the Depression revealed the true state of Frank's poverty. Even before this correspondence, Richard Hardisty no doubt had a sense that some of his brother's sons were somewhat of a disappointment. In 1884, Richard Hardisty received a letter, noting

> *Your brother William's boys also appear not to be doing well. I am very sorry for this and that they should have missed the opportunities they had—that of Thomas being an excellent one—of making their way respectively in the world.*[134]

The fact that Isabella's brothers did not succeed had little to do with the fact that their father had not provided for them, at least monetarily. As indicated in a letter to Richard Hardisty after William's death, Donald A. Smith was to be the executor of the will, which stipulated that the income from the estate be "applied to the main-tenance and education of the children." The letter also advised that William's widow, Mary Allen Hardisty, wished to relocate from Lachine to be nearer to Richard, and that Donald Smith's advice would be heeded in regard to a "good boarding school" for the boys. There were also sufficient funds so that, at the time of the letter, Isabella had just sailed to England for a month's visit.[135]

As noted earlier, it is not clear whether or not Mary Allen Hardisty ever visited Calgary after Isabella married James. However, the economic management of the Lougheed and Hardisty estates was eventually taken over by James, when he assumed the role as exec-utor of William Hardisty's estate from Donald A. Smith. Later, Clarence Hardisty managed the estate from his position with McLaws Redman Lougheed and Cairns, and there was some correspondence between Clarence and his grandmother, Mary Allen Hardisty. The correspondence is always written with a tone of respect and some affection, suggesting that there was a personal relationship.

The executors of William Hardisty's estate had continued to acquire assets in the form of land and stock in companies such as the Bank of Montreal and Bell Telephone, and Clarence continued to update his grandmother regarding the estate. In 1929, Clarence wrote to "My dear Grandmother" at Inwood, Manitoba, to advise her of finances,

> You will notice that there are four payments of $100.00 each listed as having been made to Lady Lougheed under dates of March 1st., April 1st., May 27th and July 13th. These payments were not made to my Mother, as it was agreed by her and the late Mr. Taylor that she be credited with these amounts on the books of the Estate and payment be made later on when there might be more funds on hand in the Bank.[136]

Aside from confirming a familial caring on the part of Clarence for his grandmother, this letter suggests that Isabella's mother may have been making some inquiries about the state of her late husband's estate. The letter also confirms that Isabella was not able to withdraw money from her father's estate in 1929, when she was a widow and experiencing financial difficulties herself. It also suggests that Isabella could not have helped her mother at this time, even had she wanted to.

Even before the difficulties of the Great Depression, Isabella's mother was likely not any wealthier than her sons appeared to be. The 1901 Census of Canada shows Mary, Edwin, and Ellen Thomas living in the District of Selkirk, Manitoba, in the St. Laurent subdistrict. Also living in that same district at the time were Isabella's sister, Mary Louise, and her husband, Alfred Hackland.[137] By 1911, both the Hackland and Thomas families were living in the District of Dauphin, Manitoba, Sub-District Township 18. At this time, Mary and Edwin Thomas had William Laurence Thomas, perhaps a grandson, given that he was born in 1909, living with them.

Isabella's brother, William Lucas Hardisty Jr., also lived in the same district as his mother in 1911.[138] Clearly, Isabella's siblings kept in closer geographic proximity to their mother than she had. When she died at the age of ninety, the funeral notice for Mary Allen Hardisty Thomas indicated only that she was the wife of Edwin S. Thomas and mother of Mr. Thos. Hardisty of Woodlands.[139] Thomas Hardisty may have had a closer connection to his mother, since his wife was the sister of Mary Allen Hardisty's second husband, Edwin Thomas. Yet, although Mary Allen Hardisty's daughter Isabella had achieved a position of considerable importance in the new North West as Lady Lougheed, she was not mentioned in her mother's obituary notice.

The lack of success of Isabella's brothers likely instigated the disputes that are documented in the files of McLaws Redman Lougheed and Cairns. The files contain the affidavit of Archbishop Samuel Pritchard Matheson, which indicates there were some contentious claims made against the estate of Isabella's father. Matheson said of Richard Robert Hardisty, Isabella's brother who was killed at Duck Lake, that he

knew him intimately from his boyhood and I would have known of
it had he been married...I have reason to believe and do believe that
the said Richard Robert Hardisty was never married.[140]

A letter to Isabella's son, Clarence Lougheed, also stated that
Richard Hardisty was not married and that there could be no legitimate claim on his behalf on the estate of Isabella's father. Clarence
also disputed another claim, made by Jessie Hardisty, widow of
Isabella's brother, Donald Alexander Hardisty. In his letter, Clarence
noted that Jessie Hardisty was the adoptive mother of Rae Hardisty,
a child who was never adopted by Isabella's brother, Donald.[141]
Despite all the protestations, Clarence advised Royal Trust, the
administrators of the estate in 1933, that "neither Mrs. Jessie
Hardisty nor her adopted child has any interest, and we suggest
that you should write her accordingly."[142]

Another claim against the estate of Isabella's father was $283.50,
payable to Mrs. Thomas Bird of Inwood, Manitoba, for the board
and care of Mrs. Mary Thomas, Isabella's mother.[143] Clarence
Lougheed's law firm initially refused to acknowledge the request
made by A.S. Morrison, Esq., on behalf of Mrs. Bird, writing,

Mrs. Thomas was entitled to the income of the estate, and up to
the time of her death this was paid, partly to her, and partly, under
her directions, to her children. Not only was the entire income
distributed up to the time of her death, but the amount distributed
exceeded the income. After the death of Mrs. Mary Thomas the
balance of the Estate was to be distributed to the children of the
testator. We do not see how the trustee can recognize any creditors
of Mrs. Thomas.[144]

The writer went on to note that a "considerable distribution was
made recently to: W.L. Hardisty, Esq., Frank A. Hardisty, Esq.,
Thomas A. Hardisty, Esq.," and that "if these heirs consent to the
liabilities of Mrs. Mary Thomas being paid the Trustee has moneys

on hand to pay them."[145] In the end, it appears from various correspondence that neither Isabella nor any of her siblings objected to the payment of outstanding debts for their mother.

However, by 1931, there was some evidence of further discord in the distribution of William Hardisty's estate. In March of that year, Frank A. Hardisty threatened legal action against Clarence Lougheed after he refused his request for $125.[146] In a response from McLaws Redman Lougheed and Cairns, Frank was advised that there was only $40 on hand and that Clarence had agreed to act as trustee "without remuneration in order to keep down expenses and leave as much as possible available for distribution to the beneficiaries."[147] Again, in April of 1931, the law firm explained the status of the estate funds to Frank, noting,

> The Trustees of your father's estate have at all times endeavoured to meet the wishes and requirements of the family to the fullest extent. In doing so they have, through an agreement signed by all the beneficiaries, advanced to the beneficiaries each year sums much in excess of the income of the estate, in order to meet the pressing needs of the different beneficiaries. The Estate was not to have been distributed until your mother's death...The Estate was not inexhaustible and as the moneys drawn each year by the beneficiaries greatly exceeded the income, the capital of the estate was being continually depleted, and at the time of your mother's death it had reached the stage where we had to advise the late Mr. Edmund Taylor, who was then Trustee, that distribution would have to cease.[148]

This letter, sent during the most difficult period of the Great Depression, was to no avail, as Frank continued to plead for help, writing,

> I would ask you as an act of mercy to have a cheque forwarded to me at once...as we are in a terrible condition without food except bread. My little boy is crying all the time for food and we have to

look on in our misery. We cannot get relief from the municipality
because we are supposed to have money. I will even have to beg
postage to mail this letter.[149]

Perhaps some of the unhappiness expressed by Isabella's siblings with regard to her son's management of William Hardisty's estate stemmed from the practice carried on by James. James had assumed the duties of executor in 1907 from Lord Strathcona, and he carried on as Donald A. Smith had, in that payments were made to the children of William Hardisty based on the "pressing needs of the Hardisty family." An affidavit filed in 1926 suggests that James also made disbursements based on pressing needs rather than income received, for he had received the sum of $142,501.81 from the estate between 1917 and 1925, and had disbursed $146,733.59.[150] In a letter dated 20 February 1929 to Lougheed & Taylor from Lougheed, McLaws, Sinclair, the writer explained that James carried on with this practice based on the assumption that William Hardisty's widow would predecease her children.[151] If Mary Hardisty had died before her children, James would have distributed the final estate less amounts already advanced to the couple's children.

However, some of William Hardisty's children predeceased his wife, and the will stated that the balance of the estate was to be distributed to grandchildren. Thus, the possibility existed that the grandchildren of Mary and William Hardisty might refuse to ratify the excess payments made to their parents. This would result in the executor, at one time James and, by default, his estate, becoming liable for any overpayments. No doubt, Clarence's response to the request made by Jessie Hardisty, referred to earlier, and to Frank Hardisty, was motivated by the fact that his grandfather's estate was already overextended, and by the fact that members of the Lougheed family themselves were now in the midst of difficult financial circumstances.

Yet perhaps Clarence felt a sense of duty not only to his mother but to his grandmother, when appeals for money continued by other family members on her behalf. In a 1930 letter, Isabella's sister, Mary Louise, who at one time had indicated that her mother was living with her, appealed to James's law firm. Mary Louise spoke in her letter of her

> *overwhelming sorrow, which is almost more than I can bear, and*
> *with the addition of continual depression and misfortune, and my*
> *large accounts, I know that I am the most unfortunate member of*
> *the family. It is needless to say that I have been compelled so often*
> *to write Mr. C.H. Lougheed...a very strange coincidence occurred*
> *yesterday, upon my arrival from Moose Jaw—The bailiff seized my*
> *new Ford car.*[152]

In this instance, it appears Clarence felt sympathy, and asked that his aunt's claim be accepted, for Mary Louise's letter continued,

> *However, upon the receipt of your pleasant surprise, I immediately*
> *had it released by paying 4100.00 which leaves a balance of $185.00...*
> *I wrote our Trustee—Mr. Lougheed and tried to explain my distressing*
> *predicament. I sincerely trust that you will soon make a further*
> *distribution, to enable me to dispose of my accounts, which too are*
> *due, to the abrupt cessation of our monthly allowance, while I had*
> *my invalid mother and step-father with me.*[153]

In the end, because Mary Thomas had died without an estate, "funds had to be sent forward privately to bury her," according to the firm of McLaws Redman Lougheed and Cairns.[154] It is not clear who forwarded funds for Mary Thomas's burial, but the only child who may have been able to do so would have been Isabella.

Although he appears to be the only son who dealt with his grandfather's estate matters, Clarence was not James and Isabella's only son who became a lawyer. James and Isabella's knowledge of the successful "kinship" network developed by lawyers in the early North West meant they supported all of their sons when they pursued careers in law. Like their father, James and Isabella's sons also became adept at managing estates that comprised primarily land. The family came by that land through various means, not only by purchasing lots from the CPR in anticipation of new settlement. James's solid cash flow had always allowed him to take advantage of opportunities such as tax arrears sales. For example, in 1897, James had acquired dozens of lots in the city for $271.18—lots that he sold in 1905 for thousands of dollars.[155] In 1911, at the "height of the urban real-estate boom" in the West, James and Isabella sold ten lots on 7th Avenue that they had acquired in the mid-1880s. The buyer of the lots in 1911 was none other than the HBC, and the sale price was $250,000, with one property alone on 8th Avenue yielding $150,000.[156]

Yet James did not fare as well as he did by investing only his own money. Reportedly, "a substantial part of the credit he extended to borrowers came from estates that he was administering, especially the estate of...William L. Hardisty (Winnipeg)."[157] Some have assessed the scruples of lawyers during this time as follows: "For most lawyers...self-interest rather than the defence of others' interests was a more compelling motive for dealing in land matters."[158] A good number of lawyers also dealt in Metis scrip, thus

> wrongfully alienating the real-estate inheritance of Metis infants... the pressure to find a legal mechanism to facilitate their sale [scrip] to speculators was enormous. This unscrupulous business was a continuation of the general purchasing of other Metis land claims, which had become so routine that going prices for scrips were advertised in newspapers.[159]

These observations refer in particular to the 1881 testimony of lawyer Heber Archibald before the Commission Inquiry into the Administration of Justice as to Infant Lands and Estates. While attempting to justify the buying of scrip for far less than it was clearly worth, Archibald stated,

It was the opinion of nine out of ten members of the [legal] profes-
sion that it was an improvident grant to the Half Breeds—in the first
place—that it would bring them more harm than good.[160]

One of the more well-known lawyers who profited from land
speculation (which included dealing in scrip) was Alexander Morris,
who served as lieutenant-governor of Manitoba and the North-West
Territories. Morris was also the principal treaty commissioner for
the renegotiation of Treaties 1 and 2 and the negotiation of Treaties
3, 4, 5, and 6. While there is some indication that Morris used his
office as lieutenant-governor to advocate on behalf of Metis land
concerns, he "nonetheless took advantage of the Metis 'sell-off' to
further his own interests. By early 1873, he had gained a reputation
as one of the busier land speculators in Winnipeg."[161]

At least one journalist who wrote about James Lougheed
believed that he also took unfair advantage of Metis scrip dealings.
Allan Hustak, who unfortunately did most of his writing without
benefit of references, wrote about James that there was "suspicion that not all of this wealth was earned legitimately."[162] Hustak
intimates that some of James's wealth came not only from insider
information about land deals but from unscrupulous dealings in
Metis scrip. Indeed, many historians have argued that the land
and money scrip certificates that were issued to the Metis population through the Manitoba Act and later through the Northwest
Halfbreed Commission were often surrendered to unscrupulous entrepreneurs for very little in return.[163] When the practice
attracted the attention of the federal government by its alarming
proportions, James initiated a bill in the Senate that imposed a
three-year statute of limitations on any charges for unscrupulous
dealings, a bill that no doubt protected a number of new western
millionaires.[164]

Later, in 1922, when a private member introduced a bill seeking
to amend the Criminal Code, which would repeal the limit of three

years placed on actions for fraud dealing with scrip, James argued vigorously against the initiative. In this case, there is a written record of James's feelings with regard to scrip prosecutions. During the Senate debates, James argued,

> Some proceedings have been taken in the city of Edmonton against a well-known resident, who was alleged to have committed a fraud touching scrip some twenty years ago...It would certainly be an abuse of justice if parties were now permitted to go back twenty years...and prosecute those who would not be able to secure evidence that must necessarily have disappeared some time ago.[165]

Lougheed then referred to allegations made by Progressive members of Parliament that the prior legislation placing limitations had been passed to protect one man in particular: Richard Secord.[166]

Secord's involvement in scrip dealing is recorded by reporter Graham Thomson, who referenced the oral testimony of descendants of Headman Moostoos and Richard Secord, both signatories to Treaty 8, as well as contemporary reports in the *Edmonton Bulletin* and the *Edmonton Journal*. Secord had formed a partnership to operate a dry goods store with John McDougall "the richest man in Edmonton," who was, perhaps not coincidentally, a member of James's extended family. Apparently, Secord, armed with a suitcase,

> stuffed with money...headed north with the government commissioners charged with negotiating the largest land deal in the history of the Dominion of Canada: the signing of Treaty 8.[167]

For three weeks in the summer of 1899,

> commissioners, policemen, secretaries, accountants, cooks, interpreters, and missionaries along with Secord spent three weeks on a

gruelling 500-km journey by wagon, by boat and by foot into the
heart of Canada's northwest interior.[168]

The report continues that Secord, who later went on to become a
member of the Alberta Legislature, bought

an estimated 150,000 acres of Metis land at discounted prices which
he, in turn, sold for a huge profit to incoming settlers. Twenty-two
years later, Secord would be charged with fraud in connection with
speculating in "script" [sic]—certificates for land and cash awarded
to the Metis as a one-time compensation for giving up title to their
traditional territory.[169]

Speaking to a newspaper reporter in 1999, Richard C. Secord, great-
grandson of the scrip dealer, and an Edmonton lawyer who at that
time defended Indigenous rights, said of his grandfather, "It's hard
to defend what he did...Nothing would surprise me in connection
with my great-grandfather. He was quite a character."[170] According
to the news report, the elder Secord was never convicted of fraud,
the charge being

conveniently quashed by sympathetic politicians in Ottawa who
rushed into law a three-year statute of limitations on scrip cases.
They applied it retroactively to Secord's case...Then, in 1981, further
scrubbing Secord's reputation clean, the province named a mountain
in his honour as a "prominent Edmonton pioneer."[171]

James was, of course, one of those "sympathetic politicians"
whose actions had protected the elder Secord. As far as his involvement in the original attempt to convict Secord, James confirmed
during Senate debates that, immediately after the statute of limitations was imposed, charges against Secord were dropped, and that

it was afterwards alleged that the Prime Minister, then Right Hon. Mr. Meighen...was playing into the hands of Mr. Secord in having this legislation passed. I likewise was charged with the offence of being a party to this proceeding.[172]

One of the men who, like Secord, "followed the Scrip Commissioner through the North, buying scrip for himself and others" was none other than Richard George Hardisty, son of the late Senator Richard Hardisty, and therefore Isabella's cousin.[173]

The whole matter of scrip originated, of course, because land occupancy was always an important aspect of Metis ethnicity in the Red River area. Subsequently, individual land ownership came to be an integral aspect of the conflict between the Metis and the government. Given that land became so important to James and Isabella's successful partnership, there is a good possibility that James was interested in scrip dealings. While it is not confirmed that James actually dealt in scrip, it is evident that men *like* James were very involved. Much of the purchasing of scrip was done by what some scholars describe as "large-scale economic operators."[174] One of the most active of "economic operators" involved in land transactions in the North West during the time of transition for the Metis was James Lougheed.[175] There is little debate that dealing in land scrip proved to be a lucrative activity for smart investors. Further, selling scrip was not illegal, although "debauching a Metis to that end was against the law. Prosecutors also frowned on the common practice of persuading Metis to apply for a second land grant under another name." Yet there was ample evidence that "participating in the dubious trade in scrip was extremely common among well-heeled businessfolk in Alberta."[176] "Well-heeled" would be an apt descriptor for James and he surely knew a lucrative deal when he saw one.

Certainly, the opportunity to trade in Metis scrip was there for any enterprising Calgary businessman. The *Calgary Daily Herald* normally featured weekly advertisements during the early 1900s, such as that by scrip dealer, C.S. Lott, who claimed, "A large saving is made by paying for Dominion Government Lands in Scrip Instead of Cash. Any amount required can be supplied."[177] It was common knowledge that the "most active area of business for lawyers" (at least in Winnipeg) in the 1880s and 1890s was arranging scrip purchases and speculating on land.[178] If James did deal in scrip, he was like many of his colleagues. In reality, it would have been unusual if James did *not* partake.

Author Marian McKenna unfortunately wrote without benefit of references when she concluded that James was just as unscrupulous as his fellow lawyers when it came to dealing in scrip. She wrote that there was

some suspicion that not all of Lougheed's activities would meet modern standards of scrupulous dealings. This suspicion was heightened by revelations that concerned Metis land claims...Metis recipients of the scrip were induced by unscrupulous land speculators to surrender their certificates for as little as a bottle of whiskey... In the Dominion these illegal practices reached scandalous proportions.[179]

Undoubtedly, James's legislation, discussed earlier, protected a "number of reputed millionaires," as McKenna and Hustak claimed. However, these authors lack the sources to support the claim that James was involved in unscrupulous dealings by inducing any land surrenders. That said, McKenna did reach the appropriate conclusion in one regard. If James was involved in unscrupulous dealings with scrip, his "role in this affair is hard to defend in view of his wife's ancestry."[180] Even James's goal to protect unscrupulous scrip dealers by way of his legislation calls into question his sensitivity to his wife's ancestry.

Whether he did deal in scrip himself, James did make inquiries about scrip applications on behalf of some Metis, including Isabella's brother Richard, who died in 1885 in Duck Lake.[181] James wrote a letter "asking to be advised of provisions made for representatives of the late Richard Hardisty re Issue of Scrip."[182] However, in July of 1901, Mary Hardisty Thomas had made an application before the North-West Halfbreed Claims Commission in Manitoba, on her own behalf,[183] and on behalf of her deceased son, Richard Thomas Hardisty.[184] At that time, Mary Hardisty Thomas was living in Oak Point, and it is possible that James was making inquiries on her behalf. If that is the case, then there was more contact between James and Isabella and her siblings and mother than is apparent in written documentation. Further, it certainly supports the argument that Isabella's mother identified as a Metis person, all those years removed from her involvement in the northern fur trade.

James was not the only member of Isabella's close family interested in making claims for scrip. It is somewhat ironic that even Chief Factor Richard Hardisty, who owned vast amounts of property, and who was known for disparaging Indigenous people for relying on government assistance, would receive government-issued scrip. Hardisty's application was approved by way of certificate No. 734.[185] No doubt the reasons for Richard Hardisty's application should be understood in a broader sense than its simple monetary value.

The same could be said for Isabella's motivations, if she was involved in her mother's and brother's applications, especially given there is no indication there was ever any financial need until well after James's death. In fact, in 1923, when many on the western Prairies were struggling to survive the droughts and downturn in the economy, Isabella and her daughter Dorothy travelled to Paris and Italy. After the trip, the *Albertan* reported that Lady Lougheed noted her "most delightful time in Paris." Isabella "told of the beautiful Bois de Boulogne and the wonderful shops they visited in Paris." Reportedly, Isabella mused, "Rome is perfectly wonderful... I would like to live there the rest of my life." On the other hand, the people of Naples gave "the impression of dirt and appalling poverty."[186] It is not clear what Isabella thought of the poverty in her own city (and Indigenous communities), which would have been difficult to ignore in 1923 when she enjoyed the European excursion. As early as the 1920s, much of the western Prairies were already enduring difficult times, given the overexpansion and extreme debt loads that wheat farmers had undertaken during the boom times of the war years.[187]

While the difficult economic times did not affect Isabella as early as they did others in the West, just a few short years after her trip to Paris, the Lougheed family fortune was but a shadow of itself. The challenges for the Lougheed estate began in 1925, when James became seriously ill. He tried to carry on and returned to Ottawa in July to prepare for an anticipated election; however, he contracted bronchitis, which progressed to pneumonia.[188] In Calgary, Isabella carried on with the responsibilities of protocol despite James's illness, and she attended celebrations in honour of the visit of Earl Haig, commander in chief of the British Army.[189] While James recovered sufficiently to see the Conservatives win the majority of seats in the election of 1925, and to be named chairman of the National Conservative Committee, he died a few days later, on 2 November, at Ottawa Civic Hospital.[190]

After the death of her husband, Isabella lived at Beaulieu with her sons, Clarence, Douglas, Edgar, and Norman.[191] While daughter Dorothy was still alive, daughter Marjorie Yolande had died in 1917 at the age of twelve.[192] By 1930, the three older sons had established their own residences in Calgary,[193] but continued to operate as a family unit for the purposes of managing the Lougheed estate. However, that family unit was increasingly challenged. After James's death in 1925, Isabella lost two sons, Douglas in 1931[194] and Clarence in 1933.[195] As noted, Norman continued to live with Isabella until her death in 1936. Although now a widow, Isabella continued, with the help of her remaining family members, to fulfill her duties as premiere hostess of the North West by opening up Beaulieu for receptions, such as that held in September of 1932 for attendees of the Canadian Law Society convention.[196]

After James's death and the ensuing global economic Depression, the estate that had been managed by James and Isabella's son Edgar reverted to the control of the Royal Trust Company. In addition to depressed land prices, James's estate was equally vulnerable because of his role as a financier and the subsequent high rate of default by debtors. Despite the severe pressures during the Depression that decimated Isabella's estate, Edgar recovered his own finances significantly with the postwar oil boom so that his estate was valued at $3 million upon his death in 1951.[197] Yet it would be the grandson of Senator James and Lady Isabella Lougheed, Peter Edgar, son of Edgar, who would return the family name to the ranks of the West's political and urban elite in the 1970s. From a similar ideological perspective as that of his Hardisty kin, who were greatly involved in diversifying after the fur trade, Peter Lougheed, when premier, was determined to diversify the western economy.[198]

Peter Lougheed also established the 1970s as the decade of energy wars against the central government. In this regard, it is interesting to note George Melnyk's observations. He argued that Peter Lougheed was following in the footsteps of the Metis leader Louis Riel in that both men "drew their lines in the sand" when they challenged central Canadian expansionists.[199] Perhaps Peter would not make the connection in the way that Melnyk did, given that Riel's men killed his grandmother's brother and that Peter was aware of Isabella's feelings about Riel. In fact, Peter Lougheed opposed granting Indigenous status to Metis people in 1982, only relenting after thousands of Indigenous people marched on the Alberta Legislature. Historian John English noted the irony that Lougheed opposed recognizing Metis people as Indigenous, given that his great-grandmother Mary Hardisty Thomas was Metis. However, in regard to the Hardisty men, English did not acknowledge that they were also Metis, writing only that Richard Hardisty had "nobly fought for the rights of the Metis in the Northwest a century before."[200]

Despite his initial opposition to granting recognition for the Metis people,[201] there is some similarity between Peter Lougheed's firm stance against Central Canada and that of the Metis, who were determined to challenge the imposition of Central Canadians upon their homeland and resources in the North West. The case for Prairie regionalism is often made by reference to moments of significant public protest, such as the Metis resistances of 1869–1870 and 1885, the rise of third parties in the 1930s and 1940s, and the emergence of provincial rights and separationist agitations in the 1970s and the early 1980s.

In many ways, Peter Lougheed's support of provincial rights and his drive to diversify Alberta's economy harkens back not only to Metis-inspired regionalism but also to the ideology of expansion that always played a large role in the development and economy of the North West, and in which his grandparents were both active participants. James had always supported any initiative that would boost the West's fortunes, even when faced with opposition. In fact, some believe that a good number of early projects, such as large irrigation initiatives (often tied to the boosterism mentality and which James supported), precluded rationality when agriculture replaced open-range ranching in parts of southern Alberta. In addition, James Lougheed embraced regionalism, joining the Provincial Rights Association, lobbying for rail lines, and becoming one of the biggest supporters of irrigation in order to encourage new agricultural settlement. Writing to the mayor and council of the City of Calgary in 1894, James had urged them of

> the immediate necessity of taking active steps to direct public attention, and particularly the attention of the Dominion Government, to the importance of promoting a proper and a vigorous system of irrigation in Central and Southern Alberta...As Macleod is equally interested in this matter with us in Calgary, I would suggest that your Council should co-operate with the Macleod Council and if

possible with the various Agricultural Societies in Southern Alberta
in forming an organization for the promotion of irrigation generally.[202]

James Lougheed was a proponent for expanding and diversifying
the economy, as well as for challenging Ottawa for provincial control
of resources. His grandson Peter Lougheed was able to restore the
family name and economic fortunes to the glory days, when Isabella
and James were members of prairie aristocracy, by championing the
same ideas. However, there were challenges for James and Isabella's
children. When Peter Lougheed's father, Edgar, was the only son left
to manage his parents' estate during the severe economic downturn
in the 1930s, one report suggests that he turned to alcohol and that
his wife suffered a nervous breakdown and was hospitalized.[203]
Researchers Pratt and Richards attribute Edgar's problems to those
"typical...of the offspring of the privileged and powerful."[204]
However, many people from varied backgrounds suffered similar
problems during the 1930s. Nonetheless, it is true that the

age of prairie elegance did not long outlive Sir James Lougheed.
Like many other members of the old mansion set of Winnipeg,
Edmonton, and Calgary, the Lougheed family did not fare well
during the Depression. Indeed, it very nearly wiped them out...The
Depression severely trimmed the values of the family properties...
Following the death of the senator's widow, the Royal Trust
Company, which held the mortgages on the Lougheed properties,
ordered the family mansion auctioned off.[205]

After James died, Edgar was expected to defer his law career in
order to manage his father's estate. Despite the challenges Edgar
faced, Allan Hustak mused that temperament and circumstances
beyond his control denied Edgar the "opportunity of coming out of
the Senator's shadow and equaling his accomplishments."[206] Edgar
did assume a difficult task in a situation over which he had little
control. The Depression was followed by the war, and, according to

Hustak, based on a conversation with Peter, his father's drinking caused "sporadic difficulties."[207] Peter went on to say that the family went through the Depression and the war in much the same way that everyone else did. That may be a slight exaggeration, given the Lougheeds continued to enjoy the services of a housekeeper throughout the period.

Although they were better off than many others during the Depression, Isabella's other sons also experienced tragedy. After his father's death in 1925, and until his own death, Clarence, as well as his brothers Edgar, Norman, and Douglas Lougheed, had become executors of their parents' vast estate, which was full-time work. The youngest Lougheed son, Douglas, was the first to die, in 1931, at the age of thirty, prior to the real downturn in family financial fortunes. The bulk of the estate Douglas left was an amount of $18,000 in life insurance.[208]

The economic depression that created severe financial problems for Isabella's family may have contributed to Clarence's sudden death in 1933 at the age of forty-eight from a heart attack.[209] With Clarence's death, Isabella lost the son who had most often accompanied her as she continued her duties when she became widowed in 1925. Despite this loss, Isabella was financially able to carry on with her duties until the 1930s.[210] However, by 1933, a lawsuit brought by the executors of the Lougheed estate against the province gives some indication of the struggles the family now faced. Following Clarence's death, the Lougheed family sought $15,000 in life insurance being withheld for payment of succession duties on Clarence's share of his father's estate. At the time of his death, Clarence was entitled to receive 20 per cent of the income from the estate. The plaintiffs in the case, Edgar and Clarence's wife, asserted that Clarence was not receiving any income from his father's estate, and that, in 1932, the estate, did not yield any income at all.[211]

In the end, the extended Lougheed–Hardisty family, which had so successfully navigated the transitional economy of the late 1800s and early 1900s, could not overcome the severe difficulties of the 1920s and 1930s. By 1938, the City of Calgary had taken possession of Beaulieu House, and all of the grand furnishings and antiques were auctioned off for depressed prices. While Isabella had lived the majority of her life as a member of the upper class and an able diplomat and networker, it was some time before her Lougheed family managed to restore their own positions to that level.

It was Isabella's own abilities as a diplomat and networker that, in the end, allowed her to remain in her grand home and maintain a semblance of her former life, even after the City of Calgary had taken possession of Beaulieu. Perhaps the best example of her success as a diplomat in the new economy of the West is in her lasting relationship with James's business partner, R.B. Bennett. Despite the bitter falling out that Bennett had with James after their law partnership ended, Bennett retained a respect and admiration for Isabella through to the end of her life. That is clear in his response to a request for aid on Isabella's behalf. It is common knowledge that many constituents appealed directly to Prime Minister R.B. Bennett for assistance during the Great Depression.[212] However, fewer know that successful appeals were also made by closer acquaintances of Bennett's who had fallen on hard times.

Isabella's daughter Dorothy was among those who appealed to Bennett on behalf of her mother. Dorothy wrote in a letter to Bennett, "My poor mother is nearly heart broken. I want her to come and live with us. It is such a tragedy to me that her last years should be filled with worry and unhappiness."[213] Bennett's response to Dorothy demonstrates his continued high regard for Isabella:

> I can only say that I have been worried more than I can tell you about your affairs...I want you to assure your mother that whatever happens I will see that she is looked after. I never forget her and her kindness to me in days that are past, and she must not be permitted to suffer because of what has transpired.[214]

It is not clear what help Bennett provided to Isabella in the end, but she was able to remain at Beaulieu until her death on 13 March 1936, two years after the city had taken possession in lieu of unpaid taxes. Even if the city allowed her to live there, the municipality would not likely have provided help with living expenses. Bennett's response to Dorothy suggests that Isabella did carry on, with his help. After Isabella's death, Bennett wrote to J.A. Hutchison, Isabella's son-in-law,

> While I am very sorry to think that I will see my dear old friend, Lady Lougheed, no more, I cannot but feel that, having regard to all the circumstances, she has escaped pain and suffering and is much better off than if she had to remain and face the sort of trouble that loomed up before her. She was a fine character.[215]

Bennett even went on to tell Dorothy's husband,

> Few people know her perhaps as well as I. Thirty-five years ago she was very, very kind to me and I cannot tell you how sorry I was that conditions should have so changed as to make her life miserable at its close. Dorothy has been a great comfort to her and I am sure Clarence would have felt exactly the same way if he were here.[216]

Bennett's response to Isabella's plight was remarkable, given that the feud between him and James upon the dissolution of their partnership in 1922 had been publicly bitter, and given Bennett's reputation for unforgiveness.[217] Aside from noting Isabella's diplomacy, Bennett's response also speaks to the fact that Isabella was as important as James to many of the networks the couple had forged, even when those networks were with James's business associates.

It is fortunate for Isabella that she had made very good connections after the fur trade transitioned. The realities in the North West after the end of the fur trade meant that different classes of

Metis emerged (or continued).[218] Compared to many other Metis women, including Marie Rose, Isabella's life speaks to this reality. While Isabella lived in one of the grandest and most talked-about homes in the North West, many Metis women spent their entire lives in log cabins, far less grand than even the log cabin in which Isabella lived when she first married James.

However, even if her log home was more than many other Metis women had, as a young wife and mother living in the rudimentary conditions of the Prairie West, Isabella would have had to rely on some of the same skills that many Metis women relied on, and with which she was familiar from her time in the North. In addition, due to the lack of help, when Isabella and James moved to their larger home, she managed the household, which would often effectively function as a hotel.

On one occasion, in a letter to her aunt, Isabella explained that her doctor had ordered her to rest as she tried to manage without the help of sufficient staff. Seven months pregnant with her sixth child, Isabella wrote to her aunt, Eliza McDougall Hardisty, that, since her return from the east, she had been kept

> so busy all day long that I always felt too tired to do anything but rest. I have had to do all the housework for nearly two months, so that my health nearly gave way. The doctor ordered me off to bed one day, and there I had to stay for a week or so, which accounts for the report that I was very ill. However I am glad to say that there was nothing in it, and I am getting quite strong again. You know there is a great deal to do in a house of this size.[219]

According to newspaper ads, there were long periods when Isabella was unable to find hired help, even when she could afford to pay for those services.

Due to James's duties in Ottawa, the public aspect of his and Isabella's relationship was clear. However, there is little to tell us about their personal relationship. In the absence of much other documentation, one way to understand personal relationships is to explore the way people determine how their estate should be managed upon their death. Despite her Indigenous ancestry, Isabella had a different stature than those Indigenous women governed by the Indian Act. James's marriage and will were sanctioned by the Christian church and state law, and for Isabella there was no stipulation that a woman could only inherit property from her husband if her character was deemed morally acceptable (as there was for Indigenous women governed by the Indian Act).[220] Yet, when James died in 1925 at the age of sixty-nine, he left control of his entire estate to his sons, with final inheritance to go to his grandchildren. The children were in line to inherit a substantial estate in the context of the time, for it was valued at $1,521,109, with Beaulieu itself valued at $30,000.[221]

James's will (executed on 16 August 1923) stipulated that, "in lieu of dower," Isabella was to receive an annual income of $8,000, along with "free use of my present residence...free of taxes, repairs and cost of grounds."[222] As executors and trustees, James named his sons Clarence and Edgar, along with business associate and former HBC man, Edmund Taylor, and the Royal Trust Company. James and Isabella's five surviving children were to receive annual incomes of $6,000, with another $1,000 per year set aside for James's brother Samuel. Samuel was the only extended family member included in the will, despite the fact that Isabella still had four remaining siblings, some in very dire need.

The wealth accumulated through their successful partnership was to be distributed among James and Isabella's grandchildren upon Isabella's death and those of her children. In fact, James allowed that, while Isabella was to have free use of his residence for the "rest of her natural life," there was a provision added that

> *if it should be thought desirable in the interests of my estate to sell or lease the same in whole or in part my Executors and Trustees shall have power so to do and shall include the proceeds in the corpus of my estate.*[223]

Thus, had the executors deemed it necessary, they could have asked Isabella to move out of Beaulieu. However, Isabella was not asked to leave her home and remained at Beaulieu while her son Edgar, despite his role as executor, lost his own home and was forced to live in an apartment overlooking Beaulieu. James had further directed that any life insurance "whether payable to my wife or my Executors to form part of my estate and be invested with my estate generally."[224] Although the estate encountered difficulties that may have been eased somewhat had Beaulieu been sold, clearly the executors ignored the provision that would have allowed them to do so. Of course, the market for the sale of mansions on the Prairies after James's death was not great.

While James did not will his estate to Isabella, Alberta law at the time would have permitted him to do so. Though women in the West could not vote until 1917 in provincial elections, and 1918 in federal elections, and they had to wait until 1929 to be legally recognized as "persons," they could, according to the North-West Territories Act of 1880, own property apart from their husbands, and women's wages were not considered in settling their husband's debts. This legislation was advanced for its time, given that, in many countries, women had no property rights whatsoever.[225] In the end, unlike Isabella's father and grandfather before him, James's will adopted a male-line inheritance strategy that relegated Isabella to nothing more than an estate dependent. Nonetheless, James followed the conventions of English Common Law and his will was totally legitimate.

To put the terms of James's will into context, it is helpful to examine other widows who were Isabella's contemporaries. Christina Grant Kinnisten, widowed in 1898 at the age of thirty-three, has been described as "one of the most obscure of the early Calgary entrepreneurs." Christina, whose husband died intestate, gained free and clear title to all family property, confirmed by the Supreme Court of the North-West Territories.[226] She then assumed control of the couple's confectionary store in Calgary, and, although the books of the company showed a healthy surplus, the store might still have collapsed had it not been for Christina's able leadership.[227] By 1903, Christina had improved the state of the store so that it showed a net worth of nearly $20,000. She raised funds for expansion by loaning money to at least one farmer and one Calgary baker for which there are records remaining. No doubt reflecting sound business judgments and trust between herself and her customers, Christina surely contributed to Calgary's prosperity.[228] Clearly, Christina's contribution was on a smaller scale than that of James and Isabella, but commendable nonetheless, considering the obstacles women often faced at that time after the death of their partners.

Isabella may have crossed paths with another prominent Calgary widow, Evelyn Albright. Evelyn's husband, Fred, once described as "one of the leaders among the young men" of the Central Methodist Church (Isabella's home church), was killed in Europe during the First World War.[229] After Fred's death, Evelyn went on to become one of the first women in Alberta to obtain a law degree. Although they had no children, based upon their extensive correspondence, it is doubtful that Fred's estate would have gone to anyone other than Evelyn.[230]

Another contemporary of Isabella's, Mary Macleod, widowed at the age of forty-two when her husband, Colonel James F. Macleod, died, managed to support her five children and remain in the family home by establishing herself as a dressmaker.[231] In 1883, Agnes Bedingfeld, a thirty-eight-year-old widow, settled in a tent on a homestead in the Pekisko area near High River with her seventeen-year-old son. In May of 1884, Agnes filed claim to a 160-acre homestead. After her son took up an adjacent homestead, Agnes lived with him for twenty-five years in the house built on her homestead and "plunged headlong into the ranching industry."[232] Mother and son built up an impressive ranching business, which, by 1899, comprised 150 Clydesdale horses and 60 head of cattle, and of which Agnes remained majority owner. While Agnes shared the duties with her son, she ran the ranch independently when her son was taken with gold fever in the late 1890s.[233]

By the early 1900s, Agnes Bedingfeld was doing well enough to lend money to local saddle maker Eneas McCormick at an annual interest rate of 8 per cent.[234] In 1911, at the age of seventy-five, Agnes retired from ranching and moved to Calgary, where she continued as a moneylender. In October of 1919, Edward, Prince of Wales, bought the Bedingfeld ranch, subsequently operating it as the E.P. Ranch.[235] It is likely that many other women ranchers were invisible in terms of historical record, when in reality they performed significant ranching tasks and operated in partnership with male ranchers.[236] In Agnes's case, because she operated the ranch as a widow, she became a more visible example of this reality. While it is not clear if these women inherited their property through the wills of husbands, these examples demonstrate that women who were contemporaries of Isabella were capable business people. They suggest it would have been possible for Isabella to assume control of the estate after James's death, assuming, of course, that she had any interest in doing that.[237]

If she had an interest in managing her own estate as a widow, then James's decision demonstrates the same paternalistic attitude he displayed toward Indigenous people during the many Senate debates pertaining to Indian Act amendments. James's version of democracy was noted by at least one newspaper, when it reported on his death. Far removed from the North West, where James spent the majority of his life, the *Sydney Record* of Cape Breton noted,

> *He was a staunch pillar of what in these days is considered to be reactionary...He tolerated democratic methods, but he never rid his mind of the idea that democracy needed very much to be kept in the leading strings of the few.*[238]

On the other hand, in regard to his estate, perhaps James continued as he had in the marriage partnership. While Isabella managed their palatial home and many of the philanthropic duties in Calgary, James managed the real estate and business aspect.

However, in the case of the property in Banff, where Isabella spent much of her time, the records list only Isabella as the owner. According to the 1911 assessment roll for District No. 102, N.W.T., Mrs. Bella C. Lougheed, who had the occupation of "Lady," was the registered owner of Lots 8, 10, 13, 14, 15, and 16, valued at $1,600.[239] By 1917, Isabella's property in Banff consisted of Lots 13–16.[240] It may be that the Banff property was listed in Isabella's name because she made use of it most often. Banff's *Crag & Canyon* often reported that Lady Lougheed had returned to Banff and "opened her Banff residence for the season."[241] Indeed, many of Calgary's society women entertained in their own Banff homes. For example, the *Crag & Canyon* reported that Mrs. P.J. Nolan "arrived in town Monday morning and has opened her charming home on Buffalo street for the season."[242] Even Lady Macdonald, wife of Sir John A., had a cottage, appropriately situated near the CPR Hotel.[243]

Despite James joining Isabella on occasion, it appears that Isabella enjoyed the property to a greater degree. The Banff home was sufficiently far removed from the public duties required of her in Calgary so it could provide Isabella with a sense of freedom. It was, after all, Isabella who ignored James's directive and joined her sons for the car excursion into the park, and it was to Banff that Isabella retreated when Beaulieu underwent its various expansions and renovations.

There is the possibility, as well, that the Banff property was purchased by Isabella with funds from her father's estate, and that is why it was listed in her name. In his own will, William Lucas Hardisty seems to have demonstrated more consideration of his wife's role than did James. Isabella's father stipulated that one-third of his estate go immediately to the Metis wife who he had once referred to as an "ignorant girl," with the remainder of proceeds being divided equally among his children. After Mary Hardisty's death and those of his children, any remaining amount was to be distributed among his grandchildren.[244]

While William retired to Quebec, his will was executed in the Red River Colony in July of 1868 at a time when many fur traders excluded their Indigenous wives from their wills altogether.[245] Further, the communication between William and Mary Hardisty's descendants demonstrates that Isabella's mother continued to enjoy more autonomy with regard to her husband's estate than was later evident for Isabella herself. In one example, in a letter to C.H. Lougheed Esq., Calgary, dated 18 October 1929, Isabella's mother advised Clarence that "I am willing, with the others of the family, to have the Royal Trust Co. act as Executors of the Estate."[246]

Isabella's grandfather, Richard Hardisty Sr., also appeared to show consideration to his wife in his will. That document stipulated that all of his property should go to his widow, except for the house in Lachine, which was to be shared by William and his sister Isabella. After Donald and Isabella Smith bought out William's share, the house always remained entirely in Isabella Hardisty Smith's name. In fact, Lord Strathcona commented that it made no difference whether it was listed in Isabella's name. To Smith's biographer, this suggests that Donald and Isabella Smith saw themselves as "an indissoluble whole."[247]

Regarding the conditions of James's will, in the end, it likely would not have affected the eventual value of his estate, no matter who served as executor. Tax returns for 1933 showed that the net income from the Lougheed estate amounted to only $18,000. This was well below the $40,000 mark established by James in his will that would have allowed the $1,000 yearly stipend for his brother Samuel, who had come west with James before he connected with the Hardisty family.[248] Regardless of the stipulations of her husband's estate, in reality, all indications are that Isabella was confident in her role as James's partner and the daughter of fur trade aristocracy who emerged as Lady Lougheed. All indications are also that Isabella's sons had great regard for her. It is interesting to note that, when Douglas, the youngest son, died, Isabella joined her son Edgar as administrator of Douglas's estate. It is not clear why Isabella was one of the administrators, given that the sole beneficiary of the estate, which comprised mainly life insurance, was Douglas's widow.[249]

James's estate in the years after his death certainly does not belie his reputation as one of the more successful businessmen of his time. Popular historian James H. Gray made an interesting observation about the importance of a man based upon the space devoted to him by local newspapers after his death. Gray observed that James merited twice as much space as his neighbour and fellow business tycoon William Roper Hull. For his part, Hull willed his entire estate to his wife, stipulating only that, upon her death, his estate should go to the orphans of Calgary. At the time of final probate of Hull's will, its worth had grown to $6 million.[250] Although this amount was far greater than the value of James's estate, Gray is correct that James seems to have attained a reputation as a man of more importance than Hull, if we are to judge by newspaper coverage.

In the case of eminent women, space devoted to their obituaries was comparably less than that of men. This is evident in the example of Mrs. W.F. Alloway of Winnipeg, who, along with her husband, established the Winnipeg Foundation. This foundation was western Canada's first charitable trust and ultimately became one of the largest funds in Canada. Upon her death, Mrs. Alloway left her entire estate of $800,000 to the foundation, yet merited only brief obituary coverage.[251] For her part, Isabella's obituary also garnered less attention than her husband's.

Yet the importance of Isabella's role in the partnership she forged with James and her importance to the economy of the West is evident in the fact that, as a widow, Isabella carried on with her role as first lady at official functions. It had come to be expected of her. Important dignitaries who had visited both James and Isabella continued to regard Isabella as an important contact. For example, the Prince of Wales carried on with the tradition of sending Christmas cards to Isabella after James's death, and during a visit in August 1927, the prince again invited Isabella to dinner at his E.P. Ranch south of Longview, along with other dignitaries.

When the Prince of Wales and Prince George visited Calgary in 1927, not all that long before her death, Isabella was again seated at the head table, along with Mrs. Edmund Taylor, the wife of James's long-time business associate and former HBC man.[252] By this time, Isabella's daughter Dorothy was Mrs. Nolen Hussey, but she still accompanied her mother, and was remembered by the *Herald* as "one of His Royal Highness' favorite dancing partners during his two previous visits to Calgary."[253]

It appears that a variety of friends, family, and former colleagues of the senator's continued to attend Isabella's New Year's Day open house, held annually at Beaulieu.[254] Right up until three months before her death, Isabella continued the fur trade tradition of keeping an open house on New Year's Day.[255] Perhaps it was these continuing public duties that inspired the city to deal with Isabella as they had. By 1934, the City of Calgary had acquired Beaulieu under the Tax Recovery Act for nonpayment of taxes on the property, and a certificate of title was issued to the city on 13 March 1934.[256] We already know that city officials allowed Isabella to remain in the house until her death in 1936.[257]

The repossession of Beaulieu by the city in 1934 was reportedly a "common enough situation." At one time, it is said that the City of Calgary had "repossessed 15 mansions."[258] While repossession by the city may have been "common enough" during the Depression, it was not as common to allow the former owners to remain in those homes. Isabella's was a unique situation and reflected the importance of her family's position. It is also indicative of the extent of the value of Isabella's "social capital." Even as a widow, the social value of Isabella's contributions was still recognized by city officials. The city's generosity in allowing Isabella to remain in Beaulieu is even more remarkable when one considers that the executors of James's estate were later prepared to appeal to the Supreme Court of Canada to challenge the city's assessment of the property for tax purposes.[259]

There are few documented details that explain how Isabella came to be in such a dire financial situation after she was widowed; however, it is reasonable to suggest that the problem lay in the fact that the estate comprised primarily real estate. With the depressed real estate prices and the demise of so many of their tenants' businesses, it would have been difficult to avoid financial ruin. When it allowed Isabella to remain in her stately home, the city enabled her to retain some semblance of her life before widowhood. While this decision also allowed her to continue with her public duties, perhaps those public duties also afforded the city an aura of prosperity in the midst of Depression conditions.

Writing at the height of depressed conditions, the *Calgary Herald* recognized the importance of Beaulieu as the official residence of the West when it reported on the reception held at Beaulieu in honour of the Canadian Law Society. The article noted that Isabella was

> *Calgary's most prominent hostess for more than thirty years...It is only suitable that this summer the Lougheed residence be the rallying ground of one of the most important gatherings of the year.*[260]

Again in 1932, the *Calgary Daily Herald* described pioneer days in the West and Isabella's role in the new economy, explaining,

> *The Lougheed home was one that always kept open house from the very beginning in the old downtown area. Then, guest accommodation was a problem. The homes of the early residents were perpetual billets for the stream of newcomers and the passers-through...when James Lougheed was made a senator, her position became that of first lady for this city and district.*[261]

The *Herald* provided some insight into the challenges Isabella had faced, as she was continually expected to eschew any semblance of a private life, for

> *throughout her residence here, she has had to adjust and arrange her household system for the entertainment of a long line of noted visitors; a list which makes her unique as a hostess in Western Canada.* [262]

The local newspaper no doubt reminded residents not only of Isabella's importance but of better times in Calgary.

Before she was able to see any financial recovery either in her own personal estate or in her beloved adopted home of Calgary, Isabella died on 13 March 1936, just six years after the death of her own mother. Isabella died at her stately home with her sons Edgar and Norman and her daughter Dorothy at her side. Like James and her children, Isabella was buried in the family plot at Calgary's Union Cemetery.[263] Shortly after her death, an auction was held to dispose of most of the collectibles Isabella had kept at Beaulieu. While it was believed the auction would raise a fair sum of money, the economy was still depressed and many invaluable items were very nearly given away.[264] Upon her death, the *Albertan* paid heed to Isabella's sacrifice, writing,

> *As nearly a thousand citizens paid tribute, Lady Isobel [sic] Lougheed, known among pioneers and younger generations for her hearty, western hospitality, a quality she shared equally with royalty and friends in humble stations in life, went to her last rest.* [265]

One particular newspaper report, titled "Colorful Life in West," hailed Isabella for her pioneer qualities of western hospitality, referring to her as the "First Lady" of the North West.[266] However, one headline that appeared after the funeral referred to Isabella as the "Gracious Albertan [who] Dies at Age of 77…Factor's Daughter."[267]

The fact that she was referred to at the time of her death in 1936 as a "Factor's Daughter" suggests that Isabella was still remembered as the daughter of fur trade aristocracy, and that her role as "first hostess" was important to the economy of the North West. Isabella was also remembered as a "gracious" woman, a characteristic first inculcated not only at the eastern school but also as the daughter of the chief factor.

Perhaps the most important contribution Isabella made to the new community of Calgary was as an agent of transition.[268] Not only did she participate in most philanthropic and cultural activities in the new emerging economy but her recreated persona was used by many in the press to demonstrate the vitality of the transformed Prairie West. Constant attention to Isabella's European dress by the local and national press, when most knew she was Indigenous, helped demonstrate the economic integration of western populations and, to some extent, the assimilation of Indigenous people. No doubt when the City of Calgary allowed Isabella to remain in her stately home, it, too, appreciated the social capital Isabella continued to contribute to the economy in the midst of the Depression era.

The term "lady" for Isabella in James's will may indicate that James felt Isabella should continue to present the persona of "lady" and not of businesswoman. In the end, though, the couple were jointly instrumental in the successful establishment of schools, churches, libraries and literary clubs, dramas and dances, and high culture and high fashion, all of which were meant to draw suitable settlers and to boost western economic fortunes, and, indeed, their own fortunes.

The Lougheeds were so economically and socially successful that they boasted a large library long before Calgary could boast a public one. In 1902, Calgary city officials bemoaned the lack of a public library, citing the need to rely on James and Isabella's extensive library for reference material.[269] The 1925 inventory of furnishings and contents, completed for the estate following James's death, suggests they

were a family "surrounded by books."[270] One of the last photographs of Isabella Hardisty Lougheed features her seated in her drawing room with a book on her lap.[271] When Isabella and James celebrated the marriage of HBC friends Charles Parlow and Miss Minnie Wheeler, rather than the typical fruit knives, silver pitchers, and card receivers, they presented the new couple with a complete set of Shakespeare's works, bound in twelve volumes.[272] In the end, Isabella continued to be important to the new Prairie West's image as a society able to equal London ballrooms—"cities beautiful" that could boast that their "first couple" were justifiable prairie "aristocrats."

William Hardisty had expressed concern that his daughter may be unhappy at that eastern school as a young girl, perhaps because he knew she was "different" than most girls there. Despite her father's concern, Isabella clearly used her "difference" to cultivate a distinct position for herself in the new economy of the Prairie West. In all aspects, James and Isabella were to be at the forefront of refined living and economic transformation.

From the time of her marriage to the time of her death, Isabella occupied her position as "First Lady" of the North West with grace. It was quite fitting, indeed, that, upon her death, Isabella would be recognized not only as a gracious lady but as the daughter of a Hudson's Bay Company chief factor, that unique pioneer status that belonged to the fur trading Metis people.

< *Lady Lougheed. Photo dated 1920s–early 1930s.*

Glenbow Alberta Museum and Archives, NA-3232-5.

5

Trader Delorme's Family

THE FIRST CHAPTER of Marie Rose Delorme's unpublished epic, "The Adventures of the Wild West of 1870," introduced readers to the untamed land that the "daring voyageurs" discovered.[1] By the second chapter, Marie Rose informed her reader that her father was a fur trader "amongst the Indians of the plains," who had in his younger days assumed the life of "a settler on the White Horse Plain" to farm on a "small scale." She continued that her father was a "clever man, full of life," who made "enough money to leave a fair estate for his wife and five children."[2]

While Marie Rose devoted much attention in her later years to writing herself into pioneer history and *not* writing her Delorme family into history, her identity formation began as a child of the fur trade. She traversed the plains with her Metis family and she learned Metis skills and culture by working alongside her Metis mother. For a short period of time, and like many Metis girls, Marie Rose was sent to a convent to be educated by Roman Catholic nuns. The goal was not necessarily that she would no longer be Metis but rather that she would retain her position as one of the higher class of Metis who were buffalo hunters and traders, and who maintained close links with the Church.

As an adult far removed from the fur trade, Marie Rose's literary work began a process of negotiating an identity in the new Prairie West and is, for the most part, truthful in its telling. Yet it is significant that Marie Rose did not explore the various conflicts in the Red River area, for she likely had some knowledge of at least the most well known—those occurring in 1869–1870 and 1885. This is especially so given that she had close family members involved in the fighting on the side of those who opposed annexationist plans by Canada in 1869–1870. In 1885, when Louis Riel again represented the Metis as they challenged the Canadian government's land policies, Marie Rose's uncles served as Riel's soldiers.

Marie Rose's family had been involved in most confrontations in Red River, beginning with the conflict in 1816 between incoming settlers and Metis hunters and traders whose families had been in Red River for generations. While there is no written documentation that he was involved in the fighting, François Delorme, Marie Rose's great-grandfather, later offered a deposition to the Coltman Commission.[3] Her family was again involved in conflict in the Red River area in 1849, when Pierre Guillaume Sayer and three other Metis traders were charged with illegally trading in furs.[4] Among those supporting Sayer was again a member of Marie Rose's family, on this occasion her grandfather, *le chef des prairies*, Urbain Delorme Sr.

It is not clear that Marie Rose's father was ever involved in the politics of Red River, but he did die a young man, leaving his widow to care for Marie Rose and her siblings. While her mother remarried, when the economy began to change with the disappearance of the buffalo and the incoming settlers, Marie Rose was to become a valuable asset for her fur trading family. As a woman who had survived for a time as a widow and who knew that the economy was changing, Marie Rose's mother chose a Euro-North American trader who appeared wealthy and whom she judged would be able to extend the family network economically. As a member of a wealthier Metis extended family, Marie Rose would also become a valuable commodity for her robe-and-whiskey-trading Euro-North American husband. Although Marie Rose vehemently opposed the marriage arrangement her mother made, she had few options as a female member of the Delorme family, whose influence was waning.

In order to understand how Marie Rose's family achieved a position of some influence, it is important to explore her early childhood and the life path of her family members. Marie Rose Delorme was born in Saint François Xavier, Red River, on 18 October 1861, to Urbain Delorme Jr. and Marie Desmarais.[5] Marie Rose was the second eldest of four surviving siblings, Elise, Urbain,[6] Madeleine, and Charlie. Elise, also known as Eliza, later married George Ness, who served as a justice of the peace in Batoche in 1885 when fighting erupted between Metis people and Canadian government forces. Madeleine married Ludger Gareau, and they also had a home in Batoche in 1885. Urbain married Nellie Gladstone, and he settled for a time in Pincher Creek. Charlie was an adopted "Sioux" boy; although he is not listed in some of the family genealogical documents, Marie Rose wrote that he was christened Charlie Ross in honour of his godfather, her uncle, Donald (Daniel) Ross.

Whatever the arrangements by which a Sioux boy was taken in by the Delorme family—by formal adoption or even sale—Marie Rose wrote that her family rescued Charlie after he was abandoned by his people. She wrote about Charlie that "he does not know he is pure Sioux Indian,"[7] and that he "called us brothers and sisters."[8] On another occasion, Marie Rose wrote, "We loved him as a true brother and he believed himself to be such."[9] There are no more specifics that could verify when Marie Rose's family informally adopted Charlie, but there is some indication that he continued to be regarded as a sibling for the rest of his life. When he married, like so many of Marie Rose's family, he settled for a time in Pincher Creek near Marie Rose.[10]

Marie Rose's mother, Marie Desmarais, was the daughter of
Joseph Desmarais and Adelaide Clairmont, both of Metis ancestry.[11]
Joseph was the son of François Desmarais and a woman described
by Marie Rose's granddaughter, Jock Carpenter, as a "full-blooded
Saulteaux maiden."[12] It was with evident pride that Marie Rose's
granddaughter communicated this ethnicity, the Desmarais family
being one of the earliest freemen families in the West.

Marie Rose's father, Urbain Jr., was the son of Urbain Delorme
Sr. and Madeleine Vivier.[13] Urbain Sr. was born in the North West,
the son of a French Canadian man, François Enos (et Hénault)
dit Delorme,[14] and a woman of the Saulteaux tribe, identified as
Madeleine Sauteuse.[15] By 1816, Marie Rose's Delorme family was
already politically active in Red River, when François Delorme was
implicated in "La bataille de Grenouillère" (Seven Oaks). When
François Delorme gave his disposition in the aftermath of the Seven
Oaks incident, he offered the names of those who gave the orders
to burn the houses of the European settlers.[16] In 1817, François
was also listed as one of the signatories on the petition drawn up
by residents of Red River when they requested Roman Catholic
missionaries for their settlement. His occupation at that time was
listed as HBC interpreter.[17] It is not surprising that François was
politically active in Red River. As the oldest Metis community west
of the Great Lakes, Red River served as the centre of Metis social
activity and political resistance until 1870, after which time many
Metis left the settlement for points west and north.

For the Metis of Red River, even prior to the exodus from Red
River, there was frequent interaction with northern Metis people
who not only travelled to Red River to trade but sent their children
to Red River to be educated.[18] Marie Rose's family would have had
interaction with the northern Metis, and they were also connected
to Cuthbert Grant Jr., the man who has subsequently been referred
to as the first leader of the Metis people. Cuthbert McGillis, who
married Marguerite Delorme (Marie Rose's aunt), had a sister

named Marie McGillis, who became Cuthbert Grant's wife.[19] When Grant was establishing his group of Metis settlers on the White Horse Plains he reportedly reserved the lots closest to him for "the bravest men and most successful hunters among his people."[20] Apparently, Marie Rose's grandfather, Urbain Delorme Sr., met those qualifications, for he is listed as one of Grant's close neighbours.[21] Grant's settlement on the White Horse Plains, initially named Grantown but later called Saint François Xavier,[22] was Marie Rose's birthplace and that of most of her fur trade family.

Not unlike many of the early traders who were stationed in fur trade country, François Delorme had sent his son (Marie Rose's grandfather), Urbain Sr., when he was four years old, to Quebec to be baptised and to live with an aunt. Although he was clearly Metis, on one occasion Marie Rose seemed to suggest that her grandfather, Urbain Sr., was a French Canadian man born in Quebec.[23] She wrote that he left that province for the West, finding a settlement of "Scotch half-breeds living on White Horse Plains...and decided to cast his lot with them."[24] Despite his long absence from fur trade country, as an adult, Marie Rose's grandfather went on to do far more than cast his lot with "half-breeds." Rather, he achieved a position of authority in Metis society and was often described as le chef des prairies. According to some historians, next to Cuthbert Grant, the elder Delorme was the "greatest of the plains hunters and traders."[25]

In comparison to many of his contemporaries, Marie Rose's grandfather could be described as a man of means. When the newspaper, Le Métis, reported his death, in error, in its 21 February 1878 edition (which it corrected in a subsequent issue on 9 May 1878), it stated that he was "l'un des plus anciens et des plus riches traiteurs de la Rivière Rouge."[26] Urbain Sr. reportedly once brought a bag of gold for safekeeping to the nuns at the convent at Saint François Xavier and advised that they would be wise to store it safely, for it was valued at "quatre mille piastres" ($4,000).[27] In his will, Marie Rose's grandfather left an impressive sum of $4,461.04,[28] which was later managed by Archbishop Alexandre Antonin Taché. A number of Urbain Sr.'s descendants, including Marie Rose, accessed funds from his estate for many years after his death.[29]

Further suggestion of the elder Delorme's status is found in oral testimony, recorded in the *Pincher Creek Echo* by Emma Lynch-Staunton, who settled on a ranch in the Pincher Creek district in the 1890s, near Marie Rose.[30] Based upon her conversations with Marie Rose, Lynch-Staunton wrote that Urbain Sr. "prospered greatly in the fur-trading business and at one time was reputed to have 90,000 (pounds) in the bank."[31] Hudson's Bay Company records confirm that, by the 1860s, Metis traders such as Norbert and Urbain Delorme earned as much as $1,000 per year in the buffalo robe trade.[32]

The brief descriptions of her life as a young girl in Red River demonstrate that Marie Rose's family followed a lifestyle that came to be viewed as more typically Metis than that of Metis born in other geographic areas. In the summer, Marie Rose's family, descendants of the Saulteaux, farmed a plot of land on the banks of the Red River, where a typical river lot

> might contain one or two dwelling houses, a barn, a stable, a storage house, a summer kitchen, and several other outbuildings, as well as ten or twenty acres of cultivated land. Behind the lot would be a second lot of equal width and depth knowns as the "hay priviliege." In many cases, the household would also possess another lot directly across the river where wood and hay could be gathered. Because few farms could have survived on the production of wheat and barley and vegetables, members of most households participated in trade, wage labour, or the annual buffalo hunts. The latter, which included 100 to 300 hunters, were essential to the survival of the settlement and have been likened to roundups in a ranch community.[33]

In fact, the Saulteaux had engaged in some form of agriculture or stock raising in southwestern Manitoba and southeastern

Saskatchewan prior to the treaties.[34] Life in the communities in the Red River area, such as the Protestant ones like St. Andrew's, where many of the Hudson's Bay Company men lived with their country wives, as well as the Roman Catholic ones, such as Saint François Xavier, where Marie Rose's family lived, was dictated by the seasons. In the summer there were fish to be caught and river traffic was steady while Indigenous families camped along the riverbank. In the fall, the Metis salt makers visited, as did Indigenous purveyors of fish oil, while many families left on their winter hunting and trading trips.[35]

As well as being early farmers, Marie Rose's family often wintered on the plains. The first description that Marie Rose provides of her memories setting out on the prairies with her Metis family was when she was seven years old, in 1868. Marie Rose is not clear whether this was a hunting expedition or strictly meant to engage in trading. However, it is possible the trip involved both activities and that her grandfather, *le chef des prairies*, was along on the 1868 trip, given that he died in 1886. By 1868, the number of carts setting out would be significantly less than at the height of the Metis-dominated economy in Red River.[36] Yet the semi-annual nomadic lifestyle that Marie Rose followed as a child remained very similar to that of her ancestors. If he was part of this particular caravan in 1868, as captain, the elder Delorme would have had soldiers serving under his command to assist in enforcing the rules of the hunt. It would have been the duty of the soldiers to set up camp, which often "occupied as much ground as a modern city."[37]

While Marie Rose did not offer specifics about the trip across the plains in 1868 to the winter hunting grounds, Norbert Welsh remembered that the trip from Saint François Xavier to the Victoria Mission northeast of Edmonton took thirty days. The traders Welsh travelled with carried supplies for trading that included items such as

> tobacco, tea, sugar, powder, shot, small bullets, Hudson's Bay blankets, all kinds of prints and cottons, vermilion (lots of vermilion),

axes, butcher knives, files, copper kettles, guns, and—the main thing—alcohol, lots and lots of alcohol. [38]

At the first opportunity, the hunt would bring in the winter's supply of meat. Indeed, at the height of the buffalo-hunting era, one hunt would often be adequate to supply needs for the entire winter. Regarding the social aspect of the hunt, Welsh noted the traders of the plains were the "aristocrats" of the fur trade, continuing, "We paid attention to class distinctions in those days, and we buffalo-hunters and traders thought quite well of ourselves." [39]

Even at a time when the buffalo were becoming more scarce, the profit on trade goods could be enough to render these traders "aristocrats." Welsh gave an example of his accounting:

> *For one buffalo robe valued at a dollar and a quarter, we gave in trade one pound of tea, which cost twenty-five cents at Fort Garry, and half a pound of sugar which cost five cents...We sold our tea for a dollar a pound, sugar for fifty cents a pound...Any kind of print or cotton measured to the extension of the arms, approximately two yards, and which cost ten cents a yard, we sold for a dollar a yard. For powder, one pint (two little tin dippersful made a pound) that cost forty cents a pound by the keg, we got a dollar a pound. Bullets that cost two dollars and a half for a twenty-five pound sack, we sold at the rate of ten for fifty cents.* [40]

According to Welsh, the "merchant princes of those times lived high," particularly when they travelled to Saint Paul with a cargo of furs. In their canteens they carried their own supplies, which included

> *all the necessaries and luxuries of camp life and travel—tea, sugar, spices, cheese, jams, jellies, marmalades, preserves, bacon and canned meats, gunpowder, shot and bullets. And then we had wild game which was plentiful along the trail.* [41]

In this instance, Welsh's descriptions do not suggest that there were no challenges for traders, no matter the size of the brigades, as they made these trips across the plains and to sell furs in the larger centres. Welsh related many instances when bridges were washed away, or times when rivers needed to be navigated with horses and carts as they swam across fast-moving waters dodging ice jams. Fur traders always had to be on the lookout as well for Indigenous people seeking to reclaim prized animals, which had been traded earlier for other goods. There were also winters when few buffalo were found and no money was made when harsh conditions had forced the movement of Indigenous groups.

For the Metis, there was strength in numbers. According to Alexander Ross, in 1840, earlier than the hunts that Welsh was on, he witnessed 1,210 carts leaving Red River for the annual hunt. On this occasion, when roll call was taken, 1,630 souls were counted. This number of carts would surely form a "strong barrier" when camp was set up. The Metis survived these challenging trips in large part because they had strict rules in place. With few variations, the laws of the hunt were generally as follows:

> no buffalo were to be run on the Sabbath; no party was to lag behind without permission; no person was to run buffalo before the general order; every captain and his men were to take turns patrolling the camp; on the first offense of these laws, the offender had his saddle and bridle cut up; on the second offence, the offender's coat was taken and cut up; on the third offence, the offender was flogged; any person convicted of theft was brought to the middle of the camp, then his or her name was called out three times, adding the word "thief" each time.[42]

While the hunt described by Ross occurred before Marie Rose's birth, and certainly long before she settled in Pincher Creek, this part of the Metis culture carried on for the Metis long past the fur trade. As Maria Campbell wrote, the annual buffalo hunt bore much similarity to the annual trips with her Metis family in the twentieth century, when they set out as a family group to pick roots and berries, and thus is one example of the continuity of the Metis history and culture. While there were no more buffalo, and no longer a Hudson's Bay Company with which to trade, the items of trade between the Metis and the farmers during Campbell's time were roots, berries, nuts, moose meat, and fish.[43]

For the Metis, there was always time for socializing on the trail. While Marie Rose did not speak much about this aspect of the annual trips with her father, Norbert Welsh wrote that there were often times when real feasts were put up. Welsh described one such feast he hosted:

> We would dance the old-time dances and the Red River Jig—reel of four, reel of eight, double jig, strip the willow, rabbit chase, Tucker circle, drops of brandy, and all the half-breed dances. There were always lots of fiddlers. Nearly every man could play the fiddle. Then we would go to another family...This feasting lasted about ten days...Some of these dances took place at the Hudson's Bay posts.[44]

It was common knowledge that there was rarely a buffalo-hunting expedition in which the fiddle was left behind. Log huts played host to festivities, in which

> jigs, reels, and quadrilles were danced in rapid succession...The men wore shirts, trousers, belts, and moccasins...A black-eyed beauty in blue calico and a strapping Bois Brulé would jump up from the floor and outdo their predecessors...In the intervals of the dance Madame Gingrais...sang some French ballads and a Catholic hymn.[45]

Indeed, along with the feasting, there was always the need to remember the spiritual aspect of the Metis culture. Often, there were priests along, but even when there were not, the hunters never left for the hunt without saying a prayer, which they believed ensured their safety. How safe they remained during the buffalo runs was also a matter of pride. As Norbert Welsh related, it was often a competition to determine who had the fastest horse in the brigade.[46] In fact, the tradition of racing horses continued for the Metis long after the buffalo disappeared and the Metis had settled in areas across the prairies.

While Marie Rose wrote about her father's trading expeditions to the prairies from Red River, which would have been much similar to those described by Welsh and Ross, she did not refer to him as a hunter. However, given her grandfather's role as captain of the hunting brigades for some twenty-five years, it is likely that her father went along on numerous hunts and that Marie Rose lived the culture of those hunts herself. Marie Rose's granddaughter, Jock Carpenter, does provide specific details of a hunt that Urbain Delorme (Marie Rose's father) was on, in which

> at a full but easy gallop, Urbain cast an eye over the plain which stretched before him...Fully-loaded guns at the ready, the riders separated to cut off the now-stampeding buffalo...Urbain shot... a cow went down...Urbain did not wait to watch the scene but, wheeling his horse, started after another animal, loading as he rode.[47]

This excerpt suggests that Carpenter believed Marie Rose's father was an experienced buffalo hunter.

Another buffalo hunter, John Kerr, describes what Marie Rose's father might have experienced on these hunts. Kerr was a soldier who came to Red River in 1870, tasked with defending against the Metis provisional government. He then elected to stay in Red River and appears to have gained the respect of Metis hunters, even claiming he was adopted into the family of Gabriel Dumont, who reportedly addressed him as "mon frère."[48] During one trip onto the plains in the spring of 1872, Kerr recalled that each family would have up to a dozen carts and extra ponies. The only ones who stayed behind were the sick or elderly. After the call of "let loose," when any number of buffalo were killed, carts were driven onto the field by the women, and

> in an incredibly short time the beast is skinned, cut up and rady [sic] for the carts...The meat was brought back to camp, where what was not for immediate use was made into dried meat and pemmican...The skins, those not used for pemmican bags or shaga-nappi, are hair scraped and flesh removed and dressed for moccasins, teepees.[49]

In regard to the trading that took Metis families on "well-worn trails from Fort Garry as far west as Edmonton," Kerr wrote,

> The usual load for a cart was about 800 pounds. Our journey from Winnipeg as far as the South Saskatchewan river took approximately one month...We averaged about 18 miles a day.[50]

By the later 1860s, when Marie Rose remembered setting out for the plains with her father, agricultural disasters in Red River had already convinced many Metis that the sale of pemmican and buffalo robes was more dependable than agriculture. Although it appears that Marie Rose's father and mother had been relatively wealthy at one time, there were numerous problems in Red River when Urbain Delorme was farming. Farmers were devastated by floods and locusts almost every year between 1821 and 1870, resulting in better survival strategies among the buffalo hunting and trading segment of the population.[51]

Marie Rose wrote that her father had farmed on a small scale until the "money wasn't coming fast enough for him." Urbain Delorme had then travelled to St. Paul, where he picked up merchandise and set out for places where he thought the "biggest camps of Indians would winter."[52] In the fall, the family would set out with a caravan of Red River carts for the plains, where they typically spent the winter hunting and trading with Indigenous groups. Marie Rose confirmed that the family ventured quite some distance onto the plains, given that it took three months to travel back to Red River with the buffalo robes and furs.[53] Although her father died a young man at the age of thirty-six, and his family may have struggled for money at some point, Marie Rose wrote that her father "made enough money to leave a fair estate for his wife and five children."[54] In addition, she wrote, "We lived mostly on wild game while travelling, father used to bank nearly all his money; thus when he died, still in the prime of his life, he left us a very considerable fortune."[55]

Marie Rose wrote little of her father's death, saying only that she was still young when he died. Her grandchildren do not know of, nor do his death records indicate, a cause. However, Urbain Delorme Jr. died prior to the fighting in 1869–1870, so he was not involved, although many members of the Delorme family were. One granddaughter thought Marie Rose's father may have died in a horse accident.[56] Many buffalo hunters died in horse accidents and, as many have observed, while the Metis of Red River may have

> sustained themselves in a variety of ways such as fishing, trapping for furs, practicing small-scale agriculture, and working as wage labourers for the Hudson's Bay Company, they were first and foremost buffalo hunters.[57]

Although Marie Rose spoke primarily of trading and farming, given the inhospitable environment and unsophisticated agricultural technology during the time her family lived in Red River,[58] there would have been an inherent need to hunt, notwithstanding the fact that hunting was an integral part of the Delorme family culture. Thus, Marie Rose's father may have died in a hunting accident, as family members came to believe.

At the start of her unpublished manuscript, "Eighty Years on the Plains," Marie Rose demonstrates a pride in her father, and perhaps unknowingly her pleasure at being introduced to eventual prairie settlement. She wrote,

> I was very excited as any other little girl might be, who, at the early age of ten years, was embarking on a winter trip over the great western plains, from the Great Lakes to the Rocky Mountains...To-day [sic], October 5th, 1871, father was taking all of us on his annual fur-trading trip into the great North-west, and for the winter months, we must bid "Au revoir" to the farm on White Horse Plains, and until our arrival back in the spring, father would now be known as Trader Delorme.[59]

As with most Metis, Marie Rose was familiar with the customs of the Indigenous people who lived on the plains and with whom her father traded when he became "Trader Delorme," some of which are described in detail in her unpublished manuscripts and referred to in other sections of this book. In her description of the Dakota boy that her family adopted, Marie Rose described rather gruesome circumstances in which the boy's mother was killed by another of the chief's wives in an act purely motivated by jealousy. As an explanation, Marie Rose reasoned, "Sioux Indians are very mean disposition and treacherous, you can't depend on them."[60] In this regard, Marie Rose's views would have been very similar to those of her Metis fur trading kinship network, given that the Metis, though trading with them by the 1870s, had often clashed with Dakota (Sioux) over contested territories and had closer links and sympathies for the Cree and Saulteaux people.[61]

Marie Rose confirmed that her father associated more often with the somewhat acculturated Cree, whom she said "mingled oftener with the White Traders from the east, thus learning white man's ways much quicker." She went on to write, "Other tribes, who were in constant contact with the Whites, and with whom Father used to trade, were the Sarcees, the Stonies, the Peigans, and the Bloods. There were also the Salteaux."[62] The fact that Marie Rose would list these various First Nation people suggests that her family's trips were quite extensive throughout the prairies, thus requiring them to travel with many supplies and experienced hunters.

According to Marie Rose, her father at one time had some forty Red River carts fully loaded, a covered democrat for "mother and children," and seventy-five head of horses.[63] If the wagons each carried eight hundred pounds, this suggests that Urbain Delorme was a trader of some worth. Among the items of trade that Marie Rose lists are prints, knives, guns, ammunition, and axes, for which her father received in return furs, buffalo hides, bladders, grease, and pemmican.[64] The children were expected to help set up camp and to gather what they could, including country foods such as eggs, berries, and roots, as well as traditional medicinal supplies.

The need to hunt would have increased when traditional transport methods that employed many of the Metis were threatened with the arrival of steamboats. Built in North Dakota, the *Anson Northrup* was the first steamboat to arrive in Red River in 1859, inspiring the HBC to experiment with steam as well. The company promptly acquired property two hundred miles south of Fort Garry, which it named Georgetown. Yet freighting by steamboat was not extensive until 1872, when the Northern Pacific Railway reached Moorehead from Duluth. By 1875, trade had increased to the point that the Red River Transportation Company carried some fifty thousand tons of freight on the river in that year alone.[65]

In addition to the technological advances inspired by the introduction of steam, there was a changing political climate in the Red River area. Thus, the HBC determined to stop using "French Halfbreeds" from that settlement, most of who supported Riel, and to make changes to the transportation system by increasingly relying on steam. Not only would steam reduce the need for Red River boatmen but it would lessen the requirements of pemmican from plains provisioners. In fact, Isabella's uncle, Donald A. Smith, had sent word to London in 1870 about the urgency to adopt the use of steamboats, reportedly vowing to hire only "English Halfbreeds and Swampy Cree from Red River," thus freezing out the French Metis believed responsible for the "general mutiny."[66]

While Marie Rose wrote that her father abandoned farming for full-time trading in 1871 (in the midst of the changes brought by the introduction of steamboats), he actually died in January of that year. Marie Rose was writing from memory, there is some indication in this particular section of her manuscript that she wrote "The Adventures of the Wild West of 1870" when she was seventy-six years old, thus in approximately 1938. Given the majority of her writing was done when she was far removed from the fur trade, there are likely errors in her recollections.[67] Nonetheless, Marie Rose repeated in her "Eighty Years on the Plains" articles published in *Canadian Cattlemen*, the story about the trip over the prairies in 1871, but now with specific details about the travel arrangements:

> *In the spring of 1871, with our train of 40 Red River carts, and the usual number of riders and 75 head of horses, led by the covered democrat, or schooner, which housed mother and us five children, we turned our course to the great prairies, seeking out the largest camps where the Indians would winter and the greatest trade in furs would take place.*[68]

If Marie Rose's dates are accurate on this occasion, her mother would have been venturing onto the plains without her husband, given that he died in January of 1871, and she did not marry Cuthbert Gervais, another Metis man, until 20 September 1872.[69] However, whether she was an independent trader on this occasion is not certain, since Marie Rose describes her mother as being "housed" in the covered democrat along with the children. Yet it would not have been unheard of for Marie Rose's mother to be an independent trader for a time, or even an accomplished hunter for that matter. Oral history tells us that Cecelia Boyer, wife of Norbert

Welsh, had her own brigade and that Isabelle Falcon had a reputation for good hunting and shooting abilities. Thérèse Schindler and Madeleine La Framboise, Metis sisters, assumed the role of trader after their husbands died.[70] These two women demonstrated themselves to be astute and capable traders when widowed.[71] However, it remains that most written records from the fur trade era do not record much trading activity on the part of women.

Maria Campbell heard stories for years in her own communities of "women who have not only raised children alone but who were also skilled hunters, trappers, and fishermen; who built their own cabins, made snowshoes, and ran dog teams." Campbell relates the story of her family member, Qui chich, who became a successful farmer, respected medicine woman, and moneylender after her husband's death.[72]

If the women were not independent traders or skilled hunters, their primary tasks on the buffalo hunt were to tend to the meat and skins. Mrs. John Norquay, wife of the Metis man who became premier of Manitoba, related the method of making pemmican on the plains when women accompanied the hunt. According to Mrs. Norquay,

> there were two ways in which pemmican was cooked. One, which
> was known as rubaboo, was made by boiling the pemmican with
> potatoes, and with onions and any other vegetables...Of course,
> there were several grades of pemmican. It was made on the plains by
> the women who accompanied the buffalo hunters. They pounded the
> buffalo meat and then poured melted buffalo fat over it and sewed it
> up in buffalo hide.[73]

This is one of the customs Marie Rose knew well, for she continued to make pemmican until the end of her life, when she was living in Edmonton in the 1950s, far removed from fur trade society.

In Marie Rose's case, after her father died, there was very likely a need for her mother to generate money by undertaking trading trips. Marie Rose explained that the land at Red River was willed to her younger brother, with her mother having the use of it as long as she needed it to support her young family. There was a fair sum of money left in the care of Roman Catholic priests; however, Marie Rose and her siblings still accessed that money when they were later married, so it is not clear if Marie Delorme continued to rely on her husband's estate. It is possible that Marie Delorme was an independent trader for a time, given that Marie Rose described her mother as owning "twenty Red River carts, a democrat and thirty head of horses."[74] However, by the time she was a widow, the economy of pemmican and buffalo robes had declined, but agricultural challenges still necessitated a nomadic lifestyle for at least part of the year. The Delormes had an extensive kinship network and Marie Rose's mother could have continued to travel the plains with them to carry on trading.

Marie Rose's mother could have continued to farm the land at Red River, as well, because Urbain Delorme had stipulated that his wife could live on the land until the children were "of age." Thus, it is also fair to assume that Urbain's wife would have had assistance with farm labour, not only from blood relatives. As Norbert Welsh related, "The traders were like one big family. They treated, and addressed each other as if they were related."[75] It is likely that Marie Rose's family carried on much as they had before her father's death—that is, they remained in Red River for part of the year and then traded for another part of the year, even when there were no longer buffalo. As Norbert Welsh put it,

> There was no more hunting on the plains...The Indians and half-breeds came to my house to trade, but business was very poor. Trading in furs was practically at an end...I began to buy cattle.[76]

After putting in a crop of wheat for three years, and losing a large portion of it to frost, Welsh, like so many other Metis at that time, concluded there was not much money in farming, so he turned to freighting.[77] According to Marie Rose, her mother did the same. She wrote that her mother was "used to roaming life so when she re-married they decided to freight for the Hudson's Bay Co." Having given up farming altogether by this time, along with her new husband, Marie Delorme Gervais transported freight from Winnipeg to Edmonton, where they would also trap and trade for whatever game could be found.[78]

Finances must have become more difficult for Marie Rose's mother as well. Marie Rose's sister Elise Delorme wrote a letter to Msg. Alexandre Antonin Taché, dated 12 November 1874, from Saint François Xavier, requesting money for her mother and family.[79] In the letter, Elise apologized for the poor quality of the paper and asked that the bishop spare a hundred dollars so that they might buy warm clothing and food for the winter. Elise indicated she had already been turned down by her grandfather, who advised her that her father's affairs were now being managed by the bishop.[80] This request for assistance could suggest that Marie Delorme Gervais and her new husband were struggling to feed her family. On the other hand, it could simply mean that Marie Rose's mother was trying to exercise assertiveness in accessing some of the funds from her late husband's estate.

A degree of assertiveness was necessary for women during the fur trade, for their duties were many. Babies were the constant companions of their mothers, and were often breastfed until the age of two or three, which undoubtedly lead to the development of a strong sense of responsibility and strong bonds between mothers and children. All indications are that Marie Rose was enthralled by her mother, and although she wrote little about Marie Delorme Gervais, her admiration was evident when she did write about her. For example, with a sense of pride, Marie Rose wrote,

> She told me the stories of the horrible practices they [young
> Indigenous men] went through, which, though they frightened me,
> yet I listened to them fascinated. I will tell you about them just as

mother told them to me, as we sat around the central fire of
the Teepee.[81]

The imagery of a close bond is striking, as Marie Rose continued,
"I snuggled up close to her, listening and inhaling the smell of the
fragrant tobacco she had bought in St. Paul...all her stories in time
occupied many winter evenings."[82]

It was on those "many winter evenings" on the trail that Marie
Rose learned of the Indigenous customs that she later related in her
writing, often from the perspective of an omniscient third party.
Around the central fire of the teepee, snuggled close to her mother,
Marie Rose learned of her mother's belief that "the Sun Dance was
the greatest ceremony these Indians could perform in worshipping
their god."[83] Although in her later years far removed from the fur
trade she eventually denounced many of the Indigenous customs
as cruel, Marie Rose still felt the need to implore readers to understand that "each ritual of this dance was carried out for a certain
purpose."[84]

Based on the stories related by her mother and in her own writing,
Marie Rose demonstrated a belief that there was a dividing line between
Metis and First Nation people, and that this was evident in many
areas, including spirituality. As an example, she wrote of her early
days on the road with her Metis family that the hunters travelled

> *day after day when Sabbath day came every body respect the day of*
> *worship the Captain would call every body attention they all gather*
> *pick an elder person lead the prayer and holy rosary if missionary*
> *amongst them they hold regular holy sacrifice of the Mass.*[85]

On the other hand, Marie Rose wrote,

> *The Indians, the old tribes they had their way of worship, some*
> *believe in Sun some believe in owls, that was a great medicine bird*
> *for them if an owl come near a camp and howl at night it was sure a*

death warning that was their belief same as a dog if he howls and
look up at the sky at the same time that another warning.[86]

Marie Rose wrote about the many medicinal practices of
Indigenous people, including the use of various roots and herbs,
which she likely learned from her mother. For example, she
described the cure for rheumatism in detail, writing that the
custom necessitated killing an older buffalo, quickly pulling out the
entrails, and placing the sick person inside so they could "absorb
the natural animal heat."[87] According to Marie Rose, First Nation
people had cured many of their elderly of rheumatism and other
"bone diseases" by following these customs. Although she admitted
that the Indigenous custom worked, she also noted this cure would
be "an awful hard thing to stand."[88] Concluding her story, Marie
Rose wrote that this was the "real Indian life of the plains."[89]

Marie Rose also shared other customs, like her mother's rendition of how the "Indians" made their bows and arrows out of "chock
[sic] cherry wood" and twisted sinew, making them "very strong with
a flint rock end. They trim the flint rock to a sharp point so it can
pierce anything that is shot."[90] On another instance, she wrote, "To
doctor themselves they used the warth of poplar tree...They have a
weed that grows in swamps...They call ki-ni-ki-nick."[91] Although they
were reportedly her mother's words, Marie Rose concluded, "Indians
are not fools, they are nature's best scholars."[92] In fact, John Norquay's
wife Elizabeth referred to "kinikinik" as the inner bark of the red
willow, which served the Metis both as a substitute for tobacco and
as a poultice against swelling.[93]

For her part, Marie Rose preferred to refer to it as something
First Nation people used, also describing how they used a baby
bag lined with moss and a sort of baby powder made of pulverized
rotten wood.[94] She went on in detail about the custom, switching to
the first person in this instance, indicating that she later relied on
these customs herself:

[I used an] Indian bag to wrap my new born babies in...I should tell
you about the moss I used in my Indian baby bag. I bought it from
the Northern Indians, and mother taught me to heat it in a frying
pan, so if there were any insects hidden in the moss they would be
driven out or killed. [95]

Johnny Grant described the work of Metis women in Red River
in the mid-nineteenth century, when Marie Rose's Delorme family
members were prominent in that settlement, work that Marie Rose
experienced herself. According to Grant, the women tanned hides
and did "all their sewing by hand...In summer they helped in the
hay-field and then in harvesting the grain." There was a pride in the
traditional work the Metis women did, for as Johnny noted, the
women had "a pleasant rivalry as to who made the finest garments
for their husbands."[96] Marie Rose confirmed that young Metis mothers

vied for one another in seeing who could make the prettiest Ti-ki-
na-ken (baby beaded bag) which is the cradle of the papoose...We
were just as proud to "show off" our bead work on the baby bag as
you are to display your knitting or embroidery. [97]

Marie Rose understood that the handiwork made by Metis women
provided a distinctive sense of pride in their culture. She continued,

Long hours were spent beading the front of vests, the cuffs of coats;
and the lad with a nicely beaded buckskin shirt was proud indeed...
and fringed, beautifully beaded trappings for the horses lent a
distinguished look to many a mounted chief. [98]

Metis women did not only sew for the sense of pride it brought
them, and they did not do it only for their own families. Rather,
they were often organized into districts, and "sewed to lighten the
domestic burden on 'other women' who could afford to purchase
[their] goods."[99] The women of Red River, where Marie Rose spent

a fair bit of her formative years, were only one example of a female economy that played a critical social role.[100] Indeed, Red River became the site for the "merger of indigenous knowledge, European notions of a lady's education, and the enduring demand for female production."[101]

Nuns in convent settings often inculcated these European notions of lady's education in Metis girls. Yet, despite the eventual importance of convent training to many Metis girls, it still was only one aspect of their education. According to Madeline Mercredi Bird, who attended the Holy Angels mission at Fort Chipewyan, her grandmother deserved the credit for teaching her practical skills, such as learning to "stitch birchbark baskets." Bird explained that her grandmother "got along well with nature and nature gave her all the important things she needed." She credited her grandmother not only with providing tools for survival but concluded that she taught her to "make life more pleasant with flowers, decoration and fancy work on clothing."[102] Not unlike Bird, Marie Rose credited much of her own knowledge of traditional Metis handiwork to her mother,[103] writing,

> The lessons I learned by mother's side were later put into use when my hand-made buckskin gloves were much sought after by the early settlers of our community, from Macleod to Pincher Creek.[104]

While Marie Rose's mother believed it important to give her daughters the education of the fur trade and life on the plains, like many Metis mothers, she also believed her daughters needed the education provided by Roman Catholic nuns. It became the duty of the Roman Catholic Metis women to educate their children in religion. The influence of the Church was always an important aspect of Metis life.[105] Writing in the context of her discussions of her time in the convent, Marie Rose made special note to "pay tribute to the memory of my mother, who...so enriched our lives with the education we received."[106]

While it does appear that Marie Rose's mother had carried on as an independent trader for a time by herself as a widow, she did remarry, and this eventually led to a change of lifestyle for Marie Rose for a few years. When Cuthbert and Marie Delorme Gervais ventured out to freight for the HBC, they took along Marie Rose's two brothers and a younger sister.[107] However, Marie Delorme Gervais took this opportunity to "enter sister Liza and me at St. Boniface boarding school."[108] Marie Rose was nine years old when she entered the convent at St. Boniface to be educated by the Grey Nuns. While Marie Rose's granddaughter, Jock Carpenter, believed her grandmother was at the convent for two years,[109] Marie Rose herself wrote that she attended for four years. According to the records consulted, this is a more probable time span, and likely happened between 1872 and 1876.[110]

Even four years would have made an important impact on the young Marie Rose. Several authors have highlighted the desire of French missionaries to assimilate their charges to French and Roman Catholic culture.[111] It is more difficult to determine the curricula for Roman Catholic girls who attended the convent schools than it is for the daughters of HBC families, who more typically attended schools such as that operated by Miss Davis in Red River. However, there are traces of information about the education Marie Rose received at the convent. For example, in 1826, Father Provencher wrote that a farmer's wife had been hired to teach the girls at school to "work the flax and [buffalo] wool" (likely in relation to the short-lived Buffalo Wool Company operating in Red River at the suggestion of John Pritchard). It is also known that the nuns viewed sewing as a priority, and that several excelled at floral embroidery.[112] The floral patterns used by the Metis women became distinctive because the schools in fur trade country not only served as "distribution points for European designs and sewing techniques" but were "also moulded by local artistic traditions." As well, the moccasins and other Indigenous clothing long remained essential items for survival in the West.[113]

There are other sources that shed light on the curricula used by the Grey Nuns. For example, Sara Riel's notebooks and letters indicated that the girls learned to spin, knit, and sew.[114] While girls at the day schools, which opened in 1844, learned reading, religion, writing, and domestic science, the girls who went to the boarding school, which began operating in 1853, also learned French, English, music, painting, history, and mathematics. It is true that Sara attended between 1858 and 1866, and took her vows in 1868, prior to Marie Rose's attendance. Yet, despite the different attendance dates, both Marie Rose and Sara likely enjoyed a comprehensive curriculum for the time, in addition to learning the handcrafts listed in Sara's diaries.

By the time Marie Rose was sent to the convent, the nuns had been at Red River for some time. The goal of the "worthy followers of Marguerite d'Youville, Foundress of the Sisters of Charity of Montreal," who had ventured west in canoes guided by voyageurs, was to "do good," for they believed that "the whole country would change if only [they] could put the sisters everywhere."[115] The arrival of the Grey Nuns to Red River coincided with the arrival of Euro-North American women who were to become wives of HBC men and Protestant clergy. In fact, George Simpson, who, like others, discarded his various Indigenous partners, finally in favour of a European one, was very supportive of the Grey Nuns establishing a presence in Red River. The support offered to the incoming nuns by authorities in Red River was assured, no doubt because, like the other Euro-North American women who were beginning to arrive in Red River, the nuns symbolized piety, purity, and domesticity, qualities that were becoming more valuable to company officers in the North West as they sought ways to further their careers.

Not long after their arrival the nuns welcomed students from among the "Saulteaux, Métis and Sioux."[116] Plans were soon underway to build a new convent that would occupy two floors and a chapel,[117] along with a boarding house for future students such as Marie Rose. The Roman Catholic Church undoubtedly hoped to prepare its young charges to be wives and mothers of large families.[118] Also, those Metis who sent their daughters to be educated at the convent in Red River were often among the wealthier. Yet the nuns and their charges still struggled under difficult conditions. The nuns were forced to adapt quickly to what would have been rudimentary conditions, in comparison to their previous lifestyles in Montreal. They were soon involved in all aspects of securing living quarters and procuring country food supplies, no doubt enduring great suffering, while literally "putting their hands to the plow." It was expected that the girls, even if they might be daughters of the wealthier families, would partake in arduous physical labour alongside the nuns. Despite inherent challenges, the fact that most of their students were drawn from the farmer/merchant/trader class, and that the central mission was to educate the Metis to a sedentary lifestyle,[119] the work of the Grey Nuns was more likely to succeed as buffalo herds disappeared.

Despite any success on the part of the nuns, by the time Marie Rose was sent to the convent school, there was concern that the missions would have to be reduced in the West when subsidies from France were affected by war costs.[120] At times surviving on dry meat, black bread, and potatoes, it was little wonder that some of the nuns became ill.[121] Little wonder, too, that some of the students became ill. However, piety would prevail among the nuns, and, by necessity, among their charges. One report claims, "Mother McMullen was especially impressed with the joy and happiness which reigned in the convent despite extreme poverty."[122] Marie Rose was to become familiar with poverty not only at the convent but also at times as an adult, and she reflected some of the piety of the nuns.

Whatever the funding restraints for the convents in the 1830s, Marie Rose received a substantial education in the 1870s compared to many other Metis girls of her time. In addition to an academic curriculum, Marie Rose learned to play musical instruments, very likely at the convent. There is evidence of some musical training or perhaps music reading in a photograph of Marie Rose as an older woman playing the accordion. As well, Marie Rose wrote that, on her many visits to Waterton Lakes National Park to visit Kootenai Brown, the first park warden, and his Cree wife, Ni-ti-mous, she accompanied Brown on the violin, as he sang his favourite song, which happened to be a well-known Metis folksong, "Red River Valley."[123]

Marie Rose was under the tutelage of the Grey Nuns just after the fighting in 1869–1870 in which her uncles were involved. The meticulous journals kept by the nuns demonstrate some sympathy for the Metis cause. Notes in the diaries indicate that prayers for Ambroise Lépine's acquittal, after he was charged with the shooting of Thomas Scott, were a regular occurrence at the convent.[124] In fact, Marie Rose would still be in the convent very near the time when the trial of Lépine was under way in 1873. In addition to prayers for Lépine, diaries from the Saint Boniface convent at various times from the 1870s to the 1880s indicate that prayers were recited regularly for Louis Riel and his various supporters (who included some of Marie Rose's family).[125]

While it would certainly have been common to pray for all sinners and the condemned, several letters written by some of the Grey Nuns at Red River, express support for the Metis provisional government. Bishop Taché's own secretary went so far in one of her letters as to say, "Louis Riel has been chosen by God to save his country."[126] Marie Rose's obedience to the Church was still evident later in her correspondence with Archbishop Taché,[127] and suggests that, during her time at the convent, she likely obeyed the calls to prayer and may have even felt some allegiance, as did many of the nuns, to the Metis cause and to Riel. The support for the provisional government witnessed at the convent by young Metis girls, in addition to the knowledge that their own families were "on the outside," with their livelihoods threatened, may have inspired some solidarity with the Metis in general, and to their own families in particular. It could also be, though, that the young girls at the convent were somewhat confused and divided, as much of Red River was at the time.[128]

The divisions in Red River led Louis Riel to choose from among the merchant/trader class when he formed his Exovedate Council. Many of those chosen had family members with a long history of involvement in the earlier conflicts in Red River.[129] Thus, it is understandable that Riel would choose one of Urbain Delorme Sr.'s sons as a member of the Exovedate, and Gabriel Dumont would choose another to serve as one of his soldiers.[130] Urbain Sr. had been active during the Sayer Trial, then on the Council of Assiniboia, and then in representing the concerns of the population that opposed the possible transfer of their land to the Dominion of Canada by the HBC. Urbain Delorme Sr. had been among the group of Metis traders and hunters who originally joined with William Dease in 1860 to articulate their Metis rights, gleaned as descendants of the Indigenous people and first residents of the area. In reality, Dease was politically active for Metis rights at a time when some note that Louis Riel was more concerned with asserting French and Roman Catholic rights.[131]

In 1869–1870, when Riel eventually emerged as the leader of the Metis to challenge Central Canadian expansionists, Marie Rose's uncle, Joseph Delorme, was living with his father, Urbain Sr.[132] Joseph Delorme was involved in the fighting, as was Marie Rose's uncle Norbert, who served on Riel's Exovedate Council. Marie Rose's sister was married to George Ness, who served as justice of the peace, and was arrested and held by the Metis fighters. Marie Rose's uncle Donald Ross was killed in the fighting as one of Riel's soldiers, and her uncle and aunt, John and Rose Pritchard, were held as prisoners by Big Bear and his people. The fighting between the Metis and the incoming government was devastating for many of Marie Rose's kin and drove a wedge between family members, likely leaving young Marie Rose to struggle with a Metis identity difficult to reconcile.

Indeed, it was not long after Marie Rose left the conflict of Red River and the convent in 1876 when her family encountered a "big, raw-boned Norwegian, of very fair complexion," named Charlie Smith.[133] According to her granddaughter, upon their first meeting, Charlie had decided that Marie Rose would make an ideal partner to complement his own nomadic lifestyle on the plains. Carpenter wrote that, as Marie Rose and her sister Elise

> *fetched water, washed the tin plates, and then prepared the teepees for the night...[and] cooked for the next day's journey...stooping to stir the roots cooking over the fire...keen senses told her she was being watched.[134]*

Carpenter continued that every time Marie Rose "looked across the fire, the trader nodded to her and smiled."[135] Moving on after that first encounter with Charlie, Marie Rose and her family had "roamed the prairie for three or four weeks, killing buffalos for our winter supply of meat, and then, choosing a suitable place we settled down for the winter...there would be several families wintering together."[136]

By the time Charlie found the Delorme family for his second visit, they were at their winter home. It would have been clear to Charlie that the survival of the Delorme family relied on the skills of every member. He would have had an appreciation for the fact that Marie Rose was quite adept and familiar with what needed to be done to ensure winter survival on the open prairie. Marie Rose explained these skills, writing that "all set to work cutting logs, putting up shacks, and plastering them with mud and hay." She went on to describe the construction of her Delorme family's winter home:

> *The windows and doors were of parchment, made from fawn skins, which were scraped very clean of hair and flesh and then stretched very, very thin. This made very good doors and windows. The fire place was also made of mud and hay. Turf was used for roofing.[137]*

No doubt Marie Rose not only observed but helped build this winter home. It is also likely that, by the time of their meeting, even though he may have been aware of impending change in the economy, Charlie still believed that a Metis girl with experience on the trail would be an asset.

Marie Rose provided details of her first encounters and "court-ship" with Charlie Smith, who appeared to her to be a "big trader," with "lots of carts, horses and...four men working for him."[138] As was the custom in many Indigenous societies, it was not Marie Rose who was courted, for Charlie "invited my father and mother to his camp. He had a supply of liquor and he offered some to my people, they were both fond of their drink."[139] Shortly after her first encounter with Charlie in 1877, at the age of sixteen, Marie Rose was "traded" to this stranger, who was approximately seventeen years older than her, for the sum of fifty dollars, paid to her mother.

There is a stirring excerpt worthy of quoting in its entirety, since it sheds some light on the fear Marie Rose felt at Charlie's "proposal":

> As we neared the house, the three of us hurried real fast, and then Charlie caught hold of me, saying something. I was so frightened I knew not what his words were, but just cried out, "Yes, yes, let me go!" Where upon he kissed me and loosed his hold. I ran like a wild antelope trying to catch up with my sister and brother before they entered the house. I was still trembling with fear as we entered the door, for we girls were not allowed alone with men..."Oh, say Mother," I cried, "you know that white man...he grabbed me and began to talk...But first he kissed me." So ended my courting days.[140]

Marie Rose then went on to explain the ensuing transaction between her mother and Charlie:

> The next day, this big Norwegian trader, with his flat sleigh and jingling harness, drove up to our house. He was warmly greeted by

my mother and step-father. There was much pleasant conversation
between the three, and then Smith asked my mother for permission
to marry me. As she looked surprised he said, "I asked her yesterday,
and she said, 'Yes'". "But I didn't know what he was saying," I
shouted at them. It made no difference. It was settled between my
parents and Charlie right then and Charlie gave my mother a
present of Fifty dollars. Was I not then sold for that sum? After
Charlie left mother called me to her, "Come here, Marie Rose, you
promised to marry that man"...I tried over and over again to
explain, but it was useless.[141]

In regard to the actual marriage ceremony of the young and
frightened Marie Rose, preparations had proceeded and the permission of the bishop was sought so Charlie, a Protestant, would be
allowed to marry this young Roman Catholic girl.[142] Although she
spoke of the broken heart her marriage arrangement brought her,
Marie Rose still acknowledged that "they" took great care of her,
when preparing her for the wedding, treating her like a "little queen."
She was wrapped in buffalo robes and provided with a driver to
take her in a flat sleigh to meet Bishop Grandin in St. Albert. When
camping en route, Marie Rose would wait in the sleigh until camp
was set up and the teepee warm, to which she was carried.

Marie Rose indicates that it was Charlie who made provision
for her transportation to the settlement of St. Albert where her
marriage was to take place. The way Marie Rose was "handled" on
the journey suggests Charlie viewed the Delorme family with respect.
While Marie Rose was apparently well accommodated on the
journey, she still wrote that she

didn't enjoy all this attention. I would rather have been out playing
in the deep snow with my brothers and sister. To such an extent was
obedience enforced among the Traders' children.[143]

Despite Charlie's apparent consideration for Marie Rose during the trip, both she and her granddaughter wrote of the fear Marie Rose experienced when she realized she must obey her mother and, as a "prairie child," marry a man she "hardly knew, much less loved, and who seemed so old to a child of sixteen."[144]

There is no indication from Marie Rose that many of the Metis wedding traditions were followed, either before or after the ceremony. There is evidence, though, that there was much merriment at typical Metis weddings, with the entire family taking part in the festivities. In settlements such as St. Albert, where the bride was transported by sleigh as Marie Rose had been, gun blasts and shouts of joy typically greeted the couple upon their exit from the church. After the wedding feast of wild game, bannock, pemmican, cake, pastries, and wine, fiddling and dancing were the norm, and for many days to follow. It is not clear if Marie Rose's marriage was celebrated in this way, nor if the couple were wrapped in the traditional sash.[145] The details of Marie Rose's wedding are impossible to know because she did not record any of them in any of the surviving documents.

Acceptance of her new situation did not come easily, for, as Marie Rose wrote, "That year was the most unhappy one of all my life. Day after day I went away by myself and cried." There was apparently only one comfort and that was that her "parents travelled with us all that summer."[146] In her unpublished writing, while Marie Rose expressed relief that her mother and family continued to travel with them, she wrote quite frankly and openly about her perception of the arranged marriage. Still exhibiting resignation as an adult, Marie Rose wrote, "So I, a little girl of sixteen years, was forced into a marriage with a man twenty years my senior, and of whom I knew nothing."[147] While Marie Rose could play at being a child during the day, she wrote,

> when night came and I was alone with my stranger husband, alone in a camp of our own, such fear seized me, that I bound my clothes about me with raw hide ropes.[148]

The young bride was aware of the embarrassment her initial behaviour was causing her husband, for she wrote that Charlie was told by others in the camp to "Beat her into submission."[149]

Although Charlie may have been viewed unfavourably by some for not acting on this advice, Marie Rose wrote that Charlie was "patient and determined to win me through love."[150] For the most part, Marie Rose wrote very little about Charlie that does not relate to what might be seen as difficult behaviour, such as his drinking or being away from home. However, the fact that she wrote in this one instance that Charlie was determined to win her through love suggests Charlie may not always have been the hard man he has been described as by at least one scholar, who wrote that Marie Rose *"endura un mari dur et un gros buveur."*[151] In the end, though, when asked by her granddaughter later in life whether she loved Charlie, Marie Rose still responded simply, "What's love got to do with it?"[152]

Researcher Maggie MacKellar believes Marie Rose's text demonstrates a double betrayal on the part of her mother, "for not only was she sold into marriage, but her husband was a white man."[153] MacKellar may be correct, given that Marie Rose noted Charlie's ethnicity when she was imploring her mother not to allow the marriage to proceed. As Marie Rose explained her first encounter with Charlie to her mother, she told her, "you know that white man, Charlie Smith, well he grabbed me and began to talk," to which her mother replied, "What did Mo-ni-ash (white man) say?"[154] His ethnicity rather than his age was the only characteristic Marie Rose used to describe Charlie in this first discussion with her mother.

There may have been several circumstances that influenced Marie Delorme Gervais to trade her daughter for fifty dollars, specifically to a Euro-North American man. Whether or not she was financially secure after the death of her husband, Marie Delorme Gervais may have felt it best to have one less mouth to feed. As Marie Rose wrote, the land her father owned prior to his death on the "White Horse Plains...was the heritage of her younger brother."[155] Marie Delorme

Gervais may also have recognized what scholars have identified, specifically the value of an Indigenous daughter at different times during the fur trade era.[156] In this respect, whatever the cultural basis of bride purchase, Marie Rose's mother might have been pragmatically considering the value of a Euro-North American man "marrying into" the family at these uncertain times.

Marie Rose may have understood some of the reasoning for her mother's choice, writing, "them days a fur trader was a big man."[157] She recognized Charlie's wealth immediately, as well as his trading abilities, noting,

> From the size of his outfit-carts and horses—we knew him to be a "big trader" He had four riders working for him...Trader Smith always carried with him a good supply of liquor—and, I must confess, more than his "permit" called for...Trader Smith invited my parents over to taste his liquid refreshments, with the result that we camped here all night.[158]

Although there is no record of such a trade in the marriage of Marie Delorme Gervais's other daughters, Madelaine and Elise Delorme both married Euro-North-American men. Both of these Euro-North American men appeared quite competent in navigating a new economy, with one operating as a justice of the peace and the other a skilled carpenter. Ness, the justice of the peace, was an Englishman who supported the Canadian government in 1869–1870. The carpenter, Ludger Gareau, a Frenchman from Quebec, was considered part of the "small bourgeoisie" that established themselves in Batoche before the resistance to central government encroachment. While openly opposed to Riel in 1885, many of these bourgeoisies were believed to secretly support him but found reason to be away during the conflict. In Gareau's case, he was in Quebec at the time. While he did indicate his support for Riel when interviewed by the local newspaper in Pincher Creek years later,[159] it appears Gareau was astute enough to be silent about that support at the time of the conflict.

While Marie Rose's sisters both eventually settled in Pincher Creek, it was the young bride, bought for fifty dollars, who first settled in 1880 "near the little stream now called Pincher Creek." Marie Rose wrote that the area was "teaming with roaming Indians." Trips to Fort Macleod twice per year for provisions took a week's travel time. Remarking on these journeys, Marie Rose noted they took the time to visit with many friends and that "so many of the white men had married young squaws,"[160] a situation that would have been very similar to circumstances during the height of the fur trade. Other similarities for Marie Rose during her early years of marriage included food and supplies, which continued to be much the same as those accessed during the fur trade, except that herds of roaming cattle now replaced buffalo. By this time, Marie Rose appeared to have come to terms with her marriage arrangement, writing that, despite living in a one-room log home as a young bride, while "dishes were few, food was plentiful."[161]

The one-room log house that served as the young bride's home, on the land that she and Charlie called Jughandle Ranch, was constructed with a "roof made of bark. The chinks between the logs were filled with mud." There was no flooring in the house and the windows were constructed of "small bits of glass." In fact, her first home as a married woman was not much different than that which Marie Rose would have helped to build when her family traversed the plains. It featured dirt floors, no beds, boxes nailed to the walls serving as cupboards, and it was situated where prairie chickens could be snared from the door, or fish caught from the nearby Pincher Creek.[162]

Marie Rose's first home as a young bride was likely even more rudimentary than that of her parents in Red River. According to the land records of Jughandle Ranch, the house and barn were originally "all one." Despite the fire that destroyed their first home in

1926,[163] there is one surviving photo of Marie Rose and her young family standing in front of it. Although material possessions were sparse in the first home she shared with her husband, throughout Marie Rose's manuscripts, she expressed a sense of pride in her role as a new wife, a role for which she earned the title "Queen of the Jughandle." Despite her initial protestations about her marriage arrangement, it appears Marie Rose eventually came to accept her destiny and the idea of a bride price.

Even though Marie Rose was clear that there was no love or courtship in her own marriage arrangement, she subsequently wrote of the First Nation custom of arranging marriages for daughters as though it were a foreign custom of a strange and savage people. Speaking as she would of a foreign people, whose customs were not in any way similar to her own, Marie Rose wrote,

> There was never any love making, no courting among them. If any young couple was fit to marry, the parents would choose the mate, no marriage ceremony. They would tell them to go together, whether they loved one another or not...They had to obey their parents.[164]

Apart from the marriage ceremony, the description Marie Rose provides for Indigenous marriages differs very little from her own. The circumstances of Marie Rose's marriage were common enough in the North West (so common that Marie Rose likely understood them well), as many fur traders sought young Indigenous women who possessed indispensable economic skills and social networks.[165] Yet there is no indication from Marie Rose that she recognized the similarities of her own marriage arrangement with those of other Indigenous women, at least in her written words intended for consumption by a Euro-North American society.

In addition to the valuable skills she possessed and that elicited a bride price, Marie Rose was born into a long-standing and elite Metis family, one with considerable status in the fur trade before 1870. However, those family connections extended to include ardent supporters of Metis nationhood, economic independence in the fur trade, political freedom at the transfer, and, finally, the Metis war against the Macdonald Government.

Thus, while the male members of her Delorme family network would no longer be an asset, Marie Rose was a valuable commodity, and she and Charlie may well have continued to live the nomadic lifestyle for which she was so well trained had it not been for the changes that were forced upon the Indigenous people as the buffalo dwindled and more Euro-North American settlers arrived. When Marie Rose exercised her only option and told her mother that, yes, she would go, and thus began her life as a married woman, she no doubt had little idea how much she would have to adapt. On the one hand, she would necessarily continue to rely on the practical skills she had learned from her Metis mother and father, skills that eventually earned her the name "Buckskin Mary." On the other hand, she would have to navigate a changing society, which grew determined to solidify racial boundaries.

Even though she became a respected pioneer in her new community, Marie Rose continued to rely on the social culture of the Metis she learned as a young girl. While she spoke little of those social aspects, at an advanced age, the old buffalo hunter, Norbert Welsh, recalled that what he liked best was to remember the exciting buffalo hunts, the long caravans of Red River carts, and every one of the old songs he enjoyed on the trails. These songs had specific cultural meaning, as they recorded the impressions of the Metis when they travelled across the plains. The Metis songs commemorated perilous buffalo hunts, holiday festivities, births, deaths, and marriages.[166] Indeed, in the only interview recorded of Marie Rose Delorme Smith, when she was ninety-five years old, she spontaneously sang a few choruses of one of those old Metis songs, "Red River Halfbreed."[167] Not only did Marie Rose clearly remember and cherish the social aspects of her Metis culture but she also had to rely on and perfect the social networking skills she had learned from her Delorme family network by expanding it to include fictive

kin, so that she could function as the Queen of Jughandle Ranch
and contribute social capital to her partnership with Charlie Smith.

6

Queen of the Jughandle

WHILE MARIE ROSE eventually referred to herself as "Queen of the Jughandle," she and Charlie began their married life "following the treaties," a phrase Marie Rose wrote was used by the fur traders who "followed the Government agents into Indian territory, as they paid the treaty money to the Indians." While she had an intimate knowledge of the Indigenous perspective of the treaty-making process, Marie Rose also understood the perspective of Charlie Smith, "the trader, and many others [who] followed the treaty from place to place."[1] According to Marie Rose, "The traders obtained money easily from the Indians at such times, for any merchandise they had to sell."[2]

However, Marie Rose expressed her disapproval of Charlie's business practices, writing, "It was regular robbery! One pound of tea, we traded for one buffalo hide; one pound of sugar for one skin... Charlie had more liquor than his permit called for." Marie Rose, describing her early days with Charlie, recalled that after loading their democrats with merchandise, they "travelled closely behind the commissioner, who paid the Indians their treaty money. Then we traded for cash or skins, some of the provisions from our loaded wagon."[3] The fact that Marie Rose would refer to Charlie's practices as "robbery" suggests he did amass what must have seemed like great wealth, as did many of the traders. Norbert Welsh noted that, although there were no more buffalo at this time, there were muskrat, wolf, lynx, bear, marten, weasel, badger, and prairie dog skins to be traded. Welsh recalled there were days that he took in five hundred dollars worth of fur, and that he doubled his money on every transaction.[4] In Charlie's case, his wealth was perhaps even more than Marie Rose had witnessed of her father's trading, who had not had the opportunity to follow the treaties and did not take in cash. Whether one saw it as robbery as Marie Rose did, by the time he decided to stop following the treaties, Charlie had earned enough profit that he was able to go to Montana, where he "bought a herd of cattle with the treaty money."[5]

As his newly purchased wife, Marie Rose had accompanied Charlie to Montana, where they lived on the treaty money during the winter of 1879. With his treaty wealth, Charlie was able to assemble a herd of "fine stock, the pick of the country."[6] The indication was always that Marie Rose and Charlie were in Montana gathering a herd for themselves only. However, Charlie declared in a scrip application for his son, Charlie Jr., in January of 1880, that he was in Montana in that year when his son was born, and that the purpose of this trip was to buy cattle for Governor Dewdney "for the Indian Department."[7] He could have been acquiring his own cattle as well as some for the government, and this could have been a second trip to Montana, given that Marie Rose and Charlie were married in 1877. Jock Carpenter wrote that Marie Rose's mother and stepfather also made the trip to Montana in 1880 when 250 head of cattle were purchased and first brought to a chosen homestead near Fort Edmonton. However, in the spring of 1881, after a bitterly cold winter, Charlie moved the herd to the Pincher Creek area.[8]

Whatever return trip from Montana Marie Rose referred to, she appeared to enjoy the journey back onto the southern plains of Alberta with the herd, writing that it was a

> wonderful life...all kinds of wild fowls, what more could any one wish. It was real life. Game was plentiful...the lakes and ponds were black with feathered game...The North West Territories was a sports-man's paradise.[9]

Around the campfire at night, according to Marie Rose, Charlie related his "interesting adventures" travelling the plains when the buffalo were plentiful.[10] No doubt these memories evoked pleasant conversations between the couple, as it was a lifestyle both had experienced.

While Marie Rose mentioned the many interesting adventures that Charlie had, in comparison to her writing about new settlers, she wrote very little about Charlie. Thus, for the most part, he remains a man of some mystery prior to his appearance in the North West, when he first set his sights on the sixteen-year-old French-Metis girl who had just left the convent. There are conflicting reports, both in a book written by his granddaughter, Jock Carpenter, and in official documents, about Charlie's background. While the 1899 census listed his nationality as German,[11] Marie Rose described him as a Norwegian who left home at the age of twelve for a life on the sea.[12] Like Marie Rose, Carpenter said that Charlie, who sported fair, shoulder-length hair and blue eyes that "twinkled under scraggy brows," spoke with the "unmistakable brand of the Norwegian."[13] At times Charlie was described as having a German accent,[14] but was also referred to as "Dutch Charlie."[15] His obituary declared he was born on the Mediterranean Sea, and he reportedly once even claimed he was Spanish.[16] The 1880 census of Missoula, Montana, where Marie Rose and Charlie gathered their herd, noted Charlie was born in Greece.[17] There are handwritten notes in granddaughter Shirley-Mae McCargar's Bible that suggest Charlie was born in Hammerfest, Norway, to Anna Peterson and Maeroward Smith. Notes further down in the Bible indicate Charlie was born "on Coast of Mediterranean."[18] In short, no one knew with absolute certainty where in Europe, or in North America, Charlie had originated, but we do know his home in Pincher Creek was a place where "no stranger was ever turned away without a good meal, as Charlie's hospitality was well known."[19]

The original homestead Marie Rose and Charlie had staked and named Jughandle Ranch was located on the southwest quarter of section 2, township 6, range 1, west of the 5th meridian of what is now the Municipal District of Pincher Creek, Alberta.[20] On this homestead the couple built their first home, which consisted of the one-room log cabin with mud floors, and was attached to the barn. Marie Rose's first years of married life with Charlie were anything but dull, and Charlie was certainly not committed to presenting himself to the new community of settlers as one of the elites.

For a large part of Marie Rose and Charlie's early lives together in the new North West, there were no saloons, which meant that drinking took place in people's homes. At times, families were given permits that allowed them to purchase Jamaica Ginger from the local drugstore. However, at Charlie's house, permit or not, there were often "barrels of beer, a few bottles of Scotch and some Montana Bourbon Whiskey."[21] As Marie Rose wrote,

> In those days men were boss and women had to obey, right or wrong.
> I obeyed to keep peace in the family. I did not like my husband
> drinking but I had to put up with it...I did the cooking and the
> work...My married life was full of trials and tribulations.[22]

Although her neighbour Ben Montgomery transcribed a version of this same sentiment, in her own words, Marie Rose wrote that child care was not made any easier by the constant revellers in her home:

*The only time I could properly feed my children was when all were
asleep. I then prepared a big meal, fed them and let them sleep, too.
Many, many nights, I sat on the end of my long cot, with the children lying crosswise of the bed, packed together like little sardines,
watching for fear the boys might upset the lamps and burn my little
ones to death, or in their stupidity wander to the bed and fall upon
it and crush one that might be sleeping.*[23]

She admitted she sometimes got "real angry," but to no avail, since
"Charlie was boss."[24] Although she acknowledged that in her own
marriage she faced many frustrations, Marie Rose still denounced
"Indian" husbands as a general rule. As a way to demonstrate the
superiority of marrying a Euro-North American man, despite all of
his faults, Marie Rose wrote,

*The Indian didn't always make a good husband. Chee-pay-tha-qua-
ka-soon (blue flash of lightning), who was once married to a young
buck and reared eight children from this marriage said, "Indian
husband no good, lazy. He beat me, see," as she showed us the marks
of punishment on her head.*[25]

Marie Rose continued her account of Blue Flash of Lightning, "Later
she married a white man and of him praised, 'White husband, good;
his squaw, a lady!'"[26]

Despite her aversion to alcohol, which may have originated with
her time in the convent, or simply because of the impact Charlie's
drinking had on her family, Marie Rose openly described Charlie's
"business practices." She wrote that he often had "more liquor than
his permit called for. It was carried in small oak barrels of two gallon
size." She remarked that, on one occasion,

*police were stationed near by [sic] and when any trader arrived
they searched his carts. When the police came to us, Charlie put the*

kegs in two large pails and said, "Go ahead and search the carts while
I go for water, and I'll give you a drink of whiskey when I come back."[27]

According to Marie Rose,

While the police searched, Charlie buried his kegs in the water and
brought back buckets of water and treated the police from the store
of whiskey, to which he was entitled by his permit.[28]

Marie Rose became well versed on the techniques of the bootleggers, no doubt in part because her husband operated as one. As
she wrote,

Some of these smugglers had a dugout near Pincher Creek. Here they
diluted their liquor with a mixture of black tea, ginger, and a little
red pepper. It was a profitable undertaking for them, but fraught
with much danger.[29]

There were a few published references to Charlie by others that
offer more insight into his character and activities. These print
references were made in regard to Charlie's partnership with prairie
character, Addison McPherson. Although Marie Rose does not
mention the family connection, Charlie's partner was a member
of her Metis fur trade family. McPherson's wife was Marie Rose's
cousin, Melanie McGillis, who was born at Saint François Xavier, on
18 August 1857, to Cuthbert McGillis and Marguerite Delorme, also
known as Marguerite dit Hénault.[30] Not unlike Marie Rose, Melanie
McGillis was enrolled in the Grey Nuns School in Saint Boniface,
however not by her parents. In Melanie's case, it was her husband
who enrolled her.[31] By 1901, Addison and Melanie McPherson had
moved further south to the Black Diamond area, where Addison
operated a coal mine.[32] It may have been Melanie McGillis, referred
to as "Mrs. McGillis," who accompanied Marie Rose on the trip to
Winnipeg when she set out in the summer of 1882. On this trip,

Marie Rose had hoped to meet up with Charlie, who had left some months earlier with the goal of taking advantage of a real estate boom in Winnipeg.[33]

When Charlie ventured out, either for wolfing or for some other activity, it could be for months at a time. During one of their wolfing expeditions, Addisson and Charlie "put up a cabin" in the Big Valley area. This suggests that the two would spend the winter there, setting up "hundreds of poison baits...already visioning a big harvest of skins." Waiting for the spring thaw and the bounty of dead wolves ready for skinning, Addison and Charlie reportedly "settled down to feast on the abundant game, smoke, play cards, darn socks, try to out-lie each other in tall stories and live the 'life of Riley' generally."[34]

During a poker game with Addison at their winter camp, Charlie was reportedly stabbed in the shoulder. Marie Rose mentioned the "crippled arm"[35] that presented mobility problems for Charlie later. However, she did not describe the specific incident. She only wrote of the scars left behind from Charlie's adventures: "Trading with the Indians oft times at the risk of losing his own life, the marks of such knives he carried to his grave."[36] No doubt the "crippled arm" of her much older husband forced Marie Rose to rely not only on her own abilities for survival but also on her kinship network.[37]

There are other references to Charlie that speak to the fact he not only carried on a nomadic lifestyle but was likely able to amass a fair bit of wealth at times, through fair or foul means. One reference to Charlie is found in the work of early local historian Edwin L. Meeres, who published one of the first local histories of the central Alberta district. He wrote of Addison McPherson and Charlie Smith's involvement in many ventures, anything that could supplement their reported love of money and nomadic lifestyles. From trading in pelts and whiskey, to hauling mail between southern Alberta and Montana, to freighting from the Red River to the Rockies, McPherson is remembered not only for his humorous antics but for his ability to succeed in the new economy.[38]

According to Elizabeth Bailey Price, McPherson told her that he first came to the North West in 1869 in search of gold. Although he did not find gold, reportedly, one winter McPherson "traded merchandise for some seven to eight thousand buffalo skins." He also related,

> We took the trail to Whoop Up, then north to the Nose Hill, near the present site of Calgary, on the forks of the Red Deer River, then to Rocky Mountain House...From there, there was a good trail to Ft. Edmonton. In our gang, was the late Charlie Smith of Pincher Creek.[39]

In addition to ranching, these stories of trading upwards to eight thousand buffalo skins lend more credence to the argument that Marie Rose and Charlie were considered wealthy for some part of their lives, at least in comparison to some of Marie Rose's Delorme family. There is a suggestion that Charlie's wealth was gained not only through trading and ranching. In one interview conducted with Charlie in the early 1900s, he indicated that Marie Rose had inherited $10,000.[40] If there was some inheritance, it likely came at the right moment, because freighting using the methods relied on by Charlie and Addison had come to an end. After the end of freighting between the Red River and the rest of the North-West Territories, Addison McPherson settled to a life of sheep ranching in the central Alberta area, and Charlie to part-time cattle ranching in southern Alberta.

During those times when Charlie was at Jughandle Ranch, it appears all were welcomed to his home. Marie Rose wrote often that, no matter who arrived at their doorstep, Charlie would tell her to put the potatoes on while he went for some fish. In fact, in the only audio recording of Marie Rose, produced a short time before her death, she still recalled this request by Charlie to "put on some potatoes." Although many of the visitors to the ranch were no doubt Indigenous, Marie Rose made only brief references to these ongoing relationships. In one example, she wrote, "in groups of twenty or more" they would appear at her doorstep, and Charlie would say, "Mary, feed the poor Indians." She explained that this is how she came by her buckskin:

> *Thus it was that I bought my buckskin from them, and I will tell you how I started to make buckskin gloves...I ripped the glove, cut a pattern from it and made my first pair of buckskin gloves, stitching them by hand. Then I branched out making buckskin shirts and bedroom slippers, drawing my own beaded designs.*[41]

Whether out of appreciation for her beaded designs or because he recognized an economic opportunity, Charlie encouraged Marie Rose:

> *When my husband saw how interested I had become in the buckskin work, he gave me a wonderful surprise. On one of his semi-annual trips to Fort Macleod for supplies, he returned at the end of the two weeks and brought me—yes—a brand new sewing machine.*[42]

Their continuing contact with Indigenous people likely led to little appreciation from both Charlie and Marie Rose of the panic that seized some new settlers during the fighting in Batoche in 1885. That year, when Charlie was called upon to protect the North West from anybody who took up arms along with the Metis, fellow volunteers in the Rocky Mountain Rangers reported,

> *A Dutchman by the name of Charlie Smith was our Lieutenant. Charlie would give the order—"Mount, Walk, Trot," then when we got in front of the little log saloon—"Halt! Everyone dismount and have a drink." That was all the drill we got.*[43]

It is interesting to note that the order Charlie gave his troop, "Mount, Walk, Trot," was the very same order given to Metis hunters by their captains during earlier buffalo hunts. The context, however, suggests Charlie was a more cavalier leader. Despite any new perceptions of Indigenous people he now encountered, Charlie (and many others) did not take their duties about protecting against Indigenous people very seriously at all. When Isabella Hardisty Lougheed's brother, Frank Hardisty, also a Rocky Mountain Ranger, was interviewed in 1945, he reported that when the fighting broke out in 1885, he "had a damn good time—and I didn't kill any Indians either."[44] A *Winnipeg Tribune* article represented Hardisty as having

> organized the Rocky Mountain Rangers and their job was to persuade Chief Crowfoot, of the Blackfeet tribe, to keep his 8000 warriors out of the uprising. He succeeded in doing so, and was quoted as saying that "The chief was a fine man. If he had given his men the word Calgary would have been wiped out in half an hour."[45]

Charlie's role as one of the commanding officers of the Rocky Mountain Rangers, whose most common order appeared to be to "dismount and have a drink," is somewhat farcical. In reality, we know the rebels that Charlie was ostensibly guarding against were the very rebels with whom he likely shared a closer affinity than members of his new community in Pincher Creek. For her part, Marie Rose seemed to see the activities of the Home Guard, the precursor of the Rocky Mountain Rangers, as farcical as well. She wrote that most of the duties for Kootenai Brown and his friends, the Rangers (one of which was her husband), consisted of being "fired up" with "Jamaica Ginger."[46] It appears that Marie Rose did not take the threat of danger by Indigenous people in 1885 any more seriously than her husband did.

Although Charlie appears only briefly in Marie Rose's writings overall, most of her writing about her husband refers to the difficulties that she, as a young wife and mother, was forced to deal with due to his extensive drinking. Writing of their early years on Jughandle Ranch, Marie Rose noted that, despite having a houseful of children,

any time the mill closed down, the boys would stampede to Charlie's
place and wait for the next cargo of liquor to arrive. They would lie
around anywhere, in the kitchen or out under the wagon...We never
seemed to be alone in those early, pioneer days.[47]

In a rare moment in which Marie Rose shared with readers her
disgust about the goings-on at the home she shared with Charlie,
she wrote, in a segment appropriately titled, "Bits of My Home
Life,"

One day I planned to get rid of the whole gang for good and the chil-
dren and I would be free of all this nonsense. I emptied the barrels,
hiding the liquor and replacing it with water, mustard, red pepper
and purgative salts. Now do you think that made them sick? No,
siree, they drank it all and never knew the difference.[48]

In another example, it appears that, in addition to writing
about her situation, Marie Rose shared her distress about Jughandle
Ranch with at least a few in her community. As her contemporary,
Ben Montgomery, wrote when describing his conversation with
Marie Rose in the late 1930s,

The only time when Mary could feed her children was when all the
visitors were asleep. She had an awful time and she used to be mad
but would not say a word because Charlie would be cross.[49]

Marie Rose (whom Montgomery referred to as "Mary") went on to
describe the lengths to which she had to go to keep her children
safe during Charlie's antics:

For the night, Mary used to put all the little folks in one cot against
the wall, just like sardines and she would sit at the foot of the cot,
watching so that the boys would not lay on her progeny.[50]

On more than one instance in her writing, Marie Rose indicated that she lacked agency as Charlie's wife, telling her readers, "You will wonder why I did not object to having the house full all the time...It was no use, Charlie was boss."[51]

The reality is that Charlie's wife was of Metis ancestry, educated by Roman Catholic nuns, and thus had some appreciation for the Western patriarchal ideology the Church adhered to. Marie Rose understood the need to be seen to be obedient to her husband, as is evident in a letter she wrote to Archbishop Taché in 1893. In that letter, Marie Rose appealed, on Charlie's behalf, and at his insistence, for an explanation of the remainder of her money willed to her by her father.[52] It is not clear if the bishop granted Charlie's request for money. However, perhaps this request had not yielded a favourable response, for Marie Rose made another inquiry in person. The journey she took to Winnipeg with Mrs. McGillis (referred to earlier) now produced a better response from the bishop, for both Marie Rose and her sister were able to withdraw a considerable sum, $1,500, from their father's estate. Marie Rose used this money in part to replace her horses so she could make the return trip to Pincher Creek on her own, having failed to connect with Charlie.[53]

When it came to Charlie's drinking, Marie Rose could not have missed the sentiments of her spiritual advisor, Father Lacombe. Lacombe was featured in the *Pincher Creek Echo*, explaining the need for a convent in Pincher Creek, the convent for which Marie Rose worked very hard to help raise funds.[54] According to Lacombe, the convent was an absolute necessity to educate children, not only with books but also with "civilization," since the children of ranchers learned the "rough" and "wild" life of the cowboy.[55] Although Charlie was not technically a cowboy, those early prairie dwellers who typically led a nomadic life as hired hands, his frequent forays away from home likely rendered his lifestyle no different in Lacombe's eyes. Marie Rose also wrote, "Father Lacombe often said that the greatest trouble-makers were the

(L–R) *Robert Gladstone, Mr. Dumont, Charlie Smith, and Kootenai Brown, in front of Brown's cabin. Photo undated.* Glenbow Alberta Museum and Archives, NA-62-1.

American whiskey traders...for the Indian becomes a savage under the influence of 'fire water.'"[56] Of course, the priest likely had no more tolerance for Canadian whiskey traders such as Charlie Smith.

While Father Lacombe may not have held Charlie in high regard, many males in his community may have respected him, or at least felt beholden to Marie Rose's generous husband. This regard is evident by the presence of other leading community members as pallbearers at Charlie's funeral, among them the first Member of Parliament for the region, local businessmen, an author, a teacher, a retired police officer, and a land agent, all of whom were notably Euro-North American.[57] Perhaps these pallbearers felt beholden to both Charlie and Marie Rose, for it was likely some of these old-timers helped pay for Charlie's funeral.

It does appear that Charlie came to gain a reputation as some-what of a folk hero. A publication that appeared in 1995, titled *Humorous Cowboy Poetry: A Knee-Slappin' Gathering*, featured a poem by Jim Green with Charlie as the main character. Green was a rancher from southwestern Alberta who also offered his services as a guide.[58] The poem, "Jughandle Smith Goes to Town," poked good fun at the fact that Charlie often returned home in a somewhat unconscious state, but no matter, because his horses knew the way back to the ranch where his young wife always waited.

Charlie's nomadic lifestyle presented challenges for Marie Rose, so she was no doubt very appreciative of the fact that Charlie had in reality joined the Delorme family. Documents confirm that her mother continued in the Metis fur trade tradition of keeping a close geographic proximity to family members. Although not confirmed in the census, other documents suggest that other members of Marie Rose's Delorme family lived for periods of time in the Pincher Creek district after Marie Rose and Charlie had settled there. For example, Marie Rose's brother Urbain does not appear on any of the census documents for the area. Two letters written in 1892 indicate that Urbain Delorme II was in Duck Lake and Batoche and was requesting funds from Bishop Taché, but, in 1894, Urbain wrote a letter from the Pincher Creek area to the bishop, again requesting money from his father's estate. By this time, Urbain had sold his land grant in the Red River area to his sister Elise Ness.[59] Also, on one occasion, Marie Rose wrote that her brother Urbain recovered her democrat after it was upset when her team of horses had spooked, leaving her to walk the five miles home.[60] Marriage records also confirm that Urbain married Nellie Gladstone in 1892 in Pincher Creek.[61]

Marie Rose's adopted brother, Charlie Ross, whom she had once referred to as the "full-blooded Sioux," was also likely living in Pincher Creek in 1889, when his daughter was born.[62] Marie Rose wrote that Charlie Ross eventually settled in the North, but the fact that his daughter was born in Pincher Creek suggests he also lived there at some point. Although it was not possible to confirm through census documents, Diane Payment wrote that Norbert Delorme, one of Marie Rose's "rebel" uncles, also settled for a time in Pincher Creek. It is very likely that Norbert was in Pincher Creek,

Marie Rose Delorme Smith and brother Urbain Delorme II, taken in Pincher Creek, Alberta. Photo dated 1900. Glenbow Alberta Museum and Archives, NA-102-12.

particularly since his wife was the sister of Cuthbert Gervais, Marie Rose's stepfather. Although he may not have taken a homestead, Norbert could have lived with any one of several family members in the Pincher Creek area. Further, given there was a warrant issued for him after 1885, family members would not likely have been forthcoming with government census workers about Norbert's whereabouts. Nor would Marie Rose have been forthcoming with this information in her manuscripts.

Another family member, Marie Rose's cousin Véronique Gervais Fidler,[63] lived for a time at Jughandle Ranch, no doubt contributing to the subsistence economy of the Smith household. Another of Marie Rose's sisters, Madeleine, and her husband, Ludger Gareau, moved to Pincher Creek in 1886, after their home in Batoche was destroyed during the fighting in 1885.[64] Like Marie Rose, Ludger and Madeleine established a ranch in the Pincher Creek district, where they raised cattle and horses.[65] Another sister, Elise, who had married George Ness (the man who served as justice of the peace in Batoche in 1885), also settled for a time to ranch in the Pincher Creek district, filing a homestead application near Beauvais Lake on 1 October 1888.[66] Apparently, when Ludger Gareau, a self-admitted "admirer of Louis Riel,"[67] headed further west to Pincher Creek in 1886, George and Elise Ness joined him and Madeleine. This means there was a two-year span between the time when George and Elise came to the Pincher Creek district and when they filed for a homestead. Many of the Delorme family could have done the same—come to the district and stay with other family members so their names would not necessarily appear in homestead records.

Marie Delorme Gervais also settled in the Pincher Creek district with her husband Cuthbert. The couple had four children, Azelda Gervais Gladstone, Nancy Gervais LeBoeuf, and Joseph and Alex Gervais, all of whom remained in the district.[68] Thus, quite a large family network eventually settled near Marie Rose and Charlie after they staked their first homestead in the late 1800s.

Marie Rose also always maintained close contact with the nuns and priests in Pincher Creek. Numerous accounts in the local newspaper confirm that Marie Rose was one of the devoted workers who raised funds so that a convent could be built in Pincher Creek. Descendants still have photos of Marie Rose with various members of the church, and recall that her close relationship with Father Lacombe allowed her to use his rail pass to access medical care. Reporting on her return visit to southern Alberta in 1955, the *Pincher Creek Echo* still drew attention to the fact that Marie Rose was a "close friend of Father Lacombe, famous missionary among the Indians in Alberta for many years."[69] Although her husband was a whiskey trader and perhaps even a one-time cattle rustler, Marie Rose continued to be held in high regard by Roman Catholic priests and nuns. However, it clearly became important to develop a wider circle of acquaintances as newcomers settled in the area.

In 1955, Marie Rose reminisced that she and Charlie were among the first settlers to the area; the only others she could recall being there were the police.[70] Marie Rose wrote that it was 1886 before the first Euro-North American women settled in the district.[71] Eventually, more settlers came and some no doubt shared the views expressed by Mary Inderwick. In 1884, this Pincher Creek rancher's wife wrote to her family in Ontario to say that she encouraged the local men to "go east and marry some really nice girls" as a way to prevent unions with the "squaw," who was described as the "nominal wife of a white man," near her ranch.[72]

While men who married Indigenous women eventually encountered racism like that expressed by Inderwick, Marie Rose indicated that, in 1882, six years after her marriage, "most of the white men had squaws for wives…There we all lived contented as lords."[73] Some of these men who had married "squaws" formed part of Marie Rose's community of friends in Pincher Creek. However, perhaps because of newcomers like Inderwick, Marie Rose eventually broadened her circle by associating with those who she perceived to be of "aristocratic" or noble birth. Included in her new circle of acquaintances was the British remittance man whom locals referred to as "Lord Lionel."[74] When Lionel Brooke arrived in Pincher Creek in the early 1880s, corporate ranches such as the Waldrond, Oxley, and Cochrane were already operational, as well as many family-based ranches. While he had partnerships in several ranching endeavours, Brooke eventually acquired the Chinook Ranch near Jughandle Ranch.[75] Although he seemed determined to "establish himself as a gentleman rancher," Brooke spent a good portion of his time "traveling around, hunting, fishing, rambling, and camping with the Stoney Indians."[76] Brooke reportedly commented that he "would rather be with the Stony [sic] Indians. To me they are 'whiter' than the White man."[77]

While they often struggled, these aristocratic remittance men still retained a sense of their own importance. In the new society of the North West, those wishing to achieve some semblance of a higher station in life often sought the company of these remittance men. In Brooke's case, there were reportedly many of the "rough and ready cowboys" who poked fun at Brooke and his "free-spending ways with money." However, many hostesses in the ranch country were apparently eager to include Brooke among their guests, likely believing he added a "flavour of aristocratic elegance to a party, for he could be very distinguished looking dressed in his best tweeds with his monocle fixed in one eye."[78]

Marie Rose appears to have been just as smitten as most local hostesses, writing that Brooke was involved in the establishment of the aristocratic sport of polo, and that he was a "big man…big Nina among the Indians." Even more importantly, Brooke had reportedly, according to Marie Rose, "traveled to different places such as Japan, South Africa, Honolulu, West Indies, China, Iceland, Norway, Bermuda, Italy, California, and many other places."[79] Marie Rose may have heard about these travels first-hand or she may have been writing directly from Brooke's obituary, which appeared in the Lethbridge Herald on 16 January 1939, and which noted some of these travel destinations.[80] Most likely, some of her esteem for Brooke

Lionel Brooke, Pincher Creek, Alberta. Photo dated 1890s.

Glenbow Alberta Museum and Archives, NA-1403-1.

came not from what he was and what he was able to produce in a
market economy (a standard that many applied at the time) but
from his family associations and his connection to distant places.

While some of the prairie characters Marie Rose identified as
historical figures, such as Lionel Brooke, are not particularly
familiar to historians now, to Marie Rose, they appeared worldly.
Although she must have had many boarders in her rooming house
in Pincher Creek, for this is how she eventually supported her family,
she does not name a single boarder other than Brooke, who spent
his last years in her home. In addition to the aristocratic air they
provided, free-spending remittance men such as Brooke were very
important to local boosters, given that many relied on the barter
and credit systems, and injections of new money were welcome news
for local, rural settlements.[81] Undoubtedly, Brooke paid for his room
and board, thus he and Marie Rose helped each other through the

barter and credit systems. However, perhaps Marie Rose also received the benefit of a sense of heightened status, for it was her home that Brooke chose for his "retiring life" and where he died in 1939, at "well over 80 years of age."[82]

Marie Rose also wanted readers to know that among her community of connections was a man who has become somewhat of a folk hero, Kootenai Brown. Impressed by Brown's "courtly manners," she wrote in her unpublished manuscript, "Eighty Years on the Plains," that she wanted to devote "a full chapter to John George Brown, better known as Kootenai Brown."[83]

Brown was born in Ireland and immigrated to Canada after serving in the British Army in India. He first travelled to the Waterton Lakes area in 1865, settling there in 1877. He was active in the Caribou Gold Rush, and often traded with the Kootenay people, a habit that likely led to his name. When the nomadic trading life-style no longer proved economically sound, Brown settled in the Waterton Lakes district, often predicting to friends that the area would one day be a major tourist destination. When the Dominion government created Kootenay Forest Reserve in 1895 as a way to preserve the Waterton Lakes and surrounding parkland for future generations, Brown became its first acting superintendent. Aside from his worldliness, there was even more reason for Marie Rose to forge her connection with Kootenai Brown, for his first wife was Olive D'Lonais, a Metis woman who had also attended the St. Boniface convent. Marie Rose was proud to refer to Olive, not because she identified her as a Metis woman but as a member of her "Alma Mater."[84]

Although she had a connection to Olive, it was on Kootenai that Marie Rose focused more of her attention. She noted that Brown was a clever, well-educated man who was to become one of the first homesteaders before the time of surveys.[85] As she wrote, Brown was a "great reader and no fool...It was interesting to listen to this man, he was well posted on any subject."[86] She pointed out that Kootenai was not merely an acquaintance but "a great friend to Charlie and me. We visited him many, many times and he came to stay with us so often." Demonstrating some admiration, Marie Rose wrote of Kootenai, "Like the rest of the oldtimers, he liked the wild life of the plains, though he never lost his gentlemanly ways and might be called a regular 'Ladies man.'"[87]

In addition to clearly enjoying his company, Kootenai Brown provided Marie Rose the opportunity to feel like one of her community's important citizens. Relating his memories also allowed her to write about Indigenous customs from the perspective of a third-person observer, as she did with her own mother's stories. According to Marie Rose, Brown and Ni-ti-mous (the Indigenous woman he married after Olive's death) would sometimes be away for "three or four weeks...On one of these trips they were compelled to go right through to Flat Head country, and they stayed with these Indians for a week."[88] According to Marie Rose, Brown

often witnessed the slaughtering of buffalo by the Indians. Out of big logs they built a round corral, very high, and on each side, at the entrance, were built wings, also very high, through which the buffalo were coaxed to enter. An Indian, called a "coaxer," dressed himself in a buffalo hide, horns and all, to resemble a buffalo as much as possible, and mingled with the herd, bellowing like one of them, and endeavouring to get them to follow him, and lead them to the entry of the corral. Buffalo run in single file, and as they followed the false leader, many riders came behind making a great deal of noise to keep the animals advancing. When all have been coaxed into the trap, a gate, made of heavy logs is dropped into place. The Indians got on top of the corral and began their slaughter. They used flint lock gun if possible, but since few had these and ammunition was scarce, they resorted to the bows and arrows to carry on the killing... The Indians called the corrals, "Buffalo ponds," and as the slaughter continued, the frightened animals ran about and piled upon one another until the last one was slain.[89]

This detailed accounting of the buffalo hunt suggests Marie Rose witnessed it herself, but she preferred to tell it as she heard it from Brown.

Although Marie Rose was smitten by newcomers, such as Lionel Brooke and Kootenai Brown, one Indigenous woman did merit some mention in her manuscripts. Kootenai Brown's "squaw wife," Ni-ti-mous, who stayed at Jughandle briefly, is the only Indigenous person Marie Rose openly identifies as part of the new network she cultivated during the transitional period. Marie Rose admired Ni-ti-mous's abilities, writing, "Mrs. Brown...made many rabbit robes which commanded a high price and I was honoured to receive one as her very good friend."[90] Despite her admiration for Kootenai, Marie Rose supported his Indigenous wife over him on at least one occasion. When Ni-ti-mous was told to leave the home she shared with Brown in favour of two Euro-North American women with whom he had been keeping company, Marie Rose encouraged her friend to stand her ground.[91]

On another extreme, but equally representative of the eclectic company she kept, Marie Rose wanted readers to know that her neighbour was Colonel James Macleod, the North West Mounted Police officer.[92] Macleod had taken a homestead near Marie Rose in the Pincher Creek area, and she often wrote about visiting his home, relating that she and others in the district referred to Macleod's "colored" housemaid as "Auntie."[93] "Auntie" was actually Annie Saunders, who served as nanny to Colonel Macleod's children after meeting Mary Drever Macleod on a steamboat travelling the Missouri River from Fort Benton, Montana. Annie lived with the Macleods from 1877 to 1880. She then became one of Alberta's earliest business people of any gender, operating a laundry, restaurant, and boarding house in Pincher Creek.[94]

< (L–R standing) Mrs. Scheer, Ed Larkin, Marie Rose Delorme Smith. (Seated) Ni-ti-mous, Kootenai Brown's wife. Photo dated 1910s. Glenbow Alberta Museum and Archives NA-2539-10, copied from Provincial Archives 385-2.

Another connection to somebody who is now a well-known historical character, but who was not so widely recognized when Marie Rose knew him, was Frederick Haultain. Marie Rose gives the sense that Haultain, as premier of the North-West Territories, was a regular visitor to Jughandle Ranch, and that he "would come up to these reunions as one of the boys."[95] Haultain was actually a highly educated man who had studied Classics and went on to achieve political success. Haultain remained a respected public figure his entire life.[96]

In another evident moment of name-dropping, Marie Rose could not help letting readers know that she knew "the Honorable Justice Ives of the Supreme Court of Alberta...from [her] youth."[97] One of the other important visitors to the ranch worthy of mention was D.W. Davis (Marie Rose spells his name "Davies") who, according to Marie Rose, was the first representative of the district in Ottawa. Interestingly, Marie Rose wrote about Davis that, although he had married a "squaw" and had three children, "Davies was very proud of his family."[98] It was on this occasion that she observed, "White blood mixed with red makes strong and healthy people."[99] It is perhaps ironic that Davis was a former whiskey trader, like Charlie, and a notorious one at that. Reverend John McDougall reportedly said of Donald W. Davis that he was "the wildest type" of trader who had promised to flood the country with whiskey.[100] Davis was an American veteran who had eventually landed at Fort Whoop-Up, and who later reworked his image so he could profit in the new era as a merchandise trader in Calgary.[101] No doubt it was this reworked image that led Marie Rose to "drop" his name in her manuscript.

Marie Rose loved to tell the stories of those she called her "true friends," who were likely seen by contemporaries as having achieved some success and notoriety. Among them was a man she called Henry Riviere, who most knew better as "Frenchy." Marie Rose repeated stories Riviere had related to her about joining the gang of "one of the most notorious cattle men in Montana, Pat Dooley, whose outfit was known as the Dooley Gang." Although she related the story as though it was personally told to her by the well-travelled Frenchy, there is a letter in her files in which Henry Riviere responds to Marie Rose's written request for details of his life. While there is no record of Riviere making the claim, Marie Rose wrote that he was a descendant of French aristocracy.[102]

Nonetheless, Marie Rose indicated that, after cutting ties with Dooley, Riviere settled in Pincher Creek, taking jobs as a park ranger, an actor in Hollywood movies, and an entertainer of tourists at the Prince of Wales Hotel in Waterton, where he told them "wild west stories of the plains in the pioneer days." Although Marie Rose referred to Riviere as "Frenchy," he had apparently openly adopted some of the Metis culture, for Marie Rose described Riviere as

> *wearing mostly buckskin garments, one of those Hudson's Bay sashes and a fire bag all beaded and heavily fringed hanging in front, his cap is made of some wild looking fur and beaded moccasins. He has travelled extensively in the country and talks French, English and Cree.*[103]

These new acquaintances to whom Marie Rose devoted so much attention in her manuscripts—Lionel Brooke, Kootenai Brown, and Frenchy Riviere—were men who most often followed a nomadic lifestyle but who garnered the respect of the transitional society of Pincher Creek.

When describing some of the activities her new community of acquaintances enjoyed, Marie Rose mostly refered to them as French rather than Metis customs. For example, she described the traditions of New Year's Day, when her family and friends in Pincher Creek followed the

> *old French custom for children to visit their parents and receive a blessing from the head of the household. There is much kissing and hand shaking as we greet one another and shout, "Happy New Year," before we sit down for breakfast...Many friends and relatives were*

there; toasts were drunk to the heads of the household and we were
soon enjoying a real French New Year's breakfast.[104]

In the published version of this excerpt, Marie Rose interjected that
the Chinook winds that melted the snow one particular New Year's
Day produced the sentiment, *"C'est pas croyable."*[105] While this New
Year's tradition was a French one, there are many instances of the
custom being followed by the HBC men, many of who were actually
country-born and who were stationed at the various northern
trading posts.

Although the persona she was constructing was that of an English-
speaking pioneer, Marie Rose still assumed many duties that were no
doubt similar to those she had witnessed of her mother on the trail.
While she may not have been skinning buffalo like her mother had,
Marie Rose continued to tan the hides she received from Indigenous
people in exchange for food. With these hides, Marie Rose made
clothing, both for her family and for sale to Euro-North American
settlers, men who worked the rail lines and the ranches, and for tourists.

Marie Rose had seventeen children (no doubt influenced by her
Roman Catholic beliefs), and her descriptions of child care suggest
her economic situation was hardly equal to some Metis women
such as Isabella Hardisty Lougheed. While she did have hired help
at times, Marie Rose explained her more traditional techniques of
child care, how she

> *raised [her] babies in the early days...I always had a hammock*
> *made of two ropes, stretched by a piece of rawhide, then we would*
> *put a blanket between the two ropes and a pillow. We never took*
> *the baby out of the hammock to feed it, we would stand near the*
> *hammock.*[106]

Marie Rose continued "When through feeding, I would give the
hammock a push and go back to my work." Marie Rose wrote that,
just as her mother had done,

We also used what we called a baby bag, laced with strings, into which we put the baby. When we untied him, about three times a day, the little fellow would stretch for all he was worth...The reason we used these bags, we had no safety pins in those days.[107]

In some instances, Marie Rose expressed the same sentiment as many around her may have. For example, she wrote, "With the coming of the settlers, coal oil lamps were introduced to us, but we would not use them as we were afraid they would explode, and moreover lamps were costly to buy."[108] Consequently, Marie Rose continued to use animal grease and rags for lamps and candles.

When she was first married, because the economy remained in transition for such a long period, Marie Rose was able to move between seasonal occupations quite successfully, and thus she had access to many items that would have been appealing for trade. During the summer, there were berries to pick and gardens to cultivate and many other duties. Most early ranchers, including some of the larger leaseholders, let their cattle graze on the open prairie, or, as historian Warren Elofson puts it, they allowed their "livestock to roam the wilds, fending for themselves most of the time."[109] Still, though, in the summer and fall, wild hay had to be gathered for winter feed. Cattle brought in from Montana were normally sold to local men such as police officers[110] or traded with Indigenous people.

Also in the fall, Marie Rose would trade with First Nation people for the material needed to maintain her cottage industry of Metis handiwork. The people she most likely traded with on a more regular basis than the Kootenai, mentioned earlier, would have been the Blood, who occupied the Milk River Ridge and the foothills southwest of Lethbridge; the Peigans of the Porcupine Hills northwest of Fort Macleod; the Stoney (likely the Bearspaw, Chiniki, and Wesley of the Nakoda nations) from the foothills west of Calgary; or the Blackfoot along the Bow River near Gleichen.[111]

Given her knowledge, experience, and extended network of connections, Marie Rose enjoyed more independence than did many new women to the area. It may seem a trivial occurrence, but given that she spoke little of her personal feelings, one moment in particular speaks to Marie Rose's increasing independence. She wrote,

> When we came into this country and settled...I had no neighbors of any kind around me so sometimes I would get very lonesome. One day I thought I would go to visit some friends who were living at the head of Mill Creek cutting logs. I asked my husband, Charlie Smith, to let me have a gentle team.

When Charlie objected, Marie Rose wrote, "Determined to go, I said, 'I will follow the tracks...I prepared for my wild trip, putting up a lunch for the children.'"[112]

The fact that Charlie agreed to let his young family venture into conditions that would have been seen as "primitive" by their new neighbours suggests that he either had confidence in Marie Rose's survival skills or he felt she would do what she wanted despite his objections. On this particular occasion, Marie Rose eventually found her friends, but not without mishap. The roads had been muddied since her last trip, and Marie Rose became disoriented on the rudimentary trails. She had to leave the children in the democrat and walk the final miles until she found the log camp. Men were sent out to recover the democrat and the children, and Marie Rose expressed relief, fear, and some degree of pride in having survived her ordeal.

For the most part, though, Marie Rose stayed on the ranch and managed the couple's livelihood in Pincher Creek. However, in 1882, she again took to the open trail without the help of her husband. The situation that led to this trip began when Charlie left in the spring to travel to Winnipeg, leaving Marie Rose with her three boys and a hired man to look after the cattle and horses. Carrying on for some time independently, Marie Rose grew "lonesome with only my small children." She decided she would "rather suffer hardships of the trail than be subjected to the ugly attentions of this hireling."[113] Clearly feeling less vulnerable on the trail than on the ranch, Marie Rose

> *made ready for the trip, heading toward Winnipeg, with a covered democrat, five head of horses, a tent, the necessary clothing and food enough to last until I would meet my husband, some where on his route back.*[114]

This was the trip mentioned briefly earlier in which Mrs. McGillis joined her.

Marie Rose never did meet up with Charlie, but she made it to Winnipeg, some nine hundred miles across country. This was a journey that few "new" pioneer women to the West would have survived. Although accompanied for part of the journey by a local man who was also headed in the same direction, that Marie Rose would undertake such a journey without her husband suggests an enduring confidence in her own abilities. On the way back at the end of the summer, her mother and stepfather, who had yet to settle in the district, accompanied Marie Rose to Jughandle Ranch. When she arrived, Marie Rose was greeted by a worried husband, clearly relieved to have his family back home safely.

Despite his methods, or perhaps thanks to them, there was a time when Charlie and Marie Rose formed a part of southern Alberta's ranching elite, at least if we are to judge by material wealth. Their proceeds allowed them to take a homestead and to amass a fair sum of property at one point. According to an interview given on his one hundredth birthday, J.R. "Bob" Smith claimed that his parents, Marie Rose and Charlie, once "ran a herd of 1,000 head of cattle on the Jughandle."[115] The one thousand head of cattle that Marie Rose and Charlie reportedly had at one time was not necessarily large compared to some of the early companies that were granted leases of land by the Canadian government. For example, shortly after the government announced a program to lease rangeland for the extremely low rate of $10 per year for every one thousand acres,[116] Senator Matthew Cochrane of Quebec leased his first 134,000 acres west of Calgary, to which he brought a herd of over 6,600 head.[117]

While their holdings were nowhere near those of absentee lease-holders like Cochrane, the 1906 census confirmed that Charlie and Marie Rose held considerable property for an individual couple compared to other Metis people in the Pincher Creek area.[118] For example, this census listed Marie Rose and Charlie's property as including two hundred horses, five milk cows, two hundred horned cattle, and four hogs. In comparison, that same year, Marie Rose's stepfather and mother, Cuthbert and Marie, had nine horses, four milk cows, six horned cattle, and four hogs. The smaller amount of stock could have been due to the fact that her parents were older and perhaps not as capable of managing a larger herd. Yet, at the same time, Marie Rose's stepsister Zilda and her husband, Robert Gladstone, had only eleven horses, eight milk cows, sixty horned cattle, and no hogs.[119] In fact, the average for new, individual home-steading couples on the prairies, a few years after the 1906 census, was still forty or fifty head of cattle.[120]

That Marie Rose and Charlie had two hundred head of horses suggests they were also likely involved in a breeding program of some sort. While some breeders exported their horses overseas, Charlie was involved in horse racing (a custom very familiar to his Metis wife) and may have been breeding horses for the local market as well. In one instance, in approximately 1902, when Charlie was making application for the adjacent homestead he had been using as pasture land, he stated that he owned four hundred horses.[121] Horse racing was a common activity for the Metis during the fur trade and Charlie's close association to the Metis would have given him some familiarity with it. Although Marie Rose did not speak at great length about Charlie's involvement in race horsing, she did say that, in a severe snowstorm in 1903, many horses and cattle were lost, including "two race horses belonging to Charley [sic] Smith...beautiful well-bred horses named Flying Fox and Wolf, both had taken good money on several occasions."[122] She also once wrote of the "splendid breeds of horseflesh, for which Pincher became noted."[123]

Conversations with Marie Rose's granddaughter, Shirley-Mae McCargar, indicate that most descendants believed her grandparents were "wealthy" when they ranched.[124] Yet Charlie and Marie Rose had settled on land that would not easily guarantee continued wealth and success. Cattle ranchers endured many setbacks due to prairie conditions, not the least of which were the extremes of weather. The particularly bad winter of 1886–1887 was referred to by some cattlemen as the worst experienced to date in southern Alberta, where some losses were especially high. Ranchers in the Pincher Creek area lost 20 to 25 per cent of their herds that year.[125] Elofson noted that years like these taught larger operators to emulate smaller operators, like those in the Pincher Creek district, who had "put up sufficient supplies of hay and had fenced in their herds," and thus "minimiz [ed] their losses."[126] While the practice of fencing and putting up hay helped, more bitter weather continued to wreak havoc on prairie stock. In 1892, ranchers endured what was later referred to as the "bitterest blizzard in twenty years."[127]

Another challenge for homesteaders in the Prairie West such as Marie Rose and Charlie was the persistent fires that often followed new rail lines. These fires were destructive to the wooden buildings of the new towns on the prairies, and could be equally devastating to cattle ranchers. With no gravel and asphalt roads or cultivated fields to serve as fire guards, early prairie fires, set off by anything from lighting to sparks from steam-driven trains, could consume much-needed pasture and ranch stock in very little time.[128] Charlie and Marie Rose would have suffered other severe losses along the way, as did most cattle ranchers. In the example mentioned above, during the winter of 1886–1887, when many in the Pincher Creek district lost the majority of their herds, Marie Rose and Charlie were surviving primarily by cattle ranching.[129]

In addition, for the better part of his life, Charlie had been a hard-drinking man. While we have no real specifics regarding the changes in their financial situation until after Charlie died, Marie Rose and Charlie may have fallen upon hard times while still on Jughandle Ranch. In 1906, a local newspaper reported that Charlie was summoned to appear before a court to answer to the charge of stealing a cow, and then released on bail of $1,500, a considerable sum at the time.[130] This charge occurred only four years after Charlie had stated in his application to claim the adjacent homestead that he owned four hundred horses. Attempts to determine whether Charlie was ever found guilty of cattle theft were unsuccessful.[131] Nevertheless, it may also be that Charlie was still operating under the rule of law of earlier ranching days, in which unbranded maverick cows were open game, a practice discussed by Marie Rose in her manuscript, "Adventures of the Wild West of 1870." Despite this example of foolhardiness, and perhaps of criminal activity, Charlie was still recognized in his obituary as one of the leading members of Pincher Creek society,[132] no doubt in part because of Marie Rose's ability to build relationships with many of the leading members of that society.

Certainly, stealing one cow did not equal the major thefts that went on in the early cattle business of southern Alberta. As Elofson found, "There was in fact so much rustling going on that it can be categorized into several clearly recognizable types."[133] Marie Rose spoke about the extensive rustling: "In those days everything looked bright and prosperous. Whereever [sic] you went, you saw riders looking for mavericks in a bunch of cattle."[134] She went on to explain,

> Some of the readers may not understand the meaning of "maverick." It means calves without a brand. The law was not very severe those days. Rustling a maverick was a joke.[135]

According to Elofson, even larger operators sometimes took possession of unmarked animals by quickly branding them.[136]

Although any suggestion of cattle theft by Charlie would be difficult for Marie Rose, there was an aspect of family life she spoke of fondly—that of being a mother. She wrote, "My happiest days were when they were all small, contented to see them around me, working for them and labouring for them."[137] As she wrote of the years raising her large family,

> I scarcely had time to pick my babies up, even to nurse them, but would stand beside the high hammock until the baby nursed his fill, then covering my breast and giving the rope a push, I went about my work while the swinging cradle lulled the baby to sleep.[138]

Aside from following the pattern of obedience in Metis families, Marie Rose also followed a pattern identified by scholars in regard to childbearing among Roman Catholic women.[139] Marie Rose's first child, Joseph, was born one year into her marriage on 12 July 1878, at Chicken Prairie, North-West Territories.[140] The 1881 "Household Census of the Bow River, North-West Territories District" indicates that Charlie and Marie Rose had two sons at that time, Joseph, aged three years, and Charles, aged one year.[141] By the time of the 1901 census, the family in the Pincher Creek district had grown to include seven sons and two daughters.[142] Marie Rose assumed the role of new mother every successive year from 1878 until 1904.

While records were not located for all of Marie Rose's children, those that were indicate she and Charlie relied on both fictive and blood kin as godparents, no doubt as a way to extend their family connections. For Jean Theodore, born in 1894, Marie Rose chose two members of her Delorme family, Ludger Gareau and Azilda Gervais, as godparents. For her younger son, Charles Frederick, Marie Rose chose James Gilruth, a local Euro-North American resident.[143] These choices suggest that, during the earlier transitional phase of the Prairie West, Marie Rose continued to rely on the fur trade connections of the Delorme family, but as more settlers arrived, she began to incorporate people other than family members as godparents.

Other than who the children's godparents were, it is difficult to learn much about her children from Marie Rose's manuscripts, so it is challenging to understand how they fared in the new economy of the North West. However, she provided some details about the deaths of three of those children, which helps us understand the family dynamics. She had consented to send one child, Mary Ann, to a convent in Valleyfield, Quebec, at the suggestion of the man who was described as her close confidant for most of her life, Father Albert Lacombe. In 1897, shortly after being enrolled by Lacombe in the Convent of Holy Names in Valleyfield, Quebec, young Mary Ann fell ill.[144] A letter dated 20 November 1897 from the nuns to Mr. and Mrs. Smith confirmed that, on 18 November, "Mary Ann was taken sick with the croup." The Sisters continued that Mary Ann's illness came on so suddenly there was no opportunity to warn the family of the "danger that threatened her life."[145] According to Jock Carpenter, Marie Rose vowed, after Mary Ann's death, that she would never again send a child away to school.[146] Most of the other children did not attend school until they could be accommodated in Pincher Creek.

Although Carpenter wrote that Marie Rose vowed to keep all of her children at home, one daughter, Françoise Josephine, was later enrolled in a school away from home at the Sacred Heart Convent in Calgary. At fifteen years of age, Françoise Josephine was older than Mary Ann had been when she was sent to Quebec, but both girls were enrolled by Father Lacombe.[147] Another daughter, Mary Hélène, was also later a resident of an institution operated by the church, albeit not far from home in the town of Pincher Creek, at Kermaria convent. This convent was a project of Father Lacombe's, for which Marie Rose helped in fundraising efforts.[148]

> *Charlie Smith, Marie Rose Delorme Smith, and daughter Mary Ann, taken in southern Alberta. Photo dated 1890s. Glenbow Alberta Museum and Archives, NA-2539-1, copied from Provincial Archives 385-15.*

Marie Rose never expressed any sort of remorse toward Father Lacombe for having advised her to send Mary Ann away, although it appears the decision was not totally hers. She wrote that she "*had to send a nice girl to school in [the] east.*"[149] Marie Rose would have understood how much it would mean to Father Lacombe that her daughter be educated at a convent in the same way she had been. Despite her extreme sorrow about the loss of the young girl she felt she had to send away, in her written texts, Marie Rose continued to demonstrate an unquestioning admiration for the priest, writing that no other man had "done as much for this country as Fr. Lacombe... in heaven he still prays for us."[150] In fact, Lacombe felt quite strongly about the need for Christian education for Indigenous children, particularly those on reserves. In 1885, he had gone so far as to urge the government to allow the industrial school near High River to remove children forcibly from reserves, because parents were "determined not to give up their younger children, unless compelled to do so."[151]

Marie Rose also spoke about her two sons, whom she lost to the First World War. She introduced readers to the fact that her sons had enlisted in the army shortly after describing the death of her husband, her "comrade of thirty-seven years," and the death of her eldest son and that of her nine-year-old daughter, all three to illness. Despite these devastating losses, Marie Rose described "her greatest sorrow" as that felt when her three youngest sons "proudly entered the house wearing red ribbons," signalling their eagerness to serve as soldiers.[152] Marie Rose wrote, "I never dreamed that I had raised boys to go to so cruel a war." She continued that she would "never forget that awful wicked war...I still carry a sore spot in my heart, will carry it to my grave."[153]

The fact that the boys enlisted in the war shortly after Charlie's death, leaving her to fend for her family alone, may have given Marie Rose even more cause to be concerned for the welfare of her sons and the stability of her family. She was in the midst of dire financial conditions and was unable to sell her land for some years after Charlie's death.

It is not clear why the three sons decided to enlist, but it may have been partly due to economics. Despite any connections that Marie Rose was able to foster, her sons were still Metis men, whose parents were no longer as wealthy as her descendants believe they once were. Other than the two sons lost to war, her other sons all pursued labouring work. Given the changing conditions of the Prairie West, there were few other options for young Metis men than to pursue labouring jobs, and often times those jobs put them at risk of physical harm. Had he not fallen from a moving train and been killed, one son, Michael, may have been following the path of "itinerant cross-border labourers" who rode the rails between Montana and western Canada, serving the natural resource industries of mining, lumbering, and grain and livestock production from 1870 and 1920.[154]

There were several factors that speak to the likelihood that Charlie was not able to assist his sons in establishing themselves: he was almost twenty years older than his wife; he was a whiskey and robe trader in a changing economy; he lacked skills to function well in a society increasingly reliant on paper transactions; and he appeared at the least inattentive to obtaining proper documentation that would ensure his family was cared for upon his death. Thus, Marie Rose's sons likely felt a need to embark on risky careers, such as riding the rails or enlisting in war. As for Marie Rose's daughters, it appears they fared at least better than the boys. One daughter, Eva, married a member of the Royal North West Mounted Police and, according to Jock Carpenter's genealogical chart[155] and other family documents, the other daughters all married Euro-North American (and, perhaps not coincidentally, non-French) men connected to the new economy.

Although it was necessary to accept independence when her older husband was ill or away, Marie Rose always described the circumstances of her married life as though she had little say in the decisions, at least in the first years of her marriage. She wrote,

He decided to take up land to homestead. After scouring the prov-
ince from north to south, he decided on a sheltered spot on the
banks of Pincher Creek...To this spot he brought two hundred and
fifty head of cattle. He brought these from Montana, thinking he
would live a quiet, independent life with his family. He called it the
Old Jug Handle Ranch..."Jug Handle" was the mark on the neck of
the cattle; the loose skin was cut left hanging like a handle. To all
friends or foe, strangers or neighbors were welcome day or night and
no one ever left the spot hungry, Indian or white man.[156]

Yet Marie Rose lived almost a lifetime, forty-six years, as a
widow in a new economy increasingly removed from the fur trade.
It is understandable, then, that not only would her children have
to establish themselves with little parental assistance but Marie
Rose, herself, would have to become fairly independent. In fact,
there were traces of independence throughout her married life that
belie the simplistic conclusion that she was always an obedient
wife without agency. Indeed, these traces of independence likely
inspired Marie Rose to refer to herself in her manuscripts as Queen
of the Jughandle.

It is informative to understand how Marie Rose managed while
Charlie was away for extended periods when they were still on the
ranch by relying on skills that enabled her to survive as a widow.
It appears the largest herd Marie Rose and Charlie may have had
was approximately one thousand head. In the days of open-range
grazing, relatively little labour needed to be expended, given that
"Cattlemen simply allowed their herds to roam the open range
summer and winter...For the most time this required a work force
of only one man per thousand head of cattle."[157] Given that Marie
Rose and Charlie's family would grow to include seventeen children,
and that many of her Delorme family lived nearby, farm labour
would have been plentiful. Furthermore, the scarcity of women on
the prairies likely gave those that were there a sense of their own
stature and potential.

For her part, Marie Rose functioned quite well as a young married woman, and she prided herself on being an able rancher. In reality, many early homesteaders and ranch women simply did what had to be done. If that meant operating the ranch while one's husband was away, as Charlie so often was, then that would simply seem a natural undertaking. Yet, even if it may have been the natural thing to do, Marie Rose noted a heightened sense of her own abilities, writing,

> With my buckskin work of shirts, gloves and all wearing garments; tents for habitation; cooking in my boarding house; and running a homestead, you will think that I never hesitated to lay my hand to any work that called for my attention.[158]

Marie Rose's relative independence, recognized by even the Roman Catholic Church authorities, was an anomaly, not only in Roman Catholic teachings at the time but in a society increasingly oriented to Victorian values. According to her granddaughter, Jock Carpenter, although Charlie was still alive at the time, it was Marie Rose who was approached by the Roman Catholic priests in Pincher Creek about investing in property in the townsite near the church, and it was Marie Rose who made the decision to do that.[159] This decision-making role is not only unusual for the times but also for Marie Rose and Charlie's own relationship because, according to Carpenter, "Charley [sic] did not like her [Marie Rose] trying to boss him. He was boss, even though she now did all the business for the ranch."[160] There is a possibility that the money to purchase the property next to the church was drawn from the inheritance of her father's estate, and this partly explains why the priests would have approached Marie Rose.

Yet it may have been her growing independence and her Roman Catholic teachings on the sanctity of marriage that inspired Marie Rose to take a position against a practice that had been common during the fur trade, that of "turning off" Indigenous partners.[161] As mentioned briefly earlier, when Kootenai Brown, a man whom she clearly admired, told his partner, Ni-ti-mous, that she would have to leave her home so he could continue keeping company with two Euro-North American women, Marie Rose came to her defence. She encouraged Kootenai's country wife, telling her, "He can't quit you, nor can he marry again...that's your home he can't put you out."[162] Marie Rose delighted in telling the story that Kootenai soon came to his senses, and that he had to give Ni-ti-mous ten dollars, his "bunch of horses," as well as his brand and "a wagon and a load of grub" to convince her to return.[163]

Marie Rose also commented on other marital arrangements she observed in her community. For example, she wrote that, even during the early years of settlement, in 1883, when "white men lived with squaws," many of these Indigenous women enlisted the help of a local dressmaker, who made "good money"[164] dressing them in ways that would be fitting for the new settlers to the area. She observed that many of these young "squaws" were "proud to dress like their white sisters."[165] While it may be so that Indigenous women were beginning to "dress like their white sisters," practicality during the early transitional period would have necessitated a continued reliance on traditional garments. It was the continued reliance on these traditional garments that allowed Marie Rose some independence and "pocket money."

Indeed, because of the many diverse ways in which she participated in the economy, Marie Rose was always able to say she had "pocket money" for herself and her children. While seamstress work was common by the nineteenth century and increasingly catered to women in the upper classes, Marie Rose also profited from seamstress work, but for the most part her work was not intended to meet the needs of the upper classes. According to her documents, she worked primarily for the men working the range and the rail lines, and to satisfy the needs of a growing tourism industry by making traditional garments.

While there are few details about Marie Rose's own clothing, there are traces that suggest some of the traditional Metis garments continued to be worn by her children; thus, she was not only producing items for sale. In one example, Marie Rose wrote that, on her way to church with three of her children on a very stormy winter Sunday, the children were "covered with badger robes." According to Marie Rose, the robes were more than adequate to keep her children warm. On the other hand, a "poor unfortunate" newcomer to the area, working in the Christie mine down the road from her home, was deemed not "very well dressed for this kind of weather." The newcomer turned down her offer of assistance when she came upon him on her return trip from church and was later "found frozen in a coulee."[166]

Jock Carpenter explained that, in addition to relying on traditional skills to feed and clothe her family, Marie Rose "let it be known that she would take in boarders and ladies-in waiting. Women, feeling that their time to deliver was near, moved into the big house." Carpenter continued,

Marie Rose's midwifery, carried on while she was at the ranch, and increased later when she had moved the family into the town of Pincher Creek. The Indians too, came to town as they had done on the ranch, seeking treatment for eye infections.[167]

Describing traditions that were no doubt relayed to her by her own mother, Carpenter wrote, "Boiling a herb the way Mother Gervais [Marie Delorme Gervais] taught her, Marie Rose bathed the infected eyes with the cooled liquid and soon the redness and draining disappeared."[168]

Eventually, the growing reliance on Euro-North American health care in the new society of the North West led the government to order Marie Rose to stop using some of her traditional skills. According to her granddaughter,

Marie Rose had put in many years of midwifery and the doctors were disgruntled at not being called to deliver the babies. Soon

Marie Rose had a letter from officials in Edmonton telling her that she must desist from this practice.[169]

It is very likely that, despite pressure from government officials, Marie Rose continued in her role as healer, given that she maintained a book filled with samples of Indigenous-inspired natural remedies until her death in 1960. While her descendants could no longer locate the medicinal book Marie Rose kept throughout her life, they recall that the book even contained samples of natural products she used when practising traditional healing.

Marie Rose did not reveal directly to readers that she relied on traditional skills to help feed her family, but the history that Mary Hélène Parfitt shared with her daughter Jock Carpenter confirms that she did. Carpenter wrote that her mother remembered being told that Marie Rose had learned many of the Metis customs from her own mother and that she carried on with those customs. Mary Hélène also recalled that her mother, in addition to her work as a midwife, "spent countless hours making buckskin articles."[170]

Mary Hélène confirmed the economic importance of Marie Rose's work when she observed that the skills Marie Rose learned "at her Mother's knee," such as "beading, cooking with native roots and herbs, tanning skins, making soap, drying meat," helped to keep the family fed and well looked after.[171] Just a few years before her death in 1960, Marie Rose was interviewed, and subsequently introduced by Harry Baalim as "this old gal...Buckskin Mary."[172]

Without the oral testimony of her descendants, we would not know that Marie Rose was a respected healer and a midwife. In fact, she wrote primarily from the third-person perspective about the childbirth experience of the first Euro-North American woman in her district, saying that Mrs. Schoening, the wife of the local blacksmith, gave birth with the help of "kind neighbor women."[173]

It is possible that Marie Rose used methods similar to those described for researcher Martha Harroun Foster when she interviewed Spring Creek Metis families. One woman had vivid memories of traditional remedies that consisted of rubbing an afflicted person's chest with "terrible-smelling goose grease, a favourite Metis remedy."[174] There are similar stories among Metis women in Ontario, including using goose grease to heal coughs, weak tea for snow blindness, black bear bile as liniment, beaver castors for poultices, oil from boiled and strained beaver castors to prevent hemorrhaging after childbirth, and brews from certain plants for various aches and pains.[175] In order to have access to the items needed to carry on as a healer, Marie Rose's social and trading network would have had to be extensive for most of her life.

Although Marie Delorme Gervais had five daughters, some of whom also settled in Pincher Creek, Marie Rose was the only one singled out by locals as having inherited the skill of working with hides. According to Marie Delorme Gervais's contemporary, she was "quite skilled at tanning hides...Wilbur Lang recalls seeing a beautiful coyote robe she had made. (This talent was inherited by a daughter, Mary Delorme Smith)."[176]

As she became more renowned for her skills, Marie Rose hired other Metis women to help meet her various contracts with the CPR and the Prince of Wales Hotel. Many of these women may have been family members, for there is some evidence from the oral testimony of her descendants that she did pass on some traditional Metis skills to her own children.[177] Family members still retain photographs of Marie Rose's handiwork, with written notations on the back indicating the models were wearing her garments. There is even one photo of a man wearing traditional First Nation clothing identified by family members as "uncle Dick playing Indian Chief."[178]

One of the most important venues at the time for Marie Rose to display her distinctive Metis handiwork may have been the Calgary Stampede. Although she did not say she had participated, Marie Rose wrote that each year the Stampede offered prizes for the "best decorated Indians and Squaws on horse back, the beaded harness aiding in the judges' decision. It would be difficult, indeed, to match the wonderful display shown there."[179] Immediately after

noting this about the Stampede, she wrote, "Much of this work I learned from my mother, and enjoy making original designs on all my buckskin work."[180] The oral testimony of her descendants suggests that Marie Rose's garments were used for venues such as the Stampede.[181]

In her manuscripts, Marie Rose confirmed that she did participate in the tourism economy, writing that she made a buckskin suit for a Miss Sharpe, the young "checking girl" at the Waterton Lakes Hotel, "at the request of the management."[182] The Prince of Wales Hotel, which opened in 1927, was intended to take advantage of the increasing tourism from the United States and helped distinguish Waterton Lakes National Park from Glacier.[183] Once seen as land that would only be good for harvesting timber, Waterton soon became a choice piece of natural parkland sought out by tourists,[184] in effect fulfilling the predictions made years earlier by Marie Rose's friend Kootenai Brown.

Marie Rose explained the process used in her preparation of the traditional clothing that was admired by tourists:

> In making my buckskin gloves, slippers and other garments, I sent to the Mission House of the Kootenay Indians, near Cranbrook, B.C. as I prefer their form of tanning to any others.[185]

Not only was she adept at recognizing quality hides, but her ongoing connections to First Nation people allowed Marie Rose to compare their work. She noted with some degree of pride that, in addition to French and English, she also retained a working knowledge of Cree for her entire life (French and Cree were the lingua franca of the fur trade).[186] Familiar with the dyeing of porcupine quills, Marie Rose

< (Back) Mary Hélène Smith (Parfitt). (Front, l–r) Kathleen Victoria Parfitt, Marie Delorme Gervais, Frances Theodora Parfitt, Marie Rose Delorme Smith, Helen Dora Parfitt (baby on lap), Alice Loretta Parfitt. Photo undated. Shirley-Mae McCargar and Donald McCargar.

also wrote, "We now can buy glass beads in almost any shade for trimming buckskin garments."[187] Pride in her skills is evident on the brief occasions when she described the skills learned during the fur trade. For example, Marie Rose continued,

> We made our own shoes or moccasins, beading in pretty designs the ones we wore for holiday wear. Long hours were spent beading the front of vests, the cuffs of coats.[188]

Marie Rose also explained the importance of her work to others:

> The lad with a nicely beaded buckskin shirt was proud indeed... Fringed, beautifully beaded trappings for the horses lent a distinguished look to many a mounted chief.[189]

Marie Rose's motivations went beyond having pocket money when she agreed to supply tents for the CPR at times when they were not available from the HBC. She wrote that she was proud to do her "bit for the two great companies," which were, by then, the primary agents of development in the Prairie West. By this time, Marie Rose had her new sewing machine. Her employees, two "half-breed women" (perhaps family members), cut out the canvas for the tents, while Marie Rose sewed from "early morning until we couldn't see on account of the dark. Besides this, cooking had to be done for my family and my help." In addition to the contract with the CPR, Marie Rose also made tents for farmers, who used them in the hay fields.[190] So not only was the southern Alberta landscape dotted with Marie Rose's handiwork, but her work established her as a business person and legitimate member of her new society. Thus, she could present herself in a different way than many Metis women, who were at this time relegated to working at menial tasks.

Despite the importance of women to the subsistence economy of the Prairie West, and this clear example of Marie Rose's important economic and social contribution, the column for occupation in early census documents was often left blank for women. Sometimes "Wife" was inserted, and, in Marie Rose's case, the 1880 census taken of their family in Missoula, Montana, listed her as "housekeeper."[191] There is no way to know whether census takers actually believed women did not work, or whether they felt married women's roles were simply too diverse and varied to be easily categorized.

Marie Rose's own view of the importance of her role as keeper of the house is evident in her observation of a Pincher Creek neighbour, who, she wrote,

> *lives in a lovely spot right along a little stream [but] the only thing that is missing is a wife...Mr. Butcher does not believe in keeping skirts around the place. Like a good many bachelors in the country, he does not know what he is missing.*[192]

She continued, "A good housekeeper is worth her weight in gold."[193]

Marie Rose clearly knew her worth because she often tended to the ranch when Charlie continued to enjoy the nomadic lifestyle that had become familiar to him when he was a robe trader. At times, Marie Rose would accompany him, first as they followed the treaties, and then as a cook for ranchers and cowboys during roundup season. However, there were many times when Charlie left Jughandle Ranch in Marie Rose's care, as he followed any of his numerous money-making schemes, from escorting settlers as far as Winnipeg to setting up winter camps to bait and harvest wolves. In the end, Charlie left Jughandle Ranch, and all of its financial and legal difficulties, for Marie Rose to deal with. After his death, the lack of clear title meant Marie Rose spent years in destitute conditions before she could sell her land to satisfy creditors. As mentioned previously, she even had to rely on her community of old-timers to provide the funds for Charlie's funeral.

That Marie Rose was able to call upon the old-timers of southern Alberta for help demonstrates that she was successful in adapting her Metis ethnicity into something more acceptable in the new era.

Likely writing during the 1920s and 1930s, her efforts to recreate her early life were impressive. This was a time when the established classes were using written records to uphold their positions, so Marie Rose was not alone in doing so. In reality, Marie Rose's husband, with his hard-drinking and nomadic ways, was somewhat of a liability as she aspired to a position in the established classes. In addition, her father's Metis family had become a liability when it decided to join forces with Louis Riel. Thus, Marie Rose needed to create a paper network of her own that would suit her need to recreate herself as a homesteading pioneer. In the end, this paper network provided people who came to her defence as she struggled to settle Charlie's estate.

Yet she was determined to protect Charlie's reputation, and her own, to the end. Although she once wrote that Charlie had many interesting tales to tell, Marie Rose related very few of them. She did not share any of the details of her poor health in the years following Charlie's death.[194] She certainly did not tell readers Charlie was a wolfer, that class of men who subsisted after the disappearance of the buffalo herds by leaving poisoned carcasses on the prairies to bait wolves. She would have known that many at this time judged wolfers to be "a grade lower than the whiskey and Indian traders...not a very outstanding class of men in the history of Alberta."[195] Yet, as Charlie's friend Kootenai Brown related it,

> Old buffalo hunters were practically driven to wolfing...The buffalo petered out and we had to do something...I suppose that is why ninety percent of the old buffalo hunters became wolfers.[196]

In the winter and spring of 1895–1896 alone, over 1,600 wolves baited by poisoning the carcass of buffalo or domestic animals were reportedly turned into cash.[197] Perhaps there were times when Charlie wolfed out of economic necessity, and it is possible this yielded a fair income at times. Yet the view on wolfers and the fact that Charlie subsisted by engaging in this activity suggests that Marie Rose's status in an increasingly agricultural economy was shifting downward long before she became a widow, and she very likely understood the need to omit some of Charlie's less acceptable behaviour from her writing.

In reality, Marie Rose's survival strategy could not include Charlie for a large part of her life, nor could she count on her husband's extended family, given that Charlie's appearance in the North West was somewhat of a mystery. As noted, there were various stories about where Charlie was born, and there was never any indication he had any family members who joined him in North America. With both a husband and a Delorme family who represented liabilities in the changing society, Marie Rose recognized the importance of securing land. While land occupancy and the concept of commons had been important to the Metis, individual land ownership became increasingly important for people like Marie Rose (perhaps even more so than to Charlie) in the new economy.

As noted, there was a time when Marie Rose and Charlie amassed a decent number of cattle and a "ranch." However, Marie Rose did not really benefit in the long term from land ownership, even though she devoted much effort to ensuring title to her land. Unfortunately, the paperwork for the property where Marie Rose lived when she was caring for her family without the aid of her older husband had not been filed properly, leaving Marie Rose with what appears to be a legal nightmare after Charlie's death. There is evidence Charlie was trying to make a second homestead entry in 1907, when he would have been approximately seventy years old, which suggests that he may have been trying to offer some assistance to his sons as he was getting older and experiencing poor health. However, Charlie was not able to obtain legal title to the property and, in the end, Marie Rose and Charlie could not offer the same assistance to their children that Metis families had been able to offer during the height of the fur trade era. While Marie Rose was eventually able to prove ownership of Jughandle Ranch, there was not much left after debts were paid.

With few assets left, Marie Rose was forced to carry on independently for a number of years after Charlie died. While she always had children living near or with her, she had to deal with the loss of many of her children without the support of her husband. As mentioned previously, Charlie was almost twenty years older than Marie Rose and, after his death, she carried on for forty-six years as a widow. While none of her activities led to any sort of material wealth, Marie Rose's skill set was diverse: she operated a boarding house; she served as a healer; she became an author. Marie Rose continued until her death to maintain important connections with her southern Alberta community, and she was recognized as an important figure—a pioneer of southern Alberta.

Despite the suggestions that he was a somewhat hard man and the reality that he had difficulty providing for his family near the end of his life, Charlie always appears to have accommodated the condition placed upon his family by Marie Rose's mother and the Roman Catholic Church that all of his children would be raised Roman Catholic. In fact, he did not seem to demonstrate much concern for religious faith at all, at least until his approaching death in 1914, when he apparently embraced his wife's religion on his deathbed. Writing with a sense of peace and accomplishment because her lifelong prayers for Charlie had come to fruition, Marie Rose explained,

> In the spring, my husband, my comrade of thirty-seven years died; but there was one consolation for me. He died in the Faith. It had been my constant prayer through all those years.[198]

These were the words of a widow reminiscing about her life partner. However, it took some years of difficulty to get to this point of reminiscence, and there is sufficient evidence to suggest Charlie was at best a questionable asset to Marie Rose.

As Marie Rose carried on as a widow for many years after Charlie died, it was fortuitous that she, though Indigenous, was not hindered by the stipulations of the Indian Act.[199] When she became widowed, Marie Rose was able to assume the position as head of her household and controller of finances,[200] even though those finances were in disarray. It was not until June of 1920, six years after Charlie's death in 1914, that she finally received confirmation from the Department of the Interior that the title on the land she was desperate to sell had finally been issued in her name. Also of great comfort would have been the letter written to her by the Great War Veterans' Association in April 1920. In this letter, she was advised that her appeal for an increase to her mother's pension and back pay for her two deceased sons was being considered, and that she "need have no fear of the mortgage being foreclosed as you are protected by law in this respect."[201] Perhaps it was the fear of foreclosure that had inspired Marie Rose to move the family from Jughandle Ranch into a house in the town of Pincher Creek, and to begin to take in boarders to supplement the family income.[202]

Writing of her time after Charlie's death, Marie Rose said that she "was left with very little, a few cows and horses after the mortgage companies got theirs." Marie Rose explained the circumstances that inspired her to take the second homestead, saying that, after Charlie died in 1914, she thought she

> would take a homestead in the south country, thinking I would make a living for the rest of my children. I had three girls and one was not very healthy. I left my girls in town to run the house, I had two boarders, and that brought me a little money. I would go to the homestead a week at a time, I put in a small garden and I would come back and forth.[203]

In addition to taking the second homestead, Marie Rose was trying to sort through the problems with the first homestead and Charlie's intent to purchase the land adjacent to that homestead. At the time of his death, no payment had been made on that second section of land, and Marie Rose pleaded for patience as she tried to sort through Charlie's estate. Signing the letter "your humble servant," Marie Rose explained she now had to conduct the business herself and was trying to sell some of the original 160 acres to satisfy her debts.[204] Further appeals were made on her behalf by some in the Pincher Creek community, which spoke to her desperate situation at the time:

> She is doing the best she can to find a purchaser, but in the depressed state of the real estate market in the West at present, this is a difficult matter. Mrs. Smith was left but little by her husband, in fact the old timers here bore his funeral expenses, and she has a large family to support, and she trusts you will be pleased to consider her case and not press for immediate settlement.[205]

By June of 1916, no payment had yet been recorded by the Land Patents Branch, and a further extension was granted, due to the fact

> the three sons of Mrs. Smith, widow of the deceased, have enlisted for active service, and that she is unable to make any further payments on this land at present. Under the circumstances, Mrs. Smith may be allowed a further extension of time until after the war.[206]

Despite her brave independence and hard work, the second homestead she was granted as a widow did not yield a great deal of wealth either. It is not clear what Marie Rose's intention was for the second homestead, but it appears all that was reaped was a "small garden." She likely chose one of the most difficult times in the Prairie West to establish a new homestead. After the overexpansion by prairie farmers during the Great War, a mass exodus ensued. Although the mass settlement and exodus had not affected Pincher Creek the way it did southern Alberta areas such as Medicine Hat, a drop in wheat prices and moisture levels had a disastrous effect on Alberta's economy in general.[207]

While she gained a somewhat "elusive independence" by taking the second homestead and operating a boarding house, Marie Rose was never as wealthy as many in the upper classes in the transitional West. Yet she was regarded as an important transitional figure. As mentioned previously, Harry Baalim took the time to record her reminiscences shortly before her death in 1960, and Marie Rose had achieved some media attention earlier, through the publication of her articles in *Canadian Cattlemen*, while her community anticipated the publication of her life history. E. Lynch-Staunton wrote in the *Lethbridge Herald* in 1941,

> *A pioneer of eighty years standing, Mary Smith (Mrs. Charlie Smith) as she is known to her hundreds of pioneer friends, is writing the memoirs of her life on the western plains, and her book may shortly be given to the publisher.*[208]

This story, written by Lynch-Staunton, a neighbour who ranched north of Lundbreck,[209] noted that Marie Rose's mother was of the "Cree Indians." The article went on to say that, after Charlie's death in 1914, Marie Rose "proved herself an astute businesswoman in building a comfortable home in Pincher Creek which has since been a home for many old friends."[210]

Marie Rose was successful enough in establishing social capital that the local newspaper, as early as 1919 (after Charlie's death), had considered it noteworthy when her daughters returned to town. With a note of deference, the newspaper noted, "Miss Frances Smith, who spent some days with her folks here, returned to Calgary last Saturday evening," and "Miss Eva Smith...is leaving for Calgary this week to be the guest of her sister, Miss Frances Smith."[211] When the local newspaper noted the return of the young "misses" to the Pincher Creek area, that return was portrayed as a novel adventure, in that "Misses Josie and Eva Smith are camping out on the ranche [sic] for a week."[212]

Still, in 1954, Marie Rose was important enough to southern Alberta history that her visit to southern Alberta from Edmonton was noted by the *Lethbridge Herald*, which wrote that Marie Rose had lived a "long and eventful life...Convent educated in Winnipeg, she was married in 1877 when 16 years of age, to Charlie Smith a noted fur trader." The skills she had learned during the fur trade were also recognized, as the article continued, "Mrs. Smith is expert in bead-work, working on buckskin, and has made countless beautiful beaded gloves, jackets, moccasins, etc." Marie Rose's storytelling skills were also recognized by the newspaper, which wrote, "She has a fund of stories of the early days."[213]

Despite her own expressed weakness and necessary obedience to her husband's will, in reality, Marie Rose viewed herself as relatively independent. She was an expert at managing her own public image and equally adept at manipulating her Metis or "pioneer" ethnicity in order to successfully extend her own and Charlie's network. Perhaps Marie Rose perceived the need to extend her network beyond her Metis family in part because her physical characteristics clearly identified her as Indigenous.

Indeed, some believe that skin colour contributed to the self-identifying process of many Metis, given that both Indigenous and Euro-North American societies were not colour blind. Thus, it may be so that, in the case of the Metis, "the fairest tended to receive the lion's share of societal rewards while the darkest were often harassed and treated like Indians."[214] It is possible, then, that skin colour could play a part in dividing Metis families. In Marie Rose's case, when she aspired to a position in the higher class of her new society, she faced the challenge that she was easily identifiable as Indigenous.

Despite being easily identifiable as a Metis woman, in becoming Charlie's wife at a time when the Prairie West was transitioning, Marie Rose perceived her only option as developing a persona as a Euro-North American homesteading pioneer. Her life as Queen of the Jughandle was not an easy one for her, nor was it an easy life for her children. It is not clear how the children eventually survived as adults, but all indications are there was very little left to prevent Marie Rose herself from being destitute, much less the children.[215] Charlie's will specified that Marie Rose was to be the sole beneficiary[216]; however, it took a good deal of time and effort for the legal mess of Charlie's homestead records to be resolved. It took some time for the mortgage companies to recover their loan. Before Marie Rose could sell the land to repay the debt, she had to prove that she was the rightful owner of the land she and Charlie had occupied since the late 1880s. The difficulty in proving ownership is likely why there is little information, both from Marie Rose and her granddaughter Jock Carpenter, about what became of Jughandle Ranch. Rather, there is simply an admission that the family moved into Pincher Creek onto property once owned by the Church. Perhaps some assistance came from the Church in making this move, but this is not documented.

Other than some reference in homestead records and census documents, there is also no way to determine the level of assistance Marie Rose might have received from her Delorme family. In the end, the appeals made on her behalf for a resolution to her property crisis after Charlie died were all made by Euro-North American agents based in Pincher Creek—her paper network. This paper network appeared to be more helpful to Marie Rose than to Charlie. All of Charlie's own appeals to the government in the hope of sorting out his homestead problems had been unsuccessful. In Marie Rose's case, there were a number of people from the Pincher Creek district who took the time to make appeals on her behalf and to stress the urgency in settling the matter of title. These appeals made on Marie Rose's behalf eventually prevailed.

Marie Rose had learned early in her marriage to rely on herself and her community of connections. When Marie Rose "thought that the whole world" was hers because Charlie had bought her a sewing machine,[217] she would have recognized that this gift would enhance her abilities to further the skills she had learned as a young girl, and to provide even more independence. The sewing machine would have enabled Marie Rose to contribute to the survival of her family, to be sure. However, perhaps as equally important during times when life might otherwise be extremely tedious and difficult was the ability to produce magnificent traditional garments that inspired tremendous pride. This pride extended to the ability to raise the status of her family through improved material wealth, while also managing a small cottage industry. No doubt there was also a quiet pride in her retention, and indeed her mastery, of Metis traditional skills.

There is enough evidence in her written diaries that Marie Rose relied, likely out of necessity, on aspects of her Metis culture, so that she was referred to not only as Queen of the Jughandle but also as Buckskin Mary. The fact that she earned these two "titles" no doubt provided a sense of some independence for Marie Rose. Her sense of independence also came because she had been relatively successful, at least if we are to judge from the manuscripts she produced, at forging valuable connections. It may have been in her later years, after Charlie's death, that these connections became even more valuable. After all, it was her community of old-timers that ensured she was able to afford her husband a proper burial suited to a respected pioneer.

However, Marie Rose's independence had limitations and could seem elusive at times. Within the parameters of her limited independence, there was a knowledge that she and her Delorme family were increasingly becoming "fenced in." This feeling was undoubtedly inspired by the growing number of physical fences erected by newcomers, but also by severe financial difficulties and the racial boundaries that were increasingly solidifying. These racial boundaries inspired an instrumental ethnicity that could be relied upon, suppressed, or repurposed as necessary for the most basic need of survival.

7

Fenced In

MARIE ROSE (DELORME) SMITH'S OBITUARY in the *Pincher Creek Echo*, on 7 April 1960, described her as one of the area's "most colorful figures," while noting she was one of southern Alberta's earliest and oldest pioneers.[1] Marie Rose witnessed the transformation of the Prairie West, which she often described as a place of beauty and unfenced freedom, to a land governed by mechanized agriculture and sedentary farm economics. Her association with legendary local personalities and her desire to record her experiences, primarily as a homesteading pioneer, likely contributed to Marie Rose's reputation as a "colorful figure." Her desire to portray herself as a homesteading pioneer no doubt assisted in diminishing the differences of being Metis as more settlers arrived in the West.

To new settlers in the West, the Metis lifestyle with which Marie Rose had been familiar as a young girl harkened back to what some have referred to as the "nomadic, Indian-like aspects of Metis society."[2] As the Prairie West was increasingly fenced in, literally, with the end of the open-range era, social fences were also being erected. Between the 1880s and the 1920s, a new world emerged in the Prairie West, and many residents reinvented themselves. People such as Grey Owl,[3] Chief Buffalo Child Long Lance,[4] and Onoto Watanna[5] embellished or even invented personal lineages in ways they imagined would render them more interesting, yet also "palatable," to the emerging society, while allowing them to profit from the new economy.

A more detailed examination of some of her writing follows, but it was in the 1920s and 1930s that Marie Rose very likely wrote most of her own manuscripts and created her persona as an old-timer and homesteading pioneer of the Prairie West. She appeared determined to write her life story and to construct a colonial discourse of sorts before anybody else did it for her. It was a time when the written record was upholding the power of the established upper classes, and Marie Rose was no longer a member of those classes as they had existed at the height of the fur trade era. Yet it seems that throughout many of her manuscripts, Marie Rose desired her story be told from the perspective of one of the new established classes, the Euro-North American wife of a rancher—a homesteading pioneer.

The motivation for this situational identity was not only a survival tactic; she also had reason to believe it would have assisted in having her manuscripts published. In her files is a letter dated 22 July 1938, addressed to A.L. Freebairn (a neighbour in Pincher Creek) from the Macmillan Company of Canada, advising that, should the author want them to consider the manuscript for publication, Freebairn should advise her that they would treat it quite confidentially.[6] However, there never was a book published and it is not clear if the manuscript was ever forwarded for full consideration. What we do know is that Marie Rose published a short series of five articles between 1948 and 1949 in the prairie ranch periodical *Canadian Cattlemen*.[7]

These published articles only touch on Metis history, focusing primarily on the lifestyle of ranching the open prairie and on stereotypical pioneer scenes such as the prairie roundup. Whether she was expressing the views of the rancher's wife or the Metis woman,

Marie Rose never seemed able to openly embrace the growing tendency to fence in the prairies. She could never be the consummate booster of large-scale settlement. Perhaps Marie Rose also had a sense of being fenced in by the number of children she was invariably responsible for due to Charlie's lifestyle. Perhaps this is why she appears to have identified with her fictional character, Georgina (discussed later),[8] who never married or had children but rather held a job and travelled the world.

When Marie Rose "agreed" to become Charlie Smith's wife, there was a sense of relief in her diaries that she was able to continue for a time to traverse the plains with her mother and stepfather, much as she had before the marriage arrangement. Yet, while Charlie and Marie Rose continued as hunters and traders, they were clearly aware of changing conditions in the North West, and the growing importance of private land ownership. This trend toward individual land ownership would eventually replace an economy that had for generations relied on the communal sharing of resources. Thus it was that Marie Rose and Charlie soon travelled to Montana, gathered a herd of cattle, and settled on land in the Pincher Creek district, with the goal to assume a somewhat sedentary lifestyle.

Although they settled on land in southern Alberta along with many newcomers, land continued to hold significance for Marie Rose in the way it had for her Metis ancestors. Both she and Charlie applied for, and received, scrip for their children, and Marie Rose received scrip for herself. In addition to the link to her past that scrip confirmed, in brief statements, such as "we had no noxious weeds in the Pincher Creek district until the c.p.r. was built and very little sickness before the railroad came through," Marie Rose revealed a sense of longing for earlier times.[9]

During the interview in the late 1950s with Harry Baalim, in which she offered her version of the Metis folksong "Red River Halfbreed," Marie Rose recalled, with pleasure, that cattle ranching on the open prairie was similar in many ways to her life as a young girl, when she had travelled with her family as part of a Metis hunting and trading caravan. Marie Rose alluded to the similarity of free-range cattle ranching in southern Alberta to the time when her people were the "Free People," noting, "Wherever you looked on the prairies you would see cattle grazing, no fences to bother with, they would roam around like buffalo."[10]

At the start of her manuscript, "Eighty Years on the Plains," it is clear Marie Rose is describing preparations for a trip onto the western plains. Her fond memories are evident:

I was very excited as any other little girl might be, who, at the early age of ten years, was on a winter trip over the great western plains, from the Great Lakes to the Rocky Mountains.[11]

Demonstrating some appreciation for metaphorical symbolism, Marie Rose continued,

The rising sun was just beginning its morning dance on the grey-white waters of the Assiniboine River, as my father, Urbain Delorme, with all his household sat down to the early morning meal.[12]

According to her recollections, Marie Rose's father was "taking all of us on his annual fur-trading trip into the great North-west." The family, with "Trader Delorme" at the helm, would winter on the open plains before returning to their small plot of land in the Red River area.[13]

The stories of her time as a daughter of "Trader Delorme" provided fond memories for Marie Rose when she wrote as a woman living out her final years in the city of Edmonton, far removed from the fur trade. It is not certain if she was writing about her father in particular in this instance, but she clearly described a Metis hunting expedition: "It was a grand sight to see them as they galloped away, their beaded shoulder straps glittering in the sun, as each loaded his gun while on full gallop."[14] Marie Rose described the duties of the women who joined the hunting brigades:

By this time the women were as excited as the men. They hustled
about, emptied the carts and made ready to drive out to bring
the meat into camp, while waiting for the men to come back from
the slaughter so all could go out together and bring back what
was killed.[15]

As Marie Rose explained

It was the women's work to cure the meat, make the pemmican
and dry the hides, tanning many for buffalo robes. If we were lucky
enough to be near a stream we would make camp for a few days
while the women completed their work.[16]

When the tents were set up, the "camp looked like a small village of
leather teepees," with carts placed in a circle to form a large corral.[17]
Although Marie Rose was writing from the perspective of an adult,
it is clear that as a young girl she was in awe of the "daring rider" who

moved in and out of the labyrinth of paths among the doomed
animals...As the hunters pressed on in a hurry, they dropped their
reins and guided their ponies by the pressure of their limbs only, by
bending their half naked, supple bodies...while the well trained pony
responded with an obedience that made rider and pony one.[18]

In reference to earlier times, Marie Rose wrote,

Wild life is a good life. Always in the open air, always breathing
fresh air and a nice clean place to camp and lots of fresh green grass
is wholesome. Oh, boy, give me the old time life, that's the life.[19]

Writing from a different perspective in another manuscript, Marie
Rose's admiration for old-timers, those first pioneers of the plains,
is evident:

There is a different class of people today compared to the oldtimers
who were so friendly and helped one another. Times have changed...
and we will never see the country like it used to be. The old pioneer
days were happy days and wants were few.[20]

Because we do not know precisely when Marie Rose wrote her narratives, both those that were published and the many that were not, it
is difficult to determine her motivation for choosing what she wrote
about and what she avoided, and whether it was the young married
woman or the elderly widow whose perspective is presented to readers.
    At times, the context gives some indication of the perspective.
In direct comparison to the early "wild life" she spoke of in the
preceding excerpts, and this time more clearly from a retrospec-
tive point of view, Marie Rose wrote of another loss: "The old time
ranching days of the northwest have vanished, those days when we
could ride the range for miles without the impediment of a fence."
Displaying a preference for ranchers over farmers, Marie Rose
continued, "When all the settlers were ranchers and everyone was
neighbourly and friendly, riding mile after mile no fences to trouble
you. Those were the days."[21] She further wrote,

When the farmers commenced to come and started farming, that
ruined our country such is life in the north west territories, it will
always be in the memory of the oldtimers.[22]

No doubt, for this "old-timer," embracing cattle ranching provided
an avenue through which she could maintain an open resource lifestyle within a private property regime.[23]
    Although she attributed farming to the ruination of the country,
Marie Rose indicated she and Charlie were eventually caught up in
the heady expansionism that contributed to the credit crisis and
the Great Depression. As she wrote,

Our financial troubles started when agriculture was encouraged to
expand using bank credit. Greed took hold of the farmers such as the
oldtimers would not have endured. We too, suffered under this new
system, though I must confess we had many thrilling moments as
our holdings expanded and we might have become "capitalists" if
the bubble hadn't burst.[24]

By this time, Marie Rose had recently lived through not only the
Great Depression but the earlier winters of 1886 and 1907, when
many ranchers and old-timers trying to survive in the new economy
suffered tremendous losses.

Marie Rose's descriptions of the "round-up time" of the new
economy (likely for the large free-range ranches),[25] invited compari-
sons to the Metis hunting camps of her youth. The organizational
work and details of the roundup had parallels to the camps. For
example, the roundup required that participants choose "a captain
to keep order in the camp,"[26] and, like the camps, the roundup had
specific duties for the women. After the captain was chosen, the
women prepared the

> *mess wagon with "grub," cooking utensils, dishes and clothing.*
> *When all was ready we started for the south end of the ranges*
> *and across the Kootenay River...usually five or six outfits travelled*
> *together...When they camped for any length of time, they formed a*
> *small village of tents.*[27]

Corrals were then made by "stringing ropes from wagon to wagon,
which were drawn up in a large circle."[28]

Again, Marie Rose had fond memories of the communal work on
the open prairie. She wrote,

> *It was a fascinating sight to see thousands upon thousands of*
> *head of cattle gathered together, with the riders weaving their way*
> *in among them, hoping to spot an animal bearing their particular*

brand. Then the dexterity of those riders, as they proceeded to "cut out" that animal from the rest of the herd, was as amazing a sight as anyone could wish for, and kept many a "green-horn" frozen to the spot in his awe.[29]

She continued to describe life before farmers and fences:

The early rancher always squatted where he could find a spring and plenty of range with good hay land. They would put shacks and corrals on his holdings and ranged his cattle for miles around. About in November before the cold weather would come, the fall roundup commenced. The rancher and his men then rode the range continuously for about two months so as to have his cattle near the place so that when severe weather set in they would be close to hand to feed...Cattle were always in good shape as grass grew abundantly and luxuriously.[30]

When cowboys travelled to different locations to "ship surplus stock," both Marie Rose and Charlie often went along as cooks and then carried on to Calgary to invest their earnings.[31] As she wrote, "No trip was too hard for us pioneer women to accompany our husbands."[32] Entertainment changed somewhat but still reflected some of the activities from previous days, when, along with new activities like polo and gymkhana, many nights were spent dancing, singing, playing games, and racing horses.[33]

Even though ranchers like Marie Rose and Charlie were intent on maintaining the distinction between ranching and farming, the reality was that, within a few years, ranchers were increasingly forced to embrace a number of farming practices to deal with the arrival of more settlers and major environmental challenges. By 1904, one of Marie Rose's neighbours indicated the Pincher Creek district was now closed to open-range ranching, with the disappearance of unappropriated land in the foothills near Pincher Creek.[34] Yet there is no evidence that Charlie and Marie Rose ever expanded into mixed farming such as seeded crops and grains, hogs, or beef in a big way, as many early ranchers had to do in southern Alberta, almost as soon as they arrived in the Prairie West.[35]

Although Jughandle Ranch was not located in the heart of the arid belt, Charlie and Marie Rose seemed to have a better understanding of true conditions in the Prairie West than the prevailing science. Their consideration for the choice of a homestead was always to find a location that would provide the best conditions for raising large herds of cattle. There is no indication they ever harvested any crops other than pasture grasses. Rather, they always relied primarily on smaller scale and family-run, free-range cattle ranching, supplemented by the survival strategies learned during the fur trade era. For Marie Rose, diversification did not mean a move to mixed farming and sheds and fences, like it did for many, but rather it meant continuing to rely on the skills she had learned from her Metis mother and expanding upon those skills. In the end, Marie Rose and Charlie were adopting what proved to be a more sustainable type of ranching—small, intensive, and family-based. The larger models were the capitalized, foreign-controlled, and distantly managed ranches that were, as historian Warren Elofson has argued, doomed. Unlike the ranches Elofson wrote about, the Smith ranch was of much smaller scale and very mixed in terms of its economy, making Marie Rose's contributions even more important.

Marie Rose felt so strongly about the ruination of the prairies with sedentary agriculture that she mentioned it often in her manuscripts. By the time she was likely doing the majority of her writing (in the 1920s and 1930s), many agreed with her, believing "soil mining" had ruined the land and created dust bowls. Farmers in general were accused of cash cropping for quick profits at the expense of the land. In slightly different wording than noted earlier, Marie Rose wrote that the richness of the country she had enjoyed in her younger days was now a "thing of the past."[36]

Commenting on Marie Rose's destiny, which was largely determined by her mother and by changing circumstances, scholar
Maggie MacKellar argued that Marie Rose experienced a "double
betrayal." Not only was she traded against her will, but the man she
had to marry was a Euro-North American. Nonetheless, MacKellar
concluded that Marie Rose retained a healthy admiration for her
Metis culture, and that she was instrumental in transmitting that
culture to her own descendants.[37] Whether she felt it to be a double
betrayal, Marie Rose may have eventually felt some gratitude to her
mother for striking a deal with a Euro-North American man. The
land to which Marie Rose's destiny had brought her was becoming
increasingly bound not only by physical fences but by racial boundaries, and it likely served her well to be married to a Euro-North
American man of Protestant background, even if his character was
questionable.

There were few settlers in the Pincher Creek area when Marie
Rose and Charlie staked their homestead in the late 1800s. However,
by the time Marie Rose was a community member of some good
standing, enough Roman Catholic buildings had been destroyed by
fires instigated by those adhering to racist beliefs in southern Alberta
that some insurance companies considered refusing policies. While
not many scholars have examined the activity of the KKK in Alberta,
those that have generally agree that the group's message

> fell on fertile ground in Alberta during the 1920s and '30s, ground
> that had been broken, ploughed, tilled and seeded by extremists in
> the Orange Lodges of central and southern Alberta.[38]

The fires that targeted Roman Catholic buildings were believed
to have been instigated by Klan members, who had by the 1920s
established a "strong foothold," with three hundred members in
Calgary and "chapters in three communities within 25 miles of the
city."[39] Cross burnings in various areas and the fact that residents of

Drumheller had elected professed members of the KKK to the town council in 1927 suggest that, at the beginning of the Depression era,

a potentially explosive atmosphere of intolerance, distrust, threatened violence, and nameless fears...made resort to such intimidation strategies both thinkable and doable.[40]

Marie Rose did not discuss the racism that was present in southern Alberta society during the early 1900s. Rather, she chose to remain safely ensconced within the boundaries of the ranching community. Yet she did confirm that many in the French and Roman Catholic communities were always important members of her social network, and she often mentioned missionaries such as Father Lacombe and acquaintances such as J.A. Rioux, secretary of the French Canadian Association of Alberta.[41]

Marie Rose continued to show reverence her entire life for at least one aspect of her personal Metis culture: her Roman Catholic faith. She wrote,

Many years elapsed before we were blessed with a convent...The saintly Bishop Legal on the occasion of his visits always congratulated the pupils of the convent for their piety and excellent conduct.[42]

Perhaps as a way to downplay any racial tensions, Marie Rose wrote that, in 1924, St. Vincent's Hospital was opened, when "Father Pilon [was] supported by the co-operation of the Catholics as well as the fine spirit and generosity of the non-Catholics and resident doctors." She continued that the re-establishment of a hospital in Pincher Creek was only possible due to "a bevy of good workers of Catholic and non-Catholic faith."[43] This perspective was in line with Marie Rose's desire to portray the pioneer spirit as conciliatory and cooperative.

Despite her understanding of French and her association with French priests, Marie Rose only wrote in French when she could attribute those words to another. Even then, those instances were very brief, as when she wrote that Father Lacombe described the "ruination of the Indian tribes" by observing, "'Les pauvres inno-cents,' he called them—'Souvent mon Coeur pleure paux [sic] eux.'"[44] It is understandable that Marie Rose would write in English for published articles, but even her handwritten notes were rarely in French. In one brief instance only, in a note to her son, is there some suggestion that Marie Rose may have retained French as her first language, when she began to tell her son that Moses Fidler "travaille" for her and Charlie. However, she then crossed the French word out to replace it with "worked" at the ranch.[45]

Census takers never mistook Marie Rose for French but seemed to know she was Indigenous, for they listed her children as "other breeds." Marie Rose inadvertently acknowledged that her own chil-dren were Indigenous when she made a note for her readers that the first "white" child was born in the area sometime after the birth of her own children. Most in her community likely knew Marie Rose's ethnicity. In fact, it was confirmed in a 1941 article in the local newspaper written by Emma Lynch-Staunton, who wrote (errone-ously) that Marie Rose's grandfather was a French voyageur and her mother was "of the Cree Indians."[46] Yet, in a later article in 1955, Lynch-Staunton wrote that "Mary Rose Smith" was the descendant of a Scottish mother and a French father, who lived on a small farm in Winnipeg and augmented his income by trading.[47]

Despite her neighbour's portrayal of Marie Rose as Euro-North American in this later article, there were instances in her unpub-lished writing that Marie Rose identified with her Metis culture. For example, she felt the song "Red River Halfbreed" important enough to Indigenous history that she recorded the words of the Metis folk song in its entirety.[48] Yet, for the most part, she maintained ethnic boundaries herself, writing that some Indigenous customs, such as the Ghost Dance and the Sun Dance, were rightfully curtailed by the government, for they had the "effect of working up the braves to a pitch of frenzy." She concluded that the custom was a "cruel, barbarous ordeal, the young Indian...was compelled to undergo."[49]

Although Marie Rose deemed some First Nation customs to be cruel, her family members speak to the resurgence of some aspects of her own Indigenous beliefs later in life that reflected her early culture. One of her grandchildren who perhaps had the most vivid memories of Marie Rose as an older woman was Shirley-Mae McCargar, whose family Marie Rose lived with in Edmonton until her death. Shirley-Mae recalled that, when she was a young girl, on three consecutive evenings, Marie Rose noted that an owl came to the window of the house. Shortly thereafter and, as predicted by Marie Rose, death visited the family when a young infant died.[50] Despite sharing similar beliefs as many First Nation people and knowing their customs well, Marie Rose still felt the need to maintain boundaries and to tell her readers that "they" were a "queer" people.[51]

The majority of her writing is not dated, but reasoned speculation suggests that Marie Rose began to write only later in life. Even up to the 1920s, she was preoccupied with raising her family and would likely only have had the freedom to begin writing after this time. Marie Rose indicated in "The Adventures of the Wild West of 1870" that she wrote the manuscript when she was seventy-six years old.[52] We know that Marie Rose's articles were published in the ranch periodical *Canadian Cattlemen* in 1948–1949 and that the letter from a possible publisher was received in 1938. Thus, it is fair to say that the majority of Marie Rose's writing was not done much earlier than 1930.[53] By this time, she seems to have determined to write her own story for the most part from the perspective of homesteading pioneer.

Jock Carpenter's memoir of her grandmother, *Fifty Dollar Bride— Marie Rose Smith: A Chronicle of Métis Life in the 19th Century*, largely adhered to Marie Rose's version of her life. More determined to portray Marie Rose as a Metis woman than a pioneer, Carpenter romanticized Metis people as a "hearty race" with "charcoal faces," who adopted the best of two cultures.[54] Although she does note that her grandmother's marriage was not her own choice, Carpenter tends to romanticize the circumstances of the marriage trade as well. She suggests Charlie's patience won out, and that Marie Rose, shedding the robes with which she had bound herself nightly since her wedding, finally accepted her marriage as "God's will." Thus, as Carpenter wrote, "Marie Rose passed by her youth, slipping gently from a very young girl into the woman who stood beside her tall husband today."[55] We also do not learn much from Carpenter about Charlie's hard drinking and his frequent forays away from the ranch.

Perhaps even more significant is the fact that Carpenter does not explore any of the conflicts in Red River or in Batoche, which involved so many of Marie Rose's family. The only conflict mentioned, the fighting of 1885, warrants one page in Carpenter's book, where she concludes with the assessment that the Metis made a "bloody stand over land rights."[56] The only family members mentioned who were affected the fighting are Madeleine and Ludgar Gareau and Elise and George Ness. The Gareaus had left Batoche for Montreal before the fighting started, and, according to Carpenter, returned to find their house burnt on orders of the Metis. Like Marie Rose, Carpenter makes no mention of the fact that Gareau was actually a Riel supporter. In 1952, some years before the publication of Carpenter's book, Ludger Gareau told the *Pincher Creek Echo* he was an admirer of Louis Riel and contended that it was "Riel's influence that often held the Metis and Indians in check."[57]

In regard to George and Liza Ness, Carpenter wrote, "Word filtered back to Marie Rose" that Ness was a prisoner of the Metis.[58] Carpenter did not write at all about Marie Rose's uncles, Donald Ross and Joseph and Norbert Delorme, despite the fact she did make inquiries about the two Delorme men, in particular, in a letter to a genealogical researcher.[59] For the most part, Carpenter adhered primarily to the narrative of Marie Rose's texts, while noting she also shared some oral history with other family members. However,

Carpenter did not place the same emphasis on her grandmother's adopted Sioux brother as Marie Rose did, even leaving him off the genealogical chart at the end of her book.

Although she more openly acknowledged her affection for her Sioux brother as a family member than did Carpenter, Marie Rose devoted even less time than Carpenter to traditional Metis culture. Even when discussing her life on the plains, the inclination from readers would be to view Marie Rose as a homesteading pioneer rather than a daughter of the fur trade. For the most part, Marie Rose's writing depicts a woman happy to assume the life of a pioneer, even if that life may have presented a number of challenges. Other than her lamentations about Charlie's drinking, it might not appear in her manuscripts that Marie Rose was often unhappy or "suffering." Certainly, she made no mention of the struggles she faced after Charlie died and which carried on for some years. Yet, since we do know that Marie Rose overcame many challenges, perhaps suffering was the catalyst that served as the inspiration for her life writing, as has been suggested of life writing in general.[60] Another perspective offers, "A published story can be seen as a way to take part in civil society, to exercise citizenship and democratic participation."[61] Perhaps this wish for inclusion was the catalyst for Marie Rose's life writing—a desire to be seen as a rightful citizen of the changed society in which she was forced to negotiate her identity.

Today's life writers are sometimes criticized for either not telling the whole truth or telling *too much* truth.[62] We might level one aspect of this same critique at Marie Rose's work, for it is not entirely truthful in its telling. However, the reality for Marie Rose was that, if she had any hope of having her manuscripts published (and we know she did),[63] she had to write to the expectations and demands of a reading public of different ethnicity and class, and one with only a limited interest and stake in the earlier fur trade era.

There are details missing from Marie Rose's life writing, to be sure. In life writing we can never know the whole truth, yet it does not follow that there is "no truth to be had."[64] What we have with Marie Rose's life writing is a representation of the events she witnessed. The manner in which she chose to represent those events provided protection for her, as well as for those whose stories she was either telling or failing to tell—life writing that was at times memoir, at times fiction, at times historical narrative. For Marie Rose did not have the luxury of writing a memoir after the death of key persons in her own life story.[65]

If she felt any pride in her connection to Metis history, it would be private, given that her "historical" accounts of the Metis actions of 1869–1870 and 1885 do not connect her to some of the soldiers and do not show any support for those soldiers. It is not clear who her sources were, but as a child of eight years of age, who lived in the Red River area, Marie Rose may have known of the shooting of the Orangeman from Ontario, Thomas Scott, by a Metis firing squad on 4 March 1870, when it happened. However, it is more likely Marie Rose solidified her opinion of both the events of 1869–1870 and 1885 later, when she lived in the Pincher Creek district, by relying on the oral testimony of some of her family members who were involved, and even more so through the judgments of her mainly English-speaking community.

Marie Rose did write that her version of Thomas Scott's shooting, which she may have hoped to publish, was told to her by her brother-in-law, George Ness, a justice of the peace in Batoche in 1869–1870 and an "Englishman by birth."[66] Ness appears as the only family member who openly opposed Riel and his soldiers. In regard to Scott's shooting, Marie Rose concluded Riel made a "grave mistake" when he permitted that to happen. In her version of the events, the firing squad consisted of five Metis men, after one "refused to be a member of such a party, which he declared was really murder." Marie Rose then described how

every member of that squad was an expert marksman and at such close range could not have failed in his aim, yet of the five bullets

fired, only one struck the victim. He fell to the ground, wounded...
While still living, he was placed in a rough board coffin.[67]

This version gives the sense that the Metis guards and marksmen, who actually had close connections to her Delorme family, did not wish to follow Riel's directive to kill Scott. In another of Marie Rose's accounts of the same historical event, although commenting that Riel was a "remarkable man of his race," she concluded that, because of the cruel deed of Scott's murder, the hanging was "too good for him."[68]

There is some suggestion the Delorme men who supported Riel spent some time in Pincher Creek, but little documentation exists to support that. However, there is confirmation that many of Marie Rose's Delorme family followed the pattern of fur trade Metis families when they settled in Pincher Creek after the conflict of 1885, including her mother and stepfather, her sisters and brothers-in-law, Madeline and Ludger Gareau and Elise and George Ness,[69] and her brothers Urbain and Charlie. Yet Marie Rose makes no mention of even these family members living in Pincher Creek, instead focusing primarily on her English-speaking acquaintances. Given that her writings are often in the form of diaries, the omission of most family members is noticeable, particularly since she does mention other rebels by name. If she sought only to record "historical" characters, then, certainly, some of her family members meet that criterion. Riel's soldiers, Norbert and Joseph Delorme, Donald Ross, and Metis hostages John and Rose Pritchard were all historically significant at the time. One can only speculate on her omissions. Marie Rose may have been trying to protect family members, whom she feared incriminating, but almost certainly she feared for her own position in the community if she drew attention to the connections between her family and Louis Riel.

Marie Rose may have been inspired in her writing by her membership in the Southern Alberta Women's Pioneer Association, whose members had an interest in recording local history. For Marie Rose, who had a desire to have her manuscripts published, the tendency was to focus on the "great" people around her, primarily male subjects. Not many of the great men she wrote about were Indigenous. However, one was the legendary Chief Crowfoot. We know Marie Rose and Charlie followed the treaties for a period of time, so she was familiar with the treaty-making process. On one occasion, she described in detail the proceedings of Treaty 7,[70] when Chief Crowfoot addressed the treaty commission. Using an omniscient third-person narrator, her description began with the observation that First Nation people were "selfish" in their demands. Yet, shortly thereafter, Marie Rose concluded they were a "wonderful people. They never look for riches as long as they have something to eat and wear, they are satisfied."[71]

Marie Rose's retelling of a meeting between her father and Chief Crowfoot is one of the instances in which she inserts dialogue.[72] Reportedly, the legendary chief had told her father,

> I have heard many white men preach of their goodness and truth, but to the Indian, White Man's religion is love of money and fear of death. White man thinks his reading and writing has lifted him above the native of the prairie and made him clever. He learns from books, but the Indian learns from nature. Nature taught him how to doctor the sick...Nature also taught them to brew medicinal tea from the barks and roots...Since the white traders would see no doctors from the time they left Winnipeg, they were glad to learn what nature had already taught the native tribes. Besides the use of roots and herbs, we adopted the use of the buffalo bladder for a syringe, for medical uses.[73]

Even in her published account, Marie Rose repeated the irony noted by the chief, writing that he said, "I have heard many white men preach of their goodness and truth, but to the Indian, White Man's religion is love of money and fear of death."[74] This time, in her own words, Marie Rose echoed the words of the legendary chief, writing that the "old timers" "stood their hardships—with a smile."[75]

For the most part, though, Marie Rose's writing did not feature Indigenous people as the heroic characters. Rather, the heroes were more often Euro-North Americans such as her neighbour, Colonel Macleod. She told of his legendary meetings with the Blackfoot tribes, writing that Macleod (Stamiotokon) "had many dealings with the Blackfeet and had won their confidence and good will."[76] According to the dialogue she inserts into her narrative at this point, the chiefs who attended the treaty talks expressed the belief,

The advice given me and my people by the Queen Mother's officers has proved to be good. Bad white men and their evil fire-water were killing us so fast that very few, indeed, would have been left today, if the Red Coats (police) had not protected us. I wish them good! I trust our hearts will increase in goodness from this time on. I am satisfied! I will sign the Treaty.[77]

Marie Rose concluded with the observation, "And thus it was that the Red Men and their descendants became the wards of the British Government in Canada."[78] Whatever her source, in relaying this last sentence, Marie Rose displayed some political awareness, given the relationship between Indigenous people and Europeans had evolved by this time from that of trading partners and military allies to one of wardship.

However, Marie Rose's political awareness did not extend to, or perhaps she did not allow herself to display, a sophisticated analysis of the reasons why First Nation people had sought treaties in the first instance and why some of them were drawn into the fighting that began in Batoche in 1885. Although Marie Rose acknowledged on one occasion that she had regular contact with First Nation people, often offering them a meal at Jughandle Ranch, she made no mention of food shortages or increasingly repressive measures undertaken by government officials against First Nation people, measures that included withholding food rations, prohibitions against selling their own stock, and attempts to establish joint territory. Rather, Marie Rose wrote,

> For a long time, after the signing of the Treaties, the Red Man could not accustom himself to the White man's civilization. He fretted in the close confines of his house on the Reserve, longing to roam the plains once again and erect his cozy Teepee. It was not long before a restlessness broke out among the young men of the tribes, which later was fanned into open rebellion.[79]

Marie Rose also publicly revealed little appreciation for the historic role of Indigenous women in the fur trade. At times, she offered the same sort of assessments that many of the early traders had made regarding the role of Indigenous women within their society, regarding them as no more than beasts of burden.[80] There is little difference between fur traders' assessments and that of Marie Rose, who wrote,

> The squaws would have to do all the work while the bucks did the hunting and smoked their pipe. The squaws with a papoose on their back would have to put up the lodges, get the wood and water, cook the meals and make the dry meat.[81]

She continued, "After the buck killed his game, he would lie down and take his comfort. The squaw, the poor slave, did the work but never grumbled." Her conclusion was that "they respected their men and called them 'Nina' Big Man. There was never any love making, no courting among them."[82] This evaluation is really not all that different than her telling, on several occasions, of her own need to obey her husband. Yet it seemed important to Marie Rose that readers recognize a difference between her own marriage arrangement and those of First Nation people.

Although she may not have intended to reflect the diversity of Metis identity, Marie Rose inadvertently did that by inviting readers to entertain the idea that there were degrees of Metisness. It appears that way of life, rather than ancestry, was the methodology she used to determine that there were different classes of Metis. She identified some Indigenous people as "quarter breeds," others as "half breeds," and still others as "squaws," apparently depending on lifestyle or level of material wealth as a way to determine these distinctions. Metis activist Jim Brady, who worked to organize Alberta's Metis people for political action in the 1930s (and whom Marie Rose may have heard of), believed the two classes of Metis people that could be identified were the class of nomadic, destitute Metis, and that of the progressive, land-owning Metis. According to Brady, the nomadic Metis were the uneducated, who constituted the "half breed problem."[83] Marie Rose might have agreed with Brady, for it was these more nomadic Metis that she often identified as "Indian halfbreeds," who were of a lower social status.

Despite the fact that she accepted Metis scrip and clearly was connected to family and homeland, the portrait of Marie Rose featured in the June 1948 edition of *Canadian Cattlemen* pictured her in a matronly dress and a dainty hat upon her head,[84] not really dressed the way many in the older generation of Metis women continued to dress into the 1950s. These Metis women tended to wear long, dark dresses and grey shawls, and they often donned large crosses.[85] Marie Rose did not devote much attention to describing her own attire in her manuscripts, but she did write there was one aspect of her early apparel that she carried on into adulthood:

> We liked to decorate ourselves with fancy shells or other ornaments; perhaps that is why when a baby girl was born, they immediately pierced the lobes of her ears so she could when grown, wear ear rings. Today I never feel fully dressed unless my ear rings are in place.[86]

However, for the most part, Marie Rose dressed later in life as we might expect a Euro-North American author to dress at the time. A picture of Marie Rose in a Lethbridge newspaper in 1954, after she had become a recognized author in southern Alberta, featured her in a calico dress and beaded necklace.[87] Another photo featured her on the streets of Edmonton with her daughter in a European-inspired coat and fur hat.

While some have argued the Metis communicated their identity on "several levels: in the way they dressed, how they made their clothing, and the meanings this clothing conveyed to other people,"[88] Marie Rose could have had many inspirations to dress in a manner that was little different than Anglo-speaking, Euro-North American pioneer women, and to determine to write herself into history. The mail order catalogues that were available at the turn of the century may well have been an influence. Indeed, by the time her articles appeared in *Canadian Cattlemen*, the population of Alberta had grown well past the seventy-three thousand that was still recorded in 1901.[89]

However, this was over twenty years after Marie Rose first settled in the province, demonstrating that the net growth in population was a slow process. Perhaps it was the slow growth that led many of the newcomers in the Prairie West to see themselves as pioneers. Some argue there was a "cult-like worship of the pioneer," which inspired many to write their memoirs.[90] It could be that the proliferation of memoirs by those who might not rightly be considered genuine old-timers of the North West was one inspiration for Marie Rose to write her own life story. Marie Rose noted that the "oldtimers," which undoubtedly included the Metis pioneers, "blazed the trail for the new settler who has reaped the benefit. It is really sad that one forgets the life of the oldtimer."[91]

Even if Marie Rose did wish to record her personal history as an old-timer, it was not really possible to record her entire history because she was hesitant to fully and publicly embrace her Metis culture. Although Marie Rose had a reputation because of her

Marie Rose Delorme Smith, seen here sometime after her marriage to Charlie Smith. Photo undated. Shirley-Mae McCargar and Donald McCargar.

ability to produce Metis-inspired handiwork, it was not a reputation she promoted when writing her own life story. Rather, it was others who recognized her handiwork in their brief articles about her or in their interviews with her. For example, when he interviewed Marie Rose at the age of seventy-two, Ben Montgomery obviously felt her life was important enough to document, not only as a pioneer but as a Metis woman, for he still referred to her as Buckskin Mary.[92]

Writing from the perspective of a pioneer, Marie Rose concluded that, as a youngster, "our wants were few and simple; home industries supplied our need."[93] Life in the Prairie West as one of the first homesteaders necessitated that wants would have to be simple, and home industries must be made to supply basic needs. Even if one had great wealth, the availability of supplies necessitated a reliance on home industry. Yet readers really had little to suggest that Marie Rose's home industries were in any way different from those relied upon by the new settlers to the Prairie West, and that those home industries were actually inspired by her Metis culture.

Although she seemed hesitant to identify herself as Metis and any of her home industries as linked to Metis culture, Marie Rose still wished to record intimate details of Indigenous culture, most often from the third-person perspective. Her descriptions of cultural practices such as the Sun Dance and Ghost Dance, and the rituals to honour a dead chief, were at times elaborate. One example includes her detailed description of sweat lodges:

> There were some great medicine men and women among them. They built a round sweat house, making a hole in the middle. The frame was made of willow sticks and covered with buffalo hides so no steam could escape...They heated big rocks in the fire until red then rolled them into the house in this hole. They then poured cold water over these red hot rocks...They crawled in and you could hear them making all kinds of noise, groaning and singing. After they came out they would go to the lake or stream and jump in. It did not seem to hurt them, in fact it was healthy.[94]

There are glimpses of Marie Rose's own travel and trading activities, in which she would have obtained her traditional remedies and home supplies, and where she likely witnessed the customs she described in various parts of her manuscripts. For example, there is one occasion when she began to tell readers about a trip her friend Kootenai Brown's second wife, Ni-ti-mous, took, in which she travelled as far as Flathead country. In the midst of relating the story of Ni-ti-mous's travels, the narration reverted to first person, and Marie

Rose wrote, "We would be gone for three or four weeks. Sometimes a snow storm would catch us and then we would see hard times, no grass for the horses." She continued,

> On one of these trips we went right through to the Flathead country.
> We stayed with Flathead Indians for a week. They gave me some
> skins all ready tanned and a horse for paying them a visit. This is
> an Indian Custom.[95]

This excerpt provides some understanding of how she accessed her materials for traditional works when she lived in Pincher Creek, but it also demonstrates she was always hesitant to take full ownership of her close ties to Indigenous people.

Although Marie Rose's articles were published when she was living in Edmonton, she did not write in either her published or unpublished accounts about carrying on later in life with some aspects of Metis culture. Only the oral testimony of family members again confirms that Marie Rose carried on with activities such as making pemmican, which she did until the 1950s.[96] No doubt pemmican remained an item of subsistence and trade for Marie Rose when she assumed a sedentary ranching lifestyle. Yet it would not have been necessary for the same reasons by the time she was living in Edmonton. Rather, making pemmican would have been a way to remain connected to her Metis culture.

When Marie Rose made pemmican in Edmonton, the process likely involved the whole family and some sharing of the cultural significance of the Metis staple.[97] Marie Rose also did not write of another Metis tradition, that of jigging, but there is ample evidence she always enjoyed music.[98] Family members proudly share a photo of Marie Rose dancing at a very advanced age, and she could still recall the lyrics of the Metis folk song "Red River Halfbreed" until a few months before her death at the age of ninety-nine.

While she did not write about some of the aspects of her Metis culture she continued to enjoy, Marie Rose never disguised her devotion to her Roman Catholic faith and its leaders. For example, she may have been aware that Lacombe had urged the government to impose restrictions on some Indigenous cultural activities.[99] Yet Marie Rose also shared with her readers Father Lacombe's belief that

> white people spoiled the Indians. Civilization did not agree with them. They were happy roaming the plains...It was the worst thing that ever happened to this country when that treaty came in force in 1876.[100]

It appears from this excerpt that Lacombe may have openly shared his own ambivalence as to the coming of settlers. Although instrumental in ensuring successful treaty negotiations, it seems from Lacombe's own words that he sensed the great loss that treaties really represented for Indigenous people. He reportedly wrote,

> I would look long in silence at that road coming on—like a band of wild geese in the sky—cutting its way through the prairies; opening up the great country we thought would be ours for years. Like a vision I could see it driving my poor Indians before it, and spreading out behind it the farms, the towns and cities you see to-day.[101]

Marie Rose seemed at times to agree with Father Lacombe's assessment, at least in the portions of her manuscript that were never published. In a rare instance of assertiveness against what soon became the majority in the West, Marie Rose wrote,

> When the white people came in, the Indian thought the white people came and take the plains from them, which they did in time, they took the free life and land...So when they thought the white people came to rob them of their country in a way they were right.[102]

Despite glimpses that Marie Rose felt some regret for the loss of Indigenous freedom and culture, she rarely placed herself in the Indigenous world in her writing. However, there was one instance when she did so in a published article: "We were just as proud to 'show off' our bead work on the baby bag as you are to display your knitting or embroidery."[103] Just a few paragraphs later, she again placed herself in the category of Euro-North American, when she asked readers to reminisce with her: "Do you remember our old 'quilting bees'? We must have adopted the idea from the elderly squaws, who held 'Teepee Bees.'"[104]

At times, Marie Rose's published articles reflect the same stream of consciousness evident throughout her personal, unedited manuscripts. For example, she began an excerpt by discussing her home life on Jughandle Ranch, and then very soon followed with a discussion of life on the trail, first with her husband, then earlier still with her stepfather, shortly after her time at the convent:

> To all, friends or foes, neighbors or strangers, there was a welcome here. I was often tired or angry at the extra work involved, yet no one ever left the place hungry, whether he be White man or Indian... [we would] go back to our winter quarters, on Tail Creek, when Trader Smith was hunting for the camp of freighter Gervais, who was traveling with two daughters just out from Convent.[105]

This excerpt would no doubt be somewhat confusing to her readers and really did not expand the knowledge of Metis life on the trail. For the majority of the articles, Marie Rose was clearly writing for an audience of cattlemen. As such, her story in *Canadian Cattlemen* culminated with the rancher's wife relating "bits of [her] home life," and the experiences of what became the stereotypical prairie scene—the roundup. She was apparently enthralled with the dexterity of the ranchers and cowboys. Settlers were not often spoken of in admirable terms. Rather, it is the old-timers (really, the

Metis pioneers), those who endured the hardships in order to make the country habitable, who are the real heroes to Marie Rose:

There will be a day when the oldtimers will be forgotten altogether. They are dying fast, one by one crossing the great divide. The new settlers do not realize what the oldtimer had to endure to make this country liveable for them.[106]

Marie Rose does not disguise the fact that even her aristocratic and well-travelled friends, such as Lionel Brooke and Kootenai Brown, were more nomadic than they were settlers.

Perhaps in large part because of her published articles, and also because she was able to build an extensive network, it appears Marie Rose's contemporaries accepted her as a rightful member of their new society. Her obituary garnered as much print space as did Charlie's in the local newspaper, and her death was also mentioned in the newspapers of several surrounding communities. The amount of space devoted to her obituary was quite extraordinary for an Indigenous woman, even considering that she died in 1960, a time when there was increasing awareness of Indigenous history and culture. In the end, then, Marie Rose appears to have done an admirable job of writing herself into the early local history of the Prairie West.

Indicating her interest in both fiction and life writing, Marie Rose wrote, "How can heaven be dull if its angelic inhabitants have access to the past."[107] Yet writing about her past did not really afford Marie Rose the luxury of exploring the political climate of her times and the increasing racial and class boundaries. It was only in her brief fictional narratives that Marie Rose could question the actions of the government and incoming settlers, whose arrival displaced Indigenous people. This approach is really not so unlike writers who publish today. Some theorists argue fictional litera-ture allows one to "vividly imagine forms of moral and immoral behavior,"[108] and to gently and less didactically inspire moral decision making from the audience.

Marie Rose produced two brief unpublished texts that are more easily identifiable as fiction. One is titled, "The Twenty Warnings," and the other, "Does God Know His Business?" The first indicator that these particular works were intended as fiction is that the manuscripts, which were more likely intended for publication, were typed and arranged in chapters, while the nonfiction were either handwritten or not arranged in any particular order. The other indicator is that Marie Rose's fiction features the main elements of this literary genre: plot, action, character development, conflict, and resolution.

The title, "The Twenty Warnings," given to her account of the fighting beween the Metis and the Canadian government in 1885, was likely chosen because Marie Rose writes about a number of appeals made prior to the fighting: "In 1878 the Metis sent a carefully worded petition to Ottawa, signed also by English-speaking settlers." She continued that the bishop had tried to intercede, as had the "Mounted Police" and the "lieutenant governor," all to no avail, as "Ottawa remote and busy, maintained unbroken silence."[109]

In some ways, this particular story could be termed "philosophical fiction,"[110] in the sense that Marie Rose seeks to inspire her readers to question the motives of church and government officials. It is also evident that, unlike the majority of her other writing, Marie Rose was trying to inject symbolism into this short story, as one would do in literary fiction:

> "Riel is back"...This message...sent a ripple of execration around the land...and fell like a cold rain on the ripening harvest of security. Only where the spruce forests of the North Saskatchewan devoured the sunlight...the fruit of a decade's toil and peril hung visible, and peace lay in as Indian summer haze over the region where life had so lately been a universal brawl...Riel was back.[111]

A character named Elliot then comments, "I have fifteen dollars that says it means fighting before spring." Marie Rose goes on to describe her character Riel: "a man of no marked significance in aspect barely five feet six inches in height—with a pale flabby face, close set dark gray eyes, a long neck, and a soft voice."[112] Symbolism abounds as Marie Rose concludes, "Indians...might indeed have been tempted to try fishing for their rights in a lake of blood."[113]

As a way to have her reader understand the setting for the conflict, Marie Rose wrote that, when Central Canadian government surveyors came to stake claims on previously occupied Metis land, the Metis protested this as a "deprivation of their rights, in vain they protested that the ties of their little farms were dear to them. Claim-jumpers took advantage of the turmoil." As she told the potential readers of her fiction, "It all seems incomprehensible and unimportant now, but to the few half starving Metis then it was a matter of life."[114] In this instance, Marie Rose displayed an understanding of the realities for some classes of Metis as more English-speaking settlers arrived in the West. Marie Rose even identified the hypocrisy of officials, writing,

> If a half-breed purloined a pair of stockings from the Hudson's Bay store he was punished quickly enough; but if some body trespassed on his land and cut his timber, he was informed that there was no redress, that he had no property right in the soil or trees.[115]

It is helpful to compare Marie Rose's fictional writing about the conflicts with her more factual texts, which may have been perceived by her as more acceptable to her contemporary audience. While her fiction revealed an appreciation for Metis concerns, her factual accounts ignored the hardships many Metis faced as more and more settlers arrived from Central Canada and established farms on what had long been considered Metis-occupied lands. Marie Rose wrote,

In the previous year the half-breeds began a series of meetings,
discussing their rights and acknowledging their fear of White Man's
law. When George (Ness) heard of these gatherings, he attended
them and said, "Brothers, you can't buck the White Man's govern-
ment, it is of no use to try. They are the Great White Mother's
servants; you are her children. Let us send a message to the Great
Teepee."[116]

In this excerpt from her unpublished manuscript, as she did in
the published version, Marie Rose concluded with the statement,
"The rest of the story is history,"[117] suggesting, at least in her quasi-
historical accounts, that there was no need to discuss the matter
with more depth. Rather, relying upon the oral testimony of her
brother-in-law, George Ness, Marie Rose judged the Metis foolhardy,
writing,

The famous Gabriel Dumont and a few others said that they would
stir up something and that would make the government notice
them. So at a meeting they all agreed to go across to Montana and
get Louis Riel. Poor simple half breeds, they had great faith in Riel,
he being pretty well educated.[118]

In contrast to this excerpt, Marie Rose's "The Twenty Warnings"
demonstrates the author to be astute and politically aware. As the
author of fiction, Marie Rose asked the questions,

What was the reason for such deafness [?] Had [sic] the legisla-
tors forgotten 1870—was Prince Albert so far away as to diminish all
meanings to a whisper or had the public interest ceased to come or
did they suppose that because the Police had handled all previous
situations, they could handle this [?][119]

Marie Rose's conclusion to the questions she raises about the
folly of war is worth quoting in its entirety, for the observation

reveals an intelligent, perceptive, and philosophical person. In addition, it suggests she continued to identify, at least privately, with her Metis community:

> *That fateful year had a quality of turning all it touched to misapprehension and farce. The very credit for success was distorted to historical inaccuracy. The work of the police was minimized to nonexistence...Official sagacity (meant that) Middleton was voted twenty thousand dollars...Riel was hanged after a famous trial at the Police barracks in Regina, and he died bravely, refusing to resort to the subterfuge of insanity...When the bill was presented, the Canadian people discovered that the neglect of 1884 had cost the lives of thirty nine brave and loyal men, wounds to one hundred and twenty and a hundred thousand dollars a piece to kill each rebel who had so bravely fought. But the men whose criminal incapacity had brought on the trouble escaped any punishment whatever— perhaps the greatest folly of all.*[120]

Although she did not name the rebels in this narrative, and contemporaries may or may not have made the connection, readers (if there were any) might have guessed from the empathy shown that some of the rebels included Marie Rose's fur trade family.

Immediately following the excerpt quoted above, Marie Rose provided a version of an 1884 letter, supposedly written by Father André to Riel. In this letter, the priest urged Riel to return from Montana. In reality, some believe Father André, the parish priest at Prince Albert, was reportedly "one of the few who had regarded Riel's return with misgivings and who was not impressed by Louis's demonstration of piety and religious devotion."[121] It seems André actually wrote to Riel, asking him *not* to go to Prince Albert.[122]

Nonetheless, in her fictional account, identifying some hypocrisy on the part of the priest, Marie Rose noted the irony of Father André's request that Riel return to the North West, when André "was later to watch him [Riel] being hanged." She continued that for the "school teacher living in a crowd of snakes," receiving a letter from "such a pressing delegation" would represent the "earnest desire of Providence."[123]

When Marie Rose moved into the discussion of the fighting, she provided details of battles between General Crozier's men and the Metis in 1885. She even included descriptions of Riel's interactions with his Exovedate Council. These excerpts are provided, complete with dialogue, and claim that, at one point, Riel shrieked, "'It is blood, blood we want blood...It is a war of extermination,' whereupon the Exovede rose abruptly mentioned a committee meeting and left the room."[124]

Marie Rose lived in a world touched by the life and work of literary tricksters, such as Pauline Johnson,[125] and *literal* tricksters such as Long Lance, and she may have tried to emulate them in her writing. Since Johnson published her work before Marie Rose, it is helpful to have some understanding of the impact of some of that work, and the fact that Johnson may have been a role model for Indigenous women. Johnson, also known as Tekahionwake,[126] was born in 1861, the same year as Marie Rose and Isabella, near present-day Brantford, Ontario, and was the daughter of a Mohawk chief and an English Quaker mother.[127] Johnson may have displayed a sense of "indigeneity" when she performed with an assembly of props not specific to any particular tribal tradition, as some have argued. However, some view her as a "trickster" who had an ability to "conjure up, sometimes simultaneously, a host of cultural images," thus demonstrating how "individual identity is lived as a matrix of subject-positions," who presents as a "shape-shifting humorist with a sharp sense of irony."[128]

While she may have been manipulating her audience through reverse appropriation, Johnson offered direct repudiation of negative stereotyping in some of her work. For example, her 1882 essay "A Strong Race Opinion on the Indian Girl in Modern Fiction," challenged authors to create characters who showed respect for the diversity of Indigenous communities.[129] The woman of Johnson's prose and poetry was very clearly not the "squaw" of others' stories. Certainly, Johnson's heroines were not likely to be the Indigenous women of Marie Rose's texts, often times referred to as "squaw." However, both Johnson and Marie Rose could be seen as literary tricksters who moved in and out of their Indigenous pasts.

Winnifred Eaton, a friend of Isabella Lougheed's, was a woman of "mixed ancestry" who wrote fiction and was successfully published during this period.[130] However, Eaton published under the pseudonym, Onoto Watanna, a name intended to have readers believe the author was Japanese. While she created heroines who were Japanese, Eaton was, in fact, born in Montreal to Chinese and English parents, a member of a "large, impoverished family." After marrying in New York in 1917, she and her husband moved to the Cochrane area to ranch.[131] Eaton's writing was ignored by critics for many years, likely because they felt disdain for what they perceived as her deception, and the "rather disturbing fact...that Winnifred Eaton was not merely capitalizing on the western stereotypes of Asia and Asian women, she was instrumental in creating them."[132] Yet Eaton was the first and most prolific author of Asian descent to publish novels in the United States.

More recently, critics have characterized Eaton's stereotypical representations of Asians and the subsuming of her own ancestry as acts of subversion, depicting her as a trickster figure who actually undermined racist and patriarchal ideologies, even though it seemed she adopted those ideologies. It is plausible that Eaton used the perceived faults of "chicanery, cheating, and lying...clever deviousness and deception" in order to achieve "victory or a balance of the scales."[133] Perhaps she relied on Japanese heroines because, prior to Japan's involvement in the First World War,[134] the Japanese were not generally subjected to the same level of extreme racial prejudice that the Chinese were. In reality, Eaton, had she portrayed heroines that were part Chinese, would likely never have been published during her lifetime.

It is from a perspective based on "present-day cultural or political needs"[135] that many often discount the difficulties women of mixed ethnicity, like Eaton and Johnson, and like Marie Rose, faced as they negotiated their identity and sought to have their voices heard in the increasingly Anglo-dominated society that emerged after the fur trade gave way to agriculture and industrialism. While it may appear to current-day scholars that Johnson, Eaton, and even Marie Rose *created* harmful stereotypes, had it not been for women such as Johnson and Eaton, the only literary voices heard at all during the later 1890s and early 1900s might have been those who relied totally on uncomplimentary stereotypes, such as that of poet Duncan Campbell Scott. As noted earlier, authors can often explore injustices through fiction, and gently and less didactically inspire moral decision making from the audience.

The title Marie Rose chose for her second work of fiction, "Does God Know His Business?" suggests that the character (and likely the author) question the circumstances of life and God's plan. In this regard, "Does God Know His Business?" could also be viewed from the perspective of philosophical fiction in that Marie Rose exposes the emotional struggles born of great loss. It appears it was only in this short fiction that Marie Rose felt some freedom to explore her immense grief. This story also demonstrates some respect for the oral tradition of her Indigenous ancestors, since, for Georgina, the best hours were those spent at night around the fire, when her mother would tell stories.[136] Indeed, although Georgina never married and seems happy enough "enjoying life to the fullest," the fact is that "her chances of ever having grandchildren to whom she could relate her escapades and romances are becoming slimmer every day."[137]

It appears the biggest regret in Georgina's life is that she has no family with whom she can share her stories, something Marie Rose was blessed with. Despite having no family, in the end, Georgina comes to demonstrate a strong and independent character, after much heartache. It is perhaps in Georgina's independence and Marie Rose's own eventual independence, both achieved after great loss, that the similarities are most evident. Like Marie Rose, Georgina has a hard life, in that she loses all of her family members. However, Marie Rose's heroine apparently

> knows that by being left to her own resources so young, she has developed more stamina, and self-reliance than she ever would have done, had she always had her family to shoulder her responsibilities and to shelter her from the hard knocks that we are all bound to receive from this world of ours.[138]

The reader can hardly miss the similarities to Marie Rose's own life. Although she continued to appreciate the presence of her mother for the first part of her married life, Marie Rose felt betrayed by her mother for disregarding her objections to her marriage. Thus, at such a young age, Marie Rose likely felt herself to be quite alone, much the same way Georgina felt.

Perhaps the grief in Georgina's life served as a foil for Marie Rose's extreme grief at the loss of so many of her children. After the death of her mother and only brother, Georgina asks the question, "Does God know his business?" and then offers the answer, "It is rather a difficult feat to bow to God's will when He alone has taken that which one values most."[139] This exchange leaves little doubt that Marie Rose, along with Georgina, questioned God's plan, as she lost child after child. In the end, though, Georgina eventually becomes a nurse and is so busy she has no time to think of her troubles and her losses, having little time for "fretting."[140] Georgina's busy life mirrors that of Marie Rose, in which she assumed the roles of mother, homesteader, ranch manager, cottage industry craftsperson, medicine woman, midwife, and hostess, a busy life that allowed little time for fretting and for processing grief.

Near the end of her life Georgina "developed more stamina, and self-reliance, [than she would have] had she always had her family to shoulder her responsibilities."[141] Marie Rose wrote her fictional pieces later in her life, when perhaps she, like Georgina, had developed more stamina and self-reliance and felt the freedom to write about her own experiences. In her old age, Marie Rose, seemed to feel some sense of peace, as noted by Ben Montgomery, who transcribed some of her history when she was seventy-two years old. As Montgomery wrote, after having passed some time in "Hell Creek," Marie Rose later took up "residence in an earthly paradise."[142] Georgina also found a sense of peace, for as Marie Rose wrote of her heroine,

> *Many times she would find herself comparing her own happy home life with the lives of the people with whom she came in contact, who seemed to have so much more financially than she had had, but who could not boast of being happier or even as happy as she had been in the all too short years that she had spent with her family and their lack of luxuries.*[143]

In the end, Marie Rose, like Georgina, felt a sense of accomplishment. While there is some suggestion in the archival material that she desired to have a manuscript published, Marie Rose surely recognized that having a series of articles published as a Metis woman writing during the 1930s was a significant achievement. She would also have appreciated, though, that her success at publishing in a ranch periodical came primarily from her success in portraying herself as an English-speaking wife of a Euro-North American rancher—a homesteading pioneer.

Near the end of her life, when she reflected on her history, Marie Rose commented that life is the "greatest of all riddles."[144] With regard to her married life, she observed that whether it was worth it depended "altogether upon how much love is between each other and how gallantly we can play the game."[145] The "riddle" of life assumed a role in her writing, as though Marie Rose felt opposition to the cards life dealt was fruitless—one was best to learn to "play along." On faith, Marie Rose related the metaphor of games again: "After all what do you get after death, a box and a good long rest... Life is the greatest of riddles because everyone of us is compelled to give it up."[146] Marie Rose's words demonstrate that, much like her fictional character Georgina, she knew how to "play the game."

Perhaps her references to the riddles of life offer some support for the argument that Marie Rose assumed a trickster role in her private writing, in that she played along with the new proscriptions of her society, intent on erecting racial boundaries, as a way to perhaps expose those proscriptions in the fiction that she was likely aware would remain private, at least until after her death.

Examining some of Marie Rose's documents, literary critic Helen Buss believed the words of pioneer women, those

> so-called naïve accounts, lacking polish and linguistic complexity, can become more interesting than traditional literary texts. They seem to invite the reader to construct the story herself rather than live inside an already constructed world.[147]

Marie Rose's manuscripts, although perhaps written in a style that could be classified as "naive" in their literary presentation, are often quite complex and thought-provoking. These qualities appear in the brief fictional accounts she left behind, particularly her account about the Metis wars, "The Twenty Warnings." Only in this short, fictionalized, and unpublished version of the fighting, in which she inserted dialogue, did Marie Rose offer a supportive view of the Metis concerns of 1885 over land occupancy, and an equally unsupportive view of government officials and Roman Catholic authorities.

In the end, Marie Rose's society paid her a measure of honour by recognizing her as an important transitional figure, an author, and a "pioneer," who earned the name Buckskin Mary. Her family network also demonstrated immense respect for Marie Rose in several ways, including by having her live with family members until her death. Members also ensured her manuscripts would be forever preserved in a public archive. Yet another measure of respect is that family members remain committed to sharing her story.

For obvious reasons, given the political climate in which she wrote, Marie Rose did not describe sharing the traditional Metis skills she had learned from her mother with her own children and grandchildren. Marie Rose likely felt fenced in by this restriction, as well as by the physical fences that were appearing and by the hardening social boundaries that were becoming more evident. In her writing, for the most part, Marie Rose demonstrated instrumental ethnicity, only really acknowledging her Metis culture from a third-person perspective.

However, her descendants confirm that she did share some of her traditional Metis skills and culture. In an original interview with her granddaughter, Shirley-Mae McCargar, there was little to suggest that Shirley-Mae embraced her own Indigenous ancestry. However, without much prompting, Shirley-Mae indicated she had some exposure to the Metis culture of her grandmother, and she was eager to share photographs and stories. A photograph that surfaced later confirmed Shirley-Mae had dressed at least one of her children, her son Donald, in the traditional Metis garments made by her grandmother. Yet Shirley-Mae also indicated that she had warned Donald of the potential dangers of revealing his Metis identity. As an adult, he chose to embrace his Metis ethnicity, while Shirley-Mae concluded, for her part, that she was of Dutch descent. That said, she was sufficiently aware of the importance of Marie Rose's history and Metis culture to the building of the Prairie West that she later directed the interviewer to Donald, so that he could continue sharing her family's stories..

It was only in a later interview with Donald McCargar, Shirley-Mae's son and Marie Rose's great-grandson, that the generational transmission of a healthy and vibrant Metis identity and culture was evident. Donald spoke with pride about his long involvement in the legal struggle to gain hunting rights for Metis people that would equal those of First Nation people. Donald cherishes vivid memories of tanning hides on the balcony of his childhood Edmonton home with his grandmother, Eva Forsland, Marie Rose's daughter. He notes Eva was quite adept at making traditional Metis garments, most of which were sold to private collections years ago. In the summer of 2011, when Donald campaigned to become the president of the Métis Nation of Alberta, his website featured the photo of him as a young child wearing traditional beaded Metis clothing, with a notation that the clothing was made by his great-grandmother.[148]

There are shades of other Metis leaders in Marie Rose's great-grandson Donald. Clearly an astute, educated, and successful businessman in the new economy of the Prairie West, and having spent some time as a missionary, Donald proudly speaks of raising his five children on wild game. Next to the elaborate house he lives in, Donald's plans are for a cabin in the bush as a reminder for his children of his family's links to the fur trade. If Donald McCargar represents any sort of standard by which to measure the transmission of Metis culture by Marie Rose to her descendants, then the conclusion would have to be that she did an admirable job, as privately as she felt that must be. Indeed, perhaps in her old age, Marie Rose felt more freedom about her Metis ethnicity.

This does not negate the reality that, for a large part of her adult life, Marie Rose did not feel free to fully and publicly embrace her Metis ethnicity. She perceived the need to build strategic new links that would enhance her persona and her family's standing in their community of southern Alberta. It was perhaps this lack of freedom that induced Marie Rose to write her own story as a pioneer who still longed for the days of the open prairie, when cattle (like buffalo) could be seen roaming freely, unfettered by fences.

8

Many Voices—One People

CANADA'S CONSTITUTION ACT, although it now considers the
Metis as Indigenous (Aboriginal) people, has yet to determine who
can, from the government's perspective, rightfully identify as Metis.
Indeed, this is not a definition that can be determined by the
Canadian government. Yet nor have the Metis people and their organizations agreed on this point, or even reached agreement about
the proper spelling of "Metis" (Métis; metis). It is likely that the
historical community has contributed to, and perhaps even created,
some of the ambivalence surrounding the term "Metis." Beginning
in the 1970s, when more scholars turned their attention to the Metis,
there was a focus on demonstrating the divisions in the geographic
area of Red River. Since the 1970s, whether examining religion,
class, company structures, or geographic territories, historians have
argued either for or against the reasons behind those divisions.

These debates certainly drew attention to the history of the
Metis, which had largely been ignored until the 1970s. However,
there is also the possibility that the focus on conflict and disunity
among the Metis has actually presented challenges for them as

they struggle for rights that would equal those of other Indigenous people.[1] Certainly, the tendency to focus on differences in the Metis community might lead some to argue that it is not logical to compare Isabella and Marie Rose, given the divergent paths their lives followed for most of their adult lives. As scholar Brenda Macdougall notes, because Metis ancestry is drawn from both Indigenous and European heritages, "their stories are not told in one voice or by one group. Rather the stories are layered."[2] Although the stories are clearly not told in one voice and are layered, this book has demonstrated that there were many parallels in Marie Rose's and Isabella's lives and as many similarities, both in how they adapted to their changing worlds and in how they managed their identities as the fur trade drew to a close. Thus, much can be learned by conducting close case and comparative studies about the survival strategies of other Metis people as the fur trade transitioned.

Indeed, in an interesting discussion about the challenges for scholars of defining one Metis culture and identity, Nicole St-Onge and Carolyn Podruchny note that, despite difficulties, it is important that scholars continue their work. In part, this importance rests on the fact that Canada's Constitution Act of 1982 recognized Metis people and confirmed their "aboriginal" rights. These scholars argue the claims processes that have forced the Metis to define territories risk dominating the definition of a Metis Nation and do not reflect the reality of the Metis people in the eighteenth and nineteenth centuries, the time when Marie Rose and Isabella, and their families before them, were internalizing their own identities. They argue that focusing on territorial claims distorts the reality that, for many "Metis," their identity and culture were more rooted in "extended kin lineages, reciprocal ties, and access and use of common resources" than in "abstract identities with central authority and clear territorial boundaries."[3]

Some also argue that kinship has not received the attention it needs when studying the history of the Indigenous people of North

America. Indeed, kin connections were a very important component of Metis life and identity, where traders were "born into a fluid
and mobile fur trade world" in which small hunting camps and
trading posts were connected to vast geographic and global systems
of trade.[4] At a time when Metis people were often defined by their
link to the fur trade, it was this link and the kinship connections
on both the maternal and paternal sides of the two Metis women,
Isabella and Marie Rose, that established them and their Euro-
North American husbands as community members of important
social standing in southern Alberta after the fur trade transitioned.
Even more importantly, Marie Rose and Isabella devoted a good
deal of effort to extending their fur trade kinship connections by
developing fictive kin networks that would serve to solidify their
own status in this transitional period.

This book confirms that both Isabella and Marie Rose were
publicly silent about their Metis identities. Yet some of Marie Rose's
and Isabella's descendants have openly acknowledged their Metis
ancestry. This fact certainly suggests that a pride in that history
and culture may have persisted privately for both women and their
web of kinship networks. That Isabella and Marie Rose did not
publicly embrace their ethnicity, as there was certainly no clear
evidence of Metis sashes, fiddle music, a Metis flag, or the Michif
language, does not mean they privately denied that Metis ethnicity.
Indeed, this study of their lives suggests that any ambivalence was
not born of a lack of a sense of self as Metis women but rather of a
need to accommodate the increasing racism in their society.

Because they were apparently publicly silent about their Metis
identity—we might ask of both Marie Rose and Isabella—what made
them Metis? In its most basic sense, both women had mothers,
fathers, and grandparents who were ethnically Metis. However,
categorizing Isabella and Marie Rose as Metis simply because they
had ancestors who were Indigenous and ancestors who were Euro-
North American would be to priviliege racial categorization above
cultural categorization and, ultimately, to continue the historical

fallacy of understanding the Metis as a people "in between." As Brenda Macdougall argues, implying that "mixed blood, mixed ancestry...is all that is required to be Metis" negates the authenticity of the Aboriginality of the Metis, potentially reducing them to an "in-between, incomplete, 'not-quite-people.'"[5]

Indeed, the Metis identity, history, and culture of Isabella and Marie Rose moved beyond the fact that they were ethnically Metis. Both had a history and a connection to the fur trade. As young girls, both lived the collective experiences of their fur trade families,[6] Marie Rose in Red River and on the western plains, and Isabella at the northern fur trade posts and in the care of her Metis paternal grandparents. The close presence of their Metis mothers was an important component of the identity formation for both Marie Rose and Isabella. Marie Rose recalled the many times she spent at the side of her Metis mother, listening to the oral history of her people and learning the culture. While Isabella said little that was documented about the importance of her Metis mother, it was her mother who knew the customs of the northern Metis and who was the primary caregiver during Isabella's formative years when Isabella's father tended to his duties as chief factor of the vast Mackenzie district.

As adult women, both Isabella and Marie Rose achieved a good measure of success in the Euro-North American world in large part by continuing to rely, as Metis women married to Euro-North Americans, on their fur trade families. At a time when locale was not as important as kin to the Metis identity, both Marie Rose and Isabella established their marital homes near their fur trade kin group in southern Alberta. At various times, Marie Rose's parents and many of her siblings lived in the Pincher Creek area near Marie Rose's Jughandle Ranch, and they no doubt contributed to her ability to operate a ranch, raise seventeen children, maintain a small cottage industry, and publish some articles, all while her husband maintained a semi-nomadic lifestyle. As a girl of marrying age, Isabella was sent to live with her fur trade chief factor uncle in the sparsely settled hamlet of Calgary, at a time when her uncle was an HBC man who nonetheless still recognized that his right as a Metis man entitled him to receive government-issued Metis scrip. Isabella always relied on the Hardisty kin group to expand her own network, and to ensure the success of her husband. Due to her Metis family's contributions, Isabella was able to establish herself as an important member of her new community, manage a stately home, and raise five children, all while her husband was often away.

The fur trade Metis were always closely tied to mercantile capitalism, which remained the case for both Marie Rose and Isabella. As a chief factor for the Hudson's Bay Company, Isabella's father, and then her uncle, with whom she lived in Calgary, were both adept at realizing profits for the company and for themselves. When the fur trade transitioned, the Hardisty family incorporated the outsider, James Lougheed, whose skills as a lawyer were useful in the new economy that became reliant on paper transactions. In Marie Rose's case, her father was a fur trader of some worth with an extensive trade network, as was the Delorme family that continued to support Marie Rose's mother after the death of her husband. There is some indication her mother continued as an independent trader, no doubt within the context of the Delorme family trading network, until she married another Metis man. When the marriage trade was effected that saw Marie Rose marry the robe and whiskey trader Charlie Smith, her Metis kin continued to traverse the plains with the couple, trading and following the treaties, eventually settling in southern Alberta along with them. It is clear the fur trade Delormes had incorporated the outsider Charlie Smith into their kinship web, as had the fur trade Hardistys incorporated the outsider James Lougheed into theirs.

There are documented cases, such as that of Johnny Grant, in which the Metis settled in areas in which they had never lived because they knew they would find a web of kinship. These connections or "webs as mental spaces and physical realities could be resilient and robust."[7] No doubt these connections were crucial for both Marie Rose and Isabella, who successfully transitioned because those webs of kinship, both real and fictive, supported them in their new homes in southern Alberta. Not unlike the fur trade business that needed the Metis for their skills as entrepreneurs, labourers, and middlemen, James Lougheed and Charlie Smith needed the skills and connections of their Metis wives and their kin connections to thrive in the transitional period after the fur trade. At the same time, the Metis families of Isabella and Marie Rose needed the newcomers, who had skills—James as a lawyer and Charlie as a rancher and horse breeder—that were necessary in the new economy. Also, not unlike the Metis at the height of the fur trade, identity based on expansive kinship networks allowed Marie Rose and Isabella to adapt and prosper in situations that were at times hostile, to recover from financial and personal setbacks, and to demonstrate a resilience that reflected that of their Metis fur trade families.

Both Charlie Smith and James Lougheed clearly recognized the value of being incorporated into the family networks of their Metis wives. Charlie's granddaughter acknowledged that Charlie had determined upon his first encounter with the Delorme winter camp that he should work out an arrangement to forge a partnership through marriage. In his own words, James Lougheed acknowledged that, in marrying Isabella, he had himself become a "company man." In the end, this book has confirmed, as have others, that being Metis, "whether one formally labelled oneself as such or not—was an intrinsically adaptive social construct" that "ebbed and flowed given specific conditions in specific moments and places."[8]

This book has also shown that, as Isabella and Marie Rose negotiated a changing society, the adaptive social construct common to the Metis also changed. Their higher status during the fur trade had enabled them to enjoy Euro-North American educations. Marie Rose's grandfather, known as le chef des prairies, had been a captain of a Metis hunting brigade, while Isabella's grandfather and father were chief factors in the HBC, assuring both a higher status. It is true that, between 1885 and 1925, a number of Alberta's bourgeoisie very likely had ties to the fur trade, and more specifically to the HBC. Thus, the class system that was becoming more apparent during the latter part of the fur trade, in which those affiliated with the HBC achieved more influential positions and thus more wealth, would persist.

However, despite the higher status that both had enjoyed during the fur trade, and which was more likely to continue for Isabella due to her HBC connection, both Isabella's and Marie Rose's social status was threatened as adult women. Most basically, both were Metis at a time when many Metis were relegated to lower-status lifestyles. More specifically, for Marie Rose, there was a time when the men in her Delorme family network aligned themselves with Louis Riel, and thus they needed to be silenced in her manuscripts when Riel's armies were defeated. For Isabella, beyond her Metis ethnicity, which some argue affected her husband's political aspirations, her social standing was threatened when the vast estate she and James had been able to amass, based on business partnerships with the Hardisty family, was devastated and Isabella was left virtually penniless. Yet the semblance of higher status remained for both Isabella and Marie Rose all of their lives, due in large part to the social capital both continued to contribute to their respective communities, as well as their ability to create new personae.

While early historians of Metis identity argued class distinctions played a role in that process, some suggest that, in studying Indigenous history, it is more appropriate to understand identity formation from the perspective of kinship and gender than it is to focus on class and race.[9] While this book has only briefly examined the histories of the male members of Isabella's and Marie Rose's fur trade families, it is clear Isabella and Marie Rose were able to rely on their Metis kin, identity, culture, and gender in order to transition more successfully than their male siblings.

In terms of using gender to discuss Metis identity, Brenda Macdougall argues that Metis people defined their relationship to each other based on their maternal *and* paternal ancestors, and that the act of applying for scrip demonstrated an assertion of rights that "flowed from their maternal ancestry to land."[10] Although not all Metis in North America were eligible for scrip, and, therefore, the application for scrip is certainly not the only signifier of Metis identity, those Metis who did make application (as did both Isabella's and Marie Rose's families) were asserting a belief in their rights as "a people" apart from First Nations and Euro-North Americans.

While this book has examined identity primarily through culture, gender, and kinship, there are some who argue that, for an individual or a community to rightfully identify as Metis, they must not only self-identify as Metis but must have a "connection to the historical core in the Red River region." The argument continues that to discuss Metis identity in terms other than "nationhood" reduces the discussion to one of race.[11] This perspective discounts the possibility that a community or individual could be culturally and historically Metis, even if they had no connection to the Red River region. This perspective then naturally raises the question of the Metis families and communities that developed in and around the HBC trading posts that had little or no known connection to the Red River region, and, thus, to the "nation" of Metis that was claimed by Louis Riel and his supporters. To suggest the Indigenous people connected to northern fur trade posts were not culturally and historically Metis (because they may not have experienced a "gravitational pull" to the Red River region for "Métis collective self-identification")[12] would be to view them as "mixed-bloods." This perspective reduces the discussion about the history of these particular Indigenous people to one of race, and thus forces us to demonstrate ambivalence about them as Metis people.[13]

Further, to suggest the Metis began to perceive themselves as an Indigenous people primarily as a result of specific events in Red River, such as the conflicts in 1816 and 1869–70, is to discount that the Metis (*bois brulé*, *gens libre*, freemen, country-born, mixed-blood, or half-breed) understood themselves to be distinct Indigenous people, even if they were not referring to themselves as "Metis." This perspective risks perpetuating colonial discourses that proposed Indigenous people had no agency, and that their very identities must be categorized and inspired by outsiders. At the very least, this perspective denies that one can identify as a Metis person without formulating a "national consciousness."

Both the Hardisty and Delorme families asserted their Metis rights (and identity) through cultural practices and, indeed, scrip applications. However, the argument is not that all members, or Marie Rose and Isabella, ascribed to a Metis nationalism in the same way the Metis of Red River did after the conflicts of 1816, 1869–1870, and 1885. Indeed, it should be noted that Metis nationalism largely went underground after the defeat of 1885. Simply because both Isabella and Marie Rose did not appear to publicly identify as Metis, and there was certainly no indication of Metis nationalism, does not negate the reality that they capitalized on their Metis identity and the Metis culture of their youth as necessary in order to successfully transition. This very ability is at the root of Metis identity as it is understood by many scholars and in this book. That Isabella and Marie Rose understood the challenges of publicly embracing a Metis identity in a society that was increasingly focused on racial categorizations and boundaries does not mean they stopped relying on their Metis culture and kin—it simply means they adapted and they compromised. Rather than focus on race or nationalism as a method of understanding the history of the Metis, a greater understanding is found in examining the role of women, the reciprocal relationships that were integral to Metis communities, their participation in the fur trade and in transitioning economies, their ability to adapt, and the compromise the Metis always sought between "European and Indian ways."[14]

As they adjusted to the new realities of their southern Alberta homes, Marie Rose and Isabella compromised and adapted. At the Euro-North American boarding schools, Marie Rose and Isabella learned the ideology of "gracious womanhood." These schools provided skills that assisted in Marie Rose's and Isabella's transition when the fur trade gave way to more sedentary lifestyles. Yet, in some ways, these schools also confirmed both girls were "different" from Euro-North Americans. As this book has suggested, it was not only their Euro-North American educations that enabled their transition. In reality, neither Marie Rose nor Isabella "married out." As part of transition planning, there was family involvement in the choice of their marriage partners, but those partners were really without influential connections themselves. It was actually Marie Rose and Isabella, relying on their Metis culture, identity, and families, who carried the class distinctions into their marriages and who provided the social capital to enable a successful transition, both for themselves and for their Euro-North American husbands.

In Marie Rose's case, her marriage arrangement to a Euro-North American man was more apparent, largely because we are privy to her innermost thoughts about her lack of agency. While the man chosen as Marie Rose's husband may have appeared wealthy enough by the standards of the day, he was still a nomadic robe and whiskey trader with no family connections in the North West. It was a fortuitous trade on Charlie's part because not only was Marie Rose a member of the hunter and trader class of Red River Metis society but she proved adept at using her Metis culture to adapt to a sedentary economy. Charlie made few adjustments when he and Marie Rose chose a homestead in southern Alberta. For a large part of the year, he continued to traverse the plains, either as a wolfer, trader, or guide to newcomers. Indicative of his social standing was the fact that Charlie could not deal in scrip but was relegated to "obtaining money from the Indians" at treaty time. It was Marie Rose who assumed the more sedentary lifestyle, managed the ranch, and gave birth to seventeen children, while trading with First Nation people for supplies and earning pocket money for herself and her children. More importantly, it was Marie Rose who seems to have assumed the primary duty of social networking with new arrivals to southern

Alberta, and who was able to establish herself as a respected home-steading pioneer.

Although she proved adept at networking, Marie Rose faced several challenges. In addition to the challenges of living with a nomadic and hard-drinking husband, Marie Rose had to contend with the fact that her Delorme family had made the choice to fight alongside Louis Riel. Thus, whereas her Metis culture had served her well, the Metis family that had held influence during the height of the fur trade era, even though some settled near her, became somewhat of a public liability. It turned out that there were no male family members with whom Charlie could publicly forge econom-ically advantageous business connections. Further, Marie Rose was of French ancestry in a society that was becoming increas-ingly Anglocentric. Marie Rose continued to rely on the culture of her youth, and even privately on her fur trade family. She would have had to in order to survive the rudimentary conditions of the West as Charlie's wife. However, Marie Rose perceived the wisdom of subsuming her Metis ethnicity, and even her French ethnicity, as the demographics of the West changed. She increasingly preferred to present herself as a homesteading pioneer, an old-timer, rather than as a French-Metis woman. At this time, with the conflicts arising from the Manitoba schools question in 1896 which became a national crisis, there were problems presenting as a Metis and as a French person. At the same time, Marie Rose expanded her network, her Metis web, by incorporating outsiders through prac-tices such as godparenting, and through marriages for her children to English-speaking, Euro-North Americans, thus maintaining a class position that began for her during the fur trade era.

In Isabella's case, her mother continued to rely on her Metis fur trade family network when she dispatched Isabella and her brothers to live with their uncle in Calgary. By this time, Richard Hardisty was well on his way to becoming one of the wealthiest men in the North West. The HBC remained a viable entity in the new economy, enabling officers and their families to transition more successfully than the French Metis. Richard was the area's first senator while he was still an HBC man, demonstrating the advantage company men continued to enjoy. After Richard Hardisty's death, the man who had become the patriarch of the Hardisty fur trading family, Donald A. Smith (Lord Strathcona), would also preside over the long transitional economy in the West. Smith would emerge as one of the wealthiest men in that new economy, as he diverted his investments, and those of many of the Hardisty family, to rail and land.[15] Due to the positions of her family members, both in the company and in the new economy, when Isabella's mother sent her to live with her uncle in the tiny hamlet on the open prairie, it was a natural assumption that Isabella would maintain her social standing. Indeed, the connection to the Hardisty family accomplished what was intended for Isabella, who was able to maintain her social standing, while her own mother lost both her connection to the Hardisty family and her social status. Like Marie Rose, through various practices such as godparenting and marriages for her children with Euro-North Americans, Isabella maintained the class distinctions she had enjoyed as the daughter of a chief factor in the fur trade.

When Isabella married James Lougheed, his legal training was complementary to the changing economy, in which it was no longer trading chiefs that served as useful connections but lawyers able to negotiate land deals and commercial ventures. James provided skills the Hardisty family needed, thus ensuring he and Isabella maintained higher social standing. Unlike Charlie, James rose to a high enough class that he did not need to rely on trading for treaty money; rather, James was able to trade in land scrip. James's economic success enabled Isabella to be well positioned to emulate her father's role as a chief factor, adept at hosting dignitaries and boosting her own social network, thus contributing social capital to the partnership. It soon fell upon Isabella to manage the couple's networking in Calgary when James stepped into Richard Hardisty's position in Ottawa, a situation that also raised Isabella's own status in the community.

However, as ethnic boundaries increasingly solidified in the West, Isabella, like Marie Rose, chose to recreate her public persona by subsuming her Metis ethnicity. Isabella, too, determined to portray herself as a homesteading pioneer, an old-timer. Marie Rose's and Isabella's ethnicity appeared very much to be an instrumental one that could be highlighted or downplayed as need be, or adapted, as had always been the case for the Metis. Their public personae, depicted in the photographs that were used by newspapers, were those of English-speaking, Euro-North American women. These public personae, developed for the sake of successful transition, in no way suggest Marie Rose's and Isabella's private personae were indicative of a "mixed people in between" but rather confirm their identity was very much diverse, fluid, and resiliently "Metis." Both were able to adapt and expand their network to incorporate outsiders as a way to ensure their social status was not threatened.

In the public realm, it appears both Isabella and Marie Rose had their homesteading pioneer (rather than Metis) identities confirmed by their contemporaries. In a 1922 article about Canadian women that appeared in *Saturday Night*, Isabella's life was described as having "all the background of romance, adventure and hardship of the pioneer life of the frozen north—on down to the comforts and civilization of the 'Boom Days.'"[16] Marie Rose's obituary in the *Pincher Creek Echo*, on 7 April 1960, described her as one of the area's "most colorful figures," while noting she was one of southern Alberta's "earliest and oldest pioneers."[17]

While Marie Rose and Isabella were recognized as pioneers of some note, their degree of financial success for a large part of their lives as married women was vastly different. Isabella lived in a palatial home, where servants often helped raise the children, the first home on the prairies to enjoy the luxury of electric power. James was a gentleman, adept at networking with princes and prime ministers. On the other hand, Marie Rose raised her seventeen children in a log home, where she continued to rely on wood stoves and cupboards made of boxes. At times, Charlie was a wolfer, the class of men who subsisted after the disappearance of the great buffalo herds by poisoning carcasses and harvesting the spoils. Try as she might, and despite permeable boundaries during the boom and bust days of early settlement, Marie Rose could never really be considered a "rightful" member of the upper class. Yet both Isabella and Marie Rose relied on a classification system for the Metis, viewing themselves as of a higher status and some Metis as lower class "half-breeds." Both were proponents of the image of a new "civilized" Prairie West, in which they were respected pioneers of higher social status, unlike other Indigenous people.

In maintaining social status, based simply upon their life occupations, the financial capital offered by Charlie and James is more apparent than that of their partners. The labour Marie Rose and Isabella expended had social value but unidentifiable monetary value. There are no documents to tell us how much material worth their labour contributed.[18] Yet, just as reasoned speculation confirms that female partners in the fur trade were valuable contributors to both the company's and the hunters' and traders' activities, their lives speak to the fact that Isabella and Marie Rose were equally important to the financial and social success of their respective partnerships, not only by way of their physical labour but by the social capital they contributed. They were managing the households and creating their personae while their husbands were away for extended periods of time. Isabella and Marie Rose were forging relationships with important members of their respective societies by entertaining visitors and new settlers in their respective homes. While the guests Isabella was entertaining were actors on the political stage, who virtually guaranteed her social status, to Marie Rose, her guests were equally important to the social fabric of her community and, indeed, contributed to her social status.

Because the economy had changed, rather than trade in furs, cooking utensils, and beads, Marie Rose and Isabella now traded primarily in hostess skills, community-building skills, mothering skills, boosterism skills, and really anything that could contribute to the success of their respective social and familial kinship networks, while also contributing to the image of a new Prairie West. In reality, Isabella and Marie Rose provided many of the technical skills necessary for survival in the new economy, as had their own mothers during the fur trade era. Given the realities of their new homes, it is even more likely that both Marie Rose and Isabella continued to rely on the social and economic relations, obligations, and exchange traditions that are traceable to the process of "being and becoming" Metis.

Although their family fortunes were vastly different for the majority of their lives, Marie Rose and Isabella lived their last days in houses they no longer owned. Yet the webs of kinship they had developed came to their aid at the hour of their greatest need and speak to the success and status that both Isabella and Marie Rose were able to maintain their entire lives. Indeed, it was their community of connections that assured both Isabella and Marie Rose a semblance of respectability in their final years, and a semblance of retaining the land that had become important to them. For Isabella, the municipality heeded the call for assistance and responded by allowing her to remain as hostess of her grand home. Also, a former prime minister very likely ensured the funds were available so she could manage that grand home. For Marie Rose, support followed when at least one of her aristocratic friends stayed in her boarding house and thus enabled land ownership. Also, the old-timers came to her aid, making countless appeals to the government so she was finally able to sell her land, and even providing funds so Charlie could have a respectable burial.

Despite somewhat similar conditions near the end of their lives, for the greater part of their adult lives, Marie Rose must have been more concerned about the social capital of her new connections. Her family presented more challenges for a successful transition, due partly to their political activity as the fur trade drew to a close, and partly to their ethnicity as French Metis, and partly to the fact they were not part of the HBC culture. Yet, as both women negotiated a new society founded in paper transactions, they had to be cognizant of the image they projected. For Marie Rose, that awareness meant writing herself into history as a homesteading pioneer and creating a paper kinship network. For Isabella, as it had for Marie Rose, that awareness meant distancing herself from some members of her fur trade family, such as her siblings, and even her mother, who had not successfully transitioned. For Isabella, it also meant managing her image through various media outlets and establishing herself as a pioneer community builder through leadership roles in various social organizations.

In 1983, Jennifer Brown identified a need for further study of the detailed family histories of Metis women to understand how the economic roles some of them assumed afforded them the opportunity to maintain a sense of continuity with their past.[19] While reflecting on her life after being diagnosed with cancer, renowned Prairie author Margaret Laurence (whose main characters were often Metis people living on the prairies after the end of the fur trade) observed that the kind of history that

> has the most powerful hold over us in unsuspected ways, the names or tunes or trees that can recall a thousand images...this almost-family history can be related only to one's first home.[20]

Laurence continued of her first home in Neepawa,

> This was my territory in the time of my youth, and in a sense my life since then has been an attempt to look at it, to come to terms with it.[21]

Due to a paucity of sources, the challenge presented by Brown, and the quest to understand the ways in which Metis women came to terms with their first home (as identified by Laurence), have been difficult to accomplish in the case of Metis women. While many scholars likely believed the Metis continued, in the transitional period, to rely on the culture and extended networks, or the "webs of real and imagined kin,"[22] established during the fur trade, it has often been difficult to reach definitive conclusions. However, this close study of Marie Rose and Isabella confirms that their transitional lives relied on a certain continuity with their fur trade lives, their "first homes." This conclusion, upon further study, might be extended to many Metis who negotiated their survival as the fur trade was waning, and whose lives have yet to be studied.

Marie Rose and Isabella may have chosen to come to terms with their perceived need to obscure some of the culture of their first homes through the organization that held their interest for so long, the Women's Pioneer Association of Southern Alberta.[23] This organization proudly displayed its connection to former times in many ways, not the least of which included singing the Metis folk-song "Red River Halfbreed" at all of its public gatherings until at least the 1930s.[24] This association also had a mandate to record the "local history" of the pioneers, that group of people defined by the fact that they were living in the North West prior to 1884.[25] It is clear the pioneer association was not referring to the homesteading pioneer but rather the fur trade pioneer. We know that Marie Rose had an interest in history and, if the conclusion reached by the first researchers at the restored Beaulieu House is correct with regard to Isabella's passion for history, then it would be an interest she had in common with Marie Rose.

In 1927, when Isabella was again elected president of the Women's Pioneer Association of Southern Alberta, the member for Pincher Creek was Mrs. C. Lynch-Staunton, while the member representing Macleod was Mrs. G.C. Ives.[26] Marie Rose knew both women quite well and spoke of them in her manuscripts. It is altogether possible that membership in the pioneer association brought

Isabella and Marie Rose together on some occasion. Even when the group stopped meeting at Beaulieu in favour of the Palliser Hotel, Isabella continued to

> *greatly enjoy these meetings...where old friends and acquaintances join with her in recalling the days of the prairie schooner, the buffalo herds, the wide ranges and also many departed pioneers of the seventies, eighties and nineties in Southern Alberta.*[27]

Given their backgrounds, if Isabella and Marie Rose met through the pioneer association, they would have had a great deal to reminisce about. Because the pioneer association was formed and grew in popularity in the 1920s, during the economic slump in Alberta the resiliency and importance of the Metis "pioneer,"[28] in particular, may have been accentuated. Indeed, Isabella's and Marie Rose's communities recognized them as Metis pioneers, and so did their family members.

When Isabella's daughter related the automobile trip into the mountains, she noted that Isabella had demonstrated her "pioneer spirit" by walking the seven miles to the train station. Her family member knew Isabella was not a homesteading pioneer, but rather that she was a pioneer of the northern fur trade posts, when she spent her formative years primarily in the company of the Metis mother who had also spent her own formative years in fur trade country. In Marie Rose's case, her unpublished manuscript, "Eighty Years on the Plains," confirmed that she, too, was not simply the homesteading pioneer that her brief published manuscripts described, but rather that she was a Metis pioneer.

Perhaps Isabella's and Marie Rose's conversation, if they met in person, may have even strayed to fur trade families. Had their conversation been frank and private, Isabella and Marie Rose might have commented that they both continued to rely on those family networks when they first settled in southern Alberta. They may have commented on their work to maintain the social positions they had enjoyed during the fur trade, but that faced challenges due, in part, to emerging racial boundaries. Had their conversations carried on to siblings, they might have found more similarities.

This book touched only briefly on Marie Rose's and Isabella's brothers, in part because that information is not as easily accessible, and in part because comparative studies of the adaptive strategies of men from the French-Metis tradition and the English-speaking tradition have not yet been undertaken. However, the intital information suggests their male siblings were not nearly as successful as Marie Rose and Isabella in negotiating the changing economy of the Prairie West. While both Marie Rose and Isabella achieved some considerable attention from their contemporaries and the local media, their brothers did not. There is some evidence Isabella's brothers did not continue to enjoy material wealth, even though they were from the H B C tradition. Despite the Hardisty family's extensive connections during the fur trade and into the early transitional period, Isabella's brothers all appear to have faded into obscurity, some in very dire financial conditions and certainly without the social status that they enjoyed because they were sons of an H B C chief factor. This book did not delve into this reality for Isabella's brothers, and further study could shed light on the value of Metis culture and identity for men in comparison to women during the transitional period. The same could be said of Marie Rose's brothers as is said of Isabella's, which might be more the expected outcome because of the French-Metis ancestry of one and the Sioux ancestry of the other. It appears that both of them lived briefly in the Pincher Creek area but had little hope of carving social positions for themselves as respected homesteading pioneers in the way Marie Rose did. This book did not delve into these circumstances, which invites further study as well.

In a close case study of one Metis man, Gerhard Ens argued that, when the dualistic economy disappeared from the plains,

343

Many Voices—One People

Metis identity was no longer instrumentally advantageous. It was during this period that many Metis began drifting back to their native roots (entering treaty or reserves), or assimilating to a Euro-Canadian identity...Being Metis during these decades was no longer economically nor socially advantageous.[29]

It may have been the case that it was no longer advantageous to be Metis for men, and more comparative studies may confirm that and explore the reasons for it. However, "being Metis"—that is, relying on the social and practical skills Metis women learned during the fur trade era—was of considerable advantage to Marie Rose and Isabella, as it may well have been for other Metis women at the time. What was not advantageous for Marie Rose and Isabella was to openly embrace the fact they were Metis.

We can clearly see through her own words the manipulation of Marie Rose's persona. She was successful at writing herself into homesteading pioneer history, even though little of that history was published during her lifetime. The gaps in Marie Rose's history served to distance her from the Metis conflicts of 1869–1870 and 1885. It was only in Marie Rose's brief fictional accounts that she flirted with publicly embracing a Metis identity and summoned the courage to chastise the governing forces for their inattention to Metis territorial land rights.

Isabella's manipulation of her persona must be deduced from the many contemporary publications that paid her attention because of her position as the wife of the area's senator. A great deal of space was devoted to elaborate descriptions, often by male journalists, of Isabella's clothing and her hostess skills. Pictures and descriptions of Isabella as a gracious Euro-North American lady, while most were aware of her Indigenous ancestry, suggest she may have been viewed as a commodity of boosterism and successful assimilation. However, Isabellas participation in the media also suggests that she not only allowed herself to be such a commodity but manipulated the management of her own image. During the few public interviews she granted, while dressed as a gracious woman, Isabella ensured that readers were aware she had endured many "privations" at a northern fur trade post but had successfully transitioned.

In addition to their ability to manage their own personae, Marie Rose and Isabella also shared some external cultural factors, such as traditional Metis clothing, socials, music, jigging, and country food. More importantly, there were social factors evident in the manifestations of their early identities: a common history of duality and distinctness emanating from the fur trade, family collectivity shaped by common employment and reciprocal responsibility, as well as religious beliefs, historical knowledge, adaptability, and the incorporation of outsiders as real and fictive, or imagined, kin that allowed them to "survive and refine themselves,"[30] as the Metis had done throughout the fur trade era.

Yet self-identity is not found only in itemized lists of cultural attributes or in census documents. In addition to sharing the cultural identifiers of the Metis, both Isabella and Marie Rose were physically identifiable as being of Indigenous ancestry. Contemporaries knew Isabella was Metis. Chief Buffalo Child Long Lance confirmed it in an article for the *Mentor*, writing that Lady Lougheed, wife of Minister of the Interior Sir James Lougheed, was a "half-breed."[31] In her interviews with pioneers conducted in 1935, Edna Kells described Marie Rose: "Of Indian blood. Yellow complexioned, brown eyes that seem to penetrate, dark hair, sharply modelled features, lined face. Erratic—kindly."[32] According to a recent study, Metis ethnicity and identity were often a function of the beliefs of "historical actors who [were] both 'insiders' and 'outsiders,'" so that whether one saw oneself as Metis could at times be dependent upon how others viewed that person or group.[33]

We cannot ignore both biological and historical realities, and how those impacted self-identity for many Indigenous people. For some, increasing racism and the categorizations imposed by governments and "outsiders" were major catalysts in embracing a Metis identity,[34] and this may have been the case for the men in Marie Rose's and Isabella's fur trade kinship network. Further research may confirm their own Metis identity contributed to the lack of financial success for both Isabella's and Marie Rose's siblings. However, Marie Rose and Isabella were negotiating a changing society and they were women who married Euro-North American men. At the beginning of their married lives, there was nothing very unusual about interracial unions. Both Isabella and Marie Rose might even have initially assumed their Metis ethnicity was advantageous and neither a matter to be denied or asserted. However, as more settlers arrived, both women astutely recognized the need to establish new economic pathways, to embrace the new era of the paper transaction, and to recreate their public personae as gracious "pioneer" women, something their marriage to Euro-North American men facilitated. Their physical appearance may have provided even further incentive to forge new connections with Euro-North American people. Indeed, their new communities of connections clearly recognized the social capital Marie Rose and Isabella contributed, not only to their marriage partnerships but to their communities as well. Yet, while all knew Marie Rose and Isabella were Metis, most public accounts supported Isabella's and Marie Rose's homesteading pioneer personae while downplaying any Indigenous ethnicity.

If we were to base our conclusions of successful transition on economics, then we would have to conclude that Marie Rose, a woman of French-Metis ethnicity, did not transition as successfully as Isabella, a woman from the country-born tradition. However, if we are to judge by their own perceptions of their distinctness and the pride in their own abilities to transition and to position them-selves as "pioneers," there can be no doubt that both Marie Rose and Isabella successfully negotiated the changing economy. In fact, they were validated as important pioneers by their societies. For Marie Rose, her influential connections were forged in the pioneer ranching and agricultural community, while Isabella forged her connections in the emerging commercial real estate and political community. These important new connections assisted Marie Rose and Isabella in retaining positions of importance in their respective communities.

In the end, though, there are no real and permanent fixed boundaries when considering culture, identities, and kinship networks. This fluidity was particularly so for the Metis, whose history demonstrates an ability to both incorporate outsiders and to adapt. The lives of Isabella and Marie Rose are a testament to the importance of appreciating the reality of fluid boundaries of identity, which are nonetheless diverse but in no way "in between" or "mixed." In Isabella's case, she appeared equally at ease hosting in her stately home the aristocracy of Europe, while they enjoyed the strains of classical piano, as she did in hosting the pioneers of southern Alberta, with whom she enjoyed the tunes of the Red River Jig and reputedly gladly shared the smoking of a pipe.[35] Yet, while on the one hand explaining the privations that she, as a daughter of the fur trade, endured at northern posts, Isabella could just as quickly express disdain that the only hired help available to her as she managed her stately mansion were "halfbreeds," who were none too reliable.

In the same way, Marie Rose felt equally comfortable continuing to trade with First Nation people for hides and ministering to their ailments as she did in forging links with the emerging aristocracy of early prairie ranching society. She could publicly refer to "Indian halfbreeds" with a disdain that suggested they were dirty and unreliable, while privately referring to Indigenous people as nature's children, capable of caring for their sick with the wisdom of ages. Marie Rose could publicly refer to the foolhardy half-breeds who followed Riel, while privately and "fictionally" pointing out the irony of the Metis being held to account for purloining stockings while the government was not accountable for encroaching on the small plots of land that had, for generations, rightfully belonged to the Metis.

If we are to believe the words Marie Rose wrote, and the words her contemporaries wrote about Isabella, for the majority of their adult lives both women lived like Euro-North Americans. Yet both women served as living examples of the bridge that allowed for the transition of the North West from nomadic fur trade economy to sedentary agriculture and the beginnings of industrial capitalism, in effect serving as major contributors to the building of the new Prairie West. By providing the technical and social skills necessary for their families' survival in the new economy, Marie Rose and Isabella not only increased their own power, status, and influence, but they remained distinct, in the same way Metis women did during the fur trade era when their identities were situational, inclusive, fluid, and complex. Yet that distinctness for Marie Rose and Isabella must, for the most part, be viewed publicly in the vein of "gracious womanhood," of homesteading pioneer, of old-timer, rather than of Metis matriarch. Indeed, their respective societies confirmed that they were, in the end, respected "pioneers" of the new Prairie West. Their status suggests that further study will confirm that many other Metis "pioneers" relied on the same cultural, adaptive, and situational survival strategies that these two intelligent, resourceful, and strong Metis women did as the fur trade transitioned and the Prairie West was built.

Notes 349

NOTE ON TERMINOLOGY

1. John Giokas and Paul L.A.H. Chartrand, "Who Are the Métis in Section 35? A Review of the Law and Policy Relating to Métis and 'Mixed-Blood' People in Canada," in *Who Are Canada's Aboriginal Peoples? Recognition, Definition, and Jurisdiction*, ed. Paul L.A.H. Chartrand (Saskatoon: Purich Publishing, 2002), 86.

2. Murray Dobbin, *The One-and-a-Half Men: The Story of Jim Brady and Malcolm Norris, Metis Patriots of the Twentieth Century* (Vancouver: New Star Books, 1981) provides a history of the political organization of the Metis in Alberta.

3. Gerhard Ens and Joe Sawchuk, *New Peoples to New Nations: Aspects of Métis History and Identity from the Eighteenth to Twenty-First Centuries* (Toronto: University of Toronto Press, 2016), 3. The authors refer to the case of *Daniels v. Canada*, 2013 FC6 para 619, and note that this case was challenged by Metis organizations and had not yet been settled, 514. On 14 April 2016, the Supreme Court ruled in the case of *Daniels v. Canada* that both Metis and non-status Indians are within the scope of federal jurisdiction over "Indians" under section 91(24) of the Constitution.

4. Jacqueline Peterson, "Red River Redux: Métis Ethnogenesis and the Great Lakes Region," in *Contours of a People: Metis Family, Mobility, and History*, ed. Nicole St-Onge, Carolyn Podruchny, and Brenda Macdougall (Norman: University of Oklahoma Press, 2002), 25.

5. Michel Hogue, *Metis and the Medicine Line: Creating a Border and Dividing a People* (Chapel Hill: University of North Carolina Press, 2015), 13. See also Nicole St-Onge and Carolyn Podruchny, "Scuttling Along a Spider's Web: Mobility and Kinship in Metis Ethnogenesis," in *Contours of a People: Metis Family, Mobility and History*, ed. Nicole St-Onge, Carolyn Podruchny, and Brenda Macdougall (Oklahoma: University of Oklahoma Press, 2012), 61.

6. Brenda Macdougall, "*Wahkootowin*: Family and Cultural Identity in Northwestern Saskatchewan Metis Communities," *Canadian Historical Review* 87, no. 3 (2006): 434.

NOTE ON SOURCES

1. Sarah Carter and Patricia McCormack, "Lifelines: Searching for Aboriginal Women of the Northwest and Borderlands," in *Recollecting: Lives of Aboriginal Women of the Canadian Northwest and Borderlands*, ed. Sarah Carter and Patricia McCormack (Edmonton: Athabasca University Press, 2011), 17. The authors discuss the distinctions between oral history and tradition. In the case of this book, there were few people available who had first-hand memories of Isabella and Marie Rose.

INTRODUCTION

1. Doris J. MacKinnon, "'I am alone in this world'—The Identities of Marie Rose Smith" (MA thesis, University of Calgary, 2006). Some of the research supporting this thesis was published under the title, *The Identities of Marie Rose Delorme Smith: Portrait of a Métis Woman, 1861–1960* (Regina: University of Regina Press, Canadian Plains Research Center, 2012).

2. For the purpose of this study, ethnicity means identifying with a group because of shared culture and history.

3. St-Onge and Podruchny, "Scuttling Along a Spider's Web," 70.

4. MacKinnon, "'I am alone in this world'"; MacKinnon, *The Identities of Marie Rose Delorme Smith*.

5. Doris Jeanne MacKinnon, "Métis Pioneers: Isabella Hardisty Lougheed and Marie Rose Delorme Smith" (PHD dissertation, University of Calgary, 2012).

6. Gloria Jane Bell, "Oscillating Identities: Re-presentation of Métis in the Great Lakes Area in the Nineteenth Century," in *Métis in Canada: History, Identity, Law & Politics*, ed. Christopher Adams, Gregg Dahl, and Ian Peach (Edmonton: University of Alberta Press, 2013), 8.

7. Christopher Adams, Gregg Dahl, and Ian Peach, *Métis in Canada: History, Identity, Law & Politics* (Edmonton: University of Alberta Press, 2013), xv.

8. Ens and Sawchuk, *New Peoples to New Nations*, 4.

9.   Adams, Dahl, and Peach, *Métis in Canada*, xviii.

10. Laura-Lee Kearns, "(Re)claiming Métis Women Identities: Three Stories and the Storyteller," in *Métis in Canada: History, Identity, Law & Politics*, edited by Christopher Adams, Gregg Dahl, and Ian Peach (Edmonton: University of Alberta Press, 2013), 59–92.

11. Ibid., 60.

12. Carter and McCormack, "Lifelines," 5.

13. Ibid., 10–11.

14. Beverly Boutilier and Alison Prentice, eds., *Creating Historical Memory: English Canadian Women and the Work of History* (Vancouver: UBC Press, 1997), 20n11 and 24.

15. Jean Barman, "Writing Women into the History of the North American Wests, One Woman at a Time," in *One Step Over the Line: Toward a History of Women in the North American Wests*, ed. Elizabeth Jameson and Sheila McManus (Edmonton: University of Alberta Press; Athabasca: Athabasca University Press, 2008), 100.

16. Patricia Roome, "Remembering Together: Reclaiming Alberta Women's Past," in *Standing on New Ground: Women in Alberta*, ed. Catherine A. Cavanaugh and Randi R. Warne (Edmonton: University of Alberta Press, 1993), 185.

17. Carter and McCormack, "Lifelines," 10. The editors provide examples of more recent publications, including their own, that have relied on biography to explore the lives of Indigenous women. Yet they conclude, "Despite the advances in this field, our knowledge of Aboriginal women of the past is limited,"112.

18. Ibid., 8.

19. Allan Sheppard, "Undercurrents of Intolerance: Swimming in KKK Waters," *Legacy* (Summer 2000): 26–29, accessed 10 May 2011, http://www.abheritage.ca/albertans/articles/kkk.html. Reference *The Albertan*, 6 December 1924.

20. Donald B. Smith, "The Original Peoples of Alberta," in *Peoples of Alberta: Portraits of Cultural Diversity*, ed. Howard Palmer and Tamara Palmer (Saskatoon: Western Producer Prairie Books, 1985), 67. Reference Archibald Oswald MacRae, *History of the Province of Alberta*, vol. II (n.p.: Western Canadian History Co., 1912), 50–64. See photo (dated 1906), Glenbow–Alberta Institute Archives NA-3899.2, which includes the young Norman Lougheed and his teammates with the schoolmaster Archibald Oswald MacRae.

21. Joan M. Jensen, "The Perils of Rural Women's History: (A Note to Storytellers Who Study the West's Unsettled Past)," in *One Step Over the Line: Toward a History of Women in the North American Wests*, ed. Elizabeth Jameson and Sheila McManus (Edmonton: University of Alberta Press; Athabasca: Athabasca University Press, 2008). Jensen notes that if she wrote "only about settlers and not Indigenous

people, native born and not immigrant, white and not people of color, I miss the vital edges where people come together, mix, and clash or cooperate," 171.

22. Elizabeth Jameson and Sheila McManus, eds., *One Step Over the Line: Toward a History of Women in the North American Wests* (Edmonton: University of Alberta Press; Athabasca: Athabasca University Press, 2008), 310.

23. Raymond Williams, *The Long Revolution* (New York: Columbia University Press, 1961), 47–49. Williams's argument is that the most difficult thing to get hold of when studying any past period is the sense of the quality of life at a particular place and time: a sense of a way of thinking and living. Even when we restore the outlines of a particular organization of life, or the social character (a valued system of behaviour and attitudes), this is usually abstract. The closest we come to understanding the actual experience through which these valued systems of behaviours and attitudes were forged is through the arts of a period (i.e., the written texts in the case of this book) but also the social activities that the main characters enjoyed.

1   BEING AND BECOMING METIS

1. Harold Innis, *The Fur Trade in Canada: An Introduction to Canadian Economic History* (1930; repr., Toronto: University of Toronto Press, 1999).

2. Arthur Ray, *Indians in the Fur Trade* (1974; repr., Toronto: University of Toronto Press, 1998). Also Carol M. Judd and Arthur J. Ray, eds., *Old Trails and New Directions: Papers of the Third North American Fur Trade Conference* (Toronto: University of Toronto Press, 1980). This anthology demonstrated the quickening pace of fur trade research, which was now becoming interdisciplinary, with studies within archaeology, economics, ethnohistory, geography, history, and anthropology.

3. Sylvia Van Kirk, *"Many Tender Ties": Women in Fur-Trade Society, 1670–1870* (Winnipeg: Watson & Dwyer Publishing Ltd., 1980).

4. Jennifer S.H. Brown, "Women as Centre and Symbol in the Emergence of Métis Communities," *Canadian Journal of Native Studies*, 3 no. 1 (1983): 39–46. Another major study was Brown's *Strangers in Blood: Fur Trade Company Families in Indian Country* (Vancouver: UBC Press, 1980).

5. Jacqueline Peterson, "Many Roads to Red River: Métis Ethnogenesis in the Great Lakes Region, 1680–1815," in *The New Peoples: Being and Becoming Métis in North America*, ed. Jacqueline Peterson and Jennifer S.H. Brown (Winnipeg: University of Manitoba Press, 1985), 37–72. Peterson saw the interrelationships of family and community as personal and social constructs.

6. John Foster, "The Métis: The People and the Term," *Prairie Forum* 3, no. 1 (1978): 79–90.

7.   Lucy Eldersveld Murphy, *A Gathering of Rivers: Indians, Métis and Mining in the Western Great Lakes, 1727–1832* (Lincoln: University of Nebraska Press, 2004).

8.   Tanis C. Thorne, *The Many Hands of My Relations: French and Indians on the Lower Missouri* (Columbia: University of Missouri Press, 1996).

9.   Susan Sleeper-Smith, *Indian Women and French Men: Rethinking Cultural Encounter in the Western Great Lakes* (Amherst: University of Massachusetts Press, 2001).

10. Susan Sleeper-Smith, "Women, Kin, and Catholicism," *Ethnohistory* 47, no. 2 (2000): 423–452.

11. Ibid.

12. Sarah Carter, *The Importance of Being Monogamous: Marriage and Nation Building in Western Canada to 1915* (Edmonton: University of Alberta Press, 2008). As many historians have now concluded, the concept of punishing Indigenous women for "marrying out" was a manifestation of the Indian Act, instituted in 1876, and aimed at both saving money and forcing Indigenous people to adopt Christian European standards of patriarchal and monogamous marital unions.

13. Sylvia Van Kirk, "Toward a Feminist Perspective in Native History," *Centre for Women's Studies in Education Occasional Papers*, no. 14 (1987), 6.

14. For one recent study, see Nathalie Kermoal, *Un passé métis au féminin* (Québec: Les Éditions GID, 2006).

15. Heather Devine, *The People Who Own Themselves: Aboriginal Ethnogenesis in a Canadian Family, 1660–1900* (Calgary: University of Calgary Press, 2004).

16. Brenda Macdougall, *One of the Family: Metis Culture in Nineteenth-Century Northwestern Saskatchewan* (Vancouver: UBC Press, 2009), 242.

17. Martha Harroun Foster, *We Know Who We Are: Métis Identity in a Montana Community* (Norman: University of Oklahoma Press, 2006), 205. Foster studied the group of Red River and Pembina Metis who went to the Judith Basin area of central Montana to found Lewisten in 1879. The US government negotiated with these people as a segment of Chippewa society.

18. Ibid.

19. Ibid., 207.

20. Ibid., 220.

21. Thorne, *The Many Hands of My Relations*. Thorne studied kinship networks between Creoles and Central Siouan tribes along the lower Missouri River up to the removal era in the 1870s.

22. Foster, *We Know Who We Are*, 220.

23. Ibid., 9.

24. Melinda M. Jetté, "Ordinary Lives: Three Generations of a French-Indian Family in Oregon, 1827–1931" (MA thesis, Université Laval, 1996), 127.

25. Marcel Giraud, *The Métis in the Canadian West*, trans. George Woodcock (1945; repr., Edmonton: University of Alberta Press, 1986).

26. Brenda Macdougall, "The Myth of Metis Cultural Ambivalence," in *Contours of a People: Metis Family, Mobility, and History*, ed. Nicole St-Onge, Carolyn Podruchny, and Brenda Macdougall (Norman: University of Oklahoma Press, 2012), 433. Reference to Marcel Giraud, *Les Métis Canadiens*, 329.

27. W.L. Morton, "The Canadian Métis," in *Contexts of Canada's Past: Selected Essays of W.L. Morton*, ed. A.B. McKillop (Toronto: Macmillan of Canada, 1980), 61.

28. Ibid., 62.

29. Gerald Friesen, *The Canadian Prairies: A History* (Toronto: University of Toronto Press, 1984), 113–114.

30. Juliet Pollard, "The Making of the Metis in the Pacific Northwest Fur Trade Children: Race, Class, and Gender" (PHD dissertation, University of British Columbia, 1990), 203–204.

31. Dobbin, *The One-and-a-Half Men*. Dobbin discusses the activism by some Metis in the 1930s that aimed to address the challenges that political and economic realities presented for various groups of Metis people. For the challenges faced by the Metis after 1885, see Diane Payment, *The Free People—Li Gens Libres: A History of the Métis Community of Batoche, Saskatchewan* (Calgary: University of Calgary Press, 2009); Bruce D. Sealey and Antoine S. Lussier, *The Métis: Canada's Forgotten People* (Winnipeg: Manitoba Métis Federation Press, 1975); Joseph Kinsey Howard, *Strange Empire: Louis Riel and the Métis People* (1952; Toronto: James Lewis and Samuel, 1974); D.N. Sprague, *Canada and the Métis, 1869–1885* (Waterloo, ON: Wilfrid Laurier University Press, 1988).

32. Gerald Friesen, *River Road: Essays on Manitoba and Prairie History* (Winnipeg: University of Manitoba Press, 1996), 11. Friesen writes that, although Norquay had proudly stated in the legislature in the 1870s that Indigenous blood flowed through his veins, his descendants objected to a plaque that described him as a "Halfbreed."

33. Friesen, *The Canadian Prairies*, 211.

34. Ibid., 214.

35. Ibid., 202.

36. Ibid., 225.

37. Ibid., 226.

38. Frank Tough, *"As Their Natural Resources Fail": Native Peoples and the Economic History of Northern Manitoba, 1870–1930* (Vancouver: UBC Press, 1996), 187.

39. Sarah Carter, *Lost Harvests: Prairie Indian Reserve Farmers and Government Policy* (Montreal: McGill-Queen's University Press, 1990). This was an important new study that examined Indigenous farming.

40. Ibid., 301.

41. Morris Zaslow, *The Opening of the Canadian North: 1870–1914* (Toronto: McClelland & Stewart, 1971), 234.

42. Scrip originated with the Manitoba Act of 1870 and was originally to be issued to the children of residents of the Red River Colony as compensation for loss of territory when the H B C handed control over to the Canadian government.

43. The term "First Nation" came into use in the 1980s and largely replaced the term "Indian Band." Collectively, First Nation, Metis, and Inuit constitute the Indigenous peoples of Canada. Although the term was not widely used during the period studied, it is used here as a way to distinguish between those Indigenous people who were Metis and those who had accepted treaty, and/or who were viewed by Marie Rose and Isabella as continuing in a more traditional "Indian" lifestyle. While Marie Rose used the term "Indians" largely to refer to those Indigenous people who lived a different lifestyle than hers, unless she is being quoted directly, the term "First Nation" will be used.

44. Payment, *The Free People*, 24.

45. Ibid., 26.

46. W.L. Morton, ed., *Alexander Begg's Red River Journal and Other Papers Relative to the Red River Resistance of 1869–1870* (Toronto: The Champlain Society, 1956), xxi.

47. For a comprehensive study of Irene Spry's economic theories, see Duncan Cameron, ed., *Explorations in Canadian Economic History: Essays in Honour of Irene M. Spry* (Ottawa: University of Ottawa Press, 1985). Other scholars at various times have agreed with the concept of class as the signifier of Metis identity, including John Foster, Jennifer Brown, Gerhard Ens, and Brenda Macdougall.

48. St-Onge and Podruchny, "Scuttling Along a Spider's Web," 81.

49. Ibid.

50. Payment, *The Free People*, 27.

51. Ibid.

52. Brenda Macdougall, "'The Comforts of Married Life': Metis Family Life, Labour, and the Hudson's Bay Company," *Labour/Le travail*, no. 61 (Spring 2008): 24.

53. Ibid., 31.

54. Robert R. Janes, *Preserving Diversity: Ethnoarchaeological Perspectives on Culture Change in the Western Canadian Subarctic* (New York: Garland Publishing, 1991), 133.

55. Macdougall, "'The Comforts of Married Life,'" 31.

56. Susan Armitage, "Making Connections: Gender, Race, and Place in Oregon Country," in *One Step Over the Line: Toward a History of Women in the North American Wests*, ed. Elizabeth Jameson and Sheila McManus (Edmonton: University of Alberta Press; Athabasca: Athabasca University Press, 2008), 63.

355

Notes

57. Peter Bakker, *A Language of Our Own: The Genesis of Michif, the Mixed Cree-French Language of the Canadian Métis* (New York: Oxford University Press, 1997), 53.

58. Chris Anderson, *"Métis": Race, Recognition, and the Struggle for Indigenous Peoplehood* (Vancouver: U B C Press, 2014), 24.

59. St-Onge and Podruchny, "Scuttling Along a Spider's Web," 80.

60. Bakker, *A Language of Our Own*, 53.

61. Theda Perdue, introduction to *Sifters: Native American Women's Lives*, ed. Theda Perdue (New York: Oxford University Press, 2001), 5.

62. Naomi E.S. Griffiths, *The Splendid Vision: Centennial History of the National Council of Women of Canada, 1893–1993* (Ottawa: Carleton University Press, 1993), xii.

63. Marjorie Griffin Cohen, *Women's Work: Markets and Economic Development in Nineteenth-Century Ontario* (Toronto: University of Toronto Press, 1988), 5–6. Also see the importance of women in dairying, 96.

64. Sherry Farrell Racette, "Sewing for a Living: The Commodification of Métis Women's Artistic Production," in *Contact Zones: Aboriginal & Settler Women in Canada's Colonial Past*, ed. Katie Pickles and Myra Rutherdale (Vancouver: U B C Press, 2005), 17–46.

65. Macdougall, "'The Comforts of Married Life,'" 24.

66. Brown, "Women as Centre," 41.

67. Racette, "Sewing for a Living," 5.

68. Sleeper-Smith, *Indian Women and French Men*, 4.

69. Valerie Maher, family member of Marie Allen Hardisty Thomas (mother of Isabella), interview by author, Calgary, AB, October 2006.

70. Saint François Xavier Parish Records, Accession No. M38, B114, Archives of Manitoba (AM).

71. Marie Rose Smith Fonds, File 6: 18, Glenbow–Alberta Institute Archives (GAIA).

72. Donald B. Smith Collection, Lougheed # 1, Box 1, James Lougheed Medicine Hat File, Lougheed House National Historic Site Archives (LHA). Reference John H. Warkentin, "Western Canada in 1886," papers read before the Historical and Scientific Society of Manitoba, Series III, Number 20, 1963–1964, ed. Thelma Jean Call, Winnipeg, 1965.

73. Ibid.

74. Sheila McManus, *The Line Which Separates: Race, Gender, and the Making of the Alberta–Montana Borderlands* (Lincoln: University of Nebraska Press, 2005), 149. Reference Mary Inderwick to sister-in-law Alice, ca. fall 1884, correspondence 1883–91, M559, Glenbow Archives (GA).

75. Jennifer S.H. Brown, "Linguistic Solitudes and Changing Social Categories," in *Old Trails and New Directions: Papers of the Third North American Fur Trade Conference*, ed. Carol M. Judd and Arthur J. Ray (Toronto: University of

Toronto Press, 1980), 150–151. By the time that Inderwick arrived in 1833, the terms "squaw" and "half-breed" had become more commonplace and uncomplementary. The terms first appeared in written records in New England in the 1630s, first among Nor'Westers and only sporadically until after the 1790s. It appears that Peter Fidler may have been the first HBC man to use the term "Metis" in his writing in 1815. At this time his terminology was changing perhaps as a result of the competition and the fact that many "native North West Company sons were beginning to see themselves as a distinct group with shared interests" and increasingly identifying with the term "Metis."

76. McManus, *The Line Which Separates*, 150. Another early settler, Carolyn Abbott Tyler, while denouncing the "Indians" as "savage," provided elaborate descriptions of Indigenous customs and artefacts but did not identify how she came to know those details. By not revealing her sources, perhaps Tyler was inadvertently admitting she had witnessed some of those customs herself but preferred to maintain a physical separation for the benefit of her readers, 153.

77. Sarah Carter, *Capturing Women: The Manipulation of Cultural Imagery in Canada's Prairie West* (Montreal: McGill-Queen's University Press, 1997), 159.

78. McManus, *The Line Which Separates*, 143.

79. Ibid., 140.

80. Sheila McManus, "Unsettled Pasts, Unsettling Borders: Women, Wests, Nations," in *One Step Over the Line: Toward a History of Women in North American Wests*, ed. Elizabeth Jameson and Sheila McManus (Edmonton: University of Alberta Press; Athabasca: Athabasca University Press, 2008), 38. Reference Inderwick, diary entry 29 October 1883, M559, GA.

81. McManus, *The Line Which Separates*, 141.

82. Ibid., 144.

83. Ibid., 116.

84. Judith Hudson Beattie and Helen M. Buss, eds., *Undelivered Letters to Hudson's Bay Company Men on the Northwest Coast of America, 1830–1857* (Vancouver: UBC Press, 2003), 42.

85. Payment, *The Free People*, xvii.

2 THE TIES THAT BIND

1. Newspaper Clippings File, "Canadian Women in the Public Eye," *Saturday Night*, 16 September 1922, n.p., LHA.

2. Ibid.

3. Ibid.

4. Lougheed Family Bible, LHA. The Bible lists two different years for Isabella's birth, 1860 and 1861. Also Reel T6551, *Census of Canada, 1901*, Province of Alberta,

District of Central Alberta, 13, Library and Archives Canada (LAC). This census lists Isabella's date of birth as 18 April 1861. Also Reel T6425, Census of Province of Alberta, District No. 197, 34, LAC notes that Isabella's mother was born in British Columbia and her father was born in Quebec. Also Donald B. Smith collection, Lougheed #1 Box 1, Lougheeds of Britannia File, LHA. This file contains documents stating that James's grandfather, James Lougheed Sr., also married a "Miss Allen," when he immigrated to the United States from Ireland in 1804. Reference Jopie Loughead, Viviane McClelland, and Frank Ellis Wickson, *The Lougheeds of Britannia*, no publisher.

5. Beckles Willson, *The Life of Lord Strathcona and Mount Royal G.C.M.G., G.C.V.O., 1820–1914* (London: Cassell, 1915), 83. Willson wrote that Isabella's grandfather, Richard Sr., married Marguerite Sutherland, a "dark, petite woman of remarkable beauty, undoubtedly derived from her mixed-blood or Indian mother." Willson also references Kipling Records 62. Also Donald B. Smith Collection, Hardisty Box 1, Hardisty Family File, LHA. Reference MG25G Volume 14 Scrip certificate No. 734, application made in Edmonton in 1885, LAC. Scrip application references the marriage.

6. "Hardisty, William Lucas," Hudson's Bay Company Archives (HBCA), Biographical Sheets, accessed 2 May 2012, http://www.gov.mb.ca/chc/archives/hbca/biographical/html. Also Carol M. Judd, "'Mixt Bands of Many Nations': 1821–70," in *Old Trails and New Directions: Papers of the Third North American Fur Trade Conference*, ed. Carol M. Judd and Arthur J. Ray (Toronto: University of Toronto Press, 1980), 128. Judd notes that the exact meaning of the term "native" is not recorded, but she assumes that the word "parish" referred to the place from which the contracting employee derived his cultural traits. She continues that employees from Rupert's Land were almost always identified as native, an umbrella term that included "Indians, mixed bloods, and theoretically at least, also Europeans. Because very few natives of Rupert's Land at that time were of European descent, and fewer still probably worked for the Hudson's Bay Company, it is reasonable to assume that 'native' employees were either mixed bloods or Indians," 138.

7. Charles Camsell, *Son of the North* (Toronto: Ryerson Press, 1954), 5.

8. "Hardisty, William Lucas. Biographical Sheets."

9. Michael Payne, *The Most Respectable Place in the Territory: Everyday Life in Hudson's Bay Company Service, York Factory 1788–1870* (Ottawa: National Historic Parks and Sights, Environment Canada, 1989), 83. Payne notes that, although much attention has focused on alcohol consumption and its impact on First Nation people, "the drinking habits of traders themselves are worthy of some scrutiny." While Payne's research looked at York Factory in particular, it is reasonable

to assume that many of the same drinking habits were evident at most of the remote posts, given that often the same HBC men moved frequently between northern posts. Payne notes that social events and church services were often disrupted by alcohol, and that accidents and deaths did occur as a result of alcohol abuse, for fur traders were not known for their moderation, 84. Alcohol was often a major item of trade, and it was used extensively to reward dangerous and demanding work. It would not even have been unusual because, in the eighteenth and nineteenth centuries, alcohol consumption in Britain was also high and drunkenness was commonplace at all levels of society, 85–86.

10. Debra Lindsay, ed., *The Modern Beginnings of Subarctic Ornithology: Correspondence to the Smithsonian Institute, 1856–1868* (Winnipeg: Manitoba Record Society, 1991), 200.

11. Donna McDonald, *Lord Strathcona: A Biography of Donald Alexander Smith* (Toronto: Dundurn Press, 1996), 354. Reference to various correspondence, including Roderick McKenzie to Roderick MacFarlane, 14 December 1879; Richard Hardisty to MacFarlane, 28 February 1880 and 10 January 1881, MG29, A11, Volume 1, LAC; Grahame to Armit, 20 January 1881, D. 13/5, HBCA. Also F983-1 Microfilm MS35 Reel 8, #1926, Strachan Jones, Fort Youcon, to John Strachan, 2 October 1864, Archives of Ontario (AO). In this letter to his father John Strachan, Strachan Jones, who served in the Mackenzie district along with William Hardisty, bemoaned the conditions in the northerly posts but expressed his gratitude for William Hardisty, imploring his father to send Mr. Hardisty "a tin jar of *good* whiskey. I hope you will send it I am under considerable obligations to him and was really glad when he asked me to write to you for the whiskey for I saw that I had an opportunity to oblige him."

12. Lindsay, *Subarctic Ornithology*, xiv. By the time William Hardisty attained the post of chief trader in the Mackenzie district, the HBC no longer feared competition for trade, and thus employees were happy to assist openly with scientific expeditions. Kennicott's expedition was one of the first, and was deemed a "large-scale, apolitical, and non-commercial scientific study of Rupert's Land." As Lindsay notes, the Smithsonian was not concerned with territorial expansion, transport routes, or resource exploitation but sought specimens "for research, for enumeration, and for display." Of the HBC men who submitted the bulk of the Smithsonian's specimens, William Hardisty sent a fairly small amount, 6 per cent compared with other northern men, xix.

13. Donald B. Smith Collection, William Hardisty File, LHA. Reference *Dictionary of Canadian Biography* (Toronto: University of Toronto Press, 1982), 384–385; Jennifer S.H. Brown, "William Lucas Hardisty," *Dictionary of Canadian Biography*, vol. 11, 1881–1890 (Toronto: University of Toronto Press, 1982), 385.

14. Donald B. Smith Collection, William Hardisty File, *Annual Reports of the Board of Regents of the Smithsonian Institution,* 1866, 312, LHA.

15. Donald B. Smith Collection, Hardisty File, LHA. Reference Clifford Wilson, ed., *Papers Read before the Historical and Scientific Society of Manitoba: Private Letters from the Fur Trade* (Winnipeg: Advocate Printers Ltd., 1950), 23. James Anderson to Mr. Wm. McMurray, 28 November 1854.

16. Lindsay, *Subarctic Ornithology,* 59.

17. Ibid., 64.

18. Ibid., 170. James Lockhart to Robert Kennicott, 21 November 1864.

19. Ibid., 191. James Lockhart to Robert Kennicott, 26 June 1865. Lockhart was chief trader at Fort Yukon until moving to Fort Resolution in 1863, where he stayed until outfit 1866–1867, xix.

20. Ibid., 161–162. James Lockhart to Spencer Baird, 1 July 1864.

21. Ibid., 198. Roderick MacFarlane to Spencer Baird, 20 January 1866.

22. Camsell, *Son of the North,* 2. In 1868, Camsell's mother, Sarah, had been invited by Isabella's mother to return with her to the Mackenzie district, where Sarah met her future husband, Captain Julian Stewart Camsell. Camsell's surname was Onion when he was first engaged by the HBC, but he soon took his mother's surname of Camsell. Camsell succeeded William Hardisty as chief factor at Fort Simpson, where Camsell met and married Sarah, 5. Also William J. Healey, *Women of Red River: Being a Book Written from the Recollections of Women Surviving the Red River Era* (Winnipeg: Women's Canadian Club, 1967), 169–170. Apparently, Sarah had nothing but good memories of the North, noting that she "never found life in the Mackenzie District hard," despite living there for thirty-two years. Julian Camsell had signed on with the HBC in 1859, and he ended his career as chief factor of the Mackenzie district in 1882, a post that Isabella's father had also held.

23. Camsell, *Son of the North,* 5.

24. Ibid., 6.

25. Ibid., 6, 7.

26. Ibid., 7.

27. Ibid., 8.

28. Ibid., 9.

29. Ibid., 9.

30. Ibid., 10. Another building was used for storing bales of dried meat and fish. Nearby were thousands of sticks of frozen white fish hung on fences in the fall to be used for both human consumption and dog food. This was where a five o'clock bell summoned servants of the company to get their daily rations.

31. William Hardisty, Fort Simpson, to My Dear Miss Davis, 20 November 1869, Davis Family Correspondence, General #22, Hardisty Family File 1, P1110-1122 (1869–70), AM. Also Donald B. Smith Collection, Hardisty Box 2, Isabella Hardisty Lougheed Timeline File, LHA, contains a copy of this letter.

32. Camsell, *Son of the North*, 18.

33. Ibid., 19.

34. Paul Laverdure, Jacqueline Moir, and John S. Moir, eds., *Travels around Great Slave and Great Bear Lakes, 1862–1882* (Toronto: The Champlain Society, 2005), 163–164. Petitot, who spent many years at northern posts, provides an appealing description of something that Isabella may have encountered as a child, along with other Indigenous children. Even to Petitot's eyes, the "considerable quantity of eggs from all kinds of birds" was like "manna," coming in "pink, pearl grey, white, olive green, beige, and mauve." One only had to scoop down to pick up a handful of "pretty" eggs, some with patterns delicately outlining a "geographic map." If a priest who had likely experienced some hardships could appreciate this beauty, then that much more could a young child like Isabella.

35. Ibid., xx.

36. Ibid., 248.

37. Ibid., 118.

38. Ibid., 149.

39. Ibid., 151.

40. J. Russell Harper, ed., *Paul Kane's Frontier: Including Wanderings of an Artist among the Indians of North America* (Toronto: University of Toronto Press, 1971), xi. Although some have questioned the authenticity of some of Kane's observations, both written and pictorial, Kane's work does serve as another indicator of the close relations between "white, Metis and Indians alike" at the northern fur trade posts where Isabella spent her formative years.

41. Ibid., 172.

42. Donald B. Smith Collection, Hardisty Box 2, Isabella Hardisty Lougheed Timeline File, LHA. Reference *Saturday Night*, 16 September 1922, Elizabeth Bailey Price Fonds, M1000 Price, Elizabeth Bailey Clippings, 1920s–1950s Biographies, L–Z Alberta, GAIA.

43. Beckles Willson, *The Great Company (1667–1871): Being a History of the Honourable Company of Merchants-Adventurers Trading into Hudson's Bay*, vol. 1 (London: Smith, Elder & Co., 1900), 510–511.

44. Payne, *The Most Respectable Place*, 27.

45. Ian MacLaren, "Paul Kane and the Authorship of *Wanderings of an Artist*," in *From Rupert's Land to Canada: Essays in Honour of John E. Foster*, ed. Theodore Binnema,

Gerhard Ens, and R.C. MacLeod (Edmonton: University of Alberta Press, 2001), 138.

46. Kerry Abel, *Drum Songs: Glimpses of Dene History* (Montreal: McGill-Queen's University Press, 1993), 150. Reference Andrew Flett to W.L. Hardisty, Peels River, 1 February 1866, B.200/b/36,40, HBCA.

47. Ibid., 50. Reference W.L. Hardisty to Governor Mactavish, Fort Simpson, 27 November 1866, B.200/b/35, Folder 103d, HBCA. It is not clear what caused the death of so many in this instance, but by this time many Indigenous people had suffered tremendous losses due to a variety of epidemics.

48. Donald B. Smith Collection, James Lougheed #1 Box 1, James Lougheed Overview File, "James Alexander and Isabella Lougheed A Chronological History," LHA. Reference James Grierson MacGregor, *Senator Hardisty's Prairies, 1849–1889* (Saskatoon: Western Producer Prairie Books, 1978), 46–47. Reference Chief Trader William Lucas Hardisty to Sir George Simpson–Fort Yukon, 10 November 1857, D./45, Folder 264d, HBCA, AM. Also Beattie and Buss, *Undelivered Letters*. Reference D./45 Folder 263d-4d, HBCA, AM.

49. Beattie and Buss, *Undelivered Letters*, 43. The editors offer no references upon which they base their conclusion.

50. Donald B. Smith Collection, Hardisty Box 2, Belle Hardisty Timeline File, LHA. Reference William Hardisty, Fort Simpson, to My Dear Miss Davis, 20 November 1869, Davis Family Correspondence, General #22, Hardisty Family File 1, P1110-1122 (1869–70), AM.

51. Martha McCarthy, "Northern Métis and the Churches," in *Picking Up the Threads: Métis History in the Mackenzie Basin* (Winnipeg: Metis Heritage Association of the Northwest Territories and Parks Canada–Canadian Heritage, 1998), 135. Reference OAGP Faraud to Hardisty, 8 July 1863.

52. Charles D. Denney Fonds, W.L. Hardisty to Dear Sister, En Route to Portage La Loche 10 July 1870, GAIA. Denney references Richard Hardisty Fonds M7144 File #330,000.

53. MacGregor, *Senator Hardisty's Prairies*, 60. Reference C.D. Denney papers, Marriage of Eliza McDougall and Richard Hardisty, 20 September 1866, GAIA. Richard no doubt met Eliza after providing travel accommodations for her father, George McDougall, and his son, John, on their early missionary trips as the Methodists struggled to keep up to Roman Catholic missionaries. As MacGregor writes, John McDougall, a "muscular young Methodist," was to give Father Lacombe a "hard race towards the pinnacles of fame...but also one whose family history was destined to run hand in hand with Richard Hardisty's," 44–45.

54. Richard Hardisty Fonds, Accession No. M5908-1458, Series 23-1, Richard Hardisty Sr. to Richard Hardisty, 28 March 1859, GAIA.

55. Richard Hardisty Fonds, Accession No. M5908-1469, Series 23-1, Richard
     Hardisty Sr. to Richard Hardisty, 14 April 1863, GAIA; Richard Hardisty Fonds,
     Accession No. M475, H264A, Richard Hardisty Sr. to Richard Hardisty, 23 January
     1860, GAIA. In this earlier letter, Richard Sr. said of William that he did not
     "think that there can be any necessity for his sending his wife to Canada to be
     educated, he is well enough able to educate her himself if he likes." Perhaps
     William took advantage of the educational material forwarded by England in
     order to do just that.

56. Abel, *Drum Songs*, 151n26. Reference W.L. Hardisty to James Grahame, Portage la
     Loche, 19 August 1877, B.200/b/39, Volume 2 Folder 39, HBCA. William Hardisty's
     comments were not that unusual and are similar to those of Alexander Ross.
     Alexander Ross, *The Red River Settlement: Its Rise, Progress, and Present State* (1856;
     repr., Minneapolis: Ross and Haines, 1957). Ross was a fur trader who had also
     married an Indigenous woman and his book was the first published account by
     an author from that region.

57. Donald B. Smith Collection, Hardisty Box 2, Belle Hardisty Timeline File, LHA.
     Reference William Hardisty, Fort Simpson, to My Dear Miss Davis, 20 November
     1869, Davis Family Correspondence, General #22, Hardisty Family File 1, P1110-
     1122 (1869–70), AM.

58. Willson, *The Life of Lord Strathcona*, 119.

59. Ibid., 125.

60. Parish Records Saint Stephen's, F.36, 70, Diocèse de Montreal Eglise Anglicane
     du Canada Archives.

61. He fulfilled this duty for both Marguerite Sutherland Hardisty and Thomas
     Hardisty, who died in 1875.

62. MacGregor, *Senator Hardisty's Prairies*, 183.

63. Willson, *The Life of Lord Strathcona*, 360.

64. Ibid. Appendix A in Willson's book shows a photo of William Hardisty as he
     might have looked when hosting the splendid parties.

65. Donna McDonald, *Lord Strathcona: A Biography of Donald Alexander Smith*
     (Toronto: Dundurn Press, 1996), 354. McDonald refers to various correspondence,
     including Roderick McKenzie to Roderick MacFarlane, 14 December 1879;
     Richard Hardisty to MacFarlane, 28 February 1880 and 10 January 1881, MG29,
     A11, Volume 1, LAC; and Grahame to Armit, 20 January 1881, D.13/5, HBCA.

66. McDonald, *Lord Strathcona*, 354; Donald B. Smith Collection, William Hardisty
     File, LHA. Reference *Dictionary of Canadian Biography* (Toronto: University of
     Toronto Press, 1982), 384–385. Also Christina Jorup-Ronstrom, "Epidemiological,
     Bacteriological and Complicating Features of Erysipelas," *Scandinavian Journal
     of Infectious Diseases* 18, no. 6 (1986): 519–524, doi:10.3109/00365548609021656.

The illness Isabella's father died from, erysipelas, is a bacterial infection often occurring in those suffering from diabetes or alcoholism. Also *Manitoba Daily Free Press*, 18 January 1881, n.p. The *Manitoba Free Press* noted that the "Veteran Nor'Wester" had died suddenly in Lachine, leaving a widow and several children who resided in Winnipeg.

67. MacGregor, *Senator Hardisty's Prairies*, 183. Reference *Edmonton Bulletin*, 4 March 1882.

68. McDonald, *Lord Strathcona*, 354.

69. Ibid., 355. Reference Smith to Richard Hardisty, 7 October 1885, M5908, Box 8, GAIA.

70. Ibid., 357. Reference Jim Hill papers, Smith to Hill, 2 February 1884.

71. Ibid., 356. Reference Hardisty to Smith, 24 October 1884, D.18/5, HBCA; Smith to Richard Hardisty, 7 October 1885, Glenbow, M5908, Box 8; Joseph Hardisty to Richard Hardisty, 17 December 1885, Glenbow M477, Box 7.

72. Donald B. Smith Collection, Lougheed #1 Box 1, Lougheed Toronto Directories File, footnote 31, LHA refers to an email to Donald B. Smith from Judith H. Beattie, keeper of the HBCA on 10 June 1999, about Mary Allen. Also Notman, William & Son Photographic Studio Collection, Accession No. C343, McCord Museum, Montreal, Glenbow catalogue number NA 2758-1, GAIA, photo of Mary Allen Hardisty Thomas, who married Edwin Stuart Thomas, in 1881. Mary Allen is also identified in the photo as the daughter of Robert Allen and Charlotte Scarborough, Metis.

73. Donald B. Smith Collection, Hardisty Box 1, Hardisty Family File, LHA. The file notes correspondence from Bruce Watson via Jean Barman. Also Beattie and Buss, *Undelivered Letters*, 40–43. Reference undelivered letter dated 4 June 1833 from Mary Allan (Allen), mother of Robert Allen, who was distraught and out of money. Also Edwin Ernest Rich, ed., *The Letters of John McLoughlin from Fort Vancouver to the Governor and Committee*, vol. 1 (Toronto: The Champlain Society, 1941), 190. Rich lists Robert Allen as a carpenter on board the *Nereide* on 26 October 1837.

74. Beattie and Buss, *Undelivered Letters*, 40. Reference 4 June 1833, C.7/21, Folder 7-8d, HBCA, AM.

75. Donald B. Smith Collection, Allen Richard Cadboro File, LHA. Reference Rich, *The Letters of John McLoughlin*, 355. Also Donald B. Smith Collection, Hardisty Box 1, Captain James Allen Scarborough File, LHA. Reference for Captain Scarborough's wife in the *Sunday News Tribune*, Tacoma, WA, 10 August 1958.

76. Beattie and Buss, *Undelivered Letters*. They provide details of the *Isabella's* sailing on 30 October 1829, arriving on the Columbia via the Sandwich Islands on 2 May 1830, when she was wrecked with no loss of life. Reference C.1/355, HBCA, AM.

77. Rich, *The Letters of John McLoughlin*, 277.

78. Ibid., 102.

79. Edmond S. Meaney, *Origin of Washington Geographical Names* (Seattle: University of Washington Press, 1923), 259.

80. Donald B. Smith Collection, Hardisty Box 1, Captain James Allen Scarborough File, LHA. Reference "Scarborough's Pioneer Home, Pacific Northwest 100 Years Ago," *Seattle Sunday Times*, 21 September 1947, 2.

81. Pollard, "The Making of the Metis," 1.

82. Ibid., 43. Pollard writes that the children of Chinook and European ancestry numbered in the thousands by 1850.

83. Ibid., 3-4.

84. Mikell De Lores Wormell Warner, *Catholic Church Records of the Pacific Northwest: Vancouver Volumes I and II and Stellamaris Mission*, trans. Harriet Duncan Munnick (St. Paul, OR: French Prairie Press, 1972), 25, 26, 27, M9.

85. Beattie and Buss, *Undelivered Letters*, 424n10.

86. Warner, *Catholic Church Records*, A88. Also Rich, *The Letters of John McLoughlin*.

87. Warner, *Catholic Church Records*, A8. James Birney was at Fort George in 1842.

88. United States, Work Projects Administration, Washington State, *Told by the Pioneers*, vol. 1 (Olympia, WA: n.p., 1937-1938), 113.

89. Warner, *Catholic Church Records*, A5. In November of 1842, Alexandre Burney, son of James Burney and Charlotte Beaulieu, was baptised by Father Blanchet. This was one year before the marriage of James Birney and Charlotte Beaulieu and, at the time, Birney was listed as a clerk in charge of Fort George, in the service of the HBC, 7, 8, and 9, B27.

90. Warner, *Catholic Church Records*, 3 and 4, B16. In November of 1842, James Scarborough and Paley Temaikamae Tchinouk had their son, James, three and a half months old, baptised by Father Blanchet. In May of 1848, Charlotte Beaulieu and James Birney had two children baptised at Fort Vancouver, a son, Archibald, seven months old, and a daughter, Caroline, four years, Stellamaris Point Register 972, 95 and 96, B643.44. In November of 1851, James Birney and "Mistress Charlotte Beaulieu" of Cathlamet city, had a son, Thomas Lowe, aged three months, baptised, Register 121, 122, 126, and 124, B29. On 30 October 1843, Paley was baptised as Anne Elizabeth by Father Modeste Demers, and her godparents were Forbes Barclay, esquire and doctor, and his wife Maria Pambrun. On that same day, Paley and James Scarborough were married, Register 25, 26, and 27, B105 and M9. On 24 November 1848, Xavier Scarborogt (Scarborough), son of Anne Elizabeth (Paley Temaikamae, Chinook), and Jacques A. Scarborough were baptised by Father Lionnet at Stellamaris Point Chinouk, Register, 1 and 2, B1. There was a baptism by the same priest on 17

May 1850, of a four-year-old boy named Philippe, the son of a female slave at the house of Scarboeoth (Scarborough), Stellamaris Point Chinouk Register, 4 and 5, B41. On 14 January 1851, Robert Skarboroth (Scarborough), four days old, son of Anne Elizabeth and Jacques A., was baptised. On the same day, an infant, Marthe, born of a slave woman in the house of Scarboroth (Scarborough) was also baptised, Stellamaris Point Chinouk Register, 5, 6, and 7, B48.

91. Warner, *Catholic Church Records*, Stellamaris Point Register, 10, 11, and 12.

92. Ibid., 12 and 13, B98.

93. Pollard, "The Making of the Metis," 20.

94. Richard Somerset Mackie, *Trading beyond the Mountains: The British Fur Trade on the Pacific, 1793–1843* (Vancouver: UBC Press, 1997), 303. Reference Alexander Ross, *Adventures of the First Settlers on the Oregon or Columbia River: Being a Narrative of the Expedition Fitted out by John Jacob Astor, to Establish the Pacific Fur Company* (London: Smith, Elder and Co., 1849), 94.

95. Ibid., 310.

96. Ibid., 308.

97. Ibid., 306.

98. Ibid., 306.

99. Ibid.

100. "Allen, Robert," HBCA, Biographical Sheets, accessed 7 January 2010, http://www.gov.mb.ca/chc/archives/hbca/biographical/a.html.

101. Rich, *The Letters of John McLoughlin*, 356.

102. Fort Dunvegan was established by the North West Company in 1805 as a trading post on the Upper Peace River, and as a base for exploration and development of New Caledonia (northern British Columbia). By the time of Mary Allen's arrival in the area as a child, the post was already in the control of the HBC. Thus, if there was a trade brokered for Mary Allen, it is highly likely there was an HBC connection.

103. Beattie and Buss, *Undelivered Letters*, 41. Reference A.10/19 Folder 166, HBCA, AM.

104. Ibid., 424. Reference E.69/1, Folder 68, HBCA, AM.

105. "Hardisty, William Lucas," Biographical Sheets.

106. Chief Trader William Lucas Hardisty to Sir George Simpson, Fort Yukon, 10 November 1857, D5/45, Folder 264d, HBCA, AM. Also Robin Fisher, *Contact and Conflict: Indian–European Relations in British Columbia, 1774–1890* (Vancouver: UBC Press, 1992), 26. Fisher wrote that Fort Simpson, where Hardisty married Mary Allen, was the most important coastal station of the HBC. The schooner *Cadboro* was acquired in 1827 and was used in the establishment of Fort Simpson. It is interesting that Isabella's great-grandfather, Captain Scarborough, commanded the schooner that would help establish Fort Simpson, the post at which her

father, William Hardisty, would serve in 1862, and the post where he would marry the granddaughter of Captain Scarborough.

107. John S. Galbraith, "Simpson, Sir George," in *Dictionary of Canadian Biography*, vol. 8, University of Toronto/Université Laval, 2003–, accessed 2 May 2012, http://www.biographi.ca/009004-119.01-e.php?id_nbr=4188.

108. Beattie and Buss, *Undelivered Letters*, 42.

109. Ibid., 42. Beattie and Buss note the irony that William Hardisty felt he needed to explain his marriage to a woman of Indigenous ancestry, given that he was himself the product of a country marriage.

110. Donald B. Smith Collection, Hardisty Box 1, William Hardisty File, LHA. Reference D S/12//0093-94 Simpson Correspondence, 1857, Chief Trader William Lucas Hardisty to Sir George Simpson, Fort Youcon, 10 November 1857, HBCA.

111. Donald B. Smith Collection, Hardisty Box 1, Mary Allen Hardisty 1840–1930 File, LHA. Reference Charles Denny Papers, Richard Hardisty, Accession No. M7144, File 330,000 (1 and 2), Valerie Dartnell to unknown, 11 September 1973. Dartnell wrote that Mary Allen "said she was French, but my mother didn't think so. She looked like a native."

112. Donald B. Smith Collection, Mary Allen Correspondence File, LHA. Reference McCord Museum, Notman Collection, catalogue number NA-2758-1, source Mrs. L. Morrison, Calgary.

113. Gerhard J. Ens, ed., *A Son of the Fur Trade: The Memoirs of Johnny Grant* (Edmonton: University of Alberta Press, 2008), x.

114. Established in 1786, Fort Resolution was originally a North West Company post but was renamed after the amalgamation in 1821.

115. K.S. Coates and W.R. Morrison, "More Than a Matter of Blood: The Federal Government, the Churches and the Mixed Blood Populations of the Yukon and the Mackenzie River Valley, 1890–1950," in *1885 and After: Native Society in Transition*, ed. F. Laurie Barron and James B. Waldram (Regina: Canadian Plains Research Center, 1986), 255.

116. Martha McCarthy, *From the Great River to the Ends of the Earth: Oblate Missions to the Dene, 1847–1921* (Edmonton: University of Alberta Press, 1995), 16–17.

117. Janes, *Preserving Diversity*, 185.

118. Hudson's Bay Company Collection, C099, Fort Simpson Journal 1862–65, 1 February 1863, McCord Museum Archives (MMA).

119. Jennifer L. Bellman and Christopher C. Hanks, "Northern Métis and the Fur Trade," in *Picking Up the Threads: Métis History in the Mackenzie Basin* (Winnipeg: Metis Heritage Association of the Northwest Territories and Parks Canada–Canadian Heritage, 1998), 63.

120. Tough, *"As Their Natural Resources Fail,"* 19.

121. Janes, *Preserving Diversity*, 79.

122. Ibid., 84.

123. Jennifer Bobrovitz, researcher, Lougheed House National Historic Site, interviews by author, Calgary, AB, 2007–2009.

124. Van Kirk, *"Many Tender Ties,"* 97. Also Payne, *The Most Respectable Place*, 108. Reference B.239/b/78, Folder 5, annual letter to York Factory, 29 May 1794, HBCA. It seems that the central office of the HBC in England had similar concerns. As early as 1794, London had shipped "one hundred Primers or Spelling Books for the use of the Children" to York Factory, and some were also shipped to other posts.

125. Abel, *Drum Songs*, 94.

126. Ibid., 146.

127. Donald B. Smith Collection, Hardisty Box 1, Mackenzie River File, LHA. Reference Chris Hanks, "Francois Beaulieu II: The Origins of the Metis in the Far Northwest," in *Selected Papers of Rupert's Land Colloquium 2000* (Winnipeg: The Centre for Rupert's Land Studies, 2000), 9. Hanks refers to the writings of Mendez, n.d.

128. Clifford Wilson, ed., *Papers Read before the Historical and Scientific Society of Manitoba: Private Letters from the Fur Trade* (Winnipeg: Advocate Printers Ltd., 1950), 41. Reference W.L. Hardisty, Fort Providence, 24 December 1869, to William McMurray Esq., Fort Chipewyan.

129. Ibid., 45. Reference W.L. Hardisty to Mr. McMurray, 12 January 1870 [1871].

130. McCarthy, *From the Great River*, 116.

131. Innis, *The Fur Trade in Canada*, 342.

132. McCarthy, *From the Great River*, 116. Reference B.200/e/14, Folder 3d, Mackenzie District Report, 1875, HBCA.

133. Ibid., 108.

134. Ibid., 123. Reference AASB T11274-76 Gascon to Taché, 1 December 1872.

135. McCarthy, *From the Great River*, 110. McCarthy relies on the *Annales de la Propogation de la Foi* when she writes that George Simpson believed that François, in the end, refused to carry out the crime. Reference Annales 37 (1865), Petitot to Faraud, 22 June 1864. McCarthy likely refers to the 1816 incident in which MacKintosh used his influence to prevent Clarke from encountering Indigenous people in order to trade. The result was that fifteen men, one clerk, and a woman and child died of starvation. Also Philip Goldring, "MacKintosh, William," in *Dictionary of Canadian Biography*, vol. 7, University of Toronto/ Université Laval, 2003–, accessed 27 April 2012, http://www.biographi.ca/009004-119.01-e.php?id_nbr=3522.

136. McCarthy, *From the Great River*, 114. One example, which again involved William Hardisty, was the situation with Catherine Beaulieu, daughter of François, who married Joseph Bouvier of Red River. In 1878, Catherine, reacting to the anti-Catholicism of the HBC postmaster, John Reid, used her influence with Indigenous peoples in Providence so that they gave their grease and good meat to the Roman Catholic mission. Thereafter, William Hardisty "withdrew his recommendation that a pension be awarded to Mme Bouvier following the death of her husband," 110.

137. Hudson's Bay Company Collection, C099, Fort Simpson Journal 1862–65, 30 June 1863, MMA.

138. Ibid., journal entry for 4 August 1863.

139. Kerry Abel, "Bompas, Charlotte Selina (Cox)," in *Dictionary of Canadian Biography*, vol. 14, 1911–1920 (Toronto: University of Toronto Press, 1998), 247.

140. Hudson's Bay Company Collection, C099, Fort Simpson Journal 1862–65, 16 May 1864, MMA.

141. Ibid., 28, journal entry for March 1863.

142. Donald B. Smith Collection, Hardisty Box 2, Belle Lougheed File, Madeline Johnson, "Lady Isabella Lougheed," 6, LHA.

143. Lougheed House Research Files, "Beaulieu (the name)," LHA. Also "Beaulieu: Palace House and Abbey," accessed 14 April 2011, http://www.beaulieu.co.uk/ bealieupalace/introduction.cfm. Palace House, formerly the fourteenth-century Great Gatehouse of Beaulieu Abbey, was owned by Lord Montagu's family since 1538, when Sir Thomas Wriothesley, the first Earl of Southampton, bought the estate after the dissolution of the monasteries. Also Old Files, Letter to Vera Appletree (a Calgary resident) from Beaulieu Abbey & Exhibition, Hampshire, 28 January 1998, LHA. The letter is obviously a reply to an inquiry about a link between Isabella's "Metis ancestors" and "the Montagus of Beaulieu." The archivist explains that, while she cannot confirm a link, the abbey adopted the French meaning of "Beau Lieu" after the monks, and Lord Montagu retained the French spelling. The archivist goes on to explain that one of Lord Montagu's ancestors did subscribe to an expedition of the Northwest Passage in 1746 in association with the HBC.

144. Newspaper Clippings File, "Canadian Women in the Public Eye." In Lachine, as Isabella recovered from the illness that had forced her to leave Miss Davis's school, she would have worshipped at Saint Stephen's Anglican Church, which still stands today next to the cemetery, where, according to church records, her father is buried. Reference Quebec Family History Society, Burial 1881, St. Stephen Anglican, accessed 6 October 2007, http://www.qfhs.ca. Also personal correspondence with St. Stephen Anglican. Unfortunately, the cemetery has

fallen into ill repair and very few markers are left to indicate the exact location of William Hardisty's burial (confirmed after a visit I made to Lachine, Quebec, in July 2009, and through correspondence with Bob Smith, church historian).

145. Matilda Davis School Folder, Research Files, Robert Hunter, Architectural History Branch, "Historic Sites and Monuments Board of Canada Agenda Paper," 253, LHA. Matilda was sent to England to be educated, and when she returned to Red River was reportedly regarded as a "distinguished member of the community, invited to the governor's balls, complimented on the quality of her French by the Roman Catholic bishop and noted for her integrity."

146. Pollard, "The Making of the Metis." Pollard wrote that the closest the Metis children ever came to an "all-Metis" education was when the HBC fort schools were established in the late eighteenth and early nineteenth centuries, 280–281. She refers to the journal of Reverend John West, who established the first Anglican school at Red River in 1820, to write that the purpose was to maintain, clothe, and educate a "number of half-breed children running about, growing up in ignorance and idleness," 281. Reference John West's journal, 12–13. Although most of the children were of mixed-blood heritage, Pollard argued that the goal was still to maintain a class system and to reproduce gentlemen and ladies in the children of officers, while the children of labourers were intended to become good Christians and useful labourers, 282. As to curricula, the HBC issued a directive that children be instructed in "A B C" and schools could be sanctioned for not doing so. As early as 1798 there is reference in post journals to children being "at their books" at Moose Factory, 284. Reference H.A. Innis, ed., "Notes and Documents: Rupert's Land in 1825," CHR, no. 4, 1926, 320.

147. Matilda Davis School Folder, Research Files, LHA. From Matilda Davis School Collection, MG2C24, Box 2 File 2, Notebook, 3, AM. Also Matilda Davis School Collection, Accession P4724/3, Correspondence, 1861–65, Letter, 12 November 1865, Hardisty Family to Isabella Hardisty, from Fort Simpson to Davis School, AM. The letter is dated 1865, but this suggests that Isabella would have been at Miss Davis's School at the age of four. Further, there are only records confirming tuition for Isabella at Miss Davis's school for the year 1867. Regardless if the date is correct, the letter does reveal concern on the part of Isabella's mother and father with her being so far from home. Her mother asks William if Isabella cried when she was left at the school, while William implores Isabella several times in the letter to be a "good girl" continuing that she must "never be cross never do anything that is bad, and never forget your Papa, Mamma, Dick &; Little Ned."

148. Richard Hardisty Fonds, Accession No. M5908, Series 23-2, 1489, GAIA. Margaret Hardisty to Richard Hardisty, 3 September 1867.

149. Newspaper Clippings File, "Canadian Women in the Public Eye." Also Waymarking, accessed 20 January 2010, http://www.waymarking.com/waymarks/ WM9XH_OHP_ONTARIO_LADIES_COLLEGE_Whitby. Whitby College was operated by the Methodist Church in the former residence of Nelson Gilbert Reynolds, a man appointed to serve as sheriff of Whitby, Ontario. Also Whitby Public Library, Online Historical Photographs Collection, accessed 2 May 2012, http://images.ourontario.ca/whitby/43652/data. It is not clear if Isabella might have been referring to the son of the owner of the house, Reynolds, or to Rev. Dr. John James Hare, who served as the principal of the Ontario Ladies' College from 1874 to 1915.

150. Donald B. Smith Collection, Hardisty Box 1, William Hardisty File, LHA. William Hardisty to Miss Davis, 10 July 1870, from En Route to Portage La Loche. Reference Barbara Johnstone Collection, Prepared by J. Pentland, August 1986, P2342 111, Davis Family Correspondence General #22, Hardisty Family File 1, P1110-1122 1869–1870, AM.

151. Donald B. Smith Collection, Hardisty Box 2, Belle Lougheed File, Madeline Johnson, "Lady Isabella Lougheed," 4, LHA. Also Matilda Davis Family Fonds, P2342, AM.

152. For most of the girls at Red River, the goal was no doubt that they would take their rightful place as wives of officers and mothers of future officers, and, in so doing, increase the earning potential, strength, and stability of the extended family network.

153. Donald B. Smith Collection, Hardisty Box 1, William Lucas Hardisty File, LHA. William Hardisty to Miss Davis, 10 July 1870, from En Route to Portage La Loche. Reference Barbara Johnstone Collection, prepared by J. Pentland, August 1986, P2342 111, Davis Family Correspondence General #22, Hardisty Family File 1, P1110-1122 1869–1870, AM.

154. Parish Records Saint Stephen's, F.39, 76, ACA. William Lucas Hardisty was present and served as witness to the burial.

155. George Heath MacDonald, *Edmonton: Fort, House, Factory* (Edmonton: Douglas Print Company, 1959), 155. Reference Donald A. Smith to Richard Hardisty, Montreal, 27 December 1872. The author does not indicate where he accessed the letter.

156. Ibid., 193.

157. Hamilton Public Library File, R376.8 W516 1871/72, Wesleyan Female College, Tenth Annual Catalogue, Wesleyan Ladies' College Archives File, Hamilton Public Library Archives (HPLA). The majority of Isabella's schoolmates this year were from Ontario, Quebec, or the eastern United States.

158. Richard Hardisty Fonds, Accession No. M 477-72, Series 6-7, GAIA. W.L. Hardisty to "Dear Sister," 10 July 1870.

159. Ibid.

160. Richard Hardisty Fonds, Accession No. M 5908, Series 23-2, 1505, GAIA. Margaret Hardisty to Richard Hardisty, 8 April 1872.

161. Archives Files, R376.8 W 518 W H, *Literary Club in connection with the Hamilton Ladies' College Alumnae Association*, 1, HPLA. The minute books of the Wesleyan Alumnae Association for the period prior to 1915 are missing, thus I cannot confirm if Isabella was involved in any way after she left Hamilton.

162. Archives Files, R376.8 W 518 W H, *Literary Club in connection with the Hamilton Ladies' College Alumnae Association*, Annual Report 1962–63, 1070, HPLA.

163. Hamilton Public Library File, Hamilton Wesleyan College Archives File, Louise E. Purchase to Miss Waldon, 26 October 1962, "A Sketch of Janet (Nettie) T. Coatsworth Ramsey Mistress of English Literature, 1875–1879," LHA.

164. *Hamilton Herald*, 29 June 1927, 12.

165. Richard Hardisty Fonds, Accession No. M 5908, Series 23-3, 1572, Bella Hardisty to Dear Aunt Eliza, 10 December 1877, GAIA.

166. Elizabeth Bailey Price Fonds, Accession No. M1000, File 2, "Lady Lougheed," 5, GAIA.

167. Arthur Ray, *The Canadian Fur Trade in the Industrial Age* (Toronto: University of Toronto Press, 1990), 26.

168. Newspaper Clippings File, "Canadian Women in the Public Eye." Also Donald B. Smith Collection, Lougheed #1 Box 1, James Lougheed Overview File, LHA. Excerpt written by Jennifer Bobrovitz. Also Elizabeth Bailey Price Fonds, Accession No. M1000, File 2 "Lady Lougheed," 3, GAIA.

169. Donald B. Smith Collection, Hardisty Box 2, Hamilton College File, LHA. Also Jennifer Cook-Bobrovitz and Trudy Cowan, *Lougheed House: More Than a Century of Stories* (Calgary: Lougheed House, 2006). Reference Hamilton Public Library, Special Collections Dept., to M.H. Exton, Lougheed House Conservation Society, 6 March 1996.

170. Richard Hardisty Fonds, Box 5, Item 8983, GAIA. John Bunn, Fort Calgary, to Bella Hardisty, 5 September 1877. The letter refers to her safe arrival and that "I am sure that you are both happy together at school."

171. Brown, "William Lucas Hardisty," 385. Also Elizabeth Price, "Alberta Women Pioneers Will Form Organization," *Calgary Herald*, 21 March 1922. Isabella confirmed this information in her interview with Price.

172. MacGregor, *Senator Hardisty's Prairies*. Members of Isabella's kinship network assisted the Central Canadian government both in 1869–1870 and in 1885. When fighting erupted in 1869 in Red River, Isabella's uncle, Donald A. Smith, was

appointed by the Canadian government to travel to Red River in an attempt to resolve the dispute. Her other uncle, Richard Hardisty, interrupted his furlough and joined his brother-in-law in Fort Garry, where he was promptly arrested by Riel's men, 70–71. Also Beckles Willson, *The Life of Lord Strathcona and Mount Royal* (Boston: Houghton Mifflin Company, 1915). While some accounts claim that both Donald A. Smith and Richard Hardisty were held prisoner when they arrived in Red River, Willson claimed that Hardisty, because he had "Indian blood in his veins," was allowed to consort freely with his Metis friends in the settlement. Willson continued that this freedom allowed Richard Hardisty to carry out Smith's mission to "secure partisans amongst the half-breeds" by offering them cash or promissory notes from the HBC, 327–328. Willson wrote that many old-timers later remembered that Donald Smith's life had been at great risk because he was an HBC man, 343. Also Ens, *A Son of the Fur Trade*. Ens writes in the introduction that, according to Grant, who was in Red River in 1869–1870, Richard Hardisty was not allowed to "consort freely," but rather his life was in as much danger as that of Donald Smith's, with violence only averted "through the mediation of the Catholic clergy," xviii.

173. Deborah Lougheed Research Disc, *Manitoba Free Press*, 21 May 1885, 1–4, LHA. Also McLaws Redman Lougheed and Cairns Fonds, Fond 37, File 173, Folder 2, William Lucas Hardisty Estate, Certificate of death for Richard Hardisty, Province of Manitoba, Dept of Health and Public Welfare, 12 May 1885, issued 12 April 1930, the Legal Archives Society of Alberta (LASA).

174. Deborah Lougheed Research Disc, *Manitoba Free Press*, 21 May 1885, 1–4, LHA.

175. Ibid., 22 May 1885, 5.

176. Ibid., 28 May 1885, 2.

177. Lougheed House Research Files, Chief Buffalo Child Long Lance, "Indians of the Northwest and West Canada," *The Mentor* 12, no. 3 (March 1924): 6, LHA. Also Donald B. Smith, *Chief Buffalo Child Long Lance: The Glorious Impostor* (Red Deer: Red Deer Press, 1999). Smith explores Long Lance's real identity.

178. Richard Hardisty Fonds, Accession No. M477, File 137, #808, letter to My dear Hardisty, 22 December 1876, GAIA. The author may have been R. MacFarlane, since other letters found in Richard Hardisty's files from the same location and with the same date are signed by MacFarlane.

3   GRACIOUS WOMANHOOD

1.   Carole Gerson and Veronica Strong-Boag, "Championing the Native: E. Pauline Johnson Rejects the Squaw," in *Contact Zones: Aboriginal & Settler Women in Canada's Colonial Past*, ed. Katie Pickles and Myra Rutherdale (Vancouver: UBC Press, 2005), 50.

2. Lougheed House Research Files, Accession No. 2000.12.1, LHA. Also Dr. B.J. Charles Fonds, Accession No. M8949, GAIA. *The Albertan*, 28 January 1965, "Man About Town," explains that Dr. Charles was a dentist with an interest in the Pioneers Association and that he spent hours in the 1930s recording its stories. Also Eva Reid, "Eavesdrop with Eva," *The Albertan*, 18 February 1961, Dr. B.J. Charles Fonds, Accession No. M8949, GAIA. Reid writes that the footage, the only surviving one of Isabella, shows her strolling through her beautiful garden with her son Edgar (Peter Lougheed's father).

3. LHA Archivist Cassandra Cummings notes that filming began in 1933. Reference "Unique Film Collections Shows Many Oldtimers," *The Albertan*, 8 July 1950.

4. "Hardisty, William Lucas," Biographical Sheets.

5. Donald B. Smith Collection, Hardisty Box 2, Isabella Hardisty Lougheed Timeline File, *Saturday Night*, 16 September 1922, LHA. Reference Accession No. M1000, Elizabeth Bailey Price & clippings, 1920s–1950s Biographies, L–Z Alberta, GAIA.

6. Jennifer Bobrovitz Files, LHA. Reference Charles Denney Papers.

7. David J. Hall and Donald B. Smith, "Lougheed, Sir James Alexander," in *Dictionary of Canadian Biography*, vol. 15, University of Toronto/Université Laval, 2003–, accessed 26 April 2011, http://www.biographi.ca/en/bio/lougheed_james_ alexander_15E.html.

8. *Calgary Herald*, 23 November 1883.

9. Donald B. Smith Collection, Hardisty Box 2, Isabella Hardisty Lougheed Timeline File, *Saturday Night*, 16 September 1922, LHA. Reference Accession No. M1000, Price, Elizabeth Bailey Ms. & clippings, 1920s–1950s Biographies, L–Z Alberta, GAIA.

10. Hall and Smith, "Lougheed, Sir James Alexander."

11. Jennifer Bobrovitz Files, LHA. Reference *Calgary Herald*, 5 October 1883, personals, "James A. Lougheed. Barrister, Solicitor, Conveyancer. Notary Public. Calgary and Medicine Hat. Office at Wilson's Dental Rooms, north of new post office."

12. James Lougheed Biographical Dictionaries File, 31–40, LHA. Reference David J. Hall and Donald B. Smith, *Dictionary of Canadian Biography* vol. 15, 1921–1930, 608. Also J.M.S. Careless, "The Emergence of Cabbagetown in Victorian Toronto," in *Gathering Place: Peoples and Neighbourhoods of Toronto, 1834–1945*, ed. Robert F. Harney (Toronto: Multicultural History Society of Ontario, 1985), 25.

13. Hall and Smith, "Lougheed, Sir James Alexander."

14. Alan L. Hayes, *Holding Forth the Word of Life: Little Trinity Church, 1842–1992* (Toronto: Corporation of Little Trinity Church, 1991), 11.

15. Samuel's brother, Edward, later became premier of Ontario and leader of the federal Liberals.

16. Donald B. Smith Collection, Lougheed #1 Box 1, James Lougheed 1854–1925, Newsletter Volume 4, No. 2, November 1993, LHA. Also Donald B. Smith Collection, James Lougheed Biographical Dictionary File, 608, LHA. These reminiscences were reportedly by cousins Jane and Elizabeth in 1936. Also Lougheed Correspondence James & Bell File, Box 1, letter from Donald Smith to Peter Lougheed, LHA. Smith writes that Perkins Bull Papers Archives of Ontario interviewed Jane Lougheed (1850–1939) and Elizabeth Lougheed (1861–1947) in 1936. Reference Lougheed Archives P36705. Also Donald B. Smith Collection, Lougheed #1 Box 1, Lougheed Toronto Trip File and Lougheeds of Britannia File, LHA. Reference Ontario Archives Perkins Bull Collection Series A. This file contains a copy of the interview.

17. Donald B. Smith Collection, Lougheed #1, Box 1, James Lougheed Overview File, LHA. Jennifer Bobrovitz "James Alexander and Isabella Lougheed: A Chronological History," 19 August 2003. Bobrovitz quotes Certificate, M4843, File 13, GAIA. Also Donald B. Smith Collection, Lougheed #1 Box 1, Lougheeds of Britannia File, Correspondence of 11 February 1999, LHA. Correspondence dated 2 March 1999 notes that Sam continued in the family trade, becoming a carpenter and, for a time, teaching shop at residential schools established to house Indigenous students, both in Red Deer and Battleford. Also Donald B. Smith Collection, Samuel Lougheed File, LHA. Reference Walter J. Wasylow, "History of Battleford Industrial School for Indians" (M.ED. thesis, University of Saskatchewan, 1972), 346, 350, 354, 358. Wasylow included copies of the school's newsletter, "The Guide," in his thesis. These newsletters indicate that Sam Lougheed was the carpenter and Mrs. S. Lougheed the instructress at Battleford Industrial School starting in 1895. This is supported by the Denney Papers, Richard Hardisty Fonds, Accession No. M7144, File #330,000 (1 and 2), GAIA, which indicate that Sam Lougheed was transferred in the spring of 1895 to Battleford from Red Deer Industrial, where he had been since its opening in 1889.

18. Diary of James Lougheed, 11 June 1882, LHA.

19. Jennifer Bobrovitz Files, LHA. Reference Medicine Hat Archives, Thomas Tweed Family Fonds, 1884–1913.

20. Donald B. Smith Collection, Lougheed #1 Box 1, Lougheeds of Britannia File, 35, LHA.

21. Marian C. McKenna, "Sir James Alexander Lougheed: Calgary's First Senator and City Builder," in *City Makers: Calgarians after the Frontier*, ed. Max Foran and Sheilagh S. Jamieson (Calgary: The Historical Society of Alberta, Chinook Country Chapter, 1987), 95–116. Reference Senate Debates, Vol II, No. 3, 12 January 1926, 9. According to Senator G.D. Robertson, Lougheed's deskmate in the Senate, James told him he arrived in Calgary on foot.

22. Ibid. Although some accounts claim that James was the first lawyer to come to Calgary, McKenna writes there were at least three lawyers already in business in Calgary when James opened his practice, 98.

23. Donald B. Smith Collection, Calgary 1883–1889 File, LHA. Reference J. Fraser Perry, ed., *They Gathered at the River* (Calgary: Central United Church, 1975), 123.

24. Donald B. Smith Collection, Lougheed #1 Box 1, Lougheeds of Britannia File, LHA. Reference newspaper article, no newspaper source listed.

25. Allan Hustak, *Peter Lougheed: A Biography* (Toronto: McClelland & Stewart, 1979), 12.

26. *Calgary Herald*, 17 September 1884, n.p. Also Jennifer Bobrovitz Files, chronological notes, 5, LHA. Reference McDougall Family Papers, Accession No. M732, File 12 or Folder 13, Methodist Church Mission, Morleyville, North West Territories, Marriage Register, GAIA.

27. George and John McDougall Fonds, Accession No. M729-74, GAIA. Also Donald B. Smith Collection, Calgary 1883–1889 File, LHA. Reference M485 Mrs. Wm Pearce, GAIA.

28. Donald B. Smith Collection, Lougheed #1 Box 1, James Lougheed 1854–1925 File and Lougheed Drafts of Article File, LHA. Reference MacGregor, *Senator Hardisty's Prairies*, 194.

29. MacGregor, *Senator Hardisty's Prairies*, 223. While MacGregor does not provide footnotes for this, he does speak about a statement submitted by James Lougheed covering the period from May 1884 to April 1886, which lists several items that refer to debts owed to Richard Hardisty and to mortgages held on Calgary property.

30. Ibid., 137. Reference William Newton, *Twenty Years on the Saskatchewan* (London: Elliot Stock, 1897), 16. Given the partnership the McDougall family had with Richard on trading ventures, it is likely the Roman Catholic Church was right to say that Richard Hardisty was influenced by the McDougall family to eject Roman Catholic missionaries from inside the Fort Edmonton palisades.

31. Donald B. Smith Collection, Lougheed #1 Box 1, Lougheed Drafts of Article File, LHA. Smith writes, "In a statement submitted by his lawyer, James A. Lougheed, covering the period from May, 1884 to April, 1886, there are glimpses of some of [Hardisty's] personal dealings. Several items in Lougheed's statement refer to debts owed to Richard Hardisty and to mortgages he held on Calgary property." Reference MacGregor, *Senator Hardisty's Prairies*, 223.

32. McKenna, "Sir James Alexander Lougheed," 100.

33. Grant MacEwan, *Calgary Cavalcade: From Fort to Fortune* (1958; repr., Saskatoon: Western Producer Prairie Books, 1975), 78.

34. McKenna, "Sir James Alexander Lougheed," 101. Reference *Calgary Herald*, 13 March 1936.

35. Newspaper Clippings File, Emil Longue Beau, "No. 45—Sir James Lougheed," *Star Weekly*, 31 July 1921, n.p., LHA.

36. Newspaper Clippings File, *Calgary Tribune*, 18 December 1889, n.p., LHA.

37. Ibid. There is some discrepancy in the source material regarding the value of the land owned by James Lougheed in 1889. Whatever the exact figure, the sizeable amounts listed in the sources reveal that Hardisty invested heavily in land over a short period of time.

38. R.C. MacLeod and Heather Rollason Driscoll, "Natives, Newspapers and Crime Rates in the North-West Territories, 1878–1885," in *From Rupert's Land to Canada: Essays in Honour of John E. Foster*, ed. Theodore Binnema, Gerhard Ens, and R.C. MacLeod (Edmonton: University of Alberta Press, 2001), 257.

39. Donald B. Smith Collection, Lougheed #1 Box 1, LHA. Draft article for *Dictionary of Canadian Biography* online Aug. 1999, 3. Smith did not publish this comment in the online version of the biography on James. Also Donald B. Smith, *Calgary's Grand Story: The Making of a Prairie Metropolis from the Viewpoint of Two Heritage Buildings* (Calgary: University of Calgary Press, 2005), 36. In this book, Smith writes of this particular letter, suggesting that it demonstrated how well connected James now was. Just "three years removed from Toronto," James had a "surprising new acquaintance, his wife's uncle, Donald A. Smith."

40. Richard Hardisty Fonds, M5908/1688, Letter from James A. Lougheed to My Dear Mr. Hardisty, 25 November 1885, GAIA. Also Donald B. Smith Collection, Calgary 1883–1889 File, LHA.

41. Richard Hardisty Fonds, Accession No. M5908-1788, Series 23-7, GAIA. Edmund Taylor, "Ye Olde Tyme Tales and Valuable Historical Data," n.d. Also Shirlee Anne Smith, "Hardisty, Richard Charles," in *Dictionary of Canadian Biography*, vol. 11, University of Toronto/Université Laval, 2003–, accessed 25 April 2012, http://www.biographi.ca/en/bio/hardisty_richard_charles_11E.html. Smith writes that in January 1888, Hardisty was appointed acting inspector of the northern department of the HBC. Then in February 1888 he was appointed as the first senator for the district of Alberta, after having run unsuccessfully in the election of 1887 as an independent candidate.

42. Richard Hardisty Fonds, Accession No. M5908-1788, Series 23-7, GAIA. Taylor, "Ye Olde Tyme Tales"; Smith, "Hardisty, Richard Charles."

43. Deidre Simmons, *Keepers of the Record: The History of the Hudson's Bay Company Archives* (Montreal: McGill-Queen's University Press, 2007), 157.

44. Grant MacEwan, *He Left Them Laughing When He Said Goodbye: The Life and Times of Frontier Lawyer Paddy Nolan* (Saskatoon: Western Producer Prairie Books,

1987). As James became more involved in politics, Isabella was called upon to entertain many visiting politicians. A good number of those visits demonstrate the close links that many in the North West maintained well beyond the transition from fur trade economy. Just one example was the 1898 visit by Nicholas Flood Davin, when a "worthy reception" was held at Beaulieu, 59. Davin, who came to play such an important role in the education of Indigenous children at residential schools, had worked in the same law office as James in Toronto. Also Donald B. Smith Collection, Lougheed #1 Box 1, Lougheed Toronto Area Peel File, LHA. James recalled later in life Davin's disappointment with his loss in defending the man accused of murder in the death of George Brown, the leader of the Reform movement that so strongly advocated annexation of the North West. Reference Davin File, Saskatchewan Archives Board, University of Regina, SHS14. Also Donald B. Smith Collection, Lougheed #2 Box 2, Davin File, LHA. Reference Zachary MacCaulay Hamilton and Marie Albina Hamilton, *These Are the Prairies: Saskatchewan Jubilee Edition 1905–1955* (Regina: School Aids and Text Book Publishing Co. Ltd., 1948), 206–207.

45. Donald B. Smith Collection, James Lougheed #1 Box 1, James Lougheed Overview File, Draft by Donald B. Smith and David Hall for "Sir James Alexander Lougheed" for *Dictionary of Canadian Biography* online, LHA. Reference Sir John A. Macdonald Papers, 7980, Leonard Gaetz to G. Foster, 25 October 1889, LAC.

46. Graeme Mercer Adam, *Prominent Men of Canada: A Collection of Persons Distinguished in Professional and Political Life, and in the Commerce and Industry of Canada* (Toronto: Canadian Biographical Publishing Co., 1892), 118.

47. Ibid., 119.

48. Donald B. Smith Collection, Lougheed #1 Box 1, Lougheed Toronto Directories, Assessment Rolls File, LHA. Reference Smith and Hall Draft. Reference Paul Whitely, Patrick Seyd, and Jeremy Richardson, *True Blues: The Politics of Conservative Party Membership* (Oxford: Clarendon Press, 1994), 64. Also reference Adam, *Prominent Men of Canada*, 118. It should be noted that these references do not confirm *Herald* ownership for James. Also Donald B. Smith Collection, Calgary 1883–1889 File, LHA. Letter from Peter McCarthy, 21 October 1889. The Conservatives felt it so important to keep the *Calgary Herald* solvent that McCarthy noted he and James had "within the last two weeks been forced to purchase the plant and franchises of the Calgary Herald to prevent it [going insolvent?]." Reference Sir John A. Macdonald Papers, 238100-102, provided by David Hall; Rev. Gaetz to G. Foster, 25 October 1889, LAC; Leishman McNeill, *Tales of the Old Town* (Calgary: Calgary Herald, 1950), 75. According to McNeill, writer for the *Calgary Herald*, James Lougheed, Alex Lucas, and M.S. McCarthy bought the *Calgary Herald* from Hugh Cayley in 1886.

49. Richard Hardisty Fonds, Accession No. M5908, Series 23-6, 1762, GAIA. James Lougheed to Mrs. Hardisty, 24 December 1889.

50. Donald B. Smith Collection, Hardisty Box 2, Isabella Hardisty Lougheed Timeline File, LHA. Reference *Saturday Night*, 16 September 1922, Elizabeth Bailey Fonds, M1000 Price, Elizabeth Bailey Clippings, 1920s–1950s, Biographies, L–Z Alberta, GAIA. Also Todd Paquin, Darren R. Préfontaine, and Patrick Young, "Traditional Métis Socialization and Entertainment," 30 May 2003, Gabriel Dumont Institute of Métis Studies and Applied Research, accessed 15 July 2012, http://www.metismuseum.ca/media/document.php/00724.pdf. Traditional Metis celebrations included gatherings for Christmas and New Year's when foods such as wild game, bannock, and pemmican were enjoyed, often for several days. Children were an integral part of the celebrations, often receiving gifts and treats.

51. Jennifer Bobrovitz Files, #11, *Calgary Weekly Herald*, 6 January 1892, n.p., LHA.

52. *Calgary Tribune*, 17 February 1892, 8.

53. Larry Pratt and John Richards, *Prairie Capitalism: Power and Influence in the New West* (Toronto: McClelland & Stewart, 1979), 154.

54. Jennifer Bobrovitz Files, 10, LHA. Reference *Toronto Mail*, 17 October 1891; *Calgary Weekly Herald*, 6 January 1892; *Toronto Globe*, 17 October 1891.

55. Lougheed House Fonds, Research Comm, old files, LHA. Reference Janet Wright, "Beaulieu Revitalized," *Heritage Canada* (January/February 1998): 6.

56. Lougheed Family Bible, LHA.

57. Clarence would later be christened by the Reverend John McDougall, also a member of the Hardisty extended family.

58. Lougheed Family Bible, LHA. Also *Calgary Tribune*, 6 February 1889.

59. Lougheed Family Bible, LHA.

60. Ibid. Also Matilda Davis School Collection, Accession P4724/3, Correspondence, 1861–65, Letter, 12 November 1865, Hardisty Family to Isabella Hardisty, from Fort Simpson to Davis School, AM. In this letter to Isabella, her father refers to himself as "Papa," his wife as "Mamma," and Isabella's grandmother as "Grandmamma." This might suggest the influence of the Beaulieu family on Mary Anne Allen as a young girl in northern fur trade country.

61. Donald B. Smith Collection, Hardisty Box 2, Belle Lougheed File, LHA. Trudy Cowan was the first director of Lougheed House National Historic Site, and instrumental in obtaining the designation as a historic site. Jennifer Bobrovitz was the first archivist and researcher.

62. Donald B. Smith Collection, Hardisty Box 2, Beaulieu House File, LHA. Reference "A Daughter of the West Who Made a Difference," *Calgary Herald*, 30 December 2001.

63. Ibid.

64. Donald B. Smith Collection, Lougheed #1 Box 2, Norman Lougheed File, LHA.
Reference *Golden West Magazine*, St. Andrews 1914 File, 197. Also Donald B.
Smith Collection, Lougheed #2 Box 1, LHA. Reference *Morning Albertan*, 5 April
1912. This article was one of many that spoke of Mary and Isabella attending
public functions together, such as this one, which noted Isabella accompanied
both Norman and Mary Stringer Lougheed to a bridge party. Also Donald B.
Smith Collection, Lougheed #2 Box 1, Lougheed 1912 File, LHA. Reference
Morning Albertan, 10 April 1912. This article speaks of Isabella hosting a "box
party" in honour of the daughter of fellow Senator Watson, when again Mrs.
Norman Lougheed is listed in attendance. Also Donald B. Smith Collection,
Lougheed #2 Box 1, Lougheed 1912 File, LHA. Reference *Morning Albertan*, 28 May
1912. This article speaks of a second trip to Banff by motor car, which included
Mr. and Mrs. Norman Lougheed. It was reported, "Mrs. James A. Lougheed is
arranging for a party to motor to Banff...While there they will be the guests of
Mrs. Lougheed at her charming summer cottage."

65. Donald B. Smith Collection, Mary Stringer Lougheed File, unnamed source,
LHA.

66. Donald B. Smith Collection, Hardisty Box 2, Beaulieu House File, LHA. Reference
"A Daughter of the West Who Made a Difference."

67. Ibid.

68. Donald B. Smith Collection, Lougheed # 2 Box 2, LHA. Reference Bob Edwards,
Calgary Eye Opener, 16 June 1906, c1. Also Donald B. Smith Collection, Lougheed
#2 Box 1, Keith Regular File, LHA. Reference George F.G. Stanley, "From New
Brunswick to Calgary—R.B. Bennett in Retrospect," in *Frontier Calgary: Town, City
and Region 1874–1914*, ed. A.W. Rasporich and Henry Klassen (Calgary: McClelland
& Stewart West, 1975), 250.

69. Bobrovitz, interview by author, 6 October 2008.

70. Donald B. Smith Collection, Edgar Lougheed File, LHA. Reference *Calgary
Herald*, 30 December 2000.

71. Grant MacEwan, *Mighty Women: Stories of Western Canadian Pioneers* (1975; repr.,
Vancouver: Douglas & McIntyre, 1995), 43.

72. Peter Laslett, *The World We Have Lost* (New York: Charles Scribner's Sons, 1984).
This applied to society in general in the pre-industrial period, when women
clearly contributed social capital.

73. Henry Cornelius Klassen, *Eye on the Future: Business People in Calgary and the
Bow Valley, 1870–1900* (Calgary: University of Calgary Press, 2002), 332. Reference
assessment roll for 1887, City of Calgary Archives; Supreme Court of the
Northwest Territories, Calgary, Civil Cases, File 2303, Peter McCarthy v. James A.

Lougheed, 15 January 1895, Provincial Archives of Alberta (PAA). See also, note 73, this volume.

74. Robert Lougheed, communication with author, 9 August 2011.

75. Donald B. Smith Collection, Calgary 1883–1889 File, LHA. Letter from P. McCarthy, 21 October 1889. Reference Sir John A. Macdonald Papers, 238100-102, LAC. Also Donald B. Smith Collection, Calgary 1883–1889 File, LHA. Rev. Gaetz to G. Foster, 25 October 1889.

76. Donald B. Smith Collection, Hardisty Box 1, William and Mary Children File, LHA. Reference *Morning Albertan*, 4 April 1912.

77. Newspaper Clippings File, *Morning Albertan*, 4 April 1912, quoting the *Montreal Star*, LHA.

78. Ibid.

79. Ibid.

80. Alison Prentice et al., eds., *Canadian Women: A History*, 2nd ed. (Toronto: Harcourt Brace & Company, 1996), 100.

81. Jennifer Bobrovitz Files, notes, 6, LHA. Reference "Alberta Women Pioneers Will Form Organization," *Calgary Daily Herald*, 20 March 1922. Also Perry, *They Gathered at the River*, 176. Perry confirms that James was church superintendent from 1884 to 1888.

82. Jennifer Bobrovitz Files, notes, 6, LHA.

83. *Calgary Herald*, 17 July 1886 and 24 July 1886. Also David Bly, *Calgary Herald*, 30 December 2000.

84. McKenna, "Sir James Alexander Lougheed," 103–104. Reference Hustak, *Peter Lougheed*, 9–10; *Calgary Herald*, 17 January 1900.

85. Donald B. Smith Collection, Lougheed 1921 File, LHA. Reference "Some Senate Leaders Are Very English," *Toronto Star Weekly*, 21 May 1921, 10, c.1. Also "The Spotlight: Sir James Lougheed," *Toronto Star*, 21 June 1923, 6. This newspaper wrote, "What some people choose to regard as his English accent is as English as it ever was—which is scarcely at all."

86. Max Foran, *The History of Canadian Cities: Calgary, an Illustrated History* (Toronto: James Lorimer & Company, 1978), 36.

87. Donald B. Smith Collection, Lougheed #2 Box 1, Lougheed 1914 File, LHA. Reference "The Borden Cabinet—X. The Government Leader in the Senate," *The Canadian Liberal Monthly*, July 1914, 123.

88. "Some Senate Leaders Are Very English," *Toronto Star Weekly*, 21 May 1921, 10, c.1. The *Star Weekly*, which dismissed the claim that some made about James trying to sport a British accent, instead judged him to be quite humble. The *Star Weekly* noted, "Lawyer Lougheed occasionally received fees from remittance men, but accents never. He doesn't talk quite like the old Cabbagetowner he is, but that is

381

Notes

not because he forgets that he came from the same quarter of the globe as Bob Fleming, Judge Coatsworth...If you drive around with Sir James next time he comes to the city of his youth, and you approach the Don bridge from the west, he will point out the circular plot in the thoroughfare which connects King and Queen, he will tell you that here's the exact location of his parental home."

89.   Sir James Alexander Personal Biography Folder 3 of 4, LHA. Reference Robert Haig, *Ottawa: City of the Big Ears* (Ottawa: Haig and Haig Publishing, 1975), 173. Also Jennifer Bobrovitz Files, notes, 20, LHA. Bobrovitz confirms that Lougheed lived at 26 Roxborough Apartments. Also Sir James Alexander Lougheed Personal Biography Folder 3 of 4, LHA. Reference Lucien Brault, *Ottawa...the Way We Were* (Toronto: Nelson, Foster & Scott, 1975), 41. No doubt James knew the Roxborough was "the" place to live while in Ottawa, given that Mackenzie King, Louis St. Laurent, and General George Vanier had all lived there at one time during their careers.

90.   Donald B. Smith Collection, Lougheed #1 Box 1, Lougheed Toronto Directories, LHA. Reference "Religion Half Century Ago Simple, Stern, Says Judge," *Toronto Star*, 26 February 1940. Justice Emerson Coatsworth, a close childhood friend of James, recalled the strict upbringing that both boys had while members of Berkeley Street Methodist, commenting they did "not play cards or dance. We did not attend the theatre or the races."

91.   P.B. Waite, "Sir Oliver Mowat's Canada: Reflections on an Un-Victorian Society," in *Oliver Mowat's Ontario*, ed. Donald A. Swainson (Toronto: Macmillan, 1972), 26.

92.   Smith, *Calgary's Grand Story*, 37. Reportedly, James said of patronage, "What reason is there why a good party man should not get a good public office provided he is equal to the duties of the post?" Reference "James Lougheed," 10, cited by Beau. It does appear that James had more of a reputation for being straight-laced than did Isabella. Also Desmond Morton, *Winning the Second Battle: Canadian Veterans and the Return to Civilian Life, 1915–1930* (Toronto: University of Toronto Press, 1987). In 1916, when the Senate debated the addition of soldiers' pensions to include "unmarried wives," Senator Raoul Dandurand turned to Lougheed and asked, "Does this payment to the concubine of the soldier do any violence to my hon. friend's sense of propriety?" 157. Also Donald B. Smith Collection, Lougheed #2 Box 1, Lougheed 1917 File, LHA. When his fellow attorney, Paddy Nolan, continually defended Mother Fulham, Calgary's infamous "pig lady," during her numerous run-ins with the law and other citizens, James complained that her presence was devaluing his property. Also "Lougheed Is Old Toronto Boy," *Toronto Star Weekly*, 29 September 1917. This newspaper article noted that James "has none of the characteristics of the blustering politician...He is never dogmatic or o'er positive. He knows a great

deal but he never knows it all...In manner Senator Lougheed is dignified, but it is the dignity of a gentleman. He can be sarcastic when occasion demands it, but it is not the loud and offensive description. It is quiet, but pointed," 13. Certainly, politics and, no doubt, Isabella, softened the early views that had made James a welcome addition to the Orange Order. See also Smith, *Calgary's Grand Story*. It was said that later in life, James "enjoyed a warm relationship with Quebec Senator, Raoul Dandurand, a Liberal and a Roman Catholic," 30.

93. MacEwan, *He Left Them Laughing*, 38. Reference *Calgary Tribune*, 23 November 1892.

94. Ibid., 38. Reference *Calgary Tribune*, 30 November 1892. Nolan was a fellow lawyer, but he focused on criminal law. His gregarious personality helped him achieve much notoriety.

95. Foran, *The History of Canadian Cities*, 40.

96. Sarah Carter, "Britishness, 'Foreigness,' Women and Land in Western Canada," *Humanities Research Britishness & Otherness* 13, no. 1 (2006): 49. Well known for his oratorical skills, many, including Edwards, recognized James's influence on the younger Richard Bedford Bennett. Also Donald B. Smith Collection, Lougheed # 2 Box 2, LHA. Edwards wrote, "We have often fancied that Bennett picked up that affected style of grandiose speech from his partner Lougheed, to whom this style comes natural." Reference *Calgary Eye Opener*, 16 June 1906, c1. Also Hugh A. Dempsey, ed., *The Wit and Wisdom of Bob Edwards* (Edmonton: Hurtig, 1976). Dempsey notes that Edwards's wit was appreciated by Calgarians when he attacked the "crooked politicians, Sanctimonious preachers and social snobs." Edwards was one of the "most widely read journalists of his day, quoted in newspapers and magazines all across Canada, as well as in Britain and the United States." His style earned him the reputation as a "tireless crusader on behalf of the 'little man,'" 7–8.

97. Donald B. Smith Collection, Lougheed #2 Box 2, Bob Edwards File, LHA. Reference *Calgary Eye Opener*, 14 July 1906.

98. Donald B. Smith Collection, Lougheed #2 Box 2, Bob Edwards File, LHA. Reference *Albertan*, 18 May 1912. Also *Calgary Eye Opener*, 23 August 1919, 2. Despite the many snide remarks at James's expense, Edwards was not above paying respect to Sir James when he approved of something the senator had done. Edwards related the prompt response received for appeals to drop charges of misconduct against a sergeant-major who had taken "one too many" drinks. In this instance, Lougheed was described by *Calgary Eye Opener* as "a great administrator, shrewd as the devil and full of the milk of human kindness." Whether being facetious or not, Edwards did note that James was a "good

deal of a man" in comparison to Sam Hughes, the "temperance crank and super-disciplinarian."

99.   Jennifer Bobrovitz Files, notes, 17, LHA.

100. Ibid.

101. Donald B. Smith Collection, Donald B. Smith and David Hall, Draft article for *Dictionary of Canadian Biography* online, LHA. Lougheed's work with soldiers continued after the war, when Robert Borden responded to complaints about the treatment of returning wounded soldiers by establishing a Military Hospitals Commission, appointing James as the chair. James was later appointed as Minister of Soldier's Civil Re-establishment, a position he held from 1918 to 1920, 7.

102. MacGregor, *Senator Hardisty's Prairies*, 249. Also Harry Max Sanders, *The Story behind Alberta Names: How Cities, Towns, Villages and Hamlets Got Their Names* (Calgary: Red Deer Press, 2003), 200.

103. Newspaper Clippings File, *Calgary Herald*, 30 December 2001, 1, LHA.

104. Donald B. Smith Collection, Lougheed #1 Box 1, Lougheed Toronto Directories File, LHA. Quoted in *Morning Albertan*, 3 November 1925, after the death of Sir James.

105. Donald B. Smith Collection, Lougheed #2 Box 1, James Lougheed 1917 file, LHA. Reference *Toronto Star Weekly*, 29 September 1917, p. 13, C5.

106. Donald B. Smith Collection, James Lougheed #1 Box 1, James Lougheed Overview File, Draft by Donald B. Smith and David Hall for "Sir James Alexander Lougheed" for *Dictionary of Canadian Biography* online, LHA. Reference *Senate Debates*, 1894, 338–339 (9 May 1894); 1906, 833 (20 June 1906); 1914, 518–527 (26 May 1914); 1918, 353 (29 April 1918); 1920, 442–498, 772–774 (28 May; 2, 9, 28 June 1920); 1922, 557–562 (23 June 1922).

107. Ibid.

108. Donald B. Smith Collection, Lougheed #1 Box 1, LHA. Correspondence from David Hall to Donald Smith, 2, refers to *Senate Debates* 1894, 338–339, 347 (9 May 1894). Also Hall and Smith, "Lougheed, Sir James Alexander."

109. *Calgary Weekly Herald*, 11 December 1889, n.p.

110. *Calgary Weekly Herald*, 19 April 1893, n.p. Also William Beahen, "Campbell, Andrew," in *Dictionary of Canadian Biography*, vol. 12, University of Toronto/ Université Laval, 2003–, accessed 22 July 2012, http://www.biographi.ca/en/ bio/campbell_andrew_12E.html. Campbell arrived in Calgary in 1891 and presented himself as a doctor, but there was no evidence he had any professional qualifications. When he was arrested for offering a noxious substance to Maggie Stevensen, James Lougheed was successful in having him moved from the town jail, which was considered unsanitary, to the NWMP guardroom.

111. *Calgary Semi-Weekly Herald*, 3 November 1893, n.p. Also Beahen, "Campbell, Andrew." Campbell was charged in 1894 in Lethbridge, Alberta, for once again providing an "abortifacient drug," this time to a sixteen-year-old girl. Because charges of performing abortions were "rarely laid in the pioneer west, Campbell was unsusual in his notoriety."

112. Prentice et al., *Canadian Women*, 179. The authors write that the Criminal Code stated it was unlawful for anyone to offer to sell, advertise, or have at their disposal "any medicine, drug or article intended or represented as a means of preventing conception or causing abortion."

113. *Medicine Hat News*, 26 March 1903, 5.

114. *Calgary Herald*, 23 March 1903, 5.

115. *Medicine Hat News*, 25 June 1903, 1.

116. Brenda McCafferty, archivist, Legal Archives Society of Alberta, correspondence with author, 10 August 2012. McCafferty confirms that the archives have the notebook kept by Justice Arthur Sifton when he heard the case and convicted Lougheed in 1903. According to the notes kept by Sifton, Jas. A. Lougheed was twenty-three years of age in 1903. Thus, this was not the same Sir James Lougheed who was born in 1854. Also Philip Pype, archivist, City of Medicine Hat, correspondence with author, 15 August 2012. Pype writes that census data for 1901 confirms a James A. Lougheed, occupation as a brakeman, was a lodger in a household with two daughters, eight sons, and six lodgers. He was listed as twenty-one years of age in 1901, and thus this was the man who was twenty-three when he faced charges in 1903. This James was also listed as Irish and born in Ontario.

117. Pratt and Richards, *Prairie Capitalism*, 154. The authors provide no reference for this statement. They may have been referring to an article that appeared in *Canadian Forum* in October/November 1978, "The Lougheeds and the Age of Prairie Elegance," no author, which made this claim in exactly the same wording. Reference Lougheed, Sir James Alexander, Personal Biography Folder 4 of 4, LHA. Also Donald B. Smith Collection, Lougheed #1 Box 1, Lougheed James 1854–1925 File, LHA.

118. Donald B. Smith Collection, Lougheed #1 Box 2, Edgar Lougheed File, LHA. Reference untitled online article, 14 September 1997, c1.

119. McDonald, *Lord Strathcona*, 402.

120. Donald B. Smith Collection, Lougheed Box 2, James Lougheed 1890–1911 File, LHA. Reference *Debates of the Senate of the Dominion of Canada*, 20 June 1906, 833.

121. Ibid.

122. Ibid., 669–671.

123. Donald B. Smith Collection, Lougheed #2 Box 1, Lougheed 1920 File, LHA.
Reference *Debates of the Senate of Canada*, 442–444.

124. Ibid., 473.

125. Donald B. Smith Collection, Lougheed #2 Box 1, Lougheed 1920 File, LHA.
Reference *Debates of the Senate of Canada*, 489–498. On 9 June 1920, James
argued strenuously that Indigenous people who wanted to appear before
the Senate committee should not be heard because that would render their
claim illegitimate and hearing them would only increase agitation. As many
historians have noted, when Fred Loft was attempting to organize Indigenous
people for political activity, Duncan Campbell Scott mounted an aggressive
campaign, not only to discredit him but to force enfranchisement upon him.
Also Donald B. Smith Collection, Lougheed #2 Box 1, Lougheed 1921 File,
LHA. Duncan Campbell Scott to James Lougheed, 21 February 1921. Much of
Scott's correspondence when he served as deputy superintendent general of the
Department of Indian Affairs with regard to Loft was directed to his superior,
James Lougheed. In this letter, Scott wrote about Loft, "I have proposed to him
that he should be enfranchised, which, I think, accounts for this sudden activity
on his part. What he ought to get is a good snub! He volunteered for the war and
looked very well in a uniform, but he was cunning enough to evade any active
service, and I do not think his record in that regard is a very good one."

126. Smith, "The Original Peoples of Alberta," 67. Smith references Archibald Oswald
MacRae, *History of the Province of Alberta* (The Western Canada History Co., 1912),
430.

127. Donald B. Smith Collection, Lougheed #2 Box 1, Lougheed 1921 File, LHA.
Reference F.O. Loft to Hon. Sir James Lougheed, Minister of the Interior, 9
February 1921. Reference Indian Affairs, RG10, Volume 3211, File 527, 787 pt.
1, 551227, LAC. In this letter, Fred Loft had set out his own case for refusing
enfranchisement. Loft said, "For the sake of my race, I hold exceptional pride in
my present status; for the simple reason so few of our people are able to prove to
the outside world the advantages of higher education...If it should serve nothing
more than as an example to others, it is something. To this extent we should
be encouraged rather than discouraged by being made alien by force of law to
foreswear our nationality; to be forced to renounce the blood of a father and
mother."

128. Donald B. Smith Collection, Lougheed #2 Box 2, Lougheed 1922 File, LHA.
Reference *Debates of the Senate of Canada*, 23 June 1922, 557–558.

129. Isabella may or may not have been more in tune to the Indigenous concept of
learning, which often relied on the ideology of experiential learning and the
concept of the three Ls: look, listen, and learn, with an emphasis on the natural

consequences of allowing children the freedom to learn by making mistakes. On the other hand, all indications about James Lougheed's upbringing are that he followed the strict guidelines of devout and pious parents, who were determined he should not make mistakes that required atonement.

130. *Banff Crag & Canyon*, 21 August 1909, 6.

131. Donald B. Smith Collection, Lougheed #1 Box 2, Norman Lougheed File, LHA. Reference *Golden West Magazine*, St. Andrews 1914 File.

132. Donald B. Smith Collection, Lougheed #1 Box 2, Norman Lougheed File, LHA. Reference *Golden West Magazine*, 1977, St. Andrews 1914 File.

133. Ibid.

134. Ibid.

135. Ibid.

136. Ibid.

137. Ibid.

138. Ibid.

139. Jennifer Bobrovitz Files, notes, LHA. Reference Jennifer Howse, *Letters of Richard Hardisty*.

140. Donald B. Smith Collection, Lougheed #1 Box 2, Norman Lougheed File, LHA. Reference *Golden West Magazine*, 1977, St. Andrews 1914 File. Also Robert Collins, "With Dust, Joy, Mud and Anguish the Car Transformed Alberta," in *Alberta in the 20th Century: The Boom and the Bust, 1910–1914*, ed. Ted Byfield (Edmonton: United Western Communications Ltd., 1994), 51. Referring to an article in the *Albertan*, Collins noted that, by 1913, women had prevailed and many owned "cars built especially for their private use, and not a few of these handle a car with the skill of an expert...One was Mrs. James A. Lougheed (who as owner of Calgary's first large automobile was hardly typical)." Quoting from the *Albertan*, Collins wrote, "Mrs. Lougheed is very fond of motoring and one of her pet luxuries is her garage and her motor-driven equipages. Her cars are probably the finest in this province," 52. Also Lougheed House Fonds, Collections: 1912 Peerless Car File, LHA contains a photo of a car enclosed in a letter from Rick Harris to Trudy Cowan, 25 April 2001. In 2001, the Western Development Museum in Saskatoon had on display a 1912 Peerless, with an original purchase price of $6,000, which was reputedly ordered by Isabella. With only one hundred original miles registered, it is not clear whether Isabella ever took delivery of this particular car, but it is likely that she did.

141. Collins, "With Dust, Joy, Mud," 34. When the Conservatives were later returned to office, it was Senator Lougheed who reportedly persuaded the Minister of the Interior to lift the ban on vehicle traffic in national parks. Also Hustak, *Peter Lougheed*, 18. Hustak does not provide references, but he writes that Mary

Lougheed, who was present on the fated trip, recalled that, when Laurier was defeated a few years after this incident, James approached the new Minister of the Interior in the Borden Government, explaining the "inconvenience of the park statute." Donald B. Smith Collection, Lougheed #1 Box 2, Norman Lougheed File, LHA. Reference *Golden West Magazine*, St. Andrews 1914 File. Also *Banff Crag & Canyon*, 13 August 1910, 4. The newspaper reports that, prior to 1912, boosters from the Calgary Automobile Association had lobbied to have the prohibition lifted.

142. Bobrovitz, interviews by author, 2007–2009.

143. Ranchmen's Club, *A Short History of the Ranchmen's Club* (Calgary: Calgary Centennial Project, 1975). Organized in 1891, the original roster of the Calgary club included primarily ranchers. The original constitution stipulated that members were men divided into two classes: ordinary and privileged. Privileged members were "officers in His Majesty's Army and Navy and persons holding military and civil appointments under the Imperial Government who may be stationed in Canada," 31. Also Ranchmen's Club, *Officers, Members, Constitution and Rules of the Ranchmen's Club of the City of Calgary: Established 1891, Amended to 11 April 1913* (Calgary: McAra Press, 1913), 50. This book notes that the Calgary club differed from its British counterparts in that the Ranchmen's Club in Calgary stated "politics and religious matters were to be excluded from discussions within the Club." Also Ranchmen's Club, *A Short History*, 3, 18. By 1958, there was still a rule that "business is not discussed in the lounges of the Club," although special rooms were available for such discussions. At a time when public libraries were not available, the reading rooms provided by the club were of great advantage to members. Another advantage was a result of some creative thinking, when a private room was set up during prohibition, where members could enjoy liquor, for "medicinal purposes." According to local histories of the Ranchmen's Club, these men's clubs followed the "flag of the Empire" into Canada during the Victorian Era, ii. The Calgary club remained exclusive, allowing a maximum of 250 ordinary members, with James Lougheed being among its first in 1891.

144. Ranchmen's Club, *A Short History*, 31. It was not until 1925 that "Lady Associate members" were allowed and a "Ladies Lounge" set aside to accommodate women, and not until 1968 that women were actually allowed into the main dining room, 19.

145. Elizabeth Bailey Price Fonds, Accession No. M1000, File 1, GAIA. Reference *Calgary Herald*, 18 November 1933, n.p. Also Sherrill MacLaren, *Braehead: Three Founding Families in Nineteenth Century Canada* (Toronto: McClelland & Stewart, 1986), 48. MacLaren notes that Christen Drever was the daughter of William

and Helen (Rothney) Drever. William was born in the Orkney Islands and signed on to work for the HBC in 1821. William then met Helen, who had come to fur trade country as a nanny for Adam Thom after he was appointed as the first judge of Rupert's Land. Helen Rothney Drever was involved in a scandal in Red River when she became pregnant by Drever and broke her contract with Thom, and then brought her case for lost wages before the magistrates. After marrying, William and Helen built a log cabin at the Lower Fort in 1843, where Helen gave birth to five children with the help of a Metis midwife. Like Isabella, some of the Drever girls attended Miss Davis's school.

146. Elizabeth Bailey Price Fonds, Accession No. M1000, File 1, GAIA. Reference *Calgary Herald*, 18 November 1933, n.p.

147. WEDC Translation File, Lougheed House newsletter, undated, 23, LHA. Also Charles M. McCullough Article 1, 20 March 1937, R376.8 W517 CANA H Reel #111, HPLA. This article recorded the reminiscences of some of the former students, which demonstrate it was not all seriousness for students, and that Isabella likely enjoyed many of the social aspects of Wesleyan and the camaraderie of other students. The journalist wrote, "What gay times we had at the 'conversats' remarked an animated member of the class of the mid-eighties...The word Wesleyan in the title of the college meant something in those days—no dancing at any school function...'There were compensations, however,' broke in a third 'old girl'—Think of the romantic tete-a-tetes under shelter of the spreading palms and in remote corners where the gas wasn't 100 per cent efficient."

148. Newspaper Clippings File, *Calgary Daily Herald*, 14 January 1914, 10, LHA.

149. Smith, *Calgary's Grand Story*, 126. Reference *Calgary Herald*, 5 October 1912.

150. Ibid. Reference "Bishop McNally," *Calgary Herald*, 19 March 1914.

151. Ibid. Reference *Morning Albertan*, 3 January 1914, 4.

152. *Morning Albertan*, 5 January 1914, 5. By this time, furor over the tango was beginning to subside in other areas. Also *Morning Albertan*, 17 January 1914, 4. As the *Albertan* reported, the "Naughty Tango" received the approval of an audience of "Duchesses, countesses, and bishops" who deemed the version they witnessed as "so modest it bored...to tears."

153. Calvin Demmon, "The Arts: Enter the Professional," in *Alberta in the 20th Century: The Boom and the Bust, 1910–1914* (Edmonton: United Western Communications Ltd., 1994), 61.

154. Maida Parlow French, *Kathleen Parlow: A Portrait* (Toronto: Ryerson Press, 1967), 2. Kathleen's father, Charles Parlow, was a factor for the HBC stationed at Fort Calgary when Kathleen was born in 1890, and the man who stood as James's best man during his wedding. According to her friend and cousin, Maida Parlow French, Kathleen and her father "loved Indians," and Kathleen spent hours

listening to Indigenous legends told to her by her father, much to her mother's annoyance. Also Smith, *Calgary's Grand Story*, 310n61. It was in Isabella's home where Kathleen and her mother stayed during her first stop in Calgary as a celebrated and world-renowned performer. Kathleen Parlow's diary, held by the University of Toronto Music Library, also confirms this visit to Isabella's home. *Calgary News Telegram*, 22 February 1911 reported on a reception held in honour of Kathleen. Apparently, Kathleen once mused that she might have "six or seven Indian half-brothers and –sisters," (Smith, *Calgary's Grand Story*, 54). Before she was five, Kathleen Parlow's mother took her to live with relatives in San Francisco, and she never saw her father again. Although she had severed her connection to her fur trade father, it was Kathleen Parlow's connection to her father and to the HBC that provided her the opportunity to succeed on the world stage. It was Isabella's uncle, Lord Strathcona, who provided funds that allowed Kathleen to study in Russia with the renowned violinist Leopold Auer (French, *Kathleen Parlow*, 9–10).

155. Jennifer Bobrovitz Files, 14, LHA. Reference "Calgarians at Big Function," *Calgary Daily News*, 4 October 1909.

156. *Morning Albertan*, 2 October 1909, 2.

157. Ibid.

158. Donald B. Smith Collection, Lougheed #1 Box 1, James Lougheed 1854–1925 File, LHA. Reference Perry, *They Gathered at the River*, 87.

159. Jennifer Bobrobitz Files, 13, LHA. Reference *Calgary Daily News*, 27 July 1907, 1.

160. Ibid., 14. Reference "Social and Personal," *Calgary Daily Herald*, 12 September 1908, 2.

161. Jennifer Bobrovitz Files, 18, LHA. Also *Calgary Herald*, 15 September 1919, 14; *Morning Albertan*, 15 September 1919, 4.

162. *Morning Albertan*, 15 September 1919, 4.

163. Ibid.

164. Bobrovitz, interviews by author, 2007–2009.

165. Jean Leslie, *Glimpses of Calgary Past* (Calgary: Detselig Enterprises Ltd., 1994), 98. Also "Prince Chooses Own Partners at Big Dance," *Morning Albertan*, 9 September 1919, 5. The newspaper makes it clear that Dorothy Lougheed was thought of as the "belle" of the ball by Calgarians for having been chosen by Edward to be his dancing partner. Also Rupert Godfrey, ed., *Letters from a Prince, Edward, Prince of Wales to Mrs. Freda Dudley Ward, March 1918–January 1921* (London: Brown and Company, 1998), 190–191. Dorothy may not have made the same impression on the prince, or perhaps the prince simply knew his audience. Writing to Wallace Simpson, his "beloved little Madonna," after one of the dance marathons in Calgary, Edward noted, "Some of the Calgary girls of last night have followed

us up here...There are 1/2 dozen nice Canadian girls here, darling, all of them hideous but good dancers & cheery & great fun & good for anything I should say, though that doesn't interest this little boy...guess if you asked in the right way, why, you'd get just anything you wanted!!" Also *Morning Albertan*, 17 September 1919, 9. Given that the *Morning Albertan* reported that the Prince of Wales declined to leave the ball in Calgary until a late hour, telling his aide to "Please don't bother me. I'm having a good time," we might assume the dashing young prince quite astutely knew his audience, not only in Calgary but with his "little Madonna."

166. *Morning Albertan*, 23 September 1919, 4. Also *Morning Albertan*, 18 September 1919. Isabella would have been in attendance when Prince Edward had the name Chief Morning Star bestowed upon him by the "Stoney Cree Indians," 10.

167. Donald B. Smith Collection, Lougheed #1 Box 2, James Lougheed 1890–1911 File, LHA. Reference *Calgary Herald*, 26 November 1898.

168. Ibid. Reference *Alberta Magazine*, December 1981, from Charles D. Denney Papers. The article in *Alberta Magazine* referenced the earlier edition of the *Calgary Herald*.

169. Donald B. Smith Collection, Mary Stringer Lougheed File, LHA. Reference *News Telegram*. The article was hand-dated 5 October 1911. However, this date must be wrong as it refers to a ball held in 1914.

170. Newspaper Clippings File, *Calgary Herald*, 17 June 1913, 7, LHA.

171. Donald B. Smith Collection, Lougheed #2 Box 1, Lougheed 1912 File, LHA. Reference *Morning Albertan*, 10 April 1912.

172. Donald B. Smith Collection, Lougheed #2 Box 1, Lougheed 1914 File, LHA. Reference *News Telegram*, 20 June 1914. The family photo shows Isabella as matriarch in the front row (see figure in Chapter 3 of this volume). One might be inclined to think that James was somewhat irrelevant, given that it is not immediately apparent he is even in this family photo. He is not seated by Isabella, where we might expect to find him, but is somewhat lost in the back row.

173. *Morning Albertan*, 13 January 1911, 5.

174. Ibid., 13 November 1909, 9.

175. Leslie, *Glimpses of Calgary Past*, 100. Although being dubbed the "cream of Calgary society [as] the official dance band at the Palliser Hotel for 15 years," Josephine Trainor reportedly played for every strata of Prairie society. She described her greatest pleasure as being when she played for the service men and women of both wars, noting that, during the "bleak days of the '30s when there was no money, any free entertainment was welcome."

176. Newspaper Clippings File, *Calgary Daily Herald*, 6 January 1914, 12, LHA.

177. Newspaper Clippings File, *Morning Albertan*, 3 January 1914, 4, LHA.

178. Ibid., 3 January 1914.

179. Newspaper Clippings File, *Calgary Herald*, 15 January 1913, 10, LHA.

180. Newspaper Clippings File, *Calgary News Telegram*, 4 September 1912, LHA.

181. Lougheed House Research Files, Duke and Duchess of Connaught Folder, LHA. *Calgary Daily Herald*, 30 March 1912.

182. *Calgary News Telegram*, 4 September 1912.

183. Carter, *The Importance of Being Monogamous*, 280. Reference "Editorial," *Western Standard Illustrated Weekly*, 12 June 1913, n.p.

184. Ibid., 282.

185. McDonald, *Lord Strathcona*, 423.

186. Carter, *The Importance of Being Monogamous*. Carter writes that Lady Strathcona was referred to as a "squaw wife" by Governor General Lord Minto. There is no reference for this, but it may be McDonald, *Lord Strathcona*. According to Carter, it is ironic that the article in *Western Standard Illustrated Weekly* ignored Isabella's ancestry when it noted that she hosted many royal visitors. This irony is heightened given that an article on the same page criticized another Indigenous woman for her lack of hosting skills. The Indigenous woman was not named in the article, but it was noted that she "knew nothing of how to serve" when hosting the Marquis of Lorne.

187. McDonald, *Lord Strathcona*, 448. Reference letter from Minto to Peter Elliot (his brother), 30 November 1901, MG 27 II BI, Volume 35, LAC.

188. Ibid., 358–362. Isabella Hardisty Smith and her husband Donald worked hard at carving a position of importance for themselves. Part of that networking involved making rather large endowments to many causes. For example, in 1883, Isabella and Donald donated $30,000 to the Trafalgar Institute, a boarding school for Protestant girls in Montreal. In 1884, when the board of McGill University still hesitated to admit women as students, the couple donated $50,000 to establish an endowment fund for women's education. In 1886, the Smiths provided a further $70,000 so that the third and fourth years of women's degrees could be offered. They continued as benefactors through the establishment of the Royal Victoria College for Women.

189. Donald B. Smith Collection, Hardisty Box 2, Isabella Hardisty Lougheed Timeline File, LHA. Reference *Calgary News Telegram*, 7 February 1912.

190. Ibid.

191. Donald B. Smith Collection, Hardisty Box 2, Isabella Hardisty Lougheed Timeline File, LHA. Reference Jack Peach, "Historic Theatre Stately Old Lady with Grand Past," *Calgary Herald*, 6 April 1985.

192. National Council of Women of Canada, accessed 2 May 2012, http://www.ncwc. ca/aboutUs_history.html. Also Veronica Strong-Boag, *The Parliament of Women: The National Council of Women of Canada, 1893–1929* (Ottawa: National Museums of Canada, 1976), vii. Strong-Boag notes that some historians have suggested that Lady Aberdeen (married to Lord Aberdeen, Governor General of Canada from 1893 to 1898), in her role with the National Council of Women, actually hindered the liberation of women. However, some believe that the largely middle-class women who joined the council were able to effect reforms that corrected some of the abuses of capitalism and sexism, even though they were somewhat responsible for perpetuating both systems.

193. Marjorie Norris, *A Leaven of Ladies: A History of the Calgary Local Council of Women* (Calgary: Detselig Enterprises Ltd., 1995), 29–30. Norris writes that Madame Rouleau, wife of Justice Rouleau who fled to Calgary after the conflict in 1885, was president of the Calgary local.

194. John T. Saywell, ed., *The Canadian Journal of Lady Aberdeen, 1893–1898* (Toronto: The Champlain Society, 1960), 134, entry for 13 October 1894. Lady Aberdeen writes, "I went to Senator & Mrs. Lougheed's to meet a number of ladies, a gathering which was supposed to be social, but which ended in its being decided to have a meeting for the Women's Council on our way back. Mrs. Pinkham, the Bishop's wife, initiated the idea, & seemed interested."

195. Ibid., 269, entry for 10 August 1895.

196. Jennifer Bobrovitz Files, notes, 11, note 71, LHA. Reference Norris, *A Leaven of Ladies*; Saywell, *Journal of Lady Aberdeen*. Also *Calgary Tribune*, 30 November 1895; *Calgary Herald*, 29 November 1895.

197. Elise A. Corbet, "A Do-Gooder, Not a Suffragette: A. Maude Riley," in *Citymakers: Calgarians after the Frontier*, ed. Max Foran and Sheilagh Jameson (Calgary: The Historical Society of Alberta, Chinook Country Chapter, 1987), 209.

198. Leslie, *Glimpses of Calgary Past*, 47–48. Reference oral testimony of Pansy Pue, former Calgary alderman and Conservative Party worker, who attended and worked with Nellie McClung to found the Calgary branch of the Canadian Federation of Business and Professional Women. This group would later install a bronze plaque at the entrance of the Senate chambers to honour the Famous Five, with money raised solely from Alberta women.

199. *Calgary Daily Herald*, 28 May 1895, 1–2.

200. Historians have characterized maternal feminists in particular as harbouring a belief that women have a duty to "mother," and therefore nurture and ensure proper moral standards not only for their own households but for society in general.

201. Norris, *A Leaven of Ladies*, 26.

202. Main catalogue search results, 21 January 2009, GAIA.

203. Calgary Local Council of Women Fonds, Accession No. M5841, File 24, Minutes 1919–1924, GAIA. Also Griffiths, *The Splendid Vision*, 14. The aim of the local council in Calgary, which reorganized in 1912, was to achieve "political equality for men and women...a speaking knowledge of either the English or French... equal moral standards in public and private life." Local council meetings were normally held monthly, with the president maintaining contact with members through regular visits. Griffiths believes that the provincial presidents of certain locals, including the one in Calgary, had a "significant role in developing policies of the National Council," 160. In 1938, a time when we know Isabella was no longer involved, Calgary's local included groups such as the WCTU, the Business and Professional Women's Club, the Calgary section of Jewish women, the Unemployed Women's Association, the women's section of the Dominion Labour Party, and the Women's Labour League, 190. This suggests the club's ideology became more progressive or even radical when compared to earlier times.

204. Norris, *A Leaven of Ladies*, 34–35.

205. Ibid., 60. Reference "No Militant Methods Necessary for Vote in Canada," *Minneapolis Sunday Tribune*, in *Morning Albertan*, 28 February 1913, 44.

206. Richard Langworth, ed. *Churchill by Himself: The Definitive Collection of Quotations* (New York: PublicAffairs, 2011), 332. This brings to mind Churchill's remarks about his mother, Lady Randolph Churchill: "My mother made the same brilliant impression upon my childhood's eye. She shone for me like an Evening Star. I loved her dearly, but at a distance...[In my career she] cooperated energetically from her end. In my interest she left no wire unpulled, no stone unturned, no cutlet uncooked."

207. Strong-Boag, *The Parliament of Women*, 80.

208. Donald B. Smith Collection, Lougheed #2 Box 1, James and Belle Lougheed 1914 File, LHA. Reference *Senate Debates*, 17 June 1920, 589.

209. Donald B. Smith Collection, Lougheed #2 Box 1, James Lougheed 1917 File, LHA. Reference *Calgary News Telegram*, 27 November 1917.

210. Jennifer Bobrovitz Files, notes, 15, LHA. Reference *Morning Albertan*, 28 October 1909.

211. Perry, *They Gathered at the River*, 249. Isabella served as president of the Ladies' Aid in 1890.

212. Rosemary R. Gagan, *A Sensitive Independence: Canadian Methodist Women Missionaries in Canada and the Orient, 1881–1925* (Montreal: McGill-Queen's University Press, 1992), 22.

213. Ibid., 254.

214. Arty Coppes-Zantinga and Ian Mitchell, *The Child in the Centre: Seventy-Five Years at the Alberta Children's Hospital* (Calgary: University of Calgary Press, 1997), 44. Also John Murray Gibbon, *The Victorian Order of Nurses for Canada: Fiftieth Anniversary, 1897–1947* (Montreal: Southam Press, 1947), 1. Organized in 1897 by Lady Aberdeen, the Victorian Order of Nurses (VON) was fashioned after the Queen's Institute of District Nursing in England. Given that it was the connection of Lady Aberdeen that first drew Isabella and James to the National Council of Women and to the Imperial Order Daughters of the Empire, it is likely this connection also drew Isabella to the VON. Also VON Fonds, M2645, FF7A, GAIA. In 1909, Isabella served as the first president of the VON's Calgary branch. From 1909 to 1915, the Calgary chapter of the VON was served by one district nurse, who, most times, had to make her way to visits without the assistance of the bicycle acquired by the VON in 1916. The bicycle enabled the nurse to visit 432 patients, for a total of 2,175 visits, and collect fees of $432.00, Report of 1932. By 1925, the Gyro Club, of which Isabella's son, Clarence, was a founding member, bought and maintained one car for the VON and paid the salary of one nurse, Inventory Listing, 4.

215. Gibbon, *The Victorian Order of Nurses*, 7–8. Reference Lady Aberdeen's "What Is the Use of the Victorian Order?"

216. Ibid., 8–9. The VON was originally conceived by Lady Aberdeen in part as a way to commemorate the Diamond Jubilee, 5. No doubt both Isabella and James again recognized the value of affiliating themselves with another British-inspired institution.

217. VON Fonds, M2645, Inventory Listing, 5, GAIA. Also Alberta History Magazine Folder, LHA. Marianne M. Molyneaux, "Early Days in Alberta," *Alberta History* 8, no. 2 (Spring 1960): 8. Isabella was also involved in the organizational work to establish a cottage hospital in 1889. She was one of only three women who turned out for the inaugural meeting of the Women's Hospital Aid Society. One of the other women was Bishop Pinkham's wife, the former Jean Drever, who joined Isabella on most new endeavours. Also Tyler Trafford, *Calgary Golf and Country Club: More Than 18 Holes, 1897–1997* (Calgary: The Calgary Golf and Country Club, 1997), 34. As with most everything else in Calgary, Isabella was involved with organizing the Calgary Golf and Country Club and, in 1913, served as honorary president of the Ladies' Section. Just as the golf courses of today often serve as venues for networking, they did in Isabella's time. Trafford noted that, while golf was primarily thought of as a sport for men at the beginning of the 1890s, by early 1897, the "Ladies of Golf" in Calgary were "energetic and interested in competition" and "a regular Saturday event was a round of golf

with tea served afterwards." One of the major competitions for ladies was, perhaps quite appropriately for Isabella, the HBC Cup, 32.

218. Coppes-Zantinga and Mitchell, *The Child in the Centre*, 42. On the Prairies, the VON was involved in both hospital and home visit nursing, often providing education on hygiene and food preparation. Eventually, the organization developed into providing community-based nursing, and was among the "first to offer scholarships to their nurses to take the degree in public health nursing as soon as it was available," 44. Perhaps this ideology appealed to many women at the time because it allowed them to pursue independent careers, even though they were careers that were seen as employing women's special skills as mothers.

219. Donald B. Smith Collection, Hardisty Box 2, Isabella Hardisty Lougheed Timeline File, LHA. First draft of the VON history forwarded to Lougheed House Conservation Society from Victorian Order of Nurses Calgary Branch, Helen English, 160, 4411-16 Avenue NW, Calgary, T3B 0M3 286-8200, note, 3.

220. VON Fonds, M2465-7A, List of Board 1909, GAIA.

221. Gibbon, *The Victorian Order of Nurses*, 60.

222. Wesleyan Ladies' College Archives File, R376.8W517 CANA H Reel #11, HPLA. *Globe and Mail*, 29 October 1946, n.p.

223. Donald B. Smith Collection, Lougheed #1 Box 2, James Lougheed 1890–1911 File, LHA. *The Calgary Club Woman's Blue Book* (Calgary: Calgary Branch of the Canadian Women's Press Club Publishers, 1915), 14–17.

224. *Morning Albertan*, 21 October 1909, 1.

225. Newspaper Clippings File, *Morning Albertan*, 14 March 1936, n.p., LHA.

226. Katie Pickles, *Female Imperialism and National Identity: Imperial Order Daughters of the Empire* (Manchester: Manchester University Press, 2002), 1.

227. Ibid, 273. Pickles wrote that where non-Protestant or non-Anglo-Celtic members were concerned, those identities were contained within particular chapters, so that while such chapters emphasized the possibilities of assimilation, they could be "containers" of religion (as in the Quebec chapter of primarily Roman Catholics), or ethnicity (as in the club in Winnipeg made up of Icelandic immigrants), or class (such as the blue-collar Ross Rifles chapter), 32. One chapter of the IODE was named the Lady Douglas Chapter, in honour of the wife of Captain James Douglas, and one was named the Pauline Johnson Chapter. While records are scarce that could confirm other members of the Macleod Chapter that Isabella joined, charter members of the Municipal Chapter in Calgary formed in 1918 include Elizabeth Turner Bone, Mary Spence, and Edith Robie. Elizabeth's husband, P. Turner Bone, an engineer with the CPR, had bunked with James when they lived in Medicine Hat and again when they arrived in Calgary. Also Sylvia Van Kirk, "Tracing the Fortunes of Five Founding Families

of Victoria," *BC Studies*, 115/116 (Autumn/Winter 1997): 149–179. Van Kirk's study of the five founding families of Victoria features Josette Work, who was part Cree, and who once dressed as Queen Victoria for an IODE meeting, no doubt with the goal to be accepted by Victoria's elite.

228. Newspaper Clippings File, "Canadian Women in the Public Eye."

229. Ibid.

230. Pickles, *Female Imperialism*, 8–9.

231. Ibid., 9.

4   WITH THIS ECONOMY WE DO WED

1. Pratt and Richards, *Prairie Capitalism*, 152.

2. Careless, "The Emergence of Cabbagetown," 29. The settlement adopted the name "Cabbagetown" because of the "poor Irish settlers of the day, both Protestant and Catholic, who traditionally raised the humble green vegetable."

3. Paul Voisey, *Vulcan: The Making of a Prairie Community* (Toronto: University of Toronto Press, 1988), 28. Voisey writes that many municipalities passed laws forbidding "rowdy behaviour, for only a respectable population could build progressive, civilized communities."

4. Annie L. Gaetz, *Trails of Yesterday: Folklore of the Red Deer District* (Red Deer: self-published, 1952), 32.

5. Donald B. Smith Collection, Lougheed #2 Box 2, Leonard Gaetz File, LHA. Reference Red Deer and District Archives MSS 446, Annie L. Gaetz, "Rev. Leonard Gaetz, D.D.—Maker of History," 4.

6. Ibid., 5.

7. Ibid., 6.

8. Ibid. Reference Red Deer and District Archives, Annie L. Gaetz Papers, Publishing Dept. Agriculture, Gov't Canada, Alberta, N.W.T., Rev. Leo. Gaetz, "Report of six years experience of a farmer in the Red Deer District, 1890," 3.

9. Ibid.

10. MacGregor, *Senator Hardisty's Prairies*, 105. Reference Constance Kerr Sissons, *John Kerr* (Toronto: Oxford University Press, 1946), 203.

11. Ibid., 148. Richard Hardisty was not only well placed to extend patronage to the free traders of his choice but was cognizant of the fact that the HBC would face competition from new investors. By 1877, he had been watching the progress of the cattle industry around Fort Macleod and Calgary. When his brother-in-law, Reverend John McDougall, moved cattle from Edmonton to Morley in 1873, and the next year added another thirty animals he had brought in from Montana, Hardisty no doubt realized they would flourish in the southern foothills.

12. MacGregor, *Senator Hardisty's Prairies*, 169.

13. Ibid., 171. Reference *Calgary Herald*, September 1881. Confirmed in Hardisty to MacFarlane, 14 March 1882, MacFarlane Papers, MG29, A11, Folder 876-879, LAC.

14. Ibid., 176. Reference *Edmonton Bulletin*, n.d. (however, it should be 26 February 1881).

15. Ibid., 175. Reference *Canada Sessional Papers*, vol. XVIII, no. 7, paper 18.

16. Ibid., 176. Reference *Edmonton Bulletin*, 7 January 1882.

17. Geoff Ironside, "Slopes and Shafts," in *Edmonton: The Life of a City*, ed. Bob Hesketh and Frances Swyripa (Edmonton: NeWest Press, 1995), 193.

18. Ibid., 194.

19. MacGregor, *Senator Hardisty's Prairies*, 172. Reference *Edmonton Bulletin*, 15 April 1882.

20. Ibid., 174. Reference Hardisty to MacFarlane, 14 March 1882, MacFarlane Papers, MG29, A11, Folder 876-879.

21. Ibid. Reference *Canada Sessional Papers*, vol. XV, no. 9, paper 22, 1882.

22. Ibid., 224.

23. Ibid., 128.

24. Ray, *The Canadian Fur Trade*, 12.

25. Ibid., 13.

26. Simmons, *Keepers of the* Record, 164–165. Simmons writes that there are "virtually no records of the land commissioner's office during Donald Smith's tenure, and any that are written in his hand are almost impossible to read because of his illegible handwriting."

27. Ray, *The Canadian Fur Trade*, 13.

28. Ibid., 14. Also Simmons, *Keepers of the Record*. Although Smith became very wealthy, Simmons writes that Smith was negligent at the helm and notorious in record keeping, which the HBC placed a premium on.

29. MacGregor, *Senator Hardisty's Prairies*. Reference *Victoria Times Colonist*, 10 February 1884. The *Colonist* noted that the elder Hardisty had an estate substantial enough so that he could leave the sum of $15,000 to one son in particular, George.

30. Foran, *The History of Canadian Cities*, 25. From the extensive ranching industry came investments in other manufacturers, such as brewing, malting, tannery, soapworks, cold storage, and commercial blocks, such as the Alberta Hotel, 30.

31. MacGregor, *Senator Hardisty's Prairies*, 175. Reference Hardisty Papers, Box 7, File 210, Folder 1355, GAIA.

32. Ibid., 175. Reference *Edmonton Bulletin*, 16 December 1882.

33. Thomas S. Burns and George B. Elliot, eds., *Calgary, Alberta, Canada: Her Industries and Resources* (Calgary: Glenbow Museum, 1974), 48.

34. McKenna, "Sir James Alexander Lougheed," 95–116. Reference letter from Lougheed to "fatherinlaw," 25 November 1885, Lougheed Family File, in which he talked of his cattle. James's father-in-law died in 1881, but perhaps he referred to Richard as his father-in-law.

35. Newspaper Clippings File, "Senator James Lougheed Was Famous Adopted Son," hand-dated 2 November 1925, LHA. This date cannot be accurate as the article notes Isabella's passing in 1936.

36. Klassen, *Eye on the Future*, 288. In 1891, as company lawyer, James helped the HBC raise its profile, when it finally outmanoeuvred the I.G. Baker & Co., assuming control of its stores in Calgary, Fort Macleod, and Lethbridge, 273–274.

37. Donald B. Smith, "Color Conscious: Racial Attitudes in Early 20th Century Calgary," in *Remembering Chinook Country: 1905–2005 Centennial Edition*, ed. Chinook Country Historical Society (Calgary: Detselig Enterprises, 2005), 144. Edmund Taylor was the son of Thomas and Elizabeth Margaret Kennedy Taylor, both of "leading Hudson's Bay Company families." Edmund Taylor's aunt, Margaret Taylor, was the "country-born" wife of George Simpson. Also Klassen, *Eye on the Future*, 285–286. Edmund was born in Manitoba in 1871, and joined the HBC as an apprentice clerk in 1885, then served at several of its posts in the North-West Territories. Taylor then moved up to the position of accountant and, finally, to manager of the company's new department store in Calgary. Also Smith, *Calgary's Grand Story*, 59. When he shared his experiences during an address to the Calgary Historical Society in 1924, Taylor noted that, for three generations, his family had been intimately connected with both the HBC and North West Company. Reference Edmund Taylor, "Western Canada in the Making," reprinted in Calgary Historical Society under title "Something of Life of Early Factors," January 1924; George B. Coutts Papers M279, File 41, GAIA. Also Lougheed House Research Files, E.L. Taylor Folder, LHA. Reference *Calgary Daily Herald*, 3 October 1929. No doubt Edmund would have been very familiar with the Hardisty family, which very likely played a part in his ensuing business association with James Lougheed. The partnership with Taylor would become another fortuitous connection for James, since Taylor went on to become a prominent financier and was very active in all aspects of the Calgary economy, including serving as president of the Calgary Stock Exchange and on the boards of many corporations. Also Lougheed House Research Files, E.H. Taylor Folder, LHA. Reference *Calgary Daily Herald*, 3 October 1929. Taylor made another major contribution to Calgary society, one that would have been appreciated by Isabella, who showed her own interest in preserving historical records through her membership in the Southern Alberta Pioneer Association. In 1929, Taylor is

credited with establishing the first historical collection of records of the HBC in Canada.

38. Jennings Publishing Company, *Merchants' and Manufacturers' Record: Calgary, Sunny Alberta, the Industrial Capital of the Great West* (Calgary: Jennings Publishing Co., 1911), 98.

39. Jennifer Bobrovitz Files, notes, 16, LHA.

40. McNeill, *Tales of the Old Town*, 34.

41. Ibid., preface. Although McNeill claimed to be a founding member, the Southern Alberta Pioneer Association was founded prior to his membership. Isabella Lougheed was a founding member in 1896, the year of McNeill's birth. Even though his memory is somewhat inaccurate, McNeill's book, *Tales of the Old Town*, reprinted by the *Calgary Herald*, relies on memory and oral testimony of other "old-timers." McNeill wrote that the basement of one of the Lougheed buildings housed the Plaza, a "long, narrow room, decorated with palms and soft-colored lights," with a beautiful dance floor. In the background, "soft dance music of the highest quality played from 10 oclock till about 2 A.M.," 34.

42. Demmon, "The Arts," 59.

43. MacEwan, *Calgary Cavalcade*, 112.

44. Bruce Hutchinson, "5000 to 75,000 in 12 Years—That's How Calgary Came to Be," in *Alberta in the 20th Century: The Boom and the Bust, 1910–1914*, ed. Ted Byfield (Edmonton: United Western Communications Ltd., 1994), 88. Census figures from Calgary Municipal Handbook Online, accessed 30 April 2012, http://www.calgary.ca/CS/CSC/Pages/Municipal-handbook.aspx.

45. Foran, *The History of Canadian Cities*, 67.

46. Ibid., 74.

47. Ibid., 76.

48. Klassen, *Eye on the Future*, 332. Also Canada Life, accessed 3 May 2012, http://www.canadalife.com/003/Home/CorporateInformation/CompanyOverview/EarlyYears/index.htm. This company was established in Ontario by Hugh C. Baker in 1847 and was the first independent insurance company in the colony. By the time James was dealing with this company, it was headed by Senator George Cox, who established a Calgary branch in 1900 and installed Canada Life as the first Canadian company operating with full branches in Great Britain. Also Michael Bliss, "Cox, George Albertus," in *Dictionary of Canadian Biography*, vol. 14, University of Toronto/Université Laval, 2003–, accessed 3 May 2012, http://www.biographi.ca/en/bio/cox_george_albertus_14E.html. Although not a Conservative like James, George Cox (appointed to the Senate by Laurier) was an ardent Methodist and temperance campaigner.

49. Klassen, *Eye on the Future*, 333.

50. Ibid., 334. It is also true that the years from "the 1870s to the 1890s spanned an era of amazing economic growth in Calgary and the Bow Valley...Those who remained as permanent settlers left the imprint of their work upon a region once devoted to the buffalo hunt and the fur trade," xix.

51. *Morning Albertan*, 26 January 1914, 5.

52. Ibid., 14 February 1914, 9.

53. Ibid., 8 March 1911, 1.

54. P. Turner Bone, *When the Steel Went Through: Reminiscences of a Railroad Pioneer* (Toronto: Macmillan, 1947), 44.

55. Ibid., 50.

56. Ibid., 49.

57. Ibid., 50.

58. McKenna, "Sir James Alexander Lougheed," 99.

59. Author Marian McKenna and journalist Alan Hustak both questioned the ethics of these transactions.

60. Pratt and Richards, *Prairie Capitalism*, 154.

61. Donald B. Smith Collection, Lougheed #1 Box 2, James Lougheed 1890–1911 File, LHA. Senator J.A. Lougheed, "Why Go to Canada: The City of Calgary," supplement to *Calgary Daily Herald*, June 1910.

62. Ibid.

63. Ibid.

64. This term is taken from Maxwell Laurence Foran, "The Civic Corporation and Urban Growth: Calgary, 1884–1930" (PHD dissertation, University of Calgary, 1981), 71.

65. Donald B. Smith Collection, Lougheed #1 Box 2, James Lougheed 1890–1911 File, LHA. Senator J.A. Lougheed, "Why Go to Canada: The City of Calgary," supplement to *Calgary Daily Herald*, June 1910. If James's practices were anything like those of his junior partner R.B. Bennett, then special privileges borne of their relationship with the CPR were extremely profitable for Bennett, and for James and Isabella. Also Louis A. Knafla, "Richard 'Bonfire' Bennett: The Legal Practice," in *Beyond the Law: Lawyers and Business in Canada, 1830 to 1930*, ed. Carol Wilton (Toronto: The Osgoode Society, 1990), 354. Relying on the recollections of John Brownlee, Knafla noted that Brownlee recalled his early days as a young law student working in Bennett's office, and concluded that Bennett did profit from private information obtained from the CPR. Some of this information allowed Bennett to buy parcels of land from the CPR on five- to seven-year instalments, well before the company's announcement of plans for new branch lines, stations, roundhouses, or irrigation projects. Upon public release by the rail company of the plans for new development, usually within one to three years

of his purchase, Bennett would sell the parcels for $6 per acre, which he had bought for $4 to $5 per acre. Reportedly, Bennett also arranged loans for other buyers, earning 6 per cent on instalments, while he earned a commission of twenty-five cents per acre on land sales that he brokered for these third parties. Reference MS94, A./3, 3–4, GAIA and Bennett Papers, M3140, 544, 029-42, LAC, correspondence from 21 August 1950 to 28 January 1953.

66. Foran, *The History of Canadian Cities*, 22.

67. John English, *The Conservatives and the Party System, 1901–1920* (Toronto: University of Toronto Press, 1977), 99.

68. Donald B. Smith Collection, Lougheed #2 Box 2, Harold Daly File, LHA. Daly Memoirs autobiographical notes, 14 February 1902, MG27, Series 111 F9 Volume 2 page 1 File H.M., LAC.

69. Donald B. Smith Collection, Lougheed #2 Box 1, Lougheed 1912 File, LHA. Mackenzie Papers 02399, 1 March 1912.

70. Ens, *A Son of the Fur Trade*, ix. Ens writes that Grant had ulterior motives in dictating his memoirs. Although a close partisan of Donald A. Smith from 1870 to 1878, the relationship deteriorated and Johnny "came to believe that Smith had used and manipulated him, and defrauded him of a considerable sum that was due him from the James McKay estate (Smith was the executor of the will)." Ens concludes that Grant had no problem portraying himself as "foolish and gullible," as he painted himself a victim of unscrupulous bankers, politicians, and lawyers. Ironically, perhaps, it was Johnny Grant's uncle, John Grant, who was the first husband of Isabella Hardisty (later Lady Strathcona, wife of Donald A. Smith), xlvi–xlvii.

71. Alan Wilson, "'In a Business Way:' C.J. Brydges and the Hudson's Bay Company, 1879–89," in *The West and the Nation: Essays in Honour of W.L. Morton*, ed. Carl Berger and Ramsay Cook (Toronto: McClelland & Stewart, 1976), 129.

72. Wilson, "'In a Business Way,'" 137. Also Simmons, *Keepers of the Record*, 164. Simmons writes that hiring Brydges signalled a change in business structure for the HBC, given he was not a company man but came to the company from the outside, bringing a "modern, active, aggressive, and planned" approach to land deals, 160. Reportedly, Brydges was summoned to London on more than one occasion to explain his own personal speculation on land, 163. Perhaps this explains some of the clashes with Smith, since both of them appear to have had agendas of personal profit.

73. McKenna, "Sir James Alexander Lougheed," 99.

74. Ibid. Reference *Edmonton Journal*, 12 October 1983 (possibly an error and should be *Calgary Herald* 1883).

75. Ibid., 99. Reference *Edmonton Journal*, 12 October 1983.

76. James H. Gray, *R.B. Bennett: The Calgary Years* (Toronto: University of Toronto Press, 1991), 42. Reference *Calgary Herald*, 25 September 1897.

77. Henry Cornelius Klassen, "Lawyers, Finance, and Economic Development in Southwestern Alberta, 1884–1920," in *Beyond the Law: Lawyers and Business in Canada, 1830 to 1930*, ed. Carol Wilton (Toronto: The Osgoode Society, 1990), 299.

78. Ibid., 300. At the height of its economic success in 1920, the firm of Lougheed and Bennett operated with eleven partners, 302.

79. Ibid., 305. Reference MG26, K, Bennett Papers, Volume 877, Calgary, R.B. Bennett to C.H. Barker, 5 March 1903, LAC; Calgary, R.B. Bennett to D. Shannon Bowlby, 8 April 1903.

80. Ibid., 304.

81. Ibid., 298. Klassen identifies three groups of lawyers who practised in Alberta at the same time as James Lougheed. Of these, the first group consisted of a small number of men of great wealth whose involvement in diverse commercial and industrial activity formed the basis of such wealth. Both Lougheed and Bennett belonged to this first group. The second group consisted of men of lesser wealth who focused primarily on real estate investment, and had a net worth of between $38,000 to $71,000. The largest group consisted of lawyers with the lowest net worth, but Klassen notes that boundaries were permeable, with the fairly steady movement of newcomers into the legal community.

82. Ibid., 304.

83. Ibid., 305.

84. Ibid., 313.

85. Ibid., 310. Despite the decline in their prestige during difficult economic times, Klassen argues that lawyers occupied an

> *ever more significant position in the southwestern Alberta economy during the period 1884 to 1920...many, along with merchants and other businessmen, were responsible for increasing the region's financial resources and for delivering prosperity despite a number of downswings in the business cycle. These lawyers developed close links with the commercial, agricultural, and industrial sectors and through networks of friends and business associates gained detailed information that was vital to the conduct of their complex operations.*

Lawyers assumed a significant role in directing capital, particularly when banks were hesitant to extend credit. Thus, lawyers contributed to the growth of trade in urban centres and the development of agriculture in the larger region.

86. Ibid., 313.

87. Ibid., 314.

88. Ibid., 315.

89. David C. Jones, *Empire of Dust: Settling and Abandoning the Prairie Dry Belt* (Calgary: University of Calgary Press, 2002), 25.

90. Donald B. Smith Collection, Lougheed #2 Box 2, Bob Edwards File, LHA. *Calgary Eye Opener*, 5 May 1906.

91. Ibid.

92. Jonathan S. Swainger, "Ideology, Social Capital, and Entrepreneurship," in *Beyond the Law: Lawyers and Business in Canada, 1830 to 1930*, ed. Carol Wilton (Toronto: The Osgoode Society, 1990), 388.

93. Ibid., 389. As the few who continued to enjoy prosperity during difficult economic times, lawyers "came to symbolize for many Albertans the ills, not only of the Canadian economy, but of the entire Canadian political structure," 393. However, with the rise of agricultural groups and the election of the United Farmers of Alberta (UFA), there was less room for the participation of lawyers, based on the fact that the UFA's "economic and political philosophy was at the root of its distrust of the legal profession," 390.

94. Hustak, *Peter Lougheed*, 17.

95. Ibid.

96. Unlike James, Bennett liked to portray himself as an independent Conservative, for whom the interests of the West and the small producer were paramount. Also McKenna, "Sir James Alexander Lougheed," 108n34. Whatever image Bennett chose to cultivate, he was closely associated with CPR interests, earning annual retainers in the area of $10,000 in the early 1900s. Also Stanley Bruce Gordon, "R.B. Bennett, M.L.A., 1897–1905: The Years of Apprenticeship" (MA thesis, University of Calgary, 1975), 40–42. Bennett talked of his business connections with the CPR in the *Calgary Herald*, 28 September 1898 and 31 October 1898. He was the solicitor and vice-president of its subsidiary irrigation company.

97. Klassen, *Eye on the Future*, 227–228. The growing opposition to Macdonald's deal with the CPR led to an anti-monopoly provincial government in Manitoba, led by a Metis man, John Norquay.

98. Jones, *Empire of Dust*, 21.

99. Ibid.

100. Jennifer Bobrovitz Files, 19, LHA. Reference Archives Files RG 15 B2A, Volume 175.

101. Ibid. Reference *Morning Albertan*, 11 November 1920, 12.

102. Foran, *The History of Canadian Cities*, 60. Reference *Calgary Tribune*, 21 October 1885 and 3 April 1886.

103. David H. Breen and R.C. Macleod, eds., *William Stewart Herron: Father of the Petroleum Industry in Alberta* (Calgary: Alberta Records Publication Board, 1984), xxvi.

104. Ibid.

105. It was Peter Lougheed's belief that the difficult times only served to strengthen the resolve of his family, and thus he would have it no other way. Despite their significant wealth, Isabella and James were not members of the "Big Four" of Calgary business, which included Pat Burns, owner of Burn's Meats; Alfred Ernest (A.E.) Cross, rancher and owner of Calgary Brewing and Malting; Archie McLean, rancher and politician; and George Lane, rancher and first supplier to the North West Mounted Police. It was these four who joined together in 1912 to finance what has become perhaps the best symbol of early Prairie boosterism, the Calgary Stampede. The Calgary Stampede did much to preserve the image of Calgary as home of the "Old West" and the ranching capital of Canada before the decline of the old cattle empires. Perhaps the reason James is not normally considered a member of this particular group is that ranching was a minor enterprise for him. While he preferred to cultivate an image of British aristocracy, the Big Four promoted an image of Calgary as the defender of the Old West and pioneer hospitality. Also Pratt and Richards, *Prairie Capitalism*, 46. The first resource boom in Alberta in 1914 at Turner Valley was directed by some of these four, but, as noted earlier, also included James. Since Alberta did not at that time control its own natural resources, "vast quantities of gas, for which there was little market, were flared at rates as high as 600 million cubic feet per day" at a location dubbed "Hell's Half Acre." It was no doubt the resource boom that convinced James to become an enthusiastic supporter of provincial autonomy, even in the face of opposition from fellow Albertans. Also Douglas R. Owram, ed., *The Formation of Alberta: A Documentary History* (Edmonton: Historical Society of Alberta, 1979). The *Macleod Gazette* castigated the *Calgary Herald*'s "desperate" support for such a movement, writing that the *Herald* had apparently at last recognized the hopelessness of securing home rule, as it was called, for Alberta. Its insanity had not taken much serious hold, but it could see the absurdity of agitating for provincial autonomy, with the great mass of people opposed to it, 110. Reference *Macleod Gazette*, 13 November 1896. Also *Calgary Herald*, 22 March 1895, 86. The *Herald* indicated that James was in favour of the "insanity" of autonomy. Also *Calgary Herald*, 28 September 1898, 113. Apparently, Calgarians always believed it would be more to their advantage to achieve political autonomy, since they believed, as Bennett articulated, "We should remember that with provincial autonomy Calgary would become the capital. In the east Calgary is always spoken of in terms of praise as an enterprising city

with fine buildings and energetic citizens." Also Paul Voisey, "Unsolved Mysteries of Edmonton's Growth," in *Edmonton: The Life of a City*, ed. Bob Hesketh and Frances Swyripa (Edmonton: NeWest Press, 1995), 321. In the end, Edmonton's business community proved a little more adept at boosterism. It certainly did not hurt Edmonton's case that it was a Liberal federal government that finally granted autonomy, and that Calgary's Member of Parliament served in opposition, while Edmonton's Frank Oliver sat with the Liberal administration.

106. Klassen, "Lawyers, Finance," 304.

107. Ibid., 305.

108. Foran, *The History of Canadian Cities*, 30.

109. *Calgary Daily Herald*, 22 January 1891, n.p.

110. *Calgary Daily Herald*, 26 December 1900. Also Klassen, *Eye on the Future*, 244. It was the incessant prairie fires that no doubt inspired Calgary to become the "Sandstone City" (between 1886 and 1914), made possible because of an abundance of sandstone in the "high hills surrounding it...underlaid with a very superior quality of sandstone, easily worked, and which hardens when exposed to the air."

111. Richard Cunniffe, *Calgary in Sandstone* (Calgary: Historical Society of Alberta, Calgary Branch, 1969), 20.

112. Paul Voisey, "Entrepreneurs in Early Calgary," in *Frontier Calgary: Town, City, and Region, 1875–1914*, ed. Anthony W. Rasporich and Henry Cornelius Klassen (Calgary: McClelland and Stewart West, 1975), 238.

113. Trudy Soby, *Be It Ever So Humble* (Calgary: Century Calgary Publications, 1975), 9.

114. Voisey, "Entrepreneurs in Early Calgary," 240.

115. Ibid., 238.

116. As her Christmas greeting card, Isabella chose not a winter scene but one of her standing in front of a lilac in full bloom.

117. Jason Patrick Bennett, "'Nature's Garden and a Possible Utopia': Farming for Fruit and Industrious Men in the Transboundary Pacific Northwest, 1895–1914," in *The Borderlands of the American and Canadian Wests: Essays on Regional History of the Forty-Ninth Parallel*, ed. Sterling Evans (Lincoln: University of Nebraska Press, 2006), 231. Also Jean Barman, "Ethnicity in the Pursuit of Status: British Middle and Upper-Class Emigration to British Columbia in the Late Nineteenth and Early Twentieth Centuries," *Canadian Ethnic Studies* 18, no. 1 (1986): 38. Barman writes that, although Lady Aberdeen referred to Coldstream Ranch as "a really high-class little community," in which they sold plots of land to "selected Englishmen and Scots," at least one resident described the new residents as a collection of "English school boys whose parents sent them to the 'colonies' with their blessings because they would not fit into anything at home."

118. McKenna, "Sir James Alexander Lougheed," 79. James was favoured with this position, despite the fact that Bennett was the only Conservative from Alberta to hold a federal seat.

119. Ibid., 110. As noted earlier, James and Isabella shared Beaulieu with the duke, the duchess, their daughter, Princess Patricia, and an entourage of thirty.

120. Donald B. Smith Collection, Lougheed #1 Box 2, James Lougheed 1890–1911 File, LHA. Also *Banff Crag & Canyon*, 12 June 1991 features a picture of Lougheed house built by James and Isabella in 1910, located at 137 Spray Avenue in Banff National Park.

121. McKenna, "Sir James Alexander Lougheed." Reference Hon. W.B. Willoughby, Senate Debates, 12 January 1926, 10.

122. James Lougheed Family Fonds, Accession No. M4843, File 13, copy of originals held in oversize files, GAIA. Also Hustak, *Peter Lougheed*, 19. The Governor General, the Duke of Connaught, wrote to Princess Louise, "Lougheed has done admirably; he is an honourable gentleman, a businessman, and all the militia council are delighted to work under him."

123. The Military Hospitals Commission's recommendations served as forerunners of the social welfare state and current-day veterans' hospitals, training programs, pensions, and disability allowances and represent one of the first instances of government-led programs for citizen care. With Canada unprepared for the scale of wounded and disabled after the First World War, and no previous experience with such massive casualties, it fell upon James to supervise the building of hospitals and convalescent homes to care for the wounded. He was also tasked with establishing programs to retrain and find employment for those able to work, and to solicit help from nongovernmental relief organizations. No doubt James's work with this commission was bolstered by Isabella's involvement in numerous philanthropic organizations such as the Red Cross.

124. Smith, *Calgary's Grand Story*, 21. Smith writes that Griesbach said of Lougheed that he "could meet a delegation and be as sweet as pie, but finally having made up his mind he became a boss and was vigorous and sometimes ruthless in carrying out his ideas."

125. Foran, *The History of Canadian Cities*, 32.

126. Ibid., 34.

127. Ibid., 56.

128. Ibid., 54. Reference *Calgary Tribune*, 18 December 1889.

129. Ibid., 54. Reference *The Western World*, August 1890, 143.

130. Ibid., 56.

131. *Calgary Weekly Herald*, 16 February 1893, n.p.

132. *Calgary Daily Herald*, 11 August 1897, n.p.

133. Donald B. Smith Collection, Hardisty Box 1, Mary Hardisty 1840–1930 File, LHA. Reference *Winnipeg Tribune*, May 1945 and Charles D. Denney Papers, GAIA.

134. Richard Hardisty Fonds, Accession No. M5908, Series 23-5, 1683, GAIA. Letter to Mr Hardisty from unknown person (last page missing), 4 October 1885, Montreal.

135. Richard Hardisty Fonds, Accession No. M5908, Series 23-4, 1618, GAIA. James Bissett to Richard Hardisty, 16 February 1881. Also Richard Hardisty Fonds, Accession No. M477-874, Series 16, GAIA. Indenture between William Lucas Hardisty and Donald A. Smith, no date.

136. Donald B. Smith Collection, Hardisty Box 1, Mary Hardisty 1840–1930 File, LHA. Reference Clarence Hardisty to Mrs. Mary Thomas, c/o Mrs. Thomas Bird, Inwood, Manitoba, 29 October 1929. Also reference Denney Papers, Accession No. M7144, File #330,000 Statement of earnings from Richard Hardisty. There are no letters to Clarence from Mary Thomas, thus perhaps she relied on family to read the letters to her because it has not been established that she had the benefit of a Euro-Canadian education.

137. Donald B. Smith Collection, Hardisty Box 1, William and Mary Children File, LHA. Also notes provided to the author by Val Maher (descendant of the Thomas family), October 2006, indicate that Mary Louise and Alfred Hackland lived there as well.

138. Donald B. Smith Collection, Hardisty Box 1, William and Mary Children File, LHA. Also notes provided by Val Maher, October 2006.

139. Donald B. Smith Collection, Hardisty Box 1, Mary Hardisty 1840–1930 File, LHA. News clipping not dated or identified by newspaper source; provided by Val Maher to Donald Smith.

140. Donald B. Smith Collection, Hardisty Box 1, William and Mary Children File, LHA. Reference W.L. Hardisty Estate, McLaws Fonds, The Legal Archives Society of Alberta, Fonds 37, File 173, Folder 2.

141. Donald B. Smith Collection, Hardisty Box 2, William Hardisty Estate File, LHA. Reference letter from unknown author to C.H. Lougheed, Esq., Lougheed & Taylor Ltd., 19 May 1930, W.L. Hardisty Estate, McLaw's Fonds, The Legal Archives Society of Alberta, Fonds 37, File 173, Folder 2. Also letter to Clarence Lougheed from William Lucas Hardisty Jr. (Isabella's brother), 21 October 1929. This letter stated, "If she had a claim on Donald her mother or the law could have had Donald arrested for bigamy." Also Jessie Hardisty (Donald's wife) to Clarence Hardisty, 16 November 1929. This letter explained that, when she married Donald, Jessie was a war widow and they adopted a girl together.

142. Donald B. Smith Collection, Hardisty Box 2, William Hardisty Estate File, LHA. Reference McLaws, Redman, Lougheed & Cairns to Royal Trust Company, 20 June 1933 in Wm Lucas Estate McLaws Fonds, Folder 37, File 52.

143. Donald B. Smith Collection, Hardisty Box 2, William Hardisty Estate File, LHA. A.S. Morrison, Winnipeg, to McLaws, Redman, Lougheed & Cairns, 19 June 1930. Reference W.L. Hardisty Estate, McLaws Fonds, Legal Society Fonds 37, File 173, Folder 2.

144. Donald B. Smith Collection, Hardisty Box 2, William Hardisty Estate File, LHA. McLaws, Redman, Lougheed & Cairns to A.S. Morrison, Esq., 8 July 1930. Reference W.L. Hardisty Estate, McLaws Fonds, Fond 37, File 173, Folder 2.

145. Ibid.

146. Donald B. Smith Collection, Hardisty Box 2, William Hardisty Estate File, LHA. Frank A. Hardisty to Clarence Lougheed, 16 March 1931. Reference McLaws Fonds, Fond 37, File 173, Folder 2.

147. Donald B. Smith Collection, Hardisty Box 2, William Hardisty Estate File, LHA. McLaws, Redman, Lougheed & Cairns to Frank A. Hardisty, Esq., 30 March 1931. Reference Hardisty Estate McLaws Fonds, Fonds 37, File 173, Folder 2.

148. Donald B. Smith Collection, Hardisty Box 2, William Hardisty Estate File, LHA. McClaws, Redman, Lougheed & Cairns to Frank A. Hardisty, 8 April 1931. Reference McLaws Fonds, Fond 37, File 173, Folder 2.

149. Donald B. Smith Collection, Hardisty Box 2, William Hardisty Estate File, LHA. Frank Hardisty, St. Vital Manitoba, to W.H. McLaws, 19 April 1931. Reference Hardisty McLaws Fonds 37, File 173, Folder 2.

150. Donald B. Smith Collection, Hardisty Box 2, William Hardisty Estate File, LHA. Affidavit filed 10 June 1926. Reference McLaws Fonds, Folder 54.

151. Donald B. Smith Collection, Hardisty Box 2, William Hardisty Estate File, LHA. Reference McLaws Fonds, Fond 37, File 173, Folder 1. Lougheed, McLaws, Sinclair & Redman to Lougheed & Taylor, 20 February 1929.

152. Donald B. Smith Collection, Hardisty Box 2, William Hardisty Estate File, LHA. M. Louise Hackland to Mr. N.H. McLaws, 8 July 1930. Reference McLaws Fonds 37, File 173, Folder 2.

153. Ibid.

154. Donald B. Smith Collection, Hardisty Box 2, William Hardisty Estate File, LHA. Letter dated 25 May 1933 to Collector of Succession Duties, Edmonton.

155. Klassen, "Lawyers, Finance," 305.

156. Ibid.

157. Ibid.

158. Richard A. Willie, "'It Is Every Man for Himself': Winnipeg Lawyers and the Law Business, 1870 to 1903," in *Beyond the Law: Lawyers and Business in Canada, 1830–1930*, ed. Carol Wilton (Toronto: The Osgoode Society, 1990), 269.

159. Ibid. Reference Gerhard Ens, "Métis Lands in Manitoba," *Manitoba History*, no. 5 (Spring 1983): 6.

160. Ibid., 270. Reference GR174, Box 19, Report of Commission of Inquiry into Administration of Justice as to Infant Lands and Estates, Testimony of Heber Archibald, 23 Nov 1881, AM. The commissioners were Frederick McKenzie and Thomas A. Bernier, both lawyers.

161. Robert J. Talbot, *Negotiating the Numbered Treaties: An Intellectual and Political Biography of Alexander Morris* (Saskatoon: Purich Publishing, 2009), 53–54.

162. Hustak, *Peter Lougheed*, 15.

163. Sprague, *Canada and the Métis*; Tough, "As Their Natural Resources Fail"; Gerhard J. Ens, *Homeland to Hinterland: The Changing Worlds of the Red River Metis in the Nineteenth Century* (Toronto: University of Toronto Press, 1996); Joe Sawchuk, *The Dynamics of Native Politics: The Alberta Metis Experience* (Saskatoon: Purich Publishing, 1998). These scholars provide thorough analyses of scrip politics.

164. Hustak, *Peter Lougheed*, 16.

165. Donald B. Smith Collection, Lougheed #2 Box 2, Lougheed 1922 File, LHA. Senate House debates, 21 June 1922, 499–500.

166. Donald B. Smith Collection, Lougheed #2 Box 2, Lougheed 1922 File, LHA. Senate House debates, 21 June 1922, 499.

167. Donald B. Smith Collection, Lougheed #2 Box 2, Lougheed 1922 File, LHA. Reference *Calgary Herald*, 26 June 1999.

168. Ibid.

169. Ibid.

170. Ibid. Secord Jr. did go on to defend his grandfather somewhat, saying, "From what I understand he was one of the few who paid a fair price for scrip." Coincidentally, Richard Secord Jr. discovered his great-grandfather's signature on Treaty 8 documents when he was appearing on behalf of Jim Badger in 1994, then chief of Sucker Creek Reserve, where the original treaty was signed, and which was challenging a hazardous waste plant near Swan Hills. Badger pointed the treaty signatories out to the younger Secord, also noting that one of those signing was Badger's own great-grandfather, Chief Moostoos.

171. Donald B. Smith Collection, Lougheed #2 Box 2, Lougheed 1922 File, LHA. *Calgary Herald*, 26 June 1999.

172. Donald B. Smith Collection, Lougheed #2 Box 2, Lougheed 1922 File, LHA. Senate House debates, June 1922, 554.

173. Donald B. Smith Collection, Hardisty Box 1, Hardisty Descendants File, LHA. Reference MacRae, *History of the Province of Alberta*, 890.

174. Ken Hatt, "The North-West Rebellion Scrip Commissions, 1885–1889," in *1885 and After: Native Society in Transition*, ed. F. Laurie Barron and James B. Waldram (Regina: Canadian Plains Research Center, 1986), 199.

175. Very near the time James was purchasing land, the Dominion Lands Act revoked much of the Metis land that had been laid out in present-day Calgary along the Bow and Elbow rivers.

176. Lougheed House Research Files, Alberta General History Folder, LHA. Reference *Tales of Two Cities*, 212, no author cited. Also Hatt, "The North-West Rebellion Scrip Commissions," 200. In response to some arguments, specifically those of Thomas Flanagan in *Riel and the Rebellion: 1885 Reconsidered*, and in reference to the vast majority of Metis who preferred money scrip to land, Hatt notes that some Metis may have preferred money scrip simply because land was inappropriate and did not suit their pressing needs. However, this does not negate the importance of land scrip, and the reality that buyers of scrip were in a position of authority and were able to set minimum prices and work within those limits, 199. Reference W.P. Fillmore, "Half-Breed Scrip," *Manitoba Bar News* 39, no. 2 (1973): 124.

177. *Calgary Daily Herald*, 13 August 1900.

178. Willie, "'It Is Every Man for Himself,'" 277.

179. McKenna, "Sir James Alexander Lougheed," 105. Reference Alan Hustak, who provides no footnotes for this.

180. Ibid.

181. 2001 Folder, Peter Lougheed correspondence to LHCS, LHA. Also RG15, Interior, Series D-11-1, Volume 451, Reel T-13140, File 119392, Access Code 90, LAC. There is also an application for scrip made by James when he had power of attorney for a man by the name of Thomas Whitford.

182. LAC, accessed 25 May 2009, http://collectionscanada.gc.ca/pam_archives.

183. Donald B. Smith Collection, Lougheed #1 Box 2, James 1890–1911 File, LHA. Reference RG15, Volume 1369, Public Archives of Canada (PAC). At that time, Isabella's mother indicated she had lived on Lot 4 at Oak Point for six years. Prior to that, she had lived in Stonewall for nine years, Lower Fort Garry for two years prior to that, in Montreal for three years prior to that, and Mackenzie River from the date of her first marriage to William Hardisty. On her application for her own scrip, Isabella's mother listed her current husband as "whiteman" and herself as halfbreed.

184. LAC, accessed 25 May 2009, http://collectionscanada.gc.ca/pam_archives.

185. MG25G, Volume 14, Kipling 62, LAC.

186. *Morning Albertan*, 3 May 1923.

187. Jones, *Empire of Dust.*

188. Jennifer Bobrobitz Files, notes, 21, LHA.

189. Ibid.

190. Donald B. Smith Collection, James Lougheed Obituaries 1925 File, LHA.
     Reference *Ottawa Evening Citizen*, 3 November 1925, and *Calgary Daily Herald*, 10
     November 1925.

191. Jennifer Bobrovitz Files, notes, 22, LHA. Reference Henderson's City Directory
     1926, 460.

192. Jennifer Bobrovitz Files, notes, 18, LHA. Reference Lougheed Family Bible;
     indicates burial at Calgary Union Cemetery.

193. Ibid. No reference.

194. Jennifer Bobrovitz Files, notes, 22, LHA.

195. Ibid., 18.

196. Ibid., 22. Reference *Calgary Herald*, 27 August 1932; *Edmonton Journal*, 29 August
     1932.

197. Pratt and Richards, *Prairie Capitalism*, 162.

198. Ibid., 155. In his case, Peter aimed to free Alberta from its reliance on foreign
     oil companies through the development of domestic entrepreneurial ambitions
     and skills. Whether it is so that Peter Lougheed "obsessed" about diversifying
     the economy, he was determined to transfer decision-making powers from
     Central Canada to the resource-rich western periphery. In so doing, Peter
     aimed to "nurture the development in Alberta of a strong indigenous class of
     entrepreneurs and managers capable of running a more complex and diversified
     economy. With this has come a pronounced ideological emphasis on people's
     capitalism," 242.

199. Gerald Melnyk, *Riel to Reform: A History of Protest in Western Canada* (Saskatoon:
     Fifth House Publishers, 1992), 6.

200. John English, *Just Watch Me: The Life of Pierre Elliott Trudeau, 1968–2000* (Toronto:
     Alfred A. Knopf Canada, 2009), 514. Also Elizabeth Bailey Price, "The
     First White Girl Born in Alberta," *Lethbridge Herald*, 23 October 1926. Even
     contemporaries seemed to sometimes forget Hardisty's Indigenous ancestry, as
     evidenced by Price's claim that Richard's daughter was the first white girl born in
     Alberta.

201. Not unlike his own grandmother, Peter Lougheed recreated himself as a member
     of the elite, downplaying his own Metis ancestry until after retiring from his
     political career.

202. Donald B. Smith Collection, Lougheed #1 Box 2, James Lougheed 1890–1911 File, LHA. Letter from James Lougheed, 20 February 1894. Reference City Clerk's Papers, Box 1, File 8.

203. Pratt and Richards, *Prairie Capitalism*, 155.

204. Ibid.

205. Ibid., 54.

206. Hustak, *Peter Lougheed*, 22.

207. Ibid., 28.

208. Hustak, *Peter Lougheed*, 25. Hustak speculates Douglas's death was a suicide but provides no references. Also "D.G. Lougheed Dies in City," *Calgary Herald*, 16 October 1931. Newspaper reports at the time simply stated that Douglas died in hospital "after an illness which had kept him in bed most of the summer."

209. "Clarence Lougheed, Prominent Native Calgarian, Is Dead: Son of Pioneer Family Expires in Bed Thursday Morning," *Calgary Daily Herald*, 2 February 1933; "Clarence Lougheed, Calgary Native Son Found Dead in Bed," *Morning Albertan*, 3 February 1933. Also *Morning Albertan*, 6 February 1933. Reportedly, "every walk of life" was represented at the graveside service held for Clarence, a man described as having a "warm heart and unselfish spirit."

210. Donald B. Smith Collection, Lougheed #1 Box 1, Clarence Lougheed File, LHA. Reference David Mittelstadt, no book title.

211. *Morning Albertan*, 14 October 1933.

212. Linda M. Grayson and Michael Bliss, eds., *The Wretched of Canada: Letters to R.B. Bennett, 1930–1935* (Toronto: University of Toronto Press, 1971). Also Gray, *R.B. Bennett*, 248. Gray wrote, "Bennett was a patron of the Red Cross, the YWCA, YMCA, and of all the organized sports groups for miles around...With Bennett, however, giving was more than dropping money into outstretched hands. He frequently developed a genuine interest in the affairs of beneficiaries of his largesse. One of his earliest projects was to provide medals each year for outstanding students of the Calgary public schools. In early December 1928 he wrote to Alice Millar (his assistant) from Ottawa to remind her not only to send out the medals but to get the names of all the winners so that...he could write each one a personal note of congratulations...he reminded her to...ask Mrs. Kirby to drop into the office and give her a $50 bill." Despite his contributions to charity, Bennett had a reputation for rudeness, arrogance, and a lack of compassion during his time as prime minister.

213. R.B. Bennett Fonds, MG26, K, Volume 956:060536-060537, LAC. Dorothy Lougheed Hutchison to R.B. Bennett, 15 October 1935. Also Reel M3179 M-605-386-436, LAC.

214. R.B. Bennett Fonds, MG26, K, Volume 956:0605390, LAC. R.B. Bennett to Dorothy Lougheed Hutchison, 6 November 1935.

215. Donald B. Smith Collection, Hardisty Box 2, Isabella Hardisty Lougheed Timeline File, LHA. R.B. Bennett, Ottawa, to J.A. Hutchison, Edmonton, 2 May 1936; R.B. Bennett Fonds, MG26, K, Volume 956: 0606501 P-450, LAC.

216. Donald B. Smith Collection, Hardisty Box 2, Isabella Hardisty Lougheed Timeline File, LHA. R.B. Bennett, Ottawa, to J.A. Hutchison, Edmonton, 2 May 1936; R.B. Bennett Fonds, MG26, K, Volume 956: 0606501 P-450, LAC.

217. Donald B. Smith Collection, Lougheed #2 Box 2, Lougheed Bennett Legal Feud 1922 File, LHA. Reference *Newsletter*, 1995, Legal Archives Society of Alberta. Reference *Newsletter*, 1995, Legal Archives Society of Alberta, 4–5. In excerpts from the speaking notes of Mr. Justice J.C. Major, the degree of enmity between James and Bennett becomes clear, if the oral testimony is to be believed. Major noted that legal action meant that

> *all files were under the eye of a custodian for the next 3 years. When either firm required access to a client's file, it was necessary to get a court order and a sheriff's deputy to retrieve it from storage...Even when the seizure was complete, Bennett was not satisfied. Walking past the old office one day he noticed the firm's polished brass plate attached to the building. He went to the receiver's office and insisted that the plate be seized. He wanted, but failed, to have the awning from the office windows removed. Lougheed refused saying that they were fixtures. Bennett sued. Bennett's anger was intense. For years members of the Lougheed McLaws and Bennett Hannah firms would pass on the street without speaking. Twenty years after the fact, Bennett would not accept an invitation from Carson MacWilliams in England during the war to attend a party at which the Calgary Highlander's Band, of which he had been the first Honorary Colonel, was playing. He refused because MacWilliams had been one of the students with Lougheed and Bennett who had gone with the Lougheed side some 20 years before...That Bennett would fight with such rage, that he would go back full time to building a practice as a result of the dispute, is inexplicable.*

According to Major's article in the *Newsletter* of the Law Society of Alberta, had it not been for Bennett's hatred of James Lougheed, and "had Lougheed not precipitated the dispute, however valid he felt it was, Bennett would likely have retired and moved within that year. For better or worse, he may not have returned to politics and been Prime Minister."

Also James H. Gray, *Talk to My Lawyer: Great Stories of Southern Alberta's Bar and Bench* (Edmonton: Hurtig Publishing, 1987), 18. Gray went even further in noting the importance of the Lougheed–Bennett dispute to the history of Canada, writing, "When, if ever, would there have been a Bank of Canada, or a Canadian Broadcasting Corporation, a Canadian Wheat Board?...It was the Lougheed–Bennett confrontation that made all this possible." According to Gray, Lougheed and Bennett, although partners for twenty-five years, had always shared an "impersonal, arms-length relationship." While both were millionaires before the age of fifty, the similarities reportedly ended there. Lougheed was described as "an enthusiast, the booster-joiner type of pioneer that Calgarians thought of first when casting about for people to head up new committees. He had a genius for making friends and a passion for becoming involved," while Bennett is described as the "cold, calculating, ruthless, thinking-machine who almost never made a friend," 19. In the end though, it was Bennett's firm that went on to become one of Alberta's most successful. Also Law Society of Alberta, *Just Works: Lawyers in Alberta, 1907–2007* (Toronto: Irwin Law Inc., 2007), 30. Without noting the irony, this text notes that it was Bennett's firm where Lougheed's grandson Peter returned to practise in 1987 after sixteen years as premier of Alberta.

218. Dobbin, *The One-and-a-Half Men.*

219. Richard Hardisty Fonds, Accession M5908/1779, Series 23-7, GAIA. Belle C. Lougheed to Eliza (McDougall) Hardisty, 24 November 1903. Also Strong-Boag, *The Parliament of Women*, 194. Isabella's sentiments about her many responsibilities are similar to those expressed by one "prominent Kingstonian," who worried that "the middling rich will soon be debarred raising children it is so hard to get a servant to stay where there are children." Reference Shortt Papers, Elizabeth Shortt to Mother & Gertrude, 12 September 1895. As Strong-Boag notes, mistresses persisted in their often vain attempts to get satisfactory domestic substitutes from among the lower classes at home or abroad. The ideal, at least in the West, was the "Chinaman, who may be dismissed at any time without responsibility," 237. Reference Mrs. Skinner, "Immigration from a Western Point of View," NCWC Report (1900), 43.

220. Sarah Carter, *Aboriginal People and Colonizers of Western Canada to 1900* (Toronto: University of Toronto Press, 1999), 117.

221. Jennifer Bobrovitz Files, notes, 21, LHA. Reference Alberta probate office. Also Donald B. Smith Collection, Lougheed #2 Box 2, James Lougheed Will Aug. 16, 1923 File, LHA. Also Pratt and Richards, *Prairie Capitalism*, 154. Pratt and Richards write that James Lougheed actually left an estate worth some $12 million on his death in 1925; however, they provide no documentation to support

this statement. Like his daughter Marjorie, James was laid to rest at Calgary's Union Cemetery in what had become the Lougheed family plot.

222. Donald B. Smith Collection, Lougheed # 2 Box 2, James Lougheed Will Aug. 16, 1923 File, LHA. Original will.

223. Ibid.

224. Ibid.

225. Catherine Philip, "The Fair, Frail Flowers of Western Womanhood," in *Frontier Calgary: Town, City, and Region, 1875–1914*, ed. Anthony W. Rasporich and Henry Cornelius Klassen (Calgary: McClelland and Stewart West, 1975), 114.

226. Klassen, *Eye on the Future*, 339. Reference Calgary Court House, Surrogate Division, Estate of W.H. Kinnisten File, 29 December 1898.

227. Ibid., 339.

228. Ibid., 340.

229. Perry, *They Gathered at the River*. Reportedly, Fred Albright was one of the young men who helped to repair Central Methodist after a fire on 29 February 1916, 37. Reference excerpt by Dr. G.W. Kerby, Pastor, Central Methodist Church, 1903–1911. In 1917, when the church undertook a financial drive, a list of members of the legal profession was drawn up, and both James Lougheed and Frederick Stanley Albright appear on that list, 169.

230. Lorna Brooke, Correspondence of Evelyn and Fred Albright, accessed 5 February 2011, http://www.oocities.org/echoinmyheart@rogers.com/contents.htm. Even though circumstances forced Evelyn to carry on independently after Fred's death, there is no indication she would have been a dependent partner even if Fred had returned to Calgary after his tour of duty. In their correspondence, Evelyn and Fred debated most major social issues of the day, including temperance, Indigenous peoples, and the franchise for women. While it was clear that both Fred and Evelyn respected the gender-specific roles their society assumed to be natural, it is also clear that both appreciated one another's intelligence and their abilities to contribute equally to society. This is very likely why Fred encouraged Evelyn in her pursuit of a law degree. While Evelyn, who remained a widow for the remainder of her life, did obtain that degree, she worked in a field that was at the time more acceptable for women, that of teaching.

231. Klassen, *Eye on the Future*, 301–302.

232. Ibid., 305.

233. Ibid., 308.

234. Ibid., 309.

235. Ibid.

236. Klassen, *Eye on the Future*, 310. Also see Rachel Herbert, "Ranching Women in Southern Alberta, 1880–1930" (MA thesis, University of Calgary, 2011), which offers a recent study of the contributions of ranching women.

237. Although James could have willed his entire estate to Isabella, women still faced some restrictions in regard to property ownership. Nanci Langford, *Politics, Pitchforks and Pickle Jars: 75 Years of Organized Farm Women in Alberta* (Calgary: Detselig Enterprises, 1997), xv. It was only in 1978 that the government of Alberta introduced the Matrimonial Property Act, which recognized that each partner had a legal right to an equal share of assets accumulated during the marriage. This law, which came into effect 1 January 1979, was the result of a long period of lobbying by groups like the Women of Unifarm (the new name of the United Farm Women of Alberta as of 1970). This group supported Irene Murdoch in 1973 when she asked the courts to recognize her twenty-five years of unpaid farm labour on the family farm that was legally owned by her husband, 54. While a man could will his estate to his wife by the time of James Lougheed's death, there was still the possibility of widows being left destitute if a husband chose to will land and possessions to sons or other male relatives. See also Faye Reineberg Holt, "Magistrate Emily Ferguson Murphy," in *Edmonton: The Life of a City*, ed. Bob Hesketh and Frances Swyripa (Edmonton: NeWest Press, 1995), 143–144. Edmonton's Local Council of Women, with the help of Emily Murphy as its convenor, lobbied successfully for amendments that were enacted in December 1910. Yet the legislation only allowed women to petition for one-third of the homestead. Also *Morning Albertan*, 30 November 1909, 4. No doubt Isabella was aware of the campaign launched by "the women of the province of Alberta," which aimed to give women the right to "share in the benefit of their husband's property." Regardless of what he could have done in his will, at the time of James's death, women had limited rights. While single or widowed women could acquire, hold, and dispose of property as a man could, they could not homestead unless they were the sole head of a family. Married women could not dispose of or acquire land without their husband's permission until 1906. Until the adoption of the Dower Act by the Alberta government in 1917, women could be left with nothing upon their husband's death.

238. Donald B. Smith Collection, Lougheed #2 Box 2, James Lougheed Obituaries 1925 File, LHA. Reference *Sydney Record*, C.B., 3 November 1925, DF 36774.

239. Assessment Role, National Park School District No. 102, N.W.T., 1911, 160–61, no. 146–147, Whyte Museum of the Canadian Rockies Archives.

240. Assessment Role, National Park School District No. 102, N.W.T., 1917, 107, no. 206. The home on the property was built in 1910 after leasehold title was obtained from the federal government and just one year prior to new "eligibility resident"

legislation that granted the Lougheeds exemption. Also *Banff Crag & Canyon*, 12 June 1991. Isabella and James's home remains as one of Banff's oldest residential buildings. The original property belonging to Isabella was located at 137 Spray Avenue in Banff but was subdivided in 1991 after an application by Isabella's descendants. The original house was moved and incorporated into a much larger home on what is now called Lougheed Circle.

241. *Banff Crag & Canyon*, 14 June 1919, n.p.; *Banff Crag & Canyon*, 25 July 1914. James did accompany Isabella on occasion. The *Crag & Canyon* reported on those visits, writing, "Senator and Mrs. Lougheed entertained…at their charming home," n.p.

242. *Banff Crag & Canyon*, 4 July 1914, n.p.

243. Ibid., 8 August 1908, 5.

244. Donald B. Smith Collection, Hardisty Box 1, William Hardisty File, LHA. Reference Reels 425, 426, A36-2 (1823–1881), 7, 8, HBCA, AM.

245. A.36/7, Folders 61–66, Officers and Servants Wills G-H, Hardisty, William Lucas (d. 1881), HBCA.

246. Donald B. Smith Collection, Hardisty Box 1, William and Mary Hardisty Children File, LHA. Mary Thomas to C.H. Lougheed, Inwood Manitoba, 18 October 1929. The letter appears to be handwritten by someone other than Mary Thomas, who signed her name rather tentatively. The salutation is "Dear Sir," also suggesting it was not written by Mary Thomas.

247. McDonald, *Lord Strathcona*, 125. Reference various correspondence between attorneys and William Hardisty, Donald Smith, and Richard Hardisty found in HBCA.

248. Donald B. Smith Collection, Lougheed #1 Box 1, Sam Lougheed (1857–) File, n.p., LHA.

249. Newspaper Clippings File, *Calgary Herald*, 5 December 1931, n.p., LHA.

250. James H. Gray, *The Roar of the Twenties* (Toronto: Macmillan of Canada, 1975), 88.

251. Ibid.

252. Newspaper Clippings File, *Calgary Daily Herald*, 15 August 1927, LHA.

253. Ibid., 13 August 1927, 32. After visiting with the royal party in Calgary, Isabella and Dorothy were again invited to lunch at the E.P. Ranch, 5.

254. Donald B. Smith Collection, Hardisty Box 2, Belle Lougheed File, LHA. Draft by Jennifer Bobrovitz and Trudy Cowan.

255. Donald B. Smith Collection, Hardisty Box 2, Isabella Hardisty Lougheed Timeline File, LHA. "Lady Lougheed Called by Death," newspaper source not identified.

256. House General File, Title Search, LHA. This file contains a copy of the original certificate of title filed by the municipality when it took possession.

257. Jennifer Bobrovitz Files, 22, LHA.

258. Publications More than a Century of Stories Folder, draft by Jennifer Bobrovitz, 11, LHA.

259. Donald B. Smith Collection, Lougheed #2 Box 3, Lougheed Estate File, LHA. "Lougheed Estate would go to High Court," *Morning Albertan*, 27 August 1935.

260. Donald B. Smith Collection, Hardisty Box 2, Isabella Hardisty Lougheed Timeline File, LHA. Reference "Prominent Canadian Hostess Opens Home for Law Reception," *Calgary Herald*, 27 August 1932. Also "Lady Lougheed Noted Hostess," *Edmonton Journal*, 28 August 1932.

261. Donald B. Smith Collection, Hardisty Box 2, Isabella Hardisty Lougheed Timeline File, LHA. "Alberta Women We Should Know," *Calgary Daily Herald*, 17 December 1932.

262. Ibid.

263. Hustak, *Peter Lougheed*, 146. Also Jennifer Bobrovitz Files, 23, LHA. Reference *Albertan*, 17 March 1936; unknown newspaper, 17 March 1936; *Calgary Herald*, 14 March 1936; *Albertan*, 14 March 1936.

264. "'Going, Going, Gone'—Peter Explores Mansion," *Morning Albertan*, 26 August 1938. One of the most surprised by the low prices was the young Peter Lougheed, who told reporters he had snuck into Beaulieu prior to the beginning of the auction, discovering "secret balconies" from which he could watch the auction. Disappointed with prices on the first day, Peter was certain people would be returning the next day "with money, not just $5 or $10," to bid on the large oil paintings. Peter would be disappointed when paintings went for as low as $0.35 and hand-carved solid mahogany chairs for $24, while a walnut bedroom suite went for $45 and a solid oak table for $2. One woman who bought a large framed portrait of Sir Robert Borden, no doubt a personal gift to the Lougheeds, paid $0.25 and told reporters she really only bought it for the frame and intended covering the photo.

265. Donald B. Smith Collection, Hardisty Box 2, Isabella Hardisty Lougheed Timeline File, LHA. *Morning Albertan*, no date referenced.

266. Donald B. Smith Collection, Hardisty Box 1, Mary Hardisty 1840–1930 File, LHA. Reference "'First Lady' of Early Days Succumbs After Colorful Life in West," *Albertan*, 14 March 1936.

267. Jennifer Bobrovitz Files, notes, no reference, LHA. After Isabella's death, her son Norman continued to live at Beaulieu with his family until August 1938, when the contents of the house were disposed of in a two-day auction. Also Jennifer Bobrovitz Files, notes, 23, LHA. After it was repossessed, Beaulieu House assumed many roles, including housing the Dominion-Provincial Youth Training Plan, the Women's Army corps, and the Canadian Red Cross, before

its restoration began in 1993. In 2005, Lougheed House National Historic Site opened its doors.

268. Van Kirk, "Tracing the Fortunes." Van Kirk studied the women in these founding families, arguing that they served as agents of transition.

269. *Calgary Daily Herald*, 12 June 1902.

270. Presentation CLA Folder, LHA. Reference presentation by Jennifer Bobrovitz to Canadian Library Association Conference, 18 June 2005. Also "'Going, Going, Gone.'" The auction of Beaulieu's contents listed among items sold many books valued in the hundreds of dollars, and one lot that included several hundred books sold for twenty two dollars.

271. Other photos held by the Lougheed House Archives confirm the portrait of Isabella and James as a couple surrounded by books. There was a wall of bookcases on the main floor of Beaulieu, one library on the ballroom level, six sectional bookcases in the second-floor sitting room, a bookcase in the second-floor senator's bedroom, three sectional bookcases in the third-floor sitting room, as well as bookcases in the Ottawa apartment.

272. *Alberta Tribune*, 11 September 1889.

5   TRADER DELORME'S FAMILY

1. Marie Rose Smith, "The Adventures of the Wild West of 1870," Marie Rose Smith Fonds, Box 1, File 3: 1, GAIA. It is difficult to determine exactly when this was written, but some of the details in her manuscripts suggest that it was likely written in the later 1930s.

2. Ibid.

3. The conflict in 1816 originated in 1812, after the HBC gave Lord Selkirk a land grant of 116,000 acres near the confluence of the Red and Assiniboine rivers to which he brought settlers from Europe. The North West Company, for their part, suggested that the Metis lay claim to a "new nation" on the land that was their birthright from their "Indian" mothers.

From the beginning, the Metis feared this land grant would threaten the land on which they had settled. There was further concern when Miles Macdonnell, acting as governor of Assiniboia, issued a proclamation prohibiting the export of the Metis staple, pemmican. Conflict ensued in 1816 when Cuthbert Grant's men were intercepted by the new governor, Robert Semple, in an attempt to seize their pemmican. In the end, Semple and twenty-one settlers were killed in what was later called the Battle of Seven Oaks. The battle was immortalized by Pierre Falcon, and some believe this confrontation inspired Metis nationhood.

4. Devine, *The People Who Own Themselves*, 134–135. Sayer had worked in territories controlled by the North West Company until the merger with the HBC in 1821. After working for the HBC until 1829, Sayer again engaged with a competing fur trade company in North Dakota. When brought to trial, Sayer was supported by Louis Riel Sr. and other Metis who surrounded the courthouse. Under pressure, Justice Adam Thom found Sayer guilty but levied no penalty, leading the Metis to declare that free trade was won. There were three other Metis arrested and charged with illegally trading furs. Sayer was the first and only brought to trial. As Devine notes, these free traders had succeeded in undermining the HBC monopoly. However, the decline in big game populations forced woodlands people onto the plains where buffalo herds soon disappeared as well. Thus, free traders from Red River were really not able to capitalize on their victory.

5. Saint François Xavier Parish Records, Accession No. M38, B114, AM.

6. Jock Carpenter, *Fifty Dollar Bride—Marie Rose Smith: A Chronicle of Métis Life in the 19th Century* (Sidney, BC: Gray's Publishing, 1977), 22. Carpenter notes that Urbain was referred to as "Pezzan," so as not to confuse him with his father and grandfather. Marie Rose does not mention this.

7. Marie Rose Smith Fonds, untitled, File 4: 29 and File 3: 12, GAIA.

8. Marie Rose Smith Fonds, untitled, File 6: 23, GAIA.

9. Marie Rose Smith, "Eighty Years on the Plains," Marie Rose Smith Fonds, Box 1, File 4: 30, GAIA. Also Marie Rose Smith, "Eighty Years on the Plains," *Canadian Cattlemen* 12, no. 1 (June 1949): 34. Marie Rose wrote of an incident in which she was almost swept away in the current, just as "brother Charlie called out, 'Marie Rose, you'll get drowned!'" Also Carpenter, *Fifty Dollar Bride*, 39. Carpenter wrote that Marie Rose had but three siblings, and that Mother Delorme only acted as the Sioux boy's godmother. The genealogical chart at the end of her book leaves Charlie out completely.

10. Clarence Kipling Fonds, Accession No. M7144, GAIA, noted that Charles Delorme dit Ross married Marie Desjarlais and they had a child born in Pincher Creek on 14 December 1899. In 1900, Charles was reportedly in Havre, Montana. Also St. Michael's Parish, Records of Baptism, Pincher Creek, AB, provided by Rosalie Lévesque on 28 September 2005 and 9 March 2006. These records confirm that Adele Delorme Ross, child of Charles Delorme Ross and Marie Desjarlais, was baptised on 16 December 1899.

11. Fonds Paroisse, Saint François Xavier, Accession No. 0103-001, B267, Archives de la Société historique de Saint-Boniface (ASHSB). Jock Carpenter lists the birth date of her great-grandmother as 14 August 1838. However, the Marie Desmarais born on that date to Joseph and Adelaide died five days later (S141). Marie Desmarais, who later became Marie Rose's mother, was born on 17 August 1839.

Joseph Desmarais was the son of François Desmarais and a woman identified as "Marie de la tribu des Sauteux." Adelaide Clairmont Desmarais was the daughter of Joseph Clairmont and Louise Crise. Various sources confirm this information, including parish records, and the Charles D. Denney Fonds, Accession No. M7144, GAIA.

12. Carpenter, *Fifty Dollar Bride*, 17. Reference Margaret MacLeod and W.L. Morton, eds., *Cuthbert Grant of Grantown: Warden of the Plains of Red River* (Toronto: McClelland & Stewart, 1974), 93, 153.

13. Fonds Paroisse, Saint François Xavier, Accession No. 0103-001, B75, ASHSB. Urbain Sr. was married in 1823. Also Le Centre du Patrimoine, accessed 29 August 2005, http://www.shsb.mb.ca/bulletin/delorme.html. Reference Provincial Archives of British Columbia. Also Charles D. Denney Fonds, Accession No. M7144, GAIA. Madeleine Vivier Delorme was the daughter of Alexis Vivier and Marie-Anne of the Assiniboine Nation.

14. Devine, *The People Who Own Themselves*, Appendix 2, provides a thorough explanation of French naming practices and the use of the term "dit." In New France, the use of surname aliases, sometimes referred to as "dit", added to the complications of using multiple and hyphenated first names. As Devine explains, "the term 'dit' was used to differentiate between non-related families sharing identical surnames, or to differentiate between descendant branches of the same family. A family would have their primary surname, and then a secondary surname would be attached by the word 'dit.'" Since the Roman Catholic Church dictated given names, and there might be several branches of a family living in the same area, the use of "dit" proved a necessary strategy, 223–225.

15. Delorme File, Riel-Delorme Papiers, ASHSB. Scrip application made by Urban Sr., dated 7 July 1870, at Saint François Xavier. Urbain wrote that his mother was "Madeleine an indian woman of Sauteaux Indians."

16. Thomas Douglas Selkirk, 5th Earl Papers, Accession No. M185, 61,16192, AM. François's testimony lists the names of those from the North West Company who gave orders to burn the houses of settlers.

17. Le Centre du Patrimoine. Also Le Dossier Delorme, Riel-Delorme Papiers, ASHSB, notes that François Delorme signed the petition addressed to Mgr. Plessis. Also Alfred Fortier, "Urbain Delorme: L'Homme riche des prairies." *Bulletin de la Société historique de Saint-Boniface* 3 (Printemps 1995): 3–8. Fortier refers to François's political activity. Also Le Dossier Delorme, ASHSB. In 1814, Peter Fidler listed a Delorme married to an Amerindian who lived as a freeman in Red River. It is believed this was François. Also Calendar of Lord Selkirk

Papers, Part II, Volume 2, Index of Papers, PAC, lists the deposition of François Eno dit Delorme, given 2 September 1817.

18. Diane Payment, "Métis People in Motion: From Red River to the Mackenzie Basin," in *Picking Up the Threads: Métis History in the Mackenzie Basin* (Winnipeg: Metis Heritage Association of the Northwest Territories and Parks Canada–Canadian Heritage, 1998), 93.

19. Marie McGillis became Cuthbert Grant's wife after his first wife, Bethsy, disappeared with his son, and after he ended his short marriage, *a la façon du pays* (in the custom of the country), with Madeline Desmarais. Also the LAC website confirms scrip was issued to Marguerite Delorme dit Henault, sister of Urbain Delorme Jr., married to Cuthbert McGillis.

20. MacLeod and Morton, *Cuthbert Grant of Grantown*, 93.

21. Ibid., 153.

22. This section of land was given to Grant after he left the HBC in 1823 with the intention that he would encourage Metis to settle on river lots. In 1824, the settlement became Saint François Xavier.

23. Some of Marie Rose's descendants continue to refer to her ancestry as French Canadian rather than Metis. In her Bible, Marie Rose's granddaughter, Shirley-Mae McCargar, keeps a record of family history. When she shared the Bible with me in October 2010, Marie Rose's father was listed as French Canadian and her mother as French.

24. Marie Rose Smith, "Eighty Years on the Plains," Box 1, File 4: 2, GAIA.

25. L.A. Prud'homme, "Urbain Delorme: Chef des prairies," *Revue canadienne* 23 (1887): 270–279. Also Fortier, "Urbain Delorme."

26. "One of the oldest and richest traders in the Red River."

27. Prud'homme, "Urbain Delorme," 279. Also Fortier, "Urbain Delorme," 8. Fortier refers to a letter from Bishop Taché to Charles-Felix Cazeau, diocese of Québec, asking that money be invested on behalf of Urbain, "*l'homme le plus riche et le plus généreux de sa paroisse*" ("the richest and most generous man in his parish").

28. Fortier, "Urbain Delorme," 8. Also Recherches Généalogiques, 4/66, ASHSB, Testament de Urbain Delorme, lists assets as $4,461.05.

29. Fonds Antonin Taché, ASHSB. Grandson Urbain Delorme seemed to be the most prolific in his requests for funds as he moved throughout the territories.

30. Lynch-Staunton was a local historian who published a few articles and one book on the history of ranching in southern Alberta.

31. Ludger E. Gareau Fonds, Kootenai Brown Pioneer Village Archives (KBPA). Reference *Calgary Herald*, 6 October 1934.

32. Gerhard J. Ens, *Homeland to Hinterland: The Changing Worlds of the Red River Metis in the Nineteenth Century*, 84. Ens does not distinguish between Urbain Jr. or Sr., so it is not clear whether this was Marie Rose's grandfather or father.

33. Friesen, *River Road*, 6.

34. Carter, *Lost Harvests*, 3. Carter writes that Indigenous people are not often credited with the pioneering efforts to farm the prairies, but, in fact, they were the first pioneer farmers in the West. Carter's well-made point does not negate the likelihood that, despite their resourcefulness and ability to adapt to their environment, many Indigenous people, Marie Rose included, harboured conflicting views of their changing lifestyles as buffalo herds dwindled and more settlers arrived.

35. Friesen, *River Road*, 7–8.

36. It was in 1840 that Alexander Ross described the 1,200 carts that set out on the biannual hunts.

37. Foster, *We Know Who We Are*, 38. Reference Ross, *The Red River Settlement*, 246–248. Foster noted that the Metis hunting and trading camps were similar in organization to those of the Plains Chippewa, except for the use of carts, 38. The Plains Chippewa are sometimes called Ojibwe, while the Saulteaux were a branch of the Ojibwe.

38. Mary Weekes, as told to her by Norbert Welsh, *The Last Buffalo Hunter* (Toronto: Macmillan Company of Canada, 1945; repr., Calgary: Fifth House Publishers, 1994), 16.

39. Ibid., 23.

40. Ibid., 27.

41. Ibid., 59–60.

42. Alexander Ross, "The Red River Buffalo Hunt from Red River Settlement," *Manitoba Pageant* 5, no. 2 (1960): 1–5.

43. Maria Campbell, "Charting the Way," in *Contours of a People: Metis Family, Mobility, and History*, ed. Nicole St-Onge, Carolyn Podruchny, and Brenda Macdougall (Norman: University of Oklahoma Press, 2012), xxi–xxv.

44. Weekes, as told to her by Welsh, *The Last Buffalo Hunter*, 74–75.

45. William J. Healy, *Women of Red River: Being a book written from the recollections of women surviving from the Red River era* (Winnipeg: The Women's Canadian Club, 1923), 206–207.

46. Weekes, as told to her by Welsh, *The Last Buffalo Hunter*, 162.

47. Carpenter, *Fifty Dollar Bride*, 33. It is not clear where Carpenter gets this description because there is no such description of her father in Marie Rose's papers.

48. Sissons, *John Kerr*, 88.

49. John Kerr, "Hunting Bison on the Plains," *Winnipeg Tribune Magazine*, 23 June 1934, 1–3.

50. Ibid.

51. Arthur J. Ray, "The Northern Great Plains: Pantry of the Northwestern Fur Trade, 1774–1885," in *The Western Métis: Profile of a People*, ed. Patrick Douaud (1984; repr., Regina: Canadian Plains Research Center, 2007), 62. Also G. Herman Sprenger, "The Métis Nation: Buffalo Hunting vs. Agriculture in the Red River Settlement (Circa 1810–1870)," in *The Other Natives: The Métis*, vol. 1: 1700–1885, ed. Antoine S. Lussier and D. Bruce Sealey (Winnipeg: Manitoba Métis Federation Press, 1978), 120–122. Sprenger writes that throughout the history of the Red River Settlement (1812–1870), "agricultural productivity was consistently hampered by a variety of natural hazards, such as frosts, floods, droughts, excessive dampness, mice, blackbirds, wild pigeons, locusts and mites." In addition, farming operations such as seeding relied on archaic and time-consuming methods, given that agricultural machinery and adequate facilities for preparation and storage were not available. Seeds more appropriate for the climate, such as Red Fife wheat, only became available after 1876.

52. Marie Rose Smith, "The Adventures of the Wild West of 1870," Box 1, File 3: 1, GAIA.

53. Ibid., 2.

54. Ibid., 1.

55. Marie Rose Smith, "Eighty Years on the Plains," Box 1, File 4: 14, GAIA.

56. Shirley-Mae McCargar, interviews by author, St. Albert, AB, 3 October 2005–28 March 2006.

57. Sprenger, "The Métis Nation," 116.

58. Ibid., 124. Sprenger lists thirty reported crop failures between 1812 and 1870, noting these are only the failures that were reported.

59. Marie Rose Smith, "Eighty Years on the Plains," Box 1, File 4: 1, GAIA.

60. Marie Rose Smith, "The Adventures of the Wild West of 1870," File 6: 23–24, GAIA.

61. W.L. Morton, "The Battle of the Grand Coteau: July 13 and 14, 1851," in *The Other Natives: The Métis*, vol. 1: 1700–1885, ed. Antoine S. Lussier and D. Bruce Sealey (Winnipeg: Manitoba Métis Federation Press, 1978), 47–62. In 1851, the Metis had clashed with the Dakota on the slopes of the Grand Coteau in what is now North Dakota, defeating the Dakota soundly. Some say this established the Metis as the "masters of the plains," who could march wherever they chose in the aftermath of this battle. Morton relied on correspondence between various missionaries and the accounts of Alexander Ross and Henri de Trémandan for his descriptions of the battle. In general, the Metis occupied territories in the

western Great Lakes (now American Midwest), north to Alberta, Saskatchewan, Manitoba, and the Pacific Northwest south of the Great Lakes to the Great Plains of the United States.

62. Marie Rose Smith, "Eighty Years on the Plains," Box 1, File 4: 38, GAIA.

63. Marie Rose Smith, "The Adventures of the Wild West of 1870," Box 1, File 3: 1, GAIA.

64. Marie Rose Smith, "Eighty Years on the Plains," Box 1, File 4: various pages, GAIA.

65. Lewis G. Thomas, ed. *The Prairie West to 1905: A Canadian Sourcebook* (Toronto: Oxford University Press, 1975), 319–320. Reference John Macoun, *Manitoba and the Great North-West* (Guelph, 1882), 579–580.

66. Tough, *"As Their Natural Resources Fail,"* 54. The charge of mutiny stemmed from an incident in the summer of 1870 when the crews of four boats left their "lading behind and returned to Red River on three boats which they appropriated for their own use." Reference A.11/51 (1 August 1870), Folder 100, HBCA.

67. Marie Rose Smith, "The Adventures of the Wild West of 1870," Box 1, File 3: unnumbered final page, GAIA.

68. Marie Rose Smith, "Eighty Years on the Plains," *Canadian Cattlemen* 11, no. 1 (June 1948): 30.

69. Payment, *The Free People*, 25. Payment noted that Marie Desmarais Delorme was "among a number of prosperous independent traders at Red River by the mid-nineteenth century." There is no reference for this.

70. Prentice et al., *Canadian Women*, 70. Reference two studies of the Great Lakes trade.

71. See John E. McDowell, "Madame La Framboise," *Michigan History* 56, no. 3 (Winter 1972): 271–286, and John E. McDowell, "Thérèse Schindler of Mackinac: Upward Mobility in the Great Lakes Fur Trade," *Wisconsin Magazine of History* 61 (Winter 1977–1978): 125–143.

72. Campbell, "Charting the Way," xxiv.

73. Healy, *Women of Red River*, 155–156.

74. Marie Rose Smith, "Eighty Years on the Plains," Box 1, File 4: 64, GAIA. Also Marie Rose Smith, "The Adventures of the Wild West of 1870," Box 1, File 3: 7, GAIA. On this occasion, Marie Rose wrote that her mother was a widow for two years before remarrying.

75. Weekes, as told to her by Welsh, *The Last Buffalo Hunter*, 171.

76. Ibid., 205.

77. Ibid., 217–218.

78. Marie Rose Smith, "The Adventures of the Wild West," Box 1, File 3: 7, GAIA.

79. Fonds Antonin Taché, Accession No. CACRSB, T15046-47, ASHSB. Saint François Xavier, Elise Delorme to Archbishop Taché, 12 November 1874.

80. Ibid.

81. Marie Rose Smith, "Eighty Years on the Plains," Box 1, File 4: 40–42, GAIA.

82. Ibid.

83. Marie Rose Smith, "Eighty Years on the Plains," Box 1, File 4: 44–46, GAIA.

84. Ibid.

85. Marie Rose Smith, untitled, File 6: 15, GAIA.

86. Ibid.

87. Marie Rose Smith, "Eighty Years on the Plains," Box 1, File 4: 45–46, GAIA.

88. Marie Rose Smith, "The Adventures of the Wild West of 1870," Box 1, File 3: 28, GAIA.

89. Ibid., 29.

90. Ibid., 48.

91. Marie Rose Smith, untitled, File 6: 93, GAIA.

92. Ibid., 48.

93. Healy, *Women of Red River*, 154.

94. Marie Rose Smith, "Eighty Years on the Plains," Box 1, File 4: 46, GAIA.

95. Ibid., 82.

96. Racette, "Sewing for a Living," 17. Reference Johnny Grant, *Very Close to Trouble: The Johnny Grant Memoir*, ed. Lyndel Meikle (Pullman: Washington State University Press, 1996), 153. Also Ens, *A Son of the Fur Trade*, 245. Ens's work is an updated annotation of the diary, including Grant's time in Canada. It was reportedly to his wife Clothilde Bruneau that Grant dictated his memoirs. There are several instances in which Grant noted that Clothilde worked very hard at things such as boarding men so they could have money to furnish their house.

97. Marie Rose Smith, "Eighty Years on the Plains," Box 1, File 4: 22–23, GAIA.

98. Ibid.

99. Racette, "Sewing for a Living," 17.

100. Ibid., 17–18. Racette writes that this female economy also occupied an essential aspect of the overall economy of the fur trade and the numerous initiatives undertaken by free traders and family groups.

101. Ibid., 20.

102. Ibid., 22.

103. Ibid. Reference Marie Rose Smith, "Eighty Years on the Plains," Box 1, File 4: 2, GAIA.

104. Marie Rose Smith, "Eighty Years on the Plains," Box 1, File 4: 2, GAIA.

105. Antoine S. Lussier, "The Métis," in *The Other Natives: The Métis*, vol. 1: 1700–1885, ed. Antoine S. Lussier and D. Bruce Sealey (Winnipeg: Manitoba Métis Federation Press, 1978), 18.

106. Marie Rose Smith, "Eighty Years on the Plains," Box 1, File 4: 65, GAIA.

107. The two brothers here obviously included the Sioux boy, Charlie, and demonstrate that, when speaking casually, Marie Rose viewed him as a genuine member of her family.

108. Marie Rose Smith, "Eighty Years on the Plains," Box 1, File 4: 64, GAIA.

109. Carpenter, *Fifty Dollar Bride*, 44.

110. Church records could not confirm the exact length of time she attended, just that Marie Rose contracted whooping cough while at the convent. Efforts to confirm the exact date of attendance with the Grey Nuns in Montreal, where all of the records from St. Boniface are now stored, were unsuccessful. However, Archivist Mylène Laurendeau was able to confirm that Marie Rose, when a student of the boarding school, was treated by nursing staff for whooping cough from 14 March 1872 until 17 April 1872 (correspondence with author, 23 March 2006). While Marie Rose did not mention whooping cough, she wrote that she and "Liza" learned to read and write in both French and English, which demonstrates a diligence to study, even if she was there for four years rather than two as Carpenter thought. Also Accession No. CACRSB, T15046-47, ASHSB. Elise Delorme to Msg. Alexandre Antonin Taché, Saint François Xavier, 12 November 1874. In this letter, Elise requested money for her mother and family, writing in French, demonstrating the skills she would have acquired at the convent. Marie Rose indicated that she and Elise attended the convent at the same time, and that they were enrolled only after their father's death and their mother's remarriage. Also marriage certificate, M5, Parish Records, the Catholic Archdiocese of Edmonton confirms that Marie Rose married Charlie Smith shortly after she left the convent, on 26 March 1877. Further, it was reported in the *Pincher Creek Echo*, in 1955, that Marie Rose had been at the convent for four years. Thus, it appears that the girls were being cared for by the nuns sometime between 1872 and 1876, a somewhat longer time than thought by Carpenter.

111. Diane P. Payment, "'On n'est pas métchifs nous autres': Un aperçu des relations entre les Femmes francophones au Manitoba durant les années 1810–1920" (Conference pour Collège Universitaire de Saint-Boniface, 8 Février 1992), 51. Payment argued that Métis women were the "keepers of the faith," a role assigned them by the Roman Catholic missionaries.

112. Racette, "Sewing for a Living," 21.

113. Ibid., 21–22.

114. Lesley Erickson, "At the Cultural and Religious Crossroads: Sara Riel and the Grey Nuns in the Canadian Northwest, 1848–1883" (MA thesis, University of Calgary, 1997), 60.

115. Estelle Mitchell, *The Grey Nuns of Montreal and the Red River Settlement: 1844–1984*, trans. J.F. O'Sullivan and Sister Cecile Rioux (Montreal: Grey Nuns of Montreal, 1986), preface.

116. Ibid., 29.

117. Ibid., 31.

118. Payment, *The Free People*, 94. Payment writes that the priests particularly sought the support of Metis women who were the educators and transmitters of culture in the home and thus the greater influence on children and future generations.

119. Raymond J.A. Huel, *Proclaiming the Gospel to the Indians and the Métis: The Missionary Oblates of Mary Immaculate in Western Canada, 1845–1945* (Edmonton: University of Alberta Press, 1996), 99.

120. Mitchell, *The Grey Nuns of Montreal*, 93.

121. Ibid., 94.

122. Ibid., 70.

123. Marie Rose Smith, "The Adventures of the Wild West," Box 1, File 3: 46–47, GAIA. Also Edith Fowke, ed., *The Penguin Book of Canadian Folk Songs* (Markham, ON: Penguin Books Canada, 1986), 204. "Red River Halfbreed," sometimes also referred to as "Red River Valley," was believed by some to be a reworking of a popular American song of 1896, entitled, "In the Bright Mohawk Valley." However, research by Fowke suggests that the folk song was known in at least five Canadian provinces before 1896. Marie Rose used the phrase "half breed that loves you so true," while the "cowboy that loves you so true" is the more familiar version of the lyric in American folk history.

124. Sisters of Charity (Grey Nuns), MS Chronicles 1843–1893, Accession No. MG7D2, Reel 1, AM.

125. Sisters of Charity (Grey Nuns), MS Chronicles 1843–1893, Accession No. MG7D2, Reel 1, AM. The diaries list various dates when prayers were recited for Sara Riel, Louis Riel, and later for prisoner Ambroise Lépine during his trial. Also Mitchell, *The Grey Nuns of Montreal*, 89.

126. Erickson, "At the Cultural and Religious Crossroads," 97. Reference Elizabeth de Moissac, "Les Soeurs Grises et les événements de 1869–70," *La Société Canadienne d'Histoire de L'Église Catholique*, Sessions D'étude (1970): 215.

127. Fonds Antonin Taché, Accession No. CACRSB-TA1995-TA-2009, ASHSB. Marie Rose Smith to "A la Grace Monseigneur A. Taché," 15 September 1893. In the letter, Marie Rose assumes an apologetic tone for having to bother Taché

but nonetheless indicates that she must satisfy Charlie's inquiries about her inheritance.

128. Gerhard J. Ens, "Prologue to the Red River Resistance: Pre-liminal Politics and the Triumph of Riel," *Journal of the Canadian Historical Association* 5, no. 1 (1994): 111–123. Ens argues that the early phase of conflict in Red River was led by two opposing Metis leaders, Louis Riel and William Dease. He writes that Dease stressed Metis Indigenous rights, while Riel, aided by the Roman Catholic clergy, stressed French and Catholic rights. Ens argues that it was surprising that Louis Riel emerged as leader in 1869, given he had no natural constituency among the Metis, having left the settlement in 1858 at the age of thirteen and, when he returned in 1868, did not farm, hunt, trade, or haul freight. Also Gerhard J. Ens, "Dispossession or Adaptation? Migration and Persistence of the Red River Métis, 1835–1890," *Canadian Historical Association Historical Papers* (1988): 120–144. In this article, Ens argues that changes in the Metis economy after 1850 not only integrated the Red River Settlement into a wider capitalist economy but divided Metis society along economic and occupational lines.

129. Ens, "Prologue to the Red River Resistance," 111–123. Ens argues that Riel's view of land and Metis rights was different from many of the Metis in the Red River Settlement. Whereas Riel approached the issue from a French Roman Catholic view of land, many Metis understood land in terms of territory and common use. The loss of commons is also explored by Irene Spry, "The Great Transformation: The Disappearance of the Commons in Western Canada," in *Canadian Plains Studies 6: Man and Nature on the Prairies,* ed. Richard Allen (Regina: Canadian Plains Research Center, 1976), 21–45.

130. Fortier, "Urbain Delorme," 7.

131. Ens, "Prologue to the Red River Resistance," 115. Reference "The Land Question," *Nor'Wester,* 14 March 1860.

132. Le Dossier Delorme, ASHSB, notes that in 1870 Joseph Delorme lived on Lot 181 at Saint François Xavier, with his father Urbain Sr.

133. Marie Rose Smith, "Eighty Years on the Plains," Box 1, File 4: 65, GAIA.

134. Carpenter, *Fifty Dollar Bride,* 46.

135. Ibid.

136. Marie Rose Smith, "Eighty Years on the Plains," Box 1, File 4: 66–67, GAIA.

137. Ibid.

138. Marie Rose Smith, "The Adventures of the Wild West of 1870," Box 1, File 3: 7, GAIA.

139. Ibid., 8.

140. Marie Rose Smith, "Eighty Years on the Plains," Box 1, File 4: 69–70, GAIA.

141. Ibid.

142. Marie Rose Smith, untitled, File 6: 20, GAIA.

143. Marie Rose Smith, "Eighty Years on the Plains," Box 1, File 4: 72, GAIA.

144. Ibid.

145. Leah Dorion, "Métis Family Life," Gabriel Dumont Institute, 30 May 2003, accessed 15 July 2012, http://www.metismuseum.ca/resource.php/01262.

146. Ibid., 73.

147. Ibid., 71.

148. Ibid., 73.

149. Ibid.

150. Marie Rose Smith, "Eighty Years on the Plains," Box 1, File 4: 73, GAIA.

151. "Endured a difficult and drunken husband." See Diane Payment, "Un aperçu des relations entre les missionnaires catholiques et les métisses pendant le premier siècle de contact (1813–1918) dans l'ouest canadien," *Études oblates de l'ouest* 3 (1994): 155.

152. Shirley-Mae McCargar, interviews by author, 3 October 2005–28 March 2006.

153. Maggie MacKellar, *Core of My Heart, My Country* (Melbourne, Australia: Melbourne University Press, 2004), 109.

154. Marie Rose Smith, "Eighty Years on the Plains," *Canadian Cattlemen* 11, no. 4 (March 1949): 217.

155. Ibid., 213.

156. Van Kirk, *"Many Tender Ties."* See also Brown, *Strangers in Blood*; Carter, *Aboriginal People*; Juliet Pollard, "A Most Remarkable Phenomenon Growing Up Metis: Fur Traders' Children in the Pacific Northwest," in *An Imperfect Past: Education and Society in the Pacific Northwest*, ed. Donald J. Wilson (Vancouver: Centre for the Study of Curriculum and Institution, UBC, 1984): 120–140.

157. Marie Rose Smith, untitled, Box 1, File 6: 18, GAIA.

158. Marie Rose Smith, "Eighty Years on the Plains," Box 1, File 4: 65, GAIA.

159. Pincher Creek Historical Society, *Prairie Grass to Mountain Pass: History of the Pioneers of Pincher Creek District* (Pincher Creek, AB: Pincher Creek Historical Society, 1981), 229–232. Also Ken Liddell, "Pincher Creek Man Remembers Batoche," *Pincher Creek Echo*, 30 May 1953. Gareau told the reporter that when the couple left St. Boniface in February 1885, they were "well aware they were leaving a state of unrest behind them." Also "Riel Admirer to Mark 97th Birthday Soon," *Lethbridge Herald*, 7 November 1952. It appears that Gareau gained a reputation as an admirer of Riel's.

160. Marie Rose Smith, "Eighty Years on the Plains," Box 1, File 4: 169, GAIA.

161. Ibid., 161.

162. Marie Rose Smith, transcribed by Ben Montgomery, "Tribulations of Mrs. C. Smith of Pincher Creek Alberta," Marie Rose Smith Fonds, Box 1, File 6: 2, GAIA.

163. Beauvais District Buildings and Sites, Accession No. 988-57-2, KBPA. Compiled by John Daeley, Alberta Culture Historic Sites, 988-57-1, SW1/4 Sec2 Twp6 R1 W5.

164. Marie Rose Smith, "The Adventures of the Wild West of 1870," Box 1, File 3: 29, GAIA; italics added.

165. Diane Payment, "Marie Fisher Gaudet (1843–1914): 'La providence du fort Good Hope,'" accessed 2 June 2011, http://www.ecclectica.ca/issues/2003/2/gaudet.asp.

166. Weekes, as told to her by Welsh, *The Last Buffalo Hunter*, 294–296.

167. Marie Rose Smith, interview by Harry G. Baalim, late 1950s, Accession No. RAT-2-3, audiotape, GAIA.

6   QUEEN OF THE JUGHANDLE

1. Marie Rose Smith, "Eighty Years on the Plains," Box 1, File 4: 66–67, 34, GAIA.

2. Ibid., 80.

3. Marie Rose Smith, "Eighty Years on the Plains," Box 1, File 4: 171, GAIA. Also Weekes, as told to her by Welsh, *The Last Buffalo Hunter*. While Marie Rose does not go into the dollar amounts of the profit that Charlie or her father made, Norbert Welsh described his first trading journey from Fort Garry in 1862, when one buffalo robe valued at "a dollar and a quarter" was traded for one pound of tea (which cost the traders twenty-five cents) and half a pound of sugar (which cost five cents), representing a decent profit for traders, 9.

4. Weekes, as told to her by Welsh, *The Last Buffalo Hunter*, 290.

5. Marie Rose Smith, "Eighty Years on the Plains," Box 1, File 4: 34, GAIA.

6. Marie Rose Smith, "The Adventures of the Wild West of 1870," Box 1, File 3: 35, GAIA.

7. Notes addendum to scrip application for Charles Smith Jr., dated 6 August 1900, provided by Donald McCargar, Marie Rose's great-grandson.

8. Carpenter, *Fifty Dollar Bride*, 69.

9. Marie Rose Smith, "The Adventures of the Wild West of 1870," Box 1, File 3: 35, GAIA.

10. Ibid.

11. Family Search, accessed 5 July 2011, http://www.familysearch.org. Transcribed from original census data. Original census documents left the ethnicity of the children blank, and listed the whole family as Roman Catholic, as were all other residents of Bow River. This suggests that census takers may have been filling in the blanks as they saw fit.

12. Marie Rose Smith, "person," File 6: 14–19, GAIA. The inventory site forms of Jughandle Ranch, compiled by Alberta Culture Historic Sites in 1981, also list Charlie Smith's country of origin as Norway. See also Charlie Smith to Secretary,

Department of the Interior, 11 March 1908, Homestead Records, Accession
No. 1970.313, File 434151, Document 1550683, PAA. This letter was part of the
ongoing correspondence in which Charlie was attempting to prove title on his
first homestead. In this letter, Charlie wrote, "I have been in the country since
1867 and is the fault of the Government hoping you will look into this matter as
I came to stay and I want my right. It was the Government fault I was delayed
on my First Homestead." Also Homestead Records, Accession No. 1970.313,
Film 2022, File 361944, PAA. Statement Made and Confirmed by Statutory
Declaration by Charles Smith. In this claim for the adjoining homestead, Charlie
claimed he was born on the Mediterranean coast, had came the North West from
Dakota Territory, and that he had been a rancher prior to his arrival.

13.   Carpenter, *Fifty Dollar Bride*, 45.

14.   William Bleasdell Cameron, "Ad McPherson, Old Timer of '69," *Canadian
      Cattlemen* 12, no. 4 (November 1949): 8.

15.   Gordon E. Tolton, *Rocky Mountain Rangers: Southern Alberta's Cowboy Cavalry in
      the North West Rebellion—1885, no. 28*, ed. Gregory Ellis (Lethbridge: Lethbridge
      Historical Society, 1994), 51.

16.   Edna Kells Fonds, "Pioneer Interviews," ca. 1935, Accession No. M4026, GAIA.
      Kells was women's editor for the *Edmonton Journal* between 1910 and 1933.

17.   *Pincher Creek Echo*, 13 February 1914, "Roped his last steer and has gone to his
      long rest." Also Census 1880, Accession No. 34, Montana Historical Society,
      Missoula, MT.

18.   Shirley-Mae McCargar, interview by author, St. Albert, AB, 2 October 2010.
      Efforts to confirm any of the ancestral information on Charlie through various
      ancestry sites and Norwegian records were unsuccessful.

19.   Pincher Creek Historical Society, *Prairie Grass to Mountain Pass*, 248.

20.   Beauvais District Buildings and Sites, Accession No. 988-57-2, KBPA. Compiled
      by John Daeley, Alberta Culture Historic Sites, 988-57-1, SW1/4 S2 T6 R1 W5.
      The Jughandle Ranch property, as it was at the time that Marie Rose lived on it,
      was subdivided years ago. Also Daniel Byrne, telephone interview by author, Red
      Deer and Nanton, AB, 2 January 2006, 1 April 2006. The "Jughandle" name lives
      on through Danny Byrne, great-grandson of Marie Rose and Charlie, who owns a
      ranching operation under that name in southern Alberta.

21.   Marie Rose Smith, "The Adventures of the Wild West of 1870," Box 1, File 4: 163,
      GAIA.

22.   Marie Rose Smith, "The Adventures of the Wild West of 1870," Box 1, File 3:
      63, GAIA. According to Georgia Green Fooks, Charlie Smith had a daughter,
      Rosie Davis, who was born in Montana to an Indigenous woman (Double Gun
      Woman). Fooks writes that the year of Rosie's birth is not clear, but she once

said that she was born in 1877, and on another occasion her birthday appeared on treaty lists as 1880. Rosie's mother married a man named Joe Healy (an Indigenous man adopted by John Healy), and they eventually lived in southern Alberta as members of the Blood people. Fooks references the *Lethbridge Herald*, 6 November 1976, 13, when she writes that Jock Carpenter confirmed that Rosie was Charlie's daughter. See Georgia Green Fooks, "The First Women: Southern Alberta Native Women before 1900," *Alberta History* 51, no. 4 (Autumn 2003): 23–28.

23. Marie Rose Smith, "Eighty Years on the Plains," Box 1, File 4: 166, GAIA.

24. Ibid., 167.

25. Marie Rose Smith, untitled, File 4: 37, GAIA.

26. Marie Rose Smith, untitled, File 4: 37, GAIA. Since Marie Rose injects dialogue into her narrative, and does not always attribute the origin of her quotes, it is left to her audience to decide on its factual content. See also Gordon E. Tolton, *The Cowboy Cavalry: The Story of the Rocky Mountain Rangers* (Victoria: Heritage House Publishers, 2011), 128. Tolton writes that Blue Flash of Lightning (Che-Pay-Dwa-Ka-Soon) was Kootenai Brown's second wife, who he often referred to as Nichemoos, meaning "Loved One." He also writes that Kootenai had acquired Blue Flash of Lightning through a trade deal in which her father received "five Cayuses." Reference W. McD. Tait, *Recollections of Kootenai Brown as He Related Them to W. McD. Tait*, xvi.

27. Marie Rose Smith, "Eighty Years on the Plains," Box 1, File 4: 171, GAIA.

28. Ibid.

29. Marie Rose Smith, "Eighty Years on the Plains," *Canadian Cattlemen* 12, no. 5 (December 1949): 48.

30. The LAC website confirms scrip was issued to Marguerite Delorme dit Hénault, married to Cuthbert McGillis. Also McPherson File, Red Deer Public Archives, contains a newspaper article written by E.L. Meeres, 18 August 1982, which provides the ancestry of McPherson's wife. Also Clarence Kipling Fonds, GAIA. Kipling is a descendant of the McPherson family and confirms the McGillis/Delorme connection. These documents confirm that Marguerite was a daughter of Urbain Delorme Sr., hence the sister of Urbain Jr., and thus an aunt of Marie Rose.

31. Clarence Kipling Fonds, Accession No. M6069, D920.M172, File 4, "Addison McPherson," 2, GAIA. According to researcher Charles Kipling, descendant of the McGillis family, Cuthbert and Marguerite McGillis, Marie Rose's aunt and uncle, had settled in Calgary in 1887, before the time that Addison and his wife Melanie purchased land there. The kinship connection between Marie Rose and Addison McPherson is further indication that Charlie "married into" his wife's family,

and not the other way around. It suggests, too, that Charlie relied on his wife's kinship connections in order to further his economic activities, in the same way that so many Euro-North American traders had done during the fur trade era.

32. GAIA, Clarence Kipling Fonds, Accession No. M6069, D920.M172. C. Kipling to unknown "Dear Sir."

33. Marie Rose Smith, "Eighty Years on the Plains," Box 1, File 4: 73–74, GAIA.

34. Cameron, "Ad McPherson, Oldtimer of '69," 8.

35. Marie Rose Smith, untitled, File 4: 68, GAIA.

36. Marie Rose Smith, untitled, File 6: 15, GAIA.

37. Carpenter, *Fifty Dollar Bride*, 86. Carpenter writes that Charlie's arm remained "forever stiff" and that he could not even raise it to light his pipe, thus it would have presented many challenges for his ranching duties.

38. Edwin L. Meeres, *The Homesteads That Nurtured a City: The History of Red Deer, 1880–1905* (Red Deer: Fletcher Printing Company, 1984), 32.

39. Elizabeth Bailey Price Fonds, "A Western Pioneer of the Sixties, "Accession No. M1002, File 4, 2, GAIA.

40. Edna Kells Fonds, "Pioneer Interviews," ca. 1935, Accession No. M4026, GAIA. This was the same interview in which Charlie claimed to be Spanish, so perhaps he was embellishing his wealth for this interview.

41. Marie Rose Smith, "Eighty Years on the Plains," Box 1, File 4: 170, GAIA.

42. Ibid.

43. Tolton, *Rocky Mountain Rangers*, 51. See also Tolton, *The Cowboy Cavalry*, 9. The Rocky Mountain Rangers were a group of 114 cowboys, army officers, ex-Mounties, ranchers, settlers, and trappers who Tolton contends were "resolutely prepared to fight, as mounted cavalry, should the rebellion spread to involve the discontented Blackfoot tribes or border-jumping American Indian raiding parties." Tolton provides a roster of the 1885 Rocky Mountain Rangers, which lists Charlie as a lieutenant in Number 3 Troop, Pincher Creek Home Guard, 106. Reference Charles Boulton, *Reminiscences of the North-West Rebellions* (Toronto: Grip Printing and Publishing, 1886).

44. Donald B. Smith Collection, Hardisty Box 1, Mary Hardisty 1840–1930 File, LHA. Reference *Winnipeg Tribune*, May 1945 and Charles D. Denney Papers, GAIA.

45. Ibid.

46. Marie Rose Smith, untitled, File 6: 80, GAIA. Marie Rose spoke briefly about the Home Guard, not as a way to explain its role but to describe the members of the group as "having the best of times" while they enjoyed their "Jamaica Ginger." Also Tolton, *Rocky Mountain Rangers*, 65. According to Tolton, clashes occurred regularly between the Rocky Mountain Rangers and, not the Metis, but the Halifax Provisional Battalion, stationed at Medicine Hat during the conflict.

Tolton quoted William Tupper, son of Sir Charles Tupper, as saying that the Rangers did nothing but "go through the town firing revolvers and swearing like fiends."

47. Marie Rose Smith, "Bits of My Home Life," Marie Rose Smith Fonds, File 4: 161–162, GAIA.

48. Ibid., 166.

49. Marie Rose Smith, transcribed by Ben Montgomery, "Tribulations of Mrs. C. Smith of Pincher Creek Alberta," Box 1, File 6: 7, GAIA.

50. Ibid.

51. Marie Rose Smith, "Bits of My Home Life," File 4: 167, GAIA. Also Payment, *The Free People*, 355. Payment writes that, despite the desires of the church, Metis women had agency, that they were "bosses in the homes and were responsible for the education and survival of future generations."

52. Fonds Antonin Taché, Accession No. CACRSB, TA1995-TA 2009, ASHSB. This letter may have been transcribed by someone on behalf of Marie Rose, since the handwriting is slightly different than that used in the postcard addressed to her son before his death during the First World War. However, the letter was written sixteen years before the postcard, and the handwriting is similar to other handwritten notes in her files held at the Glenbow–Alberta Institute Archives.

53. Marie Rose Smith, "The Adventures of the Wild West of 1870," Box 1, File 3: 16, GAIA.

54. *Pincher Creek Echo*, 21 February 1905.

55. Ibid., 14 December 1906.

56. Marie Rose Smith, "Eighty Years on the Plains," *Canadian Cattlemen* 12, no. 2 (September 1949): 16.

57. Pincher Creek Historical Society, *Prairie Grass to Mountain Pass*. Various family histories provide details of some of the pallbearers who were: John Herron, sergeant-major in the NWMP and first representative to the federal Parliament for the Macleod riding; A. Christie, owner of the Christie Coal Mine; A. Freebairn, local businessman and author; A.E. Cox, first school teacher; and land agent, A. Rouleau. See also Tolton, *Rocky Mountain Rangers*. Tolton provided biographical information on Charlie. Also *Pincher Creek Echo*, "Obituary," 13 February 1914, 8.

58. Jim Green, "Jughandle Smith Goes to Town," in *Humorous Cowboy Poetry: A Knee-Slappin' Gathering* (Layton, UT: Gibbs Smith Publishers, 1995), 62.

59. Fonds Antonin Taché, Accession No. CACRSB, T47636 and T47706, ASHSB. Two letters written in 1892 indicate that Urbain Delorme Jr. was in Duck Lake and Batoche and was requesting funds from Taché. After her purchase from Urbain, Elise Ness then requested of Archbishop Taché, in a letter dated "26 août 1893,"

from Jack Fish Lake, that the bishop sell her land for her so she might have money to enrol her two daughters in a convent.

60. Marie Rose Delorme, "Eighty Years on the Plains," Box 1, File 4: 176, GAIA.

61. Geoff Burtonshaw Genealogical Collection, Accession No. M8450, File 74, GAIA. Also Carpenter, *Fifty Dollar Bride*. Carpenter's geneaological chart indicates there were no children born to Urbain and Nellie. Also Image No. NA-184-23, GAIA. The caption for this photo reads "William Gladstone and granddaughter Nellie (later Mrs. H.A. Riviere) Pincher Creek, Alberta." Also Image No. NA-3187-18, GAIA. The caption for this photo identifies George Riviere, Pincher Creek, Alberta, son of Henri (Frenchy) Riviere and the former Nellie Gladstone. It is not clear if this is the same Nellie Gladstone who had married Urbain Delorme. Neither Marie Rose nor Jock Carpenter mention any remarriage for Nellie, nor any marriage for Frenchy Riviere.

62. Charles D. Denney Fonds, Accession No. M7144, #90000, GAIA. Denney notes that Charlie married Marie Desjarlais and daughter Adele Delorme dit Ross was born on 14 December 1889 in Pincher Creek. Also Geoff Burtonshaw Genealogical Collection, Accession No. M8450, File 74, GAIA.

63. Geoff Burtonshaw Genealogical Collection, Accession No. M8450, File 74, GAIA.

64. Smith, "Eighty Years on the Plains," *Canadian Cattlemen*, 12, no. 2 (September 1949): 16.

65. Pincher Creek Historical Society, *Prairie Grass to Mountain Pass*, 232.

66. E. Lynch-Staunton, "Picturesque Pioneer Recalls the Old Days," *Calgary Herald*, 10 June 1934, accessed at KBPA, in the Ludger E. Gareau Fonds. Also Beauvais District Buildings and Sites, Accession No. 988-57-2, compiled by John Daeley, Alberta Culture Historic Sites, SE1/4 S27 TWP5 R1 W5, KBPA. The house was listed as abandoned in 1980. According to the letter referenced earlier, by 1893, Elise Ness was in Jackfish Lake.

67. *Calgary Herald*, 7 November 1952. Accessed at KBPA, in the Ludger E. Gareau Fonds.

68. Pincher Creek Historical Society, *Prairie Grass to Mountain Pass*, 559.

69. *Pincher Creek Echo*, 15 September 1955.

70. *Pincher Creek Echo*, 15 September 1955. Also Farley Wuth, "Early History of the NWMP Horse Ranch," *Pincher Creek Echo*, 28 July 1998. Wuth writes that the North West Mounted Police established their horse ranch along the creek in 1878.

71. Marie Rose Smith, "The Adventures of the Wild West of 1870," Box 1, File 3: 82, GAIA.

72. Sarah Carter, "Categories and Terrains of Exclusion: Constructing the 'Indian Woman' in the Early Settlement Era in Western Canada," *Great Plains Quarterly*

13, no. 3 (Summer 1993): 147–161. Carter quotes Inderwick. Also Hugh P. MacMillan, *Adventures of a Paper Sleuth* (Toronto: Penumbra Press, 2004), 156–157. It appears that Inderwick's life was not as idyllic as one might think when she assumed this rather authoritative position on acceptable marriage partners. According to MacMillan, after coming west, Mary Ella Lees married Charlie Inderwick, a "charming remittance man with some bad habits." After tiring of ranching, the couple returned to Ontario, where Charlie "continued to drink and gamble" until, finally, Mary Inderwick's husband was sent off by his father to the tea plantation in Ceylon, "never to see Mary and their three sons again." Also Hugh A. Dempsey, ed. *The Best from Alberta History* (Saskatoon: Western Producer Prairie Books, 1981), 197n10. Dempsey references a letter written by Inderwick to her sister-in-law in 1884 that he cross-referenced with her diary. In her diary, Inderwick referred to women that Marie Rose also referred to, such as Mrs. George Ives, Mrs. J. Heron, and Mrs. Charles Kettles.

73. Marie Rose Smith, "The Adventures of the Wild West of 1870," Box 1, File 3: 65, GAIA.

74. Farley Wuth, "Lionel Brooke's Role as a Remittance Man" (presented at Lethbridge Historical Society, Lethbridge, AB, 19 October 2004), accessed at KBPA, 12 November 2005. Lionel Brooke was the son of Sir Reginald and Lady Brooke, owners of a large estate in Cheshire, England. Remittance men like Brooke were often the younger sons of aristocratic families in England, not eligible for inheritance of the physical property at home. Without such eligibility, these remittance men were often shipped to the colonies with a quarterly stipend. The western prairies in the 1880s and 1890s tended to attract many remittance men from England, given there was vast amounts of land available, and that many of the existing ranch owners had British or eastern Canadian origins. While they were expected to find meaningful work, primarily as ranchers, few had the practical skills that would allow them to succeed. Even had they been able to acquire such skills, remittance men had often been reared with free-spending ways and many of them eventually experienced financial difficulty. Also Mark Zuehlke, *Scoundrels, Dreamers & Second Sons: British Remittance Men in the Canadian West* (Vancouver: Whitecap Books, 1994; repr., Toronto: Dundurn Press, 2001), 151–152. According to Zuehlke, after travelling abroad for two years, Brooke came to western Canada to visit his friends who owned Jughandle Ranch. Zuehlke writes (without footnotes) that in the 1930s, near the end of his life, quarterly cheques from England to Brooke were about five thousand dollars, 163.

75. Wuth, "Lionel Brooke's Role as a Remittance Man."

76. Ibid.

77. Smith, "Eighty Years on the Plains," *Canadian Cattlemen*, 12, no. 2 (September 1949): 36.

78. Wuth, "Lionel Brooke's Role as a Remittance Man."

79. Marie Rose Smith, untitled, File 6: 69, GAIA.

80. Newspaper Archive, *Lethbridge Herald*, 16 January 1939, accessed 4 February 2012, http://newspaperarchive.com/searchresultsv3.aspx.

81. Wuth, "Lionel Brooke's Role as a Remittance Man."

82. Ibid. While some of the oral history claimed that Brooke died penniless, Wuth wrote that others believed Brooke had "$14,000 to his name when he passed away, and left much of it to some of those locals who not only assisted him at the end but who may have need of the money as well." Marie Rose would meet those qualifications as one who both helped Brooke and who needed assistance herself. In addition to their importance to the barter and credit systems, remittance men like Brooke provided much appreciated relief from the isolated landscapes and difficult times by hosting and attending social functions, and "many a social get together, be they polo games, parties, or ranching bees, were held by Brooke at his Chinook Ranch." In addition to his socializing with those who viewed themselves as the middle to upper classes, Brooke spent a great deal of time travelling the plains with Indigenous people, who named him "Man with a Pane," in reference to his monocle. Regardless of his Indigenous companions, Brooke continued for the most part to be regarded as an aristocrat. Also Zuehlke, *Scoundrels, Dreamers & Second Sons*, 201. Wuth may be right about Brooke's financial fortunes, for Zuehlke writes that, although some remittance men lost their stipends after the war, Brooke's continued through the Depression and until his death in 1939.

83. Marie Rose Smith, "Eighty Years on the Plains," Box 1, File 4: 120, GAIA.

84. Marie Rose Smith, "Eighty Years on the Plains," *Canadian Cattlemen* 12, no. 3 (October 1949): 15.

85. Marie Rose Smith, "The Adventures of the Wild West of 1870," Box 1, File 3: 41, GAIA.

86. Ibid., 64.

87. Ibid., 120.

88. Ibid., 129–131.

89. Marie Rose Smith, "Eighty Years on the Plains," Box 1, File 4: 137–138, GAIA.

90. Ibid., 137.

91. William Rodney, *Kootenai Brown: His Life and Times 1839–1916* (Sidney, BC: Gray's Publishing Ltd., 1969), 217. Rodney discounted Marie Rose's criticisms of Brown, writing that while "most recollections of Kootenai Brown are highly favourable," Marie Rose's accounts measured Brown "in feminine terms," painting him in

one instant as heartbroken and full of remorse over the death of Olive and in the next breath as a man who neglected Isabella (his Cree wife) and whose eye wandered in the presence of young white girls. Although he discounted Marie Rose's opinion, Rodney's is perhaps the only instance where we get an "outside view" of Marie Rose.

92. Hugh A. Dempsey, "One Hundred Years of Treaty Seven," in *One Century Later: Western Canadian Reserve Indians since Treaty 7*, ed. Ian Getty and Donald B. Smith (Vancouver: UBC Press, 1978), 20. Reference Richard Hardisty, "The Blackfoot Treaty," *Alberta Historical Review* 5, no. 3 (1957): 20–22. Macleod was present at the signing of Treaty 7 at Blackfoot Crossing in 1877 (as was Isabella Lougheed's uncle, Richard Hardisty). Also Hugh A. Dempsey, "1870: A Year of Violence and Change," in *Alberta Formed, Alberta Transformed*, vol. 1, ed. Michael Payne, Donald Wetherell, and Catherine Cavanaugh. (Edmonton: University of Alberta Press, 2006), 211.

93. Marie Rose Smith, "Eighty Years on the Plains," Box 1, File 4: 100, GAIA. Marie Rose wrote that "Old Auntie" was "wont to claim that 'The Colonel's Lady' and herself were the first ladies 'ob de land.'"

94. Cheryl Foggo, "Assembling Auntie: Illuminating a Long-Forgotten Pioneer," *Alberta Views* 12, no. 1 (January/February 2009): 34–39. Foggo studied the elusive Annie Saunders and believes she likely spent some thirty years as a slave before meeting Mary Macleod and "impulsively" accepting her invitation to come to Canada. Foggo surmises that Annie had a keen sense of humour and was fond of saying, "Me and Mrs. Macleod...were the first white women in the region," 36.

95. Marie Rose Smith, "Premier for NWT," File 3: 64, GAIA.

96. Gayle Thrift, "'By the West, for the West': Frederick Haultain and the Struggle for Provincial Rights in Alberta," *Alberta History* 59, no. 1 (Winter 2011): 2–11.

97. Marie Rose Smith, "The Adventures of the Wild West of 1870," Box 1, File 3: 66, 67, GAIA. Justice William Ives was born in Quebec in 1873, but his family moved to the Alberta District of the North-West Territories shortly thereafter. Marie Rose writes that the family came west in 1882. See also Franklin Foster, *John E. Brownlee: A Biography* (Lloydminster, AB: Foster Learning Inc., 1996). After studying law at McGill, Ives returned to Lethbridge in 1901 to practise, earning the nickname "Cowboy Judge" when he was appointed to the bench. Ives was the presiding judge over the trial of Premier John Brownlee, when he was charged with seducing a young female employee in 1934. Also Law Society of Alberta, *Just Works*, 30. Justice Ives also heard portions of the case following the bitter dissolution of the partnership of Lougheed and Bennett.

98. Marie Rose Smith, "The Adventures of the Wild West of 1870," Box 1, File 3: 64, GAIA. Also Hugh A. Dempsey, *Firewater: The Impact of the Whisky Trade on the*

Blackfoot Nation (Calgary: Fifth House Publications, 2002), 104. Dempsey writes that Davis's wife was Revenge Walker, daughter of Red Crow, head chief of the Blood tribe.

99. Marie Rose Smith, "The Adventures of the Wild West of 1870," Box 1, File 3: 64, GAIA.

100. Dempsey, *Firewater*, 102. Reference John McDougall, *On Western Trails in the Early Seventies* (Toronto: William Briggs, 1911), 69, 151.

101. Howard Palmer and Tamara Palmer, *Alberta: A New History* (Edmonton: Hurtig Publishers, 1990), 35. The authors write that Davis was by no means the worst offender at Whoop-Up.

102. Marie Rose Smith, "The Adventures of the Wild West of 1870," Box 1, File 3: 72, GAIA. There is no indication in any of the source material that Henry Riviere was born into an aristocratic family.

103. Marie Rose Smith, "The Adventures of the Wild West of 1870," Box 1, File 3: 72, GAIA. Marie Rose did provide a birthdate of 9 January 1869, in Paris, for Frenchy, and wrote that he left home at the age of fourteen, arriving in the North-West Territories in 1886, with a desire to become a cowboy, 70. Also Image PA-3433-2, GAIA. This photo confirms the attire described by Marie Rose and features Riviere outside the Prince of Wales Hotel, adorned with the Metis sash.

104. Marie Rose Smith, "Eighty Years on the Plains," Box 1, File 4: 167–168, GAIA.

105. "It's unbelievable." Smith, "Eighty Years on the Plains," *Canadian Cattlemen*, 12, no.5 (December 1949): 5.

106. Marie Rose Smith, "The Adventures of the Wild West of 1870," Box 1, File 3: 49, GAIA.

107. Ibid.

108. Marie Rose Smith, "Eighty Years on the Plains," Box 1, File 4: 18, GAIA.

109. Warren M. Elofson, *Cowboys, Gentlemen, and Cattle Thieves* (Montreal: McGill-Queen's University Press, 2000), xviii.

110. Ibid., 4.

111. Ibid., 113.

112. Marie Rose Smith, "The Adventures of the Wild West of 1870," Box 1, File 3: 60, GAIA.

113. Marie Rose Smith, "Eighty Years on the Plains," Box 1, File 4: 73–74, GAIA.

114. Ibid.

115. 1906 Census Data, Reel T18361, LAC. Also Robert Byrne provided a copy of a Sandpoint, Idaho, news article, undated, in which J.R. "Bob" Smith, the son of Marie Rose, was celebrating his one hundredth birthday.

116. MacLeod and Driscoll, "Natives, Newspapers and Crime Rates," 257.

117. Warren M. Elofson, *Frontier Cattle Ranching in the Land and Times of Charlie Russell* (Montreal: McGill-Queen's University Press, 2004), 9.

118. Homestead Records, Accession No. 1970.313, Film 2040, File 434151, Document 2155259, PAA. Charlie Smith to Commissioner of Dominion Land, 15 June 1910. It is clear from this letter that Charlie felt he was entitled to the northwest quarter adjacent to the land he had settled on when he first arrived in the Pincher Creek district. The land was being put up for public auction as a "withdrawn stock watering reserve." He said he had "occupied" the land in question since 1886 before it was reserved for stock watering and it was always his intention to obtain it for a first or second homestead. He goes on that he had the land now being offered for public sale "under fence since about 1886, with eight acres in Timothy hay and have always pastured stock upon it. In view of these facts I beg to ask that I may be allowed, as one of the oldest settlers here, to retain this part of my old home on paying a reasonable rate per acre for it." Charlie's perspective on this reflects the ideology of common lands, so much a part of the Metis identity in earlier times. Also Document 2184703, "Auction Sale: Cancelled Stock Watering Lands," 9 July 1910, PAA, indicates that Charlie secured an agreement to purchase the land in question on that date. By 1890, homesteaders could no longer claim the second quarter. Although this provision was briefly revived in 1908, perhaps the change in regulations explains the 1910 letter from Charlie. Also Document 434151, letter dated 5 March 1914, PAA, indicates Charlie had yet to pay for this half section of land. Given that he died on 9 February 1914, this is one of the complications Marie Rose was left to deal with.

119. 1906 Census Data, Reel T18361, LAC.

120. Elofson, *Frontier Cattle Ranching*, 24.

121. Homestead Records, Accession No. 1970.313, Film 2022, File 361944, PAA. Statement Made and Confirmed by Statutory Declaration by Charles Smith.

122. Marie Rose Smith, "The Adventures of the Wild West of 1870," Box 1, File 3: 39, GAIA.

123. Marie Rose Smith, "Eighty Years on the Plains," Box 1, File 4: 94, GAIA.

124. Shirley-Mae McCargar, interviews by author, 3 October 2005–28 March 2006.

125. Elofson, *Cowboys, Gentlemen, and Cattle Thieves*, 81.

126. Ibid.

127. Ibid.

128. Elofson, *Frontier Cattle Ranching*, 94.

129. Ibid., 139.

130. *Pincher Creek Echo*, 9 November 1906.

131. No further reports appeared in the local newspaper, and the Provincial Archives of Alberta, which maintains all justice records, confirms that records from 1906 for the southern Alberta district are no longer in existence.

132. *Pincher Creek Echo*, 13 February 1914.

133. Elofson, *Cowboys, Gentlemen, and Cattle Thieves*, 121.

134. Marie Rose Smith, "The Adventures of the Wild West of 1870," Box 1, File 3: 38, GAIA.

135. Ibid. Cattle rustling was never really considered a joke; rather, theft of cattle was often punishable by hanging.

136. Elofson, *Cowboys, Gentlemen, and Cattle Thieves*, 122.

137. Marie Rose Smith, untitled, File 3: n.p., GAIA.

138. Marie Rose Smith, "Eighty Years on the Plains," Box 1, File 4: 81, GAIA.

139. Payment, "'On n'est pas métchifs nous autres,'" 13–18. Also Payment, "Un aperçu des relations."

140. Carpenter, *Fifty Dollar Bride*, 64. It is unclear where Chicken Prairie was, as it does not appear on census data. However, scrip documents (provided by Donald McCargar, Reference RG15, Interior, Series D-11-8-c, Volume 1367, Reel C-15003) for Joseph Smith, filed 6 August 1900, note that Joseph was born at Chicken Prairie, Pheasant Plains, near Touchwood Hills. Also Historic Places, accessed 12 May 2011, http://www.historicplaces.ca/en/rep-reg/place-lieu.aspx?id=3115. The HBC used its Touchwood Hills post to distribute provisions for its North West operations. At the same time that Joseph made application, Marie Rose filed applications on behalf of her deceased daughter, Mary Louise Smith, and her minor son, John Robert Smith.

141. Family Search, accessed 5 July 2011, http://www.familysearch.org. The website transcribed the census data. Original census documents left the ethnicity of the children blank and listed the whole family as Roman Catholic, as were all other residents of Bow River. This suggests the census takers may have been filling in the blanks as they saw fit.

142. According to census information, the children included Jonas, born 3 November 1881; John Robert, born 30 April 1885; William George, born 25 January 1887; Michael A., born 8 July 1890; Mary A., born 3 May 1892; John L., born 21 January 1894; Francis J., born 18 September 1895; Richard, born 17 February 1897; and Magdaline, born 25 June 1899. Also Carpenter, *Fifty Dollar Bride*. Carpenter used different spellings for some of the names, 158–159. By the time of this census, three of Marie Rose's children had died: Mary Louise in 1884, at age one; Mary Ann in 1897, at age eight, while at a convent in Quebec; and Alfred Albert in 1899, at age one. The three children born after 1901 all died at a young age: Catherine in 1902, at age one; Arthur in 1903, as an infant; and Mary Rose Alvina

in 1904, as an infant. The first-born of the family, Joseph, died in 1914; Charles died in 1907; Michael in 1909; Jonas and Theodore in 1917; and Richard in 1952.

143. St. Michael's Parish, Records of Baptism, Pincher Creek, AB. Also Pincher Creek Historical Society, *Prairie Grass to Mountain Pass*, 854. In approximately 1883, James Gilruth came to the Waterton area with his parents, where he subsequently took a homestead. Reportedly, the family were devoted Roman Catholics and perhaps this was the connection for Marie Rose.

144. Marie Rose Smith, untitled, File 4: 86, GAIA.

145. Marie Rose Smith, untitled, File 2, GAIA. The letter also stated that the nuns would be forwarding some of Mary Ann's hair and ornaments from her coffin.

146. Carpenter, *Fifty Dollar Bride*, 111.

147. Sister Elizabeth Fitzgerald, archivist, Faithful Companions of Jesus, correspondence with the author, 27 February 2006. Fitzgerald confirms that Miss Josie (Françoise Josephine) Smith attended the convent for four months starting in January 1910, and that she studied music and stenography.

148. Marie Rose Smith, "Eighty Years on the Plains," Box 1, File 4: 102, GAIA.

149. Marie Rose Smith, untitled, File 6, GAIA; italics added.

150. Marie Rose Smith, untitled, File 3: 54–55, GAIA.

151. McManus, "Unsettled Pasts, Unsettling Borders," 35. Reference "Report of Father A. Lacombe," 13 July 1885, in Canada, Department of the Interior, *Sessional Papers 1886*, vol. 4, no. 4, 77.

152. Smith, "Eighty Years on the Plains," *Canadian Cattlemen*, 11, no. 4 (March 1949): 225.

153. Marie Rose Smith, "The Adventures of the Wild West of 1870," File 3: n.p., GAIA.

154. Evelyne Stitt Pickett, "Hoboes across the Border: Itinerant Cross-Border Laborers between Montana and Western Canada," in *The Borderlands of the American and Canadian Wests: Essays on Regional History of the Forty-Ninth Parallel*, ed. Sterling Evans (Lincoln: University of Nebraska Press, 2006), 207. According to Picket, trains assumed an important role in the lives of these itinerant workers, and they came to regard trains as their "special form of free transportation." These workers took chances, and many were killed falling as they rode on top of cars, or on the "rods, blinds, bumpers, or train decks." She continues that industries in neither Montana nor Canada paid much respect to the living conditions of itinerant workers. Rather, they were viewed as "human machines who performed muscles services," 209. In reality, itinerants were seldom "ignorant misfits or begging bums" but were often young men who hoped for adventure and achievement, but for many "dreams were soon shattered by painful exploitation, bitterness, and distrust," 218.

155. Carpenter, *Fifty Dollar Bride*, 158–159.

156. Marie Rose Smith, "The Adventures of the Wild West of 1870," Box 1, File 3: 9, GAIA.

157. Elofson, *Frontier Cattle Ranching*, 20.

158. Marie Rose Smith, "Eighty Years on the Plains," Box 1. File 4: 174, GAIA.

159. Carpenter, *Fifty Dollar Bride*, 144. It is not clear when the family moved into Pincher Creek, but we do know that Marie Rose was operating the boarding house when Lionel Brooke died in 1939, for he was boarding with her at the time. The house in Pincher Creek is no longer there, but it was next to the church near Christie Avenue and Schofield Street. Also Homestead Records, Accession No. 1970.313, Film 2040, File 434151, Document 454151, PAA. Department of the Interior to Messrs. Thomson & Jackson, Pincher Creek, 24 June 1920. This letter confirms Marie Rose was finally able to sell some of her land in 1920, so this suggests she ws already in Pincher Creek at that time.

160. Carpenter, *Fifty Dollar Bride*, 134.

161. Several historians have identified the practice of turning off partners, in which fur traders who were preparing to leave fur trade country would find a new trader to assume responsibility for their partners and children.

162. Marie Rose Smith, "Eighty Years on the Plains," Box 1, File 6: 186; File 4: 133, GAIA.

163. Marie Rose Smith, "Eighty Years on the Plains," Box 1, File 3: 136, GAIA.

164. Marie Rose Smith, "The Adventures of the Wild West of 1870," Box 1, File 3: 57, GAIA.

165. Marie Rose Smith, "Eighty Years on the Plains," Box 1, File 4: 169, GAIA.

166. Marie Rose Smith, "The Adventures of the Wild West of 1870," Box 3, File 1: 20, GAIA.

167. Carpenter, *Fifty Dollar Bride*, 149.

168. Ibid., 149. Also Pincher Creek Historical Society, *Prairie Grass to Mountain Pass*. This book contains a brief historical account written by Carpenter's mother, Mary Hélène Smith Parfitt.

169. Carpenter, *Fifty Dollar Bride*, 149.

170. Pincher Creek Historical Society, *Prairie Grass to Mountain Pass*, 249.

171. Ibid.

172. Marie Rose Smith, interview by Harry G. Baalim.

173. Marie Rose Smith, "The Adventures of the Wild West of 1870," Box 3, File 1: 20, GAIA. Also Eliane Leslau Silverman, *The Last Best West: Women on the Alberta Frontier, 1880–1930* (Calgary: Fifth House Publishers, 1998), 156. Silverman discovered when she interviewed pioneer Alberta women that "white women who had access to help from Metis or Indian women availed themselves of it happily." While some women brought skills of midwifery with them to the

prairies, "others learned it in their new environment, often drawing on the various medical skills of Native women."

174. Foster, *We Know Who We Are*, 203.

175. Myra Rutherdale, "'She Was a Ragged Little Thing': Missionaries, Embodiment, and Refashioning Aboriginal Womanhood in Northern Canada," in *Contact Zones: Aboriginal & Settler Women in Canada's Colonial Past*, ed. Katie Pickles and Myra Rutherdale (Vancouver: UBC Press, 2005), 234.

176. Beauvais District Buildings and Sites, Accession No. 988-57-2, compiled by John Daeley, Alberta Culture Historic Sites, SE1/4S10T6 1W4, Gervais land, KBPA.

177. Interviews by author with Donald McCargar, Spruce Grove, AB, 2 October 2010–July 2011; Shirley-Mae McCargar, St. Albert, AB, 3 October 2005–28 March 2006, 2 October 2010; and Barry McCartney, St. Albert, AB, 12 November 2005.

178. Donald McCargar, interviews by author, 2 October 2010–July 2011.

179. Marie Rose Smith, "Eighty Years on the Plains," Box 1, File 4: 23, GAIA.

180. Ibid.

181. The Calgary Stampede was intended to serve as a tool of boosterism, in that it would demonstrate the "progress" of the new West. For that reason, some historians subsequently denounced Stampede organizers for using Indigenous people as pawns of boosterism and progressivism. During interviews with the author, Marie Rose's granddaughter, Shirley-Mae McCargar, and her great-grandson, Barry McCartney, both recalled Marie Rose teaching them the art of Metis crafts. It is interesting that McCartney, although having vivid memories of working alongside his great-grandmother, still questioned whether Marie Rose was, in fact, Metis. This suggests Marie Rose did not verbalize to her descendants the cultural importance of the Metis artefacts she produced, perhaps motivated by her own perceived need to subsume her ethnicity. McCargar, in 2005, still articulated the danger for her own son, who had chosen to identify publicly as Metis. As for herself, Shirley-Mae continued to insist that she preferred a Dutch identity.

182. Marie Rose Smith, "Eighty Years on the Plains," Box 1, File 4: 25, GAIA. This portion of the manuscript is discussed in Chapter 7 because Marie Rose crossed it out with an X.

183. Catriona Mortimer-Sandilands, "'The Geology Recognizes No Boundaries': Shifting Borders in Waterton Lakes National Park," in *The Borderlands of the American and Canadian Wests: Essays on Regional History of the Forty-Nineth Parallel*, ed. Sterling Evans (Lincoln: University of Nebraska Press, 2006), 314.

184. Ibid.

185. Marie Rose Smith, "Eighty Years on the Plains," Box 1, File 4: 22, GAIA.

186. Ibid., 64.

187. Ibid.

188. Ibid., 23.

189. Ibid.

190. Ibid., 174.

191. Census data, Missoula, Montana, provided by Robert Byrne.

192. Marie Rose Smith, "The Adventures of the Wild West of 1870," Box 3, File 3: 20, GAIA.

193. Ibid. Also Homestead Records, Accession No. 1970.313, Film 2820, File 1664923, Document 3456581, PAA. Application for Entry for a Homestead, 28 July 1915. On this application, Marie Rose listed her previous occupation as "Housekeeper."

194. Homestead Records, Accession No. 1970.313, Film 2040, File 43451, PAA. There is a series of correspondence dating between 1907 and 1920 in these homestead files that show Marie Rose was destitute, in hospital at times, and desperately trying to sell land to Mr. and Mrs. Peck, but that the sale of the land was not possible until original title could be confirmed as belonging to Marie Rose and Charlie. It appears that, in 1907, Charlie was trying, among other things, to confirm his original title and obtain additional land. In a letter dated 9 September 1907, to Arthur Edgar Cox from the Department of the Interior, it advised that, because Charlie had failed to receive a certificate of recommendation for his first homestead before the end of June 1889, in fact, that he did "not even make entry for his land until the 20th of August, 1900," his request for additional land was not granted. See also Voisey, *Vulcan*, 131–133. Voisey explains that in 1890 the government stopped the practice of allowing homesteaders to acquire a second quarter of land adjacent to the first homestead. The policy was revived for some areas in 1908. When larger farmers began buying vacant lands, "many homesteaders scrambled to secure a second quarter, not to expand their operations but to preserve a unit size that they had enjoyed for years free of charge." Also Homestead Records, Accession No. 1970.313, Film 2040, File 43451, Document 2155259, PAA. One of Charlie's letters suggests this is exactly what he was doing, since he confirmed he had been using the quarter in question for years (since 1886) with no complaints from anybody, and that the land was only good for pasture. Also Homestead Records, Accession No. 1970.313, Film 2040, File 43451, Document 1444604, PAA. Arthur Edgar Cox, General Financial Agent, to Secretary Department of the Interior, 17 August 1907. This letter indicates that Charles Smith obtained his homestead through a military bounty warrant. Also Olive Tree Geneaology, Red River Military Records, accessed 14 May 2012, http://www.olivetreegenealogy.com/mil/can/rr/rref3s.shtml. The Red River Expeditionary Force lists a Charles Smith as having received bounty warrants for having served between 1870 and 1877.

This force was made up of militiamen from Ontario and Quebec who undertook an arduous journey to reach Red River. It is not very likely that Charlie was a member of this force. However, most of the men who served sold their bounty warrants that granted them 160 acres. See Thomas Flanagan, "The Market for Métis Lands in Manitoba: An Exploratory Study," *Prairie Forum* 16, no. 1 (1991): 1–20. Also Homestead Records, Accession No. 1970.313, Film 2040, File 434151, Document 2155259, PAA. Charlie Smith to Commissioner of Dominion Lands, 15 June 1910. In this letter, Charlie refers to the homestead he held "under a Military Bounty Warrant of 1885."

195. William McD. Tait, "I Remember: Recollections of Kootenai Brown as related them to W. McD. Tait," self-published, 3 August 1957. William McD. Tait Fonds, Accession No. 988.158.1, KBPA. Reference Kootenai Brown Diary.

196. Ibid.

197. Elofson, *Frontier Cattle Ranching*, 94.

198. Marie Rose Smith, "Eighty Years on the Plains," Box 1, File 4: 66–67, 87, GAIA.

199. Prentice et al., *Canadian Women*, 77, 124. Although scholars now acknowledge the important contributions of women to early prairie settlement, the "hostility to dower was particularly strong in the territories, where the right was abolished in 1886." Many farm widows found the land on which they had worked all of their lives had been left to a son. This was especially so in the West, where women had no legal right of inheritance. The rights of Indigenous women were even further thwarted, when an 1884 revision to the Indian Act stated Indigenous widows must be "of moral character" in order to inherit anything from their husbands.

200. This was stipulated by Charlie Smith in his will.

201. Marie Rose Smith Fonds, File 2, GAIA. Great War Veterans' Association to Mrs. Mary Rose Smith, 6 April 1920. Also Voisey, *Vulcan*, 132. Voisey writes there was an aggressive campaign by financial agents "begging settlers to mortgage their newly titled homesteads." Marie Rose and Charlie may have gotten caught up in this practice. Based on the provisions of the Dominion Lands Act, it is likely Marie Rose and Charlie received their first homestead for the registration fee of ten dollars. Thus, they must have mortgaged the property over the years. There is one brief note in Marie Rose's manuscripts, referred to earlier, that does indicate they got caught up in the heady days of credit expansion.

202. Beauvais District Buildings and Sites, Accession No. 988-57-2, compiled by John Daeley, Alberta Culture Historic Sites, SW1/4S2T6R1W5, KBPA. By 1920, Marie Rose had received title to the original homestead. In 1926, the house burned "by accident," and it may have become Edgewood Ranch Ltd., at some point after it changed hands. Also Alberta Geneaological Society, Homestead Records, accessed 3 May 2012, http://abgensoc.ca/. This website notes Marie Rose filed

her homestead under the name "Mary Rose Smith." Also Homestead Records, Accession 1970.313, Film 2820, File 1664923, PAA. Marie Rose's homestead application was received on 18 July 1915, and her sworn statement on 27 July 1915. There is no obvious sign of the homestead having sold. This means Marie Rose filed for the homestead one year after Charlie's death, and she wrote that she was already living in the town of Pincher Creek at that time.

203. Marie Rose Smith, "The Adventures of the Wild West of 1870," File 3, n.p., GAIA. Also Carter, "Britishness," 1. The only reason Marie Rose was allowed to take the second homestead after Charlie died was because she had now become the head of her household in the eyes of government officials. Had she been a single woman, she would not have qualified as a homesteader. Marie Rose might have been aware of this "privilege," given that women of western Canada brought a petition to the Parliament of Canada in 1913 asking that "unmarried women of British citizenry" be allowed to take a free homestead, the same right afforded male immigrants. Reference Library and Archives Canada Records of the Dept. of the Interior, Record Group 15 (RG 15) D-11-1, Volume 1105, File 2876596, Parts 1 and 2. The fact that she said there was little left except a few horses and cows suggests the Jughandle may have reverted back to the mortgage company. It was while she was on the homestead that Marie Rose received the sad news that her two sons had been killed in France.

204. Homestead Records, Accession No. 1970.313, Film 2040, File 434151, Document 3118483, PAA. Mrs. Charlie Smith, widow, to Department of the Interior, 9 March 1914.

205. Homestead Records, Accession No. 1970.313, Film 2040, File 434151, Document 3254061, PAA. Kemmis, Thomson & Jackson to The Controller—Land Patents Branch, 27 October 1914.

206. Homestead Records, Accession No. 1970.313, Film 2040, File 434151, Document 1664923, PAA. Memorandum, Mr. N.O. Cote, Land Patents Branch, 17 June 1916. Also Homestead Records, Accession No. 1970.313, Film 2040, File 434151, Document 4102012. Memorandum to Controller Land Patents Branch from Thomson & Jackson, 23 October 1918, stated that Marie Rose had found a buyer for the land, but the sale was in jeopardy because she still had not retained the necessary title from the Land Patents Branch, and she was now in hospital and in "needy circumstances." Also Homestead Records, Accession No. 1970.313, Film 2040, File 434151, Document 3818108. W.A. Ross, Secretary Treasurer, Beauvais S.D. No. 18, 26, to Department of the Interior, December 1916. The writer advised that there were school taxes outstanding for the past five years. Also Homestead Records, Accession No. 1970.313, Film 2040, File 434151, Document 434151. Department of the Interior to Thomson & Jackson, 24 June 1920. It was

not until this date that the matter of title was settled and Marie Rose was able to sell the land.

207. Jones, *Empire of Dust*, 108. Jones writes that an assortment of plagues "like those of Biblical Egypt poured down upon the people without mercy." Jones wrote about the Medicine Hat area, which featured mixed grasses and not the fescue foothills where Jughandle Ranch and the new homestead were situated. Although located more in the dry belt than Marie Rose's homestead (which she filed in July 1915), the southern Alberta town of Alderson, upon the first visit by Jones in 1984, elicited his observation: "The story of this ghost town and of the enormous surrounding tracts of a life-sized sage of frothy boosterism, lightning expansion and utter miscalculation—It is the tale of the disaster that befell the prairie dry belt after the Great War, the untold sorrow of...southeastern Alberta, an empire of dust," 3. Perhaps, Marie Rose was initially inspired by the back to the land movement that invigorated many after the "mammoth crops of 1915 and 1916" in Alberta and Saskatchewan, following years of bad crops. By 1916, the dry belt of Alberta had seen a population increase to 101,679 from 4,415 in 1901, 88. However, with the crop failures of 1917, it soon became clear that many communities in the dry belt had overextended themselves, 93. For the dry belt of Alberta and Saskatchewan, the Great Depression began well before the Dirty Thirties. Between one-fifth and one-quarter of all townships in southeastern Alberta, an area covering 3.2 million acres, would lose "at least 55 percent of their population" between 1921 and 1926, 117. The Roaring Twenties were anything but a roaring success in two-thirds of Alberta's dry belt, where there was over four times the number of abandoned farms in 1926 as there was in 1936, 221. By the 1920s, the "bubbly local correspondence" of scores of boosters was thinning to a trickle, 101.

208. *Lethbridge Herald*, 14 November 1941, 16.

209. Farley Wuth, archivist, Kootenai Brown Pioneer Village Archives, correspondence with author, 21 March 2006.

210. *Lethbridge Herald*, 14 November 1941, 16.

211. *Pincher Creek Echo*, 14 November 1919; italics added.

212. *Pincher Creek Echo*, 2 August 1918. While this was three years after Marie Rose had claimed her second homestead and she may have already been living in Pincher Creek, the girls may have been at the new homestead.

213. *Pincher Creek Echo*, 24 September 1954.

214. Pollard, "The Making of the Metis," 373.

215. Homestead Records, Accession No. 1970.313, Film 2040, File 434151, PAA. Various appeals were made to the Department of the Interior on Marie Rose's behalf, pleading that the matter of title for Jughandle Ranch be settled so she

could sell the land and pay her creditors. Some of the correspondence referred to her being hospitalized and to the fact that she had sons away at war.

216. "Last Will and Testament of Charles Smith," Accession No. 1970.313, Film 2040, File 434151, Document 4124068, PAA. The will was confirmed by the district court of the District of Macleod on 27 February 1914, as was Marie Rose's role as "executrix."

217. Marie Rose Smith, "Eighty Years on the Plains," Box 1, File 4: 170, GAIA.

7 FENCED IN

1. *Pincher Creek Echo*, 7 April 1960, 1.

2. Foster, *We Know Who We Are*, 57.

3. Archibald Belaney (1888–1938) was born in England but assumed the name Grey Owl after marrying an Indigenous woman in Ontario. He became a conservationist and respected author who even gained an audience with the queen as Grey Owl.

4. Sylvester Clark Long (1890–1932), born in North Carolina to a family of black slaves, he assumed the name Buffalo Child Long Lance when he came to Canada in 1919, after serving in the war and when black immigration was discouraged.

5. Onoto Watanna was the pen name of Winnifred Eaton, a woman born in Montreal to Chinese and English parents. Eaton came to Cochrane, Alberta, in 1917 with her husband to ranch. As an author, she chose a pen name intended to portray herself as being of Japanese ethnicity at a time when Chinese were the subject of racism.

6. Marie Rose Smith Fonds, File 2, GAIA. The Macmillan Company of Canada to A.L. Freebairn, Esq., Pincher Creek, Alberta, 22 July 1938. Archivist Carl Spadoni, with the William Ready Special Collection Library at McMaster University, Hamilton, Ontario, which holds the Macmillan Archives, confirms that no further records exist that could confirm whether the manuscript was ever received. Also Marie Rose Smith Fonds, File 2, GAIA. Mrs. Hyrum Ririe, Lewiston Utah, to Mrs. Charles Smith, 21 November 1941. Ririe requested a copy of the book when published and referred to an article in the *Lethbridge Herald*, 14 November 1941, which was actually written by Emma Lynch-Staunton, in which Staunton spoke of the anticipated publishing of Marie Rose's book.

7. Marie Rose's writings, prepared for publication, invite greater scrutiny and a separate study, as the excerpts communicating her ideas in her manuscripts varied stylistically. The syntax differences in some of them suggest a very heavy editorial hand, if not a complete borrowing from another secondary source. It may also be that some of the quotes referenced throughout this study originate in all of the sources available on Marie Rose, including handwritten notes, typed

manuscripts, and published articles. Thus, it is difficult to determine if the editing was by Marie Rose or by others.

8. The discussion in this chapter of Marie Rose's writing is brief and meant simply as a way to understand how her writing facilitated her persona as a homesteading pioneer, and to understand how the emerging racial boundaries served to "fence" her in. For a more detailed analysis of Marie Rose's writing, and her role as an author of both fiction and nonfiction, please see my previous publications as cited in the bibliography of this book.

9. Marie Rose Smith, "The Adventures of the Wild West of 1870," Box 1, File 3: 65, GAIA.

10. Ibid. Also Spry, "The Great Transformation." Marie Rose's perceptions are similar to those discussed by Spry, who argues the eventual disappearance of common land on the prairies after 1870 was a tragedy. Also Peter Erasmus, *Buffalo Days and Nights*, transcribed by Henry Thompson (Calgary: Fifth House Publishing, 1999). Erasmus was born in 1833 and trained for missionary work, but instead became a guide, interpreter, and buffalo hunter. He, too, spoke fondly of the abundance and easy living at the height of buffalo-hunting days.

11. Marie Rose Smith, "Eighty Years on the Plains," Box 1, File 4: 1, GAIA.

12. Ibid.

13. Ibid.

14. Ibid., 12.

15. Ibid.

16. Ibid.

17. Ibid.

18. Ibid., 139.

19. Ibid., 3.

20. Marie Rose Smith, "The Adventures of the Wild West of 1870," Box 1, File 3: 74–75, GAIA.

21. Ibid., 73.

22. Ibid., 51.

23. Spry, "The Great Transformation," 33. Spry noted that in the early ranching days, the small number of operators and homesteaders on a quarter section could turn their cattle loose and let them graze on the adjacent land, the "commons." It was important that new settlers have the right to collect hay from untitled land in order that cattle could survive the cold winters. As private ownership extended, common rights to resources such as hay and wood were extinguished.

24. Smith, "Eighty Years on the Plains," *Canadian Cattlemen*, 12, no. 1 (June 1949): 12.

25. Marie Rose Smith, "Eighty Years on the Plains," *Canadian Cattlemen* 12, no. 4 (November 1949): 15.

26. Smith, "Eighty Years on the Plains," *Canadian Cattlemen*, 12, no. 1 (June 1949): 11.

27. Ibid., 141.

28. Ibid.

29. Ibid., 142.

30. Marie Rose Smith, "The Adventures of the Wild West of 1870," Box 1, File 3: 74, GAIA.

31. Ibid.

32. Marie Rose Smith, "Eighty Years on the Plains," Box 1, File 4: 172, GAIA.

33. Ibid.

34. Elofson, *Cowboys, Gentlemen, and Cattle Thieves*, 138. Reference *Pincher Creek Echo*, 24 May 1904.

35. Elofson, *Cowboys, Gentlemen, and Cattle Thieves*, 134. Under the provisions of the Dominion Lands Act there would have been the requirement to cultivate at least forty acres, but there is no mention made of working the land at all in either Marie Rose's writing or that of Jock Carpenter's. Also Homestead Records, Accession No. 1970.313, Film 2040, File 434151, Document 4170741, PAA. Thomson & Jackson to Department of the Interior, 22 April 1919. As part of the correspondence that sought to allow Marie Rose to sell some of the property for which proper titles had not been obtained while Charlie was alive, Marie Rose's representatives noted the land was fenced and "70 acres" had been "broken and ploughed in each year for several years past." They noted they would be glad to hear "after inspection by the homestead inspector will be sufficient fulfillment of the homestead requirements."

36. Marie Rose Smith, "The Adventures of the Wild West of 1870," Box 1, File 3: 38, GAIA.

37. MacKellar, *Core of My Heart*, 108.

38. Sheppard, "Undercurrents of Intolerance," 2.

39. Ibid. Reference *The Albertan*, 6 December 1924.

40. Sheppard, "Undercurrents of Intolerance," 4. Also William Peter Baergen, *The Ku Klux Klan in Central Alberta* (Red Deer: Central Alberta Historical Society, 2000), 13. Baergen notes that Alberta was the only Canadian jurisdiction to accept formal registration of the KKK under its Societies Act. He contends that although "Canada's use of public schools to assimilate non-Anglo-Saxons to the British way, its active discouragement of Black immigration, and the placing of Indians on reserves, appear mild [in comparison to the Jim Crow laws of the United States], such government support gave official sanction to the notion that some races were second-class. In granting the Ku Klux Klan a charter, the Alberta government sanctioned its activities, even though one of its stated objects was 'racial purity.'" As Baergen argues, the goal of "white supremacy"

might have been more subtly pursued by the KKK in Canada, but that goal was still "boldly stated as an object in their key documents such as application forms, their charter, brochures, and their manual, *The Kloran*."

41. Marie Rose Smith, "Eighty Years on the Plains," Box 1, File 4: 104, GAIA. Also Diane Payment, "Marie Fisher Guadet (1843–1914: 'La providence du fort Good Hope,'" accessed 2 June 2011, http://www.ecclectica.ca/issues/2003/2/gaudet.asp. In the 1920s, Metis women in western Canada were pressured to integrate and many would increasingly claim that *"on n'est pas mitchifs nous-autres"* ("we are not Metis"). Marie Rose's awareness of the political climate made it that much more important that she prove to have extended her network if she hoped to retain any semblance of the position as a member of the higher class that her family had enjoyed during the fur trade era.

42. Marie Rose Smith, "The Adventures of the Wild West of 1879," Box 1, File 3: 75, GAIA. The convent she speaks of is Kermaria Convent in Pincher Creek, where three of her children attended.

43. Ibid., 79–80.

44. "My poor innocents, often my heart cried for them." Marie Rose Smith, "Eighty Years on the Plains," Box 1, File 4: 105, GAIA.

45. Postcard to "My dear Son Joe," 4 June 1909. Courtesy Shirley-Mae McCargar.

46. *The Lethbridge Herald*, 14 November 1941. Both of Marie Rose's parents were of Metis ancestry and had ancestors from the Saulteaux people (associated with the Ojibwe people).

47. *Pincher Creek Echo*, 15 September 1955.

48. Marie Rose Smith, "The Adventures of the Wild West of 1870," Box 1, File 3: 46–47, GAIA.

49. Ibid. In 1885, the Indian Act was amended to prohibit several traditional Indigenous ceremonies; in 1905, the act was amended to allow the government to remove Indigenous people from reserves that were near towns with populations over eight thousand; in 1914, there was a requirement that western Indigenous people seek permission before appearing in Indigenous "costume" in order to take part in any dance, show, public exhibition, or pageant. Likely, there were many in Marie Rose's society that were adopting the ideology that Indigenous ceremonies were "barbarous ordeals."

50. Shirley-Mae McCargar, interviews by author, October 2005–July 2011. These are also Metis beliefs. For example, if a woodpecker sits on the corner of a house, this is understood by many Metis to mean impending death.

51. Marie Rose Smith, "The Adventures of the Wild West of 1870," Box 1, File 3: 26, GAIA.

52. Ibid., n.p.page. Also Marie Rose Smith, "The Adventures of the Wild West of 1870," File 3:83, GAIA. In this excerpt, she indicated that "Yesterday (was) June 2nd 1938."

53. Southern Alberta Pioneers and Descendants Fonds, Accession No. M2077 B1.6.5727, GAIA. The Southern Alberta Women's Pioneer and Old Timer Association Constitution, Article 1. The Southern Alberta Women's Pioneer and Old Timer Association was formed in 1922, and one of its major goals was to preserve and "rescue from oblivion the memory of its early pioneers." This initiative, which Marie Rose joined, may have been the inspiration for writing and publishing what she could of early pioneer experiences.

54. Carpenter, *Fifty Dollar Bride*, 17.

55. Ibid., 63.

56. Ibid., 88.

57. Ludger E. Gareau Fonds, KBPA.

58. Carpenter, *Fifty Dollar Bride*, 88.

59. Charles D. Denney Fonds, Accession No. M7144, GAIA. Jock Carson Carpenter to Mr. Charles Denney, 8 January 1984. This letter is dated some years after the publication of *Fifty Dollar Bride*, so there is a possibility Carpenter was not aware at the time of publication that Norbert and Joseph were involved in the conflict of 1885.

60. Arthur W. Frank, "Moral Non-Fiction: Life Writing and Children's Disability," in *The Ethics of Life Writing*, ed. Paul John Eakin (Ithaca, NY: Cornell University Press, 2004), 174.

61. Marianne Gullestad, "Tales of Consent and Descent: Life Writing as a Fight against an Imposed Self-Image," in *The Ethics of Life Writing*, ed. Paul John Eakin (Ithaca, NY: Cornell University Press, 2004), 239.

62. Paul John Eakin, "Introduction: Mapping the Ethics of Life Writing," in *The Ethics of Life Writing*, ed. Paul John Eakin (Ithaca, NY: Cornell University Press, 2004), 1–4.

63. While she was not able to have the majority of her manuscripts published during her lifetime, her descendants recognized their value and ensured they would be deposited with the archives at the Glenbow–Alberta Institute Archives after her death.

64. Paul Lauritzen, "Arguing with Life Stories: The Case of Rigoberta Menchú," in *The Ethics of Life Writing*, ed. Paul John Eakin (Ithaca, NY: Cornell University Press, 2004), 31.

65. Claudia Mills, "Friendship, Fiction, and Memoir: Trust and Betrayal in Writing from One's Own Life," in *The Ethics of Life Writing*, ed. Paul John Eakin (Ithaca, NY: Cornell University Press, 2004), 117.

66. Marie Rose Smith, "Eighty Years on the Plains," Box 1, File 4: 56–58, GAIA.

67. Marie Rose Smith, untitled, Box 1, File 4: 56–57, GAIA.

68. Marie Rose Smith, untitled, Box 1, File 3: 60, GAIA.

69. Homestead Records indicate Ness settled on SE-27-5-1-W5, filed 1 October 1888, KBPA.

70. Treaty 7 was signed in 1877 and included territories of the Blackfoot, Peigan, Sarcee, Blood, and Stoney in the Rocky Mountain foothills. Indigenous people viewed it as a peace treaty meant to protect them from whiskey traders and other Indigenous groups after rampant smallpox epidemics and the loss of buffalo.

71. Marie Rose Smith, "The Adventures of the Wild West of 1870," Box 1, File 3: 34, GAIA.

72. Chief Crowfoot died near Blackfoot Crossing in 1890, thus Marie Rose may have encountered him as a married woman living in southern Alberta.

73. Marie Rose Smith, untitled, File 4: 35–36, GAIA.

74. Marie Rose Smith, "Eighty Years on the Plains," *Canadian Cattlemen* 11, no. 3 (December 1948): 144.

75. Marie Rose Smith, "The Adventures of the Wild West of 1870," File 3: 67, GAIA.

76. Marie Rose Smith, untitled, File 4: 50–54, GAIA.

77. Marie Rose Smith, "Eighty Years on the Plains," Box 1, File 4: 55, GAIA.

78. Ibid.

79. Ibid., 56.

80. Van Kirk, *Many Tender Ties.*

81. Marie Rose Smith, "The Adventures of the Wild West of 1870," File 3: 29, GAIA.

82. Ibid.

83. Dobbin, *The One-and-a-Half Men*, 91.

84. Smith, "Eighty Years on the Plains," *Canadian Cattlemen*, 12, no. 1 (June 1949): 19.

85. Foster, *We Know Who We Are*, 204.

86. Marie Rose Smith, "Eighty Years on the Plains," Box 1, File 4: 16, GAIA.

87. Unidentified newspaper, 24 September 1954, KBPA. The article noted Marie Rose was visiting in Lethbridge and also featured a photo of a young Marie Rose with a caption that read she was twenty-one years old in the photo. The article also suggested Charlie had built the fine home in Pincher Creek, likely referring to the boarding house. This is the only indication Charlie was well enough to build the house sometime between 1910 and 1914, when the family likely moved into town before Charlie's death in 1914.

88. Bell, "Oscillating Identities," 14.

89. McManus, *The Line Which Separates*, 180. There was slow growth, despite extensive boosterism campaigns that accompanied the generous land grants and the growing shortage of available lands elsewhere.

90. Voisey, *Vulcan*, 29.

91. Marie Rose Smith, "The Adventures of the Wild West of 1870," Box 1, File 3: 64, GAIA.

92. Marie Rose Smith, transcribed by Ben Montgomery, "Tribulations of Mrs. C. Smith of Pincher Creek Alberta," Box 1, File 6: 2, GAIA.

93. Marie Rose Smith, "Eighty Years on the Plains," Box 1, File 4: 25, GAIA.

94. Marie Rose Smith, "The Adventures of the Wild West of 1870," Box 1, File 3: 28, GAIA.

95. Marie Rose Smith, "The Adventures of the Wild West of 1870," Box 3, File 1: 44, GAIA.

96. When she lived in Edmonton with her family, Marie Rose's granddaughter Shirley-Mae McCargar remembered that Marie Rose always kept her pemmican in her own room and that, often, as a young girl, Shirley-Mae would sneak in to enjoy a taste. It was only near the end of her life that Shirley-Mae's mother insisted Marie Rose stop making pemmican, for she appeared to have lost the ability to make it so it would not spoil.

97. Cora Taylor, *Victoria Calihoo: An Amazing Life* (Edmonton: Eschia Books, 2008), 123. Reference Naomi McIllwraith, historical interpreter at Fort Edmonton Park, who explained the pemmican-making process.

98. Foster, *We Know Who We Are*, 259n20. Foster noted her own personal experience in witnessing the enthusiasm of the Spring Creek Metis for all aspects of the Metis culture, including not only oral history and the making of pemmican but one woman in her nineties who "rolled her wheelchair onto the floor to jig."

99. Maureen K. Lux, *Medicine That Walks: Disease, Medicine, and Canadian Plains Native People, 1880–1940* (Toronto: University of Toronto Press, 2001), 83. Reference M2816, Volume 8, Dewdney Papers, Lacombe to Dewdney, 7 April 1889, 2187, GAIA. There is evidence that Father Lacombe once demanded of government officials that they use their power to stamp out Indigenous ceremonial practices and healings, when he wrote, in a letter to Edgar Dewdney, "It is to be regretted that the govt doesn't stop that demonstration altogether—You are strong enough by your moral influence and your mounted police to make the Sun Dance Die out." There is no way to know if Marie Rose was aware of Lacombe's petition to the government.

100. Marie Rose Smith, "The Adventures of the Wild West of 1870," File 3: 29, GAIA. This reference is to Treaty Number 6, which covered over 120,000 square miles of what are now parts of Alberta and Saskatchewan.

101. Katherine Hughes, *Father Lacombe: The Black-Robe Voyageur* (Toronto: William Briggs, 1911), 273. Hughes relied on her association with Bishop Legal and his access to the archives at St. Albert, as well as his correspondence with Father Lacombe.

102. Marie Rose Smith, untitled, File 6: n.p., GAIA.

103. Marie Rose Smith, "Eighty Years on the Plains," *Canadian Cattlemen* 11, no. 2 (September 1948): 73.

104. Ibid. Many of the Plains Metis drew firm distinctions between the Metis and "Indians."

105. Smith, "Eighty Years on the Plains," *Canadian Cattlemen*, 11, no. 4 (March 1949): 217.

106. Marie Rose Smith, "The Adventures of the Wild West of 1870," File 3: 67, GAIA.

107. Marie Rose Smith, "The Twenty Warnings," Marie Rose Smith Fonds, File 5: 45, GAIA.

108. Lauritzen, "Arguing with Life Stories," 23.

109. Marie Rose Smith, "The Twenty Warnings," File 5: 6, GAIA.

110. Philosophical fiction typically devotes a significant portion to ethics or morals by using a simple story to explain difficult aspects of human life.

111. Marie Rose Smith, "The Twenty Warnings," File 5: 1, GAIA.

112. Ibid.

113. Ibid., 18.

114. Ibid., 7.

115. Ibid.

116. Marie Rose Smith, "Eighty Years on the Plains," Box 1, File 4: 58, GAIA.

117. Ibid., 59.

118. Marie Rose Smith, "The Adventures of the Wild West of 1870," File 3: 59, GAIA.

119. Marie Rose Smith, "The Twenty Warnings," File 5: 19, GAIA.

120. Ibid., 8. Some historians have also been critical of the Roman Catholic clergy's hypocrisy in its dealings with Riel.

121. George F.G. Stanley, *Louis Riel* (Toronto: The Ryerson Press, 1963), 277.

122. Ibid.

123. Marie Rose Smith, "The Twenty Warnings," File 5: 8–9, GAIA.

124. Ibid., 29.

125. Tricksters in the Native American spiritual world and in mythology can be in the form of gods, goddesses, spirits, or animals that typically play tricks or disobey normal rules and conventional behaviour with positive results. They have the ability to transform themselves, as in the Coyote, which can be the creator in some creation stories. In the literary world, the trickster dismantles the master's house by using the master's tools in unconventional ways. This is the understanding of trickster used in this book, specifically that the master's

house for authors such as Johnson, Onoto, and Marie Rose was the Euro-North American world in which they sought to be published. They used whatever tools they could in order to publish their work, perhaps as a way to dismantle some of that world.

126. Marilyn J. Rose, "Johnson, Emily Pauline," in *Dictionary of Canadian Biography*, vol. 14, University of Toronto/Université Laval, 2003–, accessed 16 April 2011, http://www.biographi.ca/en/bio/johnson_emily_pauline_14E.html. Tekahionwake was the name of Johnson's great-grandfather.

127. Penny Petrone, ed., *First People, First Voices* (Toronto: University of Toronto Press, 1983), 140.

128. Veronica Strong-Boag and Carole Gerson, eds., *Paddling Her Own Canoe: The Times and Texts of E. Pauline Johnson (Tekahionwake)* (Toronto: University of Toronto Press, 2000), 114.

129. Rose, "Johnson, Emily Pauline." While the essay was originally published in Toronto's *Sunday Globe*, there is no indication it received much attention at the time.

130. George Melnyk, *The Literary History of Alberta: Volume One from Writing-on-Stone to World War Two* (Edmonton: University of Alberta Press, 1998), 105. Also Smith, *Calgary's Grand Story*, 61. Both reference Margaret P. Hess Collection, Special Collections, University of Calgary Library. The book held by the Special Collections at the university library is Isabella's copy of Eaton's 1923 novel, *Cattle*, set in Alberta, in which the author wrote the inscription, "To Lady Lougheed—a picturesque and delightful personality with the regard of the author. Onoto Watanna, Calgary, December 22, 1922. The world is just as a person's heart makes it."

131. Jean Lee Cole, *The Literary Voices of Winnifred Eaton: Redefining Ethnicity and Authenticity* (New Brunswick, NJ: Rutgers University Press, 2002), 104.

132. Ibid., 3. Reference Eve Oishi, in the 1999 reprint of Eaton's first novel, *Miss Nume of Japan* (1899).

133. Ibid., 2. Reference Jinqui Ling, *Creating One's Self*, 312–313.

134. The growing anti-Japanese nativism led to the Gentleman's Agreement in 1907, which aimed to stem immigration. In an attempt to stop emigration to the United States, and as a way to prevent anti-immigration laws such as the Chinese Exclusion Acts of 1882, Japan "agreed" not to issue passports. However, Japan continued to issue passports to Hawaii, from where many Japanese people continued to enter the United States.

135. Cole, *The Literary Voices of Winnifred Eaton*, 9.

136. Marie Rose Smith, "Does God Know His Business?" Marie Rose Smith Fonds, File 6: 5, GAIA.

137. Ibid., 11.

138. Ibid.

139. Ibid., 9.

140. Ibid.

141. Ibid., 11.

142. Marie Rose Smith, transcribed by Ben Montgomery, "Tribulations of Mrs. C. Smith of Pincher Creek Alberta," Box 1, File 6: 1, GAIA.

143. Marie Rose Smith, "Does God Know His Business?" File 6: 11, GAIA.

144. Marie Rose Smith, "The Adventures of the Wild West of 1870," File 3: 52, GAIA.

145. Ibid., 73.

146. Ibid., 54.

147. Beattie and Buss, *Undelivered Letters*, 406.

148. Donald McCargar campaign website, accessed 29 July 2011, http://www.donformetis.com/.

8 MANY VOICES—ONE PEOPLE

1. Brenda Macdougall, *One of the Family: Metis Culture in Nineteenth-Century Northwestern Saskatchewan* (Vancouver: UBC Press, 2009), 14. Macdougall argues the focus on debates about French or British Metis negates the Indigenous connection to the culture of their homeland.

2. Ibid., 3.

3. St-Onge and Podruchny, "Scuttling Along a Spider's Web," 60.

4. Ibid., 67.

5. Macdougall, "The Myth," 422. Also Anderson, "Métis," 12. Anderson agrees, writing, "To speak of our mixedness is to speak of our comparative inauthenticity."

6. Devine, *The People Who Own Themselves*. Devine argued that within one family, children could assume dramatically different identities based on their life experiences. By tracing the Desjarlais family, Devine demonstrated it was the collective that determined Metis ethnogenesis.

7. St-Onge and Podruchny, "Scuttling Along a Spider's Web," 82.

8. Ibid., 82–83.

9. Nancy Shoemaker, "Categories," in *Clearing a Path: Theorizing the Past in Native American Studies*, ed. Nancy Shoemaker (New York: Routledge, 2002), 55–56. Also Anderson, "Métis," 12. Anderson argues racialized discourses about the Metis are "dangerous" because they "foreclose on conversations that put Métis on more equal political footing with the Canadian state and with other Indigenous peoples."

10. Macdougall, "The Myth," 437–438.

11.　Anderson, "Métis," 6.

12.　Ibid., 18. Anderson argues it has "become fashionable to scorn what has been termed 'Red River myopia,'" but he does concede that his book "touches upon the relationship between kinship and nationhood...though there are no neat or definitive answers to this question." He is unapologetic about his privileging of the term "Métis," referencing exclusively the "history, events, leaders, territories, language, and culture associated with the growth of the buffalo hunting and trading Métis of the northern Plains, in particular during the period between the beginning of the Métis buffalo brigades in the early nineteenth century and the 1885 North West Uprising," 24.

13.　Macdougall, "The Myth," 424–429. Macdougall argues scholars such as Sylvia Van Kirk were ambivalent about their own understanding of Metis identity. Macdougall references Van Kirk's portrayal of Alexander Ross's "Anglophone mixed-blood" children as ambivalent about their identity because they were not French Metis.

14.　Sealey and Lussier, The Métis, 13.

15.　Wilson, "'In a Business Way,'" 115. Wilson wrote that, by 1879, Smith had concluded the "Company's and the North-West's future would primarily be affected by the railroad, and by the relationship established between the federal government, the successful railroad syndicate, and the Bay Company."

16.　Newspaper Clippings File, "Canadian Women in the Public Eye."

17.　Pincher Creek Echo, 7 April 1960, 1.

18.　Griffiths, The Splendid Vision. Also Cohen, Women's Work.

19.　Brown, "Woman as Centre," 41.

20.　Donez Xiques, Margaret Laurence: The Making of a Writer (Toronto: Dundurn Press, 2005), 42.

21.　Ibid., 44.

22.　St-Onge and Podruchny, "Scuttling Along a Spider's Web," 81.

23.　The Southern Alberta Pioneers and Their Descendants, accessed 18 February 2012, http://www.pioneersalberta.org/profiles/d.html. In 1901, the Calgary Old Timer's Association formed with membership limited to those who resided in Calgary prior to 1884. In 1920, this organization expanded to become the Southern Alberta Old Timers Association, with the requirement that members must be males (or their male descendants) who were living just north of Red Deer to southern Alberta prior to 31 December 1890. In March 1922, the Women's Pioneer Association of Southern Alberta formed, and the two groups held many joint meetings until their amalgamation in 1964. In 1974, the name became the Southern Alberta Pioneers and Their Descendants and the group still has a presence, maintaining a memorial building at 3625-4 Street s w in

Calgary. It also publishes a website, historical books, and magazines, and offers an informational booth at the Calgary Stampede, that celebration of pioneer days that began during Isabella's and Marie Rose's time and continues as an important tool of boosterism. Also "Lady Lougheed Again President of Southern Alberta Women," *Morning Albertan*, 22 January 1925. This article explained the group was active in the Calgary Stampede, and entered "into the affair with a real zest, contributing to the parade and the Old Timers' hut in splendid manner." Isabella was the first president and served in that role until 1928. Also Voisey, *Vulcan*, 29. It is interesting that some pioneer associations had different qualifications, such as the Cleverville Pioneer Club, which stipulated membership was restricted to those "present in the district before 31 December 1910." The southern Alberta association had first stipulated members must be residents of their district in 1884, twenty-six years earlier, making it more likely they would be people with some connection to the old economy.

24. Elizabeth Bailey Price Fonds, Accession No. M1002, File 19, GAIA. "The Red River Valley." While Edith Fowke provides a more scholarly review of this folk song, Price was a contemporary of many in the Old Timers Association. She had come to Calgary as an infant in 1893, trained as a teacher, and joined the editorial staff of the *Calgary Albertan* in 1911. Price wrote that the author of the song is unknown but that the song was sung by traders and Metis and that, according to old timers, the story was that "Louis Riel fell madly in love with a beautiful visitor...poured forth his passionate declaration of love." She continues that the original word "half-breed" became "maiden" to accommodate the "world-wide sensitiveness of the half-caste." Price was the first secretary of the Southern Alberta Old Timers Association.

25. Southern Alberta Pioneers and Descendants Fonds, Accession No. M2077 B1.6.5727, GAIA. The Southern Alberta Women's Pioneer and Old Timer Association Constitution, Article 1. In 1922, when the Women's Pioneer Association of Southern Alberta was formed, its mandate was, as with so many clubs of that era, to be a benevolent association meant to cultivate social intercourse. However, another major component of its mandate was to "rescue from oblivion the memory of its early pioneers and to obtain and preserve narratives of their exploits, perils and adventures; to promote the study of the history of the Province and to diffuse and publish information as to its past and present condition and resources and in all appropriate matters to advance the interests and perpetuate the memory of those whose sagacity, energy and enterprise induced them to settle in the west," 1.

26. Donald B. Smith Collection, Isabella Timeline File, LHA. Reference "Lady Lougheed Popular President Southern Alberta Women Pioneers," *Morning Albertan*, 27 January 1927.

27. *Calgary Daily Herald*, 17 December 1932.

28. Voisey, *Vulcan*, 28. Voisey's pioneers were the "progressive minded people bent on emulating the city, fostering civilized behavior, and recreating former ways of life," who nonetheless did not deny the influence of the frontier on their lives. One of these new prairie dwellers who fancied herself a pioneer wrote home that "Out West usually calls to mind great stretches of land...This abundance of space gives every man a chance to become a property owner and to be his own master." Although both Marie Rose and Isabella became property owners, their view of themselves as pioneers would be different than this one articulated by a "new pioneer," who did not have the qualifications to become a rightful member of the Southern Alberta Pioneer Association. Not only was she not born in the West prior to 1890, but she was taken with the concept of private property ownership, which was a foreign concept to the pioneer Metis families of Isabella and Marie Rose. The pioneer days for Isabella and Marie Rose were not those that had transformed "the wilderness into 'smart little cities'" but the days of Metis pioneers, long before this later period, when the landscape was unfettered by fences and fur trade girls endured the privations of northern lands, 32.

29. Gerhard J. Ens, "Metis Ethnicity, Personal Identity and the Development of Capitalism in the Western Interior: The Case of Johnny Grant," in *From Rupert's Land to Canada: Essays in Honour of John E. Foster*, ed. Theodore Binnema, Gerhard Ens, and R.C. MacLeod (Edmonton: University of Alberta Press, 2001), 174.

30. St-Onge and Podruchny, "Scuttling Along a Spider's Web," 81.

31. Lougheed House Research Files, LHA. Chief Buffalo Child Long Lance, "Indians of the Northwest and West Canada," *The Mentor* 12, no. 2 (March 1924): 6. For an understanding of Long Lance's deception and his real identity, see Smith, *Chief Buffalo Child Long Lance*.

32. Edna Kells Fonds, "Pioneer Interviews," ca. 1935, Accession No. M4026, GAIA.

33. Ens and Sawchuk, *New Peoples to New Nations*, 5.

34. Pollard, "The Making of the Metis," xxiii.

35. While the former director of the Lougheed House National Historic Site, Trudy Cowan, once stated Isabella did smoke a pipe, archivist Amanda Kriaski noted this has not been confirmed in any documentation and may be an example of "folklore."

PRIMARY SOURCES

Manuscript Collections

Alberta Women's Institute Fonds. Glenbow–Alberta Institute Archives.

Assessment Roll, National Park School District No. 102, N.W.T. Whyte Museum of the
    Canadian Rockies Archives, Banff, AB.

Assiniboia District Court Records. Archives of Manitoba.

Beauvais District Buildings and Sites. Compiled by John Daeley. Alberta Culture
    Historic Sites. Kootenai Brown Pioneer Village Archives, Pincher Creek, AB.

Belleau Collection. Transcripts of Letters of Catholic Missionaries in the Red River
    and Pembina District 1867–1925. Archives of Manitoba.

Calgary Local Council of Women Fonds. Glenbow–Alberta Institute Archives.

Canada Department of Justice. List of Prisoners 1885, Warrants 1885. Archives of
    Manitoba.

Canadian Genealogy Centre—North West Mounted Police. Library and Archives
    Canada.

Cemetary List, updated 20 June 2004. Alberta Genealogical Society, Edmonton, AB.

Census 1880. Montana Historical Society, Missoula, MT.

Census Data, 1881, 1891, 1901, 1906, 1911. Library and Archives Canada.

Charles D. Denney Fonds. Glenbow–Alberta Institute Archives.

Clarence Kipling Fonds. Glenbow–Alberta Institute Archives.

Deaths and Births Table. Quebec Family History Society, Pointe-Claire, QC.

Donald B. Smith Collection. Lougheed House National Historic Site Archives.

Dr. B.J. Charles Fonds. Glenbow–Alberta Institute Archives.

Edna Kells Fonds. Glenbow–Alberta Institute Archives.

Elizabeth Bailey Price Fonds. Glenbow–Alberta Institute Archives.

Ernest Watkins' R.B. Bennett Research Collection. Glenbow–Alberta Institute
    Archives.

Eva Reid Fonds. Glenbow–Alberta Institute Archives.

Faithful Companions of Jesus Archives, Calgary, AB.

Filles de Jésus Archives, Calgary, AB.

Fonds Antonin Taché. Archives de la Société historique de Saint-Boniface, MB.

Fonds Corporation Archiépiscopale Catholique Romaine de Saint-Boniface. Archives
    de la Société historique de Saint-Boniface, MB.

Fonds Paroisse. Saint François-Xavier. Archives de la Société historique de Saint-
    Boniface, MB.

Fonds Pierre Picton. Archives de la Société historique de Saint-Boniface, MB.

Geoff Burtonshaw Genealogical Collection. Glenbow–Alberta Institute Archives.

George and John McDougall Fonds. Glenbow–Alberta Institute Archives.

Government of Canada Files. Library and Archives Canada.

Grants to Half-Breeds Register Saint François-Xavier. Métis Culture and Heritage
    Resource Centre, Winnipeg, MB.

Hamilton Public Library Collection. Lougheed House National Historic Site Archives.

Henry "Frenchy" Rivière Fonds. Glenbow–Alberta Institute Archives.

Homestead Records. Provincial Archives of Alberta.

Hudson's Bay Company Collection. McCord Museum Archives.

James A. Lougheed Folder. Lougheed House National Historic Site Archives.

James Kennedy Cornwall Fonds. Glenbow–Alberta Institute Archives.

James Lougheed Family Fonds. Glenbow–Alberta Institute Archives.

J.E.A. Macleod Fonds. Glenbow–Alberta Institute Archives.

Jennifer Bobrovitz Files. Lougheed House National Historic Site Archives.

John Strachan Papers. Archives of Ontario.

Lougheed House Fonds. Lougheed House National Historic Site Archives.

Lougheed House Research Files. Lougheed House National Historic Site Archives.

Louis Riel Papers. Archives of Manitoba.

Ludger E. Gareau Fonds. Kootenai Brown Pioneer Village Archives, Pincher Creek, AB.

Luxton Family Fonds. Whyte Museum of the Canadian Rockies Archives, Banff, AB.

Marie Rose Smith Fonds. Glenbow–Alberta Institute Archives.

Marie Rose Smith Fonds. Kootenai Brown Pioneer Village Archives, Pincher Creek, AB.

Matilda Davis School Folder, Lougheed House National Historic Site Archives.

Matilda Davis Family Fonds, Archives of Manitoba.

Maude & Harold Riley Fonds. Glenbow–Alberta Institute Archives.

McLaws Redman Lougheed and Cairns Fonds. Legal Archives Society of Alberta, Calgary.

Meeres, Edwin L. "Addison McPherson began area Settlement with a search for gold," 16 August 1982. McPherson Family File. Red Deer & District Archives.

Newspaper Clippings File. Lougheed House National Historic Site Archives.

North West Halfbreed Claims Commission 1900. Métis Culture and Heritage Resource Centre, Winnipeg, MB.

North-West Territories Gazette. Kootenai Brown Pioneer Village Archives, Pincher Creek, AB.

Notman, William & Son Photographic Studio Collection. McCord Museum Archives.

Parish Records. Catholic Archdiocese of Edmonton.

Parish Records Saint Stephen's. Diocese Fonds. Diocèse de Montreal Eglise Anglicane du Canada Archives.

Parmelle, Lea E. Fonds. McCord Museum Archives.

Patrick McPherson Fonds. Glenbow–Alberta Institute Archives.

The Portfolio Collection. Hamilton Public Library Archives.

Rare Books Collection. University of Calgary.

R.B. Bennett Fonds. Library and Archives Canada.

Recherche Généalogiques par localité. Fonds Pierre Picton. Archives de la Société historique de Saint-Boniface, Manitoba.

Richard Bedford Bennett Fonds. Glenbow–Alberta Institute Archives.

Richard Hardisty Fonds. Glenbow–Alberta Institute Archives.

Riel-Delorme Papiers. Archives de la Société historique de Saint-Boniface, Manitoba.

Saint François Xavier Parish Records. Archives of Manitoba.

Scrip Affidavit No. 1240 Claim 2608. Métis Culture and Heritage Resource Centre, Winnipeg, MB.

Sisters of Charity (Grey Nuns). MS Chronicles 1843–1893. Archives of Manitoba.

Soeurs Grises Archives, Montreal, QC.

Soldiers of the First World War (RG 150). Library and Archives Canada.

Southern Alberta Pioneers and Descendants Fonds. Glenbow–Alberta Institute Archives.

Special Collections. Hamilton Public Library Archives.

Thomas Douglas Selkirk, 5th Earl Papers. Archives of Manitoba.

Victorian Order of Nurses (VON) Fonds. Glenbow–Alberta Institute Archives.

Wesleyan Ladies' College Archives File. Hamilton Public Library Archives.

William McD. Tait Fonds. Kootenai Brown Pioneer Village Archives, Pincher Creek, AB.

Young Women's Christian Association Fonds. Glenbow–Alberta Institute Archives.

Theses and Dissertations

Ens, Gerhard. "Kinship, Ethnicity, Class and the Red River Metis: The Parishes of St. Francois Xavier and St. Andrew's." PHD dissertation, University of Alberta, 1989.

Erickson, Lesley. "At the Cultural and Religious Crossroads: Sara Riel and the Grey Nuns in the Canadian Northwest, 1848–1883." MA thesis, University of Calgary, 1997.

Foran, Maxwell Laurence. "The Civic Corporation and Urban Growth: Calgary, 1884–1930." PHD dissertation, University of Calgary, 1981.

Forget, Simone. "Beauvais School: A Collected and Living History." M.ED. thesis, University of Lethbridge, 2003.

Foster, John Elgin. "The Country-Born in the Red River Settlement, 1820–50." PHD dissertation, University of Alberta, 1973.

Gordon, Stanley Bruce. "R.B. Bennett, M.L.A., 1897–1905: The Years of Apprenticeship." MA thesis, University of Calgary, 1975.

Herbert, Rachel. "Ranching Women in Southern Alberta, 1880–1930." MA thesis, University of Calgary, 2011.

Jetté, Melinda M. "Ordinary Lives: Three Generations of a French-Indian Family in Oregon, 1827–1931." MA thesis, Université Laval, 1996.

Kermoal, Nathalie J. "Le « Temps de Cayoge » : La Vie Quotidienne des Femmes Métisses au Manitoba de 1850 a 1900." Doctorate histoire, Université d'Ottawa, 1996.

MacKinnon, Doris J. "'I am alone in this world'—The Identities of Marie Rose Smith." MA thesis, University of Calgary, 2006.

MacKinnon, Doris Jeanne. "Métis Pioneers: Isabella Hardisty Lougheed and Marie Rose Delorme Smith." PHD dissertation, University of Calgary, 2012.

Moodie, Donald Wayne. "The St. Albert Settlement: A Study in Historical Geography." MA thesis, University of Alberta, 1965.

Pollard, Juliet. "The Making of the Metis in the Pacific Northwest Fur Trade Children: Race, Class, and Gender." PHD dissertation, University of British Columbia, 1990.

Wasylow, Walter J. "History of Battleford Industrial School for Indians." M.ED. thesis, University of Saskatchewan, 1972.

Published Primary Sources

Ahenakew, Edward. *Voices of the Plains Cree.* Edited by Ruth M. Buck. Toronto: McLelland and Stewart, 1973.

Atkins, Beryl, et al., eds. *Collins Robert French Dictionary.* Glasgow: HarperCollins Publishers, 1995.

Begg, Alexander. *The Creation of Manitoba; or a History of the Red River Trouble.* Toronto: A.H. Hovey, 1871.

——. *Red River Journal and Other Papers Relative to the Red River Resistance of 1869–1870.* Edited by W.L. Morton. New York: Greenwood Press, 1969.

Bompas, Charlotte Selina. *Owindia: A True Tale of the Mackenzie River Indians, North West America.* London: Wells Gardner, Darton, 1886.

Bone, P. Turner. *When the Steel Went Through: Reminiscences of a Railroad Pioneer.* Toronto: Macmillan, 1947.

Breland, Pascal. "To the Editor." *The Nor'Wester,* 28 September 1860.

Burtonshaw, Geoff. *Back in the Bush: The Life and Times of Geoff Burtonshaw.* Edited by Gerald T. Conaty. Calgary: Geoff Burtonshaw, 2010.

Cameron, Agnes Deans. *The New North: An Account of a Woman's 1908 Journey through Canada to the Arctic.* Saskatoon: Western Producer Prairie Books, 1986. First published 1909.

Cameron, William Bleasdell. "Ad McPherson, Old Timer of '69." *Canadian Cattlemen* 12, no. 3 (October 1949): 16–17.

——. "Ad McPherson, Oldtimer of '69." *Canadian Cattlemen* 12, no. 4 (November 1949): 8–9, 32–34.

——. *Blood Red the Sun.* Edmonton: Hurtig Publishers, 1977.

Campbell, Maria. *Half-Breed.* Halifax: Formac Publishing, 1973.

Censuses of the Red River Settlement: An Index to the Censuses for the Years 1827; 1828; 1829; 1830; 1831; 1832; 1835; 1838; 1840 and 1843. Pawtucket, RI: Quinton Publications, 1999.

Charette, Guillaume. *Vanishing Spaces: Memoirs of Louis Goulet.* Translated by Ray Ellenwood. Winnipeg: Éditions Bois-Brûlés, 1976.

Delorme, Urbain. "To the Editor." *The Nor'wester,* 14 June 1860.

Dion, Joseph F. *My Tribe the Crees.* Calgary: Glenbow–Alberta Institute, 1979.

Elliot and Brokovski. *Preliminary Investigation and Trial of Ambroise D. Lepine for the Murder of Thomas Scott, Being a full report of the proceedings in this case before the Magistrates' Court and the several Courts of Queen's Bench in the Province of Manitoba.* Montreal: Burland-Desbarats Co., 1875.

Ens, Gerhard J., ed. *A Son of the Fur Trade: The Memoirs of Johnny Grant.* Edmonton: University of Alberta Press, 2008.

Erasmus, Peter. *Buffalo Days and Nights.* Transcribed by Henry Thompson. Calgary: Fifth House Publishing, 1999.

Forsland, Eva. "Without Stripes." In *Red Serge Wives*, 138–141. Edmonton: Lone Pine Publishing, 1974.

Gladstone, William. *The Gladstone Diary: Travels in the Early West*. Edited by Bruce Haig. Lethbridge: Historic Trails Society of Alberta, 1985.

Griesbach, William Antrobus. *I Remember by W.A. Griesbach*. Toronto: Ryerson Press, 1946.

Healy, William J. *Women of Red River: Being a book written from the recollections of women surviving from the Red River era*. Winnipeg: The Women's Canadian Club, 1923.

Johnson, Pauline. *Legends of Vancouver*. 8th ed. Vancouver: Saturday Sunset Presses, 1913.

Kerby, George W. *The Broken Trail: Pages from a Pastor's Experience in Western Canada*. Toronto: W. Briggs, 1910.

Kerr, John. "Hunting Bison on the Plains." *Winnipeg Tribune Magazine*, 23 June 1934, 1–3.

Laverdure, Paul, Jacqueline Moir, and John S. Moir, eds. *Travels around Great Slave and Great Bear Lakes, 1862–1882*. Toronto: The Champlain Society, 2005.

Lynch-Staunton, Emma. "Eighty Years on the Plains: The Story of Mrs. Charles Smith, Pincher Creek." *The Lethbridge Herald*, 14 November 1941.

McDougall, John. *In the Days of the Red River Rebellion*. Edmonton: University of Alberta Press, 1983. First published 1903.

Miller, Jay, ed. *Mourning Dove: A Salishan Autobiography*. Lincoln: University of Nebraska Press, 1994.

Morin, Gail. *Metis Families: A Genealogical Compendium, Volume 2 Dahl to Gunn*. Pawtucket, RI: Quinton Publications, 2001.

Mosionier, Beatrice. *Come Walk with Me: A Memoir*. Winnipeg: Highwater Press, 2009.

Munnick, Harriet Duncan. *Catholic Church Records of the Pacific Northwest: St. Paul, Oregon 1839–1898*. Portland, OR: Binford & Mort, 1979.

Pritchard, John. "Letter to the Editor." *The Toronto Daily Mail*, 8 August 1885.

Ross, Alexander. "The Red River Buffalo Hunt from Red River Settlement." *Manitoba Pageant* 5, no. 2 (1960): 1–5.

Smith, Marie Rose. "Eighty Years on the Plains." *Canadian Cattlemen* 11, no. 1 (June 1948): 1; 30–31; 34.

——. "Eighty Years on the Plains." *Canadian Cattlemen* 11, no. 2 (September 1948): 72–73; 76–77.

——. "Eighty Years on the Plains." *Canadian Cattlemen* 11, no. 3 (December 1948): 144–145; 148–149.

——. "Eighty Years on the Plains." *Canadian Cattlemen* 11, no. 4 (March 1949): 212–225.

——. "Eighty Years on the Plains." *Canadian Cattlemen* 12, no. 1 (June 1949): 12–13; 40–41.

——. "Eighty Years on the Plains." *Canadian Cattlemen* 12, no. 2 (September 1949): 16–17; 36–37.

——. "Eighty Years on the Plains." *Canadian Cattlemen* 12, no. 3 (October 1949): 15; 18–19.

——. "Eighty Years on the Plains." *Canadian Cattlemen* 12, no. 4 (November 1949): 15; 18–19.

——. "Eighty Years on the Plains." *Canadian Cattlemen* 12, no. 5 (December 1949): 4–5; 49–50.

Stanley, George F.G., ed. *The Collected Writings of Louis Riel.* Vols. 1–5. Edmonton: University of Alberta Press, 1985.

Steele, Samuel Benfield. *Forty Years in Canada: Reminiscences of the Great North West, with Some Account of His Service in South Africa.* New York: Dodd Mead, 1913. Reprint, Toronto: Coles Publishing Company, 1973.

Strong-Boag, Veronica. *The Parliament of Women: The National Council of Women of Canada, 1893–1929.* Ottawa: National Museums of Canada, 1976.

Tyman, James. *Inside Out: An Autobiography of a Native Canadian.* Calgary: Fifth House Publishers, 1989.

United States. Work Projects Administration, Washington State. *Told by the Pioneers.* Vol. 1. Olympia, WA: n.p., 1937–1938.

Warner, Mikell De Lores Wormell. *Catholic Church Records of the Pacific Northwest: Vancouver Volumes I and II and Stellamaris Mission.* Translated by Harriet Duncan Munnick. St. Paul, OR: French Prairie Press, 1972.

Weekes, Mary. As told to her by Norbert Welsh. *The Last Buffalo Hunter.* Toronto: Macmillan Company, 1945. Reprint, Calgary: Fifth House Publishers, 1994.

Wilson, Clifford, ed. *Papers Read before the Historical and Scientific Society of Manitoba: Private Letters from the Fur Trade.* Winnipeg: Advocate Printers Ltd., 1950.

SECONDARY SOURCES

Books

Abel, Kerry. *Drum Songs: Glimpses of Dene History.* Montreal: McGill-Queen's University Press, 1993.

Adam, Graeme Mercer. *Prominent Men of Canada: A Collection of Persons Distinguished in Professional and Political Life, and in the Commerce and Industry of Canada.* Toronto: Canadian Biographical Publishing Co., 1892.

Adams, Christopher, Gregg Dahl, and Ian Peach. *Métis in Canada: History, Identity, Law & Politics.* Edmonton: University of Alberta Press, 2013.

Albers, Patricia, and Beatrice Medicine, eds. *The Hidden Half: Studies of Plains Indian Women.* Lanham, MD: University Press of America Inc., 1983.

Alberta Genealogical Society. Edmonton Branch. *Index to the 1901 Census District of Alberta* (No. 202). Edmonton: Alberta Genealogical Society, 1999.

Ambrose, Linda M. *For Home and Country: The Centennial History of the Women's Institutes in Ontario.* Guelph, ON: Federated Women's Institutes of Ontario, 1996.

Anderson, Chris. *"Métis": Race, Recognition, and the Struggle for Indigenous Peoplehood.* Vancouver: UBC Press, 2014.

Anderson, Mary. *The Life Writings of Mary Baker Mcquesten: Victorian Matriarch.* Waterloo, ON: Wilfrid Laurier University Press, 2004.

Backhouse, Constance. *Colour Coded: A Legal History of Racism in Canada, 1900–1950.* Toronto: University of Toronto Press, 1999.

——. *Petticoats and Prejudice: Women and Law in Nineteenth-Century Canada.* Toronto: The Osgoode Society, 1991.

Baergen, William Peter. *The Ku Klux Klan in Central Alberta.* Red Deer: Central Alberta Historical Society, 2000.

Bakker, Peter. *A Language of Our Own: The Genesis of Michif, the Mixed Cree-French Language of the Canadian Métis.* New York: Oxford University Press, 1997.

Barkwell, Lawrence J., Leah Dorion, and Darren R. Préfontaine, eds. *Metis Legacy: A Metis Historiography and Annotated Bibliography.* Winnipeg: Pemmican Publications Inc., 2001.

Barman, Jean. *French Canadians, Furs and, Indigenous Women in the Making of the Pacific Northwest.* Vancouver: UBC Press, 2014.

——. *Maria Mahoi of the Islands.* Vancouver: New Star Books Ltd., 2004.

——. *Sojourning Sisters: The Lives and Letters of Jessie and Annie McQueen.* Toronto: University of Toronto Press, 2003.

Barman, Jean, and Bruce McIntyre Watson. *Leaving Paradise: Indigenous Hawaiians in the Pacific Northwest, 1787–1898.* Honolulu: University of Hawai'i Press, 2006.

Barnholden, Michael, trans. *Gabriel Dumont Speaks.* Vancouver: Talonbooks, 1993.

Barron, F. Laurie, and James B. Waldram, eds. *1885 and After: Native Society in Transition.* Regina: Canadian Plains Research Center, 1986.

Beal, Bob. *Prairie Fire: The 1885 North-West Rebellion.* Toronto: McClelland & Stewart, 1994.

Beattie, Judith Hudson, and Helen M. Buss, eds. *Undelivered Letters to Hudson's Bay Company Men on the Northwest Coast of America, 1830–1857.* Vancouver: UBC Press, 2003.

Berger, Carl. *The Sense of Power: Studies in the Ideas of Canadian Imperialism, 1867–1914.* Toronto: University of Toronto Press, 1970.

Binnema, Theodore, Gerhard Ens, and R.C. MacLeod, eds. *From Rupert's Land to Canada.* Edmonton: University of Alberta Press, 2001.

Bougnet, Georges. *Nipsya*. Translated by Constance Davies Woodrow. New York: L. Carrier & Company, 1929.

Boutilier, Beverly, and Alison Prentice, eds. *Creating Historical Memory: English Canadian Women and the Work of History*. Vancouver: UBC Press, 1997.

Braroe, Neils Winther. *Indian & White: Self-Image and Interaction in a Canadian Plains Community*. Stanford, CA: Stanford University Press, 1975.

Breen, David H., and R.C. Macleod, eds. *William Stewart Herron: Father of the Petroleum Industry in Alberta*. Calgary: Alberta Records Publication Board, 1984.

Brennan, Brian. *Building a Province: 60 Alberta Lives*. Calgary: Fifth House Publishing, 2000.

Brown, Jennifer. *Strangers in Blood: Fur Trade Company Families in Indian Country*. Vancouver: UBC Press, 1980.

Brownlie, Robin Jarvis, and Valerie J. Korinek, eds. *Finding a Way to the Heart: Feminist Writings on Aboriginal and Women's History in Canada*. Winnipeg: University of Manitoba Press, 2012.

Bumsted, J.M. *Lord Selkirk: A Life*. Winnipeg: University of Manitoba Press, 2008.

——. *Louis Riel v. Canada: The Making of a Rebel*. Winnipeg: Great Plains Publications, 2001.

Burley, Edith I. *Servants of the Honourable Company: Work Discipline and Conflict in the Hudson's Bay Company, 1779–1879*. Toronto: Oxford University Press, 1997.

Burns, Thomas S., and George B. Elliot, eds. *Calgary, Alberta, Canada: Her Industries and Resources*. Calgary: Glenbow Museum, 1974.

Byfield, Ted, ed. *The Boom and the Bust*. Edmonton: United Western Communications Ltd., 1994.

——. *The Great War and Its Consequences*. Edmonton: United Western Communications, 1994.

Cameron, Duncan, ed. *Explorations in Canadian Economic History: Essays in Honour of Irene M. Spry*. Ottawa: University of Ottawa Press, 1985.

Camsell, Charles. *Son of the North*. Toronto: Ryerson Press, 1954.

Carpenter, Jock. *The Bootlegger's Bride*. Calgary: Gorman Publishers Ltd., 1993.

——. *Fifty Dollar Bride—Marie Rose Smith: A Chronicle of Métis Life in the 19th Century*. Sidney, BC: Gray's Publishing, 1977.

Carter, Sarah. *Aboriginal People and Colonizers of Western Canada to 1900*. Toronto: University of Toronto Press, 1999.

——. *Capturing Women: The Manipulation of Cultural Imagery in Canada's Prairie West*. Montreal: McGill-Queen's University Press, 1997.

——. *The Importance of Being Monogamous: Marriage and Nation Building in Western Canada to 1915*. Edmonton: University of Alberta Press, 2008.

———. *Lost Harvests: Prairie Indian Reserve Farmers and Government Policy*. Montreal: McGill-Queen's University Press, 1990.

Carter, Sarah, and Patricia A. McCormack, eds. *Recollecting: Lives of Aboriginal Women of the Canadian Northwest and Borderlands*. Edmonton: Athabasca University Press, 2011.

Cavanaugh, Catherine A., and Randi R. Warne, eds. *Standing on New Ground: Women in Alberta*. Edmonton: University of Alberta Press, 1993.

———. *Telling Tales: Essays in Western Women's History*. Vancouver: UBC Press, 2000.

Centenary United Church. *Centenary United Church of the United Church of Canada Photo Directory 2001*. Hamilton, ON: Centenary United Church, 2001.

Chan, Sucheng, Douglas Henry Daniels, Mario T. Garcia, and Terry P. Wilson, eds. *Peoples of Color in the American West*. Lexington, VA: D.C. Heath and Company, 1994.

Chartrand, Paul L.A.H., ed. *Who Are Canada's Aboriginal People? Recognition, Definition, and Jurisdiction*. Saskatoon: Purich Publishing, 2002.

Cohen, Marjorie Griffin. *Women's Work: Markets and Economic Development in Nineteenth-Century Ontario*. Toronto: University of Toronto Press, 1988.

Cole, Jean Lee. *The Literary Voices of Winnifred Eaton: Redefining Ethnicity and Authenticity*. New Brunswick, NJ: Rutgers University Press, 2002.

Cook-Bobrovitz, Jennifer, and Trudy Cowan. *Lougheed House: More Than a Century of Stories*. Calgary: Lougheed House, 2006.

Coppes-Zantinga, Arty, and Ian Mitchell. *The Child in the Centre: Seventy-Five Years at the Alberta Children's Hospital*. Calgary: University of Calgary Press, 1997.

Cott, Nancy F. *Public Vows: A History of Marriage and the Nation*. Cambridge, MA: Harvard University Press, 2000.

Coutts, George Ballantine. *The Ranchmen's Club: A Short Historical Sketch, 1891–1952*. Calgary: Calgary Ranchmen's Club, 1953.

Cruikshank, Julie. *Life Lived like a Story*. Lincoln: University of Nebraska Press, 1990.

Culin, Stewart. *Games of the North American Indians—Volume 1: Games of Chance*. Lincoln: University of Nebraska Press, 1992.

Cunniffe, Richard. *Calgary in Sandstone*. Calgary: Historical Society of Alberta, Calgary Branch, 1969.

Daschuk, James. *Clearing the Plains: Disease, Politics of Starvation, and the Loss of Aboriginal Life*. Regina: University of Regina Press, 2013.

Demos, John. *The Unredeemed Captive: A Family Story from Early America*. New York: Alfred A. Knopf, 1994.

Dempsey, Hugh A. *Firewater: The Impact of the Whiskey Trade on the Blackfoot Nation*. Calgary: Fifth House Publications, 2002.

Dempsey, Hugh A., ed. *The Best from Alberta History*. Saskatoon: Western Producer Prairie Books, 1981.

——. *The Wit and Wisdom of Bob Edwards*. Edmonton: Hurtig, 1976.

Den Otter, A.A. *Civilizing the Wilderness: Culture and Nature in Pre-Confederation Canada and Rupert's Land*. Edmonton: University of Alberta Press, 2012.

Devine, Heather. *The People Who Own Themselves: Aboriginal Ethnogenesis in a Canadian Family, 1660–1900*. Calgary: University of Calgary Press, 2004.

Dickason, Olive Patricia. *Canada's First Nations: A History of Founding Peoples from Earliest Times*. 3rd ed. Don Mills, ON: Oxford University Press, 2002.

Dictionary of Hamilton Biography, Volume III: 1925–1939. Hamilton, ON: Dictionary of Hamilton Biography, 1981.

Dobbin, Murray. *The One-and-a-Half Men: The Story of Jim Brady and Malcolm Norris, Metis Patriots of the Twentieth Century*. Vancouver: New Star Books, 1981.

Dye, Eva Emery. *McDonald of Oregon: A Tale of Two Shores*. Chicago: A.C. McClurg & Co., 1906.

——. *McLoughlin and Old Oregon: A Chronicle*. Portland, OR: Binfords & Mort Publishers, 1936.

Eakin, Paul John, ed. *The Ethics of Life Writing*. Ithaca, NY: Cornell University Press, 2004.

Elias, Peter Douglas. *The Dakota of the Canadian Northwest: Lessons for Survival*. Winnipeg: University of Manitoba Press, 1988.

Elofson, Warren M. *Cowboys, Gentlemen, and Cattle Thieves*. Montreal: McGill-Queen's University Press, 2000.

——. *Frontier Cattle Ranching in the Land and Times of Charlie Russell*. Montreal: McGill-Queen's University Press, 2004.

English, John. *The Conservatives and the Party System, 1901–1920*. Toronto: University of Toronto Press, 1977.

——. *Just Watch Me: The Life of Pierre Elliott Trudeau, 1968–2000*. Toronto: Alfred A. Knopf Canada, 2009.

Ens, Gerhard J. *Homeland to Hinterland: The Changing Worlds of the Red River Metis in the Nineteenth Century*. Toronto: University of Toronto Press, 1996.

Ens, Gerhard, and Joe Sawchuk. *New Peoples to New Nations: Aspects of Métis History and Identity from the Eighteenth to Twenty-First Centuries*. Toronto: University of Toronto Press, 2016.

Epp, Marlene, Franca Iacovetta, and Frances Swyripa, eds. *Sisters or Strangers? Immigrant, Ethnic, and Racialized Women in Canadian History*. Toronto: University of Toronto Press, 2004.

Evans, Sterling, ed. *The Borderlands of the American and Canadian Wests*. Lincoln: University of Nebraska Press, 2006.

Fisher, Robin. *Contact and Conflict: Indian–European Relations in British Columbia, 1774–1890*. Vancouver: UBC Press, 1992.

Flanagan, Thomas, ed. *The Diaries of Louis Riel*. Edmonton: Hurtig Publishers, 1976.

Foran, Max. *The History of Canadian Cities: Calgary, an Illustrated History*. Toronto: James Lorimer & Company, 1978.

Foran, Max, and Sheilagh S. Jamieson, eds. *Citymakers: Calgarians after the Frontier*. Calgary: Historical Society of Alberta, 1987.

Foster, Franklin. *John E. Brownlee: A Biography*. Lloydminster, AB: Foster Learning Inc., 1996.

Foster, Martha Harroun. *We Know Who We Are: Metis Identity in a Montana Community*. Norman: University of Oklahoma Press, 2006.

Fowke, Edith, ed. *The Penguin Book of Canadian Folk Songs*. Markham, ON: Penguin Books Canada, 1986.

French, Maida Parlow. *Kathleen Parlow: A Portrait*. Toronto: Ryerson Press, 1967.

Friesen, Gerald. *The Canadian Prairies: A History*. Toronto: University of Toronto Press, 1984.

——. *Citizens and Nations: An Essay on History, Communication and Canada*. Toronto: University of Toronto Press, 2000.

——. *River Road: Essays on Manitoba and Prairie History*. Winnipeg: University of Manitoba Press, 1996.

Gaetz, Annie L. *The Park Country: History of Red Deer (Alberta) and District*. Red Deer: self-published, 1960. First published 1948.

——. *Trails of Yesterday: Folklore of the Red Deer District*. Red Deer: self-published, 1952.

Gagan, Rosemary R. *A Sensitive Independence: Canadian Methodist Women Missionaries in Canada and the Orient, 1881–1925*. Montreal and Kingston: McGill-Queen's University Press, 1992.

Gardner, Don. NWMP *Police Outposts of Southern Alberta, 1874–1904: A Report in Four Volumes Compiled for Alberta-RCMP Century Committee*. Vol. 2. 1975.

Garroutte, Eva Marie. *Real Indians: Identity and the Survival of Native America*. Berkeley: University of California Press, 2003.

Getty, Ian, and Donald B. Smith, eds. *One Century Later: Western Canadian Reserve Indians since Treaty 7*. Vancouver: UBC Press, 1978.

Gibbon, John Murray. *The Victorian Order of Nurses for Canada: Fiftieth Anniversary, 1897–1947*. Montreal: Southam Press, 1947.

Giraud, Marcel. *The Métis in the Canadian West*. Translated by George Woodcock. Edmonton: University of Alberta Press, 1986. First published 1945.

Gleason, Mona, and Adele Perry, eds. *Rethinking Canada: The Promise of Women's History*. Toronto: Oxford University Press, 2006.

Godfrey, Rupert, ed. *Letters from a Prince, Edward, Prince of Wales to Mrs. Freda Dudley Ward, March 1918–January 1921*. London: Brown and Company, 1998.

Gray, James H. *Booze: The Impact of Whisky on the Prairie West*. Toronto: Macmillan of Canada, 1972.

——. *R.B. Bennett: The Calgary Years*. Toronto: University of Toronto Press, 1991.

——. *The Roar of the Twenties*. Toronto: Macmillan of Canada, 1975.

——. *Talk to My Lawyer: Great Stories of Southern Alberta's Bar and Bench*. Edmonton: Hurtig Publishing, 1987.

Grayson, Linda M., and Michael Bliss, eds. *The Wretched of Canada: Letters to R.B. Bennett, 1930–1935*. Toronto: University of Toronto Press, 1971.

Green, Joyce, ed. *Making Space for Indigenous Feminism*. Black Point, NS: Fernwood Publishing, 2007.

Greer, Allan. *The People of New France*. Toronto: University of Toronto Press, 1997.

Greer, Allan, and Ian Radforth, eds. *Colonial Leviathan: State Formation in Mid-Nineteenth-Century Canada*. Toronto: University of Toronto Press, 1992.

Griffiths, Naomi E.S. *The Splendid Vision: Centennial History of the National Council of Women of Canada, 1893–1993*. Ottawa: Carleton University Press, 1993.

Hamilton, Zachary MacCaulay, and Marie Albina Hamilton. *These Are the Prairies: Saskatchewan Jubilee Edition 1905–1955*. Regina: School Aids and Text Book Publishing Co. Ltd., 1948.

Harper, J. Russell, ed. *Paul Kane's Frontier: Including Wanderings of an Artist among the Indians of North America*. Toronto: University of Toronto Press, 1971.

Hartz, Louis. *The Founding of New Societies*. New York: Harcourt, Brace & World Inc., 1964.

Hayes, Alan L. *Holding Forth the Word of Life: Little Trinity Church, 1842–1992*. Toronto: Corporation of Little Trinity Church, 1991.

Healey, William J. *Women of Red River: Being a Book Written from the Recollections of Women Surviving the Red River Era*. Winnipeg: Women's Canadian Club, 1967.

Henley, Brian. *The Grand Old Buildings of Hamilton*. Hamilton, ON: The Spectator, 1994.

Hesketh, Bob, and Frances Swyripa, eds. *Edmonton: The Life of a City*. Edmonton: NeWest Press, 1995.

Higham, Carol L. *Noble, Wretched, and Redeemable: Protestant Missionaries to the Indians in Canada and the United States, 1820–1900*. Calgary: University of Calgary Press, 2000.

Hogue, Michel. *Metis and the Medicine Line: Creating a Border and Dividing a People*. Chapel Hill: University of North Carolina Press, 2015.

Houghton, Louise Seymour. *Our Debt to the Red Man: The French-Indians in the Development of the United States*. Boston: The Stratford Company, 1918.

Howard, Joseph Kinsey. *Strange Empire: Louis Riel and the Métis People*. Toronto: James
Lewis and Samuel, 1974. First published 1952.

Howse, Jennifer. *The Métis*. Calgary: Weigl Educational Publishers, 2008.

Huel, Raymond J.A. *Proclaiming the Gospel to the Indians and the Métis: The Missionary
Oblates of Mary Immaculate in Western Canada, 1845–1945*. Edmonton: University of
Alberta Press, 1996.

Hughes, Katherine. *Father Lacombe: The Black-Robe Voyageur*. Toronto: William Briggs,
1911.

Hustak, Allan. *Peter Lougheed: A Biography*. Toronto: McClelland & Stewart, 1979.

Innis, Harold. *The Fur Trade in Canada: An Introduction to Canadian Economic History*.
Toronto: University of Toronto Press, 1999. First published 1930.

Jameson, Elizabeth, and Sheila McManus, eds. *One Step Over the Line: Toward a History
of Women in the North American Wests*. Edmonton: University of Alberta Press;
Athabasca: Athabasca University Press, 2008.

Janes, Robert R. *Preserving Diversity: Ethnoarchaeological Perspectives on Culture Change in
the Western Canadian Subarctic*. New York: Garland Publishing, 1991.

Jenness, Diamond, ed. *The American Aborigines: Their Origin and Antiquity*. New York:
Russell & Russell, 1933.

——. *The Indians of Canada*. Ottawa: Ministry of Supply and Services, 1977. First
published 1932.

Jennings Publishing Company. *Merchants' and Manufacturers' Record: Calgary, Sunny
Alberta, the Industrial Capital of the Great West*. Calgary: Jennings Publishing Co.,
1911.

Jones, David C. *Empire of Dust: Settling and Abandoning the Prairie Dry Belt*. Calgary:
University of Calgary Press, 2002.

Judd, Carol M., and Arthur J. Ray, eds. *Old Trails and New Directions: Papers of the Third
North American Fur Trade Conference*. Toronto: University of Toronto Press, 1980.

Kealey, Linda. *Enlisting for the Cause: Women, Labour and the Left in Canada, 1890–1920*.
Toronto: University of Toronto Press, 1998.

Kells, Edna. *Elizabeth Mcdougall, Pioneer*. Toronto: United Church Publishing House,
1934.

Kermoal, Nathalie. *Un passé métis au féminin*. Québec: Les Éditions GID, 2006.

Kermoal, Nathalie, and Isabel Altamirano-Jiménez, eds. *Living on the Land: Indigenous
Women's Understanding of Place*. Edmonton: Athabasca University Press, 2016.

Klassen, Henry Cornelius. *Eye on the Future: Business People in Calgary and the Bow Valley,
1870–1900*. Calgary: University of Calgary Press, 2002.

La Société historique de Saint-Boniface. *Histoire de Saint-Boniface: Tome 1 A l'ombre des
cathédrales des origines de la colonie jusqu'en 1870*. Saint-Boniface, MB: La Société
historique de Saint-Boniface, 1991.

Langford, Nanci. *Politics, Pitchforks and Pickle Jars: 75 Years of Organized Farm Women in Alberta.* Calgary: Detselig Enterprises, 1997.

Langworth, Richard, ed. *Churchill by Himself: The Definitive Collection of Quotations.* New York: PublicAffairs, 2011.

Lape, Noreen Grover. *West of the Border: The Multicultural Literature of the Western American Frontiers.* Athens: Ohio University Press, 2000.

LaRocque, Emma. *Defeathering the Indian.* Agincourt (Toronto), ON: The Book Society of Canada, 1975.

Laslett, Peter. *The World We Have Lost.* New York: Charles Scribner's Sons, 1984.

Law Society of Alberta. *Just Works: Lawyers in Alberta, 1907–2007.* Toronto: Irwin Law Inc., 2007.

Lawrence, Bonita. *"Real" Indians and Others: Mixed-Blood Urban Native Peoples and Indigenous Nationhood.* Vancouver: UBC Press, 2004.

Lee, Mary Madeline (Bobby). *The New Nation: Christ's Chosen People.* Calgary: self-published, 1987.

Leslie, Jean. *Glimpses of Calgary Past.* Calgary: Detselig Enterprises Ltd., 1994.

Lewis, Oscar. *Anthropological Essays.* New York: Random House, 1970.

Lindsay, Debra, ed. *The Modern Beginnings of Subarctic Ornithology: Correspondence to the Smithsonian Institute, 1856–1868.* Winnipeg: Manitoba Record Society, 1991.

Lischke, Ute, and David McNab, eds. *The Long Journey of a Forgotten People: Métis Identities and Family Histories.* Waterloo, ON: Wilfred Laurier University Press, 2007.

Lussier, A.S., ed. *Riel and the Metis: Riel Mini-Conference Papers.* Winnipeg: Manitoba Métis Federation Press, 1979.

Lutz, Hartmut. *Contemporary Challenges: Conversations with Canadian Native Authors.* Saskatoon: Fifth House Publishers, 1991.

Lux, Maureen K. *Medicine That Walks: Disease, Medicine, and Canadian Plains Native People, 1880–1940.* Toronto: University of Toronto Press, 2001.

MacDonald, George Heath. *Edmonton: Fort, House, Factory.* Edmonton: Douglas Print Company, 1959.

Macdougall, Brenda. *One of the Family: Metis Culture in Nineteenth-Century Northwestern Saskatchewan.* Vancouver: UBC Press, 2009.

MacEwan, Grant. *Calgary Cavalcade: From Fort to Fortune.* Saskatoon: Western Producer Prairie Books, 1975. First published 1958.

——. *Eye Opener Bob: The Story of Bob Edwards.* Edmonton: Institute of Applied Art, 1957.

——. *He Left Them Laughing When He Said Goodbye: The Life and Times of Frontier Lawyer Paddy Nolan.* Saskatoon: Western Producer Prairie Books, 1987.

———. *Mighty Women: Stories of Western Canadian Pioneers.* Vancouver: Douglas & McIntyre, 1995. First published 1975.

MacGregor, James Grierson. *Senator Hardisty's Prairies, 1849–1889.* Saskatoon: Western Producer Prairie Books, 1978.

MacKellar, Maggie. *Core of My Heart, My Country.* Melbourne, Australia: Melbourne University Press, 2004.

Mackie, Richard Somerset. *Trading beyond the Mountains: The British Fur Trade on the Pacific, 1793–1843.* Vancouver: UBC Press, 1997.

MacKinnon, Doris J. *The Identities of Marie Rose Delorme Smith: Portrait of a Métis Woman, 1861–1960.* Regina: University of Regina Press, Canadian Plains Research Center, 2012.

MacLaren, Sherrill. *Braehead: Three Founding Families in Nineteenth Century Canada.* Toronto: McClelland & Stewart, 1986.

MacLean, Andrew Dyas. *R.B. Bennett: Prime Minister of Canada.* Toronto: Excelsior Publishing Co., 1934.

Maclean, John. *McDougall of Alberta.* Toronto: Ryerson Press, 1927.

MacLeod, Margaret, and W.L. Morton, eds. *Cuthbert Grant of Grantown: Warden of the Plains of Red River.* Toronto: McClelland & Stewart, 1974.

MacMillan, Hugh P. *Adventures of a Paper Sleuth.* Toronto: Penumbra Press, 2004.

Macpherson, C.B. *Democracy in Alberta: Social Credit and the Party System.* Toronto: University of Toronto Press, 1953.

MacRae, Archibald Oswald. *History of the Province of Alberta.* Vol. II. N.p.: Western Canadian History Co., 1912.

Marks, Lynne. *Revivals and Roller Rinks: Religion, Leisure and Identity in Late 19th Century Small Town Ontario.* Toronto: University of Toronto Press, 1996.

McCarthy, Martha. *From the Great River to the Ends of the Earth: Oblate Missions to the Dene, 1847–1921.* Edmonton: University of Alberta Press, 1995.

McDonald, Donna. *Lord Strathcona: A Biography of Donald Alexander Smith.* Toronto: Dundurn Press, 1996.

McKillop, A.B., ed. *Contexts of Canada's Past: Selected Essays of W.L. Morton.* Toronto: Macmillan Company of Canada, 1980.

McManus, Sheila. *The Line Which Separates: Race, Gender, and the Making of the Alberta-Montana Borderlands.* Lincoln: University of Nebraska Press, 2005.

McMillan, Alan D. *Peoples and Cultures of Canada: An Anthropological Overview.* Vancouver: Douglas & McIntyre, 1995.

McNeill, Leishman. *Tales of the Old Town.* Calgary: Calgary Herald, 1950.

Meaney, Edmond S. *Origin of Washington Geographical Names.* Seattle: University of Washington Press, 1923.

Meeres, Edwin L. *The Homesteads That Nurtured a City: The History of Red Deer, 1880–1905.* Red Deer: Fletcher Printing Company, 1984.

Melnyk, George. *The Literary History of Alberta: Volume One from Writing-on-Stone to World War Two.* Edmonton: University of Alberta Press, 1998.

——. *Riel to Reform: A History of Protest in Western Canada.* Saskatoon: Fifth House Publishers, 1992.

Metis Heritage Association of the Northwest Territories. *Picking Up the Threads: Métis History in the Mackenzie Basin.* Winnipeg: Metis Heritage Association of the Northwest Territories and Parks Canada–Canadian Heritage, 1998.

Meyer, George, Bill Holmes, and Don Tanner, eds. *The Best of Times: The War Years, 1912–1918.* Calgary: Century Books, 2001.

Meyers, Melissa L. *The White Earth Tragedy: Ethnicity and Dispossession at a Minnesota Anishinaabe Reservation, 1889–1920.* Lincoln: University of Nebraska Press, 1994.

Mitchell, Estelle. *The Grey Nuns of Montreal and the Red River Settlement: 1844–1984.* Translated by J.F. O'Sullivan and Sister Cecile Rioux. Montreal: Grey Nuns of Montreal, 1986.

Mittlestadt, David. *Foundations of Justice: Alberta's Historic Courthouses.* Calgary: University of Calgary Press, 2005.

Morgan, Henry James. *The Canadian Men and Women of the Time.* 2nd ed. Toronto: Briggs, 1912. First published 1898.

——. *Types of Canadian Women and of Women Who Are or Have Been Connected with Canada.* Toronto: William Briggs, 1903.

Morton, Arthur S. *A History of the Canadian West to 1870–71.* Toronto: University of Toronto Press, 1973. First published 1939.

Morton, Desmond. *Winning the Second Battle: Canadian Veterans and the Return to Civilian Life, 1915–1930.* Toronto: University of Toronto Press, 1987.

Morton, Desmond, ed. *The Queen v Louis Riel.* Toronto: University of Toronto Press, 1974.

Morton, W.L., ed. *Alexander Begg's Red River Journal and Other Papers Relative to the Red River Resistance of 1869–1870.* Toronto: The Champlain Society, 1956.

Mountain Horse, Mike. *My People the Bloods.* Edited by Hugh Dempsey. Calgary: Glenbow-Alberta Institute, 1979.

Munro, K. Douglas, ed. *Fur Trade Letters of Willie Traill, 1864–1894.* Edmonton: University of Alberta Press, 2006.

Murphy, Lucy Eldersveld. *A Gathering of Rivers: Indians, Métis and Mining in the Western Great Lakes, 1727–1832.* Lincoln: University of Nebraska Press, 2004.

Nelles, H.V. *The Art of Nation-Building: Pageantry and Spectacle at Quebec's Tercentenary.* Toronto: University of Toronto Press, 1999.

Norris, Marjorie. *A Leaven of Ladies: A History of the Calgary Local Council of Women.* Calgary: Detselig Enterprises Ltd., 1995.

Owens, Louis. *Mixedblood Messages: Literature, Film, Family, Place.* Norman: University of Oklahoma Press, 1998.

Owram, Douglas R. *Promise of Eden: The Canadian Expansionist Movement and the Idea of the West, 1856–1900.* Toronto: University of Toronto Press, 1992.

Owram, Douglas R., ed. *The Formation of Alberta: A Documentary History.* Edmonton: Historical Society of Alberta, 1979.

Palmer, Howard, and Tamara Palmer. *Alberta: A New History.* Edmonton: Hurtig Publishers, 1990.

Palmer, Howard, and Tamara Palmer, eds. *Peoples of Alberta: Portraits of Cultural Diversity.* Saskatoon: Western Producer Prairie Books, 1985.

Pannekoek, Frits. *A Snug Little Flock: The Social Origins of the Riel Resistance of 1869–70.* Winnipeg: Watson & Dwyer, 1991.

Parr, Joy. *Domestic Goods: The Material, the Moral, and the Economic in the Post War Years.* Toronto: University of Toronto Press, 1999.

——. *The Gender of Breadwinners: Women, Men and Change in Two Industrial Towns, 1880–1950.* Toronto: University of Toronto Press, 1990.

Patterson, Ida Smith, ed. *Montana Memories: The Life of Emma Magee in the Rocky Mountain West, 1866–1950.* Pablo, MT: Salish Kootenai Community College, 1981.

Payment, Diane. *The Free People—Li Gens Libres: A History of the Métis Community of Batoche, Saskatchewan.* Calgary: University of Calgary Press, 2009.

——. *"The Free People—Otipemisiwak": Batoche, Saskatchewan 1870–1930.* Ottawa: Minister of Supply and Services Canada, 1990.

Payne, Michael. *The Most Respectable Place in the Territory: Everyday Life in Hudson's Bay Company Service, York Factory 1788–1870.* Ottawa: National Historic Parks and Sights, Environment Canada, 1989.

Payne, Michael, Donald Wetherell, and Catherine Cavanaugh, eds. *Alberta Formed, Alberta Transformed.* Vol. 1. Calgary: University of Calgary Press, 2006.

Peers, Laura. *The Ojibwa of Western Canada: 1780–1870.* Winnipeg: University of Manitoba Press, 1994.

Perdue, Theda, ed. *Sifters: Native American Women's Lives.* New York: Oxford University Press, 2001.

Perreault, Jeanne, and Sylvia Vance, eds. *Writing the Circle: Native Women of Western Canada.* Edmonton: NeWest Press, 1990.

Perry, Adele. *On the Edge of Empire: Gender, Race and the Making of British Columbia, 1849–1871.* Toronto: University of Toronto Press, 2001.

Perry, J. Fraser, ed. *They Gathered at the River.* Calgary: Central United Church, 1975.

Peterson, Jacqueline, and Jennifer S.H. Brown, eds. *The New Peoples: Being and Becoming Métis in North America*. Winnipeg: University of Manitoba Press, 1985.

Petrone, Penny, ed. *First People, First Voices*. Toronto: University of Toronto Press, 1983.

Pickles, Katie. *Female Imperialism and National Identity: Imperial Order Daughters of the Empire*. Manchester: Manchester University Press, 2002.

Pickles, Katie, and Myra Rutherdale, eds. *Contact Zones: Aboriginal & Settler Women in Canada's Colonial Past*. Vancouver: UBC Press, 2005.

Pincher Creek Historical Society. *A History of Pincher Creek Ranches and the People Involved*. Pincher Creek, AB: Pincher Creek Historical Society, n.d.

——. *Prairie Grass to Mountain Pass: History of the Pioneers of Pincher Creek District*. Pincher Creek, AB: Pincher Creek Historical Society, 1981.

Podruchny, Carolyn. *Making the Voyageur World: Travellers and Traders in the North American Fur Trade*. Toronto: University of Toronto Press, 2006.

Pratt, Larry, and John Richards. *Prairie Capitalism: Power and Influence in the New West*. Toronto: McClelland & Stewart, 1979.

Prentice, Alison, Paula Bourne, Gail Cuthbert Brandt, Beth Light, Wendy Mitchinson, and Naomi Black, eds. *Canadian Women: A History*. 2nd ed. Toronto: Harcourt Brace & Company, 1996.

Preston, Richard J. *Cree Narrative: Expressing the Personal Meanings of Events*. Montreal: McGill-Queen's University Press, 2002.

Racette, Sherry Farrell. *Aboriginal Cultures and Perspectives: Making a Difference in the Classroom*. Saskatoon: Saskatchewan Professional Development Unit, 1996.

Raibmon, Paige. *Authentic Indians: Episodes of Encounter from the Late-Nineteenth Century Northwest Coast*. Durham, NC: Duke University Press, 2005.

Ranchmen's Club. *Officers, Members, Constitution and Rules of the Ranchmen's Club of the City of Calgary: Established 1891, Amended to 11 April 1913*. Calgary: McAra Press, 1913.

——. *The Ranchmen's Club: A Slight Historical Sketch, 1891–1952*. Calgary: The Club, 1953.

——. *A Short History of the Ranchmen's Club*. Calgary: Calgary Centennial Project, 1975.

Rasporich, Anthony W., and Henry Cornelius Klassen, eds. *Frontier Calgary: Town, City, and Region, 1875–1914*. Calgary: McClelland and Stewart West, 1975.

Ray, Arthur. *The Canadian Fur Trade in the Industrial Age*. Toronto: University of Toronto Press, 1990.

——. *Indians in the Fur Trade*. Toronto: University of Toronto Press, 1998. First published 1974.

Rees, Tony. *Polo, the Galloping Game: An Illustrated History of Polo in the Canadian West*. Cochrane, AB: Western Heritage Centre Society, 2000.

Rich, Edwin Ernest. *The Fur Trade and the Northwest to 1857*. Toronto: McClelland and Stewart Limited, 1967.

Rich, Edwin Ernest, ed. *John Rae's Correspondence with the Hudson's Bay Company on Arctic Exploration, 1844–1855.* London: Hudson's Bay Record Society, 1953.

———. *The Letters of John McLoughlin from Fort Vancouver to the Governor and Committee.* Vol. 1. Toronto: The Champlain Society, 1941.

Rodney, William. *Kootenai Brown: His Life and Times 1839–1916.* Sidney, BC: Gray's Publishing Ltd., 1969.

———. *Kootenai Brown: The Unknown Frontiersman.* Surrey, BC: Heritage House Publishing, 1996.

Rogers, Edward S., and Donald B. Smith, eds. *Aboriginal Ontario: Historical Perspectives on the First Nations.* Toronto: Dundurn Press, 1994.

Rooney, Elizabeth, and Linda Trinh Moser. *A Half-Caste and Other Writings: Watanna, Onoto, 1879–1954.* Chicago: University of Illinois Press, 2003.

Ross, Alexander. *The Red River Settlement: Its Rise, Progress, and Present State.* Minneapolis: Ross and Haines, 1957. First published 1856.

Ross, George William. *Getting into Parliament and After.* Toronto: Briggs, 1913.

Said, Edward. *Culture and Imperialism.* New York: First Vintage Books Ltd., 1994.

Sanders, Harry Max. *Calgary Historic Union Cemetery: A Walking Guide.* Calgary: Fifth House, 2002.

———. *The Story behind Alberta Names: How Cities, Towns, Villages and Hamlets Got Their Names.* Calgary: Red Deer Press, 2003.

Sangster, Joan. *Regulating Girls and Women: Sexuality, Family and Law in Ontario, 1920–1960.* Toronto: Oxford University Press, 2001.

———. *Transforming Labour: Women and Work in Postwar Canada.* Toronto: University of Toronto Press, 2010.

Sawchuk, Joe. *The Dynamics of Native Politics: The Alberta Metis Experience.* Saskatoon: Purich Publishing, 1998.

Saywell, John T., ed. *The Canadian Journal of Lady Aberdeen, 1893–1898.* Toronto: The Champlain Society, 1960.

Schneider, David. *A Critique of the Study of Kinship.* Ann Arbor: University of Michigan Press, 1984.

Sealey, Bruce D., and Antoine S. Lussier. *The Métis: Canada's Forgotten People.* Winnipeg: Manitoba Métis Federation Press, 1975.

Selles, Johanna M. *Methodists and Women's Education in Ontario, 1836–1925.* Montreal: McGill-Queen's University Press, 1996.

Sharp, Paul. *Whoop-up Country: The Canadian-American West, 1865–1885.* Norman: University of Oklahoma Press, 1973.

Shiels, Bob. *Calgary: A Not Too Solemn Look at Calgary's First 100 Years.* Calgary: Calgary Herald, 1974.

——. *The Calgary Herald "Takes the Lid Off Calgary": What and Why Is Calgary?* Calgary: Calgary Herald, 1957.

Shoemaker, Nancy, ed. *Clearing a Path: Theorizing the Past in Native American Studies.* New York: Routledge, 2002.

Silverman, Eliane Leslau. *The Last Best West: Women on the Alberta Frontier, 1880–1930.* Calgary: Fifth House Publishers, 1998.

Simmons, Deidre. *Keepers of the Record: The History of the Hudson's Bay Company Archives.* Montreal: McGill-Queen's University Press, 2007.

Sissons, Constance Kerr. *John Kerr.* Toronto: Oxford University Press, 1946.

Sleeper-Smith, Susan, ed. *Contesting Knowledge: Museums and Indigenous Perspectives.* Lincoln: University of Nebraska Press, 2009.

——. *Indian Women and French Men: Rethinking Cultural Encounter in the Western Great Lakes.* Amherst: University of Massachusetts Press, 2001.

Slotkin, Richard. *Gunfighter Nation: The Myth of the Frontier in Twentieth-Century America.* Norman: University of Oklahoma Press, 1998.

Smith, Donald B. *Calgary's Grand Story: The Making of a Prairie Metropolis from the Viewpoint of Two Heritage Buildings.* Calgary: University of Calgary Press, 2005.

——. *Chief Buffalo Child Long Lance: The Glorious Impostor.* Red Deer: Red Deer Press, 1999.

Soby, Trudy. *Be It Ever So Humble.* Calgary: Century Calgary Publications, 1975.

——. *A Walk through Old Calgary.* Calgary: Century Calgary Publications, 1975.

Sprague, D.N. *Canada and the Métis, 1869–1885.* Waterloo, ON: Wilfrid Laurier University Press, 1988.

Srigley, Katrina. *Breadwinning Daughters: Young Working Women in a Depression-Era City.* Toronto: University of Toronto Press, 2010.

St-Onge, Nicole J.M. *Saint-Laurent, Manitoba: Evolving Métis Identities, 1850–1914.* Regina: Canadian Plains Research Center, 2004.

St-Onge, Nicole J.M., Carolyn Podruchny, and Brenda Macdougall, eds. *Contours of a People: Metis Family, Mobility, and History.* Norman: University of Oklahoma Press, 2012.

Stanley, George F.G. *The Birth of Western Canada: A History of the Riel Rebellions.* Toronto: University of Toronto Press, 1961. First published 1936.

——. *Louis Riel.* Toronto: Ryerson Press, 1963.

Stonechild, Blair. *Loyal till Death: Indians and the North-West Rebellion.* Calgary: Fifth House Publishing, 1997.

Strong-Boag, Veronica, and Carole Gerson, eds. *E. Pauline Johnson (Tekahionwake): Collected Poems and Selected Prose.* Toronto: University of Toronto Press, 2002.

——. *Paddling Her Own Canoe: The Times and Texts of E. Pauline Johnson (Tekahionwake).* Toronto: University of Toronto Press, 2000.

Swainson, Donald, ed. *Oliver Mowat's Ontario: Papers*. Toronto: Macmillan of Canada, 1972.

Talbot, Robert J. *Negotiating the Numbered Treaties: An Intellectual and Political Biography of Alexander Morris*. Saskatoon: Purich Publishing, 2009.

Taras, David, Beverly Rasporich, and Eli Mandel, eds. *A Passion for Identity: An Introduction to Canadian Studies*. Scarborough, ON: Nelson Learning Canada, 1993.

Taylor, Cora. *Victoria Calihoo: An Amazing Life*. Edmonton: Eschia Books, 2008.

Thomas, Lewis G., ed. *The Prairie West to 1905: A Canadian Sourcebook*. Toronto: Oxford University Press, 1975.

Thorne, Tanis C. *The Many Hands of My Relations: French and Indians on the Lower Missouri*. Columbia: University of Missouri Press, 1996.

Titley, Brian E. *A Narrow Vision: Duncan Campbell Scott and the Administration of Indian Affairs in Canada*. Vancouver: UBC Press, 1986.

Tolton, Gordon E. *The Cowboy Cavalry: The Story of the Rocky Mountain Rangers*. Victoria: Heritage House Publishers, 2011.

———. *Rocky Mountain Rangers: Southern Alberta's Cowboy Cavalry in the North West Rebellion—1885, no. 28*. Edited by Gregory Ellis. Lethbridge: Lethbridge Historical Society, 1994.

Tosh, John. *The Pursuit of History: Aims, Methods, and New Directions in the Study of Modern History*. London: Longman, 2002.

Tough, Frank. *"As Their Natural Resources Fail": Native Peoples and the Economic History of Northern Manitoba, 1870–1930*. Vancouver: UBC Press, 1996.

Toyo Eiwa Jogakuin. *Toyo Eiwa Jogakuin*. Tokyo, Japan: self-published, 2004.

Trafford, Tyler. *Calgary Golf and Country Club: More Than 18 Holes, 1897–1997*. Calgary: The Calgary Golf and Country Club, 1997.

Trémaudan de, Anguste-Henri. *Histoire de la nation métisse dans l'oeust canadien*. Saint-Boniface, MB: Éditions des Plaines, 1979. First published 1928.

Trigger, Bruce G. *Natives and Newcomers: Canada's "Heroic Age" Reconsidered*. Montreal: McGill-Queen's University Press, 1985.

Valverde, Mariana. *The Age of Light Soap and Water: Moral Reform in English Canada, 1885–1925*. Toronto: McClelland & Stewart, 1991.

Van Kirk, Sylvia. *"Many Tender Ties": Women in Fur-Trade Society, 1670–1870*. Winnipeg: Watson & Dwyer Publishing Ltd., 1980.

Venne, Sharon Helen, ed. *Indian Acts and Amendments 1868–1975: An Indexed Collection*. Saskatoon: University of Saskatchewan Native Law Centre, 1981.

Voisey, Paul. *Vulcan: The Making of a Prairie Community*. Toronto: University of Toronto Press, 1988.

Wachowich, Nancy. *Saqiyuq: Stories from the Lives of Three Inuit Women*. Montreal: McGill-Queen's University Press, 1999.

Walker, James W. St. G. *"Race," Rights and the Law in the Supreme Court of Canada: Historical Case Studies*. Waterloo, ON: Wilfrid Laurier University Press, 1997.

Ward, Tom. *Cowtown: An Album of Early Calgary*. Calgary: McClelland and Stewart West, 1975.

Warrender, Susan. *Alberta Titans: From Rags to Riches during Alberta's Pioneer Days*. Canmore, AB: Altitude Publishing Canada, 2003.

Watanna, Onoto. *Cattle*. New York: A.L. Burt, 1924.

Watkins, Ernest. *R.B. Bennett: A Biography*. Toronto: Kinswood House, 1963.

Weaver, Sally M. *Medicine and Politics among the Grand River Iroquois: A Study of the Non-Conservatives*. Ottawa: National Museums Canada, 1972.

Whitely, Paul, Patrick Seyd, and Jeremy Richardson. *True Blues: The Politics of Conservative Party Membership*. Oxford: Clarendon Press, 1994.

Whyte, Jon. *St. George's-in-the-Pines: The Anglican Church in Banff*. Banff, AB: Parish of St. George's-in-the-Pines, 1990.

Williams, Raymond. *The Long Revolution*. New York: Columbia University Press, 1961.

Willson, Beckles. *The Great Company (1667–1871): Being a History of the Honourable Company of Merchants-Adventurers Trading into Hudson's Bay*. 2 vols. London: Smith, Elder & Co., 1900.

——. *The Life of Lord Strathcona and Mount Royal*. Boston: Houghton Mifflin Company, 1915.

——. *The Life of Lord Strathcona and Mount Royal G.C.M.G., G.C.V.O., 1820–1914*. London: Cassell, 1915.

Wilson, Clifford, ed. *Northern Treasury: Selections from the Beaver*. New York: Devon Adair, 1954.

Wilson, Donald J., ed. *An Imperfect Past: Education and Society in Canadian History*. Vancouver: Centre for the Study of Curriculum and Institution, University of British Columbia, 1984.

Wilton, Carol, ed. *Beyond the Law: Lawyers and Business in Canada, 1830–1930*. Toronto: The Osgoode Society, 1990.

Woodcock, George. *Gabriel Dumont: The Métis Chief and His Lost World*. Edmonton: Hurtig Publishers, 1975.

Xiques, Donez. *Margaret Laurence: The Making of a Writer*. Toronto: Dundurn Press, 2005.

Zaslow, Morris. *The Opening of the Canadian North: 1870–1914*. Toronto: McClelland & Stewart, 1971.

Zolf, Larry. *Survival of the Fattest: An Irreverent View of the Senate*. Toronto: Key Porter Books, 1984.

Zuehlke, Mark. *Scoundrels, Dreamers & Second Sons: British Remittance Men in the Canadian West*. Vancouver: Whitecap Books, 1994. Reprint, Toronto: Dundurn Press, 2001.

Articles, Chapters and Presentations

Abel, Kerry. "Bompas, Charlotte Selina (Cox)." In *Dictionary of Canadian Biography*. Vol. 14, 1911–1920, 247. Toronto: University of Toronto Press, 1998.

Armitage, Susan. "Making Connections: Gender, Race, and Place in Oregon Country." In *One Step Over the Line: Toward a History of Women in the North American Wests*, edited by Elizabeth Jameson and Sheila McManus, 55–79. Edmonton: University of Alberta Press; Athabasca: Athabasca University Press, 2008.

Barman, Jean. "Ethnicity in the Pursuit of Status: British Middle and Upper-Class Emigration to British Columbia in the Late Nineteenth and Early Twentieth Centuries." *Canadian Ethnic Studies* 18, no. 1 (1986): 32–51.

——. "Separate and Unequal: Indian and White Girls at All Hallows School, 1884–1920." In *Indian Education in Canada, Vol 1: The Legacy*, edited by Jean Barman, Yvonne Hébert, and Don McCaskill, 110–131. Vancouver: UBC Press, 1986.

——. "Writing Women into the History of the North American Wests, One Woman at a Time." In *One Step Over the Line: Toward a History of Women in the North American Wests*, edited by Elizabeth Jameson and Sheila McManus, 99–127. Edmonton: University of Alberta Press; Athabasca: Athabasca University Press, 2008.

Barsh, Russel Lawrence, E. Ann Gibbs, and Tara Turner. "The Metis of Lethbridge: A Microcosm of Identity Politics." *Prairie Forum* 25, no. 2 (Fall 2000): 283–295.

Bell, Gloria Jane. "Oscillating Identities: Re-presentation of Métis in the Great Lakes Area in the Nineteenth Century." In *Métis in Canada: History, Identity, Law & Politics*, edited by Christopher Adams, Gregg Dahl, and Ian Peach, 3–58. Edmonton: University of Alberta Press, 2013.

Bellman, Jennifer L., and Christopher C. Hanks, "Northern Métis and the Fur Trade." In *Picking Up the Threads: Métis History in the Mackenzie Basin*, 29–68. Winnipeg: Metis Heritage Association of the Northwest Territories and Parks Canada–Canadian Heritage, 1998.

Bennett, Jason Patrick. "'Nature's Garden and a Possible Utopia': Farming for Fruit and Industrious Men in the Transboundary Pacific Northwest, 1895-1914." In *The Borderlands of the American and Canadian Wests: Essays on Regional History of the Forty-Ninth Parallel*, edited by Sterling Evans, 222–240. Lincoln: University of Nebraska Press, 2006.

Berger, Carl. "William Morton: The Delicate Balance of Region and Nation." In *The West and the Nation: Essays in Honour of W.L. Morton*, edited by Carl Berger and Ramsay Cook, 9–32. Toronto: McClelland & Stewart, 1976.

Brown, Jennifer S.H. "A Cree Nurse in a Cradle of Methodism: Little Mary and the Egerton R. Young Family at Norway House and Berens River." In *First Days, Fighting Days: Women in Manitoba History*, edited by M. Kinnear, 19–40. Regina: Canadian Plains Research Center, 1987.

——. "Fur Trade as Centrifuge: Familial Dispersal and Offspring Identity in Two Company Contexts." In *North American Indian Anthropology: Essays on Society and Culture*, edited by Raymond J. Demallie and Alfonso Ortiz, 197–219. Norman: University of Oklahoma Press, 1994.

——. "Fur Trade History as Text and Drama." In *The Uncovered Past: Roots of Northern Alberta Societies*, edited by Patricia McCormick and R. Geoffrey Ironside, 81–88. Edmonton: Canadian Circumpolar Institute, 1993.

——. "Linguistic Solitudes and Changing Social Categories." In *Old Trails and New Directions: Papers of the Third North American Fur Trade Conference*, edited by Carol M. Judd and Arthur J. Ray, 147–159. Toronto: University of Toronto Press, 1980.

——. "Métis, Halfbreeds, and Other Real People: Challenging Cultures and Categories." *The History Teacher* 27, no. 1 (November 1993): 19–26.

——. "Partial Truths: A Closer Look at Fur Trade Marriage." In *From Rupert's Land to Canada: Essays in Honour of John E. Foster*, edited by Theodore Binnema, Gerhard Ens, and R.C. MacLeod, 59–80. Edmonton: University of Alberta Press, 2001.

——. "William Lucas Hardisty." In *Dictionary of Canadian Biography* Vol. 11, 1881–1890, Toronto: University of Toronto Press, 1982.

——. "Women as Centre and Symbol in the Emergence of Métis Communities." *Canadian Journal of Native Studies* 3, no. 1 (1983): 39–46.

Bumstead, J.M. "The Trial of Ambroise Lepine." *The Beaver* (April–May 1997): 9–19.

Bunn, John. "Smallpox Epidemic of 1869–70." *Alberta Historical Review* 11 (1963): 13–19. First published 1871.

Burk, William. "Puffball Usages among North American Indians." *Journal of Ethnobiology* 3, no. 1 (May 1983): 55–62.

Buss, Helen. "Constructing Female Subjects in the Archive: A Reading of Three Versions of One Woman's Subjectivity." In *Working in Women's Archives: Researching Women's Private Literature and Archival Documents*, edited by Helen Buss and Marlene Kadar, 10–17. Waterloo, ON: Wilfrid Laurier University Press, 2001.

Campbell, Maria. "Charting the Way." In *Contours of a People: Metis Family, Mobility, and History*, edited by Nicole St-Onge, Carolyn Podruchny, and Brenda Macdougall, xxi–xxv. Norman: University of Oklahoma Press, 2012.

Careless, J.M.S. "The Emergence of Cabbagetown in Victorian Toronto." In *Gathering Place: Peoples and Neighbourhoods of Toronto, 1834–1945*, edited by Robert F. Harney, 25–45. Toronto: Multicultural History Society of Ontario, 1985.

Carriere, Anne Acco. "Traditional Knowledge and the Land: The Cumberland House Métis and Cree People." In *Metis Legacy: A Metis Historiography and Annotated Bibliography*, edited by Lawrence J. Barkwell, Leah Dorion, and Darren R. Préfontaine, 127–131. Winnipeg: Pemmican Publications Inc., 2001.

Carter, Sarah. "Britishness, 'Foreigness,' Women and Land in Western Canada." *Humanities Research Britishness & Otherness* XIII, no. 1 (2006): 43–60.

———. "Categories and Terrains of Exclusion: Constructing the 'Indian Woman' in the Early Settlement Era in Western Canada." *Great Plains Quarterly* 13, no. 3 (Summer 1993): 147–161.

———. "The 'Cordial Advocate': Amelia McLean Paget and *The People of the Plains*." Introduction to *People of the Plains*, 1909, by Amelia M. Paget, vii–xxxiv. Regina: Canadian Plains Research Center, 2004.

———. "The Exploitation and Narration of the Captivity of Theresa Delaney and Theresa Gowanlock, 1885." In *Making Western Canada: Essays on European Colonization and Settlement*, edited by Catherine Cavanaugh and Jeremy Mouat, 31–61. Toronto: Garamound Press, 1996.

Carter, Sarah, and Patricia McCormack. "Lifelines: Searching for Aboriginal Women of the Northwest and Borderlands." In *Recollecting: Lives of Aboriginal Women of the Canadian Northwest and Borderlands*, edited by Sarah Carter and Patricia McCormack, 5–28. Edmonton: Athabasca University Press, 2011.

Cavanaugh, Catherine. "The Limitations of the Pioneering Partnership: The Alberta Campaign for Homestead Dower, 1909–1925." In *Making Western Canada: Essays on European Colonization and Settlement*, edited by Catherine Cavanaugh and Jeremy Mouat, 186–214. Toronto: Garamond Press, 1996.

Clarke, Margaret L. "The Daughters of Edward McKay and Caroline Cook." Presented at *Unsettled Pasts: Reconceiving the West through Women's History*. University of Calgary, Calgary, AB, 2 June 2002.

Coates, K.S., and W.R. Morrison. "More Than a Matter of Blood: The Federal Government, the Churches and the Mixed Blood Populations of the Yukon and the Mackenzie River Valley, 1890–1950." In *1885 and After: Native Society in Transition*, edited by F. Laurie Barron and James B. Waldram, 253–273. Regina: Canadian Plains Research Center, 1986.

Collins, Robert. "With Dust, Joy, Mud and Anguish the Car Transformed Alberta." In *Alberta in the 20th Century: The Boom and the Bust, 1910–1914*, edited by Ted Byfield, 34–55. Edmonton: United Western Communications Ltd., 1994.

Cook-Bobrovitz, Jennifer, and Trudy Cowan. "Reasoned Speculation: The Challenge of Knowing Isabella Clarke Hardisty Lougheed." In *Remembering Chinook Country: 1905–2005 Centennial Edition*, edited by Chinook Country Historical Society, 23–36. Calgary: Detselig Enterprises, 2005.

Corbet, Elise A. "A Do-Gooder, Not a Suffragette: A. Maude Riley." In *Citymakers: Calgarians after the Frontier*, edited by Max Foran and Sheilagh Jameson, 209–224. Calgary: The Historical Society of Alberta, Chinook Country Chapter, 1987.

Crawford, John. "Speaking Michif in Four Metis Communities." *Canadian Journal of Native Studies* 3, no. 1 (1985): 47–55.

Cruikshank, Julie. "Discovery of Gold on the Klondike: Perspectives from Oral Tradition." In *Reading beyond Words: Contexts for Native History*, edited by Jennifer S.H. Brown and Elizabeth Vibert, 433–453. Peterborough, ON: Broadview Press, 1996.

———. "Oral History, Narrative Strategies, and Native American Historiography: Perspectives from the Yukon Territory, Canada." In *Clearing a Path: Theorizing the Past in Native American Studies*, edited by Nancy Shoemaker, 3–27. New York: Routledge, 2002.

Dawson, J. Brian. "The Chinese Experience in Frontier Calgary, 1885–1910." In *Frontier Calgary: Town, City, and Region, 1875–1914*, edited by Anthony W. Rasporich and Henry Cornelius Klassen, 124–140. Calgary: McClelland and Stewart West, 1975.

De La Cour, Lykke, Cecilian Morgan, and Mariana Valverde. "Gender Regulation and State Formation in Nineteenth-Century Canada." In *Colonial Leviathan: State Formation in Mid-Nineteenth-Century Canada*, edited by Allan Greer and Ian Radforth, 163–191. Toronto: University of Toronto Press, 1992.

Demmon, Calvin. "The Arts: Enter the Professional." In *Alberta in the 20th Century: The Boom and the Bust, 1910–1914*, edited by Ted Byfield, 56–71. Edmonton: United Western Communications Ltd., 1994.

Dempsey, Hugh A. "1870: A Year of Violence and Change." In *Alberta Formed, Alberta Transformed*, vol. 1, edited by Michael Payne, Donald Wetherell, and Catherine Cavanaugh, 209–236. Edmonton: University of Alberta Press, 2006.

———. "Crowfoot, Bearspaw, Deerfoot and Crowchild." In *Citymakers: Calgarians after the Frontier*, edited by Max Foran and Sheilagh S. Jamieson, 47–58. Calgary: The Historical Society of Alberta, Chinook Country Chapter, 1987.

———. Foreword *Blood Red the Sun*, by William Bleasdell Cameron, 1–10. Edmonton: Hurtig Publishers, 1977.

———. "One Hundred Years of Treaty Seven." In *One Century Later: Western Canadian Reserve Indians since Treaty 7*, edited by Ian Getty and Donald B. Smith, 20–30. Vancouver: UBC Press, 1978.

———. Review of *Montana Memories: The Life of Emma Magee in the Rocky Mountain West, 1866–1950*, by Ida S. Patterson. *Alberta History* 30, no. 2 (Spring 1982): 40.

———. "The Stampede of Native Culture." *Glenbow* (Summer 1992): 4–6.

Devine, Heather. "Conversations with 'Les gens de la Montagne Tortue'—1952." Presented at *Resistance and Convergence: Francophone and Métis Strategies of*

Identity in Western Canada. Centre d'études franco-canadiennes de l'Ouest,
Institut Français, University of Regina, Regina, SK, 20–23 October 2005.

Dick, Lyle. "The Seven Oaks Incident and the Construction of a Historical Tradition,
1816 to 1970." In *Making Western Canada: Essays on European Colonization and
Settlement,* edited by Catherine Cavanaugh and Jeremy Mouat, 1–30. Toronto:
Garamond Press, 1996.

Dicken McGinnis, Janice P. "Birth to Boom to Bust: Building in Calgary, 1875–1914." In
Frontier Calgary: Town, City, and Region, 1875–1914, edited by Anthony W. Rasporich
and Henry Cornelius Klassen, 6–19. Calgary: McClelland and Stewart West, 1975.

Dorge, Lionel. "The Metis and Canadien Councillors of Assiniboia." *The Beaver* (1974):
Parts I–III, outfit 305, 1:12–19, 2:39–45, 3:51–58.

Driben, Paul. "The Rise and Fall of Louis Riel and the Métis Nation: An
Anthropological Account." In *1885 and After: Native Society in Transition,* edited
by F. Laurie Barron and James B. Waldram, 68–77. Regina: Canadian Plains
Research Center, 1986.

Driscoll, Heather Rollason. "'A Most Important Chain of Connection': Marriage in
the Hudson's Bay Company." In *Readings in Canadian History: Pre-Confederation,*
7th ed., edited by Donald B. Smith and R. Douglas Francis, 77–94. Toronto:
Thomson Nelson, 2007.

Dusenberry, Verne. "Waiting for a Day That Never Comes: The Dispossessed Metis of
Montana." 1958. In *The New Peoples: Being and Becoming Métis in North America,*
edited by Jacqueline Peterson and Jennifer S.H. Brown, 119–136. Winnipeg:
University of Manitoba Press, 1985.

Eakin, Paul John. "Introduction: Mapping the Ethics of Life Writing." In *The Ethics of
Life Writing,* edited by Paul John Eakin, 1–4. Ithaca, NY: Cornell University Press,
2004.

Edmunds, R. David. "'Unacquainted with the laws of the civilized world': American
Attitudes toward the Metis Communities in the Old Northwest." In *The New
Peoples: Being and Becoming Métis in North America,* edited by Jacqueline Peterson
and Jennifer S.H. Brown, 185–194. Winnipeg: University of Manitoba Press, 1985.

Ens, Gerhard J. "Dispossession or Adaptation? Migration and Persistence of the Red
River Métis, 1835–1890." *Canadian Historical Association Historical Papers* (1988):
120–144.

——. "Metis Ethnicity, Personal Identity and the Development of Capitalism in the
Western Interior: The Case of Johnny Grant." In *From Rupert's Land to Canada:
Essays in Honour of John E. Foster,* edited by Theodore Binnema, Gerhard Ens, and
R.C. MacLeod, 161–177. Edmonton: University of Alberta Press, 2001.

——. "Prologue to the Red River Resistance: Pre-liminal Politics and the Triumph of
Riel." *Journal of the Canadian Historical Association* 5, no. 1 (1994): 111–123.

Erickson, Lesley. "'Bury Our Sorrows in the Sacred Heart': Gender and the Métis Response to Colonialism—The Case of Sara and Louis Riel, 1848–83." In *Unsettled Pasts: Reconceiving the West through Women's History*, edited by Sarah Carter, Lesley Erickson, Patricia Roome, and Char Smith, 17–46. Calgary: University of Calgary Press, 2005.

Fausz, J. Frederick. "Anglo-Indian Relations in Colonial North America." In *Scholars and the Indian Experience*, edited by W.R. Swagerty, 79–105. Bloomington: Indiana University Press, 1984.

Fee, Margery. "Deploying Identity in the Face of Racism." In *In Search of April Raintree: Critical Edition*, by Beatrice Culleton Mosionier, edited by Cheryl Suzack, 211–226. Winnipeg: Portage & Main Press, 1999.

Flanagan, Thomas. "Louis Riel's Land Claims." *Manitoba History* 21 (1991): 2–12.

———. "The Market for Métis Lands in Manitoba: An Exploratory Study." *Prairie Forum* 16, no. 1 (1991): 1–20.

Foggo, Cheryl. "Assembling Auntie: Illuminating a Long-Forgotten Pioneer." *Alberta Views* 12, no. 1 (January/February 2009): 34–39.

Fooks, Georgia Green. "The First Women: Southern Alberta Native Women before 1900." *Alberta History* 51, no. 4 (Autumn 2003): 23–28.

Foran, Heather. "Reformer, Feminist, and First Woman Alderman in Calgary: Annie Gale." In *Citymakers: Calgarians after the Frontier*, edited by Max Foran and Sheilagh Jamieson, 197–207. Calgary: The Historical Society of Alberta, Chinook Country Chapter, 1987.

Fortier, Alfred. "Urbain Delorme: L'Homme riche des prairies." *Bulletin de la Société historique de Saint-Boniface* 3 (Printemps 1995): 3–8.

Foster, John. "James Bird, Fur Trader." In *Edmonton: The Life of a City*, edited by Bob Hesketh and Frances Swyripa, 12–20. Edmonton: NeWest Press, 1995.

———. "The Métis: The People and the Term." In *The Western Métis: Profile of a People*, edited by Patrick C. Douaud, 21–30. Regina: Canadian Plains Research Center, 2007.

———. "The Métis: The People and the Term." *Prairie Forum* 3, no. 1 (1978): 79–90.

———. "Some Questions and Perspectives on the Problem of Métis Roots." In *The New Peoples: Being and Becoming Métis in North America*, edited by Jacqueline Peterson and Jennifer S.H. Brown, 73–91. Winnipeg: University of Manitoba Press, 1985.

———. "Wintering, The Outsider Adult Male and the Ethnogenesis of the Western Plains Métis." In *From Rupert's Land to Canada*, edited by Theodore Bennema, Gerhard Ens, and R.C. MacLeod, 179–192. Edmonton: University of Alberta Press, 2001.

——. "Wintering, The Outsider Adult Male and the Ethnogenesis of the Western Plains Métis." In *The Western Métis: Profile of a People*, edited by Patrick C. Douaud, 91–103. Regina: Canadian Plains Research Center, 2007.

Frank, Arthur W. "Moral Non-Fiction: Life Writing and Children's Disability." In *The Ethics of Life Writing*, edited by Paul John Eakin, 174–194. Ithaca, NY: Cornell University Press, 2004.

Friesen, Gerald. "The Prairies as Region: The Contemporary Meaning of an Old Idea." In *The Constitutional Future of the Prairie and Atlantic Regions of Canada*, edited by James N. McCrorie and Martha L. MacDonald, 1–17. Regina: Canadian Plains Research Center, 1992.

Fur, Gunlog. "Some Women Are Wiser Than Some Men." In *Clearing a Path: Theorizing the Past in Native American Studies*, edited by Nancy Shoemaker, 75–106. New York: Rutledge, 2002.

Gallagher, Brian. "A Re-Examination of Race, Class and Society in Red River." *Native Studies Review* 4, nos. 1 & 2 (1988): 2–65.

Gerson, Carole, and Veronica Strong-Boag. "Championing the Native: E. Pauline Johnson Rejects the Squaw." In *Contact Zones: Aboriginal & Settler Women in Canada's Colonial Past*, edited by Katie Pickles and Myra Rutherdale, 47–66. Vancouver: UBC Press, 2005.

Giraud, Marcel. Foreword to *The New Peoples: Being and Becoming Métis in North America*, edited by Jacqueline Peterson and Jennifer S.H. Brown, xi–xii. Winnipeg: University of Manitoba Press, 1985.

Giokas, John, and Paul L.A.H. Chartrand, "Who Are the Métis in Section 35? A Review of the Law and Policy Relating to Métis and 'Mixed-Blood' People in Canada." In *Who Are Canada's Aboriginal Peoples? Recognition, Definition, and Jurisdiction*, edited by Paul L.A.H. Chartrand, 83–125. Saskatoon: Purich Publishing, 2002.

Graham, Donald. "Christmas, 1872." *Alberta Historical Review* 6, no. 4. (Autumn 1958): 7–9.

——. "Donald Graham's Narrative of 1872–73." Edited by Hugh Dempsey. *Alberta Historical Review* 4, no. 1 (Winter 1956): 10–19.

Grekul, Jana, Arvey Krahn, and Dave Odynak. "'Sterilizing the Feeble-Minded': Eugenics in Alberta, Canada, 1929–1972." *Journal of Historical Sociology* 17, no. 4 (December 2004): 358–384.

Gullestad, Marianne. "Tales of Consent and Descent: Life Writing as a Fight against an Imposed Self-Image." In *The Ethics of Life Writing*, edited by Paul John Eakin, 216–243. Ithaca, NY: Cornell University Press, 2004.

Hagan, William T. "Full Blood, Mixed Blood, Generic, and Ersatz: The Problem of Indian Identity." *Arizona and the West* 27 (1985): 309–326.

Hatt, Ken. "The North-West Rebellion Scrip Commissions, 1885–1889." In *1885 and After: Native Society in Transition*, edited by F. Laurie Barron and James B. Waldram, 189–204. Regina: Canadian Plains Research Center, 1986.

Hele, Karl S. "Manipulating Identity: The Sault Borderlands Métis and Colonial Intervention." In *The Long Journey of a Forgotten People: Métis Identities and Family Histories*, edited by Ute Lischke and David McNab, 163–196. Waterloo, ON: Wilfrid Laurier University Press, 2007.

Hobsbawm, Eric. "Identity Politics and the Left." *New Left Review* 217 (May/June 1996): 38–47.

——. "Language, Culture, and National Identity." *Social Research* 63, no. 4 (Winter 1996): 1065–1080.

Holt, Faye Reineberg. "Magistrate Emily Ferguson Murphy." In *Edmonton: The Life of a City*, edited by Bob Hesketh and Frances Swyripa, 142–149. Edmonton: NeWest Press, 1995.

Hunter, Frederick. "The Legend of Jimmy Smith." In *Remembering Chinook Country: 1905–2005 Centennial Edition*, edited by Chinook Country Historical Society, 109–117. Calgary: Detselig Enterprises, 2005.

Hutchinson, Bruce. "5000 to 75,000 in 12 Years—That's How Calgary Came to Be." In *Alberta in the 20th Century: The Boom and the Bust, 1910–1914*, edited by Ted Byfield, 88–117. Edmonton: United Western Communications Ltd., 1994.

Ironside, Geoff. "Slopes and Shafts." In *Edmonton: The Life of a City*, edited by Bob Hesketh and Frances Swyripa, 193–202. Edmonton: NeWest Press, 1995.

Iverson, Peter. "Indian Tribal Histories." In *Scholars and the Indian Experience*, edited by W.R. Swagerty, 205–232. Bloomington: Indiana University Press, 1984.

Jameson, Sheilagh. "The Social Elite of the Ranch Community and Calgary." In *Frontier Calgary: Town, City, and Region, 1875–1914*, edited by Anthony W. Rasporich and Henry Cornelius Klassen, 57–70. Calgary: McClelland and Stewart West, 1975.

Jenness, Diamond. "Canada's Indians Yesterday. What of Today?" In *As Long as the Sun Shines and Water Flows: A Reader in Canadian Native Studies*, edited by Ian A.L. Getty and Antoine S. Lussier, 159–163. Vancouver: UBC Press, 1983.

Jennings, John. "Policemen and Poachers: Indian Relations on the Ranching Frontier." In *Frontier Calgary: Town, City, and Region, 1875–1914*, edited by Anthony W. Rasporich and Henry Cornelius Klassen, 87–99. Calgary: McClelland and Stewart West, 1975.

Jensen, Joan M. "The Perils of Rural Women's History: (A Note to Storytellers Who Study the West's Unsettled Past)." In *One Step Over the Line: Toward a History of Women in the North American Wests*, edited by Elizabeth Jameson and Sheila McManus, 165–188. Edmonton and Athabasca: University of Alberta Press and Athabasca University Press, 2008.

Jorup-Ronstrom, Christina. "Epidemiological, Bacteriological and Complicating Features of Erysipelas." In *Scandinavian Journal of Infectious Diseases* 18, no. 6 (1986): 519–524. doi:10.3109/00365548609021656.

Judd, Carol M. "'Mixt Bands of Many Nations': 1821–70." In *Old Trails and New Directions: Papers of the Third North American Fur Trade Conference*, edited by Carol M. Judd and Arthur J. Ray, 127–159. Toronto: University of Toronto Press, 1980.

Kealey, Gregory S. "The Writing of Social History in English Canada, 1970–84." In *Workers and Canadian History*, 136–159. Montreal: McGill-Queen's University Press, 1995.

Kearns, Laura-Lee. "(Re)claiming Métis Women Identities: Three Stories and the Storyteller." In *Métis in Canada: History, Identity, Law & Politics*, edited by Christopher Adams, Gregg Dahl, and Ian Peach, 59–92. Edmonton: University of Alberta Press, 2013.

Kermoal, Nathalie. "Les Annal americaines de Louis Riel: L'Exil au Montana." *Études canadiennes* 23, no. 43 (1997): 31–42.

Klassen, Henry Cornelius. "Lawyers, Finance, and Economic Development in Southwestern Alberta, 1884–1920." In *Beyond the Law: Lawyers and Business in Canada, 1830 to 1930*, edited by Carol Wilton, 298–319. Toronto: The Osgoode Society, 1990.

———. "Social Troubles in Calgary in the Mid-1890s." *Urban History Review* (February 1974): 3–74.

Knafla, Louis A. "Richard 'Bonfire' Bennett: The Legal Practice." In *Beyond the Law: Lawyers and Business in Canada, 1830 to 1930*, edited by Carol Wilton, 320–376. Toronto: The Osgoode Society, 1990.

La Prairie, Laurent. "D'arcy Mcnickle (1904–1977)." *New Breed Magazine* (Winter 2008): 1.

Lampard, Robert. "William Morrison Mackay, MD—1836–1917." *History Now*, no. 1 (January 2005): 5–6.

Langford, Nanci. "Childbirth on the Canadian Prairies 1880–1930." Presented at the Canadian Historical Association. Calgary, AB, 1994.

Larin, Amy. "A Rough Ride: Automobiles in Banff National Park, 1905–1918." *Alberta History* 56, no. 1 (Winter 2008): 2–9.

Larocque, Emma. "The Colonization of a Native Woman Scholar." In *Women of the First Nations: Power, Wisdom, and Strength*, edited by Christine Miller and Patricia Chuchryk, 11–18. Winnipeg: University of Manitoba Press, 1996.

———. "Conversations on Metis Identity." *Prairie Fire* 7, no. 1 (Spring 1986): 19–24.

———. "Metis and Feminist: Ethical Reflections on Feminism, Human Rights and Decolonization." In *Making Space for Indigenous Feminism*, edited by Joyce Green, 53–71. Black Point, NS: Fernwood Publishers, 2007.

——. "The Metis in English Canadian Literature." *Canadian Journal of Native Studies* 3, no. 1 (1983): 85–94.

——. "Native Identity and the Metis: Otehpayimsuak Peoples." In *A Passion for Identity: Canadian Studies for the 21st Century*, edited by David Taras and Beverly Rasporich, 381–398. Scarborough, ON: Nelson Canada, 2001.

——. "Three Conventional Approaches to Native People in Society and in Literature." Presented at the Mary Donaldson Memorial Lecture Series. Saskatchewan Library Association, Saskatoon, SK, 1984.

Lauritzen, Paul. "Arguing with Life Stories: The Case of Rigoberta Menchú." In *The Ethics of Life Writing*, edited by Paul John Eakin, 19–39. Ithaca, NY: Cornell University Press, 2004.

Lee, David. "The Métis Militant Rebels of 1885." In *Readings in Canadian History: Post Confederation*, 6th ed., edited by R. Douglas Francis and Donald B. Smith, 44–62. Scarborough, ON: Nelson Thompson Learning, 2002.

Levi, Giovanni. "On Microhistory." In *New Perspectives on Historical Writings*, edited by Peter Burke, 93–113. University Park: Pennsylvania State University Press, 1991.

Long Lance, Chief Buffalo Child. "Indians of the Northwest and West Canada." *The Mentor* 12, no. 2 (March 1924): 3–6.

Lussier, Antoine S. "The Metis: Contemporary Problem of Identity." *Manitoba Pageant* (Summer 1978): 12–15.

——. "The Métis." In *The Other Natives: The Métis*, vol. 1: 1700–1885, edited by Antoine S. Lussier and D. Bruce Sealey, 15–27. Winnipeg: Manitoba Métis Federation Press, 1978.

Macdougall, Brenda. "'The Comforts of Married Life': Metis Family Life, Labour, and the Hudson's Bay Company." *Labour/Le Travail*, no. 61 (Spring 2008): 9–39.

——. "The Myth of Metis Cultural Ambivalence." In *Contours of a People: Metis Family, Mobility, and History*, edited by Nicole St-Onge, Carolyn Podruchny, and Brenda Macdougall, 422–464. Norman: University of Oklahoma Press, 2012.

——. "*Wahkootowin*: Family and Cultural Identity in Northwestern Saskatchewan Metis Communities." *Canadian Historical Review* 87, no. 3 (2006): 431–462.

MacKinnon, Doris J. "Just an Ordinary Person: The History of Dr. Ethel Taylor." *Prairie Forum* 31, no. 1 (Spring 2006): 127–140.

MacLaren, Ian. "Paul Kane and the Authorship of *Wanderings of an Artist*." In *From Rupert's Land to Canada: Essays in Honour of John E. Foster*, edited by Theodore Binnema, Gerhard Ens, and R.C. MacLeod, 225–247. Edmonton: University of Alberta Press, 2001.

MacLeod, R.C., and Heather Rollason Driscoll. "Natives, Newspapers and Crime Rates in the North-West Territories, 1878–1885." In *From Rupert's Land to Canada: Essays in Honour of John E. Foster*, edited by Theodore Binnema, Gerhard Ens, and R.C. MacLeod, 249–269. Edmonton: University of Alberta Press, 2001.

Mancall, Peter C. "The Middle Ground: Indians, Empires, and Republics in the Great Lakes Region, 1650–1815 by Richard White." *The American Historical Review* 97, no. 5 (1992): 1587–1588.

Mattes, Catherine. "Metis Perspectives in Contemporary Art." In *Metis Legacy: A Metis Historiography and Annotated Bibliography*, edited by Lawrence J. Barkwell, Leah Dorion, and Darren R. Préfontaine, 189–198. Winnipeg, Pemmican Publications Inc., 2001.

McCarthy, Martha. "Northern Métis and the Churches." In *Picking Up the Threads: Métis History in the Mackenzie Basin*, 111–136. Winnipeg: Metis Heritage Association of the Northwest Territories and Parks Canada–Canadian Heritage, 1998.

McCormack, Patricia. "Northern Métis and the Treaties: Treaties No. 8 and No. 11, and the Issuance of Scrip." In *Picking Up the Threads: Métis History in the Mackenzie Basin*, 171–202. Winnipeg: Metis Heritage Association of the Northwest Territories and Parks Canada–Canadian Heritage, 1998.

McDowell, John E. "Madame La Framboise." *Michigan History* 56, no. 3 (Winter 1972): 271–286.

——. "Thérèse Schindler of Mackinac: Upward Mobility in the Great Lakes Fur Trade." *Wisconsin Magazine of History* 61 (Winter 1977–1978): 125–143.

McKenna, Marian C. "Sir James Alexander Lougheed: Calgary's First Senator and City Builder." In *City Makers: Calgarians after the Frontier*, edited by Max Foran and Sheilagh S. Jamieson, 95–116. Calgary: The Historical Society of Alberta, Chinook Country Chapter, 1987.

McManus, Sheila. "Unsettled Pasts, Unsettling Borders: Women, Wests, Nations." In *One Step Over the Line: Toward a History of Women in the North American Wests*, edited by Elizabeth Jameson and Sheila McManus, 29–47. Edmonton: University of Alberta Press; Athabasca: Athabasca University Press, 2008.

McPherson, Kathryn. "Home Tales: Gender, Domesticity, and Colonialism in the Prairie West, 1870–1900." In *Finding a Way to the Heart: Feminist Writings on Aboriginal and Women's History in Canada*, edited by Robin Jarvis Brownlie and Valerie J. Korinek, 222–240. Winnipeg: University of Manitoba Press, 2012.

Miller, J.R. "From Riel to the Métis." *Canadian Historical Review* 69, no. 1 (1988): 1–20.

——. "Owen Glendower, Hotspur and Canadian Indian Policy." *Ethnohistory* 37 (Fall 1990): 386–415.

Mills, Claudia. "Friendship, Fiction, and Memoir: Trust and Betrayal in Writing from One's Own Life." In *The Ethics of Life Writing*, edited by Paul John Eakin, 101–120. Ithaca, NY: Cornell University Press, 2004.

Molyneaux, Marianne M. "Early Days in Alberta." *Alberta History* 8, no. 2 (Spring 1960): 6–14.

Moogk, Peter N. "*Les petits sauvages*: The Children of Eighteenth-Century New France." In *Histories of Canadian Children and Youth*, edited by Nancy Janovicek and Joy Parr, 36–56. Toronto: Oxford University Press, 2003.

Mortimer-Sandilands, Catriona. "'The Geology Recognizes No Boundaries': Shifting Borders in Waterton Lakes National Park." In *The Borderlands of the American and Canadian Wests: Essays on Regional History of the Forty-Nineth Parallel*, edited by Sterling Evans, 309–333. Lincoln: University of Nebraska Press, 2006.

Morton, W.L. "The Battle of the Grand Coteau: July 13 and 14, 1851." In *The Other Natives: The Métis*, vol. 1: 1700–1885, edited by Antoine S. Lussier and D. Bruce Sealey, 47–62. Winnipeg: Manitoba Métis Federation Press, 1978.

——. "The Canadian Métis." In *Contexts of Canada's Past: Selected Essays of W.L. Morton*, edited by A.B. McKillop, 61–68. Toronto: Macmillan of Canada, 1980.

——. Introduction to *Alexander Begg's Red River Journal and Other Papers Relative to the Red River Resistance of 1869–1870*, edited by W.L. Morton, 1–148. Toronto: The Champlain Society, 1956.

Murphy, Lucy Eldersveld. "Public Mothers: Native American and Métis Women as Creole Mediators in the Nineteenth-Century Midwest." *Journal of Women's History* 14, no. 4 (2003): 142–166.

Nicks, Trudy. "Mary Anne's Dilemma: The Ethnohistory of an Ambivalent Identity." *Canadian Ethnic Studies* 3, no. 2 (1985): 103–114.

Oake, George. "The Unbeloved 'Little Arthur' Salvages the Shattered Grits." In *Alberta in the 20th Century: The Boom and the Bust, 1910–1914*, edited by Ted Byfield, 220–239. Edmonton: United Western Communications Ltd., 1994.

O'Toole, Darren. "From Entity to Identity to Nation: The Ethnogenesis of the Wiisakodewininiwag (Bois-Brûlé) Reconsidered." In *Métis in Canada: History, Identity, Law & Politics*, edited by Christopher Adams, Gregg Dahl, and Ian Peach, 143–203. Edmonton: University of Alberta Press, 2013.

Palmer, Howard. "Ethnic Relations and the Paranoid Style: Nativism, Nationalism & Populism in Alberta, 1945–50." *Canadian Ethnic Studies* 23, no. 3 (1991): 7–31.

Pannekoek, Fritz. "The Anglican Church and the Disintegration of Red River Society, 1818–1870." In *The West and the Nation*, edited by Carl Berger and Ramsay Cook, 72–90. Toronto: McClelland & Stewart, 1976.

——. "The Flock Divided: Factions and Feuds at Red River." In *Readings in Canadian History: Pre-Confederation*, 6th ed., edited by R. Douglas Francis and Donald B. Smith, 409–416. Scarborough, ON: Nelson Thomson Learning, 2002.

——. "Metis Studies: The Development of a Field and New Directions." In *From Rupert's Land to Canada: Essays in Honour of John E. Foster*, edited by Theodore

Binnema, Gerhard Ens, and R.C. MacLeod, 111–128. Edmonton: University of Alberta Press, 2001.

———. "Some Comments on the Social Origins of the Riel Protest of 1869." In *Louis Riel & the Metis: Riel Mini-Conference Papers*, edited by A.S. Lussier, 65–75. Winnipeg: Pemmican Publications Inc., 1998.

Payment, Diane. "Combattants Métis En 1885." *The Bulletin Journal of the Saskatchewan Genealogical Society Inc.* 23 (1 March 1992): 20–25.

———. "'*La vie en rose*'? Métis Women at Batoche, 1870 to 1920." In *Women of the First Nations: Power, Wisdom, and Strength*, edited by Christine Miller and Patricia Chuchryk, 19–38. Winnipeg: University of Manitoba Press, 1996.

———. "Métis People in Motion: From Red River to the MacKenzie Basin." In *Picking Up the Threads: Métis History in the Mackenzie Basin*, 69–110. Winnipeg: Metis Heritage Association of the Northwest Territories and Parks Canada–Canadian Heritage, 1998.

———. "'On n'est pas métchifs nous autres': Un aperçu des relations entre les Femmes francophones au Manitoba durant les années 1810–1920." Conference pour Collège Universitaire de Saint-Boniface, 8 Février 1992.

———. "Un aperçu des relations entre les missionnaires catholiques et les métisses pendant le premier siècle de contact (1813–1918) dans l'ouest canadien." *Études oblates de l'ouest* 3 (1994): 139–158.

Peers, Laura. "Changing Resource-Use Patterns of Saulteaux Trading at Fort Pelly, 1821 to 1870." In *Aboriginal Resource Use in Canada: Historical and Legal Aspects*, edited by Kerry Abel and Jean Friesen, 107–118. Winnipeg: University of Manitoba Press, 1991.

Perdue, Theda. Introduction to *Sifters: Native American Women's Lives*, edited by Theda Perdue, 3–13. New York: Oxford University Press, 2001.

Peterson, Jacqueline. "Many Roads to Red River: Métis Ethnogenesis in the Great Lakes Region, 1680–1815." In *The New Peoples: Being and Becoming Métis in North America*, edited by Jacqueline Peterson and Jennifer S.H. Brown, 37–72. Winnipeg: University of Manitoba Press, 1985.

———. "Red River Redux: Métis Ethnogenesis and the Great Lakes Region." In *Contours of a People: Metis Family, Mobility, and History*, edited by Nicole St-Onge, Carolyn Podruchny, and Brenda Macdougall, 22–58. Norman: University of Oklahoma Press, 2012.

———. "Women Dreaming: The Religiopsychology of Indian White Marriages and the Rise of a Metis Culture." In *Western Women: Their Land, Their Lives*, edited by Lillian Schlissel, Vicki L. Ruiz, and Janice Monk, 49–68. Albuquerque: University of New Mexico Press, 1988.

Peterson, Jacqueline, and John Anfinson. "The Indian and the Fur Trade." In *Scholars and the Indian Experience*, edited by W.R. Swagerty, 223–257. Bloomington: Indiana University Press, 1984.

Peterson, Susan C. "'Doing Women's Work': The Grey Nuns of Fort Totten Indian Reservation, 1874–1900." *North Dakota History* 52 (Spring 1985): 18–25.

Philip, Catherine. "The Fair, Frail Flowers of Western Womanhood." In *Frontier Calgary: Town, City, and Region, 1875–1914*, edited by Anthony W. Rasporich and Henry Cornelius Klassen, 114–123. Calgary: McClelland and Stewart West, 1975.

Pickett, Evelyne Stitt. "Hoboes across the Border: Itinerant Cross-Border Laborers between Montana and Western Canada." In *The Borderlands of the American and Canadian Wests: Essays on Regional History of the Forty-Ninth Parallel*, edited by Sterling Evans, 203–221. Lincoln: University of Nebraska Press, 2006.

Pickles, Katie. "The Old and New on Parade: Mimesis, Queen Victoria, and Carnival Queens on Victoria Day in Interwar Victoria." In *Contact Zones: Aboriginal & Settler Women in Canada's Colonial Past*, edited by Katie Pickles and Myra Rutherdale, 273–291. Vancouver: UBC Press, 2005.

Pierson, Ruth, and Alison Prentice. "Feminism and the Writing and Teaching of History." In *Feminism in Canada: From Pressure to Politics*, edited by Angela Miles and Geraldine Finn, 103–118. Montreal: Black Rose Books, 1982.

Pinkham, Mrs. W.C. "Selections from the Unpublished Recollections of Mrs. W.C. Pinkham, an Early Manitoban." *Manitoba Pageant* 20 no. 1 (Autumn 1974). http://www.mhs.mb.ca/docs/pageant/20/pinkhamrecollections.shtml.

Pollard, Juliet. "A Most Remarkable Phenomenon Growing Up Metis: Fur Traders' Children in the Pacific Northwest." In *An Imperfect Past: Education and Society in the Pacific Northwest*, edited by Donald J. Wilson, 120–140. Vancouver: Centre for the Study of Curriculum and Institution, UBC, 1984.

Pomeroy, Elsie. "Mary Electa Adams: A Pioneer Educator." *Ontario History* 41, no. 3 (1949): 107–117.

Porsild, Charlene. "Coming In from the Cold: Reflections on the History of Women in Northern Canada." *Atlantis* 25, no. 1 (Fall/Winter 2000): 63–68.

Prud'homme, L.A. "André Nault." *Bulletin de la Société historique de Saint-Boniface* 4 (Été 1996): 15–27.

——. "Urbain Delorme: Chef des Prairies." *Revue canadienne* 23 (1887): 270–279.

Racette, Sherry Farrell. "Beads, Silk and Quills: The Clothing and Decorative Arts of the Metis." In *Metis Legacy: A Metis Historiography and Annotated Bibliography*, edited by Lawrence J. Barkwell, Leah Dorion, and Darren R. Préfontaine, 181–188. Winnipeg: Pemmican Publications Inc., 2001.

———. "Sewing for a Living: The Commodification of Métis Women's Artistic Production." In *Contact Zones: Aboriginal & Settler Women in Canada's Colonial Past*, edited by Katie Pickles and Myra Rutherdale, 17–46. Vancouver: UBC Press, 2005.

Ray, Arthur J. Introduction to *The Fur Trade in Canada: An Introduction to Canadian Economic History*, by Harold Innis. Toronto: University of Toronto Press, 1999.

———. "The Northern Great Plains: Pantry of the Northwestern Fur Trade, 1774–1885." In *The Western Métis: Profile of a People*, edited by Patrick Douaud, 55–71. Regina: Canadian Plains Research Center, 2007.

———. "Reflections on Fur Trade Society." *American Indian Culture and Research Journal* (Special Métis Issue) 6, no. 2 (1982): 91–107.

Rogan, Ian. "Collections Corner." *Landmark* (April 2009): 3–4.

Roome, Patricia. "Remembering Together: Reclaiming Alberta Women's Past." In *Standing on New Ground: Women in Alberta*, edited by Catherine A. Cavanaugh and Randi R. Warne, 171–202. Edmonton: University of Alberta Press, 1993.

Royal Canadian Mounted Police Quarterly 36, no. 4 (April 1971): 77–78.

Rozum, Molly P. "'That Understanding with Nature': Region, Race, and Nation in Women's Stories from the Modern Canadian and American Grasslands West." In *One Step Over the Line: Toward a History of Women in the North American Wests*, edited by Elizabeth Jameson and Sheila McManus, 129–164. Edmonton: University of Alberta Press; Athabasca: Athabasca University Press, 2008.

Russell, Peter A. "Progressive Party." Last modified 3 April 2015. Accessed 3 May 2012. http://thecanadianencyclopedia.com/articles/progressive-party.

Rutherdale, Myra. "'She Was a Ragged Little Thing': Missionaries, Embodiment, and Refashioning Aboriginal Womanhood in Northern Canada." In *Contact Zones: Aboriginal & Settler Women in Canada's Colonial Past*, edited by Katie Pickles and Myra Rutherdale, 229–245. Vancouver: UBC Press, 2005.

Sawchuk, Joe. "Negotiating an Identity: Métis Political Organizations, the Canadian Government, and Competing Concepts of Aboriginality." *American Indian Quarterly* 23, no. 1 (Winter 2001): 73–92.

Schenck, Theresa. "Border Identities: Métis, Halfbreed, and Mixed-Blood." In *Gathering Places: Aboriginal and Fur Trade Histories*, edited by Carolyn Podruchny and Laura Peers, 233–248. Vancouver: UBC Press, 2010.

Scott, Joan W. "Gender: A Useful Category of Historical Analysis." *American Historical Review* 91, no. 5 (1986): 1053–1075.

Sheppard, Allan. "Undercurrents of Intolerance: Swimming in KKK Waters." *Legacy* (Summer 2000): 26–29. Accessed 10 May 2011, http://www.abheritage.ca/albertans/articles/kkk.html.

Shoemaker, Nancy. "Categories." In *Clearing a Path: Theorizing the Past in Native American Studies*, edited by Nancy Shoemaker, 51–74. New York: Routledge, 2002.

Siadhail, Pádraig Ó. "Katherine Hughes, Irish Political Activist." In *Edmonton: The Life of a City*, edited by Bob Hesketh and Frances Swyripa, 78–87. Edmonton: NeWest Press, 1995.

Sleeper-Smith, Susan. "Women, Kin, and Catholicism." *Ethnohistory* 47, no. 2 (2000): 423–452.

Smith, Donald B. "Color Conscious: Racial Attitudes in Early 20th Century Calgary." In *Remembering Chinook Country: 1905–2005 Centennial Edition*, edited by Chinook Country Historical Society, 119–132. Calgary: Detselig Enterprises, 2005.

——. "A Good Samaritan: John Laurie." In *City Makers: Calgarians after the Frontier*, edited by Max Foran and Sheilagh Jameson, 263–274. Calgary: The Historical Society of Alberta, Chinook Country Chapter, 1987.

——. "The Original Peoples of Alberta." In *Peoples of Alberta: Portraits of Cultural Diversity*, edited by Howard Palmer and Tamara Palmer, 50–82. Saskatoon: Western Producer Prairie Books, 1985.

Spencer, Rainer. "Race and Mixed-Race: A Personal Tour." In *As We Are Now: Mixblood Essays on Race and Identity*, edited by William S. Penn, 126–139. Berkeley: University of California Press, 1997.

Sprague, Donald N. "Dispossession vs. Accommodation in Plaintiff vs. Defendant Accounts of Métis Dispersal from Manitoba, 1870–1881." In *The Western Métis: Profile of a People*, edited by Patrick C. Douaud, 125–144. Regina: Canadian Plains Research Center, 2007.

Sprenger, G. Herman. "The Métis Nation: Buffalo Hunting vs. Agriculture in the Red River Settlement (Circa 1810–1870)." In *The Other Natives: The Métis*, vol. 1: 1700–1885, edited by Antoine S. Lussier and D. Bruce Sealey, 115–130. Winnipeg: Manitoba Métis Federation Press, 1978.

Spry, Irene. "The Great Transformation: The Disappearance of the Commons in Western Canada." In *Canadian Plains Studies 6: Man and Nature on the Prairies*, edited by Richard Allen, 21–45. Regina: Canadian Plains Research Center, 1976.

——. "The Métis and Mixed-Bloods of Rupert's Land before 1870." In *The New Peoples: Being and Becoming Métis in North America*, edited by Jacqueline Peterson and Jennifer S.H. Brown, 95–118. Winnipeg: University of Manitoba Press, 1985.

St-Onge, Nicole J.M. "The Dissolution of a Métis Community: Pointe à Grouette, 1860–1885." *Studies in Political Economy* 18 (Autumn 1985): 149–172.

——. "Nationalist Perspectives: A Review Essay." *Manitoba History* (Autumn 1987): 37–39.

——. "Race, Class and Marginality in an Interlake Settlement: 1850–1950." *Socialist Studies/Études socialists: A Canadian Annual* 5 (Spring 1990): 73–87.

——. "Saint-Laurent, Manitoba: Oral History of a Métis Community." *Journal of the Canadian Oral History Association* 7 (1984): 1–4.

———. "Variations in Red River: The Traders and Freemen Metis of Saint-Laurent, Manitoba." *Canadian Ethnic Studies* 24, no. 2 (1992): 1–21.

St-Onge, Nicole, and Carolyn Podruchny. "Scuttling Along a Spider's Web: Mobility and Kinship in Metis Ethnogenesis." In *Contours of a People: Metis Family, Mobility, and History*, edited by Nicole St-Onge, Carolyn Podruchny, and Brenda Macdougall, 59–92. Oklahoma: University of Oklahoma Press, 2012.

Stanley, George F.G. "The Last Word on Louis Riel—the Man of Several Faces." In *1885 and After: Native Society in Transition*, edited by F. Laurie Barron and James B. Waldram, 3–22. Regina: Canadian Plains Research Center, 1986.

———. "Western Canada and the Frontier Thesis." In *Report of the Annual Meeting*, by Canadian Historical Association, 105–114. 1940.

Swainger, Jonathan S. "Ideology, Social Capital, and Entrepreneurship." In *Beyond the Law: Lawyers and Business in Canada, 1830 to 1930*, edited by Carol Wilton, 377–402. Toronto: The Osgoode Society, 1990.

Teillet, Jean. "200 Years of Observations on the Metis." Presented at *Canadian Issues: A National Conference on Teaching, Learning and Communicating the History of Canada*. Historica Association of Canada, Edmonton, AB, 28 October 2005.

Thom, Jo-Ann. "The Effect of Readers' Responses on the Development of Aboriginal Literature in Canada: A Study of Maria Campbell's *Halfbreed*, Beatrice Culleton's *In Search of April Raintree*, and Richard Wagamese's *Keeper'n Me*." In *In Search of April Raintree: Critical Edition*, by Beatrice Culleton Mosionier, edited by Cheryl Suzack, 295–306. Winnipeg: Portage & Main Press, 1999.

Thorner, T. "The Not So Peaceable Kingdom: Crime and Criminal Justice in Frontier Calgary." In *Frontier Calgary: Town, City, and Region, 1875–1914*, edited by Anthony W. Rasporich and Henry Cornelius Klassen, 100–113. Calgary: McClelland and Stewart West, 1975.

Thrift, Gayle. "'By the West, for the West': Frederick Haultain and the Struggle for Provincial Rights in Alberta." *Alberta History* 59, no. 1 (Winter 2011): 2–11.

Travers, Karen J. "The Drummond Island Voyageurs and the Search for Great Lakes Métis Identity." In *The Long Journey of a Forgotten People: Métis Identities and Family Histories*, edited by Ute Lischke and David McNab, 219–244. Waterloo, ON: Wilfrid Laurier University Press, 2007.

Van Kirk, Sylvia. "The Role of Native Women in the Fur Trade Society of Western Canada, 1670–1830." *Frontiers* 7, no. 3 (1984): 9–13.

———. "Toward a Feminist Perspective in Native History." *Centre for Women's Studies in Education Occasional Papers*, no. 14 (1987): 1–11.

———. "Tracing the Fortunes of Five Founding Families of Victoria." *BC Studies*, 115/116 (Autumn/Winter 1997): 149–179.

——. "A Transborder Family in the Pacific North West: Reflecting on Race and Gender in Women's History." In *One Step Over the Line: Toward a History of Women in the North American Wests*, edited by Elizabeth Jameson and Sheila McManus, 81–93. Edmonton: University of Alberta Press; Athabasca: Athabasca University Press, 2008.

——. "'What if Mama is an Indian?' The Cultural Ambivalence of the Alexander Ross Family." In *The Developing West: Essays in Canadian History in Honour of Lewis H. Thomas*, edited by John E. Foster, 125–136. Edmonton: University of Alberta Press, 1983.

Vivert, Elizabeth. "The Contours of Everyday Life: Food and Identity in the Plateau Fur Trade." In *Gathering Places: Aboriginal and Fur Trade Histories*, edited by Carolyn Podruchny and Laura Peers, 121–148. Vancouver: UBC Press, 2010.

Voisey, Paul. "Entrepreneurs in Early Calgary." In *Frontier Calgary: Town, City, and Region, 1875–1914*, edited by Anthony W. Rasporich and Henry Cornelius Klassen, 221–241. Calgary: McClelland and Stewart West, 1975.

——. "Unsolved Mysteries of Edmonton's Growth." In *Edmonton: The Life of a City*, edited by Bob Hesketh and Frances Swyripa, 316–335. Edmonton: NeWest Press, 1995.

Waite, P.B. "Sir Oliver Mowat's Canada: Reflections on an Un-Victorian Society." In *Oliver Mowat's Ontario*, edited by Donald A. Swainson, 12–32. Toronto: Macmillan, 1972.

Waldram, James B. "The 'Other Side': Ethnostatus Distinctions in Western Subarctic Native Communities." In *1885 and After: Native Society in Transition*, edited by F. Laurie Barron and James B. Waldram, 279–295. Regina: Canadian Plains Research Center, 1986.

Walker, James W. St. G. "Race and Recruitment in World War I: Enlistment of Visible Minorities in the Canadian Expeditionary Force." *Canadian Historical Review* 70, no. 1 (1989): 1–26.

Weaver, Sally M. "The Iroquois: The Grand River Reserve in the Late Nineteenth and Early Twentieth Centuries, 1875–1945." In *Aboriginal Ontario: Historical Perspectives on the First Nations*, edited by Edward Rogers and Donald B. Smith, 213–257. Toronto: Dundurn Press, 1994.

Whidden, Lynn. "Métis Music." In *Metis Legacy: A Metis Historiography and Annotated Bibliography*, edited by Lawrence J. Barkwell, Leah Dorion, and Darren R. Préfontaine, 169–176. Winnipeg: Pemmican Publications Inc., 2001.

White, Richard. "Native Americans and the Environment." In *Scholars and the Indian Experience*, edited by W.R. Swagerty, 179–204. Bloomington: Indiana University Press, 1984.

Willie, Richard A. "'It Is Every Man for Himself': Winnipeg Lawyers and the Law Business, 1870 to 1903." In *Beyond the Law: Lawyers and Business in Canada, 1830–1930,* edited by Carol Wilton, 263–297. Toronto: The Osgoode Society, 1990.

Wilson, Alan. "'In a Business Way': C.J. Brydges and the Hudson's Bay Company, 1879–89." In *The West and the Nation: Essays in Honour of W.L. Morton,* edited by Carl Berger and Ramsay Cook, 114–139. Toronto: McClelland & Stewart, 1976.

Wilton, Shauna. "Manitoba Women Nurturing the Nation: The Manitoba IODE and Maternal Nationalism, 1913–1920." *Journal of Canadian Studies* 35, no. 2 (2000). doi: 10.3138/jcs.35.2149.

Wonders, William C. "Edmonton in the Klondike Gold Rush." In *Edmonton: The Life of a City,* edited by Bob Hesketh and Frances Swyripa, 57–69. Edmonton: NeWest Press, 1995.

Wright, Janet. "Beaulieu Revitalized." *Heritage Canada* (January/February 1998): 6–8.

Wuth, Farley. "Lionel Brooke's Role as a Remittance Man." Presented at Lethbridge Historical Society. Lethbridge, AB, 19 October 2004.

Novels and Fiction

Demos, John. *The Unredeemed Captive: A Family Story from Early America.* New York: Alfred A. Knopf, 1995.

Eaton, Winnifred (Onoto Watanna). *Cattle.* New York: A.L. Burt Company, 1924.

Green, Jim. "Jughandle Smith Goes to Town." In *Humorous Cowboy Poetry: A Knee-Slappin' Gathering.* Layton, UT: Gibbs Smith Publishers, 1995.

Johnson, Pauline. *Flint and Feather: The Complete Poems.* Toronto: Hodder and Stoughton, 1974. First published 1917.

Lavallée, Ronald. *The Way of the Wolf: Tchipayuk.* Vancouver: Talonbooks, 1994.

McNickle, D'Arcy. *The Surrounded.* Albuquerque: University of New Mexico Press, 1978. First published 1936.

Mosionier, Beatrice Culleton. *In Search of April Raintree: Critical Edition,* edited by Cheryl Suzack. Winnipeg: Portage & Main Press, 1999.

Mourning Dove. *Cogewea, the Half-Blood: A Depiction of the Great Montana Cattle Range.* Lincoln: University of Nebraska Press, 1981. First published 1927.

Stringer, Arthur John Arbuthnott. *The Prairie Child.* Toronto: McClelland & Stewart, 1922.

——. *The Prairie Mother.* Toronto: McClelland & Stewart, 1920.

——. *Prairie Stories.* New York: A.L. Burt Company, 1920.

Wilson, Dot. *Canoe Lady: A Novel of Artist Frances Anne Hopkins' Years in Canada.* Olympia, WA: Boundary Line Books, 2007.

Winn, Vanessa. *The Chief Factor's Daughter.* Vancouver: Touchwood Editions, 2009.

Page numbers in italics refer to
photographs. Marie Rose refers to
Marie Rose Delorme Smith, and
Charlie refers to her husband, Charlie
Smith. Isabella refers to Isabella Clark
Hardisty Lougheed, and James refers to
her husband, James Lougheed.

Aberdeen, Lady (Ishbel Hamilton-
        Gordon)
    Coldstream Ranch, 150, 406n117
    maternal feminism, 117, 393n200
    National Council of Women,
        116–19, 393n192, 393n194
    VON founder, 395n214, 395n216
Aboriginal, terminology, xiii–xiv
    See also terminology
"The Adventures of the Wild West of
        1870" (Marie Rose Smith)
    about, 189, 286–87

date of composition, 204, 290, 297,
        420n1
    unpublished, 189
"The Adventures of the Wild West
        of 1870" (Marie Rose Smith),
        subjects
    alcohol use, 230
    arranged marriages, 224
    child care, 252–53
    father as fur trader, 189
    Frenchy Riviere, 251
    friendliness of oldtimers, 290
    Jughandle Ranch, 264
    Kootenai Brown, 246–47
    Marie Rose's independence, 254,
        263–65
    marriages of white men and
        Indigenous women, 243
    maverick cattle, 258–59
    Metis conflicts and Riel, 315
    Metis songs, 296

obedience of wives, 230, 263–64

survival skills, 267

sweat lodges, 308

transitional economy, 290

women's work, 230, 304

agriculture. *See* farms; ranches

Alberta

fur trade transitional era, xxi

land speculation, 143

oil and gas industry, 146, 405n105

population (1901), 306

western autonomy movement, 145–46, 169, 405n105

See also Calgary; Edmonton; Pincher Creek

Albright, Frederick S. and Evelyn, 177, 416nn229–30

alcohol

about, 358n9

W. Hardisty's use, 27–28, 43

HBC men's use, 27–28, 358n9

Jamaica Ginger, 230, 232, 236

Lacombe's disapproval, 238–39

traders, bootleggers, and smugglers, 227, 231–32, 250, 358n9, 358n11

See also Smith, Charlie (Marie Rose's husband), trader

Alderson, ghost town, 450n207

Allen, Charlotte Scarborough (Robert's wife, Mary Anne's mother, Isabella's grandmother), 44–45, 46, 364n72

Allen, Edwin and Robert (Mary Anne's brothers), 48–49

Allen, Mary (Robert's mother), 44, 364n73

Allen, Mary Anne (later Hardisty, later Thomas) (Isabella's mother)

birth (1840) and ancestry, 21, 44–49

life in Fort Dunvegan, 49

life in Pacific Northwest, 44–49, 364n72

marriage to W. Hardisty (1857), 38–39, 49

physical appearance, 367n111

See also Hardisty, Mary Anne Allen (William's wife, Isabella's mother); Thomas, Mary Anne Allen Hardisty (Edwin's wife, Isabella's mother)

Allen, Robert (Charlotte's husband, Mary Anne's father, Isabella's grandfather)

HBC man, 44–46, 49, 364n73

Alloway, Mrs. W.F., 181

Anderson, Chris, 460n5, 460n9, 461n12

André, Alexis, 316–17

Anglos. *See* Euro-North Americans

Archibald, Heber, 160–61

Armitage, Susan, 13

Arthur, Prince, Duke and Duchess of Connaught, 111–12, 407n122

Baalim, Harry, 268, 279, 287–88

Badger, Jim, 410n170

Baergen, William Peter, 453n40

Baird, Spencer Fullerton, 28, 30

Baker, Hugh C., 400n48

Banff National Park

British royalty visits, 107–08, 150

Isabella's auto trips, 100–03, 135, 342, 380n64, 387n140

Lougheed summer home, 179, 380n64, 407n120, 417n240, 418n241

Bank of Montreal

Hardisty kinship network, 80, 131

Barman, Jean, xxiv, 406n117

Batoche. *See* conflicts in 1885

Battle of Seven Oaks. *See* conflicts in 1816

Beattie, Judith Hudson, 21, 38, 367n109

Beaulieu family
    free traders, 55–58, 368nn135–36,
        369n136
Beaulieu House
    about, 82–83, 106–09, 135
    architecture and gardens,
        82–83, 106–07, 112, 148–49, 149,
        420n271
    auction of contents (1938), 170, 172,
        184, 419n264, 419n267, 420n270
    James's estate, 175–76
    library, 185–87, 186, 420nn270–71
    location, 82–83
    name, 58–59, 148, 369n143
    National Historic Site (2005), 148,
        379n61, 419n267
    repossession for unpaid taxes
        (1930s), 147, 173, 182–83,
        419n267
    restoration (1993), 104, 419n267
    sandstone construction, 17, 147,
        148–49, 406n110
    use after repossession (1938),
        419n267
Beaulieu House, Isabella's
    management
    about, 88–89, 110, 115, 186, 337–38
    accommodations for guests, 90,
        111–12, 174, 183, 389n154,
        407n119
    British royalty, 90, 106–08, 111–12,
        390n165, 407n119
    ceremonial events, 391n166
    clubs and organizations, 118–19,
        123–24, 126, 183, 342
    dances, 104–05, 108–09, 111,
        389n152
    dignitaries, 22, 89–90, 106–08,
        111–12, 167, 377n44
    early years, 82–83
    garden parties, 118–19, 149, 149–50

Isabella's widowhood, 22, 167,
    172–73, 175–76, 181–83, 339,
    419n267
James's absence from events,
    109–10
"Lady Belle Lougheed," 17, 22, 25–26
Lougheed children at, 85, 109, 167,
    419n267
media coverage, 71, 83, 88–89,
    104–10, 183–85
New Year's celebrations, 82, 182,
    379n50
private vs. public sphere, 125–26
pushing of protocol boundaries,
    103
servants, 125, 174, 347
social capital, 182–83, 185, 338
video of tour, 71, 374n2
Bedingfeld, Agnes, 177–78
Begg, Alexander, 8–10, 20
Bennett, Richard Bedford
    community booster, 413n212,
    414n217
    CPR interests, 401n65, 404n96
    dispute with James, 172, 173,
    414n217, 440n97
    Isabella's relationship with, 172–73
    James's law partnership, 97, 142,
    403n78, 403n81, 414n217
    land speculation, 142, 143, 401n65
    personal qualities, 173, 383n96,
    404n96, 413n212, 414n217
    prime minister, 144, 413n212,
    414n217
    views on transitional economy,
    141–42
    wealth, 140, 141, 414n217
biographies of women, xxiv–xxv, 15,
    351n17
    See also comparison of Isabella and
    Marie Rose
Bird, Madeline Mercredi, 211

509

Birney, Charlotte Beaulieu, 47, 48–49, 52, 365nn89–90

Birney, James, 46–49, 52, 365n87, 365nn89–90

"Bits of My Home Life" (Marie Rose Smith), 237

Blackfoot, 236, 253, 303, 456n70

Blake, Samuel and Edward, 74, 374n15

Blanchet, Father, 365nn89–90

Blood, 203, 253, 456n70

Bly, David, 86–87

boarding school education. See education at boarding schools

Bobrovitz, Jennifer, 84–85, 103, 107, 379n61, 382n89

bois brulé, xii
    See also terminology for Metis

Bone, P. Turner and Elizabeth, 137, 396n227

boosterism
    about, 185
    agriculture, 129–30
    back to the land movement, 450n207
    Calgary Stampede, 446n181, 461n23
    gendered images, 128
    Indigenous peoples, 446n181
    James's kinship network, 145
    land speculation, 135, 143
    Prairie regionalism, 169–70
    remittance men, 245
    self-interest, 143
    women's clubs, 151–52
    See also transitional era (1885 to 1920); transitional economy (1885 to 1920)

Borden, Robert, 93, 150–51, 384n101, 419n264

Boyer, Cecilia, 204–05

Boy Scouts, 111

Brady, Jim, 305

Breland, Marie Anne, 52

Brennan, Brian, 97

Brooke, Lionel
    about, 245, 438n74, 439n82
    Chinook Ranch, 244, 439n82
    death (1939), 244, 439n82, 445n159
    Marie Rose's social network, 244–46, 439n82, 445n159
    nomadic life, 244, 251, 312, 439n82
    public regard for, 251
    See also remittance men

Brown, Jennifer, 2, 340–41, 355n47

Brown, Kootenai
    about, 239, 246–49
    folksongs, 215
    Marie Rose's social network, 215, 246–49, 248, 265–66
    Ni-ti-mous (wife), 215, 247–49, 248, 265–66, 308–09, 434n26, 439n91
    nomadic life, 246–47, 251, 312
    Olive (wife), 246–47, 439n91
    personal qualities, 439n91
    public regard for, 251, 439n91
    in Waterton Lakes area, 215, 246–49

Brydges, John, 140–41, 402n72

Buck, Minnie, 123

buffalo hunt, 195–200
    See also fur trade

Burney, Alexandre, 365n89

Burney, James and Charlotte Beaulieu, 365n89

Burns, Pat, 405n105

Buss, Helen M., 21, 38, 322, 367n109

Byrne, Danny (great-grandson of Marie Rose)
    "Jughandle" name, 433n20

Calgary
    beer and alcohol, 405n105

cattle industry, 228, 397n11, 405n105

CPR facilities, 132, 137–40

education, 99, 99–100

federal control of natural resources, 146, 405n105

fires, 147–48, 294–95

golf courses, 395n217

government agencies, 132

insurance companies, 400n48

Isabella's life before marriage (1882), 73–74

land speculation, 134–35, 137–38, 143, 403n81

law firms, 141, 403n81, 403n85

library, 185–87, 420nn270–71

Lougheed buildings, 147–48, 400n41

meat industry, 405n105

oil and gas industry, 146, 405n105

population, 79, 134

real estate, 137–38

sandstone architecture, 147–49, 182, 406n110

veterans, 395n217, 407n123

western autonomy movement, 145–46, 405n105

wheat production, 134–35

See also Beaulieu House; CPR (Canadian Pacific Railway)

Calgary, organizations

arts scene, 91–93, 104–05, 113–14, 126, 133–34, 185, 389n154

health care, 121–23, 151–52, 395n217, 396n218, 407n123

Ku Klux Klan, xxv, 294–95, 453n40

National Council of Women, 114, 116–19, 393n194, 394n203

Ranchmen's Club, 103, 106, 388nn143–44

social reform, 116–18, 122, 394n203

social services, 120–21, 151–52

suffrage movement, 116–17

women's clubs, 114, 116–19, 123–26, 151–52

See also Calgary Stampede; Methodist Church (Central United), Calgary; Southern Alberta Women's Pioneer Association

Calgary Eye Opener, 92

Calgary Golf and Country Club, 395n217

Calgary Grain Exchange, 134–35

Calgary Herald

Conservative paper, 81, 88, 378n48, 405n105

provincial autonomy movement, 145–46, 405n105

scrip advertisements, 164–65

Calgary Petroleum Products Co., 146

Calgary Stampede

about, 405n105, 446n181

boosterism, 446n181, 461n23

Indigenous peoples, 269, 271, 446n181

Isabella's support, 461n23

Marie Rose's buckskin work, 235, 269, 271

pioneer identity, 405n105, 461n23

Campbell, Andrew, 96, 384n110, 385nn111–12

Campbell, Maria, 197–98, 205

Campbell, Robert, 27

Camsell, Charles, 31–35, 360n22

Camsell, Julian and Sarah, 360n22

Canada Life Assurance Co., 136, 400n48

Canadian Pacific Railway. See CPR (Canadian Pacific Railway)

Carpenter, Jock (Marie Rose's granddaughter)

Fifty Dollar Bride, 297–99

her mother (Mary Hélène), 267, 270,
445n168
portrayals of Metis, 297–98
pride in ancestors, 192
Carpenter, Jock (Marie Rose's
granddaughter), views on
buffalo hunts, 199
cattle purchases, 228
conflicts in 1885, 298
convent education, 428n110
her ancestors, 192
Joseph's birth place, 443n140
Marie Rose's husband, 229–30, 298,
330, 433n22, 435n37
Marie Rose's mother, 421n11
Marie Rose's Sioux brother, 421n9
midwifery, 267
move to town of Pincher Creek,
445n159
Carter, Sarah, xxiv, 92, 353n12, 354n39,
424n34
Catholics
about, 211
childbearing, 259
class and status, 10
convent education, 211–16, 238,
260–62, 261, 295, 428n110,
454n42
"dit," French naming practice,
422n14
godparents, 3, 53, 259–60, 336,
365n90
IODE chapter categories, 396n227
KKK targets, xxv, 294–95
Marie Rose's children and husband,
243, 276
Marie Rose's faith, 238, 243, 260,
276
Marie Rose's social network, 243,
265, 295, 310
Metis spirituality, 198–99, 208–09
missionaries, 362n53, 376n30

patriarchal ideology, 238, 436n51
support for free traders, 57–58
See also Lacombe, Albert
Cattle (Eaton), 459n130
cattle ranches. See ranches
Charles, Burwell James, 71, 374n2
Charlie. See Smith, Charlie (Marie
Rose's husband)
children
celebrations, 379n50
child care, 209–10, 231, 252–53, 259,
311
domestic labour, 15–16, 37, 54, 203
godparents, 3, 53, 259–60, 336,
365n90
Indigenous culture at HBC posts,
55, 386n129
See also education; education at
boarding schools; Lougheed,
Isabella, children and extended
family; Smith, Marie Rose
Delorme, children
Chinook people
M.A. Allen's early life, 45, 48,
365n82
slave trading, 47–48
churches. See Catholics; Methodists;
Protestants
Clairmont, Adelaide (Marie Rose's
grandmother), 192
Clarence Block, 147, 148
Clarke, John, 57, 368n135
class and status
about, 10–11, 127–28, 330–31
authors and writers, 286, 321
education of Isabella, 59, 333–34,
370n146
education of M.A. Hardisty, 38
education of Marie Rose, 189–90,
333–34
financial losses and changes, 331

fur trade, 11, 189–90, 196, 224–25, 330–31

HBC northern posts, 11, 37, 54, 330–31

IODE chapter categories, 396n227

Metis class system, 305, 331, 338, 355n47

nouveau riche, 148–49, 182

racial boundaries, 19, 343

religion, 10

servants, 415

skin colour, 280–81

social capital, 331, 334

successful management of transitional era, 127–28, 337–38, 346–48

transitional era, 19, 127–28, 144, 173–74, 274–75, 330–31, 343

urban elite in women's clubs, 118–19, 123–24, 393n192

See also gracious womanhood

Coatsworth, Emerson, 382n90

Coatsworth, Nettie (Janet), 64

Cochrane Ranch, 256

Coldstream Ranch, 406n117

Coltman Commission, 190

comparison of Isabella and Marie Rose

about, xx–xxiii, xxvi–xxviii, 326, 347–48

Anglo-Metis culture, xxiii, 10, 296, 335

biographical approach, xxiii–xxv, 15, 351n17

class and status, 10, 21, 330–31, 337–38

community recognition of identity, 337

critical questions on, xx–xxii, xxvii–xxviii

deaths of children, 21

education, 10, 333–34

fluid identity, xxiii, 333–34, 337, 347–48

French-Metis culture, xxiii, 10, 296, 335, 337

historical sources, xv–xvi

influence of "first homes," 340–41

kinship networks, xxvii–xxviii, 326–27

land ownership, xxvii, 463n28

languages, xxii

management of personae, xxvi, 22–23, 124–25, 337, 344–48

marriage to Euro-North American men, xxi

names, xvii

organizations, xxii

personal qualities, xxi

pioneer identity, 337, 341–42, 463n28

scrip applications, 332–33

skills for transitional economy, 338–39

social capital, xxvii, 15, 331, 338–39, 346

unpaid labour, xxv, 16, 338

widowhood, 21–23, 339–40

See also Lougheed, Isabella Clark Hardisty; Smith, Marie Rose Delorme

comparison of Metis men in transitional era

scholarship on, xxvii, 343, 346

conflicts with outsiders

about, xii–xiii, 332–33

Dakota conflicts, 202, 425n61

Delorme family, xix–xx, 190, 224–25

issues, 7, 164, 169

Metis identity, xii–xiii, xx, 332–33

Prairie regionalism, 169

property rights, 7, 164, 430nn128–29

terminology, xii–xiii

conflicts in 1816

about, xii–xiii, 190, 420n3

Delorme kinship network, 190, 192, 422n16

land policies, 420n3

North West Company's role, xiii

Seven Oaks, xii, 192, 420n3, 422n16

conflicts in 1869–1870

about, xii–xiii, 8

class and status, 10

Delorme kinship network, 190, 215–16, 222, 300

Hardisty kinship network, 66, 372n172

Marie Rose's loyalties, 215, 313–16, 344

property rights, 8, 216, 430nn128–29

Riel's leadership, 215–16, 430n128

Scott's death, 215, 300–01

conflicts in 1885

about, xii–xiii, 7

Batoche, 222, 235, 242, 298, 303, 431n159

class and status, 10

Delorme kinship network, 190–91, 222–23, 236, 242, 300, 455n59

Duck Lake, 20, 155–56, 165

in *Fifty Dollar Bride*, 298

Hardisty kinship network, 66–67, 85, 236, 372n172

historiography, 5

impact on settlers, 20

Isabella's brother's death, 66–67, 85, 155–56, 165

Marie Rose's fiction on, 313–17, 322, 344

Marie Rose's views on, 236, 300

Rocky Mountain Rangers, 235–36

underground nationalism after, 333

Connaught, Duke and Duchess of, 111–12, 150, 407n122

Conservative Party

Calgary Herald, 81, 88, 378n48

James's membership, 81, 88, 144–45, 150–51

Constitution Act, 1982

Metis terminology and rights, xi, xiii, 326

country-born, xii

See also terminology for Metis

Cowan, Trudy, 84, 379n61, 463n35

Cox, George, 400n48

CPR (Canadian Pacific Railway)

Bennett's interests, 401n65, 404n96

cancellation of monopoly, 145, 404n97

fires, weeds, and sicknesses, 147–48, 287

impact on economic development, 132

James's legal and business relations, 80, 137–40, 143–45, 160, 401n65

Marie Rose's sales of sewn goods, 265, 271

media satire on, 143–44

transitional economy, 132

travel of itinerant workers, 263, 444n154

Cree, 12, 202, 271

Cross, Alfred Ernest (A.E.), 405n105

Crowfoot, Chief, 236, 302–03, 456n72

Dakota (Sioux)

Marie Rose's adopted brother, 191, 421n9, 428n107

Metis conflicts with, 202, 425n61

Daly, Harold Mayne, 140

Dartnell, Valerie, 367n111

Davin, Nicholas Flood, 108–09, 377n44

Davis, Donald W., 250, 440n98, 441n101

Davis, Matilda, 59–60, 370n145
    See also Miss Davis's school, Red
        River
Davis, Rosie (Charlie Smith's
        daughter), 433n22
Dease, William, 216, 430n128
Delorme family
    about, xix
    ancestry, xx, 18, 192–93
    Charlie's kinship network, 329–30,
        334–35
    class and status, 11, 224–25, 275,
        331, 339–40
    conflicts with outsiders, 190–91,
        215–16, 225, 274, 300–01
    "dit," as naming practice, 422n14
    fur trade culture, 194–201
    godparents, 259–60
    Marie Rose's brothers, xxvii, 343,
        345–46
    Marie Rose's kinship network,
        xxvii, 18, 240–42, 316, 328–31,
        335, 343
    mercantile capitalism, 329
    Pincher Creek residents, 240–42
    political activism, xix, 192, 216
    scholarship on men in, xxvii
    support for Riel, 11, 215–16, 301, 331
    transitional economy, 225, 329–30
    wealth, xix
Delorme, Charles (dit Ross). See Ross,
        Charles Delorme (dit Ross)
        (Marie Rose's adopted brother)
Delorme, Donald Ross (Marie Rose's
        uncle)
    conflict of 1885, 216, 298, 301
    namesake for Charles Ross, 191
Delorme, Elise (Marie Rose's sister).
        See Ness, Elise Delorme (Eliza)
        (Marie Rose's sister)

Delorme, François Enos (et Hénault)
        dit (Marie Rose's great-
        grandfather)
    conflicts of 1816, 190, 422n16
Delorme, Joseph (Urbain Sr.'s son,
        Marie Rose's uncle)
    conflict of 1885, 216, 298, 301,
        455n59
    with father in 1870, 430n132
Delorme, Madelaine (Marie Rose's
        sister). See Gareau, Ludger and
        Madeleine Delorme (Marie
        Rose's sister)
Delorme, Madeleine Vivier (Marie
        Rose's grandmother)
    ancestry, 422n13, 422n15
    marriage (1823), 422n13
Delorme, Marie Desmarais (Marie
        Rose's mother)
    about, xix
    ancestry, 18, 192, 421n11
    birth (1839), 421n11
    children, 191
    fur trade kinship network, 190–91
    independent trader, 204–06, 212,
        329, 426n69
    Indigenous healing, 209
    Marie Rose's arranged marriage
        (1877), 190–91
    Marie Rose's love for her mother,
        211
    marriage to Cuthbert Gervais
        (1872), 204
    marriage to Urbain Delorme, Jr.,
        190–91
    storytelling, 15, 207–08
    support for education, 211
    traditional handiwork, 211
    Urbain's estate, 201, 206
    widowhood, 190, 201, 204–06, 212
    See also Gervais, Marie Delorme
        (Marie Rose's mother)

Delorme, Marie Rose (later Smith)
  about, xix
  age at marriage, 218
  ancestry, 18, 273, 296, 327–28,
    454n46
  arranged marriage (1877), 18,
    190–91, 217–21
  birth (1861), xix, 18
  brothers, 191, 343, 421n9, 428n107
  class and status as fur trade elite,
    224–25
  clothing and jewelry, 305
  convent education, 18, 189, 211–16,
    428n110
  health, 449n206
  languages (French, English, Cree),
    18, 252, 271, 296
  Metis identity formation, 328
  musical training, 214
  physical appearance, 307
  sewing and handiwork, 210–13
  as valuable commodity, 224–25
  See also fur trade; Smith, Marie
    Rose Delorme
Delorme, Norbert (Urbain Sr.'s son,
    Marie Rose's uncle)
  conflict of 1885, 216, 242, 298, 301,
    455n59
  in Pincher Creek, 240, 242, 301
  silences in Marie Rose's writing,
    301
  wealth, 194, 423n27
  wife as sister of Marie Rose's
    stepfather, 242
Delorme, Urbain, Jr. (Urbain Sr.'s son,
    Marie Rose's father)
  about, xix, 189–90, 192
  ancestry, xix, 18
  children, 18, 191
  Crowfoot meeting, 302–03
  death (1871), 190, 201, 204

farmer and free trader, 18, 200–01,
    288
  wealth and estate, 201, 203, 206,
    221, 238, 432n3
Delorme, Urbain, Sr. and Madeleine
    Vivier (Marie Rose's
    grandparents, "le chef des
    prairies")
  about, 192–94
  ancestry, 192–93
  class and status, 193–94, 330
  death (1886), 193, 195
  education in Quebec, 193
  fur trade culture, 190, 193, 195, 199,
    216
  marriage (1823), 422n13
  wealth and estate, 193–94
Delorme, Urbain II and Nellie
    Gladstone (Urbain Jr.'s son,
    Marie Rose's brother)
  in Batoche, 240
  childless, 437n61
  class and status, 343
  Marie Rose's relationship with,
    xxvii
  marriage (1892), 240
  physical appearance, 241
  in Pincher Creek, 191, 240, 301
  siblings, 191
  Urbain Jr.'s estate, 206, 221, 240,
    436n59
Dempsey, Hugh, 383n96, 437n72,
    440n98
Dené and fur trade, 12, 53
Depression
  Bennett's unpopularity, 144
  impact on Lougheed-Hardisty
    family, 147, 170–72, 180, 183
  repossession of mansions, 147, 182
Desmarais, Joseph (Marie Rose's
    grandfather)
  ancestry, 192, 421n11

Desmarais, Marie (Marie Rose's
        mother)
    ancestry, 18, 192, 421n11
    birth (1839), 421n11
    See also Delorme, Marie Desmarais
        (Marie Rose's mother); Gervais,
        Marie Delorme (Marie Rose's
        mother)
Devine, Heather, 2–3, 421n4, 460n6
Dewdney, Edgar, 81, 88, 228, 457n99
"dit," as naming practice, 422n14
Dobbin, Murray, 354n31
doctors and medicine. *See* health care
"Does God Know His Business?"
    (Marie Rose Smith), 313, 319–21
Dominion Lands Act, 145, 411n175
Dooley, Pat, 250–51
Douglas Block, 147
dower rights, 417n237, 448n199
    See also land
Drever, William and Helen, and family,
        103–04, 388n145
Duck Lake, Battle of. *See* conflicts in
        1885
Dumont, Gabriel, 239, 315

Eaton, Winnifred (Onoto Watanna),
        286, 318–19, 451n5, 458n125,
        459n130
economy, transitional. *See* transitional
        economy (1885 to 1920)
Edgar Block, 147
Edmonton
    Isabella at ceremonies, 105
    Marie Rose's life in, 22, 205, 297,
        309, 457n96
    McDougall network, 130, 376n30
    See also Fort Edmonton
education
    Catholic education, 189, 211–13,
        238, 260–62, 295
    charitable donations, 392n188

children of HBC men, 9
"civilize" children of ranchers, 238
class and status, 10, 38, 59, 189–90,
        214, 370nn145–46, 10214
curricula, 212–15, 370n146
day schools, 213
Hardisty family's belief in, 27,
        38–41, 59
M.A. Hardisty's lack of education,
        38–41, 59
HBC posts, 368n124, 370n146
Indigenous ways of learning,
        386n129
    See also Red River, education
education at boarding schools
    age at attendance, 35, 52–53, 60,
        66, 212
    assimilation of Metis, 211–12
    children from HBC posts, 35, 52,
        54–55, 59
    class and status, 214, 333–34
    convents, 211–16, 238, 260–62, 261,
        295, 428n110, 454n42
    curricula, 212–15, 428n110
    deaths of children, 260–62, 261,
        443n142, 444n145
    English and French languages,
        428n110
    gracious womanhood, 54–55,
        68–69, 333–34
    husband's enrollment of wives, 232
    Indigenous students, 213
    living conditions, 214
    musical training, 65, 91, 105, 214–15
    separation of families, 52, 61–62,
        370n147
    social capital for transition era, 32,
        333–34, 371n152
    travel to school, 35, 59
    See also Miss Davis's school,
        Red River; Wesleyan Ladies'
        College, Ontario

Edwards, Bob
  popular satire, 86, 92–93, 143–44,
    151, 383n96, 383n98
Edwards, Henrietta Muir, 116
Edward VII, Prince of Wales, 106, 178,
    182, 390n165, 391n166
"Eighty Years on the Plains" (Marie
    Rose Smith)
  about, 286–87
  Canadian Cattlemen articles, 204,
    279, 286–87, 297, 305, 311–12
  confirmation of Metis identity, 342
  Euro-Canadian identity in photos,
    305–06
"Eighty Years on the Plains" (Marie
    Rose Smith), subjects
  agricultural expansionism, 290–91
  alcohol use, 231
  buckskin work, 271–72
  buffalo hunts, 217, 247
  Calgary Stampede, 269
  Charlie's bootlegging, 231–32
  Charlie's Catholic conversion, 276
  child care, 209–10, 231, 259, 311
  courtship and wedding (1877),
    218–20, 222
  family economy, 265
  First World War, 262
  fur trade, 202
  horse racing, 256–57
  hospitality at the Jughandle, 311
  hunting expedition, 288–89
  Indigenous ceremonies, 207–09
  Kootenai Brown, 246–47
  lamps and candles, 253
  near-drowning, 421n9
  New Year's celebrations, 251–52
  Ni-ti-mous (Kootenai Brown's
    wife), 248, 249
  obedience as wife, 230–31
  pride in her father, 202
  roundup time, 291–92
  sewing and handiwork, 211–13
  simple life of pioneer, 307–08
  Smith as "big trader," 222
  storytelling by her mother, 15,
    207–08
  winter homes, 217–18
Elofson, Warren, 253, 257, 293
English, John, 168
English language. *See* languages
Ens, Gerhard, 343–44, 355n47, 402n70,
    427n96, 430nn128–29
E.P. Ranch, 178, 182, 418n253
Erasmus, Peter, 452n10
erysipelas, 43, 363n66
Esquimaux Bay district, 42
ethnicity
  as cultural construction, xxiii
  IODE chapter categories, 396n227
  kinship networks, 3–4
  terminology, 350n2
  See also race and ethnicity
Euro-North Americans
  British wives for HBC men, 9,
    49–50, 213
  Hardisty marriages to, 40–41
  Marie Rose's children's marriages
    to, 263, 335
  Pincher Creek, 243
  terminology, xiv
  before transitional era, 20
  See also education; gracious
    womanhood; marriage, Euro-
    North American men and
    Indigenous women

Faraud, Henri, 39
farms
  abandoned farms, 279, 450n207
  back to the land movement,
    450n207
  cash crops, 293
  dry belt, 279, 450n207

expansionism, 129–30, 279, 290–91

irrigation initiatives, 169–70

Metis farms, 6–8, 194, 200, 206–07, 354n39, 424n34

mixed farms, 292–93

natural hazards, 200–01, 206–07, 291, 425n51, 425n58

technologies, 425n51

See also homesteads; land

females. *See* Indigenous women; marriage, Euro-North American men and Indigenous women; Metis women; women

fences and boundaries

about, xxi, xxv–xxvi, 285–86

ethnic boundaries, 19

financial boundaries, 282

geographic boundaries, 19

Metis and Indigenous boundaries, 297

racial boundaries, xxi, 19, 282–83

social fences, 285–86

transitional era, xxi, 19–20

Fidler, Moses, 296

Fidler, Véronique Gervais, 242

Fifty Dollar Bride (Carpenter), 297–99

fires, 147–48, 294–95, 416n229

First Nations, terminology, xiii–xiv, 355n43

See also Indigenous peoples; terminology; treaties

First World War

James's political career, 93, 150–51, 384n101, 407n123

Marie Rose's sons' enlistments and deaths, 262–63, 277, 278, 449n203

military hospitals, 93, 384n101, 407n123

Foggo, Cheryl, 440n94

Fooks, Georgia Green, 433n22

Forsland, Eva Smith (Marie Rose's daughter, S. McCargar's mother)

marriage to NWMP officer, 263

Metis identity, 324

newspaper articles on, 279–80

Fort Calgary

Parlow family, 389n154

Fort Dunvegan

M.A. Allen's early life, 46, 49, 366n102

Fort Edmonton

alcohol use, 28

Big House, 43

Catholic missionaries, 376n30

Marie Rose's mother's homestead, 228

Metis social customs, 36–37

Fort George, 365n89

Fort Liard

C. Camsell's memoir, 31–32, 360n22

W. Hardisty as HBC man, 27, 32

Indigenous culture, 32, 53

location and grounds, 32, 33, 37

Fort Macleod

cattle industry, 397n11

Marie Rose's seasonal trips, 223

Fort McPherson (Peel River)

location and grounds, 33

Fort Norman

grounds, 37

Petitot's visit, 35–36

Fort Providence

Grey Nuns convent school, 39, 41

Fort Rae

Beaulieu family, 58

Indigenous gatherings, 53

Isabella's memories of, 124

location and grounds, 33

Fort Resolution

free traders, 55–56

W. Hardisty at, 27, 28, 30–31

history and location, 27, 367n114

Isabella's birth (1861), 27, 53

location and grounds, 37, 53

Lockhart as chief trader, 360n19

scientific expeditions to, 30

Fort Simpson

Beaulieu free traders, 55–58,
368nn135–36, 369n136

Big House, 34–35, 82

C. Camsell's memoir, 35–36, 360n22

children's activities, 34–35, 39

class and status, 11

country food, 33, 360n30, 361n34

food shortages, 54, 58, 65, 124

W. Hardisty as chief factor (1862–
1877), 11, 27, 30, 34, 360n22

W. Hardisty's marriage to M.A.
Allen (1857), 38, 49, 366n106

HBC centre for district, 34, 49,
366n106

Indigenous peoples, 39, 53

Isabella's life, 42, 53, 59, 65–66, 124

living conditions, 33–34, 37–38, 58,
65

location and grounds, 34, 37

New Year's celebrations, 82, 379n50

Fort Vancouver

baptisms, 365n90

Mary Anne's birth (1840), 44

schools, 46

slaves, 48

Fort Yukon

W. Hardisty at, 27, 49

Foster, John, 2, 355n47

Foster, Martha Harroun, 3–4, 268,
353n17

Freeman, Ronald, 99

freemen, xii

See also terminology for Metis

free traders

Beaulieu family, 55–58, 368nn135–
36, 369n136

class and status, 11

Desmarais family, 192

Gaetz family, 128–30

HBC relations, 55–58, 130,
368nn135–36, 421n4

marriages to Indigenous women, 11

Sayer trial, 190, 421n4

sewing, 210–12, 427n100

transitional economy, 128–30,
427n100

treaty money, 227–28, 334

French, Maida Parlow, 389n154

French language. See languages

Friesen, Gerald, 354n32

fur trade

about, 194–201

alcohol use, 358n9

buffalo hunts, 195–200, 205, 247,
249

buffalo robe economy, 206

carts, 197, 199–200, 203, 204,
424n36

class and status, 11, 189–90, 196,
224–25, 330–31

diversity of economy, 201

farms, 201, 425n51, 425n58

freighting, 207, 212, 234

histories by pioneer association
members, 341

Indigenous relations, 202–03

languages, xxii, 271, 296

laws of the hunt, 197

mercantile capitalism, 6, 16, 329

Metis identity and, 328

North West Company, 356n75,
420n3, 422n16

pemmican economy, 205, 206, 309,
420n3

seasonal activities, 194–96, 202,
210–11, 288

spirituality, 208–09

trade items, 195–96, 198, 203

transitional economy, xv, 132, 203, 206–07, 212

travel, 200–01, 204

wealth and profits, 196, 228, 432n3

widows as independent traders, 204–07, 212, 329, 426n69

winter homes, 217–18

women's work, 200, 205, 210, 217–18, 288–89

See also free traders; HBC (Hudson's Bay Company); Metis culture and society; Metis kinship

Gadsby, H.F., 90

Gaetz, Annie, 129

Gaetz, Leonard, 81, 128–30

Gareau, Ludger and Madeleine Delorme (Marie Rose's sister)

in Batoche, 191, 222, 242, 298

carpenter, 222

conflicts in 1885, 222–23, 242, 298

godparents, 259

Madeleine's marriage to Euro-North American man, 222

Madeleine's siblings, 191

Metis burning of home, 298

in Pincher Creek, 223, 242, 301

in Quebec, 431n159

gender

biographies as historical sources, xxiv

boosterism and gendered images, 128

Metis identity formation, 331

Metis maternal ancestry, 332

Metis men in transitional era, xxvii, 343, 346

See also gracious womanhood; marriage; women

gens libres, xii

See also terminology for Metis

George v, King, and Queen Mary, 113, 150, 182

Gervais, Cuthbert (Marie Rose's stepfather)

cattle, 228

children, 242

freighting, 207, 212

marriage to Marie Delorme (1872), 204, 207, 426n74

in Pincher Creek, 242, 255

property inventory (1906), 256

Urbain Jr.'s estate, 206

Gervais, Joseph and Alex (Marie and Cuthbert's children), 242

Gervais, Marie Delorme (Marie Rose's mother)

ancestry and birth (1839), 192, 421n11

arranged marriage for Marie Rose (1877), 190–91, 216–22

cattle, 228

children, 191, 242

freighting, 207, 212

marriage to Cuthbert Gervais (1872), 204, 207, 426n74

physical appearance, 270

in Pincher Creek, 242, 255

property inventory (1906), 256

Urbain Jr.'s estate, 206, 221–22

See also Delorme, Marie Desmarais (Marie Rose's mother)

Gilruth, James, 259

Giraud, Marcel, 4

Gladstone, Azilda Gervais (Zilda) (Robert's wife, Marie Rose's stepsister)

godparents, 259

in Pincher Creek, 242

property inventory (1906), 256

Gladstone, Nellie (wife of H. Riviere), 437n61

Gladstone, Nellie (wife of Urbain
        Delorme)
    marriage to Urbain (1892), 191, 240
    See also Delorme, Urbain II and
        Nellie Gladstone (Urbain Jr.'s
        son, Marie Rose's brother)
Gladstone, Robert (Azilda's husband)
    with Kootenai Brown, 239
    property inventory (1906), 256
gracious womanhood
    about, 71–72
    Anglo culture, 67–69, *115*
    avoidance of controversy, 67, 116–17,
        119–20, 124, 126
    education at boarding schools,
        54–55, 68–69, 333–34
    suppression of Metis identity,
        68–69
    See also Lougheed, Isabella,
        personal qualities
Grahame, James, 41
Grandin, Vital-Justin, 219
Grand Theatre, Calgary, 104–05, 109,
        113–14, 133
Grant, Cuthbert, Jr.
    conflicts of 1816, 420n3
    as first leader of Metis, 192–93
    marriages, 193, 423n19
Grant, John, 402n70
Grant, Johnny
    dispute with D.A. Smith, 140–41,
        402n70
    on education at boarding schools,
        52
    Ens's annotation of his diary,
        427n96
    kinship network, 329
    on Metis women's work, 210
Grant, Richard and Marie Anne, 52
Gray, James H., 181, 414n217
Great Depression. *See* Depression
Green, Jim, 239–40

Grey Owl, 286, 451n3
Griesbach, William, 151

Hackland, Alfred and Mary Louise
        Hardisty (Isabella's sister)
    in Manitoba, 155, 408n137
    Mary Thomas's life with, 159
Haig, Douglas, 167
half-breed, terminology, xii, 9
    See also terminology for Metis
Hall, David, 95
Hamilton, Ontario, college. *See*
        Wesleyan Ladies' College,
        Ontario
Hamilton-Gordon, Ishbel. *See*
        Aberdeen, Lady (Ishbel
        Hamilton-Gordon)
Hardisty family
    about, xx
    Anglo-Metis ancestry, xx
    class and status, 10, 335–36
    conflicts in 1869–1870, 372n172
    Depression's impact, 147, 170–72,
        180, 183
    education, 39, 41, 52, 59
    ethics in business, 140
    godparents, 53, 336
    gracious womanhood, 68–69
    HBC aristocracy, 17, 27, 36, 37, 80,
        335–36
    Indigenous ancestry, 168
    Isabella's brothers, xxvii, 152–54,
        343, 345–46
    Isabella's kinship network, 25–26,
        44, 136–37, 328–30, 335–36
    James's kinship network, 17, 76–80,
        82, 86–88, 329–30
    Lord Strathcona as family
        patriarch, 42–44, 136–37
    marriage of men to Euro-North
        American women, 40–41
    media coverage, 25–26, 136–37

mercantile capitalism, 329

scholarship on men in, xxvii

transitional economy, 86, 130–33, 329–30

Hardisty (town), 93

Hardisty, Edward Stewart (Isabella's brother)

death in Lachine (1868), 61, 371n154

Hardisty, Eliza McDougall (Richard Jr.'s wife)

W. Hardisty's letters to, 40, 54, 62–63

Isabella and James's letters to, 82, 174

marriage to R. Hardisty Jr., 40, 362n53

McDougall kinship network, 73, 77, 130

widowhood, 82

Hardisty, Frank Allen (Isabella's brother)

class and status, 343

conflict in 1885, 236

gold prospecting, 153

W. Hardisty's estate, 153–54, 156–59, 179–80

R. Hardisty's views on, 153–54

Isabella's relationship, xxvii, 152–53

life in Calgary, 73

poverty, 153, 157–58

Rocky Mountain Rangers volunteer, 236

Hardisty, Isabella Clark (later Lougheed)

ancestry, xx, 44–49

arrival in Calgary, 73–74

birth (1861), xx, 32, 357n4

class and status, 10

father's death, 73

Fort Liard, 32

Fort Simpson, 32–40, 42, 53, 58, 65–66, 124

gracious womanhood, 68–69

Indigenous peoples, 32

kinship network, xx, 16

Metis identity formation, 328

physical appearance, 64, 67

transitional era, 23

See also Lougheed, Isabella Clark Hardisty

Hardisty, Isabella Clark (later Lougheed), education

Miss Davis's school, 39, 41–42, 52–53, 59–61, 370n147

piano playing, 65, 105

suitability as James's wife, 68–69, 76

Wesleyan college, 16, 42, 60, 63–68, 105, 187

W. Hardisty's views on education

See also education at boarding schools; Miss Davis's school, Red River; Wesleyan Ladies' College, Ontario

Hardisty, Jessie

estate dispute, 156, 158

Hardisty, Marguerite Sutherland (Richard Sr.'s wife, Isabella's grandmother)

ancestry, 27, 62, 358n5

children, 27

Isabella's visits, 60–62, 65

James as Hardisty patriarch, 363n61

marriage to Richard Sr., 27, 357n5

Hardisty, Mary Anne Allen (William's wife, Isabella's mother)

about, xx

ancestry, 21, 44–49, 52

birth place and childhood, 357n4

children, 27, 31, 39

Chinook kinship network, 45

class and status, 11, 38

early life in Pacific Northwest, 26, 44–49

Fort Simpson, 30–31

W. Hardisty's estate, 156–59, 179–80

Isabella's relationship with, xxvi, 76–77, 152–55, 166

lack of education, 38–41, 50, 59, 363n55, 408n136

life in Lachine, 154

life in Winnipeg (1878), 42–43, 66

marriage to E. Thomas (1881), 51, 72, 155, 364n72

marriage to W. Hardisty (1857), 38–39, 41, 49, 366n106

media coverage, 87

Metis skills, 30–31, 52, 54

physical appearance, 51, 67–68, 71, 367n111

scrip application, 166, 332–33, 411n183

self-identification as Metis, 411n183

status of, 49–50

transitional era, 21

widowhood (1881), 43–44, 154

See also Allen, Mary Anne (later Hardisty, later Thomas) (Isabella's mother); Thomas, Mary Anne Allen Hardisty (Edwin's wife, Isabella's mother)

Hardisty, Mary Louise (Isabella's sister). See Hackland, Alfred and Mary Louise Hardisty (Isabella's sister)

Hardisty, Richard, Jr. (Eliza McDougall's husband, William's brother, Isabella's uncle)

cattle industry, 397n11

conflicts in 1869–1870, 372n172

death (1889), 17, 80, 82, 94

father's views on his marriage, 41

Hardisty kinship network, 25–26

HBC chief factor and inspector, 43, 80, 377n41

Indigenous ancestry, 166

Isabella's arrival in Calgary, 73–74

Isabella's kinship network, 76–78, 328–29, 335–36, 372n172

James's kinship network, 17, 76–80, 130

land holdings, 131–33

marriage to Eliza McDougall, 40, 130, 362n53

McDougall kinship network, 73, 77–78, 130

Metis identity, 329, 332–33

Protestant, 76

real estate, 80

scrip dealings, 166, 329

senator (1888), 17, 79–80, 94, 336

transitional economy, 80, 130–33, 397n11

views on William's sons, 153

wealth, 17, 73, 77, 79, 130–33, 335

Hardisty, Richard, Sr. (William's father, Isabella's grandfather)

belief in education, 27, 41

children, 27

class and status, 330–31

death (1865), 42

education in Red River, 27

home in Lachine, 180

marriage to Marguerite Sutherland, 27, 357n5

views on William's marriage, 41

wealth and estate, 132, 180

Hardisty, Richard George (Richard Jr.'s son, Isabella's cousin)

education overseas, 62

W. Hardisty's estate, 398n29

kinship network, 43–44

scrip dealings, 164

Hardisty, Richard Robert Thomas
(Isabella's brother)
class and status, 343
death at Duck Lake (1885), 66–67,
85, 155–56, 165
W. Hardisty's estate, 153–54, 155–59
R. Hardisty's views on, 153–54
Isabella's relationship, xxvii, 152–53
scrip application for, 165–66,
332–33
Hardisty, Thomas Alexander Thomas
(Isabella's brother)
class and status, 343
W. Hardisty's estate, 156–59, 179–80
Hardisty, William Lucas (Mary Anne's
husband, Isabella's father)
about, 27–30, 29
alcohol use, 27–28, 43
ancestry and birth place, 27, 30,
357n4, 367n109
children, 27, 39
class and status, 11, 330–31
death (1881), 43, 72, 363n66,
369n144
death of his young son (Edward),
61, 371n154
education in Red River, 27
education of his children, 27, 30, 35,
39, 52–53, 59, 370n147
HBC posts, xx, 11, 27–31, 29, 36,
56–58, 358n11
illnesses, 31, 37–38, 363n66
in Lachine, 16, 43, 66
languages (Yukon and Chipewyan),
30
on Loucheux people, 30
marriage to M.A. Allen (1857),
38–39, 41
media coverage, 89
physical appearance, 29, 30
siblings, 27

support for scientific expeditions,
28, 30–31, 359n12
views on Mary Anne, 11, 49–50, 55,
59, 63
views on Mary Anne's lack of
education, 38–41, 59, 363n55
wealth and estate, 17, 153–59,
179–80, 398n29
in Winnipeg after retirement
(1878), 42–43, 66, 363n64
See also Fort Simpson
Hardisty, William Lucas, Jr. (Isabella's
brother)
class and status, 343
W. Hardisty's estate, 153–59, 179–80
R. Hardisty's letter on, 153–54
Isabella's relationship, xxvii, 152–53
letters to Clarence Lougheed,
408n141
life in Manitoba, 155
Hatt, Ken, 411n176
Haultain, Frederick, 250
HBC (Hudson's Bay Company)
assistance with scientific
expeditions, 359n12
class and status, 11, 127–28, 330–31
fear of Metis strength, 56–57
James as legal counsel for, 80, 160,
399n36
kinship and corporate models,
12–13, 44
marriages as business partnerships,
127–28
mercantile capitalism, 6, 329
native, terminology, 358n6
reciprocal family model, 12–13, 16,
44
Simpson's leadership, 11, 13, 38,
49–50, 213, 399n37
HBC (Hudson's Bay Company),
northern posts
about, 32–36, 54

alcohol use, 358n9

C. Camsell's memoir, 31–35, 360n22

children's labour, 37, 54, 65

class and status, 11

country food, 33, 360n30, 361n34

education at posts, 368n124, 370n146

education away, 54–55

food shortages, 54, 58, 65, 124

free traders, 55–58

HBC men's duties, 31–32, 37, 126

Indigenous culture, 11, 32–33, 36, 39, 53–54, 55, 361n40

kinship networks, 12, 26

languages, 30

living conditions, 11, 33–34, 37–38

locations and grounds, 32–33, 37

New Year's celebrations, 251–52

slaves, 48

travel, 32, 35

women's skills, 31, 37, 40–41, 54

See also Fort Liard; Fort Simpson; Mackenzie district

HBC (Hudson's Bay Company), transitional era

cattle ranches, 80

class and status, 330–31

company records, 132, 398n26, 399n37

department stores, 133, 137, 399n36

Euro-North American wives, 213

freighting, 207, 212, 234

HBC men's personal gains, 130–32

historiography, 1–2

James's businesses, 133, 137, 141, 160

land speculation, 131–32

mining and forestry, 130–31

relations with non-HBC men, 129–30, 402n72

shift away from Metis workers, 203

health care

abortion, 96, 384n110, 385nn111–12

hospitals, 93, 122–23, 151–52, 384n101, 395n217, 396n218, 407n123

Indigenous healing, 209, 267–69, 302, 308, 347, 445n173

midwifery, 267–68, 445n173

professions for women, 121–22

VON nurses, 121–23, 395n214, 395n216, 396n218

Healy, Joe, 433n22

historiography

biographical approach, xxiv–xxv, 15, 351n17

Metis identity, 9, 325–26

oral history vs. oral tradition, xv

sources for this book, xv–xvi, xxiii–xxiv

terminology for Aboriginal, xiii–xiv

Williams on "structure of feeling," xxvi, 352n23

See also terminology

Home Guard. *See* Rocky Mountain Rangers

homesteads

claims on adjacent land, 442n118

cultivation requirement, 453n35

dry belt, 145

fires, 257

government agencies in Calgary, 132

head of household's eligibility, 449n203

Marie Rose's second homestead, 277–79, 449n203

mortgage lenders, 448n201

sale of military bounty warrants, 447n194

women's eligibility, 417n237, 449n203

See also Jughandle Ranch, title to
 homestead; land
household economy, Marie Rose's. *See*
 Smith, Marie Rose Delorme,
 transitional economy
Hudson's Bay Company. *See* HBC
 (Hudson's Bay Company)
Hull, William Roper and Mrs., 122,
 148–49, 181
Humorous Cowboy Poetry, 239–40
Hussey, Nolen and Dorothy (Isabella's
 daughter and son-in-law), 182
 See also Lougheed, Dorothy Isabelle
 (daughter of James and
 Isabella)
Hustak, Allan, 161, 165, 170–71,
 387n141, 401n59, 413n208
Hutchison, J.A. and Dorothy (Isabella's
 daughter and son-in-law), 173
 See also Lougheed, Dorothy Isabelle
 (daughter of James and
 Isabella)

The Identities of Marie Rose Delorme
 Smith (MacKinnon), xix, xxi–
 xxii, 350n1
identity, Metis. *See* Metis identity
identity as Metis, Isabella and Marie
 Rose. *See* Lougheed, Isabella,
 identity as Metis; Smith, Marie
 Rose Delorme, identity as Metis
identity as pioneer, Isabella and Marie
 Rose. *See* Lougheed, Isabella,
 identity as pioneer; Smith,
 Marie Rose Delorme, identity
 as English-speaking pioneer
Inderwick, Mary, 19–20, 243, 356n75,
 437n72
Indian Act
 assimilation strategies, 353n12,
 454n49

enfranchisement, 99–100, 386n125,
 386n127
Indigenous costume permission,
 454n49
Marie Rose's exclusion from, 277
"marrying out," 353n12
prohibition on ceremonies, 296–97,
 454n49
reserves near settlements, 98,
 454n49
status and identity under, xi, 4
women's inheritance rights, 175,
 448n199
 See also Indigenous peoples
Indian band, terminology, 355n43
 See also terminology
Indigenous peoples
 assimilation, 125–26
 farms, 6–7, 354n39
 fur trade transitional era, xxi
 Isabella and assimilation, 344–45
 kinship networks, 2–3, 22–23, 53, 57
 Marie Rose's portrayals, 302–04
 organizations, xiii–xiv
 reserves near settlements, 98
 residential schools, 262
 stereotypes, xxv, 98–100
 terminology, xiii–xiv, 355n43
 treaty money, 227–28
 See also Indian Act; Metis culture
 and society; race and ethnicity;
 terminology; treaties
Indigenous traditional culture
 buffalo corrals, 247
 ceremonies, 207–09, 296–97,
 457n99
 healing and remedies, 209, 267–69,
 308, 445n173
 oral tradition, 319–20, 458n125
 skills of chiefs, 126
 spirituality, 208–09, 297, 458n125
 storytelling, 207–08

sweat lodges, 308

tricksters, 458n125

ways of learning, 386n129

weapons, 209

Indigenous women

child care, 209–10, 259

class and status, 11

healing skills, 445n173

hide tanning, 210, 269

Indian Act and inheritance rights,
175, 448n199

Isabella as evidence of
assimilation, 114, 124–25, 185,
344–45

labour, 15–16, 30–31, 37, 304

Marie Rose's portrayals of, 304

sewing and handiwork, 210–13

stereotypes, 125

transitional economy, 16

See also marriage, Euro-North
American men and Indigenous
women; Metis women

Inuit, terminology, xiii, 355n43

See also Indigenous peoples;
terminology

IODE (Imperial Order Daughters of the
Empire), 111, 123–24, 395n214,
396n227

Iroquois freeman, xii

See also terminology for Metis

Isabella. *See* Lougheed, Isabella Clark
Hardisty

Ives, Mrs. G.C., 341

Ives, William, 250, 440n97

Jaffray, M., 99

James. *See* Lougheed, James Alexander
(Isabella's husband)

Jephson, J.P.J., 103–04

Jetté, Melinda, 4

Johnson, E. Pauline, 71, 317–18,
458n125, 459n129

Johnston, G.E.H., 99

Judd, Carol M., 358n6

Jughandle Ranch

about, 230, 264

cattle, 18, 228, 255–56, 264, 287–88,
293

fires, 448n202

"Jughandle" name, 264, 433n20

location, 18, 230, 293

one-room log cabin, 223–24, 230

property inventory (1906), 256

use of land today, 433n20

work force, 264

Jughandle Ranch, Marie Rose's
management

about, 265, 334–35, 337–38

alcohol use by Charlie and guests,
230, 237

boarders, 267

child care, 231, 237–38, 259

early years, 223–24, 230, 237, 254,
264

her independence, 254, 263–65,
273, 334–35

hospitality for all, 230, 234–35,
237–38, 264, 311

kinship network, 328

Metis sustainability skills, 293

midwifery, 267–68, 445n173

New Year's celebrations, 251–52

obedience as wife, 230–31, 237–38,
263–64

Queen of the Jughandle, 18, 224,
264, 282

Jughandle Ranch, title to homestead

about, 263, 273, 275–78, 442n118,
447n194

appeals by white friends, 278, 281

Charlie's death (1914), 442n118

Charlie's letters to/from officials,
281, 432n12, 442n118

claim on adjoining homestead,
256, 275, 278, 432n12, 442n118,
447n194
cultivation requirement, 453n35
debts, 278, 291, 448n201, 449n203,
449n206
Marie Rose's financial hardships,
262, 273, 275-78, 281, 447n194
Marie Rose's title confirmed (1920),
277, 448n202, 449n206
Marie Rose's title disputed (1915),
278, 448n202, 450n215
military bounty warrant, 447n194
policy changes, 442n118, 447n194
"Jughandle Smith Goes to Town"
(Green), 239-40

Kane, Paul, 36-37, 361n40
Kells, Edna, 345, 433n16
Kennicott, Robert, 28, 30, 359n12
Kermaria convent, Pincher Creek, 260,
454n42
Kerr, John, 199-200
Kinnisten, Christina Grant, 176-77
kinship, Metis. See Metis kinship
Kipling, Charles, 434n31
Klassen, Henry C., 403n81
Knox Presbyterian Church, 90
Ku Klux Klan (KKK), xxv, 294-95,
453n40

Lachine, Quebec
W. Hardisty's death, 363n66,
369n144
W. Hardisty's retirement to, 16, 43,
72, 363n66
Isabella's visits, 59-61, 65, 73,
369n144
Lacombe, Albert
competition with Methodists,
362n53

Marie Rose's social network,
238-39, 243, 260, 295, 296
views on convent education,
238-39, 260, 262
views on Indigenous peoples, 262,
310, 457n99
land
class and status, 275
common use, 8, 275, 287-88,
291-92, 326, 430n129, 442n118,
452n10, 463n28
dower rights, 417n237, 448n199
HBC men's personal gain in land
deals, 130-31
Indigenous territorial boundaries,
8
individual ownership, 8, 275, 287,
463n28
Metis conflicts and property rights,
7-8, 430n129
Metis identity, 8, 326
Metis ownership in fur trade era,
347
open-range grazing, 287-88
ownership and rights, xxvii
reserves near settlements, 98
Riel's views on, 430n129
scrip and land occupancy, 164-66
transitional era, 8, 130-31, 275, 287
women's ownership, 176-79,
417n237, 448n199, 449n203,
463n28
See also farms; homesteads;
ranches; scrip; treaties
Lane, George, 405n105
Lang, Wilbur, 269
languages
comparison of Isabella and Marie
Rose, 296
critical questions on, xxii
education at boarding schools
(English, French), 428n110

W. Hardisty's languages, 30

Marie Rose's languages, 18, 252, 271, 296

transitional era, xxii, 271

Lapierre House, 37

Larkin, Ed, 248

Laurence, Margaret, 340–41

LeBoeuf, Nancy Gervais, 242

Legal, Émile-Joseph, 295

Lépine, Ambroise, 215, 429n125

Leslie, Jean, 107

life writing, xv–xvi, 299–300

    See also comparison of Isabella and Marie Rose

Lindsay, Debra, 359n12

Lockhart, James, 30–31, 360n19

Loft, Fred, 100, 386n125, 386n127

Long Lance, 67–68, 286, 317, 345, 367n177, 451n4

Loucheux people, 28

Lougheed family

    Depression's impact, 18, 170–72, 183

Lougheed House. *See* Beaulieu House

Lougheed (town), 93

Lougheed, Clarence Hardisty (son of James and Isabella)

    birth (1885), 83, 379n57

    club memberships, 103, 388nn143–44, 395n214

    commercial building named for, 147

    death and burial (1933), 167, 171, 413n209

    financial hardships, 22

    W. Hardisty estate, 154–59, 180, 408n136, 418n246

    James's estate, 171, 175–76

    lawyer, 159–60

    letters to/from Mary Thomas (Isabella's mother), 154–55, 408n136, 418n246

    military service, 93

social events, 109, 150

Lougheed, Donald (grandson of James and Isabella)

    on Depression, 146–47

    memories of James and Isabella, 85, 97

Lougheed, Dorothy Isabelle (daughter of James and Isabella)

    birth (1898), 84

    British royalty visits, 107–08, 390n165

    death of her mother, 184

    letters to/from R.B. Bennett, 172–73

    marriage to J.A. Hutchison, 173

    marriage to Nolen Hussey, 182

    social events, 104, 109, 111, 166–67

Lougheed, Douglas Gordon (son of James and Isabella)

    birth (1901), 84

    commercial building named for, 147

    death (1931), 167, 171, 181, 413n208

    financial hardships, 22

    James's estate, 171, 175–76

    lawyer, 159–60, 171

    social events, 107

    wealth and estate, 171, 181

Lougheed, Edgar Donald (son of James and Isabella)

    alcohol use, 170–71

    birth (1893), 83–84

    commercial building named for, 147

    death (1951), 168

    financial hardships, 22, 170–71, 176

    his mother's death, 184

    James's estate, 168, 171, 175–76

    lawyer, 159–60, 170

    military service, 93

    social events, 107, 109

    video of, 374n2

    wealth, 168

Lougheed, Elizabeth, 375n16

Lougheed, Flora (wife of Norman
    Lougheed Jr.)
  on Isabella's personal qualities,
    85–86

Lougheed, Isabella Clark Hardisty
  ancestry, 44–49, 152, 327–28, 345
  death (1936), 167
  historical sources on, xv–xvi, xx,
    xxiii–xxiv, 84–85, 350n1
  "Lady Belle Lougheed," 25–26, 187
  management of personae, xxvi,
    22–23, 124–25, 337, 344–48
  Metis identity, 345–46
  obituary and notices, 181, 184
  physical appearance, 17, 64, 67, 71,
    110, 115, 135, 186, 345–46
  success in transitional era, 26,
    127–28, 346–48
  See also comparison of Isabella
    and Marie Rose; Hardisty,
    Isabella Clark (later Lougheed);
    Hardisty, Isabella Clark (later
    Lougheed), education

Lougheed, Isabella, children and
    extended family
  about, 83–84, 84
  automobiles, 134, 135
  children's deaths, 21
  children's marriages to Euro-North
    Americans, 336
  family trips to Banff, 100–03,
    380n64, 387n140
  godparents, 336
  overseas travel, 166–67
  relationship with her mother and
    siblings, 76–77, 152–59, 166,
    398n29
  sons' legal careers, 159–60
  See also Hardisty family

Lougheed, Isabella, community
    networks and boosterism
  about, 72, 89, 91–92
  arts scene, 91–93, 104–05, 113–14,
    126, 133–34, 389n154
  boosterism, 89, 109–10, 461n23
  Calgary Stampede, 461n23
  fundraisers, 111, 118, 121, 126
  health care, 121–23, 395n214,
    395nn216–17, 407n123
  Methodist Church, 89, 120–21
  National Council of Women, 114,
    116–19, 393n194, 394n203
  social reform, 92, 114, 116–18, 122,
    394n203
  sports clubs, 111, 395n217
  veterans, 407n123
  women's clubs, 114, 116–19, 123–26,
    151–52

Lougheed, Isabella, homes
  log hut as first home, 78
  summer home in Banff, 179,
    380n64, 407n120, 417n240,
    418n241
  See also Beaulieu House; Beaulieu
    House, Isabella's management

Lougheed, Isabella, identity as Metis
  about, xx, xxv–xxvii, 124–25
  ancestry, xx, 44–49, 327–28
  "being Metis" as adaptive social
    construct, 332–37
  fur trade family, xxvii, 124–25
  hidden pride, 23, 327
  management of personae, xxvi,
    22–23, 124–25, 337, 344–48
  media coverage, xx, 124–25, 184–85,
    344–45
  private vs. public sphere, 125–26
  Red River jigs and songs, 36

Lougheed, Isabella, identity as pioneer
  about, xxv, 125–26, 337
  community recognition, 337,
    341–42
  early memories, 59, 65, 124

fluidity of identity, 124–25, 337, 347–48

gracious womanhood, 68–69

Hardisty kinship network, 25–26, 93–94

management of personae, xxvi, 22–23, 124–25, 337, 344–48

media coverage, 25–26, 88–89, 93–94, 112, 124–25, 184–85, 337, 344–45

organizations of pioneers, 340, 341–42

private vs. public sphere, 125–26

Lougheed, Isabella, marriage

about, xxvi, 72, 86

community ceremonies, 105–06

family unit as work unit, 121

Hardisty kinship network, 10, 87, 93–94

James's knighthood (1916), 17, 92–93, 151

marriage as partnership, 86–87

metis ancestry as political liability, 97–98

personal relationship with James, 174–75

political support in Ottawa, 89

social capital, xxvii, 87, 185, 331, 334, 336, 338–39, 346, 380n72

wedding (1884), 76–78, 389n154

See also Beaulieu House, Isabella's management; Lougheed, Isabella, homes; Lougheed, James, marriage and kinship network

Lougheed, Isabella, media coverage

about, 72, 340, 344–45

arrival in Calgary, 73

dances, 104–05, 108–09

early life, 124

family trips to Banff, 100–03, 387n140

fur trade aristocracy, 184–85

government ceremonies, 105–06

gracious womanhood, 72, 124, 184–85, 344–45

Hardisty kinship network, 93–94

her views on boarding schools, 66

identity as Metis, xx, 184–85, 344–45

identity as pioneer, 25–26, 88–89, 93–94, 112, 184–85, 337

as successful woman, 112

video recording, 71, 374n2

wedding (1884), 76–77

Lougheed, Isabella, personal qualities

avoidance of controversy, 67, 116–17, 119–20, 124, 126

diplomacy, 126, 151, 172, 173

dominance, 85–86

elegance, 17, 85

gracious womanhood, 67–69, 71–72, 333–34

kindness, 173

love of dancing, 104

outgoing nature, 126

parenting style, 100–01, 386n129

private person, 84–85, 125–26, 174–75

pushing of boundaries, 102–03

strictness, 86

suppression of Metis identity, 68–69, 344–45

talented hostess, 85–86, 126

Lougheed, Isabella, views

avoidance of controversy, 116–17, 119–20, 124

Catholic faith, 60

Indigenous servants, 125, 347

maternal feminism, 117, 120–21, 393n200

women's suffrage, 120

Lougheed, Isabella, widowhood

about, 339–40

at Beaulieu House, 22, 167, 172, 175–
76, 181–84, *186*, 339, 419n267
R.B. Bennett's support, 172–73
community activities, 22, 123, 167,
181–83, 339
death (1936), 167
deaths of children, 167, 171, 181
financial difficulties, 155, 180
W. Hardisty's estate, 155, 179–80
James's estate, 168, 171, 175–76, 180,
415n221
social capital, 182–83, 339–40
Lougheed, James Alexander (Isabella's
husband)
birth (1854), 74
death (1925) and burial, 167, 175,
415n221
early career, 74–75
estate, 175–76, 180–81, 415n221
knighthood (1916), 17, 92–93, 151
life in Medicine Hat, 396n227
life in Toronto, 74–75, 90–91, 128,
381n88, 397n2
obituary, 181
physical appearance, *110*, 140
popular satire, 92–93
Protestant, 72, 74
successful management of
transitional era, 127–28
wealth, 175, 415n221
Lougheed, James, career before
marriage
about, 17, 74–76
law practice, 135–36
life in Medicine Hat, 74–75, 137,
396n227
life in Toronto, 75, 81
life in Winnipeg, 75
move to Calgary (1883), 74
wealth, 403n81, 414n217, 415n221
Lougheed, James, career in business
and real estate

about, 403n81
agriculture and irrigation, 169–70
Calgary Herald investor, 81, 88,
378n48
cattle, 79, 143
commercial buildings, 133, 147–48
CPR land, 137–40, 143–44, 160,
401n65
Depression's impact, 183
entertainment, 133
ethics and self-interest, 133,
137–41, 143–44, 151, 160–61, 165,
401n65
finance and loans, 133, 143
gold prospecting, 141, 153
HBC land and businesses, 133, 137,
141, 160
insurance loans, 136
life in Manitoba, 75
life in Medicine Hat, 75, 137,
396n227
media satire on, 143–44
oil and gas industry, 146, 405n105
partnership with E. Taylor, 80, 133,
399n37
partnership with Tweed, 75
power companies, 151
real estate, 79, 87, 133, 135–40,
377n37
resource speculation, 146
scrip dealings, 161–66, 411n181
wealth, 87, 130, 133, 141
Lougheed, James, career in law
about, 141, 336, 403n81
Bank of Montreal legal counsel, 80
CPR legal counsel, 75, 80, 137–40,
143–44, 401n65
dispute with Bennett, 172, 173,
414n217, 440n97
early law practice, 75–76, 135–36,
376n22
education, 75

fire loss, 148

Hardisty legal counsel, 136

HBC legal counsel, 80, 399n36

law firm (Lougheed and Bennett),
142, 403n78, 403n81, 414n217

legal cases, 95–96, 384n101

media coverage, 74

transitional economy, 135, 329, 336,
403n85

Lougheed, James, career in politics

about, 150–51

ambition to be prime minister, 97

Conservative Party member, 81, 88,
93, 144–45, 150–51

dispute with Bennett, 172, 173,
414n217

Isabella's ancestry as political
liability, 97–98

knighthood (1916), 17, 92–93, 151

leader of the Opposition, 144, 150

Senator, 17, 80–82, 88, 90–91,
94–95, 144

wartime service, 93, 150–51,
384n101, 407n123

western autonomy movement,
145–46, 169–70, 405n105

Lougheed, James, community networks
and boosterism

about, 91–92, 169–70, 414n217

agriculture, 169–70

arts scene, 91–93, 104–05, 113–14,
126, 133–34, 389n154

British royalty visits, 72, 106–08,
111–12, 390n165

business leaders, 72

Calgary Board of Trade, 89

ceremonial events, 105–06

health care, 121–23, 395n216

Methodist Church, 76, 89

political leaders, 72

Protestant networks, 72

Ranchmen's Club, 103, 106,
388nn143–44

school trustee, 89

social reform, 92, 114

See also Lougheed, Isabella,
community networks and
boosterism

Lougheed, James, marriage and kinship
network

about, 16–17, 87, 97

class and status, 127–28

family photo, 110

family unit as work unit, 121

Hardisty family patriarch, 154

Hardisty kinship network, 17,
76–80, 86–88, 93–94, 329, 334

Isabella's ancestry as political
liability, 97–98

marriage as partnership, 86–87,
127–28, 178–79, 185

media satire on, 143–44

personal relationship with Isabella,
165, 174–75

wedding, 76–78, 389n154

W. Hardisty estate management, 17,
154, 158–59, 179–80

See also Lougheed, Isabella,
children and extended family;
Lougheed, Isabella, marriage

Lougheed, James, personal qualities

aggressive style, 94, 407n124

ambition, 75, 94

aristocratic persona, 90–91, 382n92

authoritarian, 151

booster-joiner pioneer, 135, 414n217

British accent, 90–91, 381n85,
381n88, 383n96

clever, 151

diplomacy, 110, 151, 407n124

dominance, 407n124

executive, 110

executive abilities, 151

friendliness, 414n217
gentleman, 81, 382n92
love, 382n90
Methodist, 72, 75, 91, 381n81
Methodist faith, 382n90, 386n129
mild sarcasm, 382n92
paternalism, 178
ruthlessness, 407n124
strictness, 91, 382n92
Lougheed, James, views
becoming a "company man," 78
CPR insider information and land
speculation, 138–39
ethics, 140
Indigenous peoples, 95, 98–100,
152, 386n125, 386n127
land speculation, 140
marriage as partnership, 86–87,
127–28
patronage, 382n92
reserves near settlements, 98
sale of Indian lands, 95
scrip statute of limitations, 162
women's rights, 119–20
Lougheed, Jane, 375n16
Lougheed, Marjorie Yolande (daughter
of James and Isabella)
birth (1904), 84
death (1917), 167, 412n192
with Isabella (1911), 135
Lougheed, Mary Ann Alexander
(James's mother)
death, 76
James's admiration for, 76
religious strictness, 91
Lougheed, Mary Stringer (wife of
Norman Lougheed)
family trips to Banff, 100–03,
380n64, 387nn140–41
on Isabella's personal qualities,
85–86
social events, 380n64

Lougheed, Norman, Jr. (grandson of
James and Isabella)
oldest surviving descendant of
Isabella and James, 85
Lougheed, Norman Alexander (son of
James and Isabella)
birth (1889), 83
commercial building named for,
147, 148
education, xxv, 99
family trips to Banff, 100–03,
380n64, 387n140
financial hardships, 22
James's estate, 171, 175–76
lawyer, 159–60
life at Beaulieu House, 85, 167,
419n267
Lougheed, Peter (grandson of James
and Isabella, son of Edgar)
Alberta premier, 85, 168, 412n198,
414n217
auction of Beaulieu House's
contents (1938), 419n264,
419n267, 420n270
economic diversification, 168–70,
412n198
Indigenous ancestry, 168, 412n201
law practice, 414n217
memories of Isabella, 85
provincial rights, 169
resistance to Central Canada,
168–69
on sale of oil and gas shares in
Depression, 146–47
Lougheed, Robert (great-grandson of
James and Isabella)
views on marital partnership, 87
Lougheed, Samuel (James's brother)
carpenter, 375n17
early years in Calgary, 75–76, 79
James's estate, 175, 180

Lougheed House National Historic
Site, 148, 379n61, 419n267
See also Beaulieu House
Lynch-Staunton, Emma (Mrs. C.)
local historian, 194, 279, 296, 341,
423n30, 451n6

Macdonald, John A.
Banff summer home, 179
Calgary visit (1886), 89–90
CPR monopoly, 6, 145, 404n97
James's appointment to Senate, 81
Macdougall, Brenda, 2–3, 11, 326, 328,
331–32, 355n47, 460n1, 461n13
MacEwan, Grant, 78, 87
MacGregor, James G., 77, 376n29
MacKellar, Maggie, 221, 294
Mackenzie district
class and status, 11
convent schools, 39
Fort Simpson as headquarters, 34
W. Hardisty as HBC man and chief
factor, xx, 11, 27, 358n11
hardships, 11, 359n11
HBC fear of Metis strength, 56–57
See also Fort Liard; Fort Simpson;
HBC (Hudson's Bay Company),
northern posts
Macleod, James F.
death, 177
James's honouring of, 123
Marie Rose's social network, 249,
303
marriage to Mary Drever, 104
in Pincher Creek, 249
Treaty 7, 440n92
Macleod, Mary Drever
ancestry, 388n145
"colored" housemaid, 249, 440n94
marriage to James MacLeod,
103–04
widowhood, 177–78

MacMillan, Hugh P., 437n73
Macoun, John, 145
MacRae, Archibald Oswald, *99*, 99–100
Mactavish, William, 28
MacWilliams, Carson, 414n217
Maher, Valerie, 356n69
Major, J.C., 414n217
Manitoba
Metis terminology, xi
out-migration, 6–7
population (1881, 1886), 6
scrip, 161, 355n42
transitional economy, 6–8, 404n97
See also Red River
Manitoba Act, xi, 161, 355n42
Marie Rose. *See* Smith, Marie Rose
Delorme
marriage
British wives for HBC men, 9,
49–50
Catholic teachings, 265–66
HBC reciprocal family model, 12–13
mistresses, 50
marriage, Euro-North American men
and Indigenous women
about, 2
abandoned women, 265–66,
445n161
arranged marriages, 190–91, 224
bride purchase, 2, 221–22
class and status, 11
fur trade era, 49–50
Indigenous women in Euro-
American clothing, 266
Marie Rose and Charlie, 221–22
Marie Rose's views, 265–66
"marrying into" kinship networks,
2, 10, 222, 334–37
"marrying out" under the Indian
Act, 353n12
prevalence, 223–24, 243
racism, 243

transitional era, 49–50, 266

women as cultural mediators, 2

maternal feminism, 117, 120–21,
      393n200

McCargar, Donald (Shirley-Mae's son,
      Marie Rose's great-grandson)
   Metis identity, 323–24

McCargar, Shirley-Mae Forsland (Marie
      Rose's granddaughter)
   ancestry in family records, 423n23
   on Charlie's ancestry, 230
   descendants' beliefs on parents'
      wealth, 257
   Dutch identity, 446n181
   Edmonton home for Marie Rose,
      297, 306, 309
   on Marie Rose's pemmican, 309,
      457n96
   Metis identity, 323, 446n181

McCarthy, Martha, 57, 368n135

McCarthy, Peter, 88, 136

McCartney, Barry (Marie Rose's great-
      grandson)
   Metis identity, 446n181

McClung, Nellie, 393n198

McCormack, Patricia, xxiv

McCormick, Eneas, 178

McDougall family
   McDougall kinship network, 73,
      77–78, 130
   Protestant influence of, 376n30

McDougall, David (Eliza's brother,
      John's son)
   free trader and cattle, 130
   McDougall kinship network, 77–78

McDougall, Eliza (Richard Hardisty Jr.'s
      wife, George's daughter)
   marriage to R. Hardisty Jr., 40,
      362n53
   See also Hardisty, Eliza McDougall
      (Richard Jr.'s wife)

McDougall, Elizabeth Boyd (John's
      second wife), 87

McDougall, George (Eliza's father)
   first Methodist missionary, 73,
      362n53

McDougall, John (George's son, Eliza's
      brother)
   cattle industry, 130, 397n11
   Gaetz's friendship, 128–29
   Hardisty kinship network, 162,
      362n53, 379n57
   Methodist missionary, 87, 362n53
   Secord's business partnership, 162
   wealth, 162
   on whiskey traders, 250

McGillis, Cuthbert and Marguerite
      Delorme (dit Hénault) (Urbain
      Delorme Jr.'s sister, Rose
      Marie's aunt)
   Delorme kinship network, 192–93,
      232
   free trader, 130
   scrip, 434n30

McGillis, Marie
   marriage to Cuthbert Grant, 193,
      423n19

McGillis, Melanie (Marie Rose's cousin,
      daughter of Cuthbert and
      Marguerite)
   education, 232
   Marie Rose's travel companion,
      238, 255
   wife of Addison McPherson, 232,
      434n31
   See also McPherson, Melanie
      (Addison's wife, Marie's cousin)

McInnes, H., 99

McKenna, Marian C., 133, 165, 376n22,
      401n59

McLachlan, Irene, 118–19

McLaurin, C.C., 105

McLaws, William, 141

McLaws Redman Lougheed and Cairns
W. Hardisty's estate, 154, 155, 157,
159
McLean, Archie, 405n105
McLoughlin, John, 13
McNeill, Leishman, 134, 400n41
McPherson, Addison (Marie Rose's
kinship network)
Charlie's partnership with Addison,
130, 232–34
Marie Rose's kinship network,
434n31
wolfing expeditions, 233, 274–75
McPherson, Melanie (Addison's wife,
Marie's cousin)
Marie Rose's kinship network,
232–33, 434n31
trip to Winnipeg (1882), 232–33
McPherson, Mary Hardisty (Isabella's
aunt)
widow, 43
media coverage
Edwards's popular satire, 86, 92–93,
143–44, 151, 383n96, 383n98
Marie Rose's life, 279–80
See also Beaulieu House, Isabella's
management; Lougheed,
Isabella, media coverage
medicine. See health care
Medicine Hat
James and case of mistaken
identity, 96–97, 385n116
James's early life in, 74–75, 137,
396n227
Meeres, Edwin L., 233
Meighen, Arthur, 97, 146, 164
Melnyk, George, 168
men. See gender
Menez, Louis, 55–56
Methodists
Hardisty kinship network, 73
James as, 72, 76, 381n81, 382n90

maternal feminism, 120–21,
393n200
McDougall kinship network, 73,
77–78, 376n30
missionaries, 362n53
Red Deer, 81
Methodist Church (Central United),
Calgary
cornerstone ceremony (1904), 106
fires, 416n229
location, 106
Lougheed support, 76, 120–21,
381n81, 416n229
wedding of James and Isabella,
76–77
Metis culture and society
arranged marriages, 224
buffalo hunt, 195–200, 206
cultural preservation, 457n96,
457n98
dance, 198, 309, 457n98
as distinct social group, 57
"dit," as naming practice, 422n14
French language, 57, 296
geographic areas, 12, 425n61
historical knowledge, 14–15
historiography, 1–2, 5–7, 23, 325–26,
352n2
horses, 199, 201, 256–57, 289
kinship networks, 12, 57
music, 198, 214–15, 429n123
New Year's celebrations, 251–52
obedience to parents, 219–20, 224
Red River as political centre, 192
Roman Catholic, 57
seasonal activities, 194–95, 200,
210–11
sewing, 210–12
signifiers (clothing, dance, music,
religious beliefs, scrip), 14, 198,
327, 345
songs, 215, 225, 296, 429n123

spirituality, 198–99, 297, 454n50,
  458n125
transitional economy, 203, 206
wedding traditions, 219–20
winter hunting grounds, 194–95,
  217–18
See also conflicts with outsiders;
  fur trade; Red River; scrip;
  terminology for Metis
Metis identity
  about, xxi–xxiii, 14–15, 325–26,
    332–37
  accommodation of racism, 327
  ancestry factor, 327–28
  Anglo-Metis culture, xxiii, 10
  "being Metis" as adaptive social
    construct, xxiii, 273–74, 330,
    332–37, 344
  Catholic faith, 10
  class and status, 10, 189–90, 338
  common resources, 326, 442n118
  conflicts with outsiders, xii–xiii, xx
  critical questions on, xxi, xxvi–
    xxviii
  debates on, xx, xxiii, 14–15, 325–28
  distinct from First Nations, 208–09
  diversity of, xx, 14–15, 125, 305
  education, 10, 189–90
  fluidity of, xxiii, 14, 337, 347–48,
    454n41
  French-Metis culture, xxiii, 10
  gracious womanhood and
    suppression of identity, 68–69
  historical knowledge, 14–15
  historiography, 325–26
  identification by others, 345
  "in between" two cultures, 5, 14,
    328, 347
  integration pressures in 1920s,
    454n41
  Isabella as evidence of
    assimilation, 114

kinship and identity, xx, 326–27,
  331, 333–37
men's identity, 343–44
"mixed-bloods," 332
as political liability, 97–98, 113,
  392n186
pride in, 327
private vs. public sphere, 3–4,
  125–26, 322
scrip applications, 164–66, 332–33
self-identification as Metis, 3–4,
  332, 345–46
signifiers (clothing, jigging, music,
  flag, Michif language, religious
  beliefs, scrip), 14, 327, 345
silences on, 327, 454n41
skin colour, 280–81
transitional era, xxi, 3–4, 344
See also Lougheed, Isabella, identity
  as Metis; race and ethnicity;
  Smith, Marie Rose Delorme,
  identity as Metis; terminology
  for Metis
Metis identity and Red River history
  about, xii–xiii, xx, 14–15
  debates on, 14–15
  diversity of identity, 9, 14–15
  historical knowledge, 14–15
  historiography, 9, 325–26
  kinship ties, 10
  Metis terminology, xii–xiii
  North West Company's role, xiii
  response to conflicts with
    outsiders, xii–xiii, 332–33
  scrip applications, 332–33
Metis kinship
  about, xxii, xxvii, 2–5, 10, 326–27,
    333–37
  class and status, 10, 338
  fictive kin networks in transitional
    era, 327

fur trade culture, xxii, 22–23, 44,
206, 327–28
godparents, 3, 53, 259–60, 335–36
historiography, 1–2
identity and, xx, 326–27, 333–34
inclusivity, 3–4
location less significant than
kinship, 328
maternal and paternal links, 327
Roman Catholic networks as
parallel, 2
threat to HBC, 57
traditions, 22–23
transitional era, xxvii
value of Euro-North American men,
222
Metis organizations
history of, 354n31
Manitoba Metis Federation, 14
Métis Nation of Alberta, xi, 324
terminology, xiii–xiv
See also Southern Alberta Pioneers
and Their Descendants
Metis women
child care, 207, 209–11, 252–53, 259
domestic agency, 436n51, 436n5131
Metis skills, 31, 52, 54, 200, 204–05,
210, 289, 293
obedience to parents and
husbands, 230–31
responsibility for education,
436n51
scholarship needed on, 340, 343
successful management of
transitional era, 347–48
traders and businesswomen,
204–07
traditional handiwork, 211–13
transitional economy, 16, 206–07
unpaid labour, 15–16
women's dress, 305

See also comparison of Isabella and
Marie Rose; Lougheed, Isabella
Clark Hardisty; Smith, Marie
Rose Delorme; women
Minto, Earl of, 113, 392n186
Miss Davis's school, Red River
about, 59–60
arts, 91
backgrounds of students, 59–60, 61,
212, 388n145
class and status goals, 370n146,
371n152
curricula, 60, 91
M. Davis's education, 59–60,
370n145
Drever sisters, 103–04, 388n145
gracious womanhood ideal, 54–55,
59–60, 333–34
W. Hardisty's views on, 39, 42, 53,
60–61, 62–63
Isabella as student, 39, 41–42,
52–53, 59–60, 370n147
names of school, 59
parents' goals, 371n152
religious education, 63
travel to school, 59
See also education at boarding
schools
mixed-bloods, xii
See also terminology for Metis
Montana
Charlie and Marie Rose's life in
(1879, 1880), 228–29, 273, 287
Metis immigrants, 7
Spring Creek Metis, 3, 7, 268,
457n98
Montgomery, Ben, 230, 237, 307, 321
Moostoos, Chief, 162, 410n170
Morris, Alexander, 161
Morton, W.L., 4–5, 10, 425n61
Murdoch, Irene, 417n237
Murphy, Emily, 116, 417n237

National Council of Women, 114,
116–19, 393n192, 393n194,
394n203
national parks
automobiles in, 387n141
See also Banff National Park;
Waterton Lakes National Park
natural resources
federal control, 146, 170, 405n105
resource speculation, 146
Ness, Elise Delorme (Eliza) (Marie
Rose's sister)
convent education, 212, 428n110
in Jackfish Lake, 437n66
Marie Rose's arranged marriage,
217
marriage to Euro-North American
man, 222
in Pincher Creek, 223, 242, 300,
437n66, 456n69
siblings, 191
Urbain Jr.'s estate, 206–07, 238, 240,
436n59
Ness, George (Marie Rose's brother-
in-law)
conflicts of 1869–1870, 216, 222,
300, 315
justice of the peace in Batoche, 191,
216, 222, 242, 300
in Pincher Creek, 223, 242, 437n66,
456n69
prisoner of Metis, 216, 298, 300
Nolan, Paddy and Mrs., 91–92, 179,
382n92, 383n94
Norman Block, 147, 148
Norquay, Elizabeth, 205, 209
Norquay, John, 6, 354n32, 404n97
Norris, Marjorie, 118
Northern Pacific Railway, 203
North West Company, 356n75, 420n3,
422n16
See also fur trade

North West Mounted Police
ranch in Pincher Creek, 243, 437n70
See also Macleod, James F.
Northwest Uprising. *See* conflicts in
1885

Oakfield school, Winnipeg, 59
See also Miss Davis's school, Red
River
Oakley, R., 99
oil and gas industry, 146, 405n105
Ojibwe, 424n37
See also Saulteaux
Oliver, Frank, 7, 405n105
Orangemen, 72, 75, 300, 382n92
organization for pioneers. *See* Southern
Alberta Pioneers and Their
Descendants
Ottawa, James in. *See* Senate

Pacific Northwest
fur trade children, 45
HBC retirees, 13
M.A. Allen's early life, 26, 45–48,
365n82
slavery, 47–48
Willamette Valley, 4, 13, 48
Pannekoek, Fritz, 10
Parfitt, Kathleen, Helen, and Alice, 270
Parfitt, Mary Hélène Smith (Marie
Rose's daughter, mother of J.
Carpenter)
family photo, 270
historical account by, 268, 445n168
Parlow, Charles and Minnie Wheeler,
78, 187, 389n154
Parlow, Kathleen, 105, 389n154
Payment, Diane, 23, 429n118, 436n51
Payne, Michael, 358n9
Pearce, William, 94
Peel River (Fort McPherson)
location and grounds, 33

Peigan, 203, 253, 456n70

Perdue, Theda, 15

Person's Case, 116, 393n198

Peterson, Jacqueline, 2, 352n5

Petitot, Émile, 35–36, 361n34

Picket, Evelyne Stitt, 444n154

Pickles, Katie, 396n227

Picton, Pierre, 10

Pincher Creek
    boosterism, 245
    Catholics, 265, 295
    cattle, 228, 257
    convent, 238, 243, 260, 265, 454n42
    Delorme kinship network, 191, 223,
        240–42, 241, 301, 328, 343
    first Euro-North American women,
        243
    horse breeding and racing, 256–57
    hospital, 295
    Marie Rose's arrival (1880), 223–24
    Marie Rose's boarding house,
        245–46, 277, 279, 445n159,
        456n87
    Marie Rose's move to town, 277,
        281, 445n159, 456n87
    Marie Rose's social network,
        243–51, 248, 279–80
    marriages of white men and
        Indigenous women, 243
    NWMP ranch, 243, 437n70
    ranches, 244, 292–93
    remittance men, 244
    weather extremes, 257
    See also Brooke, Lionel; Brown,
        Kootenai; Jughandle Ranch;
        Riviere, Henry (Frenchy)

Pinkham, Cyprian, 104

Pinkham, Jean Drever, 103–04, 116, 122,
    388n145, 393n194, 395n217

Podruchny, Carolyn, 14, 326

political parties. See Conservative Party

Pollard, Juliet, 365n82, 370n146

Pratt, Larry, 170

press coverage. See Lougheed, Isabella,
        media coverage; media coverage

Price, Elizabeth Bailey, 462n24

Prince, Peter, 151

Pritchard, John and Rose (Marie Rose's
        aunt and uncle)
    prisoners of Big Bear, 216, 301

Protestants
    Euro-North American wives, 213
    Knox Presbyterian Church, 90
    social services, 152
    strictness, 104–05
    See also Methodists; Methodist
        Church (Central United),
        Calgary

Provincial Rights Association, 146, 169

race and ethnicity
    accommodation of racism, 327
    anti-immigration laws, 459n134
    "being Metis" as adaptive social
        construct, xxiii, 330, 332–37
    fluidity of racial boundaries, 19, 40,
        49–50, 337, 347–48
    HBC policies, 35, 49–50
    Indigenous stereotypes, xxv, 98–10,
        125, 231
    instrumental ethnicity, 283, 323
    intermarriage as cause of social ills,
        41
    IODE chapter categories, 396n227
    Isabella as "different" at Wesleyan
        college, 63–64, 334
    Isabella as evidence of
        assimilation, 114, 124–25, 185,
        344–45
    Isabella on Indigenous servants,
        125, 347
    Ku Klux Klan (KKK), xxv, 294–95,
        453n40

Macleod's "colored" housemaid,
249
Marie Rose on mixed blood
children, 250
Marie Rose on white vs. "Indian"
husbands, 231
Metis identity formation, 331
Pauline Johnson's transformations,
71
political liability of Indigenous
ancestry, 97–98, 113, 392n186
racial boundaries in transitional
era, 6, 49–50, 282–83, 452n8
skin colour, 280–81
stereotypes of Metis, 356n75,
357n76
trickster figures, 317–18, 322,
458n125
writers of mixed ethnicity, 317–19
Racette, Sherry Farrell, 427n100
railways
fires, weeds, and sicknesses,
147–48, 257, 287
impact on Metis, 203
Northern Pacific Railway, 203
travel of itinerant workers, 263,
444n154
See also CPR (Canadian Pacific
Railway)
ranches
about, 18, 398n30
boundary with farming, 292–93
cattle, 18, 129–30, 228, 253, 255–57
cattle theft, 258–59, 443n135
common land, 452n23
credit and loans, 143
early years, 253–54
education of children, 238
Euro-North American women, 20
expansionism, 129–30, 143, 398n30
fires, 257
grazing leases, 145, 255–56

Hardisty family network, 132
location factors, 293
Marie Rose's preference for
ranchers over farmers, 290
maverick cattle, 258–59
McDougall family, 130
Metis skills for sustainability, 293
mixed farms, 293
open grazing, 253, 264, 287–88,
291–92, 452n23
in Pincher Creek, 244
remittance men, 244, 438n74
roundup time, 291–92, 311–12
transitional economy, 132, 143,
398n30
weather extremes, 257
women ranchers, 177–78
See also homesteads; Jughandle
Ranch; land
Ranchmen's Club, 103, 106, 388nn143–
44
Red Deer
Gaetz family, 128–30
Methodists, 81
Red River
about, 192, 194–95
agriculture, 194, 200, 424n34
Catholic area (Saint François
Xavier), 193, 195, 423n22
class and status, 10
economy, 201, 210–11, 427n100,
430n128
Euro-North American women, 213
HBC retirees, 9, 13
kinship networks, 12
Metis centre, 192
out-migration of Metis, 6–7, 12, 192
petition for Catholic missionaries,
192
Protestant area (St. Andrew's), 195
river lots, 194, 423n22
seasonal activities, 194–95, 200

sewing districts, 210–11, 427n100

trade, 194, 195–96, 200–01

transitional era, 5, 192, 203, 211,
427n100

See also fur trade; Metis culture and
society; Metis identity and Red
River history

Red River, education

Anglican schools for Metis,
370n146

class and status, 370n146

convent education, 211–16, 428n110

HBC children, 9, 192, 370n146

Indigenous knowledge, gracious
womanhood, and female
production, 211

Red River Academy, 27

St. Boniface convent, 18, 211–16,
246, 428n110

St. John's College, 67

See also Miss Davis's school, Red
River

Red River Expeditionary Force,
447n194

"Red River Valley" and "Red River
Halfbreed" (songs), 225, 287,
296, 309, 341, 429n123, 462n24

Reid, Eva, 374n2

religion

IODE chapter categories, 396n227

See also Catholics; Methodists;
Protestants

remittance men

about, 244–46, 438n74

barter and credit system, 245–46,
439n82

British aristocracy, 90, 244, 438n74

Chinook Ranch, 244, 439n82

Coldstream Ranch, 406n117

Inderwick's life, 437n72

social lives, 244, 439n82

See also Brooke, Lionel

Resistance. *See* conflicts in 1869–1870

Rich, Edwin Ernest, 46

Richards, John, 170

Riel, Louis

convent nuns support for, 215,
429n125

decline in status of supporters, 11

Delorme family support for, 300

Father André's letter to, 316–17

Isabella's views on, 85

Marie Rose's fiction on, 313–17, 344

Marie Rose's views on, 300–01

property rights, 430nn128–29

provisional government, 215–16, 317

See also conflicts in 1869–1870;
conflicts in 1885

Riel, Sara, 213, 429n125

Riley, Maude, 116

Riviere, Henry (Frenchy), 250–51,
437n61, 441nn102–03

Rocky Mountain National Park, 150

See also Banff National Park

Rocky Mountain Rangers, 153, 235–36,
435n43, 435n45

Rodney, William, 439n91

Roman Catholics. *See* Catholics

Ross, Adele Delorme (child of Charles
Delorme Ross and Marie
Desjarlais), 240, 421n10, 437n62

Ross, Alexander

account of Red River, 197, 363n56,
424n36

Anglophone children, 461n13

conflicts with Dakota, 425n61

on slaves, 48

Ross, Charles Delorme (dit Ross)
(Marie Rose's adopted brother)

adopted "Sioux" boy, 191, 202, 240,
299, 421n9, 428n107

children, 240, 421n10, 437n62

class and status, 343

Delorme kinship network, 191, 240,
    428n107
    freighting for HBC, 428n107
    Marie Rose's relationship with,
        xxvii, 191, 421n9
    marriage to Marie Desjarlais, 191,
        421n10, 437n62
    in Pincher Creek, 191, 240, 301,
        421n10
    siblings, 191, 421n9
Ross, Marie Desjarlais (wife of
    Charles), 191, 421n10, 437n62
Rouleau, Charles B. and Mrs., 148–49,
    393n192
Royal Trust Company
    estate management, 168, 175

Sacred Heart Convent, Calgary, 260
Sarcee, 203, 456n70
Saulteaux
    agriculture, 194–95
    convent education, 213
    fur trade relations, 202–03
    hunting and trading camps,
        424n37
    Marie Rose's ancestors, 192,
        194–95, 422n15, 454n46
    Ojibwe, 424n37
Saunders, Annie, 249, 440n94
Sayer, Pierre Guillaume, 190, 216, 421n4
Scarboro Hill, Washington, 45
Scarborough, Anne Elizabeth(Mary
    Anne's grandmother, Isabella's
    great-grandmother), 44–47,
    365n90
Scarborough, Charlotte (Robert Allen's
    wife, Isabella's grandmother),
    44–45, 46, 364n72
Scarborough, James Allen (Mary Anne's
    grandfather, Isabella's great-
    grandfather), 44–47, 365n90,
    366n106

Scarborough, Robert, Jane, and Sarah,
    47
Scheer, Mrs., 248
scientific expeditions, 28, 30–31,
    359n12
Scott, Duncan Campbell, 319, 386n125
Scott, Thomas, 215, 300–01
scrip
    about, 355n42, 411n176
    commission inquiry, 160–61
    ethics in dealing in, 160–62, 165,
        411n176
    fraud statute, 161–65
    R. Hardisty Jr.'s dealings, 166, 329
    R. George Hardisty's dealings, 164
    James's dealings, 161, 164–65
    James's inquiries about Isabella's
        family, 165–66
    James's involvement, 161–66,
        411n181
    Marie Rose and Charlie's
        applications for children, 228,
        287
    maternal and paternal ancestry,
        332
    Metis financial need, 164, 287,
        411n176
    Metis identity, 4, 332–33
    Metis land in Calgary, 411n175
    Metis title extinguishment, 8
    Secord's scrip speculation, 162–64,
        410n170
Secord, Richard, and descendants,
    162–64, 410n170
Senate
    R. Hardisty as senator, 17, 79–80
    Indigenous issues, 95, 98, 178,
        386n125
    Isabella's visits in Ottawa, 104
    James as leader of the Opposition,
        144

James as senator, 80–82, 90–91, 94–95, 161–62

James's appointment (1889), 17, 80–81, 88

Roxborough Apartments in Ottawa, 91, 382n89

scrip issues, 161–65

Seven Oaks, Battle of. *See* conflicts in 1816

Sharpe, W.J., 99

Sherman Grand Theatre, Calgary, 104–05, 109, 113–14

Sifton, Mrs. Arthur, 109

Simmons, Deidre, 398n26, 398n28, 402n72

Simpson, George, 11, 13, 38, 49–50, 213, 399n37

   See also HBC (Hudson's Bay Company)

Simpson, W., 99

Sioux. *See* Dakota (Sioux)

Slacum, William, 48

Smith, Alfred Albert (Marie Rose's son)

   death (1891) at age one, 443n142

Smith, Arthur (Marie Rose's son)

   death (1903) at infancy, 443n142

Smith, Catherine (Marie Rose's daughter)

   death (1902) at age one, 443n142

Smith, Charles Jr. (Marie Rose's son)

   birth (1880), 228, 259

   death (1907), 443n142

   scrip application, 228

Smith, Charlie (Marie Rose's husband)

   ancestry, 229–30, 275, 432n12, 433n18, 435n40

   Catholic conversion, 276

   class and status, 334

   "crippled arm," 233, 435n37

   death and funeral (1914), 239, 262, 273, 276, 436n57, 442n118

   free trader, 130

obituary, 229, 258, 312

physical appearance, 217, 229, 239, 261

public regard for, 239–40, 258

Rocky Mountain Rangers, 435n43

will, 448n200, 451n216

   See also Jughandle Ranch; Jughandle Ranch, title to homestead

Smith, Charlie (Marie Rose's husband), children

   Catholic faith of children, 276

   his difficulties in new economy, 263–64

   Rosie Davis (daughter by Double Gun Woman), 433n22

   scrip applications for, 228, 332–33

   See also Jughandle Ranch, Marie Rose's management; Smith, Marie Rose Delorme, children

Smith, Charlie (Marie Rose's husband), marriage and kinship network

   about, 334–35

   age difference, 218, 220

   arranged marriage (1877), 18, 191, 217–22

   bride price, 18, 218

   Delorme kinship network, 18, 191, 329, 334–35, 434n31

   Marie Rose's objections to arranged marriage, 191, 320

   marriage (1877), 228, 428n110

   respect for Delormes, 219–20, 276

   silences in her writing about him, 274–75

   See also Smith, Marie Rose Delorme, marriage

Smith, Charlie (Marie Rose's husband), personal qualities

   alcohol use, 221, 233, 237, 240, 258

   hospitality, 230

nomadic lifestyle, 232–33, 238, 240, 273

patience with his young wife, 221

respect for Delormes, 221, 276

storytelling, 229, 233, 274

Smith, Charlie (Marie Rose's husband), trader

about, 130

bootlegging, 231–32

courtship of Marie Rose, 218

Lacombe's disapproval of whiskey trade, 238–39

Marie Rose's disapproval of whiskey trade, 222, 231–32

non-buffalo furs, 228, 233, 274–75

treaty money, 227–28, 334

wealth, 218, 222, 228, 233, 234, 432n3

Smith, Charlie (Marie Rose's husband), transitional economy

about, 273, 334–35

agricultural expansionism, 290–91

cattle rancher, 228, 234, 255–58, 287

cattle theft, 258–59, 443n135

cook for roundup, 291–92

difficulties with new economy, 263–64, 273, 334–35

freighting, 234

horse breeder, 256

Marie Rose's kinship network, 434n31

non-buffalo furs, 228, 233, 274–75

partnership with McPherson, 130, 232–33

real estate speculation, 233

Rocky Mountain Rangers, 153, 235–36, 435n43, 435n45

scrip applications for his children, 228, 332–33

treaty money, 227–28, 334

wealth, 255, 258

Smith, Donald A. (Lord Strathcona, Isabella Hardisty Smith's husband, Isabella Lougheed's uncle)

British royalty visits, 113

community booster in Winnipeg, 106, 392n188

conflicts in 1869–1870, 372n172

death and funeral (1914), 132, 136–37

ethics in business, 131–32, 140–41, 402n72

Hardisty family patriarch, 17, 42–44, 80, 131, 153–54, 336

Hardisty kinship network, 77, 336, 372n172

W. Hardisty's estate management by, 153–54, 158

W. Hardisty's life in Winnipeg (1878), 42–43, 66

HBC aristocracy, 42, 131–32, 140–41, 398n26, 398n28

his wife's ancestry, 97–98, 113, 392n186

James's kinship network, 77, 79–80, 144, 377n39

Johnny Grant's dispute with, 402n70

land and investment speculation, 131–32, 140–41, 402n72

marriage to Isabella (W. Hardisty's sister), 42, 97–98, 180

social networking, 112–13, 392n188

transitional economy, 131–32, 336

wealth, 17, 80, 131, 336, 392n188, 398n28

Smith, Donald B. (historian), 79, 95, 377n39

Smith, Eva (Marie Rose's daughter)

marriage to Forsland, 263

newspaper articles on, 279–80

547

See also Forsland, Eva Smith (Marie
Rose's daughter, S. McCargar's
mother)
Smith, Françoise Josephine (Marie
Rose's daughter)
birth (1895), 443n142
convent (1910), 260, 444n147
newspaper articles on, 279–80
Smith, Isabella Sophia Hardisty (Lady
Strathcona, Donald's wife,
W. Hardisty's sister, Isabella
Hardisty Lougheed's aunt)
boosterism in Winnipeg, 112–13
British royalty visits, 113
home in Lachine, 180
Indigenous ancestry, 113, 392n186
marriage to Donald A. Smith, 42,
97–98, 180
political liability of ancestry, 97–98,
113, 392n186
social networking, 392n188
support for education, 392n188
Smith, Jean Theodore (Marie Rose's
daughter)
birth (1894) and godparents, 259
Smith, John L. (Marie Rose's son)
birth (1894), 443n142
Smith, John Robert "Bob" (Marie
Rose's son)
birth (1885), 443n142
on his parents' wealth, 255
Marie Rose's scrip application,
443n140
oldest descendant, 255, 441n115
Smith, Jonas (Marie Rose's son)
birth (1881), 443n142
death in war (1917), 262–63, 277,
443n142, 449n203
Smith, Joseph (Marie Rose's son)
birth (1878), 259, 443n140
death (1914), 443n142

Smith, Magdaline (Marie Rose's
daughter)
birth (1899), 443n142
Smith, Marie Rose Delorme
about, xix–xx
ancestry, xix, 273, 296, 327–28,
454n46
arranged marriage (1877), 190–91
birth (1861), xix, 191
class and status, 243–44
convent education, 18, 189, 211–16,
428n110
death (1960), 285, 312
in Edmonton, 22, 205, 297, 306
Euro-North American clothing and
jewelry, 305–06
historical sources on, xv–xvi, xxiii–
xxiv, 350n1
languages (English, French, Cree),
252, 271, 296, 428n110
media coverage, 279–80
obituary, 285, 312, 337
physical appearance, *241*, *248*, *261*,
280–81, *307*, 345–46
transitional era, 23, 280–81
Urbain Jr.'s estate, 194, 206–07, 234,
238, 265
See also comparison of Isabella and
Marie Rose; Delorme, Marie
Rose (later Smith)
Smith, Marie Rose Delorme, children
about, 259–62, *261*, 443n142
Catholic faith and network, 243,
276
Charlie's inability to help sons,
275–76
childbearing (17 children), 252, 259,
443n142
child care, 209–11, 231, 252–53, 259
children's marriages to Euro-North
Americans, 263, 335

deaths in WWI, 262–63, 277, 443n142

deaths of children, 21, 260–63, 261, 276, 320, 443n142

education, 260–62, 261, 454n42

family trip to Winnipeg, 232–33, 254–55

godparents, 259–60

knowledge of Metis skills, 269

Marie Rose's love of motherhood, 259

oldest surviving child, 255, 441n115

silences in her writing, 260

sons as itinerant labourers, 263

Smith, Marie Rose Delorme, homes and land ownership

boarding house, 281, 456n87

second homestead in her name, 277–79, 449n203

status and land ownership, 275

See also Jughandle Ranch; Jughandle Ranch, Marie Rose's management; Jughandle Ranch, title to homestead

Smith, Marie Rose Delorme, identity as English-speaking pioneer

about, xxii, xxv, 18–19, 274, 299, 335

cattle ranch, 228

children's marriages to Euro-North Americans, 263, 335

community recognition, 21, 337, 341–42

cooperative spirit, 295

as French Canadian, 251–52, 335, 423n23

godparents, 259–60, 335

management of personae, xxvi, 22–23, 273–74, 337, 344–48

Marie Rose's social network, 243–51, 248, 334–35

persona of English-speaking pioneer, 252, 281, 286, 299–300, 321, 335, 337, 340

pioneer organizations, 341–42

support for white women, 445n173

views on "Indian" husbands, 231

winters on plains, 217–18

Smith, Marie Rose Delorme, identity as Metis

about, xix–xx, xxv, 189–90, 294, 457n96

adaptation of identity, 273–74, 330, 333, 335

ancestry, 327–28

author, 274, 282

Buckskin Mary, 225, 235, 268, 282, 307, 322

in Carpenter's *Fifty Dollar Bride*, 297–98

on census forms, 273, 296

class and status ambitions, 274, 321

Delormes in conflicts, xix, 274

as French Canadian, 251–52, 335, 423n23

fur trade culture, 189, 194–99, 309, 457n96

hidden pride, 23, 327

management of personae, xix–xx, xxvi–xxvii, 22–23, 337, 344–48

Metis songs, 225

pemmican, 205, 309, 457n96

pioneer organizations, 341–42

separation of Metis and First nations, 208–09

sewing and handiwork, 210–13, 266

suppression of Metis identity, xix–xx, 306–07, 318, 324, 344

transmission to descendants, 294, 323–24, 327

Smith, Marie Rose Delorme, marriage

about, xxvi, 18, 334–35

age at marriage, 218, 220

age difference with Charlie, 218, 220

alcohol use by Charlie and guests, 221, 230, 236–37

arranged marriage (1877), 217–21, 428n110

benefits for Marie Rose, 294

bride price, 18, 218–19, 221

Catholic faith, 259, 265–66, 276, 319–21

Delorme kinship network, 10

early years, 220–21, 254, 264, 287

her independence, 254, 263–65, 282, 321

his absences, 221

his dominance, 263–64

his whiteness, 221, 294

personal relations with Charlie, 236–37

silences in her writing, 229, 236, 274–75

social capital, xxvii, 15, 225–26, 331, 334, 338–39, 346

views on love in marriage, 221

See also Smith, Charlie (Marie Rose's husband), marriage and kinship network

Smith, Marie Rose Delorme, personal qualities

aversion to alcohol, 231, 237

Catholic faith, 238, 243, 260, 276

independence, 254, 263–65, 280, 282, 320

loneliness, 254

love of motherhood, 259

musical training, 214–15

obedience as wife, 230–31, 237–38, 263–64

private person, 221

storytelling, 280, 319

Smith, Marie Rose Delorme, transitional economy

about, 15, 225, 265

badger robes, 267

boarding house, 22, 245–46, 277, 279, 445n159, 456n87

buckskin clothing, 225, 235, 265, 268–72, 280, 282

Buckskin Mary, 225, 235, 268, 282, 307, 322

Calgary Stampede, 235, 269, 271

cattle ranch, 228, 287

class and status, 274–75

cook for roundup, 291–92

finances, 21–22, 252

hired help, 252, 269, 272

Metis sustainability skills, 334

midwifery, 22, 267–68, 445n173

sale of clothing and handiwork, 252–53, 266–67, 269, 271–72, 282

seasonal activities, 253

sewing machine, 235, 272, 282

silences in her writing, 308

small businesses, 272, 282

social capital, 15

successful management, 276, 334–35, 346–48

tanning hides, 252, 269, 271

tent-making, 265, 272

trade and barter, 252–53

traditional sewing and handiwork, 210–13, 252, 266–67, 311, 427n100

See also Jughandle Ranch, Marie Rose's management; Smith, Charlie (Marie Rose's husband), transitional economy

Smith, Marie Rose Delorme, widowhood

about, 21–22, 276–77, 339–40

boarding house, 245–46, 277, 279, 339, 445n159, 456n87

class and status, 245–46

deaths of children, 21, 276

financial hardships, 22, 276–77, 281, 449n206

health, 274, 447n194

independence, 21–22, 263–65, 282, 320

life in Edmonton, 22, 205, 297, 306, 309, 457n96

media coverage, 280

Metis culture, 225

pensions, 277

second homestead, 277–79, 449n203

social capital, 339–40

time period (46 years), 264

title to Jughandle Ranch, 339

See also Jughandle Ranch, title to homestead; Smith, Marie Rose Delorme, writer

Smith, Marie Rose Delorme, writer

about, 189, 274, 286

archives, 455n63

composition period, 290, 293, 297, 313

descendants' respect for stories, 323

diaries, 301

editorial changes, 451n7

Euro-Canadian identity in photos, 305–06

fictional narratives, 287, 312–17, 319–21

heroes of Euro-North Americans, 303, 312

motives for writing, 299–300, 306, 324, 455n53

personal book of remedies, 268

persona of pioneer, 173–74, 286, 299–300, 321, 340, 344, 452n8

publication plans, 286, 297, 321

scholarship on, 452n8

silences in her writing, 229, 260, 274–75, 300, 447n194

status as author, 274, 282, 286, 321

stream of consciousness, 311

unpublished works, 286, 290, 297

use of dialogue, 302, 303, 434n26

use of first person, 308–09

Smith, Marie Rose Delorme, writer, works

"Bits of My Home Life," 237

Canadian Cattlemen articles, 204, 279, 286–87, 297, 305, 311–12

"Does God Know His Business?," 313, 319–21

"Tales of the Wild West of 1870," 258

"The Twenty Warnings," 313–17, 322

See also "The Adventures of the Wild West of 1870"; "Eighty Years on the Plains"

Smith, Mary Ann (Marie Rose's daughter)

birth (1892), 443n142

death in convent (1897), 260–62, *261*, 443n142, 444n145

Smith, Mary Hélène (later Parfitt) (Marie Rose's daughter)

convent education in Pincher Creek, 260

with family, *270*

mother of Carpenter, 445n168

Smith, Mary Louise (Marie Rose's daughter)

death (1884) at age one, 443n142

Marie Rose's scrip application, 443n140

Smith, Mary Rose (Marie Rose's daughter)

death (1904) in infancy, 443n142

Smith, Michael A. (Marie Rose's son)

birth (1890), 443n142

death (1909), 263, 443n142

Smith, Richard (Marie Rose's son)

birth (1897), 443n142

death (1952), 443n142

Smith, Theodore (Marie Rose's son)
death in war (1917), 262–63, 277, 443n142, 449n203

Smith, William George (Marie Rose's son)
birth (1887), 443n142

Smithsonian Institution, 28, 30–31, 359n12

Soby, Trudy, 148

socioeconomic status. *See* class and status

Southern Alberta Pioneers and Their Descendants, 399n37, 400n41, 461n23

Southern Alberta Women's Pioneer Association
fur trade pioneers, 341, 455n53, 461n23, 462n25
Isabella's membership, 341–42, 347
Marie Rose's membership, 301–02, 341–42, 455n53

Sprenger, G. Herman, 425n51, 425n58

Spring Creek, Montana, 3, 7, 268, 457n98

Spry, Irene, 10, 355n47, 452n23

St. Albert
Marie Rose's wedding, 219–20

status and class. *See* class and status

St. Boniface convent, Red River, 18, 211–16, 232, 246, 428n110

stereotypes. *See* race and ethnicity

Stoney, 203, 253, 456n70

St-Onge, Nicole, 14, 326

Strathcona, Lady. *See* Smith, Isabella Sophia Hardisty (Lady Strathcona, Donald's wife, W. Hardisty's sister, Isabella Hardisty Lougheed's aunt)

Strathcona, Lord. *See* Smith, Donald A. (Lord Strathcona, Isabella Hardisty Smith's husband, Isabella Lougheed's uncle)

Strong-Boag, Veronica, 393n192, 415n219

"A Strong Race Opinion on the Indian Girl" (Johnson), 317–18, 459n129

Supreme Court of Canada
decision on Metis as "Indians," xii
Person's Case, 116, 393n198

Sutherland, Marguerite, 27, 358n5
See also Hardisty, Marguerite Sutherland (Richard Sr.'s wife, Isabella's grandmother)

Taché, Alexandre Antonin
management of Delorme estates, 193–94, 207, 238, 436n59
Marie Rose's letters to/from, 215, 238, 429n127, 436n52

"Tales of the Wild West of 1870" (Marie Rose Smith), 258

Taylor, Edmund, 80, 133, 157, 175, 399n37

Taylor, Mrs. Edmund, 182

Taylor, Nichol, 35–36

Tchinouk, Paley Temaikamae (Isabella's great-grandmother), 365n90

terminology
Aboriginal, xiii
Constitution Act (1982), xi, xiii
"dit," French naming practice, 422n14
ethnicity, 350n2
Euro-North Americans, xiv
First Nations, xiii–xiv, 355n43
Indian band, 355n43
Inuit, 355n43
native, use by HBC, 27, 358n6
for specific Indigenous groups, xiv
squaw, 19, 356n75

terminology for Metis
  about, xi–xiv, 325
  changes in personal use of, 3
  Constitution Act (1867), xii, 349n3
  Constitution Act (1982), xi, xiii, 325–26
  debates on, xii, xx, xxiii, 14
  half-breed, 9, 19, 356n75
  history of term Metis, 356n75
  native, use by HBC, 358n6
  preferred term for this book, xii
  self-identification, 3
  spelling (Metis, Métis, metis), xii, 325
Thomas, A., 99
Thomas, Edwin Stuart (Mary Anne's second husband, Isabella's stepfather)
  husband of Mary Anne, 72, 155, 364n72
  life in Manitoba, 155
  as "whiteman," 411n183
Thomas, Mary Anne Allen Hardisty (Edwin's wife, Isabella's mother)
  death (1930), 155, 159
  estate, 156, 159
  W. Hardisty's estate, 154–59, 179–80, 408n136, 418n246
  Isabella's relationship with, 152–55, 166
  letters to/from Clarence Lougheed, 180, 418n246
  life in Winnipeg, 72, 155, 159
  marriage to Edwin Thomas (1881), 51, 72, 155, 364n72
  Metis identity, 166
  physical appearance, 51
  scrip applications, 166, 332–33, 411n183
Thomas, William Lawrence, 155
Thomson, Graham, 162

Thorne, Tanis, 2, 353n21
Tolton, Gordon E., 434n26, 435n43, 435n45
Toronto
  James's early life, 74–75, 90, 128, 381n88, 397n2
  Methodist churches, 382n90
Touchwood Hills post, 443n140
Tough, Frank, 7
Trainor, Josephine, 111, 391n175
transitional era (1885 to 1920)
  about, xxi, 19
  automobile use by women, 100–03, 134, 135, 387n140
  Beaulieu House social events, 108–09
  "being Metis" as adaptive social construct, 332–37
  class and status, 127–28
  clear break vs. continuity, 1–2, 5–7, 23
  convent education, 211–16
  Euro-American women, 20
  family unit as work unit, 121
  fur trade culture shifts, 206–07, 228, 233, 274, 344
  fur trade kinship networks, xxii
  historiography, 1–7, 23, 352n2
  impact of conflicts of 1885 on, 7
  Indigenous farms, 424n34
  Isabella as agent of, 185
  isolation, 20
  men's management of change, xxii, xxvii
  Metis identity as liability, 343–44
  Metis social classes, 173–74
  political liability of Indigenous ancestry, 97–98, 113, 392n186
  Prairie regionalism, 169
  racial boundary shifts, 282–83
  reinvention of identities, 286
  research needed, 2, 351n17

settlers, 20

shift of mercantilism to industrialism, 7

social boundaries, 285–86

social capital, 15

successful transitions, 4–5, 128, 346–48

women's management of change, xxii–xxiii, xxviii, 1–2

transitional economy (1885 to 1920)

about, 346–47

agricultural expansionism, 290–91

agriculture, 129–30, 143, 206–07, 404n93, 424n34

automobiles, 134, 135

banks, 142

barter and credit system, 245–46, 439n82

boom economy in war years, 167

cattle, 253, 255–56

commercial buildings, 147–48

cottage industry trade goods, 15–16

credit and loans, 167, 448n201

economic diversification, 168–70

ethics and business, 160–61

expansionism, 167, 169, 448n201

farms, 6–8, 354n39

financial difficulties in 1920s, 167

forestry and lumber, 130–31

freighting, 203, 207, 212, 234

government workers, 222

horse breeding and racing, 256–57

innovative technology, 134

interest rates, 142

itinerant workers, 444n154

lawyers as symbols of ills of, 144, 404n93

lawyers' roles in economic development, 142, 403n81, 403n85

Metis identity as liability, 343–44

mining, 130–31

paper transactions, 128, 132, 329

Red River Metis, 5–7, 203

scrip dealings, 160–66, 336

steamboats, 203

successful transitions, 5–6, 128, 346–48

tourism, 246, 251, 269, 271

trade skills (carpentry), 222

treaty money, 227–28

wheat production, 134–35

wolfing, 274–75

women entrepreneurs, 176–78, 206–07, 249

See also boosterism; Calgary; farms; HBC (Hudson's Bay Company), transitional era; land; railways; ranches

treaties

comparison with Metis title, 8

Lacombe's views on, 310

land speculation, 162–63, 410n170

Marie Rose's portrayals of, 302–04, 310, 457n100

Morris as negotiator, 161

status determination, 4

Treaty 6, 457n100

Treaty 7, 302, 440n92, 456n70

Treaty 8, 162–63, 410n170

treaty money and free traders, 227–28, 334

tricksters, 317–18, 322, 458n125

Tupper, William, 435n46

Turner Valley, 146, 405n105

Tweed, Thomas, 75

"The Twenty Warnings" (Marie Rose Smith), 313–17, 322

Twin Oaks school, Winnipeg, 59

See also Miss Davis's school, Red River

Tyler, Carolyn Abbott, 357n76

Van Kirk, Sylvia, 2, 396n227, 461n13

Victorian Order of Nurses (VON), 121–23, 395n214, 395n216, 396n218

Voisey, Paul, 397n3, 447n194, 448n201, 463n28

Watanna, Onoto (Winnifred Eaton), 286, 318–19, 451n5, 458n125, 459n130

Waterton Lakes National Park
Kootenai Brown, 215, 246–49, 271
tourist economy, 246, 251, 269, 271

Welsh, Cecelia Boyer, 204–05

Welsh, Norbert
fur trade culture, 195–99, 204–05, 225, 240
as fur trader, 228, 432n3
kinship networks, 206
non-buffalo skins, 228

Wesleyan Ladies' College, Ontario
alumnae's community work, 123
arts and music, 91, 105
backgrounds of students, 62, 63–64, 371n157
gracious womanhood ideal, 68, 105, 333–34
W. Hardisty's views on, 60–61, 62–63
Isabella as "different," 62, 63–64, 66, 68, 187, 334
Isabella as student, 16, 42, 60, 63–66, 68, 105
social life, 388n147
tuition, 64

Western Canada College
N. Lougheed as student, 99, 99–100

wheat production, 134–35

Wheeler, Minnie, 187

whiskey. See alcohol

White, H., 99

whites. See Euro-North Americans

widowhood

See Lougheed, Isabella, widowhood; Smith, Marie Rose Delorme, widowhood

Willamette Valley, Oregon, 4, 13, 45, 48

Williams, Raymond, 352n23

Willson, Beckles, 357n5, 372n172

Wilson, Alan, 461n15

Winnipeg
W. Hardisty's life in, 42–43, 66, 363n64
IODE chapters, 123, 396n227
land speculation, 161
Mary Anne's life in, 411n183
Mary Rose's trip (1882), 232–33, 238, 254–55
Silver Heights (Lord Strathcona's home), 42–43
Winnipeg Foundation, 181
See also Smith, Donald A. (Lord Strathcona, Isabella Hardisty Smith's husband, Isabella Lougheed's uncle)

wolfing expeditions, 233, 274–75

women
automobile use, 100–03, 134, 135, 387n140
"being Metis" as adaptive social construct, xxiii, 330, 332–37
dower rights, 417n237, 448n199
higher education, 122, 392n188
homesteads in own name, 449n203
kinship networks, 333–37
maternal feminism, 117, 120–21, 393n200
Person's case, 116, 176, 393n198
professions for women, 121–22, 416n230
property ownership rights, 176–79, 417n237
Ranchmen's Club membership, 103, 388nn143–44

separate public and private
 spheres, 125–26
unpaid labour, xxv–xxvi, 15–16
voting rights, 119–20, 176
See also comparison of Isabella
 and Marie Rose; gracious
 womanhood; Indigenous
 women; marriage; marriage,

Euro-North American men
 and Indigenous women; Metis
 women
World War I. *See* First World War
Wuth, Farley, 437n70, 439n82

Zuehlke, Mark, 438n74, 439n82

Index

CPSIA information can be obtained
at www.ICGtesting.com
Printed in the USA
LVHW02s0837030618
579074LV00004B/13/P